1993

Teaching and Learning in the Middle Level School

Harvey A. Allen
The University of South Carolina—Columbia

Fred L. Splittgerber
The University of South Carolina—Columbia

M. Lee Manning
Old Dominion University

Merrill, *an imprint of*
Macmillan Publishing Company
New York

Maxwell Macmillan Canada
Toronto

Maxwell Macmillan International
New York Oxford Singapore Sydney

Editor: Linda James Scharp
Production Editor: Julie Anderson Tober
Art Coordinator: Peter A. Robison
Photo Editor: Anne Vega
Cover Designer: Cathleen Norz
Production Buyer: Patricia A. Tonneman

This book was set in Palatino and Futura by Compset Inc. and was printed and bound by Book Press, Inc., a Quebecor America Book Group Company. The cover was printed by Phoenix Color Corp.

Printed in the United States of America

Macmillan Publishing Company
866 Third Avenue
New York, NY 10022

Macmillan Publishing Company is part of the
Maxwell Communication Group of Companies.

Maxwell Macmillan Canada, Inc.
1200 Eglinton Avenue East, Suite 200
Don Mills, Ontario M3C 3N1

Library of Congress Cataloging-in-Publication Data
Allen, Harvey A.
Teaching and learning in the middle level school / Harvey A. Allen, Fred L. Splittgerber, M. Lee Manning.
p. cm.
Includes bibliographical references and index.
ISBN 0-675-21347-9
1. Middle schools—United States. 2. Middle school students—United States. 3. School management and organization—United States. 4. Middle schools—United States—Curricula.
I. Splittgerber, Fred L. II. Manning, M. Lee. III. Title.
LB1623.5.A55 1993
373.2′36—dc20 92-31113
CIP

Printing: 1 2 3 4 5 6 7 8 9 Year: 3 4 5 6 7

All photos courtesy of Donna Windham, Richland School District Two, Columbia, South Carolina.

The authors wish to dedicate this book to the middle level teachers, administrators, and students whom we have worked with over the years. Most especially, we dedicate the book to our families who have been "in the middle" of all the important things we have done.

To Judy Allen, for her love, patience, encouragement, and assistance that inspired me throughout the writing of this book.

Our sons, Andy and Cory, for their exemplary life and school experiences which made this book both possible and necessary.

To Joan Splittgerber, for her understanding and unwavering support during the writing of this book.

My children, Susan, David, and Al, for their patience and understanding while engaged in this writing project.

My parents, whose continual support and encouragement throughout my career helped make this book a reality.

To Marianne Manning, for her support, patience, and encouragement throughout the writing of this book.

My children, Jennifer and Michael, and their grandmothers, Margaret and Annie.

Preface

The young adolescent entering the middle level school in 1993 will graduate from high school in the year 2000. The middle level school is positioned as an institution between childhood and adolescence that must meet the present, compelling needs of young adolescents in the 1990s as well as prepare them for the challenge of living in the twenty-first century. The middle level school is at a unique turning point in its development as a learner-centered school designed to nurture and teach 10- to 14-year-olds. *Teaching and Learning in the Middle Level School* was written to make educators more knowledgeable about young adolescents, the urgent circumstances of their lives, and the schools they need. This textbook, written for both undergraduate and graduate students in teacher education, may also serve as a useful tool for educators desiring to become better informed about teaching and learning in the middle level school.

Teaching and Learning in the Middle Level School builds upon the authors' theoretical knowledge and firsthand experiences working with young adolescents and the vast array of research that has been assembled on the middle level. It incorporates the strengths and recommendations of *Turning Points* (The Carnegie Council on Adolescent Development), *This We Believe* (National Middle School Association), *What Matters in the Middle Grades* (Maryland State Department of Education), *Caught in the Middle* (California State Department of Education), and other relevant studies of effective middle level schools, as well as the work of many authors dedicated to improving middle level schools and the lives of young adolescents.

The authors of *Teaching and Learning in the Middle Level School* strongly advocate an ecological orientation to middle level education. An ecological orientation addresses the personal, social, and academic needs of young adolescents holistically in all of their interrelated environmental systems of family, school, peer group, church, and community. In the school setting, the student is the central focus, and curricular, instructional, organizational, and supportive systems must be directed toward establishing a living and learning community that attends to the developmental needs of young adolescents. *Teaching and Learning in the Middle Level School* presents a rationale and mandate for providing a school that meets the developmental needs of its students and, at the same time, provides them with educational experiences that prepare them for coping with the challenges of their academic, social, and personal lives.

The coverage of the textbook highlights the essential attributes of successful schools for young adolescents. Chapters deal with the origins and evolution of middle level schools. The cognitive, social, emotional, and physical characteristics of young adolescents are given comprehensive treatment. The book addresses curricular concerns such as academically effective and developmentally appropriate curriculum, integrated curriculum, specific content areas, and exploratory curriculum. Organizational issues such as interdisciplinary team organization, flexible scheduling, and school-within-a-school are examined. Teaching in the middle level school is analyzed from the perspective of the teacher as person, what the teacher knows (content), and what the teacher does (instructing, advising, managing, etc.). A chapter is devoted to the middle level guidance program in all of its various aspects, such as advisor-advisee programs, academic/career advisement, and individual counseling. A special strength of the book is the chapter on the ecological nature of home-school-community relationships. The book concludes with recommendations for how to implement best educational practice so that the middle level school we need for tomorrow can be realized today.

OBJECTIVES

Our specific objectives for the readers of this textbook are

1 To develop an understanding of the middle level concept, its origins, and how the school in the middle builds upon the efforts of the elementary school and prepares learners for the secondary school and beyond.
2 To expose educators to the personal problems and social challenges facing young adolescents in an ever-changing global society.
3 To realize how the integration of middle level school curriculum, organization, teaching and guidance functions contribute to successful educational opportunities for all young adolescents.

4 To ensure the reengagement of the family and community in the efforts to provide developmentally appropriate educational experiences for 10- to 14-year olds.

5 To provide the needed curricular, instructional, and teaching frameworks based on current research data, state initiatives, and national reports for implementing an exemplary middle level school.

SPECIAL FEATURES

To facilitate the reader's understanding of the book, special features and pedagogical aids were included, as follows:

Case Studies, appropriately arranged in the chapters on the development of physical, psychosocial, emotional, and cognitive development (Chapters 3 and 4), show educators how development and related changes are experienced by young adolescents.

Suggested Readings at the end of each chapter provide the reader with resources for additional study and information.

The **Exploration** section at the end of each chapter offers activities designed to help educators to understand young adolescents and to relate to effective middle school practices.

A **Glossary** at the end of the book provides definitions of terms related to middle level schools and young adolescents.

Appendix A contains sources for guidelines and programs for implementation in middle level schools.

ACKNOWLEDGMENTS

This book would not have been possible without the unwavering help of many people who were generous with their ideas as well as their time. The authors wish to thank the following people for their assistance and support: Mrs. Pat Carver for her willingness to prepare the manuscript and her editorial ability to put the manuscript into its final format and the librarians of Cooper Library at The University of South Carolina, who gave willingly of their time and assistance in locating documents needed for the book. We are indebted to Ms. Donna E. Windham, Coordinator of Public Information for Richland School District Two, for organizing the schedule for the chapter photographs and for her creativity, patience, and time in shooting the pictures. We also thank the administration, teachers, staff, parents, and students in Dent Middle School, E. L. Wright Middle School, and Summit Parkway Middle School of Richland School District Two for allowing us to take photographs in their schools.

We also are grateful to the individuals who reviewed the manuscript and offered numerous constructive suggestions, namely, Linda R. Kramer, SUNY–Brockport; Nancy A. Minix, Western Kentucky University; Irvin Howard, California State University, San Bernadino; S. Rex Morrow, Old Dominion University; Horace C. Hawn, University of Georgia; Dorothy Spethmann, Dakota State; Gina Schack, University of Louisville; Gordon F. Vars, Kent State University; and Donna J. Camp, University of Central Florida.

Finally, we want to thank Jeff Johnston, who helped us in the early stages of this project, and Linda Scharp and Julie Tober at Macmillan, who guided us and helped us complete the book.

H.A.A.
F.L.S.
M.L.M.

Brief Contents

Contents

CHAPTER OUTLINE

The Exemplary Middle Level School

1

OVERVIEW

Middle level schools are dynamic institutions charged by the interests, attitudes, and expectations of the young adolescents who attend them. You were probably once a student in a middle level school, you are presently studying about middle level schools, and perhaps you will teach in a middle level school. Your remembrances of middle level schools past and your perceptions of middle level schools present will contribute to the understandings you obtain from this textbook. The purpose of the book is to open to you the exciting promise and potential of what can happen to young learners when schools are responsive to their academic, social, and personal needs.

An exemplary middle level school is a school that designs its curriculum, instruction, organization, and support services to respond to the unique developmental needs of young adolescents. The school builds from a foundation of student-centeredness that places learners first and enables them to feel safe, secure, and successful. The school provides a balanced curriculum that prepares students to function effectively in society both as young adolescents and later as adults. There are many key elements that research and practice have shown to be essential to an exemplary middle level school. This chapter briefly examines some of them.

In this chapter you will read about:

1 The instructional expectations of an exemplary middle level school.

2 The personal, social, and academic dimensions of curriculum.
3 The supportive features of a responsive middle level school.
4 Developmentally appropriate curriculum and instruction for young adolescents.
5 The organizational dimension of middle level schools.

BACKGROUND

The middle level school in some form or another is entering its ninth decade of development. The first school in the middle, the junior high school, developed between 1910 and 1920, gained public and professional acceptance, and dominated until the 1960s. In the 1960s, the middle school, directed by educators like William Alexander, Donald Eichhorn, and Phillip Pumerantz, emerged as a school organized to attend to the unique needs of young adolescents, free from the overt high school influences that had characterized the curriculum of the "junior" high school. The middle school and the junior high school coexisted from the 1960s to the 1990s, with the middle school gradually surpassing the junior high school in actual numbers and philosophical orientation. Over the last three decades, the middle level school has been at the storm center of cataclysmic changes in American society. These changes have altered the expectations that people have for middle level schools and for the boys and girls who attend them.

The success of the middle school movement can be verified by the results of a survey conducted by Alexander and McEwin (1989) to determine the number of middle schools and junior high schools in the United States. They found that between 1970 and 1987 the number of middle schools (grades 6–8) grew from 1,662 to 4,329, while the number of junior high schools (grades 7–9) decreased from 4,711 to 2,191.

The junior high school and the middle school generally advocated two goals for the middle level school. These goals were to meet the unique needs of young adolescents and to provide a successful transition from elementary school to high school. However, differences have arisen over how these two essential goals can be attained. Junior high school programs have tended toward a secondary orientation while middle schools, in developing their unique middle school philosophy, have reflected elements of an elementary school philosophy.

PERSPECTIVES ON MIDDLE LEVEL SCHOOLS

There have been many different kinds of middle level schools, resulting in different definitions for them. The first middle level school, the junior high school, has been described as an intermediate school and an introductory high school. The junior high was most typically organized as a school consisting of grades 7–9 that was different academically, instructionally, and organizationally from the elementary school below and the high school above. The developmental needs of young adolescents were supposed to be the central focus of the program of study.

Gruhn and Douglass (1971) summarized the development of functions for the junior high school as they had evolved from 1910 to 1970. The six functions in Figure 1.1 represented the rationale for the exemplary junior high school and had significant implications for all middle level schools.

These functions were comprehensive and widely accepted statements of how junior high school curriculum, instruction, organization, administration, and guidance services should be developed to meet the unique needs of young adolescents in transition between elementary and high school. The perception that junior high schools were not implementing these functions effectively led to disenchantment with their approach and accelerated the development of middle schools beginning in the 1950s to the 1960s.

The modern middle level schools became more student-centered. Eichhorn (1966), building the middle school concept upon the growth and development of the learner, originated the term *transescence,* which he defined as "the period in human development which begins in late childhood, prior to the onset of puberty, and which extends through the early states of adolescence" (p. 3). The middle school follows the elementary unit and precedes the high school and includes students from grades six, seven, and eight.

Howard and Stoumbis (1970) defined the middle school as providing an educational program aimed at the 10- to 14-year-old age group, stressing curriculum flexibility rather than the acquisition of specific skills, and not emphasizing the specialization of the high school. The name *middle school* gave this institution its own standing, distinct from the image of the senior high school. The school was intended to depart drastically from the overtly high school elements of the present junior high school, which fostered an environment of early social sophistication and academic specialization. In the middle school, specialization was introduced gradually in such content areas as the arts, mathematics,

Integration:	Learning experiences are integrated into the developmental needs of early adolescents.
Exploration:	Students explore their special interests in the context of the total school program.
Guidance:	Guidance assists students toward personal and social adjustment, career planning, and decision-making.
Differentiation:	Learning activities and opportunities are differentiated to the needs, interests, and abilities of students.
Socialization:	Socialization provides for relationships with others, adjustment to social living, civic participation, and other social roles and responsibilities.
Articulation:	This function provides for a planned gradual transition from the elementary grades (childhood) to the secondary grades (adolescence).

FIGURE 1.1 Functions of the junior high school

science, and industrial arts. Middle school teachers emphasized active learning rather than passive behaviors such as sitting and listening, reading the textbook and answering the questions at the end of the chapter, and doing seatwork.

Alexander and George (1981) defined the middle school as "a school of some three to five years between elementary and high school focused on the educational needs of students in these in-between years and designed to promote continuous educational progress for all concerned" (p. 19).

For purposes of this book, the authors define the middle level school as follows:

> A school, incorporating some combination of the middle level grades, established to provide appropriate living and learning experiences for young adolescents in their passage from the elementary school to the high school. Such a school is responsive to the developmental needs of young adolescents and promotes a learning environment that is academically effective and developmentally appropriate and that fosters student self-esteem in a climate of acceptance, trust, and success.

Definitions do not make a school. Schools are made by the times and by the parents and children that need them. Schools are not conceptualized, organized, and administered as perfect, pristine models. Junior high schools were not absolutely subject-centered and middle schools were not absolutely child-centered. Instead, schools have tendencies, nuances, and gradations rather than absolute positions. Table 1.1 presents some tendencies that have characterized junior high and middle schools and have resulted in differences between the purposes and programs of the two types of middle level school.

EXEMPLARY MIDDLE LEVEL SCHOOLS TODAY

In recent years there have been national and state efforts to include all schools—intermediate, middle, and junior high—that serve the developmental needs of young adolescents in a unified movement of reform and innovation. The middle school concept with its student-centered philosophy has prevailed, but two inclusive terms, middle grade and middle level, now represent the movement. In

TABLE 1.1 Characteristics of Middle Schools and Junior High Schools

Middle School	Junior High School
Grades 6–8	Grades 7–9
Elementary philosophy	Secondary philosophy
Student-centered	Subject-centered
Integrated curriculum	Separate subjects
Exploratory activities	Mastery of subject matter
Team organization	Departmentalization
Flexible scheduling	Six-period day/Block-of-time
Active learning	Teacher-directed instruction
Intramural sports	Interscholastic sports
Unstructured social activities	Structured social activities

this book, we use the term *middle level* to avoid an overemphasis on the importance of gradedness in middle level schools. It is not the grades contained in a school that give it vitality and purpose; instead, it is the way that the educators, parents, and students interact that enable a school to make a difference in the lives of the young adolescents who attend that school.

Various goals or aims have been formulated for middle level schools. These have been both specific and general. They have emanated from national or state reports, from national associations and research centers, and from local districts. The state of Maryland identified four major goals/outcomes of middle grade education in the report, *What Matters in the Middle Grades* (1989). The goals are that middle grade education should promote (1) academic outcomes from a broad curricular framework, (2) the development of a positive self-concept, (3) respect for others and appreciation of the diversity of cultures, skills, and talents of others, and (4) a positive attitude toward learning. Additionally, different goals have been stated for the school as a whole compared with those to be attained in individual classrooms. The opinions, viewpoints, and values of a broad spectrum of society contribute to the development of appropriate goals.

This We Believe, first issued in 1982 and reissued in 1992 by the National Middle School Association, has been considered the definitive statement of what the middle level school should do for young adolescents. Such key elements as integrated curriculum, interdisciplinary teams, exploratory activities, and advisory programs are presented as responsive to the academic, social, and personal needs of students. Another important influence on the middle level school of today was *Turning Points.* This report by the Carnegie Council on Adolescent Development analyzed in broad strokes what society must do to address the needs of young adolescents coming of age in the 21st century. We urge our readers to study many of the eloquent statements of belief that have been published about young adolescents and the middle level school they need.

THE STUDENT

Figure 1.2 depicts the four essential dimensions of the ecology of middle-level schooling: curriculum, instruction, organization, and support services. The figure shows students at the center of all programs and services designed to help them develop. The emotional, intellectual, psychosocial, moral, and physical development of young adolescents influences all aspects of the middle level school. An assumption underlying the middle school would be that if the needs of students are given proper priority, the needs of parents, teachers, and society will be achieved. Certain practices, when employed in middle level schools, cause classrooms to come alive. Observation and research have indicated that such practices as exploratory curriculum, cooperative learning, interdisciplinary teams, and advisor–advisee programs broaden opportunities for student achievement, increase student interest, and enhance self-esteem. From such approaches, students not only learn the academic 3 R's—reading, writing, and arithmetic—but also the social 3 R's—respect, responsibility, and relationships.

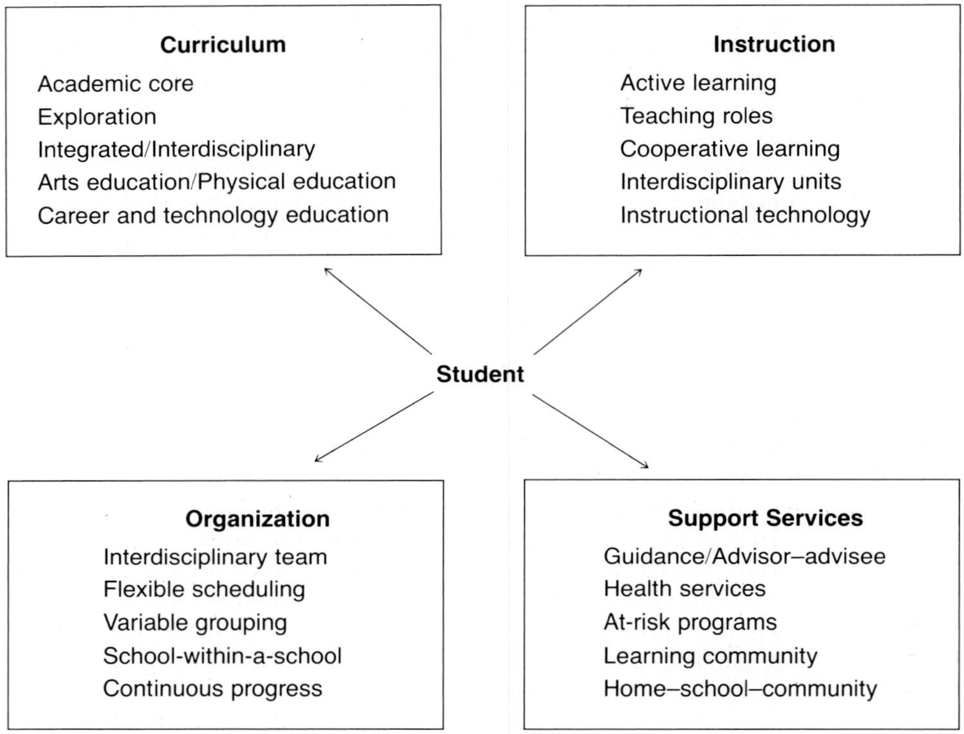

FIGURE 1.2 The four dimensions of an exemplary middle level school

Joan Lipsitz describes four such schools in *Successful Schools for Young Adolescents* (1984), a compelling book that was the culmination of her research to find effective middle grade schools in the United States. Using academic effectiveness, security, responsiveness to developmental needs, and reputation for excellence as baseline criteria, Lipsitz selected four schools for an intensive and extensive study of what made them successful. She found that they responded with sensitivity to the developmental needs of young adolescents. They were also characterized by joy and vitality, which fostered a pleasant but serious climate for students and teachers. Lipsitz concluded, "The most striking feature of the four schools is their willingness and ability to adapt all school practices to the individual differences in intellectual, biological, and social maturation of their students" (1984, p. 167). This book examines schools in a new way and provides insights into positive school contexts and strategies to implement effective middle school practice. The schools that Lipsitz describes characterize what effective middle grade schools were meant to be.

During the 1990s and into the twenty-first century, responsive middle level schools will continue to emphasize academic learning but will also increasingly concern themselves with the intellectual, physical, psychosocial, emotional, and moral development of young adolescents. In *This We Believe* (1982), the authors provide a rationale for the middle school movement and also describe the essential elements of middle schools. After discussing development among 10- to 14-year-olds, the authors write: ". . . (T)he middle school is an educational response to the needs and characteristics of youngsters during transescence and, as such, deals with the full range of intellectual and developmental needs" (p. 9). From understanding young adolescents' developmental characteristics, it becomes evident that these learners need opportunities to try out their new physical, social, and cognitive abilities and to discover what they can do successfully (Dorman, 1983). In Chapters 3 and 4, young adolescent development will be addressed in detail.

THE CURRICULAR DIMENSION

Curriculum addresses such aspects as curriculum goals, the quality and importance of the subject matter, the learning activities provided for students, and the ways that content is being taught and learned (Eisner, 1991). An appropriate middle level curriculum balances academic, personal, and social contexts to provide a developmentally sound program that matches the needs of young adolescents. Figure 1.2 shows some essential elements of the curriculum dimension, such as academic core, arts education, physical and health education, technology, integrated curriculum, and exploratory curriculum.

The academic context consists of the following basic content areas: mathematics, science, English, social studies, foreign languages, health, physical education, unified arts, technology education, home economics, and skills of reading, writing, speaking, listening, thinking, and library and information retrieval. The task of responsive middle level schools is to involve and challenge young adolescents in specific subject areas while strengthening their mastery of basic skills. Each subject contributes to broadening the individual's knowledge, social interaction, and personal experiences. Interdisciplinary approaches enable the young adolescent to observe an integrated viewpoint of content and skills as well as to appreciate the value and power of separate disciplines.

The personal context integrates content from subject matter areas, personal experiences and interests, career education and exploratory activities to assist young adolescents in constructing and creating knowledge, values, beliefs, and attitudes. It is experiential in that expanding the personal development of an individual is dependent on the prior experiences of each individual. The emphasis is on self-awareness through personal experiences. Middle level learners are encouraged to explore their own interests. The personal curriculum (1) integrates content, thinking, feelings, and actions of young adolescents, (2) recognizes that "self" is a significant area of learning, and (3) develops the whole person within the school and society.

The social curriculum is concerned with developing socially competent individuals. The focus is on citizenship and intergroup relations. The middle level curriculum provides the needed opportunities for socialization through interaction with peers, teachers, and adults outside the school in classes, extracurricular activities, and community activities. Peer acceptance and status are a critical part of each young adolescent's social development. The school and community are settings that provide opportunities for real social experiences. The social curriculum includes the recognition and appreciation of cultural diversity in young adolescents as an essential part of a democratic society. All learners should be encouraged to explore opportunities for developing and refining social skills and working with culturally diverse groups.

Integrated approaches that combine academic, social, and personal contexts are strongly recommended for middle level schools. Integrated study eliminates the boundaries that separate subjects from each other. Music and social studies, math and science, and reading and social studies are taught and studied together. For example, students might study Native Americans of the southwest United States. They study the way of life and create the music and dance of the culture they are trying to understand. The students read books, make collections, visit museums, and use resource persons to broaden their understanding and appreciation of the people they are studying. Such an approach connects art to social studies and social studies to other academic areas. Developmental theory indicates that the middle grades represent a critical time for young adolescents to engage in academic core studies. It is important for middle level schools to provide challenging and satisfying experiences with strong academic content, while connecting subject matter to other subject matter and relating subject matter to real-life situations through integrated curriculum approaches. Integrated curriculum approaches and interdisciplinary units can utilize themes of broad interest to students to provide rich experiences of an academic, social, and personal nature (Wheelock & Dorman, 1988).

A fundamental attribute of the middle level school is the exploratory curriculum. This curriculum allows young adolescents to study things they want to study and need to learn. Exploratory programs provide middle level learners with the opportunity to explore careers, personal interests, hobbies, and lifelong interests. The goal of exploratory activities is to enable young adolescents to determine who they are, what they believe, what they can do and want to be as adults. Exploratory programs must (1) provide personal, social, and academic experiences for every young adolescent; (2) focus on the future and on possible career opportunities as well as on current interests in the selection of activities and experiences; (3) utilize resources available in the community; (4) be required in all middle grade levels; and (5) offer a wide range of options for exploration.

The middle school movement has focused a great deal of attention on organizational issues, such as team teaching, the unique developmental needs of young adolescents, guidance programs such as advisor–advisee, and exploratory programs. Curriculum has not received the attention it merits. In the 1990s, that situation is being addressed by some exceptional curriculum design. James Beane (1990) has been in the forefront of the middle level curriculum rebirth with provocative ideas about integrating middle level curriculum and thereby connecting it to the lives of young adolescents.

In this book, we place considerable emphasis on the middle level curriculum. An ecological orientation is developed that links curriculum elements to the interrelated family, school, community, and peer group environments of young adolescents. This ecological link between the integrated curriculum and environmental systems seeks to establish the concept of the middle level school as a learning community. Chapters 6, 7, and 8 deal with general curriculum theory, specific subject areas, and the integrated curriculum.

THE INSTRUCTIONAL DIMENSION

Instruction is the plan to carry out the goals and objectives of the middle level curriculum. Instruction should be designed to match the structure of the subject matter and the developmental characteristics of young adolescents. Curriculum and instruction are interrelated; it is difficult to conceive of either one apart from the other. However, research shows that teaching methods are so individual and variable that the same content can be taught differently by different teachers (Eisner, 1991).

Goodlad (1982) in his observations in middle level classrooms found that instructional time was characterized by teachers lecturing and monitoring seatwork and by students preparing assignments. Though teachers recognized that they could modify their teaching methods, they tended to use techniques which resulted in passive student behavior, limited teacher–student interaction, and reduced feedback to students. Goodlad concluded that passive student behavior and repetitious teaching limited the achievement of middle level students.

The middle level teacher is the key to effective instruction. The teacher performs a variety of teaching roles, such as instructor, manager, facilitator, motivator, coach, substitute parent, collaborator, and advisor. In performing these roles and functions, the teacher promotes the broadest opportunities for young people to engage in active learning situations. Because of the dramatic physical changes they are experiencing, middle level students especially need active learning strategies as opposed to passive learning situations. Cooperative learning is a relatively new teaching–learning approach that enables students to work actively, purposely, and cooperatively to attain group and individual learning goals. Cooperative learning will be discussed later, but is emphasized here because the approach has such interesting potential for increasing student achievement, self-concept, and social skills.

Interdisciplinary units and instructional technology are highly recommended to promote active learning and positive learning outcomes. Interdisciplinary units enable students to learn holistically rather than piecemeal. Units allow subject areas to be connected to each other and learning to be linked to real-world situations. The middle level school must become part of the technology revolution sweeping our society in areas such as computers, video production, and information retrieval.

Goodlad (1982) reported that middle level students were most actively involved in classes where they learned through field trips, discussion groups, interviews, work on projects, and other active learning strategies. For the middle level school, cooperative learning, instructional technology, team learning, and interdisciplinary units hold promise for promoting student achievement and interest in learning.

THE ORGANIZATIONAL DIMENSION

The organizational dimension arranges time, space, subjects, students, and teachers to facilitate the attainment of the goals and objectives of the middle level curriculum. Organizational structures vary from elementary to middle level to high school. The elementary school has utilized a graded structure. The self-contained classroom with one teacher teaching almost all of the subjects during the instructional day has been the dominant organizational pattern. The high school has uniformly organized its instructional day into equal time units. Students then move from subject to subject through six or seven 50-minute periods, usually with a different teacher for each subject.

Interdisciplinary team organization has been a popular organizational structure of the middle level school. MacIver (1990) identifies interdisciplinary teams as "a keystone for effective education in middle grades" (p. 460). In this approach, two or more teachers work together to plan and teach the content in several subject areas. For instance, the four academic core teachers for English, social studies, mathematics, and science could work together to develop an interdisciplinary approach that would integrate the content in the four subject areas. Students benefit from this approach because they have access to teachers with subject matter expertise who have connected the elements of a particular subject to a whole curriculum program. Interdisciplinary units, exploratory activities, independent study, and personal development activities can emerge from settings where teachers have shared planning time to develop experiences and activities that connect subject areas to each other and to real-life situations. Interdisciplinary team organization should enable teachers to teach content effectively at the same time they work together to attend to the needs of young adolescents. Interdisciplinary team organization is one of the fundamental attributes of middle level practice. Interdisciplinary team organization emphasizing team teaching and team planning enables students to interact with a number of teachers representing a variety of subject matter disciplines.

Other aspects of the organizational structure of middle level schools found in Figure 1.2 are variable grouping, flexible scheduling, utilization of blocks-of-time, and continuous progress. The organizational dimension should be established in ways that allow students access to and success with the instructional program of the school.

THE SUPPORTIVE DIMENSION

Figure 1.2 shows some aspects of the support services found in many middle level schools. The supportive dimension coordinates the guidance program, health services, at-risk program, and home–school–community connections that are so vital to the well-being of young adolescents. The needs of young adolescents can no longer be adequately served exclusively by the school. Problems relating to health circumstances, family dysfunction, poverty situations, peer-group relationships, low school achievement, and other socio-personal factors require a comprehensive plan that includes home, school, community, health services, and other institutions and agencies. Middle level schools recognize the need for guidance and counseling, providing health services and information, identifying at-risk students and addressing their needs, providing special education experiences which meet all legal mandates, and taking advantage of home–school–community resources.

The guidance program in the middle level school is actually a team effort of teachers, counselors, administrators, parents, community members, and young adolescents working together in a caring manner to meet the needs of students. Responsive guidance programs address concerns and problems which may result from contemporary societal changes and also from the rapid physical, psychosocial-emotional, and intellectual-developmental changes during early adolescence.

Rather than perceiving middle level students from elementary or secondary perspectives, middle level guidance and counseling teams view 10- to 14-year-olds as unique individuals with special problems related to the developmental age. The advisor–advisee program, another essential component of responsive middle level schools, allows the classroom teacher to interact with small groups and individuals. Professionals in the guidance and counseling program play a major role in advisor–advisee sessions as they work closely with teachers in the selection of topics and strategies.

One of the most compelling recommendations of the *Turning Points* report has to do with improving the health status of young adolescents. National surveys of adolescent health (NASHS, 1988) reveal an alarming profile of poor nutrition, inadequate physical fitness, high incidence of drug, alcohol, and tobacco use, and casual attitudes toward sex education in areas such as pregnancy, sexually transmitted diseases, and AIDS. Students often possess knowledge that should prevent or remediate their health problems but this knowledge does not change their attitudes or behaviors in the face of peer pressure. The responsive middle level school must offer a comprehensive health curriculum, promote the school as a healthy workplace, and teach young adolescents decision-making skills. Additionally, the school must coordinate interaction with other community agencies and institutions to assure that young adolescents have access to the health care they need. Health education is a priority for young adolescents.

Middle level educators during the 1990s and beyond will identify young adolescents demonstrating at-risk behaviors. The task is to identify students in need while simultaneously avoiding labeling those students who are not at risk. Likewise, decisions regarding a student's propensity toward being at risk should never be based on race, ethnicity, or gender. The middle level school should (1) recognize the at-risk conditions (types and severity) confronting many young adolescents, (2) recognize that the middle school might be the most effective (and perhaps one of the last) institutions to address the needs of at-risk young adolescents, (3) avoid labeling learners as at-risk who are not, (4) provide effective in-service opportunities designed to help middle level educators be more aware and cognizant of the dangers at-risk students face, and (5) recognize the many programs available to help at-risk students.

Two of eight recommendations of the *Turning Points* report dealt with problems and issues relevant to the home, school, and community. One recommendation sought to reengage parents in the education of their middle level learners. Strategies for parental involvement in school and for assisting parents to become more effective helping teachers for their children at home have become important concerns for educators.

Middle level schools are also asked to provide opportunities for parents to participate in governance and school improvement. Parents should be able to show their support of education by volunteer service in the schools. The schools at all costs need to develop effective systems of communicating with parents. There is a high correlation between parental support of the school and the extent to which parents are kept informed about their children's progress.

Another recommendation of the *Turning Points* report was to connect middle level students with their communities. Community education has become an avenue of study in middle level schools. One of the most refreshing practices in this area is the provision by many middle level schools of community service projects for young people.

The middle level school coordinates all aspects of support services to enhance the well-being of young adolescents. A collaborative effort of home, school, and community should be engendered to promote the education and care that young adolescents need at home, at school, and in the community.

A LOOK AHEAD

This chapter has delineated the critical attributes of the exemplary middle level school. Over the past 100 years, the notion of a school between the elementary school and the high school has been discussed and a student-centered philosophy has evolved. This philosophy states that the middle level school must address the unique developmental needs of young adolescents. Additionally, the middle level school serves as a passage between the elementary school and the high school. Now is the time to look ahead to the future of middle level schools.

Dorman (1985) theorized that a middle level school must satisfy three basic requirements before it could be considered a good school by the public or by its students. The school must be: (1) physically safe and emotionally secure, (2) academically effective, and (3) developmentally appropriate. The idea of a physically safe and emotionally secure school is a prerequisite if the other two objectives are to be realized. Many of today's young adolescents are coping with significant problems occasioned by divorce, child abuse, dysfunctional families, substance abuse, poverty, peer group relationships, or myriad other contemporary problems. The middle level school needs to be uniquely prepared to help the young adolescent achieve a sense of physical safety and emotional security.

It can do this through advisor–advisee programs, improved home–school–community relationships, team organization, cooperative learning, and at-risk programs.

The middle level school must guarantee academic effectiveness by assuring a high level of academic expectation and attainment for all students. The school enables students to become proficient in the communication skills of reading, writing, listening, and speaking. Students must have high-interest, content-rich programs in mathematics, science, social studies, arts education, computer science, technology, career education, and physical and health education. The school must help students to learn to think critically and creatively, to develop a system for valuing, to become self-directed learners, and to promote a positive attitude toward lifelong learning. The curriculum programs that young adolescents need emphasize integrated and interdisciplinary curriculum study, a strong academic core, mastery of basic skills, and exploratory activities within a balanced academic, social, and personal curriculum.

A foundation objective of the middle level school is to provide a developmentally appropriate environment. Dorman (1985) proposed that middle level schools should be responsive to the seven developmental needs of young adolescents, for: (1) diversity, (2) self-exploration and self-definition, (3) meaningful participation in school and community, (4) positive social interaction with both peers and adults, (5) physical activity, (6) competence and achievement, and (7) structure and clear limits. Additionally, important physical, intellectual, socio-emotional, and psychological growth and development characteristics have implications for teaching and learning in the middle level school. The middle level school has curricular, instructional, organizational, and supportive dimensions that facilitate the total development of young adolescents. Integrated curriculum, exploratory activities, cooperative learning, interdisciplinary teams, and advisor–advisee programs are student-centered and responsive to the developmental needs of young adolescents.

In the years between the publication of *This We Believe* (1982) and *Turning Points* (1989) and *This We Believe* (1992), a sense of urgency has been introduced to the agenda of middle level schools. The middle level school is at a crucial turning point in providing programs which can enable young adolescents to live purposeful, successful, and satisfying lives.

SUMMARY

Exemplary middle level schools have young adolescents as their essential focus. Key elements of emotional, intellectual, psychosocial, moral, physical, and social development impact on all other essential features of the middle level school. To ensure a developmentally appropriate curriculum, the curriculum balances academic, personal, and social dimensions. Instruction has the challenge of motivating middle level learners and providing training for middle level teachers. In this model, the organization will enhance student achievement and provide means for placing students in settings which optimize their personal and social development. The support services ensure that equity and access exist for all middle level learners with special needs. The middle level school takes a proactive approach to meeting the academic, social, and personal needs of young adolescents.

▪ ▪ ▪

EXPLORATION

1 Review the Contents to familiarize yourself with the format of the book.
2 Select a chapter from the Contents that you would like to read first. Begin reading this chapter.
3 Identify middle level schools in your area that you might visit and observe. Be sure to make arrangements prior to your visit.
4 Start a filing system of articles, handouts, and bibliographies on aspects of middle level education.
5 Prepare a journal of your impressions, insights, and attitudes toward middle level schools. Write in your journal on a regular basis.
6 Read a book about young adolescents such as Joan Lipsitz's *Growing Up Forgotten* or her book on middle level schools, *Successful Schools for Young Adolescents.*

SUGGESTED READINGS

Caught in the middle: Educational reform for young adolescents in California public schools. (1987). Sacramento: California State Department of Education.

This task force presented an agenda of reform for addressing the needs of middle level education.

Dorman, G. (1985). *The middle grades assessment program.* Carrboro, NC: University of North Carolina, Chapel Hill, Center for Early Adolescence.

This assessment model will assist in the development of a middle level school.

Dunn, R., Beaudry, J. S., & Klavis, A. (1989). Survey of research on learning styles. *Educational Leadership, 46* (6), 50–58.

This survey helps to determine the significance of learning styles.

Lipsitz, J. (1984). *Successful schools for young adolescents.* New Brunswick, NJ: Transaction Books.

This case study examines how four middle level schools made their environments developmentally responsive and academically effective for their students.

National Association of Secondary School Principals Council on Middle Level Education. (1985). *An agenda for excellence at the middle level.* Reston, VA: NASSP.

The NASSP middle level task force proposed a blueprint for developing middle level schools.

Turning points: Preparing American youth for the 21st century. (1989). Washington, DC: Carnegie Council on Adolescent Development.

This report has become an influential force in the development of middle level schools. It was prepared by the Carnegie Council on Adolescent Development Task Force on Education of Young Adolescents. The Carnegie Council is a program of the Carnegie Corporation of New York.

REFERENCES

Alexander, W. M., & George, P. S. (1981). *The exemplary middle school.* New York: Holt, Rinehart and Winston.

Alexander, W. M., & McEwin, C. K. (1989). *Schools in the middle: Status and progress.* Columbus, OH: National Middle School Association.

Beane, J. A. (1990). *A middle school curriculum: From rhetoric to reality.* Columbus, OH: National Middle School Association.

Carnegie Council on Adolescent Development (1989). *Turning points: Preparing American youth for the 21st century.* Washington, DC: Author.

Dorman, G. (1983). Making schools work for young adolescents. *Educational Horizons, 61*(4), 175–182.

Dorman, G. (1985). *The middle grades assessment program.* Carrboro, NC: University of North Carolina, Chapel Hill, Center for Early Adolescence.

Eichhorn, D. (1966). *The middle school.* New York: The Center for Applied Research in Education.

Eisner, E. (1991). *The enlightened eye.* New York: Macmillan.

Goodlad, J. I. (1982). *A place called school.* New York: McGraw-Hill.

Gruhn, W., & Douglass, H. (1971). *The modern junior high school.* New York: Ronald Press.

Howard, A. W., & Stoumbis, G. C. (1970). *The junior high school and middle school: Issues and practices.* Scranton, PA: International Textbook.

Lipsitz, J. (1980). *Growing up forgotten.* New Brunswick, NJ: Transaction Books.

Lipsitz, J. (1984). *Successful schools for young adolescents.* New Brunswick, NJ: Transaction Books.

MacIver, D. J. (1990). Meeting the needs of young adolescents: Advisory groups, interdisciplinary teaching teams, and school transition programs. *Phi Delta Kappan, 71,* 458–464.

Making the middle grades work. (1988). Washington, DC: Children's Defense Fund.

National Adolescent Student Health Survey (NASHS) (1988). Highlights of the Survey. *Health Education, 19*(4), 4–8.

This we believe. (1982). Columbus, OH: National Middle School Association.

This we believe. (1992). Columbus, OH: National Middle School Association.

Turning points: Preparing American youth for the 21st century. (1989). Washington, DC: Carnegie Council on Adolescent Development.

What matters in the middle grades. (1989). Baltimore: Maryland State Department of Education, Maryland Task Force on the Middle Learning Years.

Wheelock, A., & Dorman, G. (1988). *Before it's too late.* Boston: Massachusetts Advocacy Center.

CHAPTER OUTLINE

The Evolving Middle Level School

2

OVERVIEW

This chapter deals with the circumstances and issues that led to the development of a school in the middle. A brief chronology of events and movements in the American educational tradition that have influenced the development of junior high schools and middle schools is presented. The junior high school and middle school are analyzed to determine the growth, purposes, and status of both movements. Contemporary efforts to implement specific "middle level" or "middle grade" practices that have been shown to assist young adolescents in meeting the challenges and demands they face in social and educational settings are examined.

The development of the junior high school and later the middle school focused on what constituted appropriate education for young adolescent learners. While there has been an evolving sentiment that the middle level school should be organized to meet the unique needs of the young adolescent and to provide a successful transition from childhood to adulthood, differences have arisen over how to attain these two purposes. These differences, currently and over time, have primarily centered on changing societal patterns and pressures, concerns for young adolescent learners, and curriculum reform and revision.

In this chapter, you will read about:

1 The two main purposes for establishing middle level schools.

2 The implications that changes in family life in the 1990s have for middle level education.
3 The main reasons for the emergence of the junior high school.
4 The six functions of the junior high school, as formulated by Gruhn and Douglass.
5 The reasons for disenchantment with the junior high school.
6 The influence of Eichhorn, Alexander, and others on the emergence of the middle school.
7 The impact of the *Turning Points* report on middle level education.
8 The significance of the National Middle School Association in the evolution of the middle school.
9 The ways that legislation in states such as Florida, Maryland, and California will affect middle grade education.
10 Some major problems and challenges confronting the middle level school.

THE FORCES INFLUENCING MIDDLE LEVEL EDUCATION

Significant social, philosophical, and curricular forces have influenced middle level education during the 100 years of its development. The middle level school has responded to an array of tumultuous social pressures, ranging from broadening the school program to include more students in the early decades of the twentieth century to providing a variety of at-risk programs in the 1990s to help students with deep and pervasive academic, social, personal, and health problems. Curriculum has been influenced by movements which promoted both the subject-centered and child-centered schools as well as cognitive and affective curricula. Child-centered movements have alternated with back-to-basics and academic reform movements. Throughout this century, advances in technology have impacted students, schools, families, and communities. Additionally, new knowledge about the learner and new concern for the learner as a person have entered the school program through behavioristic and humanistic programs. During this century, the watchword for middle level education has been *change.* The challenge has been to change schools so that they are responsive to the academic, social, and personal needs of young adolescents.

SOCIAL PATTERNS AND PRESSURES

From 1900 to World War II, the idealized American family was characterized by relatively stable and harmonious roles and relationships. The American family was the fundamental social unit, providing the primary social context for the child's care, support, socialization, nurturance, and self-esteem. The main functions of the school in this context were to provide an academic, liberal arts education for college-bound students and vocational preparation for students bound for the workplace. The school acted as an extension of the family to enhance the positive social and personal development of learners.

During this time only a relatively small percentage of American young people reached the junior high school and fewer still stayed in high school until graduation. There were high rates of failure in elementary (and junior high) school and substantial numbers of school dropouts from the high school program. The junior high was established to remedy some of these pressing educational problems. Over time, the junior high school was successful in reducing grade failure and dropouts by introducing stronger academic content programs as well as vocational and career programs. However, the junior high school, dominated by pressure from the high school, was slow to implement the changes that would enable the school to provide education appropriate to the developmental level of young adolescents.

Since 1945, and particularly in the last three decades, the social system has undergone sweeping modifications, especially in the area of the traditional American family structure. Based on trends in the 1970s and 1980s, Frost (1986) portrayed the family, social, and peer relationships that the typical American child (more than 50% of children) would experience in the year 1990. See Figure 2.1. An analysis of the Frost projections for teenagers reveals a disturbing pattern of abuse, alienation, drug use, delinquency, school failure and dropout, pregnancy, and suicide. At a time when young adolescents yearn for significant relationships with parents and other adults, the social network of family, community, school, and church is not effectively responding to the needs of young adolescents.

In addition to this unstable family context, the middle level school has been confronted with a host of challenges occasioned by the changing attitudes of

- The child will experience the divorce of his/her parents.
- The child will live in a one-parent family with the parent working outside of the home.
- The child will spend a lot of time alone.
- The child will watch a lot of television to the detriment of school achievement, physical fitness, and positive values development.
- The teenager will become a parent or have an abortion.
- The teenager will use one or more illicit drugs as well as alcohol and tobacco.
- The child will be subjected to abuse by his/her parents.
- The child will know someone who commits suicide.

FIGURE 2.1 Projections of the experiences of children and youth in 1990 *(Adapted from "Children in a Changing Society: Frontiers of Challenge" by J. L. Frost, 1986,* Childhood Education, 62, *pp. 242–249. Reprinted by permission of J. L. Frost and the Association for Childhood Education International, 11141 Georgia Avenue, Suite 200, Wheaton, MD. Copyright © 1986 by the Association.)*

children toward school, dramatic changes in social and personal values, a more liberated young adolescent subculture, increased socio-cultural diversity, and the "future shock" of technological development. In the United States, the public school has provided an accurate reflection of the values, needs, and demands of the total society, whether looking at the public schools from an historical perspective or from a contemporary context.

GROWING CONCERN FOR LEARNERS

The formative development of the public schools in the United States took its direction from changes and innovations that had occurred during the eighteenth and nineteenth centuries in Europe and the United States. In this country, beginning with Horace Mann and continuing through John Dewey, many American educators posited the notion that schools were for children. In the child-centered school, the needs, interests, and abilities of children were uppermost and curriculum and instruction were adapted to the child, instead of the opposite.

The twentieth century has witnessed significant developments in the knowledge of physical, emotional, social, and intellectual characteristics of emerging adolescents. The unique and original contributions of G. Stanley Hall in the study of the social, emotional, and mental characteristics of young people published in his acclaimed work *Adolescence* heralded a breakthrough in concern for the needs and interests of adolescents. Adolescence was seen as a period of dramatic change for individuals with significant implications for appropriate middle level schooling. Early studies of intelligence, learning, and psychology by Thorndike, Cattell, and others demonstrated the wide range of differences that could exist in the academic, social, and personal functioning of young adolescents in the middle grades. Their research gave renewed direction and dimension to freeing the schools from formalism in curriculum, instruction, and organization. In many instances, the schools did not capitalize on this research to make the changes that would have benefited the education of *all* the children attending school. For example, public schools continued to represent a traditional subject-matter curriculum, conventional teacher-directed instruction, and graded, structured organizational approaches. These practices often did not mesh with the needs, interests, and abilities of young adolescent learners.

Later research by Erikson, Havighurst, Piaget, Thornburg, and others presented new insights into stages of human development. Consequently, a new concern for developmentally appropriate education has emerged from an aggregate of socio-psychological factors typified by earlier sexual maturation, accelerated physical growth and development, new insights into cognitive development, and changing social attitudes, beliefs, and values within the family and peer groups. Lipsitz and Dorman (1985) have indicated that to be successful a middle level school should respond appropriately to specific developmental needs of young adolescents.

The humanistic movement emerging in the 1960s and represented by works of Kelley, *In Defense of Youth;* Maslow, *Toward a Psychology of Being;* Combs, *Perceiving, Behaving, Becoming;* and Rogers, *Freedom to Learn,* gave new impetus to learner-centered education. Middle school philosophy was aligned with the concern of these humanistic theorists for developing schools that would meet the personal, social, and emotional needs of young adolescents.

This new concern for young adolescent learners has evoked new purposes and functions for the middle level school. Given the problems and challenges confronting young people in contemporary American society, it is necessary for middle level schools to meet the educational and developmental needs of young adolescents in school settings and to attempt to provide experiences which are socially, emotionally, and intellectually satisfying.

CURRICULUM REFORM AND REVISION

Early in the twentieth century, the curriculum of the public school was focused on providing a college preparatory program for a relatively small number of students, and general education in basic skills for the majority. The elementary school, composed of grades 1–8, was the terminal school for most children. Few students went on to high school and still fewer to college. While several curriculum reform movements have punctuated public education during the first half of this century, the most noteworthy was Progressive Education (Squire, 1972). Progressive Education advocated that schools should be responsive to the needs, interests, and abilities of students. Curriculum would involve problem-solving experiences, social learning skills, and a variety of activities that were learner-centered and personally and socially relevant. The junior high school was in the vanguard of the Progressive Education movement.

Since World War II, various back-to-basics movements, the curriculum reforms that resulted from the former Soviet Union's launching of *Sputnik,* the educational programs of the Great Society for culturally disadvantaged learners, humanistic and open education, and the basic education/competency testing movement have caused significant and divergent changes in American public schools. The decade of the 1980s was characterized by increased regulation as state after state passed legislation which mandated what children would learn, how teachers would teach, how achievement would be measured, and what elements made a school effective. Currently, the school restructuring/decentralization movement is attempting to provide enhanced opportunities for interactive teaching and learning experiences for teachers and students. These curriculum reform efforts have had a pervasive influence on curriculum and instruction programs for the middle level years.

Some of the most challenging problems confronting the middle level school are related to developing responsive yet responsible curriculum, instruction, student services, and organization for the middle level student. While it has always been a high priority for most middle level educators to provide students with developmentally appropriate programs, events and issues of the last two to three decades have made it imperative. A wide range of concerns related to declining student achievement and behavior, changing student attitudes and values, and increased demands for personal and social freedom have emerged and demand proactive responses. Many young adolescents not only need help in adjusting and succeeding at school, but they also need help in getting along with their parents at home. Effective home–school relationships have become an integral feature of a responsive middle level school.

In summary, dramatic societal changes, new concerns for the young adolescent learner, and numerous and diverse curriculum reforms have served to exert a direct influence on education in the middle level years. These concerns either singly or in combination have caused substantial pendulum swings and fluctuations in the purposes and functions of junior high schools and middle schools. However, during the twentieth century, first the junior high school (1910 to the present) and later the middle school (1960 to the present) have attempted to implement the primary goals and functions that were viewed as important for young adolescents in the middle learning years.

The middle school, like its precursor the junior high school, was conceptualized to serve as a transition between elementary school and high school and to provide a program appropriate to the unique needs and interests of the young adolescent learner. The stated goals of exemplary middle schools corresponded closely to the goals stated for the junior high school by its advocates. That these goals were not perceived to have reached fruition in the junior high school was one of the paramount reasons for the emergence of the middle school. To understand more completely how and why middle level schooling emerged, one must examine the background of social and educational change in the United States in the twentieth century.

THE ORIGINS OF MIDDLE LEVEL SCHOOLING

Earlier we stated that the concept of an elementary school and secondary school had been established in the United States by the late nineteenth century. The school organization pattern was an eight-year elementary school and a four-year high school. This 8–4 pattern gave large numbers of students opportunities to obtain common schooling in basic skills and vocational training and gave a small, select student population formal academic preparation for college.

The next several decades were significant eras of reform and societal change in America. The reform movement dealt with the educational problems raised by more children attending school for a longer school year and a longer span of years in school. Due to protective legislation, students aged 10 to 14 who had previously worked in factories or on farms were required legally to remain in school. During this period (1900–1930), the high school became a legal tax-supported entity. Prior to 1920, because it served only a select group, high schools had developed a college preparatory pattern as the dominant curricular approach. However, industry and community leaders, highly critical of the single-track, academic, college-preparatory nature of the high school, began to demand curriculum options that would emphasize vocational preparation to accommodate more students. Finally, by 1910, there was growing concern that the eight-year elementary school did not provide a challenging and interesting curriculum for young adolescents. It was generally believed that many children did not drop out of school because of economic hardship, but because of a lack of interest in the program of study provided by the elementary school (Bossing & Cramer, 1964). A rationale and need for middle level schooling were growing in the society and the educational system.

THE JUNIOR HIGH SCHOOL EMERGES

At the turn of the twentieth century, a cadre of educational leaders published national reports and research investigations that focused attention on the emerging concept of a junior high school. During this time, the emphasis shifted from colleges and universities primarily setting the agenda for public school reform to public school educators examining the functions and relationships of the high school and the elementary school. The National Education Association (NEA), in concert with other prominent national educational leaders and groups, advocated restructuring the predominant 8–4 grade level organization to a pattern that would better meet the needs of young adolescents. The committees considered shortening the elementary school program in years and introducing more demanding academic content, such as physics, algebra, geometry, and foreign languages into grades 7 and 8 (Bossing & Cramer, 1964).

At this time, college and university leaders were concerned that students were enrolling in college at a later age and with inadequate academic preparation. Other educators were concerned with the schools' ability to keep students in school until their graduation. During this time, several studies investigated the problem of pupil attrition or elimination from school. Noteworthy studies conducted by Thorndike (1907), Ayres (1909), and Strayer (1911) found that (1) not more than 50% of students completed grade 8; (2) fewer than 10% of students graduated from high school; (3) attrition rates were highest in grades 7 and 8; (4) the number of students who were left back or dropped out varied from one city to another; and (5) the basic reason for the variation was to be found in the school curriculum. These studies argued that students from working-class and low-income families needed curriculum reforms that would attend to the vocational and academic needs of all young adolescents in grades 7–8, not just the needs of the college-bound (Bossing & Cramer, 1964).

During the decade 1910–1920, two monumental committees of the NEA made significant statements related to the school reorganization controversy that affected the status and conceptualization of the junior high school. The NEA Committee on Economy of Time in 1913 recommended a 6–3–3 reorganization plan, including a junior high school of three grade levels for 12- to 15-year-olds and a senior high school of three grade levels for 15- to 18-year-olds (Baker, 1913). In 1918, the NEA Commission on the Reorganization of Secondary

Education issued its landmark report, *Cardinal Principles of Secondary Education* (NEA, 1918). In this profound statement of purpose, the public schools declared their freedom from the domination of colleges and universities. The Commission recommended a 6–6 plan providing for six years of elementary and six years of secondary education. They further proposed a three-year junior high school encompassing grades 7 through 9 as a distinct feature of the secondary program. The functions were clearly delineated between the junior high school and senior high school by indicating that the junior high school provided for (1) a separately housed school containing grades 7, 8, and 9; (2) the needs, interests, and abilities of young adolescents; (3) prevocational and vocational training and career exploration; (4) educational and vocational guidance; and (5) departmentalization of subject matter (NEA, 1918). The junior high school consisting of grades 7–9 emerged out of the recommendations of these committees. Table 2.1 shows landmark events in the development of the junior high school, the first middle level school.

The concept of the middle level school emerged from the work of these commissions and has been refined over the years. The early reports, such as the *Cardinal Principles* (1918) and *Education for All American Youth* (1944) were broad statements representing the aims and goals that the society and the schools held for children to foster the total intellectual, social, emotional, and physical development of the child.

TABLE 2.1 The Early Development of Middle Level Schools

Date	Event	Outcome
1892	*Committee of Ten* met, chaired by Charles Eliot, President of Harvard University.	Recommended that grades 7–8 become part of secondary level.
1895	The Garfield School was established in Richmond, Indiana.	Was the first intermediate school (grades 7 and 8) especially for early adolescents.
1904	G. Stanley Hall published *Adolescence.*	Increased interest in adolescence as a developmental stage.
1909	Indianola Junior High School in Columbus, Ohio was established.	Was the first junior high school in the United States.
1910	Superintendent Frank Bunker established junior high schools in Berkeley, California.	Was the first school system to establish junior high schools.
1918	NEA Commission on the Reorganization of Secondary Education issued the *Cardinal Principles of Secondary Education.*	Identified the seven fundamental principles of secondary education and proposed a 6–3–3 grade level plan.
1920	Thomas Briggs and Leonard Koos published books about the junior high school.	Developed a theoretical rationale for the junior high school.

THE GROWTH OF THE JUNIOR HIGH SCHOOL: 1910 TO THE PRESENT

The junior high school was recognized as the appropriate school to meet the academic, vocational, and developmental needs of young adolescents. The first three-year junior high schools were instituted in Columbus, Ohio in 1909 and in Berkeley, California in 1910. Under the leadership of Superintendent Frank Bunker, the Berkeley school system reorganized its intermediate schools as "Introductory High Schools" consisting of grades 7, 8, and 9.

The early years of the junior high school movement were characterized by measured growth and a proliferation of different grade patterns and philosophical rationales. Due to the junior high school developing in so many diverse school systems and educational settings, the need arose for a clear definition of what determined a junior high school. The North Central Association of Colleges and Secondary Schools (1919) defined the junior high school as follows:

> A junior high school is a school in which the seventh, eighth, and ninth grades are segregated in a building (or portion of a building) by themselves, possess an organization and administration of their own that is distinct from the grades above and below, and are taught by a separate corps of teachers (p. 4).

There were three distinct phases in the development of the junior high school. In the 1920s, the junior high school entered into the third phase of its development. Phase one had introduced a stronger academic curriculum to grades 7 and 8 to provide students with better preparation for college. Phase two attempted to hold students in school more effectively by continuing academic preparation and by introducing vocational courses in order to prepare students for college and/or the workplace. Phases one and two coexisted as curriculum emphases and merged into phase three, which focused on meeting the unique developmental characteristics of young adolescents. The next 30 years of the movement were occupied with efforts to accomplish the institutional aims and goals of the junior high school (Perlstein & Tobin, 1988).

The junior high school fostered substantive improvements in the education of young adolescents through programs which helped to ease two pressing school problems attributed to the 8–4 school organization: the inadequate preparation of students for high school and college, and the high rate of student dropouts during grades 7–9. Noteworthy contributions of the junior high school were provision for (1) the core curriculum with its emphasis on integrated, unified, and exploratory study; (2) socialization experiences such as intramurals, clubs, and extracurricular activities; and (3) guidance services. While junior high schools were not completely successful in establishing curriculum and instruction developmentally appropriate for young adolescents, they did achieve many of the original purposes of middle level schooling by serving as a transitional school between the elementary school and the high school.

DISENCHANTMENT WITH JUNIOR HIGH SCHOOLS

During the 1960s, questions arose whether the junior high school was serving the needs and interests of young adolescents. Over the next decade, debate over these concerns would result in reorganization and reform of the junior high school and the emergence of the middle school. The Association for Supervision and Curriculum Development (ASCD) provided leadership in examining directions for the junior high school. The ASCD undertook a study entitled *The Junior High School We Need.* They proposed that the junior high school needed to consider the inclusion of the sixth grade in the junior high school grade pattern, while returning the ninth grade to the high school (ASCD Commission, 1961).

Historically, the high school had tended to dominate the junior high school. The ninth-grade program was tied to the college preparatory program, which placed emphasis on mastery of such content as mathematics and science. At the same time, the junior high school program was also expected to provide comprehensive offerings in industrial arts, fine arts, and home economics. Emphasis on social activities such as dating, dances, and clubs also reflected the influence of the high school, as did interscholastic athletic programs, marching bands, and academic honor societies.

Critics claimed that all of these manifestations of a high school program depersonalized the junior high school. Additionally, educators pointed out that earlier maturation and sophistication of adolescents suggested that sixth graders were more compatible with seventh and eighth graders than with upper elementary children. Also, ninth-grade students were felt to have more in common with high school students. While not all these generalized criticisms could be applied uniformly to the junior high school, they did represent a growing disenchantment with the junior high school and an emergent rationale for modifying middle level schooling.

In this climate, the middle school emerged essaying to maintain the gains and progress made by junior high schools while focusing attention more closely on the unique needs of young adolescents. The link between the junior high school and the middle school in their shared concern for the needs of young adolescents was traced by Wiles and Bondi (1986) in *The Essential Middle School* as follows:

> The middle school of the 1980s has emerged from the junior high school. Ironically, the stated goals of the middle school today are exactly the goals espoused for the junior high school when it began in 1910. These goals are to provide a transitional school between the elementary school and the high school and to help students bridge the gap in their development between childhood and adolescence. (p. 1)

For more than 50 years the junior high school movement established the agenda for middle level school reform and innovation. In retrospect, the junior high school was the first middle level school and is part of the ongoing development of middle level education for the 1990s and beyond.

THE BEGINNING OF THE MIDDLE SCHOOL MOVEMENT: 1960 TO THE PRESENT

In America, the middle school movement can trace its historical roots back to the junior high school. Eichhorn pointed out that the middle school movement was not new but a 70-year-old concept rededicated to the idea that the school in the middle should be designed for youngsters in transition from childhood to adolescence (ASCD, 1974). Outstanding middle or junior high schools have one common curriculum designed for the transescent learner, the learner between childhood and adolescence. Alexander observed that while there has not always been agreement about curriculum, instruction, and organization in the middle school movement, its emphasis on the transition from childhood to adolescence gives the movement purpose and significance (ASCD, 1974).

The middle school as a learner-centered alternative to the junior high school developed rapidly from the 1960s to the 1980s. The middle school philosophies of educators such as Donald Eichhorn, William Alexander, John Lounsbury, Gordon Vars, Paul George, Jon Wiles, Joseph Bondi, Joan Lipsitz, and others helped the burgeoning middle school movement to gain headway as an alternative to or modification of the academic focus of junior high school education. Much writing and research during these years emphasized identifying the characteristics, functions, and purposes that typified exemplary middle school practice. The next stage was to modify existing school practices and implement the innovative ideas and programs that characterized the best middle school practice.

THE EXEMPLARY MIDDLE SCHOOL

Eichhorn. In 1966, Eichhorn published *The Middle School,* which greatly influenced the growing middle school movement. In this book, Eichhorn established a theoretical rationale for the middle school on a socio-psychological model of young adolescent behavior. He theorized a learning environment allowing middle school students as much flexibility as the institutional setting could tolerate and still provide for student safety, welfare, and academic performance. The learning environment of the middle school was shaped by three guideposts: (1) the physical development and (2) the mental growth of young adolescents, and (3) the effect of socio-cultural forces on the development of young adolescents.

Eichhorn reviewed the reasons for the rapid rise of the middle school. He suggested that for some educators the middle school movement was simply a convenient excuse to erect new buildings or to achieve racial balance. For others, the rationale for the middle school was concern for young adolescents. Eichhorn suggested that there were three reasons for middle schools. One was the growing body of research relating to characteristics of young people in late childhood and early adolescence that reaffirmed the principle of their uniqueness, espoused by early junior high school leaders. The fact that biological maturation was occurring at an earlier age added to this factor. Second, significant changes in our culture, including population shifts, population mobility, the issue of racial equality, developments in transportation and communication, and the forces involved in a developing technology, prompted reconsideration of school buildings as well as organizational patterns. Third, there was a growing realization that schools in the middle had become rigid and institutionalized. A variety of developing educational concepts such as continuous progress, flexible schedules, nongraded classes, interdisciplinary curriculum, and team teaching appeared more likely to succeed in a revised grade framework (ASCD, 1974).

Alexander. Alexander et al. (1968) published *The Emergent Middle School,* which became the most influential book in the early middle school movement. Alexander et al. saw the middle school as a new and emergent entity, not just a reorganized junior high school. The emergent middle school was "a phase and program of schooling bridging but differing from the childhood and adolescent phases and programs" (p. 5). The authors defined three major reasons for the middle school. The first was to focus on the individual. For middle school students, this meant recognizing the ways middle schoolers differed from the children in elementary school and the adolescents in high school, and also the great diversity within the middle school student population. The second reason was to provide greater continuity of education for students throughout their school careers. The third reason was to accelerate the change process in education. The principle underlying the change process was the folk wisdom that it was easier to innovate in a new school setting than in the old one (Alexander, 1969).

THE NATIONAL MIDDLE SCHOOL ASSOCIATION

The National Middle School Association (NMSA) was established in 1973 to promote changes in middle level education. NMSA has served as a clearinghouse for educators and parents interested in the educational and developmental needs of young adolescents. The Association, through its publication *Middle School Journal,* the work of affiliated state and local associations, and its annual conference, has been in the forefront of research and scholarly writing on numerous areas essential to the implementation of exemplary middle level school practice.

This We Believe. In 1982, NMSA advanced a set of comprehensive resolutions, *This We Believe,* which established a rationale for the middle school. Middle school education is rooted in concern for human development and related principles of school learning. The challenge of the middle school is to develop a program responsive to the needs and characteristics of a unique and diverse student population. The NMSA considered the following items to be the essential elements of a "true" middle school.

1. *Educators knowledgeable about and committed to transescents.* Educators should want to teach this age group and should develop understanding of transescents.

2 *A balanced curriculum based on transescent needs.* Academic goals and developmental needs are balanced.
3 *A range of organizational arrangements.* Middle schools should utilize a variety of organization patterns, adaptable to students' needs.
4 *Varied instructional strategies.* Different methods of instruction should be used to address the unique characteristics of this age learner.
5 *A full exploratory program.* The dramatic changes in physical, social, and emotional development call for provision of short, intense, interest-based activities.
6 *Comprehensive advising and counseling.* Transescent learners have a real need for intensive and extensive guidance assistance. Each learner needs an adult who knows him/her well and can render individual attention. Home-based or advisor–advisee programs are typical advisement approaches.
7 *Continuous progress for students.* Due to wide ranges in development and achievement, students need to progress at their own rates, according to their own learning styles, and appropriate to their own developmental characteristics.
8 *Evaluation procedures compatible with the nature of transescents.* Evaluation of pupil progress, grading, and reporting to parents should help students understand aspects of their academic performance, social competence, and personal development.
9 *Cooperative planning.* Interdisciplinary subject area teams, teachers from other subject areas, and teachers and pupils should plan together to provide a developmentally appropriate curriculum.
10 *Positive school climate.* The total environment of the school should be one of warmth, caring, respect, purpose, harmony, and interdependence. (pp. 10–16)

These ten characteristics are presented as essential to the development of a responsive and responsible middle school. While other factors contribute to a positive and effective school setting, these are instrumental to an exemplary middle school. It is important not to treat these ten elements as discrete. Each element influences all of the others, either beneficially or detrimentally. School personnel, students, parents, and persons in the community must also integrate their abilities, competencies, and concerns in collaborative efforts to provide middle schools responsive to the developmental needs of young adolescents (*This We Believe,* 1982).

The National Middle School Association (NMSA) reaffirmed in *This We Believe* (1992) that the middle level school must respond to the needs of young adolescents in contemporary society. The guidelines are future-oriented, and the NMSA retained the essential attributes of a good, effective middle level school. The mandate facing middle level educators is to implement as responsibly and responsively as possible what is believed to be the best school practice. The NMSA has been a lighthouse association, providing leadership to educators through its advocacy of the needs of young adolescents.

General agreement developed among the leading proponents of the middle school concept regarding the essential characteristics of a middle school. Over time, characteristics that distinguished exemplary middle schools became evident in school practice, in the professional literature, and in research in middle level education. The middle school consisting of grades 6–8 emerged as a new institution for middle level schooling. Table 2.2 shows some of the important events of the later development of middle level schools.

THE GROWTH OF THE MIDDLE SCHOOL

The middle school emerged during some of the most sweeping changes yet seen in American education. Many middle schools were established or reconstituted, more for administrative reasons than educational or philosophical reasons—to

TABLE 2.2 The Later Development of Middle Level Schools

Date	Event	Outcome
1950	Bay City, Michigan established the first middle school.	Middle school concepts in curriculum, instruction, and organization were implemented.
1966	Donald Eichhorn published *The Middle School.*	This book pioneered the middle school movement.
1968	William Alexander et al. published *The Emergent Middle School.*	This book significantly influenced the emerging middle school.
1969	Boyce Medical Study conducted at Boyce Middle School in Upper St. Clair, Pennsylvania.	Developmental grouping was established at Boyce Middle School based on the findings of the study.
1973	National Middle School Association was organized.	The NMSA has been a strong advocate of the middle school concept.
1980	National Society for Study of Education published *Toward Adolescence: The Middle School Years.*	This yearbook represented the definitive compilation of research on the middle school.
1982	National Middle School Association committee issued *This We Believe.*	This position paper established a rationale and definition of middle schools.
1984	Florida enacted the PRIME Program.	Comprehensive legislation assured the utilization of essential middle school ideas shown by research to make a difference.
1986	NASSP issued *An Agenda for Excellence.*	This noteworthy statement established goals and objectives for middle level education.
1987	California Middle Grades Task Force issued the report, *Caught in the Middle.*	This comprehensive report made specific recommendations to implement the essential middle grades concept in California schools.
1989	Carnegie Council on Adolescent Development issued *Turning Points.*	This report developed eight guiding principles for preparing American youth for the 21st century.

resolve problems of overcrowding and understaffed classrooms, to move the ninth grade to the high school, and to enforce racial integration. The theoretical, educational reasons for the middle school, such as transition between elementary and secondary levels and implementation of innovative programs appropriate for transescent learners, received less emphasis. Consequently, many middle schools simply moved the junior high school structure, program, and schedule down a grade or two, thus perpetuating some of the secondary level characteristics, such as departmentalization, academic emphasis, and socialization pressures, that middle school advocates maintained were inappropriate for emerging adolescent learners (ASCD, 1974).

In recent years, there have been vigorous efforts to reverse the above tendencies by implementing the middle school concept in school districts throughout the United States. Each year the number of middle schools has increased in proportion to other patterns of middle level organization. In a survey of 130 exemplary middle schools, George and Oldaker found that middle school organization positively affected student achievement and personal development, learning climate, faculty morale, staff development, and parental involvement. These middle schools, to a high degree, utilized interdisciplinary teams, block scheduling, exploratory activities, home-based periods and teacher–advisor arrangements, and programs generally adapted to the nature of middle school learners (George & Oldaker, 1986).

Observation, evaluation, and research were identifying significant relationships between certain middle school concepts and positive student academic, social, and personal development. Certainly, there were middle schools and junior high schools incorporating these essential components that were providing excellent learning opportunities for the learners they served. The challenge for those charged with leadership in the area of middle level schools was to continue the work started by practitioner and theorist leaders in the junior high and middle school movements to provide the best possible school for young adolescent learners. Research findings, national reports, state initiatives, and exemplary middle school practice have begun to focus on academically effective and developmentally appropriate education for all young adolescents, whether in middle schools or junior high schools. The trend in American education is to focus on learners in middle grades or in the middle level rather than on the institutions of junior high or middle school.

In the 1980s, the middle level school movement, which had originated in the philosophy and purposes of the junior high school and which had branched into an emergent middle school emphasizing the overall development of young adolescents, culminated in a movement that included both types of schools in the concept of middle level schooling. The work of national associations, national research centers, state departments of education, college and university educators, and national commissions all contributed to this notion of seeing the junior high and/or middle school in a new light. The findings, reports, and recommendations of these interested and committed parties advocating middle level schools are discussed throughout this book.

ISSUES AND CHALLENGES FACING MIDDLE LEVEL SCHOOLS

NATIONAL REACTION

In the early 1980s, a number of national task forces and educational groups studied the condition of American education. The reports generated by these groups, such as *A Nation at Risk* and *A Place Called School,* were generally critical of American school practice and performance. *A Nation at Risk* recommended more rigorous standards for basic skills mastery, enriched/accelerated academic curricula, teacher preparation and certification, high school graduation, and many other standardizing requirements (National Commission on Excellence in Education, 1983). John Goodlad, in *A Place Called School,* attempted to provide a holistic understanding of the school. Goodlad and his research team examined the essential aspects of schools and rendered interpretations of the quantities of descriptive data they gathered. The thrust of their recommendations was that educational improvement can best emerge within each individual school (Goodlad, 1983). These recommendations, in concert with equally stringent requirements from several other national reports, exerted enormous pressure on middle level schools. Table 2.3 summarizes some reports that have influenced middle level schooling in the 1980s.

TABLE 2.3 National Reform Reports

Title	Date	Author/Group	Recommendations
A Place Called School	1982	John Goodlad	Establish common core curriculum from the "five fingers" of knowledge and experience: (1) literature and language, (2) math and science, (3) society and social studies, (4) the arts, (5) vocations.
A Nation at Risk	1983	National Commission on Excellence in Education	Raise standards for graduation emphasizing five contemporary basics. Advocate a longer school day or longer school year.
Action for Excellence	1983	Education Commission of the States	Improve curriculum and instruction at all levels. Mastery of basic skills. Programs for gifted and talented.
American Memory	1988	National Endowment for the Humanities	Assure that humanities continue to be stressed in American public schools in face of push for math, science, and technology.
The Forgotten Half	1988	W.T. Grant Foundation Commission on Work, Family, and Citizenship	Introduce success programs for young people who are not likely to attend college.
Turning Points	1989	Carnegie Council on Adolescent Development	Reform middle level education through the collaboration of all agencies and people involved in educating young adolescents.

Lively debate has resulted over how to improve the quality of American schools, including middle level schools. Concurrent with these national pressures and concerns has been a gradual shift of the locus of control from the local district or school to the state level, as state after state has passed regulatory legislation impacting on curriculum and instruction, teacher preparation and certification, and pupil and program evaluation. The clamor for increased accountability for teacher and pupil performance presented a serious challenge to the middle level school to continue its efforts to maintain and improve educational experiences for young adolescents.

STATE INITIATIVES

The latter half of the 1980s may prove to be one of the most important periods of innovation and change in the history of middle level schooling. During those years, concerns for the middle level school occupied a prominent position at the state and national level. Many states passed legislation directed toward enhancing the middle level. States also designated task force groups to study such aspects of middle level schools as at-risk students, advisor–advisee groups, teacher certification, interdisciplinary organization, and other essential areas. Though significant programs were initiated in many states, task force groups in Florida, California, and Maryland conducted studies, made recommendations, and enacted legislation that strongly illustrated the extent and diversity of the middle level movement. The programs developed in these three states could serve as models for other states in addressing the needs of middle level education. Brief descriptions of some of the most innovative state initiatives are contained in Table 2.4.

NATIONAL ASSOCIATIONS

National Middle School Association. Nationally, middle level reform was called for by national associations, national research centers, and task force commissions. Founded in 1973, the National Middle School Association (NMSA) has been an eloquent and effective advocate of a student-centered middle level school. It has been the most consistent source for implementation guidelines, descriptive monographs, and research studies relating to middle level education.

National Association of Secondary School Principals. Additionally, the National Association of Secondary School Principals (NASSP) has made important contributions to middle level education through its publications, study groups, staff development programs, and research reports. The NASSP Middle Level Task Force submitted an evocative call for doing what is right for all middle level students in its report, *An Agenda for Excellence at the Middle Level* (1985). The authors, Alfred Arth, J. Howard Johnston, John Lounsbury, and Conrad Toep-

TABLE 2.4 Selected State Initiatives in Middle Level Education

State	Date	Report	Recommendations
Florida	1984	*The Forgotten Years* PRIME	Provided philosophy and goals for middle level education in (1) organization, (2) curriculum, (3) student support services and teacher education. Enhancement objectives to facilitate development of good middle school practice were enacted.
California	1987	*Caught in the Middle*	Addressed 22 guiding principles of middle level education in (1) curriculum and instruction, (2) student potential, (3) organization, (4) teaching, (5) leadership and partnership. State-of-the-art foundation and partnership schools identified.
Virginia	1989	*Restructuring Education in the Middle School Grades*	Restructured to attain goals of positive self-esteem, meaningful learning and achievement and successful transition. State-of-the-art Vanguard schools were identified.
New York	1989	*Regents Challenge For Excellence in Middle Level Education Programs*	Recommended ten goals for middle level education with academic and personal/social focus. Accountability system to attain excellence. *Challenge for Excellence Schools* were selected to implement innovative middle level school practices.
Maryland	1989	*What Matters in the Middle Grades*	Promoted mission statement and developmental characteristics of early adolescents. Recommendations organized around seven key questions, such as self-concept, curriculum and instruction, and student support.

fer, Jr., examined the dimensions necessary for excellence and suggested a blueprint for serious, responsive, and priority action to design and implement the programs necessary for successful schools for young adolescents.

An Agenda for Excellence proposed significant changes in the way we educate young adolescents. The dimensions addressed steps to be taken at the school level to improve curriculum, instruction, teachers, school climate, community connections, student services, and student learning. While it contained many of the characteristics of previous statements of middle school philosophy, *An Agenda for Excellence* was particularly valuable because it broadened the base of middle level schooling, recommended specific implementation strategies, and invoked a sense of urgency for the cause of reform.

RESEARCH CENTERS

The National Middle School Resource Center, first located in Indianapolis, Indiana, and now housed at the University of South Florida in Tampa, has conducted surveys, action research projects, and studies on issues and concerns in middle school education. Additionally, by functioning as a clearinghouse for innovations in middle school education, the center has provided impetus for reform and innovation for the middle school movement.

The Center for Research on Elementary and Middle Schools (CREMS) at Johns Hopkins University has conducted substantive research in middle school organization, cooperative learning, patterns of grouping for instruction, advisory groups, and interdisciplinary teams. Research monographs are published on a regular basis and disseminated to schools and agencies throughout the nation and world.

In 1988, the center conducted a national survey of middle grade principals to determine the status of the education of young adolescents in the United States. Their findings, *Education in the Middle Grades: A National Survey of Practices and Trends,* were reported in a special section on middle schools in *Phi Delta Kappan* in February, 1990. Epstein and MacIver (1990) published a monograph which summarized the findings of their comprehensive 1986 survey of 2,400 middle grade principals. The findings of the national survey and other research conducted by this center hold great promise for determining best middle grade school practice and disseminating that practice to middle grade schools throughout the nation (*Phi Delta Kappan,* 1990).

The Center for Early Adolescence at the University of North Carolina at Chapel Hill has conducted research on literacy programs, at-risk students, effective school practices, and parent involvement programs. One of the most significant efforts of the center is the development by Gayle Dorman (1985) of the *Middle Grades Assessment Program* (MGAP) to guide middle level schools in self-assessment and improvement. The MGAP utilized information about early adolescence and effective schools research in conjunction with interviews and observations in schools to conduct an assessment of the total school program.

Gayle Dorman and Joan Lipsitz, in their research at the Center for Early Adolescence, proposed that middle schools should be safe and secure settings, academically effective, and responsive to the developmental needs of young adolescents. The developmental needs included in the MGAP are described in Figure 2.2.

The emphasis of the MGAP was on the developmental needs of learners rather than the middle school as an institution. The MGAP provides interviews, observations, and assessment strategies that measure the academic effectiveness and developmental responsiveness of a school. The MGAP has proven to be an effective instrument for schools to use to conduct self-assessment and initiate self-improvement.

TURNING POINTS

One of the most influential and compelling reports of the 1980s, *Turning Points: Preparing American Youth for the 21st Century,* gained national attention with its sweeping recommendations for middle level school reform. *Turning Points* made a powerful impact because it not only addressed the school needs of young adolescents, but evinced concern for the total lives of young adolescents—their

The need for diversity. Young adolescents need diversity in their academic, personal, and social lives. They need different types of learning experiences and different relationships with many different types of people.

The need for self-exploration and self-definition. Young adolescents need chances to explore and define who they are, what they believe, what they can do, and what they want to be.

The need for meaningful participation in school and community. This is a time in which young adolescents are beginning to think beyond themselves. They want to take part in their functioning social systems at school, in the family, and in the community.

The need for positive social interactions with both peers and adults. Young adolescents desire relationships with peers, parents, teachers, and other adults.

The need for physical activity. Young adolescents need physical activity. The home-school setting should be flexible enough to accommodate these diverse physical needs.

The need for competence and achievement. Young adolescents need opportunities for success which enable them to counter feelings of low self-esteem with feelings of competence and achievement.

The need for structure and clear limits. At a time when young adolescents are experiencing needs for independence, freedom, and self-regulation, they have a definite need for structure and limits.

FIGURE 2.2 Developmental needs of young adolescents *(From* Middle Grades Assessment Program *(pp. 10–13) by G. Dorman, 1985, Carrboro, NC: University of North Carolina, Center for Early Adolescence. Copyright 1985 by the Center for Early Adolescence. Adapted by permission.)*

health, welfare, self-esteem, and sense of purpose. The report called for the school to coordinate the services and resources of all agencies and institutions to meet the critical needs of young adolescents.

The goal of the *Turning Points* (1989) task force appointed by the Carnegie Corporation was to determine the qualities that would characterize a 15-year-old who had been well served during adolescence. The task force concluded that this 15-year-old would be:

- an intellectually reflective person
- a person en route to a lifetime of meaningful work
- a good citizen
- a caring and ethical individual
- a healthy person. (p. 15)

The task force presented a disturbing description of the significant choices facing young adolescents in America today. The early adolescence period was portrayed as a turning point—an opportunity for young people to make significant decisions that would have important consequences for their scholastic lives and their adult futures. Many young people handle this transition period very effectively. However, many young adolescents will get further and further behind.

Turning Points presented recommendations to modify the educational experiences of middle grade students. The task force urged that the following guiding principles for middle grade schools and services would benefit all young adolescents and would greatly help at-risk students.

1 *Create small communities for learning.* These settings would promote close, positive relationships with peers and adults as essential ingredients for personal, social, and intellectual development. The organizational patterns of the schools are schools-within-schools or house plan arrangements, interdisciplinary team organization, and small-group advising teams that ensure that each student is known well by at least one adult.

2 *Teach a core academic program.* This program would emphasize studies resulting in students who are literate, can think critically, lead healthy lives, behave ethically, and assume the roles and responsibilities of citizenship.

3 *Ensure success for all students.* The middle level school would become a success-oriented school by eliminating tracking based on achievement testing, by establishing cooperative learning programs, by maximizing resources for teachers, and by stressing flexibility in instruction, organization, and schedules.

4 *Empower teachers and administrators to make decisions about the experiences of middle grade students.* The people directly charged with instructing middle grade students, namely teachers and principals, must be given greater control and responsibility for creating learning settings responsive to the developmental needs of young adolescents.

5 *Staff middle grade schools with teachers who are expert at teaching young adolescents.* Certification, preparation, and professional development programs must be established to prepare teachers who want to teach young adolescents, are knowledgeable about them, and are competent to teach them.

6 *Improve academic performance through fostering the health and fitness of young adolescents.* The physical, social, and emotional health of young adolescents is an important priority of middle level education. Each middle level school should have a health coordinator, counseling services, and a school climate that promotes positive mental, physical, and emotional health.

7 *Reengage families in the education of young adolescents.* Schools should seek to promote parent involvement in and commitment to the school program through greater responsibilities for school governance, open communication concerning his/her child's performance, and opportunities to support his/her child's learning at home and at school.

8 *Connect schools with communities.* The middle level school must foster relationships with the total community that provide students with opportunities for community service. School-community-business partnerships need to be established to provide students with access to community health and social

services and with opportunities for meaningful interaction with business and community entities (*Turning Points,* 1989).

Turning Points encouraged state governments to build consensus at the state level and in local communities for making a major effort to improve middle level schools. Specifically, it requested every state superintendent of education or governor to convene statewide task forces to review its recommendations and determine their implications. *Turning Points* has resulted in a great deal of activity at many levels in the cause of middle grade education because of the comprehensive nature of the report and of the eloquent evocation of the futures and fateful choices facing 10- to 15-year-olds in American society. Additionally, the Carnegie Corporation made funds available to states through middle grades initiative grants to study the status of young adolescents and publish task-force reports containing specific recommendations for improving middle grade education in each state.

Turning Points was an important document, not only because of what it said and what it dreamed, but because of the commission that issued the report. The task force, with the imprint of the Carnegie Corporation, has the reputation, clout, and resources to galvanize action to make the 1990s a turning point in the way we educate and care for young adolescents.

Much energy, enthusiasm, and expertise from many different educational sources—colleges and universities, state departments of education, national associations and commissions, and middle level schools—have been focused on implementing developmentally and academically appropriate middle level schools. Thus, the mandate facing junior high schools and middle schools is related to their responsiveness to the demands of society and, more importantly, to the changing needs of young adolescents. We need the middle level school for tomorrow, today. The rich promise inherent in middle level schools must become a reality in the lives of young adolescents.

SUMMARY

In this chapter, we have examined the issues and movements that resulted in the development of middle level schools. The emergence of junior high schools and then middle schools from the context of the American educational tradition was analyzed. The functions and characteristics of exemplary junior high schools and middle schools were delineated. The challenge facing American schools resulting from basics education, effective schools, and competency testing were discussed along with the implications of these movements for middle level schools. The debate over which is better, middle school or junior high school, has to an extent been resolved by new emphasis on "middle level" or "middle grade" as being responsive to and responsible for whatever grades are housed in the school in the middle. The development of a school in the middle has been an abiding concern of educators for most of the twentieth century. In all likelihood, some of the persistent problems will remain in the year 2001, but there are fresh stirrings of reform that hold great promise for middle level education.

■ ■ ■

EXPLORATION

1 March 8–14, 1987 was the first celebration of National Middle Level Education Week. As you read this chapter and this book, list the concerns, issues, trends, programs, etc. that you feel would form the agenda for National Middle Level Education Week in your community and state.

2 Prepare a case study for an exemplary middle level school. You name the school, prepare a rationale statement, and list the recommendations that you want the school to represent. Be prepared to continue this case study throughout the rest of the book.

3 There are all types and names of middle level schools. Do a brief historical study of a middle level school in your community to trace its development, name changes, current status, etc.

4 Compare and contrast the recommendations and legislation in states such as Maryland, California, Virginia, and your own state. Specify ways that they are or are not true to middle level philosophy and purposes.

5 In *Phi Delta Kappan* (March 1990), Gene Maeroff provides "A Close Look at a Good Middle School." What elements does he suggest make this school good? Briefly describe why you agree or disagree with his assessment.

6 In this chapter, we discussed reasons for disenchantment with junior high schools. Are you aware of any disenchantment with middle schools? If yes, be able to specify some criticisms of middle schools.

SUGGESTED READINGS

Eichhorn, D. H. (1966). *The Middle School.* New York: Center for Applied Research in Education.

This early classic in the development of the middle school provided insights into organizing schools based on developmental needs of "transescents."

Epstein, J. L., & MacIver, D. J. (1990). *Education in the Middle Grades: Overview of National Practices and Trends.* Columbus, OH: National Middle School Association.

This monograph summarized the comprehensive survey of 2,400 middle grades principals conducted by the Center for Research on Elementary and Middle Grades at Johns Hopkins University.

Fenwick, J. (1986). *The Middle School Years.* San Diego: Fenwick Associates.

This book presents an analysis of the status and direction of middle level schools.

Lounsbury, J. H. (Ed.). (1984). *Perspectives: Middle School Education, 1964–1984.* Columbus, OH: National Middle School Association.

Leading authorities on middle level education document the middle school movement and discuss curriculum, organization, instruction, and other areas.

Maryland Task Force on the Middle Learning Years. (1989). *What Matters in the Middle Grades.* Baltimore: Maryland State Department of Education.

This report contained recommendations for making middle grades education emanate from the characteristics and needs of young adolescents.

Perlstein, D., & Tobin, W. (1988). *The History of the Junior High School: A Study of Conflicting Aims and Institutional Patterns.* Washington, DC: Carnegie Council on Adolescent Development.

This paper analyzed and updated the junior high school movement. The authors extended the theory that the junior high school never found its niche, due to conflicting aims, purposes, and patterns of organization.

Turning Points: Preparing American Youth for the 21st Century. (1989). Washington, DC: Carnegie Council on Adolescent Development.

This report is an eloquent statement of the uncertain future of young adolescents in America and an urgent call for establishing schools to meet the academic, social, and personal needs of young people. This report was prepared by the Carnegie Council on Adolescent Development Task Force on Education of Young Adolescents. The Carnegie Council is a program of the Carnegie Corporation of New York.

REFERENCES

Action for excellence. (1983). Atlanta, GA: Education Commission of the States.

Alexander, W., Williams, E., Compton, M., Hines, V., Prescott, D., and Kealy, R. (1969). *The emergent middle school.* New York: Holt, Rinehart and Winston.

American memory. (1988). Washington, DC: National Endowment for the Humanities.

Association for Supervision and Curriculum Development. (1961). *Middle school in the making.* Washington, DC: ASCD.

Ayres, L. P. (1909). *Laggards in our schools.* New York: Russell Sage Foundation.

Baker, J. (1913). *Economy of time in education.* Report of the Committee of the National Council of Education. Washington, DC: U. S. Bureau of Education, Bulletin No. 38, 1913.

Bossing, N., & Cramer, R. (1964). *The junior high school.* Boston: Houghton Mifflin.

Carnegie Council on Adolescent Development (1989). *Turning points: Preparing American youth for the 21st century.* Washington, DC: Author.

Caught in the middle: Educational reform for young adolescents in California public schools. (1987). Sacramento: California State Department of Education, Middle Grades Task Force.

Combs, A. W. (Ed.). (1962). *Perceiving, behaving, becoming.* Yearbook. Washington, DC: Association for Supervision and Curriculum Development.

Commission on the Education of Adolescence. (1961). *The junior high school we need.* Washington, DC: Association for Supervision and Curriculum Development.

Commission on Work, Family and Citizenship. (1988). *The forgotten half.* Washington, DC: W. T. Grant Foundation.

Dorman, G. (1985). *Middle grades assessment program.* Carrboro, NC: University of North Carolina, Center for Early Adolescence.

Educational Policies Commission. (1944). *Education for all American youth.* Washington, DC: National Education Association.

Eichhorn, D. (1966). *The middle school.* New York: The Center for Applied Research in Education.

Florida Progress in Middle Childhood Education Program (PRIME). (1984). §§230.2319

Frost, J. L. (1986). Children in a changing society. *Childhood Education, 62,* 242–249.

George, P. A., & Oldaker, L. (1986). A national survey of middle school effectiveness. *Educational Leadership, 43*(4), 79–85.

Goodlad, J. (1983). *A place called school.* New York: McGraw-Hill.

Gruhn, W., & Douglass, H. (1971). *The modern junior high school.* New York: Ronald Press.

Hall, G. S. (1904). *Adolescence* (2 vols.). New York: Appleton Co.

Kelley, E. C. (1962). *In defense of youth.* Englewood Cliffs, NJ: Prentice-Hall.

Maeroff, G. I. (1990). Getting to know a good middle school: Shoreham-Wading River. *Phi Delta Kappan, 71*(7), 505–511.

Maslow, A. M. (1962). *Toward a psychology of being.* New York: D. VanNostrand.

National Association of Secondary School Principals Council on Middle Level Education. (1985). *An agenda for excellence at the middle level.* Reston, VA: NASSP.

National Commission on Excellence in Education. (1983). *A nation at risk.* Washington, DC: U. S. Government Printing Office.

National Education Association. (1918). *Cardinal principles of secondary education. Report of the commission on the reorganization of secondary education.* Washington, DC: U. S. Bureau of Education, Bulletin No. 35.

North Central Association. (1919). *Bulletin.* North Central Association of Colleges and Secondary Schools.

Perlstein, D., & Tobin, W. (1988). *The history of the junior high school: A study of conflicting aims and institutional patterns.* Washington, DC: Carnegie Council on Adolescent Development.

Phi Delta Kappan. (1990). *71*(6), 435–469.

Regents challenge for excellence in middle level education programs. (1989). Albany, NY: New York State Department of Education.

Restructuring education in middle school grades. (1989). Richmond, VA: Virginia State Department of Education.

Rogers, C. R. (1969). *Freedom to learn.* Columbus, OH: Merrill.

Squire, J. R. (Ed.). (1972). *A new look at progressive education.* Washington, DC: Association for Supervision and Curriculum Development.

Strayer, G. D. (1911). *Age and grade census of schools and colleges: A study of retardation and elimination.* Washington, DC: U. S. Bureau of Education, Bulletin No. 5.

The forgotten years. (1984). Tallahassee, FL: Florida State Department of Education.

This we believe. (1982). Columbus, OH: National Middle School Association.

Thorndike, E. L. (1907). *The elimination of pupils from school.* Washington, DC: U. S. Bureau of Education, Bulletin No. 4.

Turning points: Preparing American youth for the 21st century. (1989). Washington, DC: Carnegie Council on Adolescent Development.

Wiles, J., & Bondi, J. (1986). *The essential middle school.* Tampa, FL: Wiles, Bondi and Associates.

CHAPTER OUTLINE

The Middle Level Student

physical and psychosocial-emotional development

3

OVERVIEW

Knowledge of the physical, psychosocial, and emotional developmental characteristics of the young adolescent provides middle level school educators with a better understanding of the individual learner and of appropriate teaching and learning practices. The unique characteristics of the 10- to 14-year-old age group place these learners in a developmental period that is neither completely child nor young adult. Teachers of young adolescents must also consider the developmental characteristics in relation to content being taught, instructional methods, and social interactions. As with all developmental periods, characteristics of children vary according to many factors such as heredity, environment, medical care, and nutrition. This chapter provides a description of the young adolescent learner and suggests implications and applications for middle level school educators. Readers are encouraged to respond to the current emphasis on and concern with early adolescence by considering 10- to 14-year-olds in their classes, families, and neighborhoods and also by remembering that "a hallmark characteristic of today's early adolescent is his/her diversity" (Thornburg, 1982, p. 272).

In this chapter, you will read about:

1 The physical and psychosocial-emotional developmental characteristics of young adolescents.

2 The implications of these developmental characteristics for middle level school teaching and learning.
3 The characteristics of a young adolescent girl and boy.
4 The health problems and issues that young adolescents are most concerned about.
5 The facts that young adolescents need to know about their developing bodies.
6 Contemporary issues affecting the physical and psychosocial-emotional development of young adolescents.
7 Sources of information about the physical and psychosocial-emotional development of the young adolescent.

MIDDLE LEVEL LEARNERS

The study of the developmental characteristics of young adolescents is relatively recent. Although first referred to nearly a half-century ago as "pre-adolescent," not much research has focused on the 10- to 14-year-old learner. Lipsitz (1979) in *Growing Up Forgotten,* contended that researchers and scholars have done little to increase our knowledge about this age span. However, recently it has achieved both recognition and respectability as a time when many complex and diverse physical, intellectual, and social changes occur. Deciding on a definition of the age group proves to be difficult, since several terms—e. g., "pubescent," "transescent," and "emerging adolescent," are being offered presently. For the purposes of this book, the authors have defined early adolescence as a stage of development in 10- to 14-year-olds characterized by dramatic physical, intellectual, emotional, and social changes with intervals of rapid or intermittent changes.

PHYSICAL AND PSYCHOSOCIAL-EMOTIONAL DEVELOPMENT DURING EARLY ADOLESCENCE

The significance of physical, psychosocial, and emotional development during early adolescence lies in two areas, both crucial to young adolescents and their educators. First, these complex and interrelated developmental changes have the potential for far-reaching consequences, in their influence on the young adolescent's developing a personal identity. Second, development in these areas influences motivation, self-concept, and overall ability to learn and to function as a socially responsible person. *Learners will benefit academically and socially when educators base teaching and learning practices on knowledge of the learner's development.* The recent emphasis on early adolescence and the growing awareness of the influence of contemporary society on these learners provide educators with clear evidence of the significance of development in teaching and learning situations.

PHYSICAL DEVELOPMENT

The young adolescent growth period ranks with the fetal period and the first two years of life for dramatic physical changes in the individual (Craig, 1986). Many of these changes begin during early adolescence (the 10- to 14-year-old growth period), while some may actually be completed during this growth period. Research on physical development during early adolescence indicates some distinct characteristics that can be considered integral to this developmental period.

CHARACTERISTICS OF YOUNG ADOLESCENTS

Developmental research allows us to paint a general portrait of young adolescents. However, it is important to remember that the growth of each individual varies according to genetic inheritances, cultural factors, and socio-economic status.

Characteristic 1: Young adolescents experience a "growth spurt"—a marked increase in the rate of growth in body size. Growth spurts and closely related physical changes are easily recognized in both boys and girls. These marked increases in the rate of growth in body size occur almost universally. Most prominent is the growth spurt that reaches its peak in girls at age 12 and in boys at age 14 (Craig, 1986). The rapid skeletal and muscular development is readily evident in young adolescents during this stage.

J. M. Tanner (1973, 1971, 1968, 1962) has conducted extensive studies on "growing up" and has provided the basis for much of the current writings on the physical development of young adolescents. From his research, Tanner (1973) concluded that these growth spurts are different for boys and girls and that, on the average, the growth spurt comes two years earlier in girls than in boys. The average boy is slightly taller than the average girl until the girl's growth spurt begins. Then, the average girl may grow taller about the ages of 11 and 13 and may be heavier and stronger.

Characteristic 2: Young adolescents experience readily apparent skeletal and structural changes. Although young adolescents are unique and different individuals, several readily apparent structural and skeletal changes serve as indicators of maturing individuals. Substantial changes in limb length, hip width, and chest breadth and depth often occur rapidly in these young people. The advent of a physically developed body, however, does not imply that other developmental changes are complete. Physical growth changes are interrelated with intellectual, social, and emotional development.

Characteristic 3: The pubertal change experienced by young adolescents is the transition time when reproduction is first possible. Closely associated with these growth spurts and changes in height and weight is the onset of puberty. Lipsitz (1979) termed this growth rate as the most intense and rapid of any stage in human development. Determining the actual beginning point of puberty is difficult since it varies for boys and girls (Tanner, 1968); however, Schuster and Ashburn (1986) considered puberty to be the entire transition period and offered a precise definition of puberty as the time when reproduction is first possible.

The most important physiological change of early adolescence is the development of the sexual reproductive system. Eichhorn (1966) reported that the female hormone develops between the ages of 9 and 12. This marks the beginning of a long series of psychological and physical changes that transform the girl into a woman. In boys, the increase in male hormones is less accentuated and occurs over a greater period of time. The exact timing of sexual development has been a complicated question, especially for boys; however, Espenschade and Eckert (1967) reported:

> The onset of puberty is difficult to assess in males and is usually based on the development of secondary sex characteristics and the growth of the genitalia. In females the menarche, or first menstrual period, is usually taken as the onset of puberty. . . . (p. 173)

Still, precise information about beginning points for sexual development continues to be elusive.

Curtis and Bidwell (1977) reported a wide range for pubertal changes, in that 88 percent of girls reach puberty by the age of 14 while 83 percent of boys attain puberty at age 15. Educators can assume that nine out of ten girls reach puberty by the time they are in the eighth grade, while more than four out of five boys will reach puberty by this time (Forbes, 1968). Although the tremendous diversity demonstrated by young adolescents makes age-developmental norms difficult to determine, teachers can expect these youngsters to be experiencing significant and possibly discomforting pubertal changes while undergoing growth spurts and rapidly increasing changes in height and muscle size.

Middle level educators might find young adolescents preoccupied with their sexual development. This could diminish the attention, motivation, and capacity of the young adolescent to focus on school learning.

Characteristic 4: The young adolescent's pubertal change includes the development of the sexual reproductive system. A contemporary issue is whether the age of puberty is occurring earlier. Although the evidence on boys' maturity is not conclusive, for girls, the age of menarche does appear to be occurring at an earlier age. In the period from 1870 to 1930, the mean age for the onset of menstruation fell from 16.5 to 14.5, a decrease of two years over a 60-year span. Another decrease to age 13.5 occurred during the years 1930 to 1950. Chamberlin and Girona (1976) stated that the age of menarche has dropped two years from 13.5 to 11.5 over the last two decades. There are reasons to believe that the age of puberty will continue to occur earlier due to improved nutrition and health care (Petersen, 1979).

DEVELOPMENTAL PATTERNS: PHYSICAL

All young adolescents experience the same developmental sequence. It is the inception and rate of development that often vary significantly. As teachers observe the physical changes signifying the transition from childhood to adulthood, understanding these two facts is of paramount importance. For example, Lawrence (1980) contended that while girls generally develop two years ahead of boys, individual children differ considerably in their development. Lipsitz (1979) reported that a six-year span in biological development was possible when a girl developed quickly and a boy developed slowly. Such factors as heredity, proper medical attention, nutrition, and exercise can contribute to one child completing a growth cycle while another of the same chronological age has not begun the growth period. Teachers need to remind young adolescents that growth rates differ and do not indicate a physical abnormality.

Of the many physical changes occurring during early adolescence, the dramatic increases in height and muscle size are among the most noticeable. Other less obvious social, psychological, and sexual changes associated with puberty may also occur simultaneously and should be considered as interrelated aspects. All of these have significant implications for middle level school educators.

Significant developmental patterns during early adolescence include the onset of puberty, a 6–8% increase in height, and a 12–15% increase in weight (Eichhorn, 1966). Chamberlin and Girona (1976), being careful to point out that there is no universal child, agreed that children are experiencing biological, intellectual, and social changes. These writers contend that several interrelated factors lead to today's earlier development and maturation. They may include improved nutrition, more and earlier immunization to disease, better medical care, and an increased use of vitamins and minerals.

TEACHING YOUNG ADOLESCENTS ABOUT THEMSELVES

Young adolescents need help not just in meeting their intellectual needs, but also in understanding the rapid changes in their bodies and realizing that the growth spurts, increase in body hair, changing voice, and development of their reproductive system are normal aspects of "growing up". It is also important for young adolescents to understand that developmental changes can vary in rate and degree and still be normal. These developing youngsters often need knowledgeable responses to questions and concerns that may appear far more important to them than the subject matter being presented in class. The responsibility of helping young adolescents understand themselves requires more than just being willing and concerned. Objective and factual knowledge of physical development continues to be a prerequisite. While some developmental characteristics are sex-specific, other changes occur in both boys and girls. Both sexes experience the growth of hair under the arms and around the pubic areas, height and weight increases, and changing voices. The above changes, of course, are only representative of the numerous changes that have the potential for causing anxiety for young adolescents.

Although physical changes are indeed normal and expected, middle level school educators must work toward teaching young adolescents about their own human development. Not accepting this responsibility and responding only to intellectual needs ignores learner characteristics which contribute significantly to academic achievement and total development. Responding to their concerns will include providing developmental benchmarks during the transition from childhood into adolescence. It is important to provide sufficient information allowing feelings of security for learners experiencing developmental changes. Teachers can provide this information in direct instruction and through informal interactions with students. A planned systematic approach can be provided during sessions with the guidance counselor or during the advisor–advisee program. Educators can invite qualified medical personnel to speak on young adolescent changes and can use charts, films, and appropriate literature designed for 10- to 14-year-old learners. Young adolescents often want information about developmental changes but are reluctant to ask parents, teachers, or other students. Consequently, an important curriculum concern of the middle level school is to provide young adolescents with knowledge of their growth and developmental changes.

IMPLICATIONS FOR MIDDLE LEVEL SCHOOL TEACHING AND LEARNING

Understanding young adolescents' physical development and related characteristics leads to several teaching and learning considerations that are crucial to middle level school education. Creative and dedicated teachers will want to consider some of the following factors when planning teaching and learning strategies.

1 Teachers should deemphasize activities where strength and stamina are stressed if there is a potential for unfavorable comparisons.
2 There is a relationship between physiological development and emotional attitudes. Early or late maturation may have repercussions on student behavior (Tanner, 1971).
3 Changing physical characteristics have a significant effect on the young adolescent's developing self-concept and sense of identity.

These factors have the potential to significantly influence levels of achievement and should be reflected in teaching and learning practices.

Several implications for middle level school practice become clear when there is a commitment to base teaching and learning decisions on physical developmental characteristics. First, the extreme variability in physical development makes learner homogeneity almost a myth. This variability, which poses significant challenges to the middle level school, is often inadequately addressed

(Lipsitz, 1979). Second, rapidly changing physical development does not provide for corresponding similar intellectual and social development. Lipsitz (1979) warned against expecting too much from rapidly developing youngsters and too little from slowly developing youngsters. Third, there is the need to respond to the concern that schools, parents, and in general, American society hurry children to grow up too fast too soon (Elkind, 1981). For example, David Elkind's *The Hurried Child* (1981) and *All Grown Up & No Place To Go* (1984), Marie Winn's *Children Without Childhood* (1981), and Neil Postman's *The Disappearance of Childhood* (1982) contended that youngsters today are not being allowed to enjoy childhood but instead are being "hurried": expected to achieve more, forced to accept responsibility earlier, pressured to wear fashions, and expected to cope with the breakup of their families. Middle level educators should place less emphasis on competitive activities such as dances and social events calling for adult-like behavior. They should focus attention on student-centered and developmentally appropriate activities for young adolescents.

CONTEMPORARY ISSUES: PHYSICAL DEVELOPMENT

Several contemporary health issues affect young adolescents and have implications for middle level school educators. First, young adolescents experiencing significant changes in their bodies are subject to considerable anxiety related to health issues (Drolet & Fetro, 1987). Middle level schools, by providing health services such as information on AIDS, sex education, and alcohol/drug abuse to young adolescents, could often alleviate needless worry, anxiety, and apprehension. Though sometimes health worries of young adolescents are exaggerated, boys and girls in this age group also encounter some very real, very serious and extremely confusing health problems. Green (1979) reported such health problems as cystic fibrosis, asthma, cancer, scoliosis, acne, obesity, excessive height in girls, and understature in girls and boys.

Contemporary health issues confronting young adolescents include AIDS (Raper & Aldridge, 1988; Olson, 1988), anorexia nervosa (Maloney & Klyklyo, 1983), fears of dentists, doctors, and of being overweight (Drolet & Fetro, 1987), and the use and abuse of alcohol, marijuana, and tobacco (Johnson, O'Malley, & Buchanan, 1985). Although the middle level school cannot accept total responsibility for helping students cope with these health problems, educators need to recognize that to the young adolescent, resolution of these problems is often just as important as academic achievement.

One of the most serious health issues facing educators in the 1990s is the AIDS epidemic. There were 3,692 children under age 13 with AIDS in the United States in March 1992 (Centers for Disease Control, 1992). This number reflects only children with AIDS and does not include children who are HIV-positive. For this age group, the incidence of AIDS was by passive receptivity with 3,133 (85%) of the exposures passed to the children by their mothers and 469 (11%) caused by blood disorders and transfusions. However, for the 13- to 19-year-olds, the incidence of AIDS was related to their own sexual behavior and drug use, as well as blood disorders. Middle level school health and guidance programs will be challenged to provide young adolescents with valid information about the circumstances and consequences of the AIDS virus.

The increasing teenage pregnancy rate represents contemporary problems that will face educators during the 1990s. It is estimated that one in five of all pregnant teenagers under the age of 15 receives little or no prenatal care. Potential developmental problems to unborn children may go undetected and untreated (Washington & Glimps, 1983). The startling number of teenage pregnancies (and the AIDS epidemic) calls for middle level school educators to provide age-appropriate learning experiences in sex education and family life education. These topics elicit controversy and angry reactions from parents, religious leaders, and others who question the school's need to provide instruction in sex-related matters. Still, responsibility must be accepted for presenting accurate and factual information, obtaining materials from professional sources, maintaining objectivity when teaching sex education, and presenting a balanced viewpoint of the controversial issues associated with sex education and family life education. Teaching rather than indoctrinating, the educator should emphasize facts, a code of ethics, and objectivity (McCary, 1978; Anspaugh, Ezell, & Goodman, 1987).

Young adolescents during the 1990s will likely experience problems once known only to adults. These problems, resulting from addictive substances, experimenting with sex, and the AIDS epidemic, will in turn pose problems for middle level school educators. Young adolescents experimenting (or experiencing the consequences from their involvement) with alcohol, drugs, and sex will likely be disruptive in class and less interested in schoolwork. However, the effects on youngsters can be multiplied, since the middle level school years might be a prime time for at-risk students making plans for dropping out of school. The crises which young adolescents sometimes face can have long-term effects extending far beyond the middle level school years.

Decisions concerning drug, alcohol, and tobacco use will confront middle level school learners and challenge professional educators. Both the general public and educators have become acutely aware of drug use as a major problem challenging the schools. When asked to identify the number one problem that public schools must deal with, those interviewed for the 1988 Gallup poll indicated the use of drugs by students (Gallup & Elam, 1988). Reasons for drug abuse include low self-esteem, peer pressure, adult modeling, mood alteration, boredom, curiosity, and alienation. The need for drug education is apparent, but what programs to use and what methods are most effective do not yield easy answers. Information must be provided that is factual, practical, realistic, and values-oriented. The middle level school must provide effective drug education programs. These must include building the learner's self-esteem and providing viable alternatives for coping with personal problems (Anspaugh, Ezell, & Goodman, 1987).

Young adolescents are, generally speaking, healthy individuals. The significant problem challenging middle level school educators, therefore, may be the problems these learners *think* they have. Middle level school learners will greatly benefit from being able to raise questions and issues in advisor–advisee programs, from meeting with guidance counselors knowledgeable of young adolescents' concerns, and from having caring and compassionate teachers who understand the health and developmental changes in young adolescents.

The following case study describes Jennifer, an 11-year-old, whose physical development characteristics are typical of young adolescent girls.

CASE STUDY

JENNIFER—AN ELEVEN-YEAR-OLD-GIRL

Jennifer, age 11, has experienced significant and often disturbing physical changes during the past year. She has grown about three inches taller as well as stronger and more coordinated, she has gained a little weight, her bones have lengthened, her muscles have increased, and her glands have begun to produce hormones. Jennifer's feelings are mixed: She is fascinated by her maturing body, yet she is anxious about being taller, stronger, and more coordinated than most boys of her age. Jennifer also wonders why her best friend, Jan, also age 11, has not experienced the same dramatic changes. Some of her other friends, however, are experiencing physical changes this year. Jan has not yet reached Jennifer's level of physical development and, therefore, she is puzzled or unable to explain the difference in physical development. Jennifer has discussed her concerns with her best friend, who does not know any more than she does. She tried talking to her parents and teachers, but they did not think her concerns and questions were of great importance, and merely assured Jennifer that "Everything will be all right." Jennifer thinks she is normal, but she still has questions about whether the physical changes in her really are normal and what other changes she may expect.

JENNIFER: A COMMENTARY FOR MIDDLE LEVEL EDUCATORS

In essence, Jennifer is in transition from childhood to adolescence. How will this affect learning? It is likely that the teachers will detect a change in Jennifer's atittude, interest, and attention span. Schoolwork might be accorded second place, while a preoccupation with her maturing body receives major attention. Professional educators in Jennifer's middle level school will recognize the need to provide Jennifer and her friends with individual attention and group discussion sessions directed toward concerns such as changing interests and attitudes, loss of interest in schoolwork, and problems caused by maturational changes.

This case study focuses on the physical changes that are experienced by young adolescents and the differences which are observed by Jennifer and Jan. Teachers and counselors can play specific roles in situations like Jennifer's. Teachers' roles could include being a strong, supportive advocate of young adolescents and also being willing to discuss Jennifer's concerns. Perceptive teachers can provide developmentally appropriate avenues such as advisor–advisee grouping, coping strategies, and individual attention before, during, and after school to discuss concerns. Counselors' roles could include being facilitators between students, parents, and teachers in the school.

PSYCHOSOCIAL-EMOTIONAL DEVELOPMENT DURING EARLY ADOLESCENCE

This section portrays the psychosocial-emotional development of young adolescents and examines appropriate middle level school practices that enhance development in these areas. Although the school's role has been popularly hailed as primarily "intellectual" and "achievement-oriented," middle level school educators face the equally important task of helping young adolescents learn about themselves.

CHARACTERISTICS OF YOUNG ADOLESCENTS

Changing social characteristics during early adolescence can have a profound and often disturbing impact on both young adolescents and their teachers. Although changes resulting from growth and development are normal aspects of early adolescence, never have so many changes occurred simultaneously. These changes hold important implications for students and middle level educators in terms of friendships, self-concepts, peer pressure, school climate, academic achievement, and teaching and learning practices (Manning & Allen, 1987).

Characteristic 1: Young adolescents become socially curious beings and strive for companionship and social interactions, while exhibiting a strong desire for peer approval. The young adolescent is described by Thornburg (1982, 1983) as a complex and diverse individual. New ways of thinking, feeling, and acting are evolving that allow reflection upon one's social experiences. These social changes, accompanied by physical and emotional changes associated with puberty, often result in atypical, drastic, daring, and sometimes aggressive behavior (Crockett, Losoff, & Peterson, 1984).

Characteristic 2: Allegiance and affiliation shift from parents and teachers toward the peer group. The peer group becomes the prime source for standards and models of behavior for young adolescents. Young adolescents become increasingly aware of the importance of peer relationships. Serious examination of long-held beliefs and allegiances begins to occur, often resulting in a move toward greater independence and freedom from authority (Alexander & George, 1981). Even without overt changes in behavior, the value system of peers remains a powerful force in a young person's actions. In some cases, the 10- to 14-year-old believes that maintaining allegiance to parents and teachers can result in loss of peer approval and acceptance (Thornburg, 1983).

Characteristic 3: Friendship formation during early adolescence is crucial to social development and includes a shift from family members to same-sex friendships, then to cross-sex friendships. Crockett, Losoff, and Peterson (1984) reported that young adolescents see friends on a daily basis and develop a system of cliques. Boys tend to congregate in groups and have a fairly extensive network of friends, while girls are more likely to become friends with one or two girls. Also, the initial same-sex friendships transform into cross-sex relationships during these critical years.

Characteristic 4: A preoccupation with self naturally develops during this period. So much is happening so fast in the bodies and minds of young adolescents that preoccupation with self and an insistent concern for how one is perceived by others becomes paramount in the lives of 10- to 14-year-olds. The powerful physical and psychosocial changes that young adolescents demonstrate can dramatically affect social interaction, peer acceptance, and personal self-esteem.

DEVELOPMENTAL PATTERNS: PSYCHOSOCIAL-EMOTIONAL

As with other developmental areas, foremost in the educator's thinking must be that psychosocial-emotional development is an individual matter. Psychosocial-emotional development is affected by such individual factors as the amount of autonomous behavior allowed by parents and teachers, whether the young person is an early or late developer, and various hereditary, environmental, and cultural factors.

Several patterns become clear as educators examine the impact of psychosocial-emotional development on young adolescents. Thornburg and Glider (1984) reported that some young adolescents experience a sense of anonymity, particularly in the transition from elementary to middle level school. These children may feel that peers and teachers do not know them, in fact, may not even know their names. Such feelings can have a relatively long-lasting and negative impact on their self-concept and level of participation in school activities. Young adolescents also often experience lower self-concepts during their transition from elementary to middle level school (Thornburg and Glider, 1984). Another pattern is for many young adolescents to demonstrate a changing personality, such as assertiveness or behavior intended to shock or surprise teachers. Young adolescents in their search for independence may rebuke authority, engage in vandalism, or become involved in sex, alcohol, or drugs. Although some may not be strongly motivated to participate in these activities, being actively involved promotes a sense of freedom from adult authority (Thornburg, 1983). Lastly, the young adolescent tends to consider the peer group as the primary reference source for attitudes, values, and behavior and as a mechanism for decision-making (Davis, Weener, & Shute, 1977).

TEACHING YOUNG ADOLESCENTS ABOUT THEMSELVES

Middle level school educators who teach young adolescents about themselves provide a valuable service that many learners may not experience elsewhere. Young adolescents who understand some of their psychosocial-emotional development may be better prepared to cope with a rapidly changing society and may be less self-absorbed. Preoccupation with self can pose a major interference with teaching and learning.

Teaching young adolescents about themselves can take several directions and can have a positive effect on their feelings about themselves as individuals, their self-image, and their developing sense of identity. First, middle level school educators can help learners to realize that their shift from a parent-centered world to a peer-centered world is the result of social developmental changes and should be viewed positively. Rather than feeling guilty or disobedient, the young learner can understand that this behavior is normal and developmentally appropriate. Young adolescents also need to be aware that friendships and cliques change. A student ignored or shunned by a clique one day might be readily accepted later in the week. It is important for young adolescents to understand that the changing nature of their friendships, including from same-sex to cross-sex, is expected and is a natural manifestation of the young adolescent years. In addition, although middle level school educators should strive to make all students feel accepted by the school and the various peer groups, young adolescents should understand that many learners still retain a sense of anonymity. The transition of moving from the elementary school to the middle level school and the transitory nature of friendships and cliques can result in students feeling "lost". Lastly, 10- to 14-year-olds should be helped to deal with peer pressure. They should learn that although not satisfying one's peers can often damage friendships, adhering to one's personal beliefs and refusing to yield to the pressure of others can often be the best decision.

Even in an already overcrowded day, responsive middle level schools can provide sessions which help young adolescents understand themselves. Approaches may include appropriate large-group or small-group classroom activities, advisor–advisee sessions, mini-courses, guidance counselors, community speakers, and other opportunities for young adolescents to discuss problems and situations important to them.

IMPLICATIONS FOR MIDDLE LEVEL SCHOOL TEACHING AND LEARNING

With the current persistent demand for more rigorous academic standards, middle level school educators should not forget crucial psychosocial-emotional aspects of early adolescence. Teachers serve an important function in the socialization of young adolescents by teaching social skills, encouraging friendships and social interaction through clubs, and allowing friends or potential friends to study together. Young adolescents frequently come from a smaller, more person-oriented elementary school to a larger, seemingly impersonal middle level school and, consequently, experience feelings of aloneness. In an effort to make all students feel they are known and an important part of the school, middle level educators should give particular attention to mobile students, unpopular or disliked students, and those just entering the middle level school from the elementary grades.

The young adolescents' search for autonomy and independence is a natural characteristic of the growth period. Allowing students independence in learning activities, encouraging independence during advisor–advisee sessions, and letting students have greater control over mini-courses to be taught will enable youngsters to know that educators understand their need for autonomy and are willing to cooperate within reasonable limits.

Peer pressure will continue to influence youngsters' behavior, attire, and speech. Additionally, educators should remember that attempts on their part to compete with peers are usually futile. Peer pressure remains a vital part of the socialization process, and a healthy self-concept still serves as the best balance to negative peer pressure. Many younger middle level school students experience a fluctuating self-concept. Being in a school where they no longer reign as the oldest and biggest, these young adolescents must reassess their standing with both peers and teachers.

CONTEMPORARY ISSUES: PSYCHOSOCIAL-EMOTIONAL DEVELOPMENT

As with physical development, contemporary issues also confront young adolescents during their psychosocial-emotional development. Several problems surface as particularly stressful: (1) Being pushed to grow up too fast academically and/or socially; (2) peer pressure to engage in sex, alcohol, and drugs; (3) stresses resulting from concerns with AIDS or other health-related matters; and (4) physical safety in schools.

Society's apparent urge to rush children through the childhood years takes a significant toll, as evidenced by teenage pregnancies, high incidence of alcohol abuse, disturbing rates of sexually transmitted diseases, and high incidence of stress-related ailments. Such issues have special significance for middle level educators, who all too often see young adolescents being hurried into adolescence and on into adulthood. Not only are young adolescents' identities becoming quasi-adult identities at earlier ages but, too often, middle schoolers are not sufficiently mature to deal with relationships with the opposite sex, substance use, academic pressure, and peer-group situations.

What practices can middle level schools implement to help young adolescents to deal with these contemporary issues? First, educators must consider the young adolescent years as an important developmental period with its own unique characteristics. Rather than viewing middle level school education as directing attention only to intellectual concerns, educators responsive to the whole child should contribute significantly to learners' self-concept and overall social and emotional growth. Second, middle level school educators can provide age-appropriate activities, e. g., intramural athletic activities, rather than interscholastic sports, and social activities such as parties involving all students, rather than boy–girl dances. Third, many contemporary issues can be treated in advisor–advisee groups, guidance programs, and special curricular areas. The challenge lies with middle level school educators interpreting their role as serving the whole child rather than accommodating only the learner's cognitive development.

As the case study of Jennifer explored the hallmark developmental characteristics of a young adolescent girl, the following case study provides a similar description of psychosocial-emotional development in a 13-year-old boy.

CASE STUDY

MICHAEL—A THIRTEEN-YEAR-OLD BOY

Michael, age 13, lives near Jennifer and attends the same middle level school. Michael is a healthy, normal young adolescent; he does have a problem, though: He is concerned about his developmental changes. Michael thinks about the person into whom he is growing and wonders what he will be like in a few years. Will I be sociable and outgoing, with lots of friends? Will I be a loner? Some days he feels capable, but on other days, he feels he cannot equal his friend's social abilities or cope with the demands of the middle level school. In his perceptions of the future, Michael looks at himself now at age 13. He has quite a few friends—mostly boys, but not many of his friends associate with girls anyway. Although he still considers his parent's wishes as a basis for his behavior, Michael does look at some of the 15- and 16-year-old boys and thinks about doing some of the things they do. So far, he has only been pressured a few times to smoke, but he wonders when he will have to choose between the wishes of his friends and those of his parents. Like most of his friends, Michael's self-concept fluctuates. Some days he feels pretty good about himself; then he looks at his awkwardness during Physical Education and the good feelings disappear. Michael is developing normally, yet he needs someone to talk with—either an understanding parent, a teacher, or someone who relates to young adolescents and is willing to take time to discuss his questions and concerns.

MICHAEL: A COMMENTARY FOR MIDDLE LEVEL EDUCATORS

Michael's psychosocial-emotional development, like Jennifer's physical development, has implications for middle level school teaching and learning. His teachers should recognize that Michael's preoccupation with social status among his peers, his questioning of his future social self, and his pressure from peers often take precedence over learning activities. His teachers should also recognize that Michael's self-concept often varies. Measures should be taken to build Michael's self-concept and make him aware of positive methods of dealing with personal problems and doubts. Other measures to address Michael's needs could include cooperative learning sessions, class schedules that maximize learning, student-teacher support teams, small-group programs, and exploratory programs. His teachers will want to assist him as needed and to provide him with opportunities to discuss problems either with the guidance counselor or during advisor-advisee sessions.

Like Michael, nearly all young adolescents are experiencing psychosocial-emotional changes which have the potential for causing major personal concerns. These learners, both boys and girls, wonder about their changes, which changes will appear next, why their best friend is not developing similarly, and what kind of person they will become. Educators will experience considerable frustration and challenges while teaching young adolescents who are more concerned with their changing bodies and identities than the subject matter being presented.

YOUNG ADOLESCENTS: RESEARCH FOUNDATIONS

Middle level school practices should be based on a credible knowledge of young adolescent development. Like learners at all levels, the developmental characteristics of young adolescents deserve careful investigation and consideration. A challenge is to base curriculum, teaching, and learning practices on research that has examined and considered characteristics of the development of the young adolescent learner. An examination of the psychosocial development theories of Erikson and Havighurst, the implications of the Boyce Medical Study, and the contributions of other significant authorities in adolescent development provide a foundation for developing middle level school practices based on the most incisive and conclusive research available.

INDUSTRY VS. INFERIORITY AND IDENTITY VS. ROLE CONFUSION (ERIKSON)

An understanding of Erik Erikson's psychosocial theories contributes significantly to middle level school educators' understanding of the young adolescent developmental period. Erikson (1963) divided the lifespan into eight psychosocial stages, each having crisis periods for social and emotional development. Although Erikson's divisions do not specifically pinpoint the 10- to 14-year-old period, two of his stages are relevant to the young adolescent: Industry vs. Inferiority (6/7–11/12 years) and Identity vs. Role Confusion (11/12–18 years). It is worth remembering that since 10- to 14-year-olds function at the latter part of the industry vs. inferiority stage and at the beginning of the identity vs. role confusion stage, young adolescents might exhibit some characteristics of both stages.

Industry vs. Inferiority. No longer content with the whims and wishes of play, the learner's aim is to be productive. The 9- to 12-year-old child wins recognition by bringing academic, social, and physical tasks to successful completion. Likewise, the child risks the danger of being dissatisfied with his or her skills, which will result in a sense of mediocrity and inferiority. The child also begins to move from a parent-centered world to a peer-centered world with peers and friends acting as socializing agents. Several steps can be taken to provide a supportive environment. Learners must be provided opportunities to be successful with academic, physical, and social tasks. But while the current demand for academic achievement must be heeded, the learner's psychosocial development must also receive priority. Feelings of inadequacy, inferiority, and frustration with tasks may result in behavior problems and "acting out."

Identity vs. Role Confusion. Erikson considered this stage to be crucial for identity formation and to represent the end of childhood. These crucial young adolescent years include the beginning of the search for an identity and both a mastery of the problems of childhood and a readiness to confront the challenges of the adult world (Maier, 1969). The many physical changes and a changing social environment present new psychosocial crises which require learners to develop a new sense of "self." Primary issues are youngsters' search for a role identity and their concern with how they appear to the eyes of others, as compared to what they feel they are. In their search for an identity, many learners during this stage begin to adopt idols, ideas, heroes, cliques, and crowds and can be remarkably clannish and cruel in their exclusion of others (Erikson, 1963). Educators working with young adolescents can take several approaches to mediate the problems of this stage. First, educators need to be aware that young adolescents function in the lower ranges of this stage. These learners should be treated neither like children nor adults. Second, young adolescents' attempts to direct their thoughts and actions toward ideal standards and values require educators to accept more realistic standards and values. Third, cliques and clans must be accepted as a part of the young adolescent's life.

DEVELOPMENTAL TASKS (HAVIGHURST)

Robert Havighurst (1972) proposed a lifespan developmental theory which held that all individuals from infancy to old age progress through a series of developmental stages, each having age-appropriate developmental tasks. Although Havighurst did not focus specifically on young adolescent development, observers of the 10- to 14-year-old group can benefit from the developmental tasks designed for the middle childhood years (6–12 years) and the adolescence period (12–18 years).

Selected developmental tasks to be mastered during the latter years (10–12 years) of the middle childhood period include building wholesome attitudes toward self as a growing organism, learning an appropriate masculine or feminine role, achieving personal independence, and developing attitudes toward social groups and institutions. Educators should encourage young adolescents to understand the positive aspects of their development, recognize the need for learners to be independent, encourage the development of positive attitudes toward social groups and other people, and arrange opportunities for students to learn age-appropriate social skills.

Likewise, curriculum planners can select age-appropriate developmental tasks from the beginning years (12–14) of the adolescent stage. Havighurst maintained that the principal lessons to be learned in this stage will be social and emotional, where students learn to work together on common interests and to place the pursuit of a common goal over one's personal interest. Developmental tasks appropriate for young adolescents include achieving new and more mature relations with age-mates of both sexes, continuing to learn an appropriate masculine or feminine social role, beginning to achieve emotional independence from parents and other adults, and working toward achieving socially responsible behavior. To help young adolescents accomplish these tasks, educators should recognize the influence of peer pressure and changing allegiances, encourage the beginning stages of achieving emotional independence, teach students to be responsible for their behavior both at home and school, and continue to teach social skills necessary for getting along with age-mates.

THE BOYCE MEDICAL STUDY: BIOLOGICAL MATURATION

The Boyce Medical Study, a landmark study of young adolescents, was a comprehensive investigation to determine the level of biological maturation and the health status of students in Boyce Middle School. This 1969 study of young adolescents resulted in detailed findings that were then analyzed for both their medical and educational implications. The investigation, conducted by Dr. Allan Drash and a team of medical specialists, sought to determine the level of biological maturation for each student by medically examining nearly 500 students and by assessing the implications of their data for education programs (Eichhorn, 1980). Drash (1980) contended that educators working with learners in junior high schools and middle schools are confronted daily with significant variations in young adolescents. Differences of 6–8 inches in height and 40–60 pounds in weight are not uncommon. This physical variability is further compounded by remarkable differences in emotional maturity, attentiveness, interest, and intellectual ability.

As a result of the study, a pattern of developmental grouping was implemented based on physical characteristics and social-psychological variables. Three major groups, pre-pubescent, pubescent, and adolescent, were established. The three developmental groups were then divided among five teaching teams. One team was composed of pre-pubescent learners, three teams were set up for pubescents, and one team was established for adolescents. The content to be studied, instructional methods used, learning theory/style employed, and activities provided were geared to the developmental level of the learners in each team.

To what extent have middle level schools implemented Eichhorn's findings? In an interview 10 years after the Boyce Medical Study, Dr. Donald Eichhorn was asked the question, "Has the Boyce Plan been implemented in any other districts to your knowledge?" Eichhorn responded that other districts had not implemented the plan even though it had been widely disseminated. The problem, Eichhorn stated, is that success cannot be guaranteed. In conclusion, Eichhorn restated his belief in the program and also that he would appreciate his findings being tested (Schuck & Garman, 1980).

CULTURAL AND GENDER DIFFERENCES: PSYCHOSOCIAL

As Thornburg (1982) made clear, the young adolescent developmental period is characterized by tremendous diversity. This diversity becomes even more pronounced when one considers cultural and gender differences. Educators planning developmentally appropriate psychosocial experiences need to remember that cultural and gender differences influence affective dimensions such as 10- to 14-year-olds' identity formation, self-concept, and friendships.

Identity Formation. The development of personal and ethnic identities is a central task of early adolescence. In the process of identity formation, African-American eighth graders think about and discuss their ethnic group membership. For example, African-American females and males usually seek ethnic group membership and generally focus on their own ethnic group (Phinney & Tarver, 1988). Asian-, African-, and Hispanic-American students often demonstrate negative ethnic identities even though a generally positive view of Asians prevails in American society. Probably because Asian-Americans lack a social movement stressing ethnic pride like that which African- and Mexican-Americans have experienced, they sometimes have trouble naming leading Asian-American personalities who might serve as role or identity models. Generally, their attitudes tend more toward assimilation than toward ethnic pride and pluralism (Phinney, 1989).

Friendships. Since the 10- to 14-year-old period is so crucial for friendship formation and the development of social networks, perceptive middle level school educators see the need to understand social networks and peer relations, especially how these dimensions are affected by culture. Friendship patterns of African- and European-American young adolescents include large numbers of both African- and European-Americans having an other-race school friend, a smaller group seeing a close other-race school friend outside of school, and African-Americans being twice as likely as European-Americans to see an other-race school friend (DuBois & Hirsch, 1990).

Gender also plays a significant role in the social contexts of young adolescents. Males and females often report the same number of best friends, but males have larger social networks than females. Attributes that young adolescents consider important in themselves and their same-sex friends differ according to sex: Males often concern themselves with attributes considered to be important for status in the peer group, while girls demonstrate concern with attributes necessary for relationships with a few friends (Benenson, 1990).

Self-Concept Development. The development of a positive self-concept is another task challenging young adolescents and their educators. For example, Asian- and Pacific-American children's physical and racial self-concepts appear to be more negative than their European-American counterparts. Japanese-American children score significantly lower than European-American children on all physical self-concept scores (Pang et al., 1985).

Significant relationships exist between gender differences, self-concept, and body image (Koff, Rierdan, & Stubbs, 1990). Generalizations concerning gender differences include males feeling more satisfied with their bodies than females, while females are more discriminating and assign different values to different aspects of their bodies. In fact, the changes affecting the female have the potential for making her disappointed in her body, while the male may be more concerned with task mastery and effectiveness than with physical appearance (Koff, Rierdan, & Stubbs, 1990).

Implications for Middle Level School Educators. A basic prerequisite for middle level school educators is to recognize that cultural and gender differences are real. Specifically, educators need to be sensitive to the tremendous cultural and gender divergences among young adolescents and not assume too much homogeneity. Once a commitment is made to base affective experiences on learners' unique cultural characteristics, middle level educators' efforts can take several directions.

First, while the importance of friendships during early adolescence has been long recognized, educators also need to provide opportunities for learners to develop other-race friendships. Second, the importance of 10- to 14-year-olds developing personal and ethnic identities cannot be underestimated, especially for culturally diverse learners developing in a majority culture and for girls who sometimes feel discriminated against by school policies and practices. Third, self-concept is crucial. Educators need to provide opportunities for culturally diverse learners to feel better about themselves, their culture, and their cultural heritages. Fourth, young adolescents are often preoccupied with their body images. How many times can one remember a boy feeling too short, a girl feeling too tall, or a student feeling his or her nose is too long? Culturally diverse learners may feel even more "different," since they may not look like majority culture youngsters. Perceptive educators encourage all cultures and both sexes to develop an accurate self-image and to realize that the majority culture does not represent a standard by which one should measure oneself.

It is important that middle level school educators consider cultural and gender diversity as strengths to be appreciated rather than weaknesses to be overcome. Young adolescents' rapidly expanding social world and their increasing ability to understand others' perspectives contribute to early adolescence being an ideal time during which to teach appreciation and acceptance of all people, regardless of cultural, gender, or other differences. Perceptive and caring middle level educators realize the benefits cultural diversity brings to classrooms and plan cognitive and social learning experiences that capitalize on this valuable resource.

SUMMARY

The considerable work on the physical and psychosocial-emotional characteristics of young adolescents emphasizes three factors to be considered: First, these often-rapid developmental changes need to be reflected in middle level school practice; to do otherwise will educationally short-change learners. Second, responding appropriately to the extreme variability and diversity in these youngsters will continue to be a major challenge for curriculum and instruction planners. Third, helping young adolescents to learn about themselves and to understand their unique problems provide a significant challenge and opportunity to professionals working with these learners.

Theorists have provided educators with a substantial body of research on the young adolescent's physical and psychosocial-emotional development and, at least in some instances, have suggested implications for educational practice. However, while research continues into how young adolescents develop, we must hearken to the idea that developmental theory is a means to an end and not an end in itself. It remains for astute developmental theorists to provide the research that creative and dedicated teachers and administrators can translate into effective classroom instruction. In the final analysis, the reason for all our efforts in education is to make it possible for the individual young adolescent to learn what he or she needs to learn.

EXPLORATION

1 Survey a group of young adolescents to determine their physical developmental characteristics. Examine specifically ages, weight, and height, and compare data between boys and girls. Compare the results to determine whether Thornburg's statement that "a hallmark characteristic of today's early adolescent is his/her diversity" (1982, p. 272) is valid. Can you expect similar results with young adolescents' psychosocial-emotional development?

2 Prepare a teaching unit designed to teach young adolescents about some aspect of their physical or psychosocial-emotional development. How will you determine the aspect of most importance to learners? What activities or materials will you use? How can you use advisor-advisee groups or guidance programs to complement your efforts?

3 A parent offers the following comment at a parent-teacher conference, "Your emphasis should be on intellectual matters. Academic achievement and test scores—that's what counts in this world! You teachers are wasting valuable time being concerned with psychosocial-emotional development. No one did that when I was in school." Outline your response—what will you say?

4 Draw up a plan for implementing an AIDS curriculum. Is an AIDS curriculum the responsibility of a middle level school? What is developmentally appropriate for young adolescents? What activities and materials will you

use? Will your curriculum be implemented with all children or just the more mature learners?

5 Consider Lipsitz's (1977) statement about early adolescence: "It is an overlooked age." In a position paper on the early adolescence period, respond to the validity of this statement. Also, outline a plan for remedying this situation. How can educators convince society to perceive early adolescence as a valid developmental period?

SUGGESTED READINGS

Beane, J. A., & Lipka, R. P. (1987). *When kids come first: Enhancing self-esteem.* Columbus, OH: National Middle School Association.

This publication examines pupil self-esteem and provides valuable information, including a sample teaching unit designed to enhance self-esteem.

Drash, A. (1980). "Variations in pubertal developmental and the school system: A problem and a challenge," in Donald Steer (ed.), *The emerging adolescent characteristics and educational implications* (pp. 15–26). Columbus, OH: National Middle School Association.

A discussion of the findings of the Boyce Medical Study.

Eichhorn, D. (1980). "Middle school developmental age grouping: A needed consideration," in Donald Steer (ed.), *The emerging adolescent characteristics and educational implications* (pp. 27–33). Columbus, OH: National Middle School Association.

A discussion of the procedures employed in the Boyce Medical Study.

Elkind, D. (1984). *All grown up & no place to go.* Reading, MA: Addison-Wesley.

An examination of problems associated with growing up too fast. Elkind contends that contemporary teens are compelled to face adult challenges too soon, which often results in behavior problems.

Johnson, M. (Ed.). (1980). *Toward adolescence: The middle school years.* Seventy-ninth yearbook of the NSSE. Chicago: The University of Chicago Press.

A collection of readings on developing 10- to 15-year-old learners, and related implications for middle level school educators.

Lawrence, G. (1980). Do programs reflect what research says about physical development? *The Middle School Journal, 11,* 12–14.

A discussion of young adolescents' physical characteristics, with implications for middle level school practice.

Lipsitz, J. (1977). *Growing up forgotten.* Lexington, MA: Heath.

Lipsitz contends in her book that the 10- to 14-year-old period has been neglected and overlooked as a developmental period.

Manning, M. L. (1988). Erikson's psychosocial theories help explain early adolescence. *NASSP Bulletin, 72,* 95–101.

This article examines in detail appropriate aspects of Erikson's Industry vs. Inferiority and Identity vs. Role Confusion stages and provides implications for educational practice.

Raper, J., & Aldridge, J. (1988). AIDS: What every teacher should know. *Childhood Education, 64,* 146–149.

This reading uses a question-and-answer format to provide a current and objective examination of AIDS.

REFERENCES

Alexander, C. (1989). Gender differences in adolescent health concerns and self-assessed health. *Journal of Early Adolescence, 9,* 467–479.

Alexander, W. M., & George, P. S. (1981). *The exemplary middle school.* New York: Holt, Rinehart and Winston.

Anspaugh, D., Ezell, G., & Goodman, K. N. (1987). *Teaching today's health.* New York: Merrill/Macmillan.

Benenson, J. F. (1990). Gender differences in social networks. *Journal of Early Adolescence, 10,* 472–495.

Centers for Disease Control. (April 1992). *HIV/AIDS Surveillance Report.* Atlanta: National Center for Infectious Diseases.

Chamberlin, L. J., & Girona, R. (1976). Our children are changing. *Educational Leadership, 33,* 301–305.

Craig, G. (1986). *Human development.* Englewood Cliffs, NJ: Prentice-Hall.

Crockett, L., Losoff, M., & Peterson, A. (1984). Perceptions of the peer group and friendship in early adolescence. *Journal of Early Adolescence, 4,* 155–181.

Curtis, T., & Bidwell, W. (1977). *Curriculum and instruction for emerging adolescents.* Reading, MA: Addison-Wesley.

Davis, A. K., Weener, J. M., & Shute, R. E. (1977). Positive peer influence: School-based intervention. *Health Education, 8,* 20–21.

Drash, A. (1980). Variations in pubertal development and the school system: A problem and a challenge. In D. Steer (Ed.), *The emerging adolescent characteristics and educational implications* (pp. 15–26). Columbus, OH: National Middle School Association.

Drolet, J. C., & Fetro, J. V. (1987). Adolescent fears: Implications for health education. *Health Education, 18,* 34–38.

DuBois, D. I., & Hirsch, B. J. (1990). School and neighborhood friendship patterns of Blacks and Whites in early adolescence. *Child Development, 61,* 524–536.

Eichhorn, D. (1966). *The middle school.* New York: The Center for Applied Research in Education.

Eichhorn, D. (1980). Middle school developmental age grouping: A needed consideration. In D. Steer (Ed.), *The emerging adolescent characteristics and educational implications* (pp. 27–33). Columbus, OH: National Middle School Association.

Elkind, D. (1981). *The hurried child.* Reading, MA: Addison-Wesley.

Elkind, D. (1984). *All grown up and no place to go.* Reading, MA: Addison-Wesley.

Erikson, E. (1963). *Childhood and society* (rev. ed.) New York: Norton.

Espenschade, A., & Eckert, H. (1967). *Motor development.* New York: Merrill/Macmillan.

Forbes, G. (1968). Physical aspects of early adolescence. In T. Curtis (Ed.), *The middle school.* Albany, NY: Center for Curriculum Research and Service.

Gallup, A. M., & Elam, S. M. (1988). The 20th annual Gallup poll of the public's attitudes toward the public schools. *Phi Delta Kappan, 70,* 33–46.

Green, M. (1979). Adolescent health care. *Children Today, 8,* 8–11.

Havighurst, R. J. (1972). *Developmental tasks and education.* New York: McKay.

Johnson, L. D., O'Malley, P. M., & Buchanan, J. G. (1985). Use of licit and illicit drugs by America's high school students, 1975–1984 (DDHS Publication. No. ADM 85–1394). Rockville, MD: National Institute on Drug Abuse.

Koff, E., Rierdan, J., & Stubbs, M. I. (1990). Gender, body image, and self-concept in early adolescence. *Journal of Early Adolescence, 10,* 56–68.

Lawrence, G. (1980). Do programs reflect what research says about physical development? *The Middle School Journal, 11,* 12–14.

Lipsitz, J. (1977). *Growing up forgotten.* Lexington, MA: D. C. Heath.

Lipsitz, J. (1979). Adolescent development: Myths and realities. *Children Today, 8,* 2–7.

Maier, H. W. (1969). *Three theories of child development* (rev. ed.). New York: Harper & Row.

Maloney, M. J., & Klyklyo, W. M. (1983). An overview of anorexia nervosa, bulimia, and obesity in children and adolescents. *Journal of the American Academy of Child Psychiatry, 22,* 99–107.

Manning, M. L., & Allen, H. G. (1987). Social development in early adolescence: Implications for middle school educators. *Childhood Education, 63,* 172–176.

McCary, J. (1978). *Human sexuality.* New York: Van Nostrand.

Olson, S. (1988). Pediatric HIV: More than a health problem. *Children Today, 17,* 8–9.

Pang, V. O., Mizokawa, D. T., Morishima, J. K., & Olstad, R. G. (1985). Self-concepts of Japanese-American children. *Journal of Cross-Cultural Psychology, 16,* 99–109.

Petersen, A. C. (1979). Can puberty come any earlier? *Psychology Today, 12*(8), 45–46.

Phinney, J. S., & Tarver, S. (1988). Ethnic identity search and commitment in Black and White eighth graders. *Journal of Early Adolescence, 8,* 265–277.

Phinney, J. S. (1989). Stages of ethnic identity development in minority group adolescents. *Journal of Early Adolescence, 9,* 34–49.

Postman, N. (1982). *The disappearance of childhood.* New York: Delacorte Press.

Postman, N. (1985). The disappearance of childhood. *Childhood Education, 61,* 286–293.

Raper, J., & Aldridge, J. (1988). AIDS: What every teacher should know. *Childhood Education, 64,* 146–149.

Schuck, R. F., & Garman, N. B. (1980). Ten years after the Boyce Medical Study: An interview with Dr. David Eichhorn. *American Middle School Education, 3,* 30–35.

Schuster, C., & Ashburn, S. (1986). *The process of human development.* Boston: Little, Brown.

Tanner, J. M. (1962). *Growth at adolescence.* Oxford: Blackwell.

Tanner, J. M. (1968). Earlier maturation in man. *Scientific American, 218*(1), 21–27.

Tanner, J. M. (1971). Sequence, tempo, and individual variation in the growth and development of boys and girls aged twelve to sixteen. *Daedalus, 100,* 907–930.

Tanner, J. M. (1973). Growing up. *Scientific American, 229*(3), 35–43.

Thornburg, H. (1982). The total early adolescent in contemporary society. *The High School Journal, 65,* 272–278.

Thornburg, H. (1983). Can educational systems respond to the needs of early adolescents? *Journal of Early Adolescence, 65,* 272–278.

Thornburg, H., & Glider, P. (1984). Dimensions of early adolescent social perceptions and preferences. *Journal of Early Adolescence, 4,* 387–406.

Washington, V., & Glimps, B. (1983). Developmental issues for adolescent parents and their children. *Educational Horizons, 61,* 195–199.

Winn, M. (1981). *Children without childhood.* New York: Penguin.

CHAPTER OUTLINE

The Middle Level Student
cognitive development

4

OVERVIEW

Though less visible than young adolescents' rapidly changing bodies and their growing desires to socialize and become independent, the cognitive development that occurs in early adolescence is no less powerful in its effect on 10- to 14-year-olds. Research in recent decades has produced important new insights into how the brain functions and develops. This research suggests that there may be several types of intelligence—not just one kind, as traditionally accepted. It also has yielded new knowledge of how learning occurs. This chapter looks at the characteristics of cognitive development in young adolescents and examines what recent research contributes to our understanding of the ways that 10- to 14-year-olds process information, think, and learn.

In this chapter, you will read about:

1. The characteristics of cognitive growth displayed during early adolescence.
2. The three major schools of thought, and their theories of cognitive development.
3. The main similarities and differences between different theories of cognitive development.
4. Recent research findings on the brain, thinking, and learning.

5 The implications for middle level school education.
6 The needs of exceptional learners in the middle level school.
7 Factors that interfere with young adolescents' cognitive development and overall school progress.
8 The effect on young adolescents of school practices, including the modern overemphasis on testing.
9 The planning of developmentally appropriate curricular practices and instructional methods by middle level school educators.
10 The implications of multiple intelligences.

THE YOUNG ADOLESCENT LEARNER

Young adolescent learners demonstrate intellectual characteristics that are age-appropriate for middle level education and differ considerably both from elementary and high school learners. During the transition from childhood to adolescence, and eventually adulthood, young adolescents progress at individual rates and display a broadening repertoire of intellectual skills. Within this age range emerges the ability for increasingly abstract and knowledgeable thought and higher levels of cognitive functions, such as complex mental manipulations and the testing of hypotheses. As with physical and psychosocial development, middle level school educators should understand the intellectual developmental characteristics of young adolescents and should plan curriculum and instruction accordingly. According to *Turning Points* (1989),

> Contrary to much conventional belief, cognitive development during young adolescence is not on hold. Belief in such claims has had substantial and damaging effects on middle grade education, by limiting innovation in curriculum development that might require new and more advanced ways of thinking. (p. 42)

Adelson (1971), two decades ago, described the thinking of 12- to 16-year-old learners as more abstract, less authoritarian, and more knowledgeable. The thinking of 10- to 14-year-old learners is not on as high a level as that of 12- to 16-year-olds; however, the transition to these higher levels has begun. An increased ability to deal with abstractions provides evidence of the gradual movement from the concrete operations stage to the formal operations stage.

As abstract thought and language develop, learners begin to represent the world internally, i.e., within their own minds, rather than depending totally upon concrete symbols and observable reference points. A predominance of concrete thought and a gradual emergence of abstract thought characterize 11- to 13-year-old learners. Educators should be careful not to overestimate the young adolescent's thought levels or mistakenly assume an ability to represent the world internally (Thornburg, 1982).

LEARNING THEORIES AND THE MIDDLE LEVEL SCHOOL

Three schools of thought—the behavorists, developmentalists, and humanists—have set out to explain the learning process and the factors that affect learning outcomes. Debate continues among them around the means and methods learners use to process information. These theories relate to all age groups and not only young adolescents. Being acquainted with the behavorial, developmental, and humanistic theories helps educators to understand contemporary theories of intelligence and cognition. However, caution must be exercised in interpreting basic principles of the three theories and applying them to the education of middle level learners. This section provides a brief introduction to the three groups of learning theories. Readers who want to study this topic in greater depth are directed to Table 4.1 and to selected sources in the list *Selected Works and Commentaries* at the end of this chapter.

BEHAVIORISM

Three outstanding behaviorists, E. L. Thorndike, B. F. Skinner, and Robert Gagné, proposed that the way to study learning was to observe how the external environment affects overt behaviors (Biehler & Snowman, 1990). The behaviorist theory holds that learning occurs through the association or bonding of a stimulus and a response. This position emphasizes a mechanical, incremental, external, and structured nature of learning. It places little importance on such nonobservable aspects of learning as perception, interest, experience, and motivation. For example, memorizing and using rules for punctuating sentences enable learners to write sentences that may be meaningful to them.

Reinforcement Theory

B. F. Skinner's (1970) most notable and significant contribution to contemporary behavioral theory was his theory of operant conditioning. This focused on experiments that attempted to shape behavior by eliciting responses to prescribed stimuli or experiences. Through appropriate reinforcement, children learn to walk, talk, perform motions, and play instruments. As reinforcement occurs, the likelihood of children repeating learned behaviors increases (Bigge, 1976).

Skinner's theories have application to teaching and learning in the middle level school. An important element of operant conditioning is proper and immediate reinforcement. The teacher who gives immediate feedback concerning student progress has provided reinforcement that will strengthen the likelihood that learning will be maintained. First, programmed instruction and later computer-assisted instruction provide a techno-psychological system of teaching and learning where subject matter is broken down into manageable steps. Such an approach may be ideal for young adolescents who have a wide diversity of cognitive abilities, intellectual skills, and interests. Skinner (1970) advocated

TABLE 4.1 Learning Theories and Their Implications for Middle Level Education

Proponents	Implications for Learners	Implications for Teachers
BEHAVIORISTS		
E. L. Thorndike 1874–1949 B. F. Skinner 1904–1990 Robert Gagné 1916–	■ Hierarchy of learning—from drill and rote to problem solving ■ Specific goals stated in behavioral terms ■ Feedback at regular intervals ■ Reinforcement techniques utilized ■ Basic skills programs and competency testing emphasized ■ Textbooks, programmed materials, skill sheets, and computer-assisted instruction	■ Teacher-directed instruction stressed ■ Diagnostic/prescriptive techniques utilized ■ Teacher as designer/manager/evaluator ■ Reinforcement techniques emphasized ■ Learning activities sequenced ■ Curriculum stress on subject matter, skills mastery
DEVELOPMENTALISTS		
John Dewey 1859–1952 Jean Piaget 1896–1980 Jerome Bruner 1915–	■ Learning through activity, direct experiences, social interaction, and problem solving ■ Thinking viewed as logical process, forming hypotheses, and using scientific methods ■ Learning adapted to needs, interests, abilities of individual ■ Socialization skills emphasized ■ Discovery learning utilized	■ Teacher as guide, resource, and collaborator ■ Teacher possesses knowledge of content, learner, and pedagogy ■ Concern for needs, interests, abilities of learner paramount ■ Curriculum stress on developmental, experiential, interdisciplinary, and relevance ■ Higher-order thinking stressed
HUMANISTS		
Arthur Combs 1912– Carl Rogers 1902–1987 William Purkey 1929–	■ Learning is perceptual, insightful, and personal ■ Learners control behavior rather than being shaped ■ Positive self-concept essential to academic achievement ■ Motivation viewed as internal, not external ■ Behavior stresses values development, independence, interpersonal relationships, and self-actualization ■ Freedom to learn emphasized	■ Teacher–pupil interaction and positive relationships stressed ■ Curriculum and instruction reflect personal developmental needs of learners ■ School climate promotes openness, equal access, security, safety, and acceptance ■ Teachers are empowered and strive to enhance learner self-concept ■ Teaching viewed as the facilitation of learning

a managed environment in which the teacher "controls" the learning situation by establishing specific goals, arranging sequential learning experiences, and providing immediate feedback. The mental, physical, and social changes that young adolescents are experiencing quite often interfere with the learning process. The middle level school based upon Skinner's principles would provide a carefully controlled environment where young adolescent learners know exactly what to do at every stage.

Neobehaviorism: The Conditions of Learning

In *The Conditions of Learning,* Gagné synthesized a learning theory drawing from behaviorism and Gestalt-field theories (Bigge, 1976). Gagné's approach divided human capabilities into five major categories and the learning process into eight hierarchical conditions. The ultimate goal of school learning is problem-solving ability. Such a goal also includes the motivation and skills to apply material learned in classrooms to situations outside the classroom. In essence, Gagné believes that students should become problem solvers, self-learners, and independent thinkers (Biehler & Snowman, 1990).

Ten- to fourteen-year-olds are beginning to develop unique abilities to function within the context of Gagné's five categories of learning. Also, the wide diversity in cognitive and physical development of young adolescents necessitates that educators be cognizant of the wide ranges of learner abilities, needs, and skills. Teachers of young adolescents should be designers, managers, and evaluators of instruction so that the proper "conditions" of learning will promote optimal learning.

DEVELOPMENTALISM

The developmentalist theories of John Dewey, Jean Piaget, and Jerome Bruner have implications for middle level school educators. Dewey's theory of learning was comprehensive and rested on philosophical, psychological, and sociological foundations of education. He wrote extensively on how children learn, how teachers should teach, and the nature of curriculum in such definitive works as *Democracy and Education* (1916), *How We Think* (1933), and *Experience and Education* (1938). Dewey espoused the view that learners do not function as passive recipients, but instead collaborate with teachers to become active partners in learning (Morris & Pai, 1976). The developmental stage theories of Jean Piaget and Jerome Bruner have also had significant influence on teaching and learning in contemporary American schools and classrooms.

Stages of Development

Piaget theorized that maturing children pass through four developmental stages: sensory-motor (birth to age two); pre-operational (ages two to seven); concrete operational (ages seven to twelve); and formal operations (ages 12 and older). Although the beginning and duration of the developmental stages vary, he maintained that the stages occur for all children in a constant, invariant sequence, with each stage having educational significance. Developmental stages having the most relevance for middle level educators are the concrete operations stage (seven to twelve years) and the formal operations stage (age twelve and older).

The *concrete operations stage* corresponds closely to the late elementary and beginning middle level school years and has significant implications for the curriculum and instruction of 10- to 14-year-olds. During the transition from the late concrete operations stage to the formal operations stage, learners develop the ability to formulate and test hypotheses (Ginsburg & Opper, 1988). Fifth- and sixth-graders order, organize, and structure information within the mind, while seventh- and eighth-graders employ deductive reasoning and reflective thinking (Thornburg, 1980).

The *formal operations stage* is exemplified by the child's capacity to conceptualize abstract relationships, to employ inductive thinking, and to expand processes of logical thinking. During this stage, the middle level learner considers all aspects of a problem and experiments, hypothesizes, and analyzes to arrive at conclusions. Active experiences in logical thinking are crucial to successful development in this stage.

Piaget's ideas on intellectual development can be a valuable resource for middle level school educators. First, teachers need to assess children's levels of thought during curriculum development and instruction to determine the appropriateness of learning experiences. Second, learning requires that children be given the opportunity to manipulate and think about objects and to develop process skills. Third, young adolescents, often with short attention spans because of preoccupations with matters other than schooling, should be motivated with experiences sufficiently unique to hold their attention. Fourth, teachers need to recognize and accept the fact that these young adolescents are developing socially and that opportunities for positive social interaction should be an important aspect of the middle level school curriculum.

Stages of Representation

Jerome Bruner (1960) in his seminal work, *The Process of Education,* combined several aspects of Piagetian learning theory with his own ideas on the structure of learning and processes for teaching and learning. His theory served as a catalyst for curriculum reform, changes in instructional methods, and appreciation for how children learn, think, and behave. Bruner, like Piaget, proposed a stage theory of cognitive development, which focused on the child's ability to think and consisted of three representation stages: enactive, iconic, and symbolic. The iconic and symbolic stages are relevant for teachers of young adolescents. In the iconic stage, the child learns through pictures and other visual representations of reality. In the symbolic stage, the child uses symbols and language to hypothesize (Yelon & Weinstein, 1977).

Bruner's contributions to the study of how children learn have implications for teachers of young adolescents. The difficulty sometimes encountered in matching Piaget's and Bruner's theories to classroom settings should not cloud the issue that the cognitive development of young adolescents must be understood and used as a basis for instruction.

HUMANISM

Humanistic theorists such as Arthur Combs, Carl Rogers, and William Purkey called for classrooms that were positive, humane, and caring; focused on the self-concept; and emphasized freedom, worth, and dignity. Their goals include accepting learner's needs and purposes, facilitating self-actualization, personalizing educational practices, and recognizing the primacy of human feelings. While Combs and Rogers focused more on the humanistic characteristics of teachers, Purkey directed attention to learners, especially their self-concepts, which he considered a significant factor in determining academic achievement. The ultimate goal, however, remained the same: teachers would facilitate learning in a school setting that stressed trust, caring, sensitivity, and empathy.

In *Perceiving, Behaving, Becoming* (1962) and *The Professional Education of Teachers* (1965), Arthur Combs presented his ideas about the behavior of teachers and students in humane classrooms. Combs thought perception to be an integral aspect of the learning process. He based his beliefs on the thesis that "all behavior of a person is the direct result of his field of perception at the moment of his behaving" (Combs, 1965, p. 12).

Combs (1982) argued that concern for student attitudes, feelings, and emotions are important facets of the learning process and must be integral aspects of educational planning and practice. Educational systems which ignore or reject such aspects run the risk of being ineffective. Four highly affective factors known to influence the learning process include: self-concept, meaningful challenge, values, and feelings of belonging. Educators should seek to apply the principles known about the nature of students and the teaching process. When these principles are applied, "students will learn *anything* better, including the time-honored basics" (p. 497).

Teachers of young adolescents can benefit from an understanding of how Combs' affective factors influence teaching and learning in the middle level school. Teachers dedicated to providing a humanistic environment will be sensitive, trusting, confident, and flexible (Biehler & Snowman, 1990). The teacher's roles will include being a facilitator, guide, and friend. Teachers should work to understand students' needs, improve self-concept, and provide a positive classroom environment. Combs considers teachers to have the dual responsibility of establishing an appropriate atmosphere for learners and of being persons capable of demonstrating humanistic characteristics.

Carl Rogers (1983) also deplored what he viewed as the mechanistic, one-dimensional nature of behaviorism. His client-centered or nondirective approach places emphasis on the learner. This theory assumes that students learn to control their own behavior and become more responsible when teachers treat them as the central figures in the teaching and learning process (Yelon & Weinstein, 1977). In books such as *On Becoming a Person* (1961) and *Freedom to Learn* (1969), Rogers conferred primacy on the concept of the individual's "freedom to learn."

Many principles of learning espoused by Carl Rogers are applicable to the middle level, since many middle level learners are in a developmental stage where they want more freedom and self-responsibility. Teachers must determine learners' interests and plan instruction accordingly, because relevant educational experiences will motivate learning. The student is the fulcrum in the teaching and learning process; the student must be helped to be self-responsible, self-motivated, self-directed, and self-evaluative. Learners must be active participants in the teaching and learning process rather than just being passive.

William Purkey (1970, 1978) considers self-concept, feelings, and emotions to be significant factors in learning. In *Self-Concept and School Achievement,* he stressed the importance of students' self-perceptions and documented the vitally important relationship between a student's self-concept and his or her level of school achievement.

Learner self-concept is particularly important to the middle level school given its relationship to academic achievement and student behavior. Experiencing far-reaching identity changes, 10- to 14-year-olds need a healthy self-concept as development progresses between childhood and adolescence and on to young adulthood. Purkey's (1970) statement that ". . . the research evidence clearly shows a persistent and significant relationship between the self-concept and academic achievement" (p. 15) provides a considerable challenge for middle level educators. This challenge requires an understanding of the relationship between self-concept and school success. Middle level educators can provide for learner success through appropriate learning environments and positive, caring relationships between learners and teachers.

IMPLICATIONS FOR MIDDLE LEVEL SCHOOL TEACHING AND LEARNING

Whether the behaviorists, developmentalists, or humanists offer the most logical explanation for how learners process information may not seem important to some middle level school educators. However, educators' opinions of how young adolescents process information and their reasons for learning have a significant influence on the curriculum, teacher behaviors, instructional and organizational decisions, and attitudes toward learners themselves. Most teachers should subscribe to more than one theory (or perhaps selected aspects of more than one theory) rather than wholeheartedly placing trust in one theory only. Another reason for being acquainted with learning theories is that having a perspective of the past permits one a better understanding of contemporary research and scholarly opinion.

EARLY ADOLESCENCE: PERSPECTIVES ON THINKING AND THE BRAIN

Research in cognitive neuroscience has documented a major educational principle: Individuals vary in their approaches to processing information. While perceptive teachers have always recognized individual differences, they have not understood the cognitive bases of these differences. Cognitive science has discovered the neural, developmental bases of differences and has demonstrated that these differences can be measured and studied (Lyons & Languis, 1985). Several areas related to thinking and the brain have been examined: brain growth periodization (Epstein & Toepfer, 1978), the triune brain (MacLean, 1977), right brain/left brain functioning (Sperry, 1974), the theory of multiple intelligences (Gardner, 1987a; Walter & Gardner, 1985), and the issue of varying learning styles among learners (Dunn, Dunn, & Price, 1986). Although this research has not focused directly on the early adolescence developmental period, the findings have considerable potential for curriculum and for instruction in the middle level school. Link (1985) wrote:

> Interest in intellectual development is no new phenomenon. Psychologists, scientists, and educators have periodically come together over the last two decades to determine the relationship of their findings and concerns to curriculum development. However, in the past five years there has been a marked increase in activity in theoretical and practical approaches to study of the human mind and the dynamics related to the development of the intellect. (p. vii)

BRAIN GROWTH PERIODIZATION

Epstein and Toepfer's (1978) research on the brain and its growth patterns has concluded that the brain, like any other organ, experiences growth spurts at specific age intervals. The occurrence of these growth spurts happens in 85% to 90% of humans at ages 3–10 months, 2–4 years, 6–8 years, 10–12 years, and 14–16 years. During these brain growth periods, Epstein and Toepfer theorize that students are able to develop higher-level cognitive skills.

As the brain experiences periods of growth, it also experiences periods in which there is little or minimal growth. These periods occur during the schooling years of 85% to 90% of the students between the ages 4–6, 8–10, and 12–14. Toepfer linked the 12- to 14-year-old plateaus to the time when most students experience seventh and eighth grade. He believed that this suggests a need to examine and reconsider educational expectations for the learner between the ages of 12 to 14. He hypothesized that a predominantly cognitive approach to curriculum presents serious problems to middle level grade students who are not ready for formal operational thinking during the brain plateau periods. This cognitive imbalance may be a primary factor in reduced cognitive learning during the middle level years (Epstein & Toepfer, 1978).

Epstein and Toepfer (1978) recommended that educators plan activities for the brain growth plateaus that review and reinforce previously learned facts and information and that allow students to consolidate capacities initiated during earlier periods of brain growth. The general tendency in the middle level years to offer students increasingly complex cognitive processes should be questioned in light of the theory of brain growth periodization (Hester & Hester, 1983).

Controversy surrounds the brain growth issue. Although Epstein and Toepfer (1978) consider their research findings to "strongly urge a searching reappraisal of the traditional approaches to cognitive learning in the middle school years" (p. 656), other writers suggest that educators must move cautiously toward implementing a middle level program based on this research. For example, the ASCD publication, *Educational Leadership* (February 1984, p. 66), in the introduction to a symposium on the brain, warned that "the implications that children cannot learn at certain ages is dangerous." One critic, McQueen (1984) had suggested that Epstein's data supports the theory of brain growth periodization "less than might be expected" (p. 68) and continued, "teachers should not begin thinking that some of their students may be unable to learn because they are in brain growth plateaus" (p. 71). Likewise, Brooks (1984) urged that school districts would be well advised to resist the temptation of basing curricular and operational decisions on Epstein's theory since hard data failed either to refute or support the theory. While Epstein's theory may have considerable potential, middle level educators probably should heed Brook's advice until more conclusive research studies have been conducted.

THE TRIUNE BRAIN

Paul MacLean (1977, 1980), the main proponent of the *triune* brain theory, argued that the human brain amounts to three interconnected biological components, each with its own special intelligence, subjectivity, sense of time and space, memory and other functions. The *reptilian* brain plays a part in aggressive behavior, territoriality and establishment of social hierarchies. Territoriality can be observed in young adolescent and adolescent behavior as they refer to *their* desk, *their* space, and *their* locker. Social hierarchies can be observed in student cliques and in typical rituals, such as affectionate slaps, strikes, and hugs that students exchange with each other in greetings and expressions of approval in sports. The *limbic* brain controls emotion, memory, and many regulatory functions of the body, such as breathing. When a student is fearful of being called on in class, for example, there may be a resulting interruption in learning the information or content being taught in the class (Quina, 1989). A third brain, the *neocortex,* primarily focuses on the outside world or on external environmental events. The primary functions of the neocortex are abstract thinking, long-range planning, and transmission of cultural knowledge; however, it is important to note that the neocortex will not function unless the primitive brains are satisfied (Schuster & Gritton, 1986; Quina, 1989).

The reptilian brain tends to be impulsive, and, therefore, explains the unpredictable behavior of middle level learners as they seek peer acceptance. The limbic brain tends to focus on emotional behavior and is important for middle level teachers to consider in planning for the emotional stability and long-term learning of the middle level student. The neocortex brain centers on rational behavior and thinking. Middle level schools have been organized for and have strongly emphasized rational thinking and behavior, thus ignoring social acceptance, peer approval, and the emotional needs of middle level learners.

Although the triune brain theory at first may sound overly philosophical or theoretical, the theory has implications for contemporary middle level school educators. First, educators work daily with young adolescents who are increasingly engaged in territoriality, ritual patterns, and social growth. Second, as teachers communicate standards and discuss information about examinations and school rules, they should remember the limbic system's potential to cut off learning when learners sense fear. Third, educators may find their young adolescents cannot engage in abstract thinking exercises until areas such as territoriality and psychological security have been satisfied (Quina, 1989). *Turning Points* (1989) states:

> . . . the young adolescent is maturing intellectually at a significant rate. Our youth will be able to analyze problems and issues, examine the component parts, and reintegrate them into either a solution or into a new way of stating the problem or issue. (p. 15)

RIGHT BRAIN—LEFT BRAIN

While the triune brain theory suggested three hierarchical levels of the brain, the theory of a right brain and a left brain assumed that the brain is divided into two hemispheres. Sperry (1974), a Nobel laureate in physiology, explained that the two hemispheres of the brain process information differently. Each hemisphere, according to Sperry (1974) and Quina (1989) has its own private sensations, perceptions, thoughts, and ideas which are separate from the corresponding experience in the opposite hemisphere. Each hemisphere has its own memories which can be recalled by the other hemisphere.

Quina (1989) provided evidence to suggest that there are distinct physical differences in the ways left and right hemispheres process visual information. For example, to recognize a face, it's necessary to take in both the details of the face—*high-frequency information*—and the overall configured pattern—*low-frequency information*. For the brain to operate at its maximum capacity, it is essential for the process to include both detail *and* overall patterns (Quina, 1989).

Springer and Deutsch (1985) maintained that left- and right-brain functions process information differently. Examples of these differences in processing are included in Table 4.2 (Springer & Deutsch, 1985; Quina, 1989).

Educators can use the left- and right-brain theory as a model for implementing learning strategies. Lesson plans, units, and other educational experiences should seek to activate both hemispheres by incorporating both left- and right-brain processes (Quina, 1989). Unfortunately, methods currently in practice tend to emphasize reading and writing—which are left-brain processes—and to neglect the right hemisphere, which emphasizes visual experiences, such

TABLE 4.2 The Left and Right Hemispheres of the Brain

Left Hemisphere	Right Hemisphere
convergent	divergent
intellectual	intuitive
deductive	imagination
historical	timeless
analytical	holistic
explicit	tacit
objective	subjective
successive	simultaneous
verbal	nonverbal
logical	gestalt
digital	spatial
Western thought	Eastern thought
rational	metaphorical
vertical	horizontal
discrete	continuous
abstract	concrete
realistic	impulsive
directed	free
differential	existential
sequential	multiple

(Table adapted from *Effective secondary teaching: Going beyond the bell curve* by J. Quina. Copyright © 1989 by Harper & Row Publishers, Inc. Reprinted by permission of HarperCollins Publishers.)

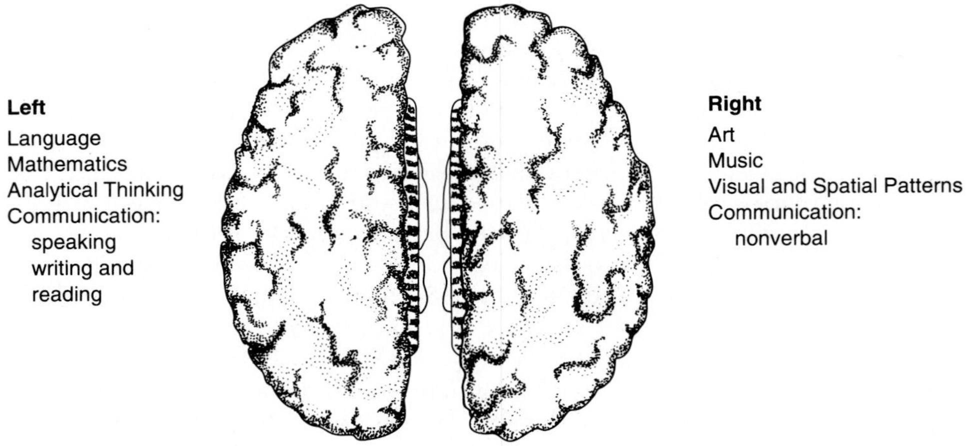

FIGURE 4.1 The two hemispheres of the brain and their cerebral functions *(Note that this does not represent an anatomically correct sketch. This figure roughly illustrates complementary dominance of left and right hemispheres for various cerebral operations.)*

as those found in art. See Figure 4.1. Other implications for educators include having teaching–learning experiences and assessment procedures that most effectively address both left- and right-brain processes, e.g., requiring both convergent and divergent thinking or providing learners with opportunities for both intellectual and intuitive thinking. Essentially, educators will be challenged to understand brain hemisphercity and to avoid teaching–learning activities which only address left-brain functioning (e.g., quantitative and verbal knowledge) at the expense of the arts (Quina, 1989).

Ornstein (1978) argued that the failure of American education results from an excessive focus on left-brain processes. In such an approach, learners have been taught to look at unconnected fragments of information rather than entire solutions. For example, a preoccupation with isolated facts has eliminated the possibility of learners grasping the relationships of parts to wholes. All knowledge cannot be expressed in words, yet the American approach to education is based almost exclusively on written and spoken forms. Such a situation neglects the artist and dancer who have learned to develop nonverbal forms of intelligence (Ornstein, 1978; Quina, 1989).

MULTIPLE INTELLIGENCES

For many years, intelligence has been defined operationally as the ability to answer items on intelligence tests. The inference from the test scores to some underlying ability is supported by statistical techniques that compare responses of subjects at different ages. The apparent correlation of these test scores across different tests corroborates the notion that a person's general intelligence does not change significantly with age nor with training nor experience. Intelligence, in essence, has been considered an inborn attribute of the individual (Walters & Gardner, 1985).

The theory of multiple intelligences (Walters & Gardner, 1985; Gardner, 1987a; Hatch & Gardner, 1988; Blythe & Gardner, 1990) questions the traditional concept of intelligence and expands it. Specifically, the theory challenges the prevailing concept of intelligence as a single general capacity which provides the individual with an ability to deal more or less effectively with any situation. The multiple intelligences theory presents a broader perspective. It proposes that each person has a number of different intelligences. It defines an intelligence as "the capacity to solve problems or fashion products which are valued in one or more cultural settings" (Blythe & Gardner, 1990, p. 33).

Several studies (Walters & Gardner, 1985; Gardner, 1987; Hatch & Gardner, 1988) have explored Gardner's theory of intelligence and have reached a consensus that the brain supports *at least seven* different abilities and intelligences. Figure 4.2 lists Gardner's seven intelligences, with examples of each.

Any new theory can be interesting and thought-provoking, but what potential or implications does the theory of multiple intelligences have for educators?

Linguistic:	the ability to use language to excite, please, convince, stimulate, or convey information (poet, novelist, editor, reporter)
Musical:	the ability to enjoy, perform, or compose a musical piece (musical performer, composer)
Logical-mathematical:	the ability to explore patterns, categories, and relationships by manipulating objects or symbols, and to experiment in a controlled, orderly way (mathematician, scientist)
Spatial:	the ability to perceive and mentally manipulate a form or object, to perceive and create tension, balance, and composition in a visual or spatial display (artist, engineer, surgeon)
Bodily-kinesthetic:	the ability to use fine and gross motor skills in sports, the performing arts, or arts and crafts production (dancer, actor, athlete, mechanic)
Interpersonal:	the ability to understand and get along with others (teacher, salesperson, clinician)
Intra-personal:	the ability to gain access to and understand one's inner feelings, dreams, and ideas (introspective novelist, lyric poet, Buddhist monk)

FIGURE 4.2 The seven intelligences *(From "New research on intelligence" by T. Hatch, & H. Gardner, 1988.* Learning88, *17 (4), p. 38. Reprinted with permission from the November/December issue of* Learning88. *Copyright 1988 Springhouse Corporation, 1111 Bethlehem Pike, Springhouse, PA 19477-0908. All rights reserved.)*

Blythe and Gardner (1990) suggested several ways that the theory of multiple intelligences could provide alternatives to current education practice:

1 *Range of Abilities Addressed.* It is important for educators to address other human abilities and talents beside the commonly considered linguistic and logical-mathematical intelligences (Gardner, 1987b).
2 *Learning Environment.* A shift in instructional conditions is called for. For example, the typical classroom, relying heavily on linguistic and logical-mathematical symbol systems, gives learners little opportunity to develop their musical intelligence.
3 *Assessment Measures.* The viability of standardized, machine-scored, multiple-choice tests, that do not allow each intelligence to be measured, is challenged.
4 *Concept of Learner.* The educator must become aware of the highly individualized ways in which each person learns since each person possesses a different combination of intelligences (Gardner, 1987b).

In light of his theory of multiple intelligences, Gardner (1987a) suggested new roles for educators. First, educators might become "assessment specialists" (p. 191) who would try to understand as sensitively as possible the abilities and interests of students. These specialists could use "intelligence-fair" (p. 191) tests to look specifically at spatial and other individual abilities rather than measuring only traditional forms of intelligence. Second, Gardner recommends the teaching of arts and humanities to young adolescents. Such efforts could include revealing and building upon students' latent abilities in the arts and the humanities. Third, the teacher's role could include matching students' profiles, goals, and interests to particular curricula and to particular styles of learning. Fourth, Gardner suggested educators (or perhaps one designated educator) being responsible for matching students to learning opportunities in the wider community. By working as apprentices or as interns, young learners can gain a feeling for the different roles offered by society.

Gardner (1987a) aptly summarized his feeling toward youngsters and their overall feelings of success at school and in the community when he stated, "I am not worried about those youngsters who are good at everything. They're going to do just fine. I'm concerned about those who don't shine in the standardized tests, and who, therefore, tend to be written off as not having gifts of any kind" (p. 192).

While Gardner's statement has direct relevance to educators at all levels, middle level educators especially should heed his concern. Middle level learners function in a vulnerable position, since they have just left the supposedly safe confines of the elementary school, they are experiencing rapid physical, psychosocial, and intellectual growth, and they are all too often bombarded with an overemphasis on testing. Perceptive middle level educators will address the needs of those young adolescents who "do everything just fine," but will also be acutely aware of young adolescents who do not appear to have "gifts of any kind."

LEARNING STYLES

Definitions. Learning styles have been defined in several ways. First, Cornett (1983) believed that learning styles are consistent patterns of behavior defined in terms of cognitive, affective, and physiological dimensions. To some degree, learning styles are indicators of how individuals process information and respond to affective, sensory, and environmental dimensions of the instruction process. A second definition came from the NASSP (1979): *Learning styles are characteristic cognitive, affective, and physiological behaviors that serve as relatively stable indicators of how learners perceive, interact with, and respond to the learning environment.* The implications of learning styles, however, extend beyond mere definitions. Style characteristics are derived from genetic coding, personality, development, motivation, and cultural and environmental influences which are relatively persistent qualities in the behavior of individual learners (Keefe, 1990). A steadily increasing body of research suggests that equating learning styles and teaching–learning activities contributes to meeting an individual's unique needs (Dunn & Dunn, 1979; NASSP, 1979; Cornett, 1983; Keefe, 1987, 1990; Stewart, 1990).

It would be a serious error to ignore developmental differences between young adolescents and adolescents. However, a study by Titus, Bergandi, and Shryock (1990) focused on adolescent learning styles and provided several conclusions with possible implications for young adolescents: (1) females were more concretely oriented than males, (2) females were more homogeneous as a group in their learning styles, and (3) slow-track students were more reflective, more active, and less abstract than fast-track students.

Space here does not allow an examination of learning styles, but interested readers may consult the *Suggested Readings* section for more detailed works. The literature on learning styles continues to expand, yet most studies are broad-based and do not deal with the young adolescent developmental period.

Assessments. Understanding what learning styles are and recognizing their potential for improving academic achievement and overall school productivity will undoubtedly be vital during the 1990s and beyond. Similarly, middle level schools will need to be able to assess an individual student's learning style. Several assessment instruments provide a means of determining specific domains of styles while still other instruments provide a more comprehensive means of assessing overall styles.

One popular instrument for assessing students' learning styles is the Learning Style Inventory (LSI) (Dunn, Dunn, & Price, 1986). The LSI incorporated many useful affective and physiological elements of learning style but lacks a definitive cognitive component. The Dunns and Price define learning style in terms of four significant learning conditions and 18 scales. Students complete a 104-item self-report questionnaire that identifies learning preferences in four learning situations: environmental conditions and emotional, sociological, and physical needs.

The NASSP Learning Style Profile (LSP) (Keefe & Monk, 1986) was developed through the combined efforts of the NASSP research department and the NASSP Learning Styles Task force. The LSP is an instrument to diagnose the learning styles of students in grades 6–12, and contains 23 scales representing four higher order factors: cognitive styles, perceptual responses, study and instructional preferences (the affective and physiological elements).

CASE STUDY

JENNIFER—AN ELEVEN-YEAR-OLD GIRL *(continued)*

Jennifer, the 11-year-old girl we met in Chapter 3, is experiencing concurrent intellectual changes that allow her to expand her mental world. Jennifer is often preoccupied with herself and often writes in her secret journal about her days at school and her thoughts about growing up. She also is beginning to develop the ability to use hypothetical reasoning and is beginning to participate in problem-solving activities. She is fascinated by her increasing ability to think and reason, but she also wonders whether she is "like other people my age." One question also bothers her: "Why can't I be really good at more than one thing?" Jennifer has been very successful at piano and has played in several citywide recitals. She wonders why she cannot be equally good at other things she tries. Jennifer sees herself as developing normally, but she still questions why some people appear to have thoughts she does not have, specifically in the problem-solving exercises in some of her classes.

JENNIFER: A COMMENTARY FOR MIDDLE LEVEL SCHOOL EDUCATORS

Jennifer's intellectual changes are closely related to her psychosocial-emotional development, rather than to her intellect developing in isolation. She is functioning in Piaget's concrete operational stage and is able to recognize and compare distinct characteristics and properties. Assuming Jennifer's teachers know her as an individual and knew her levels of cognitive development, how can they most effectively address her intellectual changes? Jennifer's school should provide an array of opportunities for critical thinking and problem-solving activities, since Jennifer is developing these cognitive abilities. Rather than memorizing information only to be given back on a worksheet, she should have numerous opportunities to think, to reason, to collect data and form hypotheses, and to reach her own conclusions without fear of teacher disapproval. Also, Jennifer's preoccupation with herself should be understood as an expected characteristic of early adolescence. A last but very important point: Jennifer should be provided opportunities to build upon her musical expertise and should be assured that learners have various abilities, skills, and intelligences. She should work on other intellectual areas and skills, though not at the expense of her music.

IMPLICATIONS FOR MIDDLE LEVEL TEACHING AND LEARNING

Knowledge and understanding of the intellectual development of the young adolescent learner will provide middle level educators with considerable insight into planning, implementing, and evaluating instruction. First, realizing the vast diversity in intellectual development is a prerequisite for choosing appropriate content and effective instruction. Second, subject matter content should correspond closely with the late concrete operational or early formal operational stages and should reflect the understanding that all learners will not be functioning at the same level. Third, learners demonstrating appropriate development should be encouraged to think in abstract terms and to develop and form hypotheses. Fourth, Thornburg (1980) suggests that learning experiences should be structured for a smooth transition to advanced levels of thought. The Middle Grades Task Force for the California State Department of Education states in *Caught in the Middle* (1987):

> The middle grades are a critical point in the development of skills for lifelong learning. The emerging intellectual capabilities of young adolescents make the use of more sophisticated learning strategies and study skills possible. (p. 27)

COGNITIVE GROWTH AND THE MIDDLE LEVEL SCHOOL

THE CHARACTERISTICS OF COGNITIVE GROWTH IN YOUNG ADOLESCENTS

As young adolescents mature physically, growing in body size and developing more motor skills, there is a concurrent growth in cognitive skills. Their world widens with each succeeding experience, and they can cope more readily with abstract ideas. They develop their ability to generalize and to discover relationships. Because of the great differences in mental and physical characteristics, educators should avoid a single, preconceived standard for all (Georgiady & Romano, 1977). Readers are reminded that although cognitive growth characteristics can be documented with some certainty, the cognitive level of individual young adolescents should be understood prior to planning curricular practices and instructional methods.

During early adolescence, cognitive development is subject to dramatic changes in capacity for processing, reasoning, and valuing. Processing involves the operations that young adolescents use as they add information to their existing cognitive structures; master concrete operations and begin formal operations and deal with the properties of the present world. Reasoning employs processes for the young adolescent to become involved with cognitively reaching a justification or an explanation. In valuing, young adolescents develop abilities for evaluating their environment and the events in their lives. Figure 4.3 describes the cognitive growth characteristics of young adolescents.

INTERRELATIONSHIPS: PHYSICAL, PSYCHOSOCIAL/ EMOTIONAL, AND MENTAL/COGNITIVE

It would be a serious error to assume that physical, psychosocial, and intellectual aspects develop in isolation. In reality, a complex and intricate process occurs as one aspect of development contributes to another. For example, as physical development occurs, the young adolescent's self-concept (a significant part of psychosocial development) changes to reflect one's developing physique. Likewise, the developing cognitive structures allow higher levels of thinking and an overall better perception of one's physical and psychosocial abilities as well as one's overall ability to cope with a rapidly changing social world. The interrelationships of physical, intellectual, and social changes can neither be overlooked nor underestimated. The kind of person the young adolescent is becoming depends significantly upon: (l) his or her previous experiences, (2) the developmental changes occurring almost daily, and (3) the developing cognitive structure which allows for increased reflection upon past and present events. Social changes, accompanied by physical and emotional changes associated with the onset of puberty (Crockett, Losoff, & Peterson, 1984), warrant a nurturing, caring, and understanding response from significant adults (Juhasz, 1982).

Cognitive developmental charcteristics include young adolescents experiencing rapid and dramatic changes in thinking and increasingly being able to:

process

Use cognitive skills to solve real-life problems
Deal with hypotheses involving two or more variables
Develop capacities to deal with abstract concepts
Deal with increasingly difficult academic concepts
Engage in the process of social analysis

reason

Think reflexively and engage in propositional thinking
Think critically, reflectively, and with reasoning skills
Argue to convince others and to clarify own thinking
Make generalizations
Use hypothetical reasoning
Consider ideas contrary to fact
Project thought into the future, to anticipate, and to formulate goals

value

Make judgments regarding behavior
Develop a sense of morality and ethical behavior
Become capable of taking another's point of view
Develop personal attitudes and perspectives
Become capable of setting realistic goals
Become capable of developing self-discipline
Develop independence and a concern for interdependence
Develop increasing recognition of cultural diversity

FIGURE 4.3 Cognitive developmental characteristics of young adolescents

COGNITIVE READINESS: PLANNING APPROPRIATE INSTRUCTION

Toepfer (1988) maintained that increased earlier intellectual maturity has not paralleled the acceleration of physical development during the young adolescent developmental period. Although some students may have the cognitive abilities for higher level challenges, Toepfer warned of introducing high school intellectual challenges into the middle level school. One should not assume that all students have the cognitive structures necessary for challenging intellectual activities. Toepfer also argued against states legislating early high school learning requirements down into the middle level. Rather than assuming that young adolescents can succeed by "trying harder" (p. 111), educators should understand that readiness, not effort alone, affects what the youngster can learn. A youngster at the concrete operations stage cannot master intellectual challenges that demand formal, abstract thinking abilities. Although some memorization might occur, learners will be unable to learn information which is beyond their cognitive ability at any given age. To assume that all young adolescents can perform at the same level as a few precocious and intellectually advanced youngsters, ignores individual differences and what is known about cognitive readiness (Toepfer, 1988).

Toepfer (1985) earlier reported that on the average, about 5% of 11-year-olds, 12% of 12-year-olds, 20% of 13-year-olds and 24% of 14-year-olds can actually do formal abstract reasoning. To determine actual cognitive readiness levels, Toepfer (1985) suggested using the Arlin Test of Formal Reasoning, which has a fifth-grade readability and can be given during a class period. The test can indicate whether students are low concrete, high concrete, low formal (abstract), or high formal (abstract) thinkers at the time. After determining the cognitive levels at which students are functioning, assignments can be arranged that match and challenge the learner's cognitive abilities (Toepfer, 1985, 1988).

According to Brooks, Fusco, & Glennon (1983), teachers can take these steps to develop a thorough understanding of a cognitive development process:

1 Identify the characteristics of each of the four stages associated with Piaget's model of cognitive development.
2 Relate the brain growth periods of Epstein to specific cognitive stages and levels.
3 Critique Piaget's stage model with respect to general educational implications.
4 Analyze student's work to determine the complexity of cognitive thinking.
5 Examine their own teaching and questioning styles in terms of learners' cognitive abilities.
6 Generate examples of the specific cognitive schemes identified in the Piagetian model through their own teaching and content areas. (p. 6)

THE NEEDS OF EXCEPTIONAL LEARNERS

All young adolescents deserve caring and qualified educators, but some learners need special attention which calls for specific expertise. The range of exceptional learners makes a listing nearly impossible, for differences which make learners exceptional are nearly endless: From the mentally handicapped to the gifted and talented, from the learning disabled to the orthopedically handicapped, and from drug and alcohol abusers to suicidal learners. Other young adolescents who may be classified as exceptional may include learners with low self-concepts, learners from poverty homes, and learners who feel unable to cope with the demands of the middle level school. It is important for educators to understand that all learners, regardless of handicapping conditions, need the most expertise and attention educators can offer; however, it is also imperative to point out that other young adolescents with less visible handicaps, i.e., low self-concept, need special and caring teachers. In a sense, all young adolescent learners are exceptional in some aspect, and it is the teacher's responsibility to determine the exceptionality and to provide appropriate curricular practices and instructional methods.

Predicting accurate numbers of exceptional needs for young adolescents is difficult at best; however, they are undoubtedly very numerous and deserve the attention of middle level educators. Three of the most common disabling conditions include social maladjustments, mental handicaps, and learning disabilities.

The *socially maladjusted learner* demonstrates behavior that violates laws or conventional standards of the school or community. This behavior may include gang- or group-related vandalism, stealing, fighting, truancy, sexual precocity, substance abuse, or other acts. To complicate the situation further, socially maladjusted youngsters impair the functioning ability of other persons, whether they are teachers or students, who are victims. A related dilemma is the socially incompetent learner; these students rarely participate in informal peer interactions and resist joining educational activities. While this behavior may not harm other learners, this learner has a reduced chance of opportunities for friendships and for profiting from classroom and informal learning activities (Cullinan & Epstein, 1990).

The *mentally handicapped learner* needs specific educational arrangements, such as regular educational placement, resource services, and self-contained classes. The instruction for mentally handicapped young adolescents and adolescents should be different from the elementary level. Many students who are mildly handicapped may also receive one or more related services, such as speech/language intervention, physical therapy, occupational therapy, and mental health counseling (Patton & Polloway, 1990).

The third exceptionality is the *learning-disabled learner.* These learners usually read poorly, often failing to apply the strategies they have. They rarely request assistance when experiencing difficulty, and they experience pervasive oral and written language problems as well as poor spelling. In addition, the problems of learning-disabled adolescents (as young adolescents) are compounded by weaknesses and shortcomings in social skills which are particularly devastating due to the importance of peer group relations (McCormick, 1990).

It is important for middle level school educators to remember that each of these exceptionalities—social maladjustment, mental handicaps, learning disabilities—as well as other exceptionalities may have a ripple effect and significantly affect the young learners' self-concept and their opinion of their ability to cope in an ever-widening social world. Not only must adequate educational programs be provided for the exceptional condition itself, but the young adolescents' related developmental areas also deserve appropriate attention.

YOUNG ADOLESCENT PREOCCUPATIONS: PHYSICAL CHANGES AND SOCIAL INTERESTS

As we saw in Chapter 3, young adolescents' preoccupation with their changing bodies and increasing social interests may make it difficult for them to listen for long periods of time, and may lessen their intellectual and scholarly efforts. Although one must be careful with generalizations, young adolescents' concerns and preoccupations about being liked or having significant friendships, without doubt, handicap attentive listening and intellectual pursuits. Teachers wanting to capitalize on friendships might want to implement cooperative learning strategies, in which friends can work together toward an established goal. In any event, middle level educators should implement curriculum and instruction that correspond to young adolescents' concerns for physical and social changes.

In Chapter 3, our Case Study examined 13-year-old Michael's physical and psychosocial-emotional development. Here, we continue the case study by examining his cognitive development, showing the intricate interrelationships between the various developmental areas.

CASE STUDY

MICHAEL—A THIRTEEN-YEAR-OLD BOY *(continued)*

Thirteen-year-old Michael's cognitive ability is expanding daily: His problem-solving abilities, his ability to think hypothetically and deductively, his reflective and abstract thinking, and his concept of volume have developed significantly. These developments have contributed to Michael's self-concept and his ability to socialize in his ever-widening world. He is able to see another person's perspective and is engaging in higher-level thinking. Michael is pleased with himself and his increasing cognitive development, yet he wonders when he will think "like an adult." In some ways, he thinks he is functioning at an adult level. For instance, his reading rate has developed almost to an adult level. Similarly, he uses charts, maps, and diagrams to communicate thoughts and messages. However, Michael still realizes his strengths and weaknesses. While his strengths include some athletic ability and the other previously mentioned skills, Michael realizes his weaknesses include music and artistic ability and a lack of development in spatial relationships. He is somewhat self-critical and wants to improve in areas of weaknesses; however, his teachers have encouraged him to understand that young adolescents have various types of intelligences and have tried to convince him to have positive feelings about his strengths. Even with his increasing cognitive development, developing a realistic picture of his abilities and skills is often difficult for Michael to accomplish.

MICHAEL: A COMMENTARY FOR MIDDLE LEVEL SCHOOL EDUCATORS

Michael's teachers need to build upon his developing cognitive abilities by giving him opportunities to participate in problem-solving activities, to think abstractly, and to work collaboratively toward a goal. Involving Michael with his peers will also contribute to his psychosocial ability and his interpersonal skills. His teachers can also help him to accept his strengths and weaknesses and to understand that he is indeed becoming an adult. Curricular opportunities should include hypothetical situations in the various subject areas, formal and informal opportunities to improve reflective thinking abilities, developmentally appropriate reading materials directed toward areas such as human relations, careers, and other areas of interest, with opportunities for both oral and written expression.

CONTEMPORARY ISSUES

Many contemporary issues affect young adolescents' academic achievement, overall school progress, and development. The wide array of issues does not allow a detailed examination of each. Therefore, it becomes necessary to select issues which have special significance to middle level learners. The three contemporary issues selected for a brief discussion include the many school pressures placed on young adolescents, the overemphasis on testing and assessment, and the current push for critical thinking and reasoning abilities.

SCHOOL PRESSURES—ACADEMIC, PERSONAL, AND SOCIAL

While it would appear that schools would be caring and humane institutions and would contribute to feelings of psychological comfort and safety, all too often the opposite scenario prevails. Schools, indeed, are considered by young adolescents to be a prime source of stress. Educators should be aware that school situations (i.e., grades, school in general, fights with peers, homework, and lost possessions) all contribute to young adolescents' stress (Greene, 1988). Research conducted by Arth (1990) documented that schools contributed to student stress. Arth's school-related concerns and pressures included: learners' fears of failure, giving presentations in front of the class, being sent to the principal's office, being picked on, and keeping up with assignments. While some pressure and stress may result from school practices, other stress may stem from pressure placed on schools to show evidence of achievement and institutional self-worth.

Middle level educators should recognize school pressures and their often detrimental effects on young adolescents' achievement and progress. Academic pressures may result from the overemphasis on testing, on overdependence on ability grouping, and educators' failure to provide curriculum practices and instructional methods appropriate to learners' abilities. Personal pressures may result from learners failing to recognize individual strengths and weaknesses and not understanding that while one "intelligence" might be low, other "intelligences" may be higher. Social pressures may result from forming friendships, peer pressures, and dealing with cliques. Although all generations have experienced pressures and stresses in one form or another, young adolescents during the 1990s and beyond will face their own unique challenges, perhaps caused in part by a rapidly changing technological society, by changing family structures, and by the educational reform movement which has placed additional demands on virtually every aspect of education.

OVEREMPHASIS ON TESTING

The overemphasis on testing and the often extreme reliance on test scores to categorize learners' abilities and to determine student achievement pose a dilemma for students, educators, and parents. Educators and parents will not be surprised to learn that most tests only measure certain abilities and intelligences and, all too often, fail to measure more abstract aspects of learning. Still, the national trend continues to test any aspect of learning which can be measured and to consider unmeasurable aspects as insignificant or unimportant. To compound the seriousness of the situation, states and school districts have used test scores as a means of holding educators accountable and as a means of justifying monetary expenditures.

While testing has been hailed by accountability advocates and test-makers, learners have not reaped the purported benefits of testing and, in some cases, have been outright harmed. First, once learners have been labeled by a score, they are likely to bear that stigma throughout their educational career. Second, tests tend to trivialize learning into multiple-choice chunks of information for the convenience of scoring (Corbett, 1990). Third, Sternberg (1990) maintained that testing and the reporting of assessment scores place value only on certain aspects of a child's education. For example, while analytical abilities—all the skills associated with acquiring and memorizing information—are the ones that most standardized and class tests measure, other abilities and skills such as creativity and practical abilities are not measured.

Most authorities on the dilemma of testing believe that the overemphasis on testing is here to stay (Brandt, 1989; Corbett, 1990; Sternberg, 1989). If this is the case, and the obsession with testing continues, what steps can be taken to provide all learners with an accurate assessment of their abilities? Sternberg (1990) recommended an assessment device which measures a broader definition of intelligence, or specifically, three types of learning: analytic learning; creativity, which may be recognized by the teacher yet cannot be tested and measured; and practical abilities, including how well learners cope with *their own* world. Sternberg (1989) also advocated that report cards should be changed to provide a better reflection of learners' overall abilities, skills, and intelligences.

Since the overemphasis on testing will probably continue during the 1990s and beyond, what specific steps can middle level school educators take to reduce the ill effects created by misuse of tests? First, it is important to point out that not all testing is misused. Diagnostic testing to determine learners' developmental or achievement levels can lead to better placement and improved instruction. Such testing is needed and should play an integral role in all middle level schools. However, the situation quickly changes when testing is misused, overemphasized, or serves only to justify grouping patterns or as a means of holding teachers accountable for situations often beyond their control. In these cases, middle level educators need to reassure learners of their self-worth and explain that while tests measure valuable information, other abilities and skills are not measured. Second, middle level educators should work through professional organizations such as the National Middle School Association to bring the testing dilemma to the attention of the public. Third, educators should insist that their districts selectively choose tests such as the Sternberg Triarchic Abilities Test (STAT) which can be group-administered and provides scores for analytic, creative, and practical abilities (Sternberg, 1990).

CRITICAL THINKING SKILLS

A third contemporary issue, that will continue at the forefront of educational interests, is students' ability to engage in problem solving and critical thinking. That students are lagging in thinking skills is apparent at all levels of education (Carr, 1988). The thinking skills issue should be especially important to middle level educators because young adolescents are experiencing rapid cognitive development, which allows critical reflection that was previously impossible. Referring specifically to young adolescents, *Turning Points* (1989) described the primary goal of effective thinking programs:

> A primary goal in choosing curricula and learning methods in the middle grades should be the disciplining of young adolescents' minds, that is, their capacity for active, engaged thinking. A student with a disciplined mind can assimilate knowledge, rather than merely recall information by rote or apply simple algorithms. The student can challenge the reliability of evidence; recognize the viewpoint or voice behind the words, pictures, or ideas presented; see relationships between ideas, and ask what-if and suppose-that questions. (p. 43)

What, then, is thinking and thought like during these critical years? Adelson (1983) argued that because of the biological and social changes occurring and because the young adolescent and adolescent years are ages of tremendous cognitive change, these groups appear particularly difficult to reach and understand. Adelson (1983) continued: "The youngster often seems to flip-flop in terms of intellectual level—at one moment concrete and rather primitive, at another moment capable of abstract and advanced thought" (p. 161). In certain aspects, cognitive modes or abilities are substantially different from those educators expect: time perspectives are generally foreshortened; a diminished sense of history characterizes thought; the ability to think into the future much beyond the present is limited; long-range consequences are not understood; and abilities to understand that social institutions are subject to modification are limited (Adelson, 1983).

Before offering suggestions on how to teach critical thinking, a definition of the term appears appropriate. Sternberg (1985) offered the following definition: "Critical thinking comprises the mental processes, strategies, and representations people use to solve problems, make decisions, and learn new concepts" (p. 46). And, *Caught in the Middle* states:

> Students in the middle grades experience a rapid unfolding of their intellectual capacities. There is a dramatic emergence of the ability to think reflectively—to think about thinking. (p. 13)

Critical thinking has been theorized in three traditions: the philosophical, the psychological, and the educational. Briefly, the philosophical tradition was concerned with the requirements of formal logical systems rather than the actual requirements of critical thinking in classrooms. The psychological tradition focused upon characterizing critical thinking as it is performed under the limitations of the person and the environment. For example, this tradition concerned itself with the differences between thinking of mentally handicapped and non-handicapped thinkers or the differences in the critical thinking of gifted and average students. The educational tradition concerned itself with the skills needed by children in the classroom for problem solving, decision-making, and concept learning (Sternberg, 1985).

Middle level educators, like educators at all levels, are under considerable pressure to prove that learners can meet assessment demands and can live satisfactorily in a democratic society. Developing appropriate critical thinking skills might be among the most effective means of accomplishing such goals. In a study focusing directly on middle level students, Straham and O'Sullivan (1988) concluded that cognitive reasoning was a significant correlate of achievement test performance and that middle level educators should identify the reasoning levels of their students and develop instructional strategies to help learners generate abstract concepts in the content areas.

Knowing how to teach critical thinking is equally important as understanding the issue and its implications for educators. Carr (1988) warned against the tendency to look for a "quick fix" (p. 64). Providing additional courses in thinking and workbook-type materials provide too-easy answers for a complex challenge. Such approaches fragment thinking skills, while failing to instill responsible attitudes toward problem solving. To avoid this situation, educators should teach students to question, to analyze, and to look beyond the superficial for possible answers (Carr, 1988).

Thinking must be applied and practiced within each content field. Rather than teaching students to memorize facts and then to assess with multiple-choice tests, educators should prepare courses with objectives that include application and analysis, divergent thinking, and opportunities to organize ideas and to support value judgements. It is impossible to explicate the many thinking programs available today; however, readers wanting more detailed information should consult more specialized information, such as the various programs presented by Sternberg (1985) and the activities and recommendations suggested by Carr (1988).

Eisner (1987) shows the importance of thinking in his article, "The Celebration of Thinking":

> One would think, given the importance of imagination, that it would be regarded as one of the basics of education. As you know, it is not on anyone's list of basics, at least not in any national report on the state of our schools that I have read. We are far more concerned with the correct replication of what already exists than with cultivating the powers of innovation or the celebration of thinking. Perhaps a little parity among these education goals would be appropriate. (p. 27)

Middle level educators are in a prime position to add thinking to the list of basics. Working with young adolescents who are experiencing significant cognitive development, middle level school educators can incorporate critical thinking into the curriculum and challenge learners to think about the various content areas, their lives, and their constantly changing worlds.

MOTIVATING LEARNERS

Motivation during the young adolescent developmental period is closely related to social development, and in many cases, a direct influence of perceptions of social events. The emergence of new cognitive abilities and the expanded competence in social situations must be considered as teachers plan motivational strategies. As children's social independence grows and their ability to evaluate statements of parents and teachers in a more critical manner, they increasingly tend to use peers as sources of wisdom and authority (Potter, 1984). Motivational techniques that once worked favorably with younger children may be ignored by the 10- to 14-year-old. Closely related to young learners' motivation and their willingness to employ *metacognitive abilities* (their own awareness of how their mind works and how they can learn better) is their expectation of success and failure. Beliefs related to one's expectations of success, to judgments about one's ability, and to emotional reactions of pride and hopelessness all contribute to the extent one is willing to use metacognitive strategies, strategies that improve one's ability to learn. Over time, learners believing that failure is caused by a lack of ability are likely to feel a sense of helplessness (Ames, 1990). This theory of the relationship between motivation, feelings of self-worth, and the willingness to use metacognitive strategies might be especially valid for middle level educators who work with learners during a developmental period when perceptions of abilities are being formed daily and at a time of intellectual development when cognitive abilities are expanding in diversity and range.

CULTURAL AND GENDER DIFFERENCES: INTELLECTUAL

For many years, educators and others assumed that everyone learned in about the same way. Such thinking resulted in cultural and gender differences being ignored and teaching–learning practices geared toward middle-class Anglo-American boys and girls. Research focusing on (1) learning styles, (2) school achievement and psychological adjustment, and (3) academic self-concept and success expectations has suggested that cultural and gender differences do, indeed, exist and affect overall achievement.

Learning Styles. In their study of Native Americans and Alaskan Native youth, Swisher and Deyhle (1989) concluded that "people perceive the world in different ways, learn about the world in different ways, and demonstrate what they have learned in different ways" (p. 2). The differences include how Native

Americans learn to learn, using visual approaches to learning, and the influence of culture such as cooperating rather than competing; and educators adapting their teaching styles to Native Americans' learning styles. Many Native Americans demonstrate strengths in visual/spatial/perceptual information; use imagery to remember concepts and words (mental associations assist in remembering); demonstrate tendencies toward being reflective rather than impulsive, or watch-then-do rather than trial and error; and exhibit tendencies toward participating in global processing on both verbal and nonverbal tasks. For instance, students might process using the whole and the relationships between the parts rather than emphasizing the parts to build the whole (More, 1987).

African Americans have the following learning tendencies: they view things in their environment in entirety rather than in isolated parts; prefer intuitive rather than deductive or inductive reasoning; approximate concepts of space, number, and time rather than aim at exactness or accuracy; and rely on nonverbal as well as verbal communication (Shade, 1982). African American seventh-grade students of varying academic levels demonstrate differing learning styles. For instance, high achievers tend to be teacher-motivated while average achievers prefer to learn in the late mornings. Also, the low achievers are more persistent and prefer nonparental authority figures present while learning (Jacobs, 1990).

For optimal academic performance, learning styles of African-, Chinese-, Mexican-, and Greek-American fourth-, fifth-, and sixth-graders indicate that classrooms should be varied, providing both quiet areas and sections for student interaction as well as conventional versus an informal seating arrangement; learners should be permitted to work either alone, in pairs, in small groups, or with the teacher; some students, like Chinese-Americans, require a variety of instructional approaches while others feel most comfortable with patterns and routines, as indicated by the responses of the African-American students (Dunn et al, 1990).

School Achievement and Psychological Adjustment. Developmental theory and research have suggested that the relationship between school achievement and psychological adjustment differs for boys and girls during early adolescence. In their study of gender differences, school achievement and self-image, Roberts, Sarigiani, Petersen, and Newman (1990) showed the link between achievement and self-image to be more positive for boys than girls and to increase for boys during the transition into adolescence. Other gender differences include: the relationship between achievement and self-image for boys at sixth grade increases as they move into the seventh grade and remains stable as they move into the eighth grade. While Roberts et al. (1990) feel the relationship is more positive for boys than for girls at sixth grade and especially at seventh grade, the relationship between achievement and self-image decreases for girls and increases for boys during the move from sixth to seventh grades. It is also interesting to note that boys show an overall increase in the relationship between achievement and self-image from sixth to eighth grade.

Academic Self-Concept and Success Expectations. Girls sometimes have substantially higher success expectations and levels of achievement than boys; however, gender differences in achievement orientation in mathematics or in general academic self-esteem usually do not exist (Skaalvik, 1990). Far too long, the popular stereotype that girls are better in reading and verbal tasks while boys excel in mathematics and the sciences has taken a toll on both boys and girls. Educators perhaps have had lower expectations for girls in mathematics and sciences and have not emphasized these academic areas as either sources of strength or possible career choices. Recent research, however, has indicated that while some gender differences do exist in motivation and learning, educators should have high expectations for both girls and boys.

Implications for Middle Level School Educators. The research on cultural and gender differences during early adolescence can help middle level school educators provide teaching–learning experiences that address the unique needs of young adolescents. Educators can glean several implications from the research on culture, gender, and the intellect, but just as with providing appropriate psychosocial experiences, there must be an accompanying commitment to provide educational experiences which address cultural and gender concerns.

First, middle level educators need to understand how cognitive perceptions differ among cultures. Approaches to learning may differ, perceptions of motivation vary among cultures, i.e., Native Americans prefer to cooperate rather than compete. Culturally diverse learners' attitudes toward motivation and learning cannot be considered through middle-class Anglo-American lenses. Second, learning styles differ among cultures. Some learners may prefer a quiet cooperative learning environment while others might prefer an atmosphere of competitiveness. Still, others may prefer to work alone on independent study projects. Third, gender differences deserve to be recognized and addressed. Boys might have strong links between school achievement and self-image while girls might have less. Fourth, culture and gender may play a role in expectations that prevent teachers from expecting all learners to do equally well.

Since everyday experiences at school and home affect young adolescents' developing self-identities, educators in responsive middle level schools should work to build accurate and realistic self-perceptions. Their efforts need to extend to both cultural and gender differences: to address stereotypes and misconceptions about boys' and girls' ability and motivation levels and to address differences in learning styles and motivations of young students from diverse cultural backgrounds.

As one reviews the research on cognitive development, it is important to realize that each theory provides a partial explanation about how the brain functions. Learning themes based on behaviorism, developmentalism, and humanism offer a balanced perspective of cognitive developmental characteristics and also show a concern for individual learners. Such balanced perspectives are essential to provide for middle level learners. Research on right- and left-brain hemispheres, multiple intelligences, and learning styles has provided insight into sequencing the curriculum and maximizing learning opportunities for middle level learners. Recognition of the diversity in the cognitive readiness and growth characteristics of young adolescents as well as of exceptional learners should suggest a middle level school that provides comprehensive instructional opportunities for all learners. These young adolescents are experiencing rapid physical changes and expanding social interests, which may make it difficult for middle level teachers to focus on cognitive learning.

SUMMARY

Theories of learning and of how the intellect develops have long interested scholars. Many researchers have directed their efforts toward understanding intellectual development and have offered several viable theories; however, reaching a firm agreement on how children and adolescents develop intellectually has proven difficult. More recent studies have sought to define intelligence and unravel the secrets of the brain. While these studies offer food for thought and interesting insights, they have not specifically addressed young adolescents and their developmental period. More efforts are needed to understand the developmental period and the inner preoccupations of young adolescents, and thus to recognize and change school policies that might actually impede young adolescents' intellectual development.

▪ ▪ ▪

EXPLORATION

1 React to Gardner's (1987a) argument that American society suffers from "testist"—a bias toward testing. Gardner stated, "If it can't be tested, it sometimes seems, it is not worth paying attention to. My feeling is that assessment can be much broader, much more humane than it is now, and that psychologists should spend less time ranking people and more time trying to help them" (pp. 192–193). Determine the types and purposes of assessment devices used during the middle level grades. Are these tests administered to rank or to help learners? How might these tests affect young adolescents during these critical formative years? How can middle level educators address the assessment problem and, generally speaking, make the entire assessment process more humane?

2 Consider the research on brain growth periodization, the triune brain, and right-brain/left-brain theory. Then, visit several middle level schools to determine the extent to which educators address these areas or recognize the extent to which the research on the brain should be incorporated into curric-

ular decisions and instructional methods. If educational practice reflects this research, tell specifically how and to what extent efforts have been successful. If educational practices do not reflect theories of brain functioning, how might middle level educators become acquainted with the research and make the transition from theory into practice?

3 Develop and administer a checklist designed to determine the intellectual characteristics of young adolescents. Which characteristics among 10- to 14-year-olds indicate brain growth periodization, the triune brain theory, or the right-brain/left-brain theory? How can such a checklist contribute to more effective curricular practices and instructional methods?

4 Review the discussion on early and late maturers in the previous chapter. How might early or late intellectual development affect other developmental areas, particularly in such areas as self-concept, motivation, and orientations toward learning and the overall school program? How might middle level educators most effectively address early and late maturers *and* their self-concept, motivation, and orientations toward learning and school?

SUGGESTED READINGS

Blythe, T., & Gardner, H. (1990). A school for all intelligences. *Educational Leadership, 47* (7), 33–36.

Blythe and Gardner explain how a school can be established to address Gardner's seven intelligences.

Carnine, D. (1990). New research on the brain: Implications for instruction. *Phi Delta Kappan, 71,* 372–376, 377.

Carnine examines recent brain research and challenges theories of localization.

Corbett, M. (1990). The testing dilemma. *The Delta Kappa Gamma Bulletin, 56 (2),* 13–15.

Corbett believes that testing has become the solution to winning public trust and gaining financial support. This has resulted in a dilemma which poses problems for both learners and educators.

Gardner, H. (1987). Developing the spectrum of human intelligence. *Harvard Education Review, 57,* 187–193.

In this readable and interesting article, Gardner proposes his theory of multiple intelligences and explains the seven different types.

Hatch, T., & Gardner, H. (1988). New research on intelligence. *Learning88, 17 (4),* 36–39.

Hatch and Gardner examine the seven intelligences, focus attention on left-brain/right-brain theories, and show how educators can apply the research.

Kane, M., & Kane, D. (1990). Right or left: Which is the right cognitive style for quality teaching? *American Secondary Education, 18 (3),* 12–15.

Kane examines the Visual/Spatial/Holistic style and the Verbal/Analytic/Detail-oriented style and explains how both styles have their advantages in the classroom.

Peterman, F. P. (1990). Successful middle level schools and the development of programs for the gifted. *NASSP Bulletin, 74 (526),* 62–65.

Peterman examines and lists the common characteristics of effective programs for gifted middle level learners.

Sternberg, R. J. (1989). The tyranny of testing. *Learning89, 17 (7),* 60–63.

Sternberg maintained that tests only measure one type of intelligence and explained his Sternberg Triarchic Abilities Test (STAT) which measures all three types of intelligence.

Sternberg, R. J. (1990). Thinking styles: Keys to understanding student performance. *Phi Delta Kappan, 71,* 366–371.

Sternberg maintains that thinking and learning styles are as important as abilities.

Titus, T. G., Bergandi, T. A., & Shryock, M. (1990). Adolescent learning styles. *Journal of Research and Development in Education, 23 (3),* 165–170.

These researchers compared male and female students of various grade levels and at both slow- and fast-learning tracks to determine adolescent learning styles.

REFERENCES

Adelson, J. (1983). The growth of thought in adolescence. *Educational Horizons, 61,* 156–162.

Adelson, J. (1971). The political imagination of the young adolescent. *Daedalus, 100,* 1013–1049.

Ames, C. A. (1990). Motivation: What teachers need to know. *Teachers College Record, 91,* 409–421.

Arth, A. A. (1990). Moving into middle school: Concerns of transescent students. *Educational Horizons, 68 (2),* 105–106.

Association for Supervision and Curriculum Development (ACSD). (February 1984). *Educational Leadership, 41* (5).

Biehler, R. F., & Snowman, J. (1990). *Psychology applied to teaching* (6th ed.). Boston: Houghton Mifflin.

Bigge, M. L. (1976). *Learning theories for teachers* (3rd ed.). New York: Harper & Row.

Blythe, T., & Gardner, H. (1990). A school for all intelligences. *Educational Leadership, 47 (7),* 33–36.

Brandt, R. (1989). On misuse of testing: A conversation with George Madaus. *Educational Leadership, 46 (7),* 26–29.

Brooks, M. G. (1984). We are not testing Epstein's ideas: A response to Richard McQueen. *Educational Leadership, 41 (5),* 72.

Brooks, M., Fusco, E., & Glennon, J. (1983). Cognitive levels matching. *Educational Leadership, 40 (8),* 4–8.

Bruner, J. S. (1960). *The process of education.* New York: Random House.

California State Department of Education, Middle Grades Task Force (1987). *Caught in the Middle.* Sacramento, CA: California State Department of Education.

Carnegie Council on Adolescent Development. (1989). *Turning points: Preparing American youth for the 21st century.* Washington, DC: Author.

Carnine, D. (1990). New research on the brain: Implications for instruction. *Phi Delta Kappan, 71,* 372–376, 377.

Carr, K. S. (1988). How can we teach critical thinking? *Childhood Education, 65,* 69–73.
Combs, A. W. (Ed.). (1962). Perceiving, behaving, becoming. Yearbook. Washington, DC: Association for Supervision and Curriculum Development.
Combs, A. W. (1965). *The professional education of teachers.* Boston: Allyn & Bacon.
Combs, A. W. (1982). Affective education or none at all. *Educational Leadership, 39 (7),* 495–497.
Combs, A. W. (1978). *Humanistic education: Objectives and assessment.* Washington, DC: Association for Supervision and Curriculum Development.
Corbett, M. (1990). The testing dilemma. *The Delta Kappa Gamma Bulletin, 56 (2),* 1315.
Cornett, C. E. (1983). *What you should know about teaching and learning styles.* Bloomington, IN: Phi Delta Kappa Education Foundation.
Crockett, L., Losoff, M., & Peterson, A. (1984). Perceptions of the peer group and friendship in early adolescence. *Journal of Early Adolescence, 4,* 155–181.
Cullinan, D., & Epstein, M. H. (1990). Behavior disorders. In N. G. Haring, & L. McCormick (Eds.), *Exceptional children and youth* (pp. 153–192). New York: Merrill/Macmillan.
Dewey, J. (1916). *Democracy and education.* New York: Macmillan.
Dewey, J. (1933). *How we think.* Lexington, MA: D.C. Heath.
Dewey, J. (1938). *Experience and education.* New York: Collier.
Dunn, R. et al. (1990). Cross-cultural differences in learning styles of elementary-age students from four ethnic backgrounds. *Journal of Multicultural Counseling and Development, 18,* 68–93.
Dunn, R. S., Beaudry, J. S., & Klavas, A. (1989). Survey of research on learning styles. *Educational Leadership, 46 (6),* 50–58.
Dunn, R. S., & Dunn, K. J. (1979). Learning styles/teaching styles: Should they . . . can they . . . be matched? *Educational Leadership, 36 (4),* 238–244.
Dunn, R. S., Dunn, K. J., & Price, G. E. (1986). *Learning style inventory manual.* Lawrence, KS: Price Systems.
Eisner, E. W. (1987). The celebration of thinking. *Educational Horizons, 66,* 24–29.
Epstein, H. T., & Toepfer, C. F. (1978). A neuroscience basis for reorganizing middle grades education. *Educational Leadership, 35 (8),* 656–660.
Gagné, R. (1974). *Essentials of learning for instruction.* Hinsdale, IL: Dryden Press.
Gardner, H. (1987a). Developing the spectrum of human intelligence. *Harvard Education Review, 57,* 187–193.
Gardner, H. (1987b). An individual-centered curriculum. In Council of Chief State School Officers and the American Association of Teacher Education (Eds.), *The schools we've got, the schools we need.* Washington, DC: Author.
Georgiady, N. P., & Romano, L. G. (1977). Growth characteristics of middle school children: Curriculum implications. *Middle School Journal, 8 (1),* 12–15, 22–23.
Ginsburg, H. P., & Opper, S. (1988). *Piaget's theory of intellectual development.* Englewood Cliffs: Prentice-Hall.
Greene, A. L. (1988). Early adolescents' perceptions of stress. *The Journal of Early Adolescence, 8,* 391–403.
Hatch, T., & Gardner, H. (1988). New research on intelligence. *Learning88, 17 (4),* 36–39.
Hester, J. P., & Hester, P. J. (1983). Brain research and the middle school curriculum. *Middle School Journal, 15,* 4–7.
Jacobs, R. I. (1990). Learning styles of Black high, average, and low achievers. *The Clearing House, 643,* 253–254.
Juhasz, A. M. (1982). Early adolescents and society: Implications from Erikson's theory. *Journal of Early Adolescence, 2,* 15–24.

Kane, M., & Kane, D. (1990). Right or left: Which is the right cognitive style for quality teaching? *American Secondary Education, 18 (3),* 12–15.

Keefe, J. W. (1987). *Learning style: Theory and practice.* Reston, VA: NASSP.

Keefe, J. W. (1990). Learning style: Where are we going? *Momentum, 21* (1), 44–48.

Keefe, J. W., & Monk, J. S. (1986). *Learning style profile examiners's manual.* Reston, VA: NASSP.

Link, F. R. (1985). *Essays on the intellect.* Alexandria, VA: ASCD.

Lyons, C. A., & Languis, M. L. (1985). Cognitive science and teacher education. *Theory Into Practice, 24,* 127–130.

McCormick, L. (1990). Communication disorders. In N. G. Haring, & L. McCormick (Eds.), *Exceptional children and youth* (pp. 327–363). New York: Merrill/Macmillan.

McQueen, R. (1984). Spurts and plateaus in brain growth: A critique of the claims of Herman Epstein. *Educational Leadership, 41* (5), 67–71.

MacLean, P. (1977). On the evolution of three mentalities. In S. Arieti, & G. Chrzanowski (Eds.), *New dimensions in psychiatry, a worldview* (2nd ed.) (pp. 305–328). New York: Wiley.

MacLean, P. (1980). A meeting of the minds: The triune brain theory. *Dromenon: A Journal of New Ways of Being, 3* (1), 12–20.

More, A. J. (1987). Native-American learning styles: A review for researcher and teachers. *Journal of American Indian Education, 27*(1), 17–29.

Morris, V. C., & Pai, Y. (1976). *Philosophy and the American school.* Boston: Houghton-Mifflin.

National Association of Secondary School Principals. (1979). *Student learning styles—diagnosing and prescribing programs.* Reston, VA: Author.

Ornstein, R. (1978). The split and whole brain. *Human Nature, 1,* 76–83.

Patton, J. R, & Polloway, E. A. (1990). Mild mental retardation. In N. G. Haring, & L. McCormick (Eds.), *Exceptional children and youth* (pp. 195–237). New York: Merrill/Macmillan.

Potter, E. F. (1984). Impact of developmental factors on motivating the school achievement of young adolescents: Theory and implications for practice. *The Journal of Early Adolescence, 4,* 1–10.

Purkey, W. (1970). *Self-concept and school achievement.* Englewood Cliffs, NJ: Prentice-Hall.

Purkey, W. (1978). *Inviting school success.* Belmont, CA: Wadsworth.

Quina, J. (1989). *Effective secondary teaching: Going beyond the bell curve.* New York: Harper & Row.

Roberts, I. R., Sarigiani, P. A., Petersen, A. C., & Newman, J. I. (1990). Gender differences in the relationship between achievement and self-image during early adolescence. *Journal of Early Adolescence, 10,* 159–175.

Rogers, C. (1961). *On becoming a person.* Boston: Houghton Mifflin.

Rogers, C. (1983). *Freedom to learn.* New York: Merrill/Macmillan.

Schuster, D. H., & Gritton, C. E. (1986). *Suggestive accelerative learning techniques.* New York: Gordon and Breach.

Shade, B. (1982). Afro-American cognitive style: A variable in school success? *Review of Educational Research, 52,* 219–244.

Skaalvik, E. M. (1990). Gender differences in general academic self-esteem and in success expectations on defined academic problems. *Journal of Education Psychology, 82,* 593–598.

Skinner, B. F. (1970). Science and human behavior. New York: Knopf.

Sperry, R. W. (1974). Lateral specialization in the surgically separated hemispheres. In F.

O. Schmitt, & F. G. Warden (Eds.), *The neuro-sciences third study program* (pp. 5–19). Cambridge, MA: MIT Press.
Springer, S. P., & Deutsch, G. (1985). *Left brain, right brain* (rev. ed.). New York: W. H. Freeman.
Sternberg, R. J. (1990). Thinking styles: Keys to understanding student performance. *Phi Delta Kappan, 71,* 366–371.
Sternberg, R. J. (1989). The tyranny of testing. *Learning89, 17* (7), 60–63.
Sternberg, R. J. (1985). Critical thinking: Its nature, measurement, and improvement. In F. R. Link (Ed.), *Essays on the intellect* (pp. 45–65). Washington, DC: ASCD.
Stewart, W. J. (1990). Learning-style-appropriate instruction: Planning, implementing, evaluating. *The Clearing House, 63,* 371–374.
Straham, D. B., & O'Sullivan, R. G. (1988). Achievement test scores in the middle grades: The influence of cognitive reasoning. *The Journal of Early Adolescence, 8,* 53–61.
Swisher, K., & Deyhle, D. (1989). The styles of learning are different, but the teaching is just the same: Suggestions for teachers of American Indian youth. *Journal of American Indian Education, Special Issue* (August), 1–11.
Thornburg, H. (1980). Early adolescents: Their developmental characteristics. *The High School Journal, 63,* 215–221.
Thornburg, H. (1982). The total early adolescent in contemporary society. *The High School Journal, 65,* 272–278.
Titus, T. G., Bergandi, T. A., & Shryock, M. (1990). Adolescent learning styles. *Journal of Research and Development in Education, 23,* 165–170.
Toepfer, C. F. (1985). Suggestions of neurological data for middle level education: A review of research and its interpretations. *Transescence: The Journal on Emerging Adolescence, 13(2),* 12–38.
Toepfer, C. F. (1988). What to know about young adolescents. *Social Education, 52,* 110–112.
Turning points: Preparing American Youth for the 21st Century. (1989). Washington, DC: Carnegie Council on Adolescent Development.
Walters, J. M., & Gardner, H. (1985). The development and education of intelligences. In F. R. Link (Ed.), *Essays on the intellect* (pp. 1–21). Washington, DC: ASCD.
Yelon, S. L., & Weinstein, G. W. (1977). *A teacher's world: Psychology in the classroom.* New York: McGraw-Hill.

SELECTED WORKS AND COMMENTARIES ON LEARNING THEORY

Anglin, J. M. (1973). *Jerome Bruner: Beyond the information given.* New York: Norton.
Biehler, R. F., & Snowman, J. (1990). *Psychology applied to teaching* (6th ed.). Boston: Houghton Mifflin.
Bigge, M. L. (1981). *Learning theories for teachers* (4th ed.). New York: Harper & Row.
Ginsburg, H. P., & Opper, S. (1988). *Piaget's theory of intellectual development.* Englewood Cliffs: Prentice-Hall.
Slavin, R. E. (1988). *Educational psychology* (2nd ed.). Englewood Cliffs: Prentice-Hall.

CHAPTER OUTLINE

The Middle Level Teacher

5

OVERVIEW

Effective teaching is essential to any middle level school setting. Reforms in the 1980s have focused on improving learning through improved instruction by the classroom teacher. Because of the developmental needs encountered in the middle level, the middle level teacher must consider those teaching characteristics that research and practice indicate are essential for dealing with the diversity found in young adolescent learners. As young adolescents cope with life's challenges, middle level teachers can promote their academic, social, and personal development. This chapter will explore different aspects of effective teaching at the middle level, and discuss the professional preparation and development of middle level teachers.

In this chapter you will read about:

1 Definitions of teaching.
2 The qualities of middle level teachers.
3 Essential teaching roles on the middle level.
4 Teaching style and essential teacher characteristics for the middle level.
5 Teacher effectiveness: essential teaching strategies and skills for a middle level teacher.
6 Reforms in teaching.

7 The certification and preparation of middle level teachers.
8 Expectations of teachers and professional development activities.

DEFINITIONS OF TEACHING

What is teaching? Teaching has been described as a series of decisions and skills and responsibilities that teachers are expected to model in their classrooms. Mostly, any list of decisions, skills, and responsibilities appears to be an ideal combination that is not found in any one teacher. It is important for middle level teachers to differentiate between essential decisions and skills required for effective teaching. Here, three approaches will be suggested toward middle level teaching: (1) teaching as decision making, (2) the dimensions of teaching, and (3) the elements of effective teaching.

TEACHING AS DECISION MAKING

Teachers have relied on their personal experiences and intuitive judgments as the basis for making most decisions about how to teach effectively. In many instances, they may not be aware of the lasting impact that their decisions could have on young adolescents. Madeline Hunter (1982) defined teaching as "a constant stream of professional decisions made before, during, and after interaction with the student; decisions which, when implemented, increase the probability of learning" (p. 3). According to Hunter, a teacher probably makes anywhere from 3,000 to 9,000 decisions in any given day. Thus, decision making is central to teaching and teachers need to be fully conscious of their decisions. A refined definition of teaching, that developed out of the Program for Effective Teaching (PET) model, stated that

> teaching is conscious decision making before, during, and after instruction that, when implemented, enhances the probability of learning.

From a series of classroom studies of teaching that she directed at the University of California at Los Angeles, Hunter grouped all teaching decisions into three areas.

1 What to teach? *(content decisions)* The decisions regarding content selection are based on the teacher's knowledge about content, skills, and learners. The teacher needs to know where the learner is—in academic, personal, and social development—and match the learner to the learning. Not all objectives should be based on academic content; they should also relate to the student's personal and social concerns.
2 How does the young adolescent demonstrate that learning has occurred?

(student behavior decisions) The emphasis is on what the young adolescent will do to illustrate learning. The teacher is faced with two difficult questions: (a) What young adolescent behavior is appropriate in a given classroom setting? (b) Is the young adolescent capable of learning the specific content (Hunter, 1982)?

3 What modeling does the middle level teacher establish to ensure learning? *(teacher behavioral decisions)* Middle level teachers exercise direct control over their own behavior. The last category is the only decision area in which teachers have the ability to establish the student's learning. The intent is consciously to focus teacher behavior on classroom decisions that result in effective learning for young adolescents.

THE DIMENSIONS OF TEACHING

The educational environment has three dimensions for which the middle level models of teaching should be designed, organized, and implemented. The concept *dimension* tends to focus directly on the personal, social, and academic imperatives of young adolescents which teachers need to address when teaching this age group. Each dimension should remain flexible and dynamic, with teachers incorporating the interrelated environments of young adolescents, family, school, and community through the interaction of integrated curriculum and instruction designed to promote a community of learners in middle level schools.

The *personal dimension* involves utilizing teacher style, characteristics, and behavior in helping the young adolescent to search for meaning and to assume part of the responsibility for his or her own development. The teacher emphasis in this dimension is focused on the unique characteristics of every young adolescent and his or her struggle for a well-rounded personality, integrating physical, personal, and emotional desires.

The *social dimension* includes the teacher's behavior, interaction between student and teacher, classroom environment and school setting, and responsibility to profession and community. Some professional aspects of this dimension would be transmitting the cultural heritage; developing competence as an international citizen in an interdependent, technological, and global world; initiating cooperative planning; and developing problem solving strategies.

The *academic dimension* assumes that the teacher is an expert in academic content and skills required for the development of knowledge, thinking, and problem solving (Joyce & Weil, 1988). This dimension emphasizes basic and occupational skills, major concepts from the disciplines (history, science, literature, etc.), inquiry approaches to thinking and broad philosophical schools (aesthetics, humanitarian issues, and ethics), and teacher competence in content. These three dimensions form the basis for discussing effective teaching in this chapter and for organizing the curriculum in Chapter 6.

EFFECTIVE TEACHING

Effective teaching suggests that there is a set of variables that can be used to analyze teacher effectiveness. Teacher effectiveness implies that teacher behavior can be identified for the improvement of student performance and outcomes. Previous research has focused on the process of *teaching*, using ratings, classroom observations, and personality tests to obtain information about what is occurring in the classroom. Only recently has the research on teaching effectiveness focused on analyzing the *student's* performance. At issue is the degree of impact that teachers have on student learning outcomes. Until the contributions of the teacher to learning can be assessed, it is difficult to determine teacher effectiveness in terms of evaluation, accountability, and/or merit pay. This section focuses on examining variables, principles of teaching for improving student achievement and performance, and the impact of learning styles on student outcomes.

Variables

Research on the relationship between teacher behavior and student outcomes has indicated some important variables. Rosenshine and Furst (1973) outlined 11 teacher process behaviors or variables that they found to correlate with student achievement. Later, Rosenshine (1979) revised his conclusions to indicate that only two variables or processes were correlated with student achievement. Those variables relate to content coverage and task orientation. The other nine processes appear to be less important in the primary grades and vary in importance depending on subject matter, instructional groups, and student's social background.

Medley (1979) found that elementary teachers who were effectively teaching lower socioeconomic status students (1) spent less time discussing matters unrelated to the lesson, (2) presented structured and sequential learning activities, (3) permitted little time on independent and small-group activities, (4) initiated low-level and narrowly defined questions that did not amplify student answers, (5) spent little time on and discouraged student-initiated questions, (6) engaged in fewer criticisms, and (7) spent less time on discipline matters. The review suggested that changing teaching strategies for different students is important. There should be a fit between teacher's teaching style and students' learning styles. Because students have different learning styles, they need different teaching techniques and learning environments. These research findings are in line with the successful teaching patterns suggested for at-risk or underachievers from lower socioeconomic backgrounds. The basic skills-and-drills approach is similar to the emphasis on content, learning time, and mastery of academic skills by the behaviorists (Ornstein, 1986). While the techniques discussed here are relevant to effective teaching, it is not suggested that they should be utilized exclusively with middle level students.

Principles of Effective Teaching

Good and Brophy (1991) have identified principles of effective teaching, but not teacher behaviors or characteristics, in Figure 5.1. Many of the principles suggested also are good classroom management techniques—probably suggesting that good discipline correlates with good teaching. The variables and principles provide guidelines for correlating student achievement and organizing, managing, and instructing young adolescents as well. Teacher behavior patterns that encourage student achievement are pacing, wait time, realistic praising, high expectations, monitoring, recognition of learner differences, obtaining the attention of learners, focusing the learner on the lesson, prompt attention to inappropriate behaviors, clarity, and knowledge of the subject matter. Teachers of middle level students need to remain aware of affective (enabling) dimensions as well as behavioral (norming) dimensions of effective teaching.

Learning Styles

Another important aspect of teaching effectiveness is learning style. Each person has a learning style or preference, which can be grouped into four dimensions: (1) *Environment* (sound, light, temperature, seating design); (2) *Emotional support*

1. **Clarity** about instructional objectives.
2. **Knowledge** about content and ways to teach it.
3. **Variety** in the use of teaching methods and materials.
4. **With-it-ness** in being aware of what is going on and in monitoring classroom activities.
5. **Overlapping** maintains an activity while doing something else at the same time.
6. **Smoothness** in sustaining proper lesson pacing and group momentum for all students.
7. **Seatwork** instructions and management produce task engagement.
8. Holding students **accountable** for learning.
9. **Realistic expectations** based on student abilities and behaviors.
10. **Realistic praise** elicits desired student behaviors.
11. **Flexibility** in planning and adapting classroom activities.
12. **Task orientation** and businesslike teacher behavior.
13. **Monitoring** of student's understanding by providing feedback, praise, and questioning.
14. Providing students the **opportunity to learn** what is to be tested.
15. **Structure learning** for concept development of learners.

FIGURE 5.1 Principles of effective teaching *(Adapted from* Looking in Classrooms, *5th ed., by T. L. Good and J. Brophy, 1991, New York: HarperCollins. Copyright 1991 by HarperCollins. Adapted by permission.)*

1 Middle school classrooms should provide alternative environments for young adolescents in the same area (quiet vs. noise, warm vs. cool, bright vs. soft light).

2 Assignments should be diversified by giving regular assignments to persistent students and breaking lessons into smaller tasks for global learners. Mobility opportunities should be provided for those who need to move about. Young adolescents who are self-structured and understand the assignment should begin to take tests when ready. The global student should be given any specialized help and encouragement to break up study tasks into units prior to any scheduled examinations.

3 The importance of peer orientation in the middle grades necessitates frequent employment of small-group techniques, such as team learning, brainstorming, role playing, and cooperative learning.

4 Young adolescents' time for studying difficult subjects should be scheduled during their best time of day, and easier subjects arranged for when they are best able to cope with learning. Teaching students when they are best able to learn is far more important than uniformity or ease of scheduling.

5 Persistent young adolescents tend to be analytic left processors who prefer continuity. Global right processors tend to work for shorter periods of time with intense energy that quickly dissipates. Global students need frequent breaks, changes in activities, a variety of patterns, prefer reading with soft light and music on a floor or bed or in an easy chair.

6 Young adolescents experience many physical changes that make them feel uncomfortable and self-conscious. They often need to snack while concentrating. Permitting middle grade students to bring raw vegetables to class should not present a problem if only vegetables or healthy foods are permitted. Each eater's grades must improve or the privilege is forfeited.

7 Motivated young adolescents with several perceptual strengths can learn through contract activities. Young adolescents who need structure and are either visual or tactile can use programmed learning approaches. Underachievers can be taught through a combination of tactile and kinesthetic materials and/or multisensory instructional packages.

(motivational support, persistence, individual responsibility, and structure); (3) *Sociological Support* (individual, pairs or teams, adult, and varied); and (4) *Personal/Physical* (modality, time, and mobility) (Dunn & Dunn, 1978). (Dunn and associates (1988) recommended 10 steps for improving middle school learning styles, which are listed in Figure 5.2.)

The environmental dimension concerns the ideal place to learn. Some learners want a bright, warm, classroom environment with desks, many peers, and much verbal interaction. Others prefer a cooler, quieter, and more informal environment with subdued lighting. The teacher's role is to be aware of and control these elements in the classroom environment.

The emotional support dimension centers around the extent to which students are self-directed learners. At one end of the continuum are self-starters who can be given a long-term project and can monitor and pace themselves. At the other end are students who need individual encouragement and teacher support and who need to have the assignment broken down into small parts with periodic due dates. This category focuses on teachers understanding the need students have for support.

The sociological support dimension is concerned with how students inter-

8 Young adolescents have a great deal on their minds. Because they do not consider schoolwork important, they cannot always concentrate on academic chores. The following techniques can help them:
1) Tell them what is important in each lesson.
2) When you mention important items, walk to the chalkboard and write a word or two that summarizes the content so that Visual Left processors can see and copy the information into their notebooks.
3) Illustrate important information when you write on the chalkboard, and encourage global students to illustrate their notes.
Visual Left learners seem to respond to words and numbers in contrast to Visual Rights who pay attention to drawings, graphs, symbols, and spatial designs. Global Rights are often tactual, and may be doodlers who pay better attention if they use their hands while listening. Since doodling helps some students listen and remember better, consider it a legitimate if somewhat unusual form of notetaking.

9 The lesson should be outlined on the chalkboard in three or four lines. This technique will help the visual learner, who cannot focus well by listening, to keep track of the lesson's focus. From time to time, show the learner that you are moving to another part of the outline.

10 Young adolescents need teachers to provide basic security—beyond helping them with their lessons—by encouraging them. Provide the opportunity for young adolescents to speak with teachers if they want to share their problems, and be sure to listen to what they have to say. Refer them if you cannot help, staying in touch. Even when they are surrounded by others, many young adolescents feel alone, and need the support of teachers. While young adolescents need to learn to compute and read well, they need to feel that their teachers care about them. "Teachers *can* make a difference between middle school success and failure. Be one who *does*."

FIGURE 5.2 Ten steps to learning *(From "Ten Steps to Better Middle Schools" by R. Dunn, T. C. DeBello, W. J. Evans, D. K. Kroon, and R. T. White.* Teaching K–8, 18 *(4), 39–41. Reprinted with permission of the publisher, Early Years, Inc., Norwalk, CT 06854. From the January, 1988, issue of* Teaching K–8.*)*

act in various classroom settings. Some dislike group work, preferring to learn by themselves; others thrive on the companionship and support generated by group activities. Still others prefer to learn from an adult. Teachers can utilize this dimension by varying teaching techniques based on different student groupings, i.e., individual, small-group, or large-group arrangements.

The personal/physical dimension is focused on modalities (visual, auditory, kinesthetic, or tactile), mobility (the need to move periodically vs. remaining stationary), and time of day (the best time for learning). Some students are morning learners, others are afternoon learners. Some students prefer working with their hands, others prefer visual and auditory activities.

Although learning styles are the result of many influences, certain style characteristics are biological and others are developed through experiences of the individual. Individual responses to sound, light, temperature, design, perception, intake, time, mobility needs, and persistence appear to be biological. In contrast, sociological preferences, motivation, accepting responsibility, and the need for structure are thought to be developmental (Dunn, Beaudry &

Klavis, 1989). Dunn and associates stated that "Despite cultural influences, however, within each culture, socioeconomic strata, and classroom *there are as many within group differences as between group differences.* Indeed, each *family* includes parents and offspring with styles that differ" (p. 56). Students should not be expected to adapt to teachers' styles. Previous research findings suggested that the closer the match between each student's and teacher's style, the higher the grade point average (Dunn et al., 1989). Identifying a reliable and valid learning style preference is extremely important today to meet the needs of a diverse middle level student population. Dunn, Dunn, and Price (1985) have developed a valid and reliable learning style inventory to assist in the assessment of learning styles.

Middle level students' responsiveness to these learning style variables aids in learners' concentration and permits them to learn more effectively. For a better understanding of Dunn et al.'s (1988) ten steps to a better middle level school (see Figure 5.2), an explanation of the terms would be useful. How learners actually process their information is referred to as *right/left hemispheres* or *processors.* Educators use such terms as *visual, auditory, tactual,* and *global/analytical* to describe which hemisphere is being employed.

These terms imply ways that teachers need to combine different learners' senses and perception in teaching them their lessons. Visual left-hemisphere learners tend to respond to words and numbers, whereas visual right-hemisphere learners pay attention to drawings, graphs, and symbols. Generally, tactual learners require manipulatives and activities that utilize their touch. Tactual learners pay better attention if they use their hands while listening. By comparison, auditory learners produce symbols, letters, and words by listening to a tape or to the teacher talking. In contrast, the visual learner should read the lesson first and will need a written outline of the lesson to keep track of the specific information that needs to be learned. Thus, these terms are employed to suggest which hemisphere and senses are being used to process the information.

Global learners are able to grasp larger concepts first and then work with the details and related facts. Many global learners tend to work for short periods of time with intense energy but need frequent breaks and changes in activities. In contrast, *analytical learners* focus on a series of facts that lead up to a concept and tend to be persistent, task-oriented students. Teachers can improve the learning of middle level learners by expanding their teaching strategies to incorporate diverse learning styles.

In summary, no learning style is better or worse than another in young adolescents. Since each style is based on biological and developmental characteristics, each young adolescent cannot be labeled or stigmatized as having any type of style. Most young adolescents can learn the content, but how well they learn the content is determined by individual learning preferences and the teacher's willingness and ability to plan for individual learning styles. Thus, some classroom techniques that hold potential for improving middle level student achievement are: (1) adapting content to learners' interests and abilities,

(2) utilizing a variety of materials, (3) assuring the pacing and sequencing of lessons, (4) employing active learning, variable group size, and individualized instruction, and (5) monitoring lessons.

THE QUALITIES OF MIDDLE LEVEL TEACHERS

Johnston and Markle (1986) identified 18 clusters of teacher behaviors that contribute to the success of middle level teachers. Table 5.1 outlines these clusters. What emerges from this list is the image of a self-confident professional who demonstrates both an awareness of young adolescent needs and varied teaching strategies. This list should be viewed as a reminder of what is unique about teaching on the middle level.

TABLE 5.1 The Qualities of Effective Middle Level Teachers

Cluster	Description
Positive self-concept	Effective teachers identify with others, demonstrate self-confidence and possess self-worth and self-esteem. They do not need to be the center of attention at all times and are comfortable with students utilizing some of the class time.
Warmth	Effective teachers seek contact with students, display concern, use affectionate words, smile, and look pleasant. Teachers who model warmth and caring tend to have classrooms where students care and show concern for each other.
Optimism	Effective teachers are optimistic in their assessment of individual student capabilities, express positive attitudes and pleasant feelings in the classroom, and tend to encourage all learners.
Enthusiasm	Middle level teachers are stimulating in their presentations, are involved in the activities of the class, tend to utilize nonverbal techniques, and avoid reading prepared lessons.
Flexibility	Middle level teachers can change the focus at any time if students become disinterested; they can adjust to changes in plans, time schedules, or student behavior; they can respond to constructive student requests for changes in classroom procedure.
Spontaneity	Spontaneous teachers utilize unexpected incidents that arise in class, tend to encourage student participation, and do not avoid situations that deviate from planned activities.
Acceptance of students	Accepting teachers avoid criticism, dignify incorrect responses, use sincere and frequent positive responses, and do not belittle young adolescents in front of others or display negative thoughts publicly.
Awareness of developmental levels	Teachers assign tasks that are developmentally appropriate to students, interests, and abilities, adjust tasks when students become confused or uncertain, are reluctant to push students into activities when they are not intellectually, personally, or socially ready and express less dismay over a learner's inability to perform tasks.

TABLE 5.1 *(continued)*

Cluster	Description
Knowledge of subject matter	Knowledgeable teachers are able to organize and revise lessons on the basis of student need, are able to monitor learning and engage students in meaningful instructional activities related to important concepts.
Variety of instructional activities and materials	These teachers are able to vary instruction in accordance with individual learning styles.
Instructional planning	Teachers who spend time discussing, explaining, and stimulating cognitive processes in organized ways stimulate greater pupil performance. They tend to review previous lessons, outline main topics of planned lessons, signal starting and closing of lessons, highlight and summarize the important points.
Monitoring of learning	These teachers check student progress on tests, work so that instruction can be adjusted, and move about the room observing students, and making suggestions. Instead of busy work, they utilize the extra class time for creative, social, or engaging activities.
Utilization of concrete materials and focused learning strategies	These teachers use models, objects, and visual aids to provoke images; attend to manipulation of concrete images before moving to formal operations; and focus student attention on problem-solving situations.
Variety of questions	Utilizing both higher order and lower order questions in appropriate situations produces improved student learning. Using a variety of questioning strategies for maximizing instructional effectiveness is preferable to reliance on a single type of question.
Indirect teaching	Indirect teachers build on student statements, praise students, encourage student talk and minimize criticism, lecturing, and confusion.
"Success-building" behavior	Success-oriented teachers use positive reinforcers, encouragement, and praise of student work. They refuse to use sarcasm, shame, and harassment.
Diagnosis of learner needs and prescription of individualized instruction	Effective teachers monitor completion of assignments and allow necessary time for completion of tasks. They design interest-based learning tasks, define expectations on an individual basis, and allow for independent and small-group activities. There is less tendency to teach the entire class the same lesson and to assess on a group standard.
Listener	Teachers who listen, attend to, and build upon student ideas and expressions. They acknowledge student input through summarizing what was said and by avoiding the appearance of preoccupation.

From "What research says to the middle level practitioner" by J. H. Johnston and G. C. Markle (1986), pp. 16–18. Columbus, OH: National Middle School Association. Adapted by permission.

THE ROLES OF THE MIDDLE LEVEL TEACHER

The qualities of middle level teachers listed in Table 5.1 suggest several behaviors characteristic of the essential teaching roles on the middle level. Middle level teachers fulfill many different roles, functioning as scientist/artist, decision maker, instructional planner, human relations specialist, classroom manager, counselor, evaluator, technologist, and person. These roles should prepare the middle level teacher for those personal, social, and academic decisions required for effective teaching. For a responsive middle level school, the counselor and technologist teaching roles were included to provide preparation needed by young adolescents in the twenty-first century. The school setting, needs of young adolescents, grade level, cultural differences, and learning style differences are all factors in the development of these roles.

Scientist/Artist

The teacher is both a scientist and an artist. Education is an applied science and teaching is one category under this heading. Scientific teaching is identifying, observing, and documenting the cause-and-effect relationships that exist between teaching and learning (Hunter, 1984). If these relationships can be observed and documented, the relationships should apply for all teaching decisions regardless of maturation, socioeconomic, or ethnic characteristics of learners. Madeline Hunter (1984) stated, "The science of teaching can be taught and predictably learned by most professionals who are willing to expend the required effort" (p. 170). If the science of teaching is known, then successful teaching is explainable and successful learning is predictable.

In contrast, the artist demonstrates the values, emotions, affect, personality, and enthusiasm that a teacher brings to the classroom. A person's intuition is highly prized. According to Costa (1984), the aesthetic responses were categorized by Harry Broudy as "formal, technical, sensuous, and expressive" (p. 201). The *formal* represents the individual's response to form, or recognition of the name or category of the object or rendition. *Technical* refers to the individual's participation in the techniques used in a play or when singing a song. The *sensuous* refers to knowing gained through senses of feel, touch, and smell. The *expressive* is where the individual learner analyzes the meaning of aesthetic experiences and incorporates these experiences into his or her schemata. Thus, teaching can be assessed for direct experiences. What avenues are there for self-actualization and self-development? Costa (1984) stated: "Aesthetics is not concerned with what learners memorize nor even with how much they *remember.* Rather, aesthetic teaching is concerned with making learning *memorable*" (p. 202).

Eisner (1983), agreeing with Costa, maintains that teaching is more an act of feelings and artistry. His premise is that behavioral psychology and educational management have reduced teaching to trivial and artificial acts. The art and craft of teaching have been lost. In his opinion, the role of the teacher should be similar to that of a conductor of an orchestra whose art arises both from innate imagination and creativity, and from knowing the established techniques of music and conducting. Teaching on the middle level cannot be based solely on scientific prescriptions. Teaching must be aesthetically rewarding. The satisfaction of teaching comes from being able to act on one's imagination, from experimenting with new forms of teaching, and from the reactions of the students, which let teachers realize that they have made an impact on young learners' lives. These rewards become the true outcomes of teaching, as of other professional artists and craftspeople. Craftspeople and artists take pride in what they do, insist on quality work, and obtain a great deal of satisfaction from their profession. This is what teaching should be in middle level schools.

The goal of middle level teaching should be to identify the science and art of teaching in language that is useful to the practitioner and focuses on the middle level learner. Both are essential to develop an effective, efficient, and relevant teacher and a positive classroom learning environment. There is a need to recognize that teaching is a synthesis of the rational/scientific analysis and one's intuition/personality. Both are dependent on each other and essential to have a comprehensive understanding of the realities of teaching and the learner. Because of the many variables, teaching always will be concerned with probability.

Decision Maker

Middle level teachers as decision makers are in control of student expectations, teaching strategies, length and difficulty of assignments, organization of materials, approaches to classroom participation, student selection for special learning groups, and strategies for encouraging slow learners. The Total Teaching Act (Figure 5.3) groups the decisions into six major categories: human relations skills, classroom management skills, instructional skills, planning, content mastery, and appropriate selection and use of instructional materials. Each of these aspects of the Total Teaching Act selects approaches that are based on knowledge and research about growth and development of the learners. No single teaching decision area is more important than the other five. The categories were modified so that selection and use of instructional materials and content were included under the role of instructional planner. At bottom, the *knowledge of human growth and development* is the foundation for effective teaching. If the developmental needs of the learner are not considered, effective teaching cannot take place. Too often, content and instructional skills are stressed instead of the learner's needs. To teach effectively, middle level teachers must balance the developmental needs of the learner with the six components of the Total Teaching Act.

Each skill component is an essential part of teaching decisions, but none is more important than any other. The teacher has the direct responsibility for decisions concerning *instructional skills*. This skill area is the one component that makes teaching different from other professions. There are explicit and implicit instructional skills that teachers are expected to demonstrate. *Human relations*

Instructional skills	Classroom management skills
Human relations skills	Selection and use of appropriate classroom materials and resources
Content mastery	Planning
Knowledge of human growth and development	

FIGURE 5.3 The Total Teaching Act

skills are necessary for dealing with students, parents, administrators, and colleagues. The same requirements of "people skills" necessary to the survival of any business or industry are just as applicable here. The only difference is that teachers are dealing with young adolescents where behavior is not consistent. *Classroom management skills* pertain to maintaining order and organizing the classroom environment for effective learning. Teachers require many types of management skills similar to those used by managers in the community and industry. *Content mastery* regarding what facts, concepts, skills, and generalizations should be taught in a given classroom are the basis for this area. Too often, the general public sees this as the only responsibility of the teacher. *Appropriate selection and use of materials and resources* is another aspect of teaching. This is one of the most abused and overlooked areas of effective teaching. Too often, the textbook is the only resource available in the classroom, while other useful print and non-print resources are neglected. Usually, school budgets are limited for materials and resources assigned to each classroom. The final component, *planning,* requires a broad range of decisions, including the daily lessons, units, instructional methods, assignments, and grading tests.

Instructional Planner

Effective planning involves establishing priorities based on (1) the general mission of the school; (2) the curriculum and objectives for the subject taught; (3) student abilities, aptitudes, needs, and interests; (4) content to be included and appropriate units into which the subject can be divided; (5) materials and resources; and (6) instructional methods for short- and long-range planning of lessons. Most teachers plan the organization and presentation of content based on knowledge of students and knowledge of how to teach the content. A second type of knowledge involves teaching activities such as diagnosing, grouping, managing, and evaluating learners. The middle level teacher emphasizes mastery of reading, writing, arithmetic, and technical skills; content from the various disciplines (history, science, literature, etc.); major concepts from the disciplines (separate or broad-based); inquiry approaches to thinking; broad philosophical schools or aesthetics (humanitarian issues and ethics); and competence. The middle level teacher as an instructional planner includes content, skills, and personal and social interaction dimensions. The middle level teacher organizes the academic learning time into specific learning tasks. This instruction is usually done by planning for the year, term, unit, week, and day. In the middle grades, a study by Brown (1988) indicated that teachers rely on previous student successes or failures, district curriculum guides, textbooks, student interests, classroom management factors, school calendar, and prior experience when they plan for yearly or term units. Classroom activity is matched to learners' prior experiences. Effective classroom learning time is organized so that students can learn academic material with a high degree of success. Myers and Myers (1990) suggested that academic time contains three measures: *allotted time* (the time given to work on academic tasks); *engaged time* (the portion of allotted time that students spend on academic tasks); and *student success* (a measure of student successes or failures at academic tasks). Young adolescents learn more if they are provided quality instructional time.

Another facet of time is the effective utilization of wait time. *Wait time,* which usually occurs when teachers ask questions during a lesson, is defined as the amount of time between the end of the question and the time when a student is expected to respond. It is recommended that teachers wait three to five seconds before calling on a student. Wait time also has been considered as the time that it takes for a student to respond once the teacher has called on the student. Depending on the complexity and difficulty of the questions, it may take the young adolescent longer to respond to more complex questions. Simple one-word or predictable factual responses may not require much wait time. Questions that require students to analyze and evaluate issues and problems will take longer. When teachers use wait time, students' responses are longer, more students respond, more academically slower students respond more frequently, and students demonstrate increased confidence in their responses (Berliner, 1985; Gage, 1984). It is not the intent of this book to deal with methods; the actual criteria for planning units and lessons can be found in several sources (Ornstein, 1990; Orlich et al., 1990; McNeil & Wiles, 1990; Muth & Alvermann, 1992).

Human Relations Specialist

The middle level teacher is described as a caring individual who is perceived by students as being concerned about their individual concerns and needs. The caring teacher promotes a comforting and nonthreatening classroom environment in which the young adolescent can develop self-esteem and self-confidence. This role always places the dignity of the student as a primary focus in the classroom. Csikszentmihalyi and McCormack (1986) suggested that teachers influence students through their personal enthusiasm, excitement about their subject, explanations accomplished in original and unique ways, their approachability in a pleasant classroom environment, promotion of student self-confidence, and demonstration that they really care about students. In this category are development of self, development of productive thinking—including creativity—development of personal meaning, self-teaching, problem-solving abilities, the development of aesthetic capacity, and the motivation to achieve (Joyce & Weil, 1988). Middle level teachers need to have high expectations of all students. Teachers need to encourage every young adolescent to achieve to maximum potential. Teachers need to reward appropriate student performance. Middle level teachers need to make students feel good about themselves. The rewards can be in the form of smiles, compliments, and recognition through reducing requirements for homework. It is important to make sure the rewards fit the middle level context in terms of peer group, instructional goals, and type of student population. Young adolescents must perceive the reward as personally valuable. The rewards can be viewed as competitive, in which some students experience success that others do not; cooperative, in which one individual's performance can increase the likelihood of rewards for others; and individual, in which the young adolescent's individual performance is recognized. The appropriate use of a reward structure is essential in middle level schools. Praise as a reward is often effective in encouraging behavior and improving academic performance, but it must be perceived as being real and meaningful to the young adolescent. Praise is more effective when directed toward specific student achievements which can reinforce a desired student behavior.

As a part of social interaction, teachers as leaders of cooperative group planning can directly affect the individual's relations with groups, society, and culture. Some of the important objectives would be transmitting cultural heritage; developing competence as international citizens in an interdependent, technological, and global world; and developing cooperative planning and problem-solving strategies. The middle level school can assist young adolescents to make commitments to community service and social advocacy. Young adolescents can be part of cooperative planning and problem solving. Another avenue might be the emphasis on economic interdependence at the international level. This focus would emphasize the skills and knowledge necessary for economic survival in a highly technical, global, and interdependent economy. Another emphasis should be on improving human relations among culturally diverse groups in the school and community. This approach could take the form of role playing and simulating such problems as conservation, pollution, and neighborhood cooperation facing groups and individuals.

Classroom Manager

The middle level teacher as a classroom manager is concerned with managing people, time, space, content, materials, and classroom climate to promote positive behavior. In managing young adolescents, attention is directed to individual characteristics and differences that motivate and develop self-responsibility for student behavior. The middle level teacher develops an effective learning environment that organizes time and space, maximizes student involvement in learning, and develops rules and procedures. The classroom climate is the psychological and social environment that exists in each classroom. Some teachers create an atmosphere that is supportive, comfortable, friendly, and relaxed while others preside over threatening, competitive, and tense classroom environments (Ryans, 1960; Tuckman, 1985). Myers and Myers (1990) suggested four "clusters" that have a positive and/or negative effect on classroom climate. *Ecology* is the physical aspects of the classroom. *Milieu* is that interpersonal atmosphere where morale is high and positive or low and threatening. *Social system* relates to formal and informal rules governing the classroom and school setting and the communication, involvement, and relationships existing between student–teacher, principal–teacher, and parents–teacher. *Culture* is the values, beliefs, attitudes, expectations, and norms existing in the classrooms and school setting.

A positive classroom climate is developed through an organization and management plan. The plan spells out rules and procedures from the first day and enforces them. Effective teachers tell and explain to young adolescents what their expectations are, model the procedures, and allow time before enforcing rules. As a part of effective classroom management, middle level teachers pace learning to accommodate student interests and abilities and create a learning environment that is success-oriented, pleasant, and purposeful. Middle level teachers need to monitor what is taking place in the classroom and know when to deal with inappropriate behavior. Teaching techniques include staying on task; varying lessons between whole-group, small-group, and individual activities; utilizing different types of instructional materials; and holding young adolescents' accountable for their work and classroom performance.

The techniques for handling misbehavior involve the middle level teacher in preventing the activity from spreading, extinguishing it, and getting the class back on track. If the behavior results in physical violence, robbery, thefts, vandalism, and drug abuse, then the teacher needs to take appropriate action to protect others, stop the behavior, and report the incident to school authorities. In this instance, the teacher should use caution and common sense and act responsibly. The focus of classroom management is centered on heading off inappropriate behavior—such as absenteeism, tardiness, verbal disruptions, inattentiveness, and skipping classes—before it happens.

Various other approaches have been proposed. In behavior modification, young adolescents are expected to demonstrate certain types of behavior and receive rewards or are punished for undesirable behaviors (Brophy, 1983). Gordon (1974), in the *Teacher Effectiveness Training* model, developed a system for analyzing conflict between teacher and student as to whether the problem (person experiencing frustration) is owned by the teacher or student. Assertive discipline (Canter & Canter, 1976) suggested that teachers should be assertive but not inhumane in establishing classroom behavioral expectations for students and should enforce those expectations with support from principals and colleagues.

On the middle level, students are oriented toward peers. Many young adolescents become resentful of or question the authority of parents and the school. Disruptions, humorous remarks, and horseplay become common behavioral responses of young adolescents as they seek peer approval. Classroom management techniques should focus on motivating and managing young adolescents who know what to do but are not always willing to do it.

There is no magic formula that works every time, but there are several common principles that can guide teachers in coping with disruptive behaviors. These are respect for individual students, willingness to understand and listen to students' problems, using instruction and persuasion rather than force, and recognizing that students are responsible for their behavior.

Counselor

Middle level teachers can serve as substitute parents, advisors, confidants, role models, and protectors. Teachers are expected to help students do the right things, and correct them when they demonstrate inappropriate behavior. Middle level students frequently need teachers' advice, guidance, and affirmation. Teachers who are readily available and are respected adults usually can help or know someone who can. Middle level teachers should become engaged in helping young adolescents resolve their personal problems, should provide a sounding board, and should offer advice confidentially. Teachers may be called into situations where they are asked to protect students from embarrassment and forms of discrimination. Middle level teachers increase the potential for personal development of self-confidence, self-esteem, and self-worth of young adolescents. Another approach in counseling is the discovery by young adolescents of personal meaning in their lives (Maslow, 1970; Combs, 1982; Rogers, 1983; and Purkey & Novak, 1984). One aspect of the teacher as counselor is encouraging young adolescents to direct their own learning and to solve problems independently. The self-directed learner will continue to seek fulfillment throughout life. Another aspect is helping young adolescents to develop a desire for self-improvement—to become self-motivated and to strive for personal success. Finally, it is important to achieve the enhancement of young adolescents' aesthetic appreciation. This challenging task is to try to instill beauty in their personal, physical, and social environments. Through a cooperative relationship, the middle level teacher and young adolescent can develop meaningful intellectual, personal, and social skills.

Part of the responsibility is communicating with parents. Middle level teachers must possess effective communication skills to inform parents of young adolescents' progress and of problem areas where improvement is needed. Interacting with parents includes informing them of progress and difficulties; consulting them on various academic, personal, and social decisions; asking for their assistance, and responding to their requests. Regardless of how much attention parents give their children or how competent the parents are, teachers must cultivate positive parental relationships in order to help young adolescents.

Currently, families are under a great deal of stress. Single-parent families or families with both parents working result in children being left alone on their own for longer periods of time. When parents do come home, they are tired and less able to concentrate on needed parenting functions. Teachers need to be understanding of parent situations and win their support for helping young adolescents. The benefactor is the middle level student. While teachers must encourage parents, they need to counsel them when their actions may hurt their children. The range of parental attitudes and skills runs the gamut from being interested, loving, emotionally secure, and understanding of their children to being frustrated, apprehensive, and too busy to care. While they show their love for their children in different ways, parents hope that teachers will guide their young adolescents to become successful human beings.

Evaluator

This role is in contrast to other roles described previously in this section. Middle level teachers are called upon to evaluate their learners. According to Slavin (1988), there are five purposes for evaluating students: to motivate students, to provide feedback to students, to provide feedback to teachers on their teaching effectiveness, to furnish information to parents, and to indicate student selection for different types of instruction. Teachers are asked to establish standards for student achievement and to motivate students to reach them. They evaluate whether students meet or fail to meet these standards. Teachers also are called upon to assess such personal qualities and characteristics as motivation, intellectual ability, and behavior. As a part of their job description, they are asked to judge students. In their judgment, teachers must be fair (objective as perceived by students) and realistic (students receive accurate information of their performance). Four types of evaluation are utilized in the middle grades: (1) placement assessment, which helps to determine student placement before classroom instruction begins; (2) diagnostic evaluation, which means determining readiness to learn and monitoring the learner's progress and learning difficulties; (3) formative evaluation, which assesses tentative student progress on a short-term basis from teacher-made tests, homework, and students' performance; and (4) summative evaluation, which is a comprehensive assessment that occurs at the end of the course and focuses on determining the degree of mastery. It is not always necessary to administer formal tests.

Technologist

Middle level teachers and learners are entering an age of changing technology and expanding information. Just what type of equipment is available, and the teacher's knowledge of the equipment and capability of using it, will determine the degree of utilization of instructional technology. Instructional technology applications can include the chalkboard, display boards, films, film strips, slides, overhead projector, television, computers, telecommunication systems, videocassettes, and videodisks. It is important to determine what types of instructional technology are available. Most middle level schools will have chalkboards, overheads, display boards, and film and slide projectors. The funding and emphasis placed on instructional technology by the school board and the community will determine the availability of educational television, computers, videotape recorders, videodisks, and telecommunication systems. Each time instructional technology equipment is used, it is important to establish a set of guidelines for using the equipment and materials in the classroom. It should be remembered that not all young adolescents enjoy visual presentations, because of learning style preferences. Some young adolescents prefer interactive modes, while others desire individual approaches to instructional technology applications. One major concern is where the equipment should be stored and whether it is easily accessible. It is highly recommended that a central location for distribution of equipment be considered. The repair, monitoring, inventory, and usage of equipment and instructional materials can be provided more effectively through a central location, and a central location makes the equipment easily available for all teachers. Disadvantages are that middle level teachers have to plan ahead and schedule equipment needed. This is not as convenient as having the equipment readily available in your classroom, and there may not be enough equipment available for use in every classroom on a given day. However, there is no guarantee that if the equipment was provided in every room it would be used more effectively.

Currently, the utilization of instructional technology centers around the role of computers on the middle level. What level of computer knowledge should be expected of young adolescents from middle level schools? Ornstein (1990) has suggested that there may be four levels of computer knowledge: (1) computer literacy (general understanding of how computers are utilized and some experience with accessing information); (2) computer competency (ability to use the computer for particular purposes; (3) computer expertise (in-depth knowledge of how computers work and the capability of programming); and (4) computer hacker (an addict who spends hours, days, and nights working on new software and programming problems, and transmitting messages to fellow hackers). On the middle level, young adolescents need to become computer literate. This objective can be accomplished through regular classroom instruction and exploratory experiences. Every young adolescent will need computer skills to access information and survive in the computerized world of banking, communication, and merchandising. Some young adolescents may already be experts.

What type of computer training should be provided for middle level teachers? The goal of middle level teachers should be to develop the degree of computer knowledge necessary to feel competent in using the computers for their classroom teaching. The biggest factor in developing computer knowledge is the attitude of the teacher. An enthusiastic and competent teacher will encourage young adolescents to utilize the computer, in contrast to a teacher who doubts his or her own ability to use the computer. With the rapid changes taking place in computer hardware and software, it is impossible to know all of the facets of any software program, let alone equipment that is constantly changing. There is a need for constant training and retraining in order to remain computer literate. There will be a continuing need for expanded budgets to purchase equipment and software. Another dilemma is how to judge the quality of computer software. Because there are no industry-wide standards, it is important to establish guidelines for evaluating computer software. In addition, guidelines need to be established for the use and availability of computers in the middle level classrooms.

Thus, the potential of instructional technology is unlimited. The limitations are imposed by availability of equipment and trained personnel to implement the materials in the classroom. Instructional technology equipment provides more opportunities for motivating young adolescents. The interactive modes of television and videodisks provide young adolescents with more involvement and control over their learning. Instructional technology is an essential competence for the middle level teacher in the twenty-first century.

Person

The teacher as a person focuses on caring, competence, and confidence. A display of warmth is demonstrated toward young adolescents. The teacher is aware of the varying developmental levels among the middle level learners in her or his classroom. The teacher displays positive self-confidence. Middle level teachers should strive for positive attitudes and the establishment of positive learning environments in their classrooms. The focus of the learning in the classroom is on the learner. Teachers are enthusiastic about middle level learners and employ instructional methods that are cognizant of the varied needs of young adolescents. There is a firm belief that all students can learn. Students are accepted for their characteristics and potential. Middle level teachers do not need to be in charge of the classroom and can be comfortable with students taking responsibility for their own learning in the classroom. This role is examined in greater detail in the following section on effective teaching.

In the next section we will examine teacher style, teacher characteristics, teacher competencies, and teacher effectiveness. These components of effective teaching should form the rationale for developing the academic, personal, and social dimensions of middle level curriculum and instruction. These three dimensions also become essential in the organization and implementation of a developmentally appropriate and responsive middle level school.

GUIDELINES FOR EFFECTIVE TEACHING ON THE MIDDLE LEVEL

No single factor can explain or describe the qualities of an effective middle level teacher. The problem of determining effective and ineffective teachers is complex. What works in one school setting may not work in another. The variations in teachers' perceptions, students, subject matter, grade levels, school setting, and social and economic backgrounds make it difficult to determine what effective teaching is. To discuss effective teaching styles on the middle level, six areas will be examined—teacher style, teacher characteristics (behavior), teacher competencies, student–teacher relationships, student expectations, and teacher expectations. These categories should be used by beginning and experienced teachers to help define more clearly those roles and qualities that make a successful middle level teacher.

TEACHING STYLES

Teaching styles encompass the teacher's stance, pattern of behavior, mode of performance, and attitudes toward self and others. Teaching styles are essential to the determination of roles, behaviors, and characteristics of middle level teachers. Teaching style has been defined as: (1) the effective utilization of classroom space (Petersen, 1979); (2) the establishment of a supportive classroom climate (Medley, 1979); (3) the freedom to express one's ideas (Ornstein & Miller, 1980); and (4) the right to select appropriate classroom instructional strategies (Ornstein & Miller, 1980). Whichever definition is selected, the notion of stability in teaching behaviors and methods is critical. There should be a predictable teaching pattern even in different classroom contexts for young adolescents. Middle level teachers can each have their own style of teaching for restructuring classroom instruction and delivery of the lesson. Some representative models of teaching styles that might be considered are: teaching descriptions, interaction analysis, leadership styles, and explicit teaching.

Teaching Descriptions. Rubin (1985) developed a teaching descriptions model with six roles: (1) *explanatory* (command of subject matter and explainer), (2) *inspiratory* (stimulating and involved), (3) *informative* (giving verbal instructions to students), (4) *corrective* (feedback for diagnosing and correcting learning), (5) *interactive* (encouraging students' ideas through dialogue and questioning), and (6) *programmed* (guiding students' independent learning). While these roles are not research based, they are suggestive of the qualities and methodologies of an effective middle level teacher. Middle level teachers need to develop their own teaching style based on their own experiences, preferences, and training. Of the teaching descriptors we have indicated, teachers should select those roles that can assist their personal approach to teaching on the middle level.

Leadership Styles. Lippitt and White (1943) found a relationship between leadership styles and teaching styles. This model has been translated into instructional leadership styles of authoritarian, democratic, or laissez-faire. The authoritarian teacher directs all activities in the classroom (directed teaching); the learners are dependent on the teacher for activities. In contrast, the democratic teacher encourages group participation, shares the decision-making process, and develops a more self-sufficient and responsible learner whose productivity is improved. This behavior appears to be conducive to fostering group decision making and problem solving. The laissez-faire teacher provides no goals or directions for learners and assumes learners are totally responsible for their learning. This allows some students to discover their creativity and their own leadership skills, but the teacher is often perceived as unorganized or ineffective (Woolfolk and McCune-Nicolich, 1988). The authoritarian–democratic–laissez-faire classification has inspired numerous empirical studies that have utilized similar teacher categories, such as direct vs. indirect teaching, formal vs. informal teaching, and teacher-centered, student-centered, and problem-centered teaching (Ornstein, 1986). An examination of the individual's leadership style is necessary to sustain effective teaching on the middle level.

Explicit Teaching. A more recent model of teaching styles, intended for use in structured classroom settings for such subjects as mathematics, social studies, reading, and science, is presented by Rosenshine (1986). This model places a high priority on goal statements, review, small increments for new learning, active practice, questioning, systematic feedback, and instruction and practice aimed toward student independence (pp. 60–61).

Rosenshine notes that for explicit teaching styles in which structured learning is preferred teachers should focus on six functions[1] that correlate with student learning. These functions are:

1 Review (homework, previous learning, and prerequisite skills and knowledge for this lesson).
2 Presentation (state lesson, teach in small steps, model procedures, use concrete positive and negative examples, use clear language, check for student understanding, and avoid digressions).
3 Guided practice (high frequency of guided practice, all students respond and receive feedback, high success rate, and continue practice until students have learned).
4 Corrections and feedback (give process feedback when answers are correct but hesitant; give sustaining feedback, clues, or reteaching for incorrect answers; and provide reteaching when necessary).
5 Independent practice (students receive assistance during initial steps, or review; practice continues until students are automatic; teacher provides active supervision; and routines are utilized for slower learners).
6 Weekly and monthly reviews.

Each of these items should be analyzed for their effectiveness in given middle level learning situations. For learners who require a structured environment, these six functions should be investigated.

In summary, teaching style is a matter of personal choice and satisfaction. What is successful for one teacher may not be useful to another teacher. Thus,

---

[1]From "Synthesis of Research on Explicit Teaching" by B. Rosenshine, 1986, in *Educational Leadership, 43*, p. 65. Reprinted with permission of the Association for Supervision and Curriculum Development and the author.

operational definitions of "good" teachers and "effective" teaching styles vary among middle level teachers and within school districts. Being aware of the various aspects of teaching styles can assist middle level teachers to be more effective in their classrooms, especially if the teaching style is employed to enhance student learning and not primarily for teacher convenience.

TEACHER CHARACTERISTICS

Teacher characteristics eventually lead to concern whether different teaching behaviors are more effective for some types of young adolescents, and about the importance of learner styles in the selection of teaching styles. It is virtually impossible to identify all the varied behaviors in any precise manner. Usually, the methods for organizing teacher behavior fall into: (1) models of teaching (Joyce & Weil, 1988), (2) interaction or instructional approaches (Ornstein, 1990), (3) teacher characteristics (Porter & Brophy, 1988), and (4) competencies (Medley, Coker, & Soar, 1984).

Models of Teaching. One may search the science of teaching without finding any one model that can be identified as the best approach to developing personal, social, or academic dimensions (Joyce & Weil, 1988). After a careful study of models during the past 20 years, Joyce and Weil maintain that a wide variety of approaches are required for effective teaching. Teaching is a process in which a cooperative environment is created and shared by teachers and students, including a consensus on important values and beliefs that shape classroom environments (Joyce & Weil, 1988). Thus, the models reflect what types of classroom environments are generated by the teacher and learner working together. While there is no perfect model of teaching that can accomplish all types of learning or work for all learning situations, Joyce and Weil proposed four "families" of models representing many types of learning and requiring different instructional methods. These families are: *information processing models, personal models, social interaction models,* and *behavioral models.* Each of the four families has serious implications for effective teaching on the middle level.

Information processing models focus on the intellectual capacity of young adolescents and methods to improve their mastery of content. Information processing refers to the "ways of enhancing the human being's innate drive to make sense of the world by acquiring and organizing data, sensing problems and generating solutions to them, and developing concepts and language for conveying them" (Joyce & Weil, 1988, p. 5). Some models are concerned with young adolescents' problem-solving and thought processes, while others focus on concepts and information from the academic disciplines. These models depend on activities that utilize young adolescents' content and skills. While all models stress the social relationships and the development of a self-concept, the emphasis is on intellectual development as the means of learning. Information processing models may be inductive (leading young adolescents through processes), deductive (providing frameworks for subject mastery), or guided discovery (a step-by-step process for accomplishing a series of tasks). The primary purposes are introduction of inquiry approaches, mastery of academic concepts and facts, and development of general intellectual skills such as thinking and problem solving. In this category, models focus on: (1) studies of thinking (deductive and inductive) such as Inductive Thinking Approach by Taba (1966) and Inquiry Training Model by Suchman (1962), (2) learning theories such as advanced organizers by Ausubel (1963), (3) concept attainment by Joyce and Weil (1988), (4) academic disciplines by Schwab (1965), and (5) cognitive developmental studies by Piaget (1952) and Sigel (1969).

Personal models focus on the unique characteristics of young adolescents in their struggle for a well-rounded personality integrating physical, personal, and emotional desires. The goal is to assist young adolescents in assuming part of the responsibility for their own development (Joyce & Weil, 1988). Teaching becomes helping young adolescents take responsibility for their own development and achieve a sense of self-worth and personal harmony. The purposes of personal models are to increase young adolescents' sense of self-worth, assist in the development of personal goals for learning, understand their emotions and the way that their emotions affect behavior, help them develop realistic learning goals, initiate plans for self-improvement, and promote increased willingness to explore new experiences. In this category, the models fall into: nondirective teaching (learner as center of learning) by Rogers (1983); synectics (enhancement of creativity) by Gordon (1961); awareness training (enhancement of self) by Schutz (1958, 1967); and classroom meeting (personalized organization of the classroom) by Glasser (1965).

Social interaction models stress the cooperative relationships that exist among young adolescents, society, and their peers and adults. Social models rely on cooperative learning strategies, group dynamics, and the processes of group interaction. In addition, social models draw on the energy of the group and utilize the outcomes that arise from dialogue on differing viewpoints. The central idea is to have young adolescents work together to identify and resolve academic, personal, or social problems. Recently, interest in cooperative models has been generated by Johnson, Johnson, and Holubec (1988, 1990) and Slavin (1987). Their studies indicate that classrooms organized into cooperative learning strategies have greater mastery of material when students work in pairs, tutor each other, and share rewards. Shared tasks and the interaction between learners produced better intergroup relations and resulted in better self-concepts. These models also are concerned with development of intellect, self-concept, and the mastery of academic content through interacting with peers, teachers, school personnel, parents, and the community. The primary goals of social models are for students to identify and solve problems, develop skills in human relations, and become aware of personal and social values.

Behavioral models utilize a common body of knowledge based on behavior modification theory. Learning theories, social learning theories, behavior modification, and behavior therapy are other terms that could be used. The key factor in these models is that young adolescents learn from receiving feedback about the effects of their behavior. These models have been used in training, therapy, and the development of interpersonal relationships. Learning tasks as a common element are broken down into a series of small sequenced behaviors. Behavioral models stress behavioral changes based on specifying behavior to be modified and practiced. Young adolescents are presented with tasks and individual and group feedback to assist them through their performance in reaching the goals they hope to achieve. Behavior is modified and revised until a satisfactory level of performance is attained. Models representative of this category are (1) mastery learning by Carroll (1963) and Bloom (1971); (2) direct instruction by Rosenshine (1973, 1979, 1986); (3) self-control (Contingency Management Model) by Rimm and Masters (1974); (4) simulations by Joyce and Weil (1988); and (5) assertiveness training by Wolpe (1969) and Wolpe and Lazarus (1966).

In summary, growth in teaching is the mastery of a variety of teaching models. Some models are more appropriate for certain middle level curricula, depending on grade and subject matter content, learner style, and teaching style. A middle level teacher's professional growth in teaching is to learn new models and combine and synthesize already learned models to create new approaches to teaching and, thereby, expand the art and craft of teaching. These models form the basis for roles that middle level teachers can utilize in curriculum planning and directing young adolescents' learning.

Interaction. Since much teaching is done through verbal and nonverbal interactive patterns, middle grade teachers communicate expectations through verbal and nonverbal means. In research studies on teacher interaction, it would appear that teachers tend to dominate the classroom, the focus of instruction is on subjects, and teaching tends to be dominated by fact-oriented presentations. The students' primary responsibilities are to respond to the teacher (Ornstein, 1990). Siegman and Feldstein (1978) concluded that nonverbal communication may be providing about 65 percent of the social meaning in the classroom. In a more recent study of 225 teachers and school principals in 45 schools, Stephens and Valentine (1986) observed that ten specific nonverbal behaviors influenced the teaching learning process. These were smiles or frowns, eye contact, head nods, gestures, dress, interaction distance, touch, body movement, posture, and seating arrangements. Distance, touch, body movement, posture, and seating are subject to personal preferences and are based on the significance attached by young adolescents to their personal and social relationships. Distance, touch, and body movement can be taken as indicators of the degree of formality and the relationship between middle level teacher and young adolescent, from intimate and personal to social and public. Middle level teachers should maintain a social and public relationship and avoid nonverbal behavior that might be interpreted to be sarcasm, harassment, or criticism.

Galloway (1984) maintains that nonverbal cues are a true reflection of the student's perceptions of the teacher's real feelings. Galloway categorized these as (1) *space* (how teachers spend time), (2) *time* (how teachers utilize class time and emphasis placed on content), and (3) *body maneuvers* (nonverbal cues that are used to control students) (pp. 411–430). Teachers either encourage or restrict student behavior through the student's perceptions of a teacher's nonverbal behavior. Students also exhibit nonverbal behavior that influences teacher behavior. Doyle (1986) characterized these as *location/proximity* (where the student elects to sit); *attentiveness* (posture, eye contact, smiling communicate attention and relate to positive evaluation of student's competence, learning, and attitude); *disruptive behaviors* (rejecting teacher's help, responding with negative nonverbal behaviors); and *timing* (students who make requests at inappropriate times) (pp. 392–431).

Good and Brophy (1991) suggested another approach to determine whether the student is attentive (engaged in an appropriate activity) or inattentive (non-engaged). For inattentiveness, they suggested observing students looking for movement in the room, doing other work during class discussion, putting their heads on their desks, daydreaming, or looking out the window. Attentive cues from students would be displayed by maintaining eye contact, working on assigned work, being prepared, acting alert, displaying positive facial expressions, and engaging in learning tasks during free activity or independent study period.

Teacher Behaviors. Teacher characteristics attempt to describe the effective teacher behaviors. There is widespread disagreement on defining what constitutes "good" teachers and "effective" teaching. Confusion exists over how to describe such teaching characteristics as traits, personality, competencies, or performance. Discrepancies between grade levels, different subjects, sex, and socioeconomic and ethnic groups have made it difficult to agree upon operational definitions, school settings, and categories for generalizing the research findings. One study has little relationship to another even though the characteristics selected may be similar. The following section discusses some studies that can be used to identify teacher characteristics for the middle level.

Research Findings. In a synthesis of research studies over the past ten years on "good teaching," Porter and Brophy (1988) found that effective teachers communicate their instructional goals, are knowledgeable about subject matter and instructional strategies, clearly state their instructional expectations and explain the reasons for these expectations to learners, and utilize existing instructional resources so that more class time can be given to practices that expand and clarify content. In addition, effective teachers are familiar with students' background, adapting instruction to their needs and anticipating minsunderstandings in their existing knowledge. They teach students metacognitive strategies (those that help learners understand how they learn and how concepts are related to knowledge), they address all levels of cognitive objectives, they monitor students' learning progress by providing regular feedback, and integrate their subject matter with other academic areas. Effective teachers also accept responsibility for student outcomes, are reflective about their teaching strategies, and are active teachers, in contrast to passive teachers.

Mitchell, Ortiz, and Mitchell (1987) found some evidence that the essential ingredient in teaching is the lesson. They concluded that teacher-led verbal lessons and those that focus on children performing an activity are the most effective for student performance, while drill work and testing are not as effective. These two studies provide a further indication of the factors that need to be considered in effective teaching on the middle level.

Treatment of Learners. As part of encouraging young adolescents, what approach should teachers employ for high achievers and low achievers? Are all students encouraged to succeed and receive equal feedback and warmth? In a study of teacher behaviors and treatment toward high and low achievers, Good and Brophy (1991) listed ways to differentiate how teachers treated high and low achievers. These differences in teacher treatment of high and low achievers are listed in Table 5.2. Probably not every middle grade teacher would demonstrate all traits, and in some instances the student treatments may not be appropriate for a specific classroom situation.

A recent list of teacher characteristics was developed by Tuckman (1985). The teacher characteristics are grouped into four dimensions. *Creative teachers* are imaginative, experimenting, and original, in contrast to noncreative teachers

TABLE 5.2 Major Differences in Teachers' Treatment of Low and High Achievers

Low Achievers	High Achievers
Shorter wait time allowed for students' responses	Longer wait time permitted for students' responses
Inappropriate behavior and responses often rewarded	Appropriate behavior and responses usually reinforced
More frequent criticism for their performance	More frequent praise for their performance
Supportive feedback infrequently provided in teacher responses	Supportive feedback frequently given in teacher responses
Lower levels of learning expectations are required	Higher levels of learning expectations are required
Students seated farther from teacher	Students seated nearer to the teacher
Interaction provided to the learner more often on an individual basis	Interaction provided to learners more often in public and group settings
Less preferential treatment given on tests and assignments	More frequent preferential treatment given on tests and assignments
Fewer nonverbal support indicators such as gestures, tone of voice, or smiles are used	More nonverbal support indicators such as gestures, smiles, and tone of voice are used
Effective, time efficient instructional strategies utilized less frequently	Effective, time efficient instructional strategies utilized more frequently
Less acknowledgement and acceptance of learners' ideas are given	Frequent acknowledgement and acceptance of learners' ideas are provided
Curriculum based on extending knowledge level through class recitation of facts and drill and practice	Curriculum based on extending higher level thinking and analysis of concepts through group interaction and discussions

Adapted from *Looking in Classrooms* (5th ed.) by T. L. Good and J. E. Brophy, 1991, pp. 122–123. New York: HarperCollins Publishers. Adapted with permission of HarperCollins Publishers.

who are routine, exacting, and cautious. *Dynamic teachers* are outgoing, energetic, and extroverted, in contrast to nondynamic teachers who are passive, withdrawn, and submissive. *Organized teachers* are purposeful, resourceful, and in control contrasted to disorganized teachers who are capricious, erratic, and flighty. *Warm teachers* are sociable, amiable, and patient, in contrast to cold teachers who are unfriendly, hostile, and impatient.

Purkey and Novak (1984) suggested that teacher behaviors can be placed into four categories for encouraging student success. These categories range from intentionally disinviting to intentionally inviting. Though teachers should intentionally invite success, many teachers are not invitational in their teaching strategies. Teaching must be carefully planned to be inviting. In these studies, some themes reoccur as characteristic of effective teaching at the middle level. They include communication of expectations; organized lessons; enthusiasm; a caring and friendly personality; familiarity with the students; practicing effective classroom management skills; teacher incentives; monitoring student's work and progress; and utilizing creative strategies. Others may be added by the reader. Some characteristics are more important for teaching on the middle level. It is essential to identify those characteristics that teachers already possess and those that individual teachers might want to practice and add to improve their teaching of young adolescents. In summary, these teacher behaviors can communicate positive or negative expectations. It is important to be aware of teacher behaviors which are discouraging to young adolescents and to take steps to avoid these behaviors in effective teaching.

TEACHER COMPETENCIES

Another approach to determining teacher behavior is the identification of teacher competencies. With the lack of agreement on defining teacher characteristics, a more precise term, *teacher competencies,* has been recommended by Medley, Coker, and Soar (1984). These competencies may be related to broad teacher characteristics, but usually they are specific definitions of teacher behavior which are placed in some type of teacher appraisal system. Examples are the lists of competencies developed by the University of Toledo and Salt Lake City School District. The 49 Toledo competencies were designed to measure five broad areas for student teaching: (1) planning teaching, materials, equipment and evaluation; (2) instructional strategies, techniques and/or methods; (3) communication with learners; (4) learner reinforcement-involvement; and (5) professional standards (Gibney and Wiersma, 1986). They reflect some 2,000 behavioral objectives that can apply to preservice and beginning teachers. In contrast, the Salt Lake City School District list contains 24 competencies in four broad categories: (1) standards of expected student performance, (2) learning environment, (3) appropriate student control, and (4) appropriate strategies for teaching (Salt Lake Teachers Association, 1988). Both sets analyze what the teacher is doing while teaching. Both utilize specific behaviors that have generated a long list of competencies.

Guidelines for Evaluation. Which of these competencies are more important to principals who evaluate teachers? In a study conducted by Arnn and Mangieri (1988) of 202 secondary schools identified for special recognition by the U.S. Department of Education because of their effectiveness in educating students, principals were asked to outline competencies that they utilized in evaluating teachers. They identified 11—in order of importance—as (1) *task orientation* (businesslike, time on task), (2) *enthusiasm and interests* (teacher's stamina and involvement), (3) *direct instruction* (establishes and assesses learning goals), (4) *pacing* (appropriate level of difficulty and pacing), (5) *feedback* (positive and negative feedback), (6) *management* (conducts class without interruptions), (7) *questioning* (poses questions at different levels), (8) *instructional time* (adequate content coverage), (9) *variability* (flexibility and adaptability of methods), (10) *structuring* (extent of teacher direction), and (11) *opportunity to learn criterion material* (criterion material is covered in class). The first five—task orientation, enthusiasm and interest, direct instruction, pacing, and feedback—are active dimensions of teaching. In general, most measurements of teacher competence focus on minimal competencies (Ornstein, 1990). Several states, including Florida and North Carolina, have developed a specific set of competencies for appraisal and merit pay plans. In addition, the national reform movement advocates have pushed for an appraisal system based on teacher competencies.

According to Wise et al. (1987), successful appraisal of competencies requires a commitment by top-level management, which must approve of the evaluation process and allocate institutional resources. In addition, competence is important; the evaluator must have expertise to perform the task of observation. Collaboration by administrators, supervisors, and teachers to develop a common understanding of goals and processes involved is another factor. Lastly, compatibility is necessary between the various support systems and between evaluation goals and processes and district goals and processes. Teachers must be given the benefit of the doubt and a chance to remediate. Any competency appraisal system denotes an understanding that there is no one preferred method and not all competencies listed can be incorporated into any given lesson.

EFFECTIVE STUDENT–TEACHER RELATIONSHIPS

The key to successful teaching on the middle level is understanding teacher and student needs and how they can be addressed. Teachers are essential because of the psychosocial needs of young adolescents and their need for nurturing and respect by adults. Teachers and adolescents need to be able to establish effective interpersonal relationships on the middle level. Many teachers discover that the transitional nature of young adolescents' personal needs is often frustrating and difficult to cope with in the classroom. In most instances, teachers trained in elementary or secondary education have not been prepared adequately for working with young adolescents. Many well-meaning middle level teachers have rigid expectations and assumptions that are better suited either for younger children or young adults. Goodlad (1984) and *Turning Points* (1989) found that many teachers of young adolescents were not satisfied teaching this age group. Less career fulfillment was experienced than was found in high schools or elementary schools. A teaching assignment to the middle level is the last choice of many teachers who were prepared for either elementary or secondary teaching assignments (*Turning Points,* 1989). The Carnegie report favored an interdisciplinary developmental approach to education for young adolescents with preparation in two academic concentrations (*Turning Points* 1989).

Certainly, many middle level teachers are excited about working with young adolescents. While the research has not been conducted in a systematic manner and is limited as to conclusive data, the available studies point to teachers who have the greatest satisfaction usually possessing the greatest understanding of adolescent developmental needs (George et al., 1992). Lipsitz (1984) from her research on four middle schools concluded that teachers are the key ingredient in successful middle level schools. Many teachers on the middle level are committed and highly competent professionals who get immense satisfaction out of teaching young adolescents. Another study, which solicited principals' viewpoints, described teachers' desire and commitment to work with young adolescents as essential. The study found that committed teachers were willing to accept all young adolescents and never gave up working with various types of learners (George & Stevenson, 1989). In summary, teachers who understand young adolescents' needs, interests, and behavior tend to be more successful. Teachers who are satisfied with middle level teaching enjoy working with young adolescents. To explore the student–teacher relationship needed for successful teaching on the middle level, an examination of teacher and student expectations will help place proper perspective on the characteristics needed by teachers.

Student Expectations

Young adolescents aged 10 to 13 appear to be more concerned about teachers' personal attributes than their teaching skills or how much knowledge the teachers demonstrate in the classroom (Beane & Lipka, 1986). According to Stevenson (1986), personal characteristics and attributes have an enormous influence on how students perceive their teachers. In a recent monograph, George et al. (1992) discussed the characteristics that young adolescents expect of their teachers. These characteristics represent some important expectations that young adolescents have of their teachers.

Respect. Middle level learners desire and need to believe in their teachers, but teachers must earn their respect. Teachers gain respect through demonstrating effective interpersonal skills in communicating with young adolescents. Teachers model their behavior in order to earn the respect of their students.

Equity. Young adolescents expect justice and fair play from their teachers. They are quick to react if they feel teachers' actions are unfair or show favoritism to some students. Teacher–student relationships that build on the tenets of equity and fair play are supported by middle level learners. Teachers must be equitable. Young adolescents cherish the opportunity to help establish rules and procedures. Teachers who are good listeners, show concerns for learners, and communicate humanely and rationally can build relationships for equity and fair play.

Order. Young adolescents have a sense of knowing how classes are to be managed and value order. While they value order and consistency, middle level learners do not hesitate to challenge teachers as part of a need to test themselves. George et al. (1992) suggested that there is a contradiction in the fact that on the one hand, students crave structure and order, while on the other extreme, they exploit teachers' weaknesses. Students need to have expectations stated and to know what consequences will result from infractions.

Sense of Humor. If young adolescents view the school as a fun place and see their teachers as having a sense of humor, then chances for learning to occur are enhanced. A sense of humor can be used to reduce tension and encourage learning. The use of comic strips and comedians from video tapes can enrich classroom teaching and student potential for learning.

Realistic Goals. Young adolescents expect that their teachers will set realistic learning goals, based on their developmental needs. Intellectual development should help the young adolescent go from experiences already learned to meaningful new experiences. Young adolescents desire to be competent, to be successful, and to be recognized for their contributions. The need for recognition and success are important in establishing realistic learning goals. Students value teachers who help them become successful and establish their individual worth and respectability among their peers and parents. Students need to be challenged, not frustrated. Students need to be assigned learning tasks that are possible to achieve, given their potential. Students who successfully manage learning challenges improve self-confidence and develop healthy mental attitudes. Teachers need to recognize the diversity in economic and family backgrounds, as well as diversity in the community, and that these factors affect learning.

Teacher Expectations

The following characteristics should provide a self-check of some of the interpersonal characteristics for meaningful teaching on the middle level. Teachers on the middle level should possess a high degree of *energy and enthusiasm* about teaching young people. Teachers serve as motivators when they demonstrate vitality and excitement about teaching. The high energy level and enthusiasm are contagious for sustaining excitement about teaching on the middle level.

The *curiosity* of the learners stimulates the teaching activities on the middle level. Teachers are challenged by the broad range of student interests, changing emotions, varied attention spans, and wide differences in intellectual sophistication. George et al. (1992) suggested that students possess a natural curiosity that teachers find personally rewarding.

A *community of learners* is fostered through collaboration and cooperation on the middle level. It involves establishing relationships among school, home, and community. Working on teams develops a spirit of cooperation and understanding and a cohesiveness among teachers and students. Student cohesiveness in schools is fostered by teams on the middle level. The establishment of common goals, close communication, and mutual support are essential for the development of a community of learners. Close communication and collaboration with students' parents to reengage the family in their children's learning are essential aspects of this category.

Middle level teachers need to plan a variety of instructional approaches and curriculum content to motivate young adolescents. Attention needs to be devoted to preparing teachers to teach integrated, interdisciplinary units. Integrated curriculum units promote the understanding of a broad range of content that is intellectually challenging and provides an opportunity for learning from colleagues. Excellence in teaching on the middle level is distinguished by personalized learning and diverse ways of presenting information for the varied developmental needs found at this level.

Middle level teachers need to balance students' work and recreation. There should be an overlap between work and recreation. Middle level teachers must balance expectations of academic performance with adolescents' developmental capacities. Academic integrity cannot be compromised, but students tend to be willing to expend effort when they are supported by teachers.

Contributing to meaningful learning experiences for young adolescents is rewarding. Teachers generally know whether they are making a contribution. Middle level schools provide an opportunity through multi-age grouping, teaming, and advisory arrangements to build a connection between student learning and teaching. These connections provide a student–teacher relationship that builds trust and understanding for forming positive and permanent bonds on the middle level.

Each of these interpersonal characteristics provides an incentive for middle level teachers. The most important issue is the type of relationship teachers desire to have with their students. Teachers who have a healthy self-concept are able to bring understanding to their classroom and a commitment for teaching on the middle level. Teachers will need support as middle level schools undergo philosophical, instructional, and curricular changes. Young adolescents do not automatically accept teachers without communication and personal effort. The best communication occurs when a teacher is a good listener, thoughtful, and reflective with young adolescents. It is important for teachers to keep students as the focal point of the middle level school. Pressures on middle level teachers tend to allow them to lose sight of the importance of maintaining a positive and optimistic learning climate that builds long-lasting student–teacher relationships. It is essential that young adolescents are supported and prized for their self-worth. Teachers communicate confidence, which in turn encourages young adolescents to accept difficult academic challenges.

The support of young adolescents should result through a friendship in which respect and honor are outcomes from mutual sharing of interests and events. Teachers must also balance their authority with affection, nurturing, and democratic control. Affection, nurturance, and democratic processes promote a healthy self-concept in young adolescents. Rational authority implies that respect is earned through dialogue, meaningful exchange of ideas and values, and a commitment to democratic processes in the school setting. Young adolescents who feel the need to question or challenge in discussions require teachers who understand their development and the sincerity of their thought. Middle level students need to have teachers listen seriously, encourage and weigh their ideas. Middle level teachers need to perceive students as partners in an effort to make living and learning as rewarding as possible. Teachers must go beyond the recognition of students' claims for respect, safety, and rationality. Teachers must make a lasting commitment of time, support, and patience. In summary, George et al. (1992) stated that:

> We will all do well to remember that in our relationships with youngsters, as in our relationships with each other, what goes around comes around. If we want a better society for future generations, we have to build it now through the trusting relationships we build with youngsters and the humanity we represent (p. 31).

Thus, what types of guidelines should be established for evaluating teacher characteristics and competencies on the middle level? Harris (1986) suggested a method for improving teaching by analyzing classroom behavior. It requires teachers and supervisors to agree on those behaviors that will be observed and analyzed. It establishes criteria for positive teacher characteristics, three separate observations, observation of teacher behaviors on agreed-upon criteria, comparison of perceptions from observers, and four types of diagnosis: (a) accomplishments—areas where all observers agree that characteristics are demonstrated; (b) need for improvements—those areas where all three sources agree that characteristics or competencies are not demonstrated; (c) uncertainty—areas where sources disagree or question, and (d) refine and upgrade—areas where observers agree that refinement or upgrading is required.

Another model by Hunter and Russell (1989) is referred to as the coaching model. A script is taken of the lesson, indicating what teachers and students said and did. This can be done by principal, teacher, department, or unit leaders. Once the lesson is over, the script is analyzed, noting objectives, teacher behaviors, instructional skills, and perceived results of students. The script becomes the essential tool in planning and conducting a teaching conference. The labeling of instructional skills and behaviors results in two categories of discussion topics: behaviors that were perceived as enabling learning and those about which the observer had questions. Next, discussion topics are prioritized for planning the conference by focusing on teacher expectations of anticipated learning and what actually happened during the lesson. The major objective of the conference is planned as the starting point. Planning the conference includes the order in which the information will be considered, selecting and marking parts of the script tape that will be needed to discuss a particular question or statement, anticipating a strategy for beginning the conference, and developing a means for closing the conference.

Next, the conference is conducted. In conducting the conference, it is important to be a good listener and dignify a teacher's potentially erroneous responses. In closing the conference, a summary of the important points of the conference, either written or verbal, is provided, and the expectations for the next observation are discussed.

In summary, while determination of teaching effectiveness is complex, middle level teachers can contribute to the research on teaching and cooperate with research studies conducted by universities and other institutions. Middle level teachers are the key to promoting realistic approaches to effective teaching studies. Through their efforts, it is possible to have an improved definition of successful teaching, even though it may never be entirely possible to have these teaching behaviors precisely measured.

REFORMS IN TEACHING

A Nation At Risk

One major implication of such reports as *A Nation at Risk* is that with the emphasis on improving teaching, there is a tendency to look only to content as the means of determining effectiveness. The commission recommended that high school graduation requirements be increased in the "five new basics": English, mathematics, science, social studies, and computer science; that standards and expectations for student performance and conduct at all age levels be raised; and that more time should be devoted to these new basics through more effective utilization of the existing school day, extension of the school day, and/or lengthening of the school year. The commission advocated making teaching a more rewarding and respected profession by setting higher standards for admission, increasing salaries, and instituting merit pay for superior teachers, creating a career ladder that distinguishes beginning, experienced, and master teachers, using incentives such as loans and grants to attract outstanding candidates into teaching, and involving master teachers in preparing and supervising probationary teachers (National Commission on Excellence, 1983). In response to this report, nearly all states have increased high school graduation requirements, raised teacher salaries, and expanded testing of new teachers. However, these recommendations divert attention from the need to attend to the social and personal interests of young adolescents. It is difficult for the middle level teacher to provide content, exploratory activities, and socialization in an atmosphere demanding basic skills, accountability for teachers, and improving standardized test scores.

The Carnegie Corporation Task Force

Three years after the publication of *A Nation at Risk,* in 1986, the Carnegie Corporation Task Force on Teaching as a Profession released *A Nation Prepared:*

Teachers in the 21st Century. It recommended a hierarchy of teachers, with a corps of "lead teachers" with leadership responsibilities in the schools; also, that teachers' salaries and career opportunities be made comparable to other professions, that teachers be given more control over their work environment, and that teachers be held accountable for student performance. The report urged the establishment of a national board to set higher standards for teacher certification and replacement of an undergraduate education major with a new professional curriculum at the graduate level, requiring a bachelor of arts or science degree before professional training. The pool of minority teachers should be expanded by providing incentives and better general education for minority students. Lastly, the report suggested that bonuses be awarded to school faculties on the basis of improved student achievement and attendance and reduced dropout rates (Carnegie Task Force, 1986). In 1987, the Carnegie Corporation helped establish a National Board for Professional Teaching Standards to issue certificates for content knowledge and effective teaching methods (Ornstein and Levine, 1989).

The Holmes Group

The Holmes Group is another national effort at reforming the teaching profession, comprised of deans at schools and colleges of education in the major research institutions nationwide. The group's first major report, *Tomorrow's Teachers,* emphasized the goals of making teacher education more demanding; creating higher standards for entry into teaching; recognizing differences in skills, commitment, and knowledge among teachers; connecting teacher training institutions more closely with elementary, middle, and secondary schools; and finally, transforming schools into better locations for teaching and learning. One of the most controversial recommendations was that undergraduate teacher education should be totally eliminated at participating teacher-training institutions (Holmes Group, 1986). As the group has formulated its policies and procedures, it has modified this position to one of encouraging an undergraduate degree before professional training.

A recent publication of the Holmes Group, *Tomorrow's Schools,* proposed a plan for a Professional Development School (PDS). The Professional Development School would provide training for beginning professionals, the continuing development of experienced professional teachers, and for the research and development of the teaching profession (Holmes, 1990). It remains to be seen if Professional Development Schools become a reality, with limited new funding initiatives an issue in a majority of states.

The Effective Schools Movement

What are the implications from the research on teaching for effective schools? In describing effective schools, the Northwest Educational Regional Laboratory (NWREL) identified five elements that lead to effective school practice. These are: (1) leadership, (2) school environment, (3) curriculum, (4) classroom instruction and management, and (5) assessment and evaluation (NWREL, 1988). The leadership of the school is vested in the principal, who is designated as the instructional leader. The instructional leader plans, organizes staff, and coordinates and directs the school improvement effort in a collaborative model of shared decision-making in which teachers participate in formulating school practices and policies. The school environment must be caring, positive, and supportive for students to learn and teachers to teach. In an effective school environment, all staff members have high expectations for all students to learn. Reasonable standards of classroom expectations are agreed on by teachers, administrators, and parents. Teachers are enthusiastic supporters of their students, pay attention to student interests, concerns, and accomplishments, and let students know they care. Teachers establish behavior expectations for students which are uniformly enforced. Student recognition should be based on specific student achievement. Student work that demonstrates high standards of excellence is displayed and reinforced by continued expectations of exemplary work. Classroom routines and processes are handled efficiently and effectively. Class interruptions are kept to a minimum, and classroom time is devoted to learning. Teachers get young adolescents ready to learn by diagnosing each learner's readiness to learn, providing instructional objectives, actively involving every young adolescent, and utilizing direct and indirect instruction depending on objectives and learners. The outcome is that teachers receive satisfaction for their teaching efforts, which have resulted in increased student achievement, and students recognize that their efforts have brought successful results.

Teacher empowerment has been proposed as a means of giving teachers more control over the curriculum, school policies, and finances. In most instances, teachers and administrators plan together to redesign educational programs and learning and teaching opportunities in their schools. In practice, faculties can determine the number of staff to be employed, how the staff will function, and how funds will be spent. Many obstacles will have to be overcome and educators must be involved in the reforms before the proposed changes will be successful. Teacher decision-making will require improved social skills to avoid the negative consequences associated with merit pay, career ladders, and differentiated approaches to curriculum and instruction.

THE PROFESSIONAL DEVELOPMENT OF MIDDLE LEVEL TEACHERS

PATTERNS OF CERTIFICATION

Because of the recent debate on teacher competence, almost every state has passed some type of competency requirement for teachers seeking initial certification. Certification is based on documentation that the candidate possesses sufficient preparation by assessing transcripts and credits or completing an approved program of study at an accredited college or university. In the past, teaching certificates were issued for life. Today, most states issue certificates for three to five years with completion of positive evaluations and/or additional in-service work to renew the certification. Certification requirements vary a great degree from state to state. Each state has its own procedures. The power to determine certification is divided among legislators, state departments of education, schools and colleges, and state boards of education. The requirements among the states vary greatly, from the number of credit hours prescribed and required in the various majors to no specification of hours. Across the country, it is usually the responsibility of the teacher training institution to determine what courses in the subject field will be used. Even when the course titles are similar, there are often wide differences in the content, intellectual level, and competencies mandated. The outcome is that state requirements and teacher training institutions do not have a uniform or universal set of courses and skills for the middle level. Some of the problem has been reduced by accreditation agencies like National Council for Accreditation of Teacher Education (NCATE) and National Association of State Directors of Teacher Education Certification (NASDTEC). In many instances, these two accrediting agencies have made significant progress in working together toward implementing similar standards and providing for reciprocity of certification. However, NASDTEC still mandates detailed evidence in writing of any standard, with little room for institutional interpretation.

Certification Requirements. In a study conducted by the Children's Defense Fund in 1988, twenty-one states indicated that they had middle level certification and 23 states reported that they did not have a middle level endorsement (pp. 15–17). Six other states indicated that they did not have certification at the present time but were investigating or in planning stages for consideration of the implementation of middle level certification. A recent survey completed by McEwin indicated that 28 states had established some form of certification or endorsement on the middle level (McEwin, 1992, p. 373). The most popular grade spans reported by these states were the 5–8 grade span in 9 of 28 states (32 percent), 5–9 grade span in 8 states (29 percent), and 4–8 grade span in 5 states (18 percent) (McEwin, 1992, p. 374). Even though over half of the states have adopted some type of middle school certification requirements, teacher training institutions have been slow to adopt pre-service training programs. Middle level teachers are either trained as elementary or secondary education teachers, and in several states have been permitted to add the endorsement for middle level with additional in-service training and/or courses. Because many state departments of education and universities have not been able to rid themselves of either elementary or secondary certification, the middle level program is placed in either elementary or secondary programs. The Carnegie Corporation is currently asking most states to assess their middle level programs. At present, many state departments are in the process of appointing a middle school coordinator. There continues to be a need for establishing leadership in the state departments of education as well as the teacher training institutions. For additional certification information, refer to: "Middle level teacher preparation and certification" by C. K. McEwin, in J. L. Irvin (Ed.), *Transforming middle level education* (1992), pp. 15–17.

Certification is based on taking courses in liberal arts, a specialized subject field major, and professional education. Liberal arts provides content in arts and sciences and seeks to give the pre-professional teacher a broad cultural background. The specialized subject area preparation usually takes the form of a specialized subject major in a content field and minor. Elementary level teachers are responsible for all subject fields and may specialize in academic content, music, art, physical education, or foreign language. On the middle level, the argument for the development of interdisciplinary units and topics implies a broad-based subject major concentration more along the lines of language arts, social studies, and general science. At the present time, these types of arrangements do not exist in a majority of teacher training institutions, and the middle level certification is usually added on to elementary or secondary majors. The major emphasis in most secondary teacher preparation programs has been placed on the subject matter. Professional studies will find most elementary majors with 30 to 40 semester hours of professional studies and secondary majors will have 15 to 20 hours, with both groups having student teaching (Ornstein and Levine, 1989). On the middle level, there is a need for courses on the young adolescent and for more clinical experiences in middle level schools. Education majors need to become aware of the opportunities and needs that exist on the middle level.

MOTIVES FOR MIDDLE LEVEL TEACHING

There are many motives for choosing a career in teaching. Readers should ask themselves why they made the choice and why they will choose the middle level. Ornstein and Levine (1989) indicated that motives for teaching may include love of children, the challenge to impart knowledge, the desire to teach, and the desire to perform a worthwhile service to society. Because of the personal and social challenges of teaching young adolescents, a careful examination of the decision to enter teaching and the middle level is essential. Individual reasons for choosing teaching will affect the teacher's attitudes and behavior toward young adolescents. If readers are currently teaching on the middle level, an awareness of early adolescents' attitudes and needs already is obvious.

PROFESSIONAL SATISFACTION

Once teachers are employed, are they satisfied with their profession? In 1987, a national poll of elementary and secondary teachers was conducted by Metropolitan Life Insurance Company. Eighty-five percent of the respondents indicated that they were satisfied or somewhat satisfied and only two percent stated that they were very dissatisfied (Harris, Kagay, & Ross, 1987). Rodman (1986) conducted a similar study of 1,144 public-school teachers and 448 private-school teachers. When respondents were asked to respond on a ten-point scale with 1 designated as "extremely satisfied" and 10 designated as "very dissatisfied," 90 percent of public-school teachers and 96 percent of private-school teachers selected ratings from one to five. Seventy-one percent of public-school teachers and 81 percent of private-school teachers rated their satisfaction as 1, 2, or 3 (Rodman, 1986, p. 4).

JOB PROSPECTS

What are the job prospects for future middle grade teachers? An oversupply of teachers was produced in the 1960s and 1970s, resulting in a decline in teacher education enrollments. There is a trend toward a slight increase in teacher enrollments that began about 1985 (Ornstein and Levine, 1989). According to Ornstein and Levine (1989), there may soon be a significant shortage of teachers, due to small numbers of students graduating annually from teacher preparation institutions. The following factors may contribute to a future teacher shortage: better opportunities for women exist than entering teaching; a significant proportion of the current teaching force is approaching retirement; mandated class size reductions; expansion of preschool education; greater emphasis on science and mathematics; and lastly, recent raised standards and requirements for entry into and graduation from teacher-education programs. Other evidence, however, suggests that there may *not* be a shortage of teachers in the 1990s. Attrition rates among teachers appear to be declining, and recent salary increases have encouraged new prospects. Some states have provided alternative certification and changes in retirement laws that may encourage older teachers to stay longer. Despite this uncertainty, there will be shortages in special needs areas, such as handicapped and remedial education, bilingual education, science, mathematics, and foreign languages. In the middle level area, there will continue to be need for specially trained middle level teachers who have broad academic preparation and specialized training in physical, psychosocial, and emotional needs of early adolescents. The current university programs are usually add-ons to an elementary or secondary teaching certificate. There is an urgent need to have a separate certification program for middle level teachers.

SUMMARY

There are three dimensions to teaching: personal, social, and academic. In the personal dimension, middle grade teachers must understand themselves and their attitudes and emotions before they can provide young adolescents with meaningful learning experiences. Middle level teachers should consider personality, level of personal confidence, and a caring attitude toward young adolescents. Communicating empathy for young adolescents and valuing each individual learner are essential aspects of the personal dimension of teaching.

In the academic dimension, middle level teachers are specialists who are capable of selecting content and using a variety of activities suited to learners' interests and abilities. The middle level teacher is enthusiastic about the subject matter he or she is teaching. Students can sense the teacher's enthusiasm toward the subject matter. Teachers who have a positive mental attitude about the content taught will be best able to provide an exciting learning environment. This dimension requires a teacher who has planning, organizational, and management skills and who utilizes direct, explicit, or indirect instruction appropriate to subject, grade level, or learner. Middle level teachers who expect young adolescents to be successful will employ classroom management techniques that ensure learner success. Classroom time is spent on pacing and sequencing lessons, employing active teaching approaches, and utilizing a variety of techniques including whole class, small-group, and individual activities. The teacher employs various levels of cognitive questioning, demonstrates enthusiastic reactions to student responses, monitors seatwork, and provides for student learning style preferences.

The social dimension of teaching includes the interaction between teacher and student, the teacher's acceptance of diverse learners, and recognition that young adolescents are preocccupied with acceptance by peer groups. Another characteristic of young adolescents is the belief that they are having unique personal and emotional experiences which they believe are important to everyone else. Being aware that young adolescents want adults, teachers, and parents to treat them as though they are unique is important in responding to their physical, psychosocial, and emotional needs. In seeking a personal identity, young adolescents want to be independent, but they do not always know what they want to be or who they are. In the social dimension, the middle level teacher needs to provide support and empathy to promote the development of socially mature young adolescents.

▪ ▪ ▪

EXPLORATION

1 Think back to one of your teachers who you can remember as being an effective teacher. What were some of the "job" characteristics that you would use to describe this teacher? The list when completed should give you some insight into effective teaching characteristics. Compare this list with those found under teacher characteristics. Do you think there are differences in job characteristics of a middle level teacher from elementary and secondary teachers?

2 From the discussion on scientists' and artists' roles in teaching, which do you think would tend to guide you? Contrast the differences between the

scientist and the artist in their approach to teaching, and consider which would be more meaningful to the young adolescent. Do not assume that either approach is good or bad.

3 Examine the list of qualities of middle level teachers in Table 5.1, and analyze which of these characteristics you already are aware of and practice. Identify which characteristics you think you might improve on in your teaching. Propose a self-development plan for improving those areas.

4 Synthesize the research on effective teaching by compiling a list of characteristics, styles, and behaviors that you would want to use in the assessment of your teaching. Are there some items that you would rank more important? If so, prioritize your list in order of importance, giving your reasons for the rankings.

SUGGESTED READINGS

Carnegie Corporation, Task Force on Teaching as a Profession. (1986). *A nation prepared: Teachers in the 21st century.* New York: Carnegie Corporation.

A national study of the teaching profession that provides insights to those entering the teaching profession and those already in the teaching profession.

Dunn, R., Beaudry, J. S., & Klavis, A. (1989). Survey of research on learning styles. *Educational Leadership, 46* (6), 50–58.

This article provides the research base and findings for learning style preferences.

Dunn, R., & Dunn, K. (1978). *Teaching students through their individual learning styles.* Reston, VA: Reston Publications.

This book provides the rationale and teaching strategies for the various learning style preferences.

Dunn, R., Dunn, K., & Price, G. E. (1985). *Learning Style Inventory.* Lawrence, KS: Price Systems. (Can be ordered from Price Systems, Box 1818, Lawrence, KS 66044–0067.)

This inventory helps teachers assess learning style preferences and plan instruction that recognizes the individual learning style preferences of their students.

George, P., Stevenson, C., Thomason, J., & Beane, J. (1992) *The middle school—and beyond.* Alexandria,VA: Association for Supervision and Curriculum Development.

This monograph presents current information on the middle level school.

Good, T. L., & Brophy, J. E. (1991). *Looking in classrooms.* New York: HarperCollins.

An excellent general source on teaching effectiveness.

Johnston, J. H., & Markle, G. C. (1986). *What research says to the middle level practitioner.* Columbus, OH: National Middle School Association.

An excellent resource on the research of teaching effectiveness on the middle level.

Joyce, B., & Weil, M. (1988). *Models of teaching.* Englewood Cliffs, NJ: Prentice-Hall.

The definitive work on teaching models.

Porter, A. C., & Brophy, J. E. (1988). Synthesis of research on good teaching: Insights from the work of the Institute for Research and Teaching. *Educational Leadership, 45* (8), 74–85.

This article provides an excellent summary of the research on effective teaching.

REFERENCES

Arnn, J. W., & Mangieri, J. N. (February 1988). Effective leadership for effective schools: A survey of principal attitudes. *National Association of Secondary School Principals Bulletin, 72,* 1–7.

Ashton, P. (1985). Motivation and teacher's sense of efficacy. In C. Ames, & R. Ames, (Eds.), *Research on motivation in education, volume 2: The classroom milieu.* Orlando, FL: Academic Press.

Ausubel, D. P. (1963). *The psychology of meaningful verbal learning.* New York: Grune & Stratton.

Beane, J., & Lipka, R. (1986). *Self-Concept, self-esteem and the curriculum.* New York: Teachers' College Press.

Berliner, D. C. (1985). Laboratory settings and the study of teaching. *Journal of Teacher Education, 36 (6),* 2–8.

Bloom, B. S. (1971). Affective Consequences of School Achievement. In J. H. Block (Ed.) *Mastery learning: Theory and practice.* New York: Holt, Rinehart & Winston.

Bondi, J., & Wiles, J. (1986). *The essential middle school.* Tampa, FL: Wiles, Bondi, and Associates.

Brophy, J. E. (1983). Classroom organization and management. *Elementary School Journal, 83 (4),* 265–286.

Brown, D. S. (1988). Twelve middle school teachers' planning. *Elementary School Journal, 89 (1),* 69–87.

Canter, L., & Canter, M. (1976). *Assertive discipline: A take charge approach for today's educator.* Seal Beach, CA: Canter and Associates.

Carnegie Corporation Task Force on Teaching as a Profession. (1986). *A nation prepared: Teachers in the 21st century.* New York: Carnegie Corporation.

Carnegie Council on Adolescent Development. *Turning points: Preparing American youth for the 21st century (1989).* Washington, D.C.: Author.

Carroll, J. B. (1963). A model of school learning. *Teachers College Record, 64,* 723–733.

Children's Defense Fund. (1988). *Making middle grades work.* Washington, DC.

Combs, A. (1982). *A personal approach to teaching.* Boston: Allyn & Bacon.

Costa, A. (1984). "A reaction to Hunter's knowing teaching, and supervising." In P. Hosford, P. (Ed.). *What we know about teaching.* Alexandria, VA: Association for Supervision and Curriculum Development.

Csikszentmihalyi, M., & McCormack, J. (1986). The influence of teachers. *Phi Delta Kappan, 67 (6),* 415–419.

Doyle, W. (1986). Classroom organization and management. In M. C. Wittrock (Ed.). *Handbook of research on teaching* (3rd ed.). New York: Macmillan.

Dunkin, M. J., & Biddle, B. J. (1974). *The study of teaching.* New York: Holt, Rinehart & Winston.

Dunn, R., Beaudry, J. S., & Klavis, A. (1989). Survey of research on learning styles. *Educational Leadership, 46(6),* 50–58.

Dunn, R., DeBello, T. C., Evans, W. J., Kroon, D. K., & White, R. T. (1988). Ten steps to better middle schools. *Teaching K-8, 18(4),* 39–41.

Dunn, R., & Dunn, K. (1978). *Teaching students through their individual learning styles*. Reston, VA: Reston Publications.

Dunn, R., Dunn, K., & Price, G. E. (1985). *Learning style inventory*. Lawrence, KS: Price Systems.

Edmonds, R. R. (1986). Characteristics of effective schools. In U. Neiser. *The school achievement of minority children*. Hillsdale, NJ: Erlbaum.

Eisner, E. W. (1983). The art and craft of teaching. *Educational Leadership, 40 (4)*, 4–13.

Engleking, J. L. (1986). Teacher job satisfaction and dissatisfaction. *ERS Spectrum, 4 (1)*, 33–38.

Flanders, N. A. (1970). *Analyzing teaching behavior*. Reading, MA: Addison-Wesley.

Gage, N. L. (1984). What do we know about teacher effectiveness? *Phi Delta Kappan, 66 (2)*, 87–93.

Galloway, C. M. (1984). Nonverbal behavior and teacher student relationships. In A. Wolfgang (Ed.), *Nonverbal behavior: Perspectives, applications, intercultural insights*. Toronto: Hogrefe.

George, P., & Stevenson, C. (1989). The 'very best teams' in the 'best schools' as described by middle school principals. *TEAM 3:* 6–14.

George, P., Stevenson, C., Thomason, J., & Beane, J. (1992) *The middle school—and beyond*. Alexandria,VA: Association for Supervision and Curriculum Development.

Gibney, T., & Wiersma, W. (1986). Using profile analysis for student teacher evaluation. *Journal of Teacher Education, 37(3)*, 43.

Glasser, W. (1965). *Reality Therapy*. New York: Harper & Row.

Good, T. L., & Brophy, J. E. (1991). *Looking in classrooms*. New York: HarperCollins.

Goodlad, J. (1984). *A place called school: Prospects for the future*. New York: McGraw-Hill.

Gordon, T. (1974). *Teacher effectiveness training*. New York: Peter H. Wyden

Gordon, W. J. J. (1961). *Synectics*. New York: Harper & Row.

Harris, B. M. (1986). *Developmental teacher evaluation*. Boston: Allyn & Bacon.

Harris, L., Kagay, M., & Ross, J. (1987). *The American teacher, 1987*. New York: Metropolitan Life.

Holmes Group. (1986). *Tommorrow's teachers*. East Lansing, MI: The Holmes Group.

Holmes Group. (1990). *Tommorow's schools*. East Lansing, MI: The Holmes Group.

Hosford, P. (Ed.). (1984). *What we know about teaching*. Alexandria, VA: Association for Supervision and Curriculum Development.

Hunter, M. (1982). *Mastery teaching*. El Segundo, CA: TIP Publications.

Hunter, M. (1984). Knowing, teaching and supervising. In P. Hosford (Ed.), *What we know about teaching*. Alexandria, VA: Association for Supervision and Curriculum Development.

Hunter, M., & Russell, D. (1989). *Mastering coaching and supervision*. El Segundo, CA: TIP Publications.

Johnson, D. W., Johnson, R. T & Holubec, E. J. (1988). *Advanced cooperative learning*. Edina, MN: Interaction Book Co.

Johnson, D. W., Johnson, R. T & Holubec, E. J. (1990). *Cooperation in the classroom*. Edina, MN: Interaction Book Co.

Johnston, J. H., & Markle, G. C. (1986). *What research says to the middle level practitioner*. Columbus, OH: National Middle School Association.

Joyce, B., & Weil, M. (1988). *Models of teaching*. Englewood Cliffs, NJ: Prentice-Hall.

Lippitt, R., & White, R. K. (1943). The social climate of childrens' groups. In R. G. Barker, J. S. Kounin, & H. F. Wright (Eds.), *Child behavior and development*. New York: McGraw-Hill.

Lipsitz, J. (1984). *Successful schools for young adolescents*. East Brunswick, NJ: Transaction.

McEwin, C. K. (1992). Middle level teacher preparation and certification. In J. L. Irvin (Ed.), *Transforming middle level education.* Boston: Allyn & Bacon.
McNeil, J. D., & Wiles, J. (1990). *The essentials of teaching.* New York: Macmillan.
Maslow, A. H. (1970). *Motivation and personality.* New York: Harper & Row.
Medley, D. M. (1979). The effectiveness of teachers. In P. L. Peterson & H. J. Walberg (Eds.), *Research on teaching: Concepts, findings and implications.* Berkeley, CA: McCutchan.
Medley, D. M., Coker, H., & Soar, R. S. (1984). *Management-based evaluation of teacher performance.* New York: Longman.
Mitchell , D. E., Oritz, F. I., & Mitchell, T. K. (1987). *Work orientations and job performance: The cultural basis of teaching rewards and incentives.* Albany: State University of New York Press.
Muth, K. D., & Alvermann, D. E. (1992). *Teaching and learning in the middle grades.* Boston: Allyn & Bacon.
Myers, C. B., & Myers, L. K. (1990). *An introduction to teaching and schools.* Fort Worth, TX: Holt, Rinehart and Winston.
National Commission on Excellence in Education. (1983). *A nation at risk: The imperative for educational reform.* Washington, DC: U.S. Department of Education.
Northwest Educational Regional Laboratory. (1988). *Onward to excellence project.* Portland, OR: Northwest Educational Regional Laboratory.
Orlich, D. C., Harder, R. J., Callahan, R. C., Kauchak, D. P., Pendergrass, R. A., Keogh, A. J., & Gibson, H. (1990). *Teaching strategies: A guide to better instruction.* Lexington, MA: Heath.
Ornstein, A. C. (February, 1989). Emerging curriculum trends: An agenda for the future. *National Association of Secondary School Principals Bulletin, 73,* 37–48.
Ornstein, A. C. (1990). *Strategies for effective teaching.* New York: Harper & Row.
Ornstein, A. C. (1986). Research on teaching: Trends and policies. *High School Journal, 68 (2),* 160–170.
Ornstein, A. C., & Levine, D. U. (1989). *Foundations of education.* Boston: Houghton Mifflin.
Ornstein, A. C., & Miller, H. L. (1980). *Looking into teaching.* Chicago: Rand McNally.
Peterson, P. L. (1979). Direct instruction reconsidered. In P. L. Peterson & H. J. Walberg (Eds.), *Research on teaching: Concepts, findings and implications.* Berkeley, CA: McCutchan.
Piaget, J. (1952). *The origins of intelligence in children.* New York: International University Press.
Porter, A. C., & Brophy, J. E. (1988). Synthesis of research on good teaching: Insights from the work of the Institute for Research and Teaching. *Educational Leadership, 45 (8),* 74–85.
Purkey, W. W., & Novak, J. M. (1984). *Inviting school success.* Belmont, CA: Wadsworth.
Riessman, F. (1967). Teachers of the poor: A five-point plan. *Journal of Teacher Education, 18 (4),* 326–336.
Rimm, D. C., & Masters, J. C. (1974). *Behavior therapy: Techniques and empirical findings.* New York: Academic Press.
Rodman, B. (May 7, 1986). Teacher's job satisfaction seen greater than that of other college graduates. *Education Week, 4.*
Rogers, C. K. (1983). *Freedom to learn in the 80's.* New York: Merrill/Macmillan.
Rosenshine, B. V., & Furst, N. F. (1973). The use of direct observation to study teaching. In R. M. Travers (Ed.), *Second handbook of research on teaching.* Chicago: Rand McNally.
Rosenshine, B. V. (1979). Content, time and direct instruction. In P. L. Peterson & H. J.

Walberg (Eds.), *Research on teaching: Concepts, findings and implications*. Berkeley, CA: McCutchan.

Rosenshine, B. V. (1986). Synthesis of research on explicit teaching. *Educational Leadership, 43 (7)*, 61–69.

Rubin, L. (1985). *Artistry in teaching*. New York: Random House.

Ryans, D. G. (1960). *Characteristics of teachers*. Washington, DC: American Council on Education.

Salt Lake Teachers Association. (1988). *A continuing contract . . . between the Board of Education of Salt Lake City . . .and Salt Lake Teachers Association, 1988–1989*. Salt Lake City, UT: Salt Lake Teachers Association.

Schutz, W. (1958). *FIRO: A three-dimensional theory of interpersonal behavior*. New York: Holt, Rinehart and Winston.

Schutz, W. (1967). *Joy: Expanding human awareness*. New York: Grove Press.

Schwab, J. (1965). *Biological Sciences Curriculum Study, Biology teachers' handbook*. New York: John Wiley.

Siegman, A. W., & Feldstein, S. (Eds.), (1978). *Nonverbal behavior and communication*. Hillsdale, NJ: Erlbaum.

Sigel, I. E. (1969). *The Piagetian system and the world of education*. In D. Elkind & J. Flavell (Eds.), *Studies in cognitive development*. New York: Oxford University Press.

Slavin, R. E. (1987). *Cooperative learning* (2nd ed.). Washington, DC: National Education Association.

Slavin, R. E. (1988). *Educational psychology: Theory into practice*, 2nd ed. Englewood Cliffs, NJ: Prentice-Hall.

Stephens, P., & Valentine, J. (1986). Assessing principal nonverbal communication. *Educational Research Quarterly, 10 (3)*, 60–68.

Stevenson, C. (1986). *Teachers as inquirers: Strategies for learning with and about early adolescents*. Columbus, OH: National Middle School Association.

Suchman, R. (1962). *The elementary school training program in scientific inquiry*. Report to U.S. Office of Education, Project Title VII, Project 216. Urbana, IL: University of Illinois.

Taba, H. (1966). *Teaching strategies and cognitive functioning in elementary school children*. Cooperative Research Project 2404. San Francisco: San Francisco State College.

Thelen, H. A. (1970). *Dynamics of groups at work*. Chicago: University of Chicago Press.

Tuckman, B. W. (1985). *Evaluating instructional programs* (2nd ed.). Boston: Allyn & Bacon.

Turning points: Preparing American youth for the 21st century. (1989). Washington, DC: Carnegie Council on Adolescent Development.

Wise, A. E., Darling-Hammond, L., Bernstein, H. T., & McLaughlin, M. W. (1985). Teacher evaluation: A study of effective practices. *Elementary School Journal, 86 (1)*, 61–121.

Wise, A. E., Darling-Hammond, L., Bernstein, H. T., & McLaughlin, M. W. (1987). Teacher evaluation: A study of effective practices. In A. E. Wise, L. Darling-Hammond, & B. Berry (Eds.), *Effective teacher selection : From recruitment to retention*. Santa Monica, CA: Rand Corporation.

Wolpe, J. (1969). *The practice of behavior therapy*. Oxford: Pergamon Press.

Wolpe, J., & Lazarus, A. A. (1966). *Behavior therapy techniques: A guide to the treatment of neuroses*. Oxford: Pergamon Press.

Woolfolk, A. E., & McCune-Nicolich, L. (1984). *Educational psychology for teachers*. Englewood Cliffs, NJ: Prentice-Hall.

Woolfolk, A. E., & McCune-Nicolich, L. (1988). *Educational Psychology for Teachers*. Englewood Cliffs, NJ: Prentice-Hall.

CHAPTER OUTLINE

An Integrated Approach to Middle Level Curriculum

6

OVERVIEW

Historically, there has been a need to develop an integrated curriculum that would consider the unique personal needs of middle level learners as well as the serious challenges found in their surrounding world. Beane (1990) stated that "the curriculum question has been an 'absent presence' in the middle school movement" (p. 1). Efforts to meet the personal and social needs of young adolescents through interdisciplinary teams and other organizational features found in the middle level school—such as flexible scheduling, exploratory activities, and advisor-advisee—have made significant progress. However, while providing an integrated curriculum has been the idealized goal, it has not really been the central focus in the evolving middle level concept. Typically, academic subject matter has been the major emphasis of the middle level curriculum rather than a balanced approach integrating the personal, social, and academic dimensions. An integrated middle level curriculum requires the conceptualization of a new direction that focuses on relevant academic content embedded in the personal needs of young adolescents both as individuals and members of society.

In the middle level school, the lack of an integrated middle level scope and sequence has made it difficult to formulate interdisciplinary teams and teaching units. (As we shall discuss in later chapters, *scope and sequence* is technical terminology for the curriculum content and the way it is placed and ordered.) Beane (1991) suggested three essential concepts for an integrated middle level curriculum. First, it should be general, and focused on "widely shared concerns of early adolescents and the larger world" rather than increasingly academic and specialized (Beane, 1991, p. 10). Second, it should be based on the unique needs of middle level learners who attend the school. Lastly, it must consider young adolescents "as real human beings" who are also participants in the societal challenges facing the world (Beane, 1991, p. 10). In this chapter, we will examine in depth how the middle level curriculum can integrate personal, social, and academic dimensions into a developmentally appropriate curriculum for young adolescents.

In this chapter, you will read about:

1. Definitions of curriculum, middle level curriculum, and instruction.
2. Curriculum frameworks for planning an integrated middle level curriculum.
3. Subject-centered and learner-centered curricula.
4. Middle school curriculum theory and development.
5. Ecological orientation for planning an integrated middle level curriculum.
6. Guidelines for planning an integrated middle level curriculum.

MIDDLE LEVEL CURRICULUM AND INSTRUCTION

Various theories of curriculum development on the middle level exist, and a wide gap still exists between theory and practice. The personal concerns of middle level learners and their participation in questions beyond the school setting calls for increased involvement by young adolescents in curriculum planning for meaningful integration to occur.

There is considerable debate on a definition for the word *curriculum* that would best suit the needs of middle level learners. Definitions found in educational literature include: (1) a plan (scope, instructional sequence, and course of study), (2) organized knowledge (academic and specialized), (3) objectives (behavioral and instructional), (4) experiences (personal and social), (5) systems/technological/competency component (a systematic framework for planning, programming, and evaluation), and (6) the total planned learning opportunities (academic, personal, and social).

There have been significant attempts to develop comprehensive curriculum theories. McNeil (1990) proposed four types of curriculum: (1) academic, (2) social functions, (3) humanistic, and (4) technological/competencies. Saylor, Alexander, and Lewis (1981) proposed a five-classification system: (1) subject matter/disciplines, (2) specific competencies, (3) human traits/processes, (4) social functions/activities, and (5) individual needs and interests/activities. Though various classification systems have broadened the curriculum framework, there is an emerging consensus that the middle level curriculum must be made more relevant by connecting the personal needs of young adolescents, their need to participate in societal questions facing the world, and their needs to master academic content into an integrated holistic curriculum.

MIDDLE LEVEL CURRICULUM

For purposes of this book, the term *middle level curriculum* is defined as "the integration of planned or intended learning experiences, formulated and organized in a given school setting specifically (1) around knowledge, (2) around the commonly shared concerns of young adolescents for their personal development, and (3) around the serious global social issues experienced by them and the world."

Because of the difficulty involved in planning systematically for the impact of all experiences on the learner, any definition of curriculum must recognize the necessity of continuously analyzing all the varied learning experiences that occur in a given school setting, including those unplanned events encountered in classrooms, in the cafeteria, and in hallways. While the faculty and administration of a given middle level school can only be held accountable for planned learning experiences in the curriculum, they may find that the unplanned learning experiences can be quite significant in the development of young adolescents.

Two other terms associated with planning an integrated curriculum are interdisciplinary and multidisciplinary curriculum. *Multidisciplinary* curriculum implies the identification of disciplines in each instructional activity so that each teacher can observe where their content is applied. As themes are identified for an integrated curriculum, each subject area is clearly identified. In the development of a theme, each content area not represented can be added easily to the integrated curriculum design. As the theme is expanded, each teacher can see a place for their content and can plan instructional activities using their content area. As the theme develops and teachers become more familiar with integrated topics, content labels may no longer be significant to the development of an integrated curriculum.

Interdisciplinary curriculum implies going from identifying the content of separate subjects into themes without establishing distinctions across subject areas. Some of the terms used previously to describe a subject-centered interdisciplinary curriculum are core curriculum, correlated curriculum, fused curriculum, and broad fields curriculum. Because of confusion over the exact meaning of these terms and the heavy emphasis on subject matter in the past, it has been difficult to implement interdisciplinary curriculum designs. At first, it may be necessary to break items and instructional activities into multidisciplinary subject matter for teachers to understand their role in planning the theme. It becomes more difficult to break subject matter down from each discipline into activities as the interdisciplinary curriculum theme evolves. But this phase may be a logical step toward having a starting point for developing an integrated unit. As the team becomes more sophisticated in its planning, subject matter area labels can be dropped. Until then, these divisions may continue to hinder the instructional activities from being developed. This evolutionary process is a logical progression that teams go through in the collaboration of an integrated interdisciplinary curriculum design.

INSTRUCTION

Another curriculum design issue is whether instructional planning should be included in a definition of the middle level curriculum. The means—the instructional strategies to be used to accomplish the ends, the curriculum objectives, often have been separated in many curriculum approaches, especially on the middle school level. While curriculum and instruction may need to be analyzed separately, they are so interrelated that it is virtually impossible to implement an integrated middle level curriculum when they are separated from each other. Curriculum and instruction should be interrelated to serve the educational needs of young adolescents.

Once the middle level curriculum design has been decided, the instructional activities need to be planned in order to implement an integrated middle level curriculum. If the instructional activities have provided young adolescents with meaningful learning experiences based on their personal concerns and societal concerns, they will have a more positive attitude about their classroom learning environment. In turn, learning will be attained, retained, and transferred to new learning situations. In the middle level school, the instruction should result in permanent learning through the acquisition of knowledge, skills, and attitudes.

In summary, there has been widespread debate on the what and how of an integrated curriculum and the relationship of instruction to curriculum. In planning the middle level program, curriculum and instruction must be interrelated to provide meaningful and relevant learning for young adolescents. In the next section, we will discuss the middle level curriculum framework, suggesting that curriculum planners consider the continuum in the selection of a developmentally appropriate curriculum for young adolescents. While a balance is needed between cognitive and affective development, it is important to keep the learner's personal and social concerns as the central focus and provide help to teachers in developing appropriate learner outcomes.

MIDDLE LEVEL CURRICULUM FRAMEWORKS

Two constructs have been used to organize middle level curriculum and instruction. The first construct organizes the curriculum around elements such as academic content, human traits and processes, social functions and activities, system/technology, and competency (McNeil, 1990). The second construct organizes the curriculum on a continuum from subject-centered approaches to learner-centered approaches (Myers & Myers, 1990). In the junior high, the focus was on coordinating learner-centered curriculum and subject-centered curriculum. Because of the junior high school's close ties with the high school, subject matter tended to dominate the curriculum. These subject matter constructs have restricted the planning of an integrated curriculum for both the junior high and middle level school. The middle level has been caught up in the demand for a strong subject matter focus from a society which is concerned about improving test scores and academic performance. The middle level must organize curriculum and instruction around both the subject-centered and learner-centered approaches, while planning for the learners' personal concerns and the larger societal issues confronting all people.

LEARNER-CENTERED CURRICULUM

The learner-centered curriculum is focused on needs, interests, and activities of learners. In Table 6.1, the learner-centered approach includes (1) core, (2) social functions, (3) experience/activity centered, and (4) humanistic. This approach stresses individuality, creativity, and the development of student learning through teacher–learner interaction.

Content selection in the *core curriculum* is determined by the needs and problems of young adolescents. Basic concepts of core programs can be organized into a number of different patterns (Vars, 1987; Lounsbury & Vars, 1978; Vars, 1969; and Van Til, Vars, & Lounsbury, 1967). From the beginnings of the junior high school at the turn of this century, various correlated courses have been referred to as block-of-time programs. Van Til, Vars and Lounsbury (1967) defined a *block-of-time* program as one where "a teacher or team meets for a block of time of two or more class periods, and that combines or replaces two or more subject areas which are required of all students and ordinarily taught separately" (p. 181). The core concept is broader than just general education and can include a problem-centered curriculum utilizing variable groups, interdisciplinary content, and individual and group guidance. Units could be developed around the broad interdisciplinary topics such as energy, pollution, careers, family, school, government, and international relations.

The most common block-of-time approach usually correlates two or more subject areas, such as language arts–social studies or science–mathematics. In this approach, a common block of time is devoted to the two subjects; each subject area retains its separate identity but provisions are made to connect them by focusing on common topics. For example, a block-of-time approach to science-social studies might explore energy, population, technology, and similar issues. In another example, language arts, social studies, art, music, dance, and home economics could be integrated into a unit on "The Roaring Twenties."

Another approach, the *multidisciplinary unit*, moves beyond the correlation of subject areas to a more comprehensive fusing of several subjects directed toward the study of a central theme. Multidisciplinary core draws from the knowledge and skills of several subject disciplines with an emphasis on resolving a thematic problem, rather than mastery of specific subject matter.

TABLE 6.1 Learner-Centered Curriculum and Instructional Framework for the Middle Level

LEARNER-CENTERED CURRICULUM	
Learning emphasizes experiences based on the felt needs, interests, and activities of the learner. The concern is with the individual student's personal development. The teacher's main responsibility is to stimulate and facilitate student activity and to focus on student individuality and creativity.	
Curriculum	Instruction
Core Curriculum: Combines subjects into broad fields but organizes the curriculum around student needs, problems and interests.	*Methods:* Utilize individual and group activities such as research writing, cooperative learning, themes and questions. Resources are cooperative planning, field trips, guest speakers, exploratory activities, etc.
Social Functions: Focuses on problems of living, individual and societal, that students will encounter in communities, requiring social action.	*Methods:* Themes and concerns for social action are identified by students in the classroom and community. Teacher acts as facilitator and cooperatively plans with students. Resources include field trips, guest speakers, community service projects, community service groups and agencies.
Open/Experience/Activity-Centered: Emphasizes continuous progress, student self-concept, personal growth, feelings, expressions, and experiences evolving from student selection and active involvement in classroom methods. Teachers facilitate instruction and establish expectations from the student selection and interaction which permit all students to succeed.	*Methods:* Focus on exploration, questioning, individual student selection of activities and personal experiences, cooperative planning and small groups, student problem solving. Resources include open and flexible spaces, student interest centers, books, field trips, video and audio tapes.
Humanistic: Fosters self-determination, independence, self-actualization, and integrity. The classroom atmosphere is based on trust, mutual respect, and cooperation. The student is the basis of the curriculum.	*Methods:* Self-exploration, cooperative learning, small-group work, dyads, and self-directed learning. Resources include books, tapes, student interest centers, video and audio tapes.

Adapted excerpts from *An Introduction to Teaching and Schools* by C. B. Myers and L. K. Myers, copyright © 1990 by Holt, Rinehart and Winston, Inc. Reprinted by permission of the publisher.

The third type of core, the *interdisciplinary unit,* utilizes predetermined problems based on the personal and social needs of adolescents, social realities, and democratic values. Students are free to select the problems that they wish to work on, and subject matter is brought in as needed to develop or help solve the problems. A problem is identified, and subject matter content is used only if it can help solve the problem. The full range of disciplines in the school's curriculum can be utilized to study broad topics such as AIDS. This core approach affords middle level learners the opportunity to express personal opinions and gain new perspectives about themselves as they study the problems under consideration. This approach usually does not attempt to replace the discipline field approach but rather tends to be complementary. Teachers and learners can plan their interdisciplinary units around problems and issues that arise from the ongoing curriculum. The units tend to be stimulating and exciting for teachers and middle level learners.

In an integrated core curriculum, the theme or problem is selected by students and teachers, and emerges from the middle level learner's experiences. This approach focuses the curriculum on young adolescents' questions and interests rather than on content determined by school or state mandates. Time is structured according to the needs of students first, and elements of the curriculum are planned around learners, rather than institutional demands. Motivation is high because the areas of study are linked to learners' lives. This approach requires tremendous effort and planning by teachers and students because the format is not based on existing curricula. Subject areas are used only if they can help solve the problem. Since there was no predetermination of problems to be studied, the teacher and students are free to select the problems they wish to pursue.

Each of the previous types of core can be seen as a continuum going from correlated curriculum to an integrated curriculum. At the middle level, some type of core has been proposed and recommended as part of the middle level curriculum. Most of the curriculum revision currently taking place on the middle level is focused on implementing some type of multidisciplinary or interdisciplinary unit.

Humanistic curriculum design is focused on the humanistic and individual traits of learners. While largely a curriculum movement of the 1970s, the emphasis on freedom, dignity, individual worth, and self-concept has continued to be important to the middle level movement. This curriculum focuses on self as a legitimate objective of learning. Some of the more critical learning traits are creativity, initiative, self-confidence, making decisions, and planning. The relevance of subject matter is centered on the young adolescent's basic life needs. Maslow (1970) and Rogers (1983) recommended this approach for the development of the total human being. Both psychologists suggested experiences to develop independence, self-determination, and self-actualization. In addition, Combs (1982) suggested that self-concept was one of the most important determiners of behavior. A healthy self-concept motivated the learner to achieve. This humanistic curriculum is designed around the development of human traits as a lifelong endeavor, and should be relevant for the transfer of these experiences over into real-life experiences. Rogers (1983) summarized the research results of humanistic curriculum as increased interests, productivity, creativity, and self-confidence among youth, with more adolescents attending school for longer periods of time.

Today, the term *confluent curriculum* is used to suggest an integration of the affective domain (emotions, attitudes, and values) with the cognitive domain (skills, knowledge, and abilities) (McNeil, 1990). Confluent curriculum stresses the integration of objective knowledge with the student's personal, imaginative, and emotional responses. Shapiro (1987) characterized the confluent curriculum as having (1) participation (consent, power sharing, negotiation, and joint responsibility); (2) integration (interaction and integration of thinking, feelings, and actions); (3) relevance (emotional and intellectual meaning for individuals); (4) self (the major objective of learning); and (5) goals (the development of a whole person). The themes presented by the confluent curriculum are important concerns in planning an integrated curriculum for young adolescents.

Eichhorn (1966, 1987) advocated implementation of the confluent curriculum in developmentally appropriate middle level schools. His curriculum, when implemented in Upper St. Clair, PA, was organized around the intellectual capabilities, personal interests, and social concerns of middle level learners. The curricula of Lounsbury and Vars (1978), Alexander and George (1981), and Beane (1990) represent more current examples of this type of curriculum. This curricular approach encompasses some of the essential elements of the developmentally appropriate curriculum proposed for the middle level by recent reform reports such as the Carnegie Corporation report, *Turning Points,* and the California State Department plan, *Caught in the Middle.*

Open/Experience/Activity-centered curricula usually are based on unstructured, often spontaneous student needs and interests rather than on planning a structured curriculum. There is less direct teacher planning because student interests cannot be anticipated in advance or planned for all learners. These activities emulating from relevant student needs and interests are essential in planning interdisciplinary units. Schools are arranged around the activities that students complete in classrooms and usually involve cooperative teacher–student planning. Activities and learning experiences are planned around student concerns and interests. Activity-oriented programs have suffered from lack of teacher expertise, the inflexible nature of school space and schedules, and the low utilization of multiple supplementary materials and community resources. The philosophy contained in this approach is being utilized currently for at-risk learners in order to make the curriculum more relevant to them. (Myers & Myers, 1990).

Social functions curriculum is focused on social living or persistent life situations that are organized around aspects of community life, social action, or global concerns. Whichever social basis is selected, the focus is on the life situations, concerns, and activities of young adolescents that directly contribute to their growing understanding of society and that deal with problems faced now or in the future (McNeil, 1990). This curriculum also is focused on activities that would carry over into real-life situations and is concerned with processes that promote future preparation for events that will shape the future of learners. Topics might include productive work experiences, health and physical wellbeing, successful family life, and wise use of leisure time. The focus is on helping the learner to analyze social, political, and economic problems found in society as well as their own individual needs and interests. The learner is the focus of the curriculum, with cooperative planning of instruction by teachers and learners and opportunities for young adolescents to direct their own learning. Middle level proponents were Eichhorn (1966), Lounsbury and Vars (1978), Alexander and George (1981), and Beane (1990). Recently, *Turning Points* (1989) has recommended that service credits be given for social service activities participated in by young adolescent learners.

In summary, each of the learner-centered approaches is essential to moving beyond traditional curricula to an integrated curriculum. The focus on learners' personal experiences and societal challenges is what makes the middle level curriculum design unique.

SUBJECT-CENTERED CURRICULUM

On the other end of the continuum, subject-centered curriculum frameworks have been around for many years and have generally dominated curriculum development on the middle level. In this approach, learning is focused on cognitive development and the acquisition of knowledge. The subject-centered framework assumes that certain subject matter should be taught to young adolescents. The teacher is expected to direct the student's learning in subject matter. In Table 6.2, three approaches to subject-centered curriculum are outlined as: (1) discipline-based, (2) broad field, and (3) structure of knowledge/spiral.

The *discipline-based* approach is focused on acquiring information and values found in the various disciplines and the development of knowledge gained from studying the separate disciplines. Each subject is taught apart from other content areas. This curriculum proposes that students can organize and classify the complex and conflicting viewpoints better in separate courses. Each discipline provides a structure for organizing the curriculum. All curriculum experiences and activities should come from disciplines rather than from the needs, concerns, and problems of learners. Thus, the curriculum, if left to this narrow interpretation of the disciplines, might not address the broader questions of personal and social needs of young adolescents.

The junior high school movement, pressure for accountability, and the recent back-to-basics movement strengthened a discipline-based curriculum on the middle level. Recent reform proposals in the 1980s also recommended discipline-based subjects as the best format for content mastery. This construct is still a dominant focus of the middle level curriculum.

The *broad fields* approach permits the blending of two or more related subjects into a single broad or unified field of study. Patterns can be structured around several subjects such as language arts, social studies, and general science. Themes and topics can be selected for units of study, such as "The Twenties", "The Great Depression", or "Pollution". This approach tends to reduce the subject boundaries and permits middle level teachers to have more flexibility in choosing content. Furthermore, the broad fields approach was supposed to reduce the fragmentation and compartmentalization found in discipline-based

TABLE 6.2 Subject-Centered Curriculum and Instructional Framework for the Middle Level

SUBJECT-CENTERED CURRICULUM	
Learning is focused on cognitive development and acquisition of knowledge for young adolescents. The teacher's main responsibility is to direct instruction in the subject.	
Curriculum	Instruction
Discipline-based: Stresses the acquisition of information, ideas, basic logic, key relationships and principles contained in various disciplines and the use of methods gained from studying those subjects.	*Methods:* Utilize expository: lecture, discussion, recitation, question and answer. Resources include teacher presentations, textbooks, video presentations.
Broad fields: Organizes content into broader content areas where subject matter is integrated and/or combined, such as English and social studies. It can be based on themes, concepts, and generalizations or problems.	*Methods:* Utilize lecture, discussion, question and answer, recitation, team teaching, inquiry, etc. Resources include team member presentations, interdisciplinary content formats, handouts, exploratory activities, etc.
Structure of Knowledge: Organizes content around concepts and generalizations of subjects and is designed for student's cognitive developmental stages and transfer of learning to new problem situations.	*Methods:* Focuses on main ideas and methods of inquiry used in the disciplines. Resources include textbooks, films, and video presentations.
Systems/Technological/Competency: Focuses on processes necessary for developing, designing, organizing, implementing, and evaluating a curriculum on a systemwide basis. It includes personnel, schedules, resources, and space.	*Methods:* Employ systems theory such as Management by Objectives (MBO) and Planning-Programming Budgeting and Evaluation System (PPBES), critical path analysis-Program Evaluation Review Technique (PERT), and competency-based formats to gather information on curriculum. Resources would include computers, system analysis, and competency-based formats.

Adapted excerpts from *An Introduction to Teaching and Schools* by C. B. Myers and L. K. Myers, copyright © 1990 by Holt, Rinehart and Winston, Inc. Reprinted by permission of the publisher.

approaches. However, the approach involves an understanding of the subject matter and the relationship among different disciplines that may go beyond the level of preparation of many middle level teachers.

The *structure of knowledge* approach focuses on concepts and generalizations to be taught and learned from subject matter and is centered on sequencing conceptual structures with the cognitive developmental stages of learners. Young adolescents are to learn main ideas and develop ways of thinking. The content begins with simple concepts and spirals to more abstract concepts as young adolescents expand their cognitive development to think on more abstract levels. This curriculum was first suggested by Bruner (1960) and Taba (1962). This approach, also, demands an in-depth understanding of the content taught and the relationship among the various subject matter disciplines that may challenge the prior academic preparation of many middle level teachers.

In summary, subject-centered approaches have continued to dominate the middle level curriculum. While subject matter cannot be ignored, a developmentally appropriate curriculum must look at all aspects of curriculum for young adolescents, including their personal and social development as well as their intellectual development.

SYSTEMS/TECHNOLOGICAL/COMPETENCY CURRICULUM

The systems/technological/competency curriculum does not fit into either the subject-centered or the learner-centered categories. For that reason, it is given a place of its own in Table 6.2. Although this approach has been popular during some decades of the twentieth century, today, it is popular mainly among industry and business leaders as a means to assess the productivity of schools. This approach should be considered neutral in that no value is placed on learner-centered or student-centered approaches except for the utilization of the existing curriculum and instructional goals and objectives to analyze the curriculum's effectiveness. Thus, a systems approach could analyze the productivity of a subject-centered curriculum approach or a learning-centered approach in the middle level. With the increasing costs of public education, this approach continues to exert influence on the middle level curriculum.

In summary, while the middle level movement has made tremendous progress in organizational features—such as interdisciplinary team organization, block/flexible scheduling, and advisory groups, the curriculum has not always been clearly defined as developmentally appropriate and responsive to the personal and social needs of young adolescents. The middle level curriculum in practice has been a more subject-centered curriculum than a learner-centered curriculum. The climate and organizational features probably have been easier to accomplish with a subject-centered curriculum (Lipsitz, 1984). While there have been additions made to existing programs to address the concerns of new curriculum expectations, there has been a noted absence of change in the curriculum design. Changes have been made in organizational structure, but the subject-matter curriculum still in place has little focus on the developmental needs of young adolescents. According to Beane (1990) "the movement has succeeded partly because it has not taken on substantive change that would touch deep subject matter loyalties" (p. 6). Middle level curriculum reform has been compounded by the external pressure from curriculum mandates, expectations of society and parents, the structures of tradition, and the interests of content specialists. In fact, the present state of the middle level curriculum is characterized by Beane (1990) as:

> A collection of specific programs intended to meet all expectations, interdisciplinary teams to create subject area correlations but still based on subject identities, "exploratory" courses to cover technical and aesthetic concerns, advisory programs to address personal-social development, activities programs to serve individual interests. . . . (p. 12)

While such a curriculum helps to maintain a balance among the various interests, the plan is a collection of diverse curriculum pieces without any clearly identified purpose or theme. Without a unifying theme or purpose, the middle level curriculum defies cogent definition.

THE EVOLUTION OF AN INTEGRATED MIDDLE LEVEL CURRICULUM

What should the curriculum of the middle school contain? The challenge is (1) to overcome the pressures exerted by competing and conflicting interests, (2) to conceptualize middle level curriculum that will satisfy the educational community, the society and parents, and (3) to provide for the developmentally appropriate needs of young adolescents.

Several approaches have been proposed for integrating the middle level curriculum. The leading theories are those of Eichhorn, Alexander and George, Wiles and Bondi, Lounsbury and Vars, the California Model, and Beane.

THE EICHHORN MODEL

One of the most comprehensive middle level school models was proposed by Donald Eichhorn. He based his model on the forces involved in young adolescents' lives: internal body changes and external forces generated by the environment. These two dimensions form an interrelated socio-psychological model that may be used as a foundation when planning an educational curriculum for young adolescents. Eichhorn (1966) proposed two curricula: the *analytical* and the *physical-cultural* (see Figure 6.1).

Analytical curriculum includes the four content divisions of language, mathematics, social studies, and science. The analytical curriculum would engage learners in the "universality of mental thought processes," particularly in terms of Piagetian types of reversibility and associativity (p. 72). These may be considered as separate or integrated subjects. The common elements creating curricular interrelations are analytical thought processes inherent in each of the four content areas. The large body of knowledge from the various disciplines should be used as a vehicle through which thought processes could be used to stimulate mental growth. Eichhorn based his curriculum in part on Piaget's stages of cognitive development. Since the range of cognitive development

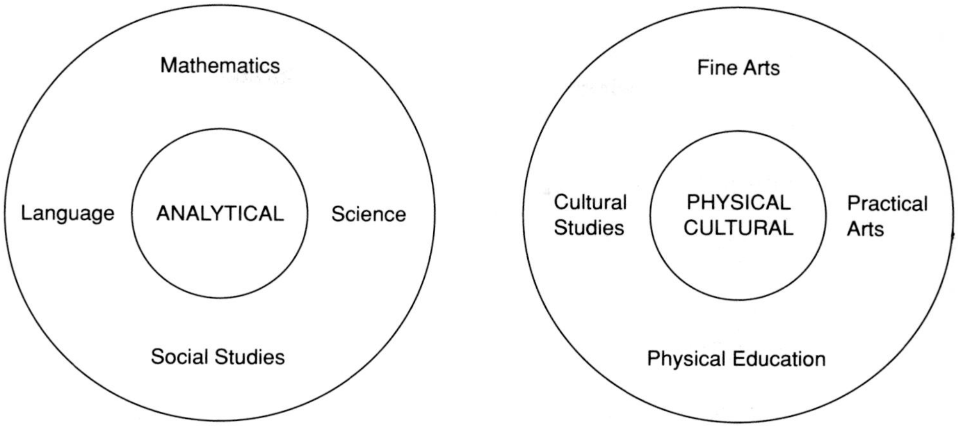

FIGURE 6.1 *Adapted from the 1987 reprint of* The Middle School *by D. H. Eichhorn, 1966, p. 65, copublished by National Middle School Association, Colombus, OH, and National Association of Secondary School Principals, Reston, VA. Adapted with permission.*

spans from pre-operations to formal operations in middle level learners, it is important to provide a broad curriculum that will recognize this vast range of cognitive differences. Because most young adolescents will be on concrete or early formative operational levels, the curriculum should structure instructional content around these two levels. The element of experience assumes a vital role in the analytical curricular sequence. These experiences are bridges to develop the transfer of knowledge from past experiences to current and future situations. Finally, young adolescents would be involved daily in instructional planning to ensure personal responsibility. Thus, Eichhorn's middle level school curriculum is organized as a socio-psychological context, with the learner as the focus of any curricular decisions.

The *physical-cultural* curriculum emphasizes aesthetic, social, practical, and physical areas, preferably in some integrated form. The four content areas Eichhorn suggests are fine arts, physical education, practical arts, and cultural studies. With these divisions, there is greater interrelatedness because each curricular structure is based on the socio-psychological model.

There would appear to be overlapping between cultural studies and social studies. The emphasis in the social studies is on thought processes, whereas in the cultural studies the emphasis is on learners gaining insight into their lives and the activities of people within a region. Within the physical-cultural grouping, curricular objectives would reflect this interrelatedness. The physical-cultural curriculum was devised to provide a more comprehensive base whereby young adolescents could gain peer approval. The curriculum features the development of independence and self-discovery as the transition is made between home-centered security to security based on peer acceptance. Middle level learners should be able to plan, research or practice, and discover in an independent and responsible manner. The curriculum attempts to provide for personal growth experiences as an important goal. Finally, the need for physical activity is seen as critical in the lives of middle level learners. Thus, the curriculum stresses physical development, individual interests, socialization, self-discovery, self-acceptance, cultural appreciation, independence, a wide range of experiences, and physical activity (Eichhorn, 1966, 1987).

When Eichhorn's model was implemented in the Upper St. Clair School District in Pennsylvania, it was modified and simplified. This curriculum had three domains: Learning Processes, Personal Development, and Knowledge (see Figure 6.2). The focus was on the developmental characteristics and needs of young adolescents. Learning processes were necessary to acquire self-education and included analytical, communication, and technical criteria. Personal development stressed self-actualization and included understanding, self-awareness, and interaction criteria. Knowledge (humanities, arts, and sciences) stressed the learner's involvement in the development of cognition through relating content to man's past contributions (Eichhorn, 1972).

THE ALEXANDER AND GEORGE MODEL

Another middle level model was first proposed by Alexander in 1968 and subsequently refined in 1981 by Alexander and George. These authors stated that "We see personal development as a very major goal of the middle school. . . ." (p. 56). In Figure 6.2, they recommended that the curriculum be based on the major educational goal statements of the middle school, with each major goal defining a domain of learning. They proposed three domains: Personal Development, Skills of Communication and Learning, and Major Knowledge Areas (1981, p. 56). Their model was based on Eichhorn's model. Each domain was broken down into key categories.

The *Personal Development* domain focused on guidance, special services, affective development, exploration, development of special interests, health and physical education, provisions for students with special needs, and alternative programs. The main focus was to have one adult advisor to whom the student could turn for guidance and special help. The advisor served as a support for special services available in and out of school. Special services included psychological, medical, social work, and exceptional children. Exploratory courses and the development of special interests were encouraged. Physical and health activities included health, sex education, and physical education.

The *Communication and Learning Skills* domain stressed reading and related study skills; speaking, questioning, and listening skills; writing skills; quantitative skills; utilization of major learning materials; and problem solving skills. Each skill was discussed in some detail and its relationship to the other two domains was presented.

The *Major Knowledge Areas* domain stressed basic studies, language arts, social studies, science, mathematics, exploratory studies in practical arts and fine arts, environmental studies, career exploration, consumer education, and

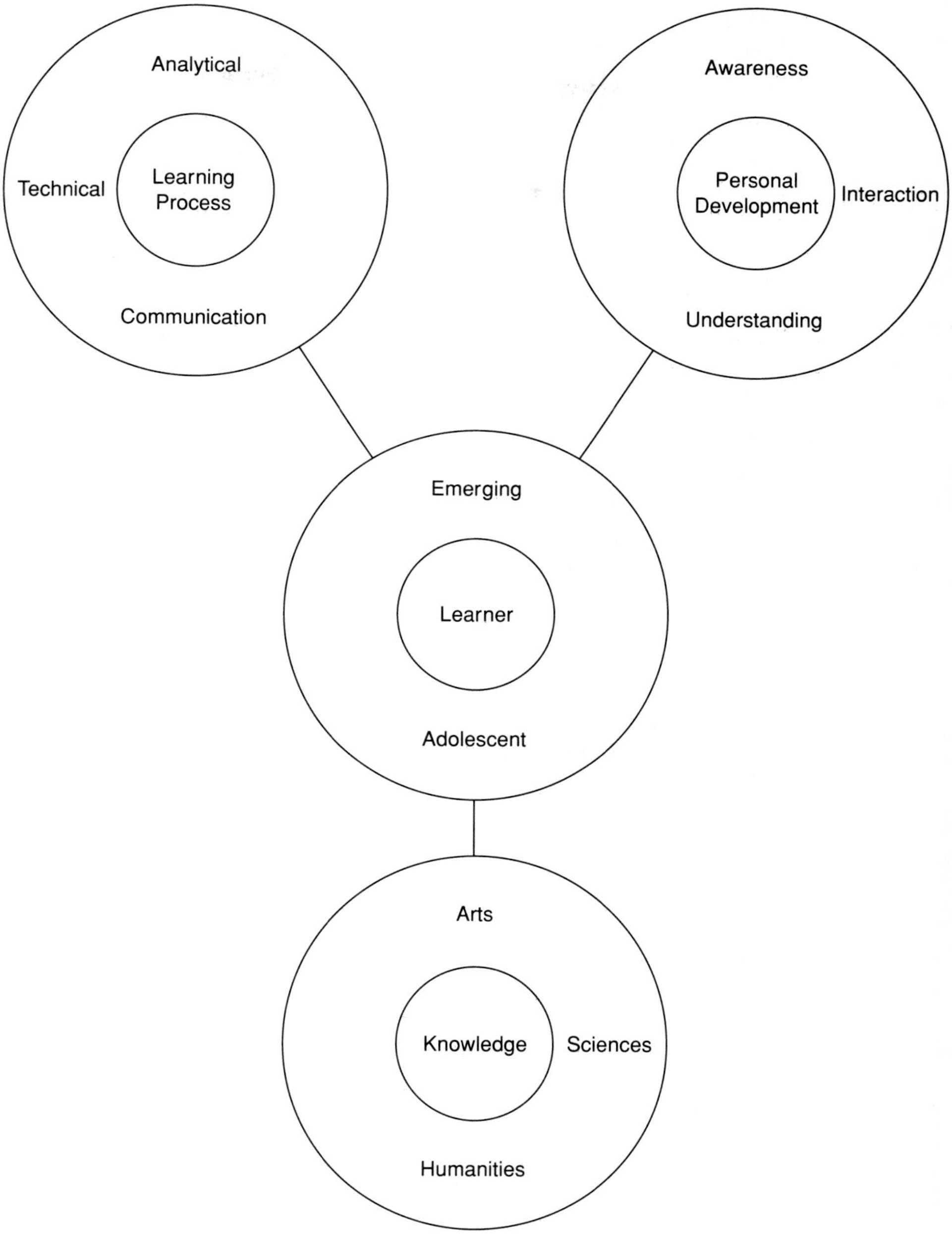

FIGURE 6.2 Emerging adolescent curriculum *(Adapted from "The Emerging Adolescent School of the Future—Now" by D. H. Eichhorn, 1972, p. 41. In J. G. Saylor (Ed.),* The School of the Future—Now. *Washington, DC: Association for Supervision and Curriculum Development. Adapted by permission of ASCD and the author.)*

media study. This domain integrated the various subjects taught on the middle level. In the model, knowledge areas were tied to personal and communication and skill domains to form a connection among the various domains. This curriculum design tried to connect the three domains into an integrated curriculum for the middle level. The idea of interdisciplinary teaming was proposed as an organizational format for developing an integrated curriculum, along with self-contained, single-subject teams and other arrangements (Alexander & George, 1981).

THE WILES AND BONDI MODEL

Wiles and Bondi (1986) also suggested a middle level curriculum with three program domains: Personal Development, Education for Social Competence, and Skills for Continuous Learning. The focus of the middle level curriculum is on the developmental characteristics of the emerging adolescents in each area. The *Personal Development* element focuses on guidance, physical education, law education, health education, provisions for students with special needs, and alternative programs. *Education for Social Competence* stresses basic studies, language arts, social studies, science, mathematics, exploratory studies in practical arts and fine arts, environmental studies, career exploration, consumer education, and media study. *Skills for Continuous Learning* are broken into communication: reading, writing, listening, and speaking; mathematics: computation, comprehension, and usage; observing and comparing; and analyzing, generalizing, organizing, and evaluating.

LOUNSBURY AND VARS CURRICULUM MODEL

The personal and social aspects of early adolescence received special emphasis in the Lounsbury and Vars (1978) middle level curriculum proposal. Lounsbury and Vars (1978) proposed that the personal and social dimensions ought to have a more significant place in the curriculum. These two authors proposed a problem-centered core curriculum using the *block of time* to emphasize the content of language arts, social studies, mathematics, and science, as well as music and art. In addition, a *continuous progress* skills development program was proposed, including skills and concepts in science, reading, mathematics, and foreign languages, and a *variable component* involving exploratory courses, independent study, interest-centered enrichment activities, electives, and student activities.

THE CALIFORNIA MODEL

The Middle Grades Task Force in the California State Department of Education (1987) proposed in *Caught in the Middle* that "every middle level student should pursue a common, comprehensive, academically oriented core curriculum irrespective of primary language or ethnic background" (p. 2). The Task Force assumed that there was a common core of knowledge that all educated citizens should possess, including "cultural literacy, scientific literacy, knowledge of the humanities, and appreciation of the values that undergird our society (p. 2). The Task Force stated that:

> The content of the core curriculum must be linked to the heightened curiosity of young adolescents about themselves—who they are, how they fit into the world around them, how that world functions, and what exciting prospects for their lives lie beyond the immediate horizons of their present knowledge and experience (pp. 2–3).

The Task Force recommended the following instructional times for grades 6 to 8:

Subjects	*Average minutes per week**
Reading/Literature	250
Language Arts	250
Mathematics	250
Science (and Health)	250
History and Geography	250
Visual and Performing Arts	125
Physical Education	200
Advisory (group guidance)	50
Elective and Exploratory	175
	1,800

*Note: The average number of minutes per week is derived from the total of the three middle level years. The actual number of minutes per week may vary for a given subject during the three-year period (*Caught in the Middle*, 1987, p. 5).

In addition, the opportunity to acquire proficiency in a second language is encouraged through the elective and exploratory curriculum. Language arts emphasizes direct instruction in writing, speaking, and vocabulary development. The study of content areas including arts should encourage students to discover the contributions of famous individuals from varied ethnic and linguistic backgrounds. Thinking and communication are stressed as essential skills for any citizen. Character development was proposed to help young adolescents personalize their ideas and to develop the capability to make reasoned moral and ethical choices. A set of performance standards was established to evaluate the effectiveness of the middle level programs utilizing these recommendations in the various school districts.

THE BEANE MODEL

Perhaps the most significant proposal in the development of middle level curriculum is James A. Beane's proposal (1990) that the middle level school be based on a general education "that focuses on the *common* needs, problems, interests, concerns of young people and the society" (p. 35). He further emphasizes that "for the middle school this means that general education is interpreted in the context of the developmental concerns of early adolescence and the social issues that do and will face these young people because they are living in a social world" (p. 36). Thus, Beane would argue that the middle level school should be a general education school based upon social and personal concerns of young adolescents.

The *personal problems* that Beane suggests should be considered include (1) understanding and coping with physical, intellectual, and socio-emotional changes; (2) developing a personal identity and wholesome self-concept; (3) exploring values, moral, and ethical questions in social contexts; (4) securing and finding a level of status in the peer group; (5) developing a personality which is balanced between independence from adult authority and dependence on adults for security; (6) coping with commercial interests related to fashion, music, and leisure activities; (7) negotiating the expectations in home, school, community, and peer group; and (8) developing commitments to people in order to obtain a feeling of self-worth, achievement, and efficacy (Beane, 1990).

The *social issues* that Beane recommends should be included in the curriculum framework are: (1) interdependence among peoples in the global society of today; (2) diversity of cultures that are formed by race, ethnicity, gender, geographic region, and other factors; (3) environmental problems; (4) political processes and organizations; (5) economic problems; (6) the significance of technology; and (7) increasing incidence of self-destructive behaviors (Beane, 1990). Beane proposed that these two categories intersect to merge personal problems and societal issues into integrated middle level curriculum themes. Beane (1990) stated, "The centerpiece of the curriculum would consist of thematic units whose organizing centers are drawn from the intersecting concerns of early adolescents and issues in the larger world" (p. 45). These themes present opportunities for integrating personal and social concerns and for connecting social issues to concrete and real experiences of young adolescents. To visualize how these two categories can intersect into curriculum themes, see Table 6.3. The curriculum suggested by Beane (1990) included (1) reflective thinking, (2) critical ethics, (3) problem solving, (4) valuing, (5) self-concepting and self-esteeming, (6) social action skills, and (7) searching for completeness and meaning. These skills are proposed because they have practical use in school and in the community. These skills are necessary to broaden our understanding of ourselves, our world, and to create a just and humane world for the future.

Beane identifies three contexts that he believes are essential to the middle level curriculum. First, "the idea of democracy ought to permeate the middle school, including its curriculum" (Beane, 1990, p. 43). The curriculum should provide opportunities for all views, content, and cultures to be recognized and examined.

Second, "the concept of human dignity and the related ideas of freedom, equality, justice, and peace ought to permeate the curriculum" (Beane, 1990, p. 44). The formation of subject matter and ideas results from human struggles and

TABLE 6.3 Intersection of Personal and Social Concerns

Early Adolescent Concerns	Curriculum Themes	Social Concerns
Understanding personal changes	TRANSITIONS	Living in a changing world
Developing a personal identity	IDENTITIES	Cultural diversity
Finding a place in the group	INTERDEPENDENCE	Global interdependence
Personal Fitness	WELLNESS	Environmental protection
Social Status	SOCIAL STRUCTURES	Class system
Dealing with adults	INDEPENDENCE	Human rights
Peer conflict and gangs	CONFLICT RESOLUTION	Global conflict
Commercial pressures	COMMERCIALISM	Effects of media
Questioning authority	JUSTICE	Laws and social customs
Personal friendships	CARING	Social welfare
Living in the school	INSTITUTIONS	Social institutions

Reprinted from *A Middle School Curriculum: From Rhetoric to Reality* by J. E. Beane, 1990, Columbus, OH: National Middle School Association. Copyright 1990 by NMSA. Reprinted by permission.

human efforts to make meaning out of one's experiences. The middle level curriculum must explore the broad themes of the curriculum "in terms of both the immediate and extended lives of early adolescents" (Beane, 1990, p. 44).

Third, "a complete curriculum must offer opportunities to explore and appreciate the workings and values of diverse cultures" (Beane, 1990, p. 45). The emphasis must be on the exciting possibilities and the richness of diversity, rather than a restricted view of ethnocentrism. The middle level school should be "a general education school with a coherent, unified, and complete curriculum" (Beane, 1990, p. 47). An authentic middle level curriculum should establish a view that general education combines the personal and social concerns of young adolescents with the larger world. Thus, the curriculum of the middle level school continues to evolve.

In summary, all middle level curricula stress the young adolescent as the focus for each curriculum, whether through academics, personal experiences, social competence, career training, or continuous progress. While knowledge is considered important in each type of curriculum, it should not dominate the middle level curriculum design. Skills are provided for as a separate category or integrated with the knowledge area, depending on the curriculum proposal. Most of these middle level curricula argue for a curriculum balanced between personal, social, and academic needs.

INTEGRATING THE CURRICULUM: AN ECOLOGICAL ORIENTATION

Given the definition of the curriculum for the middle level as the integration of planned or intended learning experiences formulated and organized specifically around knowledge, around the commonly shared personal concerns of young adolescents, and around the serious global social issues experienced by them and the world in a given school setting, there is need to explore how this definition can be translated into practice.

An ecological orientation to the middle level curriculum attends to the personal, social, and academic needs of young adolescents holistically in all of their interrelated environments of family, school, peer group, church, and community. As a rationale for a comprehensive, system approach to curriculum design, Tanner and Tanner (1980) theorized that "curriculum must be dealt with in its ecological interaction" (p. 642). These authors maintained that the curriculum design must promote the interaction of the curriculum elements instead of presenting the elements in isolation. This orientation establishes an ecological relationship among curriculum elements and environmental systems. It is important that what is taught be designed in relationship to all of the learners' continuing systems of family, school, peer group, church, and community.

One of the early proponents of an integrated curriculum was John Dewey, who proposed that the school as a social institution must be established as a form of community. In Dewey's theory, subject matter grew out of student activities. Educators often used Dewey's philosophy to form a dichotomy between the learner-centered and subject-centered school. In a sense, Dewey favored neither extreme position. Instead, he visualized that the school would be a learning community where the social, personal, and academic needs of the individual and group would be advanced. According to Squire (1972), essential principles of Dewey's theory relevant to middle level schools today are:

1. Learning through experience
2. The primacy of the individual learner
3. Learning as purposeful activity
4. Instruction directed toward pupil thinking
5. Freedom as the ability to make effective choices
6. School and curriculum as parts of an interrelated environment.

Bronfenbrenner (1979) applied the principles of human ecology in attending to the social, emotional, intellectual, and physical needs of young adolescents in their continuing environment. Bronfenbrenner's discourse dealt with a number of systems that influence the development and education of young people. Microsystems, such as the family and school, are systems in which the learner is an active participant. Exosystems, such as community agencies and businesses, have an indirect influence on children. The relationships between the various systems—such as home–school, home–agency, school–agency, and others—form the mesosystem. An ecological orientation seeks to establish positive relationships between various components of the mesosystem such as family, school, and community. Elements of the academic, social, and personal curriculum are interrelated with components of the ecological system to form a positive, relevant, and effective learning community.

Beane (1991) has made significant contributions to developing a curriculum theory for middle level schools. The middle level movement has attempted to address the unique needs of young adolescents through organizational reform, guidance programs, teacher preparation and certification, and other innovations. However, there have not been consistent and comprehensive efforts to develop appropriate and effective curriculum programs at the middle level. Beane and others are remedying this situation by formulating fresh new visions of integrated, interdisciplinary curriculum for middle level schools.

For purposes of this book, the authors have established an overarching curriculum framework, utilizing an ecological orientation that connects academic, social, and personal elements of middle level curriculum to the learner's interrelated environments of family, school, church, and community. The relationships which are formed by the ecological interaction between curriculum elements and environmental systems should promote a functioning learning community. In this learning community, the needs of the individual are the central focus. However, those individual needs are optimized in the social context of a learning community. Middle level educators must restructure the school curriculum, organization, and instruction to facilitate such learning environments for the middle level school. The idea of community builds a sense of belonging, an attitude of caring, and a concern for wholeness. When fragmentation seems to characterize curriculum, family relationships, personal adjustment, and social interaction, the concept of a learning community becomes imperative for young adolescents. There has been enormous concern for ecological awareness for rain forests, rivers, seashores, and endangered plants and animals. Restructuring the middle level school as a learning community establishes an ecological plan to "save" young adolescents.

The visual orientation for an integrated middle level curriculum is displayed in Figure 6.3. The learner is placed in the center to indicate that the focus of the middle level curriculum is on the learner. Each individual learner brings a set of personal, sociological, psychological, and cultural dynamics into the middle level school. The difficulty is in determining the various schemata being used by each young adolescent so that the curriculum can reflect the three dimensions for all learners. Each young adolescent is limited by his or her bounded rationality of previous experiences (Simon, 1957). In addition, it is important to develop empathic understanding of one's own personal needs, as well as recognizing the needs of other individuals in society (McNeil, 1990). For the middle level curriculum to meet young adolescents' needs, three key decision areas—*academic, personal, and social*—must be considered. Each dimension has a distinct set of criteria, to be considered when making decisions about the

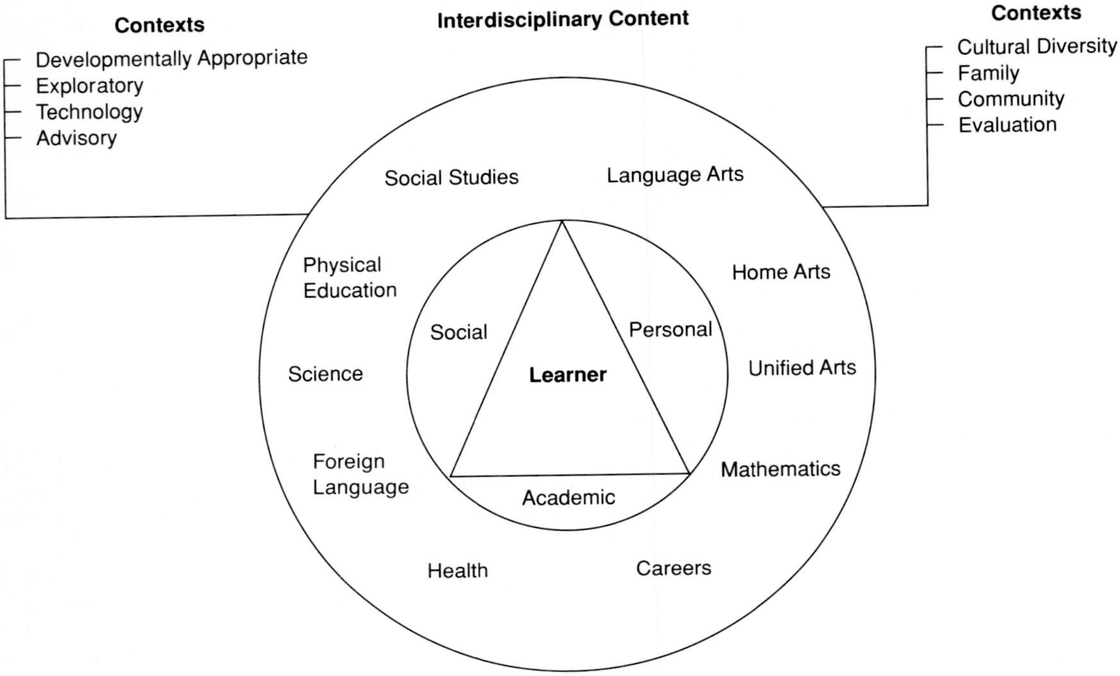

FIGURE 6.3 Integrating the middle level curriculum: an ecological orientation

middle level curriculum. Thus, each dimension is independent of the other dimensions but, yet, dependent upon the other dimensions for the full development of the learner. There is a tendency in middle level curriculum designs to focus more on one dimension and ignore the other areas. It is essential to maintain a balance among the three dimensions. For the purposes of this book, the authors have developed a comprehensive system.

In the inner circle of Figure 6.3, the three dimensions, personal, social, and academic, operate in a given school setting. The various content areas listed in the outer circle represent the possible choices of interdisciplinary content for inclusion into a given unit. The eight evaluative contexts represent decision areas that must be assessed in determining the effectiveness of an integrated curriculum. In the diagram, all aspects of the middle level curriculum are connected by the two circles. The term ecological refers to unifying and connecting of personal, social, and academic dimensions, contexts, and interdisciplinary content into an integrated middle level curriculum. The orientation model proposes to integrate by extending the planning effort to connect dimensions and content areas so that the effectiveness of the curriculum can be evaluated in each context. If middle level curriculum is to be integrated, the synthesis of these three dimensions, contexts, and interdisciplinary content must be undertaken.

A commitment must be made to providing planning time to facilitate the development of an integrated curriculum.

Personal Dimension

The personal dimension of the curriculum includes health, physical education, unified arts, career, and exploratory activities to assist the young adolescent in the development of values and attitudes. Curricular and instructional decisions are planned that draw from the experiential background of young adolescents. This dimension puts the individual learner's needs and interests at the center of the curricular decisions.

The focal point of the personal dimension is on the individual's interests, needs, and previous experiences. The idea began with John Dewey. Dewey (1938) stated that "it is a cardinal principle of education that the beginning of instruction shall be made with the experience learners already have; that this experience and the capacities that have been developed during its course provide the starting point for all further learning" (p. 88). Dewey's design focused on the child.

During this century, personalized education has been referred to as child-centered, experience-centered, progressive education and, more recently, open and humanistic education. The arguments for this dimension are that: (1) learning opportunities based on the needs and interests of the learners are more relevant; (2) the utilization of the needs and interests involves a high degree of motivation and, therefore, increases the success of the learner; and (3) the achievement of individual potential is facilitated by this design. One of the most important aspects is self-actualization. The important figure in this movement was Abraham Maslow (1968) who viewed self-actualization as encompassing several dimensions. Learners should be permitted to express, act out, experiment, make mistakes, be seen, get feedback, and discover who they are. Self-awareness is at the heart of personal experiences. Learners should be permitted to seek personal patterns in their own responses to a series of activities.

At issue is whether personal activities are developmentally appropriate for young adolescents. Can the self-interests of young adolescents be placed in perspective with common social interests of the family, community, and society? Beane (1990) states that some major concerns to be considered are that young adolescents need to:

1. Understand and be able to cope with rapid physical, intellectual, and social changes and how these changes will affect the quality of life in the present and future
2. Develop a clear self-concept, positive self-esteem, personal identity, and an understanding of how perception forms the basis of attitudes and behaviors
3. Explore personal values, morals, and ethics in various social settings, including school, home, and community

4 Obtain and maintain a level of peer acceptance, including the understanding of dynamics involved in peer groups
5 Develop a balanced perspective between independence from parents and adults and continued dependence on parents and adults for various types of support
6 Cope with a number of challenges posed by special interests, including dress, music, and recreational activities
7 Balance the numerous expectations from peer group, school, home, and community
8 Develop commitments to other persons, activities, and groups that promote a positive self-concept based on self-worth, affirmation, achievement, and efficacy (Beane, 1990).

The key to implementing the personal dimension is a wide range of exploratory activities. These should encourage young adolescents to explore special academic concerns, personal values, social opportunities, and career options to assist in their self-development. Alternatives are usually proposed when there is some need, real or imagined, that is not being met for certain learners. An important thought for personal education was the humanistic education movement. *Humanistic education* was defined by a working group of the Association for Supervision and Curriculum Development (ASCD) in 1978 as "a commitment to education and practice in which all facets of the teaching-learning process give major emphasis to the freedom, value, dignity, and integrity of persons" (p. 9). Some of its goals were to facilitate self-actualization; personalize educational decisions and practices; recognize the primacy of human feelings; utilize personal values and perceptions; establish learning environments which are perceived by all as challenging, understanding, supportive, and nonthreatening; and develop learners' concern for the worth of others and skill in conflict resolution. Thus, the focus is on the individual's experiences. Arnold (1990) catalogued exemplary middle level projects, ranging from multidisciplinary and interdisciplinary projects to special population projects, for young adolescents that might be used as models.

Further emphasis should be placed on guidance to help with learning needs, physical and mental health problems, family relationships, work, and problems outside of school. Leisure activities and the individual's special interests, health and physical activities are also a part of personal development. The exploration of home economics (family, food, nutrition, housing, and clothing), industrial arts (metalworking, woodworking, electricity, and auto mechanics), and business and distributive education (retailing, marketing, typing, data processing, and accounting) are important aspects of personal development. Other areas that should be included are fine arts: music (chorus, instrumental music, and orchestra) and the arts (ceramics, drawing, painting, film making, television, theatre, and dance).

It is important to recognize the discrepancies that often exist among the planned curriculum (formal curriculum) prescribed by state and school boards, and what teachers say they are doing (perceived curriculum); what is actually observed in the classroom (observed curriculum); and the actual experiences learners are perceiving (experiential curriculum) (Saylor, Alexander, & Lewis, 1981). Thus, it is difficult to consider all experiential factors influencing young adolescents' learning. However, while wide variation in learners' experiences makes it difficult to design curriculum for this dimension, it is essential to consider all facets of their experiences.

Social Dimension

The social dimension includes the necessary opportunities for socialization, extracurricular activities, and interaction with peers, teachers, and adults in the school, home, and community. Peer acceptance and status are critical elements of each learner's development. The social dimension involves power sharing, negotiation, and joint responsibility. The goal is to develop into a fully socially competent individual. It is important to remember that young adolescents do not live in isolation during the young adolescent stages, nor are they sheltered from the larger realities of society.

Two arguments are put forward for this dimension: that social competence is relevant to the student's needs and concerns, and that social competence can contribute to the improvement of society. The dimension includes social interaction within the schools, the participation of students in the various social groups and institutions of their schools and communities, and the specific studies and skill development activities related to particular human relations problems within the school and community. The emphasis is on developing processes for democratic participation. A key context for young adolescents is to understand that cultural diversity is an essential aspect of a democratic society. The goal is to develop a caring, morally responsive, and socially responsible individual who respects the diversity of all cultures. In the development of the social dimension, it is important not to separate for individual differences and varying academic abilities. The middle level curriculum should provide a wide range of possibilities and opportunities in order to avoid labeling students in such categories as "gifted," "vocational," and "learning disabled." All learners should be encouraged to explore social and personal concerns. In the classroom, every lesson should be organized to appeal to the unique interests, needs, and abilities that need to be developed.

Some social issues that are common to all young adolescents are:

1. The interdependence of individuals, groups, cultures, and nations in a global community
2. The cultural diversity that exists in every culture and society, arising from differences of race, ethnic groups, gender, and geographic regions
3. Environmental problems such as waste disposal, pollution, and nuclear accidents that can affect everyone's quality of life

4 Political structure and governments, including conflicting ideologies that have promoted freedom or oppression
5 Economic concerns ranging from personal financial security to the issue of inequitable distribution of wealth and related power
6 The influence of technology and science on various aspects of an individual's personal life, their value, and the moral issues they present
7 Increasing incidents of self-destructive behaviors, such as drugs, teenage pregnancies, suicides, and participation in gangs (Beane, 1990)

Poverty, homelessness, and racism are not abstractions for young adolescents. In a pluralistic society, the concept of human dignity, freedom, equality, and peace ought to permeate the middle level curriculum. Recognizing global interdependence, involving an in-depth understanding of the various cultures in the world, is a critical part of being a responsible citizen in the twenty-first century. In an interdependent global world, an integrated middle level curriculum must consider the major environmental, political, and social issues that are essential to all human beings, especially young adolescents. In sharing cultural diversity concerns with young adolescents, a better understanding of other ethnic groups and cultures and an understanding of their own culture are essential to helping young adolescents understand and cope with their future lives in a global society.

The content and organization of learning experiences are determined by the experiences of learners as they deal with everyday concerns and persistent life situations encountered on a daily basis (Simon, 1957). Student involvement in the community is encouraged. In the classrooms, teachers and learners explore specific social actions. Moral development is fostered in the class through the moral dilemmas that arise from the social activities of the class.

The core programs of middle level schools and interdisciplinary units represent an attempt to analyze social problems. Vars (1969), whom we discussed previously in this chapter, suggested that a core program could include personal problems, interests, needs, and social concerns of students. Thus, this curriculum dimension focused on social competence and social interaction in the community. *Turning Points* (1989) has recommended giving credit for participation in community projects. More recent, exemplary middle level community projects have been identified by Arnold (1990). A full discussion of home, school, and community interaction can be found in Chapter 11.

Academic Dimension

The academic dimension represents the basic content areas of mathematics, language arts, social studies, science, foreign language, health, physical education, unified arts, career, technology, home arts, and skills of reading, writing, speaking, listening, and information retrieval. It represents the traditional knowledge found in the various disciplines. An academic core program of studies results in intellectually reflective learners who are literate, can think critically, behave ethically, engage in a life of meaningful work, and assume the roles and responsibilities of citizens (*Turning Points*, 1989).

Each discipline has its distinct subject matter, tradition, methods of collecting the data base and skills that it contributes to the individuals' knowledge, social interaction, and personal experiences. This curriculum dimension is challenged to integrate academic content with personal and social dimensions.

During this century, knowledge has been the primary focus of schooling. Knowledge of subject matter as found in academic disciplines—language arts, science, social sciences, mathematics, and fine arts—has been viewed as the basis for intellectual development and has been considered necessary for man's achievement and continued survival. Academicians have justified knowledge as essential to the development of the mind. Two theories of knowledge have influenced academicians in American schools. One is that all knowledge is tentative and is subject to change, modification, and evolution. The more traditional view is that knowledge is *not* new, and is not created but already exists, is fixed and eternal (McNeil, 1990). According to Saylor, Alexander, and Lewis (1981), the curriculum plan for this dimension is based on the expert judgment of the knowledge found in various disciplines. Criteria are employed, such as difficulty or interest, in selecting subject matter for learners, and planned methods of instruction are designed to insure mastery of the subject.

The structure of knowledge was suggested by Jerome Bruner (1960) and by Schwab and Brandwein (1962). Structure refers to how the organization of each discipline differs from another, what substantive data and ideas are required in interpreting data, and how those in respective disciplines gather data, test assertions, and generalize findings. The back-to-basics movement of the 1980s strengthened the argument for academic content. Throughout the twentieth century, the academic dimension has remained the prevailing rationale for the organization of the curriculum.

An academic core has been the center of the middle level curriculum. The academic core, as proposed in this model, would include language arts, social studies, science, mathematics, unified arts (fine, practical, home arts, and technological education), physical education, health, and foreign languages. To have an interdisciplinary, integrative format, these subjects would be organized around interdisciplinary or multidisciplinary topics and themes. These themes and topics would go across the separate subject lines. In the development of the academic dimension, content must be selected that is developmentally appropriate to the intellectual abilities of young adolescents. However, on the middle level, a curriculum containing interdisciplinary content enables the young adolescent to see an integrated, holistic viewpoint of content as well as to appreciate the uniqueness of each separate discipline.

An essential part of the academic curriculum is a continuum of skills. Too often, these skills have been separated and taught apart from subject matter. For example, reading has been separated into a series of skills rather than being integrated into the content, skills, and values of subject matter being taught. For purposes of development and reinforcement, skills can be identified with one subject and/or can be attended by the various subject matter areas. Other skills are independent of any subject matter and can be employed whether content is used or not. These can be broken down into communication (writing, listening, speaking) and learning skills such as reading, quantifying, and information retrieval. With the emphasis on back-to-basics, a mandatory requirement for writing, reading, and mathematics skills has been enacted in many states. On the middle level, reading skills should be focused on corrective, developmental, and enrichment areas. Reading is divided into skills of comprehension, vocabulary, main ideas, details, inferences, and comparisons. It also may include study skills such as outlining, dictionary skills, note taking, book reporting, library skills, reading for enjoyment, and locating information in encyclopedias, atlases, and almanacs. Another skill, writing, stresses correct use of grammar, rules of punctuation, spelling and capitalization, paragraphs, main ideas, topic sentences, vocabulary, and encoding. Another skill area is mathematics, in which whole numbers, fractions, decimals, measurement by English and metric standards, geometry, percent, ratio and proportion, integers, graphing, sets, irrational numbers, probability, expressions and equations are included. Communication skills involve speaking, listening, and the use of computers, video, and television. Listening skills involve following directions, attending and responding, comprehension and analysis. Speaking involves response, delivery, organization, vocabulary, inflection, and drama. Speaking before various audiences and appearing on television or videotape are two other aspects of the skill.

Computer literacy has not yet been clearly defined and implemented. Another essential of the academic skill is the teaching of computer skills and the wise use of technology. The computer has applications to school, careers, community, and nation. The key to computers and technology is in understanding the changes that may result and the impact they may have on the lives and future careers of young adolescents in a global society. Terminology, use of commands, and word processing are important aspects of computer information retrieval, just as the knowledge of accessing libraries and media are important. Library skills represent the effective use of reference skills in the library, ranging from use of atlases, encyclopedias, reference works, the card catalogue, and the periodical guide to literature.

Skills must be integrated into all three dimensions for understanding and complete development of the skills. Too often, skills are taught as isolated processes, so that the learner may not be aware of the value of specific skills. Skills become meaningful to young adolescents when they are applied to real situations and integrated across the curriculum.

Currently, there is a move to add thinking to the list of skills. It has been referred to as reflective thinking, critical thinking, inquiry, and problem solving. There may be a question as to whether it should be referred to as a skill. Whatever term is used, thinking is broader than any one method or subject. It relies on past experiences of the individual and the schemata that each individual has developed. It is not easy to provide a simple explanation of how to arrive at thinking.

It is imperative that middle level schools provide the essential knowledge for citizens to think critically, question, inquire, and think holistically, abstractly, and yet be creative. Knowledge in a technological and scientific society undergoes rapid restructuring. World knowledge is increasing geometrically, with no single individual able to keep pace (Benjamin, 1989).

Thus, the development of thinking must be a major emphasis of the middle grade curriculum. There is general consensus that young adolescents need actual and simulated experiences in order to develop reflective thinking. Unfortunately, thinking has been accepted by teachers without careful reflection on what is meant by the thinking. According to *Making the Middle Grades Work* (Children's Defense Fund, 1988), middle grade curricula should include instruction designed "to develop students' higher order thinking skills, such as moral reasoning, critical thinking, problem solving, esthetic judgment, the use of scientific methods, and communications skills appropriate to each subject" (p. 9). Likewise, *Caught in the Middle* (California State Department of Education, 1987) called for middle level students to develop the capacities for critical thought. *Turning Points* (1989) also suggested that young adolescents develop the ability to think critically: "A primary goal in choosing curricula and teaching methods in the middle grades should be the disciplining of young adolescents' minds, that is, their capacity for active, engaged thinking" (p. 43).

The middle level curricula, using interdisciplinary approaches, provide an excellent place to teach reflective thought. Reflective thought emphasizes a conscious effort to employ criteria based on rationality and objectivity of empirical science methods in generating solutions to problems. Reflective thought always directs young adolescents back to the basis of their beliefs. Middle level teachers can use scientific method (inquiry) to involve students in observing, communicating, hypothesizing, experimenting, measuring, classifying, generalizing, and predicting. The scientific method places the responsibility on the subject matter as the structure for organizing thinking and empirical rationality. Middle level students should be encouraged to think through such relevant problems as their developing bodies, the deteriorating environment, health issues, and current societal problems.

In contrast, critical thinking comprises the mental processes, strategies, and representations that people use to solve problems, make decisions, and learn new concepts (Sternberg, 1985a). Because there are so many models of critical thinking, which often say similar things in different ways, it becomes important to develop a framework that can highlight similarities and differences. Sternberg (1985b) proposed that theories of critical thinking usually deal with one or more aspects of critical thinking: (1) its relation to the mind of the individual and to the context in which it occurs, (2) its relation to transferring past experiences of the individual to new situations requiring critical thinking, and (3) its being taught so as to maximize the probability of its transfer to real-life situations.

Reflective thinking is presumed to be based on the individual's knowledge and intuitive structures as the framework for thinking. Critical thinking relies on the thinking skills and the individual's knowledge background as the structure which frames thinking. Scientific method (inquiry) relies upon the subject matter disciplines as the structure for organizing thinking. Middle level teachers need to incorporate these approaches into the middle level curricula so that young adolescents develop competence in utilizing a full range of thinking strategies to solve problems of an academic, personal, and social nature. In summary, generalizations which should govern the development of thinking are:

Generalization 1: Thinking utilizes scientific methods (reflective thinking) as the criteria for generating solutions to problems.

Generalization 2: Thinking is based on the structure (inquiry) contained in the social science disciplines as well as other subject matter.

Generalization 3: Thinking is a set of skills (critical thinking) that could be separated from knowledge.

Generalization 4: Thinking is always limited by the individual's experiences and perceptions of the world, and thus is limited to the range of experiences that have influenced the thinker.

Newmann (1988) suggested that thoughtful classrooms would have six indicators. First, a few topics are examined in depth rather than many topics covered quickly to finish the book. Second, lessons are coherent and have continuity for the young adolescent. Third, students are allowed time to think and given time to prepare responses to challenging questions. Fourth, the teacher poses challenging questions and organizes demanding tasks. Fifth, the teacher models reflective thinking. Sixth, students are encouraged to explain and give reasons for their conclusions. Teachers need to refine their own teaching in order to become more adept organizers of higher-order thinking. A dynamic middle level curriculum must consider all needed knowledge, skills, values, and experiences, as well as instruction and curriculum, to develop a global thinking citizen.

Caution should be exercised not to limit thinking to one process, set of steps, exercises, or skills. While educators have gone to great lengths to spell out the thinking skills that young adolescents require, skills may never fully develop the intellectual understandings that are necessary for thinking. Rather than having a special unit or class on thinking, the most effective instructional approaches are to integrate thinking with daily lessons through encouraging students to think independently, through asking open-ended questions, and generally through promoting a spirit of reflective thought.

In fact, an integrated curriculum may be essential to improving thinking on the middle level. This may explain why little progress has been made in the implementation of higher-order thinking in our schools.

DESIGNING INTERDISCIPLINARY UNITS

In order to plan for the three dimensions—personal, social, and academic, Table 6.4 presents a format for organizing these dimensions, providing the team is experienced with planning integrated units. The starting place is to brainstorm and formulate characteristics of personal and social dimensions. Academic content is introduced after the categories of personal, social, and academic have been identified. The information provided in Table 6.4 represents some topics that were brainstormed for personal and social dimensions. The table should be considered as a planning document for the entire year. An integrated curriculum implies a commitment to interdisciplinary teams and a team organization that structures and integrates teaching and learning across all subject areas found in the middle level curriculum. This curriculum pattern fosters positive interactive learning environments. The personal and social dimensions become essential ingredients in an integrated middle level curriculum. The experience of the teams with interdisciplinary content and team planning will determine whether the planning should start with academic content or personal and social dimensions. Given that many teams have limited experiences with planning integrated curriculum units, it may be wise to start with subject matter first. It is important in planning integrated middle level curriculum units to start where teachers feel comfortable and confident. Inexperienced teams may need to break the content down by subject matter as the first step toward integrating interdisciplinary content.

In the following paragraphs, the four steps for integrating interdisciplinary content by middle level teachers are outlined. These are (1) organizing content

TABLE 6.4 Theme Identification

Personal Dimension	Social Dimension		Academic Dimension
Understanding physical, social, and emotional changes	Living in a constantly changing environment at home, in the school, and in the community	World is continually changing	
Finding acceptance in a peer group	Pressure from home, school, and community to conform	Pressure from peers to conform to group	
Personal health and fitness	Society pressure to protect from AIDS, drug dependency, and sexually transmitted diseases	Pressure for drug use, smoking, and sex	
Developing a sense of acceptance and personal identity	Learners interdependent on others for acceptance	Parents and adults feel need to control	

so that a theme can be identified, (2) brainstorming ideas to be integrated from the various content areas, (3) formulating these ideas into clusters for teaching the structure and relationships of interdisciplinary content, and (4) organizing activities into daily lesson plans for connecting clusters.

A reasonable starting point may be to lay out the content taught by individual teachers on the team for each nine weeks during the school year. This step will provide teachers with a beginning point for identifying themes that can be connected for integrated units. Teams that have more experience can start with personal and social issues and use these concerns as the basis for planning an integrated curriculum unit without having to start with content (see Table 6.4). For experienced teams, Table 6.4 should result in possible personal and social themes being identified across the curriculum for every grade level. Further clarification and assistance with the development of personal and social dimensions can be found in the Beane (1990) monograph. Once Table 6.4 has been broken down into what is planned to be taught in personal or social dimensions for each of the nine weeks, with integrated academic content matched to personal and social concerns, a theme can be identified for the development of an integrated unit.

Organizing Theme. Jacobs (1989) has proposed a model for developing integrated units around interdisciplinary topics. In Figure 6.4, the first step is to select an *organizing theme.* The central circle represents a theme that was developed in an actual middle level school setting. The topic can be a theme, subject area, event, issue, or problem. It should be defined and specific enough so that an event or theme issue can be investigated. The topic should be motivating and meaningful to students, and should utilize interdisciplinary content. Ideas that could be used as organizing centers include: (1) subject topics, such as climate, weather, environment, poverty; (2) events such as World War II and Desert Storm; (3) personal and social issues in students' lives, now or in the future; and (4) themes such as "The Roaring Twenties" or "The Great Depression."

Brainstorming. The second step in the model, *brainstorming,* is a flexible technique for generating ideas. In Figure 6.4, the brainstorming step is represented by the five circles with a list of items underneath each content area. Each teacher would bring his or her listing of essential content for the given time frame. A brainstorming session should generate a large volume of ideas, from which meaningful ideas can be selected.

The basic procedure of brainstorming is:

1. Every individual reflects for two minutes on the topic before the group brainstorming session begins
2. No criticism is permitted during the session
3. Every idea, however creative and novel, is encouraged
4. A large number of ideas are generated

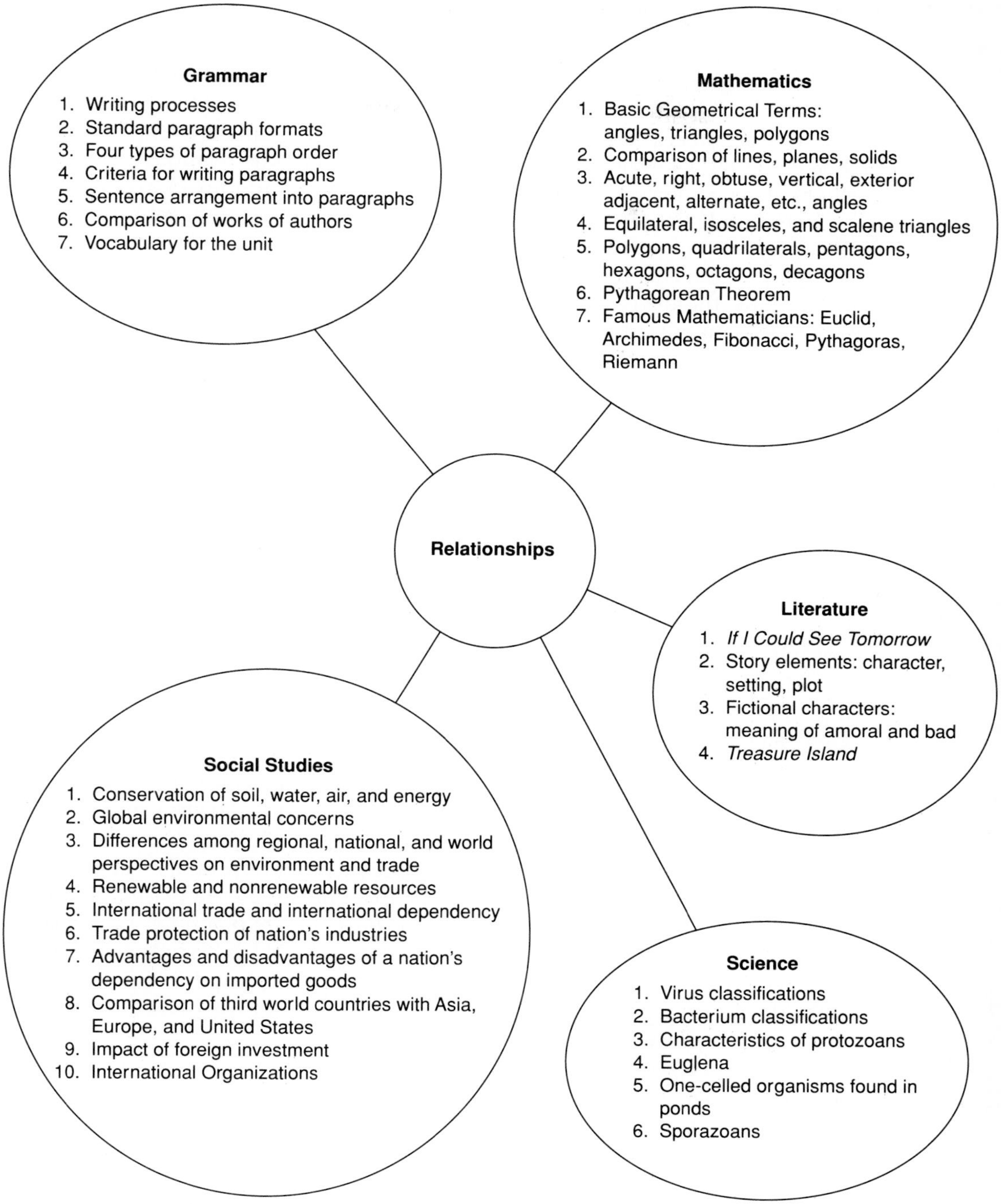
Grammar
1. Writing processes
2. Standard paragraph formats
3. Four types of paragraph order
4. Criteria for writing paragraphs
5. Sentence arrangement into paragraphs
6. Comparison of works of authors
7. Vocabulary for the unit
Mathematics
1. Basic Geometrical Terms: angles, triangles, polygons
2. Comparison of lines, planes, solids
3. Acute, right, obtuse, vertical, exterior adjacent, alternate, etc., angles
4. Equilateral, isosceles, and scalene triangles
5. Polygons, quadrilaterals, pentagons, hexagons, octagons, decagons
6. Pythagorean Theorem
7. Famous Mathematicians: Euclid, Archimedes, Fibonacci, Pythagoras, Riemann
Relationships
Literature
1. If I Could See Tomorrow
2. Story elements: character, setting, plot
3. Fictional characters: meaning of amoral and bad
4. Treasure Island
Social Studies
1. Conservation of soil, water, air, and energy
2. Global environmental concerns
3. Differences among regional, national, and world perspectives on environment and trade
4. Renewable and nonrenewable resources
5. International trade and international dependency
6. Trade protection of nation's industries
7. Advantages and disadvantages of a nation's dependency on imported goods
8. Comparison of third world countries with Asia, Europe, and United States
9. Impact of foreign investment
10. International Organizations
Science
1. Virus classifications
2. Bacterium classifications
3. Characteristics of protozoans
4. Euglena
5. One-celled organisms found in ponds
6. Sporazoans

FIGURE 6.4 Brainstorming and clustering *(Adapted from* Relationships *by F. Wann, A. Lamprey, J. Merritt, A. Sansbury, and S. Splittgerber, 1991, Columbia, SC: Irmo Middle School, Campus R. Adapted by permission.)*

5 Ideas are clustered where a relationship exists between two or more ideas—subject, event, personal problem, or social issues (Jacobs, 1989).

Teachers are free to brainstorm relationships that are linked to the organizing theme. Figure 6.4 indicates how team members noted the relationships that existed between subjects, events, individuals, readings, and materials that might be included. If the ideas or subject matter do not appear to fit into the theme, they may be omitted. If ideas and content are forced when team members do not see the rationale for including these areas in the design, the brainstorming session and the development of the integrated unit may become stymied. As teams become more experienced with planning integrated units, students become partners in planning the ideas and experiences that should be incorporated.

Clusters. The third step takes the volume of ideas generated and formulates them into *clusters for directing the structure and relationships of the unit.* A model for organizing these brainstorming techniques into clusters also is proposed in Figure 6.4. This step takes ideas that resulted from the brainstorming and places them into a visual schemata for each content area.

This model has grammar, literature, mathematics, social studies, and science because those were the content assignments of this middle level teaching team. Additional areas could include unified arts, technology, careers, etc. Additional items could be added depending on the ideas generated from the brainstorming session. As the unit is taught, items could be added by team members. It is important not to push for content areas that the team is not ready to integrate, since this could cause serious problems in getting the unit organized. The structure of the unit evolves as similar ideas are placed into clusters to guide the unit's scope and sequence. These clusters serve as an outline for related ideas to be grouped and gives a rationale and sequence for the unit. The clusters guide the integrated unit development and serve as a framework for investigating the unit. Formally, this diagram represents a description of how the relationships for the integrated unit are organized. The diagram should be placed on a large poster board or bulletin board so it is visible during team planning. Each teacher would have a smaller reproduction of this chart available in his or her classroom. Informally, as the planning and teaching of the unit proceed, team members can make the necessary adjustments due to modification of ideas, scheduling, activities, and learner needs.

Activities. The fourth step explores *procedures for connecting the clusters* generated in step three. Figure 6.5 visually organizes the interrelationships found among clusters by connecting procedures and activities with various clusters. This step describes activities and what the students will do to examine each cluster's relationship to the organizing theme.

One of the most important aspects of effective planning is that teachers encourage higher-order thinking in their daily lesson plans. Several models that facilitate higher-order thinking have been proposed. Bloom's taxonomy is used

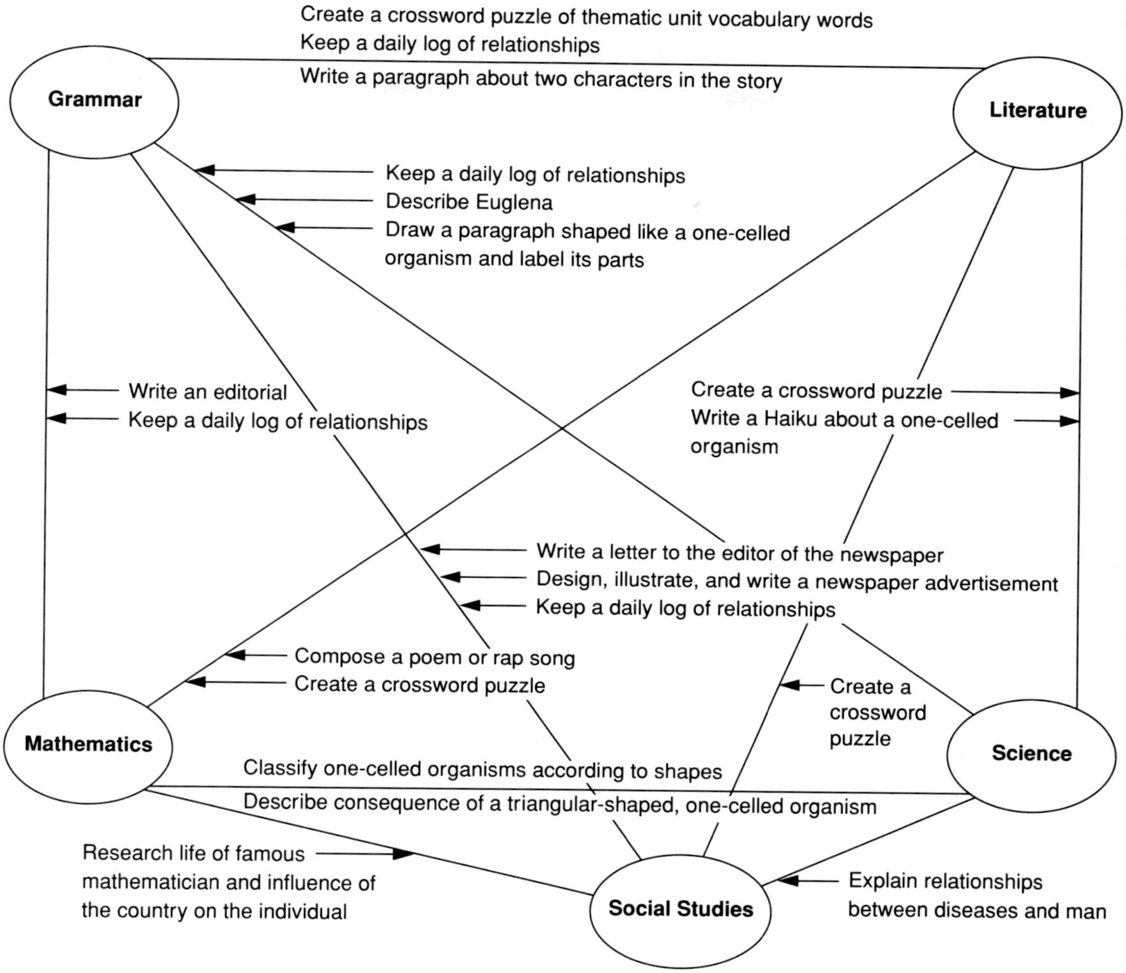

FIGURE 6.5 Connecting interdisciplinary content through activities and procedures *(Adapted from* Relationships *by F. Wann, A. Lamprey, J. Merritt, A. Sansbury, & S. Splittgerber, 1991, Columbia, SC: Irmo Middle School, Campus R. Adapted by permission.)*

to arrange each activity into performance levels in Figure 6.6. The rows represent the taxonomy of thinking processes required to gain higher-order thinking. Columns structure activities of the unit into the various taxonomic levels and form the basis for guiding activities at higher levels of thinking. If activities are planned only at the first two levels, then very little higher-order thinking will occur. A variety of activities should provide for different modalities, including auditory, tactile, and visual. A variety of heterogeneous grouping patterns may be employed, depending on the activities that are planned. The idea is to encourage individual and cooperative learning activities utilizing individual, small-

Unit: Relationships

Taxonomy	**Performance Descriptors**			
	Label:	Define:	Memorize:	Describe:
Knowledge	1) Parts of an organism 2) Parts of geometrical shapes	1) Paragraph components 2) Geometrical forms	1) Vocabulary words in thematic unit	1) Characters 2) How nations protect industries 3) Euglena
	Interpret:	Solve:	Measure:	Record:
Comprehension	1) Character traits in literature 2) Characteristics of protozoans	1) Geometry problems	1) Angles with a protractor	1) A daily record of the relationships encountered
	Record:	Solve:	Measure:	Develop:
Application	1) Observations in daily log	1) Assigned problems in geometry 2) Various angles assigned in geometry	1) Angles in Geometry	1) Paragraph using facts in daily log
	Cause & Effect:	Classify:	Investigate:	Contrast:
Analysis	1) International trade leads to international interdependency 2) International organizations	1) Geometrical shapes 2) One-celled organisms according to shapes	1) Examples of interdependency in our society	1) A real person with character in literature 2) Yourself with a friend
	Create:	Pretend:	Produce:	Develop:
Synthesis	1) Crossword puzzle of vocabulary words in thematic units	1) You are one of the main characters	1) A two-week diary 2) A mobile 3) A booklet 4) A cross stitch	1) A paragraph on the types of relationships encountered 2) Easy to learn vocabulary
	Role Play	Editorialize:	Evaluate:	Debate:
Evaluation	1) Character as plaintiff and class as jury	1) On universality of geometry 2) On timelessness of geometry	1) Long term survival of triangular shaped one-celled organisms	1) Whether U.S. Government should support protectionist legislation

FIGURE 6.6 Performance level matrix performance descriptors *(Adapted from* Relationships *by F. Wann, A. Lamprey, J. Merritt, A. Sansbury, and S. Splittgerber, 1991, Columbia, SC: Irmo Middle School, Campus R. Adapted by permission.)*

Unit: Relationships

Taxonomy **Performance Descriptors**

Identify:	Brainstorm:	Match:	Locate:
1) Story elements 2) Parts of one-celled organisms	1) Relationships studied for possible role play	1) Similar geometrical shapes	1) Congruent angles and similar parts in geometry
Chart:	Sketch:	Research:	Report:
1) Renewable & non-renewable resources	1) One-celled organisms	1) Famous mathematicians 2) Removal of rain forests 3) International organizations	1) How country of birth influenced mathematician's life
Construct:	Categorize:	Write:	Investigate:
1) A model of one-celled organism	1) The main characters in the book	1) A report on undeveloped countries	1) Effects of acid rain
Distinguish:	Compare & Contrast:	Survey:	Analyze:
1) Between an amoral character & a "bad" character	1) Writer's works to students 2) Geometrical shapes 3) Characters in the book	1) Advantages & disadvantages of dependency on imported goods	1) Third world countries in comparison to Asia, Europe & U.S.
Predict:	Compose:	Design:	Discover:
1) What a character would say if she came to this school	1) A rap, song, poem or play 2) A paragraph 3) A Haiku	1) Protozoan habitat 2) Line & compass drawings	1) Pythagorean theorem 2) Pythagorean triplets 3) Sums of angles
Assess:	Evaluate:	Measure:	Judge:
1) Impact of foreign investment 2) Impact of the removal of Iron Curtain	1) Adaptability of one-celled organisms to its environment 2) Paragraphs	1) Self-written products 2) Long-range use of thematic relationships	1) Guilt or innocence of character in book

and large-group instructional arrangements. Instructional strategies range from written assignments, debates, oral and videotaped presentations to lectures, group projects, learning centers, and discussion teams.

To assist the beginning teacher, and so that daily lessons do not overlook important concepts, a daily activity plan can be provided which shares activities and evaluation procedures required for each lesson. In Figure 6.7, an activity sheet is outlined which could serve as a daily planning sheet. This sheet communicates the lesson activities and objectives to other colleagues, to students, and to parents while providing a means to assess student learning outcomes. This activity sheet provides more structure in the planning and may help parents to understand what is taking place as the integrated curriculum format is implemented. The sheet can include behavioral objectives that can be assessed upon criterion-referenced as well as norm-referenced criteria. Criterion-referenced assessments hold each individual learner accountable for completing the learning activities without regard to a comparison with other learners. In con-

Activity Sheet

Grade: ____________________

Integrated Unit: ________________________________ Team: ____________________

Cluster:	
Objective:	
Procedures:	Materials/Resources:
	Evaluation Contexts:

FIGURE 6.7 Activity sheet *(Adapted from* Interdisciplinary Curriculum: Design and Implementation *by H. H. Jacobs (Ed.), 1989, Alexandria, VA: Association for Supervision and Curriculum Development. Adapted by permission.)*

trast, norm-referenced assessments compare the individual's learning performance to norms standardized for a larger population of students.

CONTEXTS FOR MIDDLE LEVEL CURRICULUM PLANNING

In planning the development of an integrated middle level curriculum, the authors believe that eight contexts should be embedded in all curricula of the middle level to ensure the personal, social, and intellectual development of each young adolescent. An integrated curriculum implies a commitment to interdisciplinary teams and a team organization that structures and integrates teaching and learning across all subject areas found in the middle level curriculum. This curriculum pattern fosters positive interactive learning environments. The schedule is blocked or flexible for scheduling students into subjects, exploratory activities, and guidance and career options. The team organization ensures that each young adolescent has access to a developmentally appropriate curriculum and must guarantee equal access to the academic curriculum and a broad range of exploratory, guidance, career, extracurricular, and intramural activities. The learner is the center of the curriculum and must be the focus for designing an integrated middle level curriculum. Each context provides the criteria to guide the planning of an integrated curriculum and to assess its effectiveness. Each specific context serves as the vehicle to conduct an internal assessment of the current curriculum and an external examination of the latest research. Table 6.5 outlines the contexts that should be used as a guide in developing and assessing an integrated curriculum for young adolescents.

The *developmentally appropriate* context implies that all the developmental needs of young adolescents are considered in the planning. These needs would include the establishment of a healthy self-concept toward peers and adults in order to cope with the complexities of attending large schools and living in an impersonal society, where it is difficult to develop a wholesome personal identity. The academically diverse range of learners found in the middle level should be provided equal access to the curriculum. Academic diversity should focus on mainstreaming handicapped and learning disabled students, providing a challenging curriculum for gifted and talented youth and at-risk learners, and providing for equal access to most advanced levels of the curriculum, based on the potential and interests of the individual learner. The middle level curriculum must recognize and plan for the academically diverse range of learners by ensuring they are connected to the total school program. The program of studies should result in intellectually reflective learners who are literate, can think critically, behave ethically, engage in a lifetime of meaningful work, and assume roles and responsibilities of citizenship (*Turning Points,* 1989).

The *exploratory* context should encourage middle level students to explore and select topics based on special academic, personal, social, and career interests. This context utilizes activities, real-life and/or simulated experiences and independent study. Students should be provided chances to explore and define who they are, what they believe, what they can do, and what they want to be.

TABLE 6.5 Contexts for Curriculum Planning at the Middle Level

Context	Description	Implications
Developmentally appropriate	Young adolescents have unique physical, intellectual and psychosocial and personal needs, possess academically diverse range of abilities, and must determine ethical standards of conduct in the development of a healthy self-concept.	Middle level curricula should be based on the physical, intellectual, psychosocial, academic, diversity, and personal characteristics of young adolescents and provide equal access to learning opportunities.
Exploratory	Young adolescents are encouraged to select and explore special academic, personal, social, and career interests so that they can define who they are, what they believe, what they can do and want to be, as part of the transition from childhood to adulthood.	The middle level curriculum should plan the selection and exploration to occur in classrooms, instructional activities, actual real-life and/or simulated experiences in the community or through independent study.
Technology	Young adolescents should be provided with learning experiences which integrate technology and computers into the subject areas in the middle grades in preparation for future careers and adult lives.	Computers and technology literacy should be utilized as tools to enrich the curriculum and to prepare for future careers and adulthood.
Culturally diverse learner	The cultural diversity and under-represented minorities should be addressed by developing a caring, morally responsible learner who respects the diversity of all cultures in an ever-changing interdependent society, nation, and world.	The curricula should recognize the culturally diverse range of learners by providing teaching and learning experiences to enhance the dignity of all young adolescents and guaranteeing equal access to the curriculum for all learners.

The *technology* context is focused on the utilization of computers and technology as tools for engaging the academic content and for enriching the curriculum. Technology and computer literacy should help to integrate the subject areas of the middle level curriculum. This context provides young adolescents with learning experiences that prepare them for their future careers and adult lives. Difficult ethical decisions will need to be made concerning the utilization of technology for the welfare of individuals, nations, and the world in the twenty-first century.

The *culturally diverse learner* context ensures that cultural diversity and under-represented minorities are incorporated and provided equity in any middle

TABLE 6.5 *(continued)*

Context	Description	Implications
Advisory	Information and assistance should be furnished to every adolescent about academic, career, personal and health decisions for the development of a caring, ethical, healthy, and responsible learner. Every learner should have one adult identified as an advisor in the school (advisor–advisee) and support of parents at home and school.	The middle level curriculum should provide awareness of academic options, course choices, consequences of curriculum decisions and alternatives available. Parents should be encouraged to support programs and improve their learner's performance through support of learning at home and school.
Family	The emphasis is on reconnecting the family with the school. The family must be an advocate of the young adolescent. The middle level school needs the family support to establish a meaningful learning community.	The middle level curriculum must involve parents in collaborating on learning in home through monitoring homework, tutoring and workshops on parents, teenage pregnancies, drugs, and suicide.
Community	The focus is through collaboration connecting school, home, community activities and experiences for promoting success of all young adolescents and meaningful learning situations in the community.	The middle level curriculum through collaboration must promote a learning community in which all middle level learners make relevant, meaningful, and effective connections with school, home, and community.
Evaluation	The framework for authentic evaluation includes diagnostic, formative, and summative evaluation of an instructional sequence utilizing norm-referenced, criterion-referenced, and teacher-made tests.	The middle level curriculum should be diagnostically, formatively, and summatively evaluated as to the authenticity of student mastery of an instructional sequence based on criterion-referenced, norm-referenced, and teacher-made tests.

level curriculum planning. Equal access to the curriculum is guaranteed for all learners. Young adolescents should be exposed to the various cultures of this nation and the world so that they can develop the global understanding required of citizens in the twenty-first century. The cultural diversity and under-represented minorities should be addressed in the middle level program through the development of a caring, morally responsible learner who respects the diversity of all cultures. Young adolescents must be provided an understanding of their ever-changing social status from dependence to independence and how to cope with the development of a personal identity with peers and adults within a dynamic, evolving interdependent society, nation, and world. At the same time, a dynamic, evolving interdependent society, nation, and world are continually changing the relationships among peers, parents, and adults. The middle level curriculum should recognize the culturally diverse range of learners by providing teaching and learning experiences to enhance the dignity of all young adolescents.

The *advisory* context would provide students with information about the academic program (awareness of academic options, course choices, and consequences of curriculum decisions on alternatives available in the high school) and provide assistance with making academic, career, personal, and health decisions. On the middle level, advisory services should recognize that the young adolescent is in transition from dependence to independence and is coping with the development of a wholesome personal identity with peers and adults. Every young adolescent should have access to an adult advisor who knows him or her well in an advisor–advisee relationship. Middle level schools should seek to promote parental commitment to the school program through greater involvement in school governance, open communication concerning their child's performance, and increased opportunities to support their child's learning at home and school.

The *family* context suggests that middle level schools face many challenges in educating young adolescents. Through the family, parents foster in their children the basic systems of morality, positive attitudes toward self and school, appropriate ways to demonstrate behavior, and the development of personality attributes such as honesty, integrity, caring, and compassion. Many families are having difficulty establishing successful parent–child relationships. Schools must reach out and engage parents in the learning of their young adolescent students. Positive communication needs to be maintained between the home and the school. To reengage parents, it is necessary to inform and involve them. Today, a growing number of homes have a single parent. The social and personal impact of living in a single family may have lasting effects on a young adolescent's school achievement and behavior. Also, because a large number of women are employed in the work force in order to provide an adequate standard of living, inadequate child care and lack of proper supervision for older children have resulted.

Poverty has had a detrimental effect on the young adolescent's success in school. It is extremely difficult for many families to maintain an adequate standard of living. Poor children usually have more serious health problems, more illness-related absences from classrooms, and inadequate nutrition for health and physical fitness. Poverty usually correlates with educational attainment of the parents and the student's performance in school. The middle level must reconnect the family with the school to reduce such at-risk factors among young adolescents as drug use, abuse, violence, crime, dropping out of school, teenage pregnancy, and sexually transmitted diseases, including AIDS.

The *community* context implies the need for collaboration among school, home, and community. This collaboration is needed to improve the health and fitness of young adolescents. Families need to be reengaged in the education of their children by taking an active part in the school. The school and community must collaborate to provide connections for young adolescents between schools and community through social action and community service projects. An integrated curriculum would foster a learning community in which middle level learners would value relevant, meaningful and effective social action and community service experiences. Figure 6.8 identifies ten characteristics of a learning community, as shown below.

The *evaluation* context would provide teachers, learners, parents, and the community with a framework for authentically evaluating the curriculum. Before classroom instruction begins, the teacher would use diagnostic evaluation to determine the prior knowledge and skills as well as the beliefs and interests of the young adolescent. Portfolios would contain student academic work and be used to document learner progress. The curriculum, instructional objectives, materials, and strategies would be assessed in a formative manner during instruction to find out how well students are learning and to make adjustments

Involvement	Involvement encourages participation, interaction, dialogue, and a sense of ownership. This provides opportunities for young people to become better acquainted.
Purpose	Purpose connotes good intentions, meaning, goal setting, and a goal worth striving for through individual and group action. Young adolescents need to incorporate purpose and meaning into their lives.
Commitment	Commitment evokes a sense of emotional or intellectual allegiance to a project or course of action. This trait is what keeps the group working together to attain the shared goal.
Cooperation	Cooperation is the *sine qua non* of the community. The willingness to work together builds relationships, promotes trust, and achieves goals.
Communication	Communication is the exchange of ideas and information through reading, writing, and speaking. This interaction promotes understanding, appreciation, and adjustment within the community.
Responsibility	Responsibility is personal and social accountability. This trait ensures that each member of the community knows his/her role, performs the job, and guarantees a certain behavior or performance.
Openness	Openness facilitates the give and take of ideas, invites people to participate, and keeps the door open to new ideas and new members.
Affirmation	Affirmation is concerned with accentuating the positive so that all members of the community feel a sense of acceptance, appreciation, and achievement. Young adolescents need to feel affirmed in their attitudes and behaviors.
Relationships	Relationships represent the behaviors which build a sense of wholeness, yet diversity in the community. Important relationships to promote are trust, respect, freedom, and confidence.
Continuity	Continuity is the characteristic which keeps the community energized. Continuity must provide for time stability, change, choice, and other needs of the community as it learns and works together.

FIGURE 6.8 Characteristics of an effective learning community

in objectives, materials, and strategies if necessary. Summative evaluation would be utilized at the end of each instructional sequence to determine how well students had mastered it, but it would also be part of the portfolio of each learner. The idea is to assess both short-term and long-term learning as well as mastery of higher-order cognitive knowledge levels. Criterion-referenced, norm-referenced, and teacher-made tests could be utilized to determine diagnostic, formative, or summative evaluation, but would be part of the student assessment portfolio to document all aspects of student progress. Any test results would be shared with the entire school community, including students, parents, teachers, and administrators.

MAJOR GUIDELINES

A most succinct statement concerning goals of the middle level curriculum was made by Wiles and Bondi (1986) who stated: "A well balanced program focusing on personal development, emphasizing skills for continued learning, and utilizing knowledge to foster social competence is essential if we are to serve the diverse group of youngsters found in the middle grades" (p. 81). Thus, the curriculum attempts to balance the learners' personal experiences, academics, and social competence. With this balance in mind, the following list of guidelines has been proposed for establishing a middle level curriculum:

1. Are developmentally appropriate learning experiences, based on the personal, academic, and social competence of young adolescents, proposed, designed, and implemented? Are the learning experiences comprehensive, balanced, and attainable?
2. Are learner experiences based on interdisciplinary content and designed for the young adolescent's needs and interests?
3. Are a wide variety of cognitive learning experiences balanced by affective experiences through the utilization of exploratory activities which will motivate middle level learners?
4. Are there opportunities for the development of higher-order thinking? Are all types of academic knowledge and experiences accepted as part of the development of thinking for young adolescents?
5. Are there provisions for individualized learning experiences based on the needs, abilities, and interests of young adolescents?
6. Does a balanced curriculum exist between skills, academic content, and experiences for personal, intellectual, and social development of middle level learners?
7. Is learning sequenced and is continuity maintained between levels—elementary to middle and middle to secondary?

8 Do young adolescents progress from dependent, teacher-directed learning to self-directed, independent, and cooperative learning?

9 Does the use of heterogeneous grouping criteria account for individual differences in intellectual and achievement standards, and yet appeal to varying physical, social, emotional, and personal interests and abilities as well?

10 Has special consideration been given to young adolescents' self-concept, self-responsibility, and attitudes toward school?

11 Has there been exploration of the unified arts (practical, fine, and home arts) and technology in the development of aesthetic appreciations and to foster creativity in young adolescents?

12 Is the curriculum designed to reflect the positive aspects of cultural diversity found in ethnic and socio-economic subgroups within the middle level school, community, nation, and world? Are the goals of the school clearly stated and understood by the community? Are the values and rationale underlying the goals understood?

13 Has curriculum planning involved representative groups in the community such as media, professional staff members, general public groups, and parents? Does the plan include all the resources of the school, district, community, and media?

14 Is flexibility built into the curriculum plan for alternative learning opportunities and individual learner styles and teacher styles? Does the curriculum recognize that young adolescents can have meaningful educational experiences in other settings outside the classroom?

15 Does the comprehensive curriculum plan include instruction as well as a stated scope and sequence? Does it have provisions for evaluation and feedback from learners and other concerned groups as well as provisions for making modifications if needed?

16 Who is responsible for evaluation of the curriculum? Does it rest with an advisory council, individual, community, or school group? Is there a recognizable and systematic way to make revisions and implement innovations?

These guidelines are not designed to provide a "cookbook" approach to a middle level curriculum. No hierarchy or ranking is suggested by these guidelines. Whatever curriculum is suggested for the middle level, the young adolescent should be the critical ingredient. This statement does not imply that content, skills, and social competence are not important. It suggests that a curriculum needs to maintain a balance of knowledge, personal experiences, and social competence. In no instance does an administrative or organizational pattern, in and of itself, necessarily make a difference. The focus is on an integrated curriculum planned cooperatively by teachers and learners as the key to any successful middle level school.

SUMMARY

In summary, the middle level curriculum should be focused on common educational experiences resulting from academic, personal, and social concerns of young adolescents. An interrelated balance of the three dimensions is essential. The dimensions are independent, but depend on each other for the total development of young adolescents. Personal and social dimensions focus on those critical needs which emerge in early adolescence. The personal and social concerns of young adolescents, the compelling issues facing society and the world, and the knowledge required in a global, technologically-oriented community should form the connecting points for organizing the curriculum into interdisciplinary themes and units. Taken together, these factors should help integrate the middle level curriculum. The middle level curriculum ought to assist young adolescents with personal issues emerging in their lives and at the same time connect them with the real world in which they reside. The future quality of life may in part be determined by the degree to which these social and personal concerns are addressed. The paramount goal should be to offer young adolescents a more relevant, compelling, and challenging middle level curriculum.

These three dimensions would be directed by such contexts as technology, cultural diversity, community, family, and exploratory. With this integrated approach, the middle level curriculum will be developmentally appropriate and responsive to the concerns of young adolescents and society. Subject matter would be selected for its importance to societal concerns and personal needs of young adolescents. Organizing the academic, personal, and social concerns into an integrated curriculum would help the middle level movement reach its intended goal of restructuring the middle level to meet the personal problems and social issues facing young adolescents.

▪ ▪ ▪

EXPLORATION

1 List what you believe are the important attributes in formulating a theoretical framework for a middle level curriculum. What emphasis would you place on academics, skills, personal experiences, and social interaction experiences? Assume what you already know is acceptable to the middle level school and decide what would be desirable features to have on the middle level. Please keep your list as a reference for later activities.

2 Compare and contrast the authors' definition of a middle level curriculum with those presented by other curriculum planners. Which definition in your

opinion more nearly describes the essentials for the development of a middle level curriculum? Why? What revisions would you make in the text's definition?

3 Given the various frameworks for middle level curricula (see Tables 6.1 and 6.2), compare and contrast in an outline the various approaches to a middle level curriculum. Which approach do you believe best represents what the public will support today? Since the public is concerned over the cost of public education, develop a rationale for the support of whichever curriculum you selected.

4 Design a curriculum for the middle level. What personal/experiential, social/interactive, and academic concerns would you include? You may want to review the ecological orientation (Figure 6.3), contexts (Table 6.5), curriculum frameworks (Tables 6.1 and 6.2), and the guidelines at the end of the chapter. How will you prioritize the goals and objectives? How will you convince the parents, the community, and the school board that this curriculum will make a difference?

SUGGESTED READINGS

Arnold, J. (1990). *Visions of teaching and learning: Eighty exemplary middle level projects.* Columbus, OH: The National Middle School Association.

This monograph catalogues eighty exemplary curricular and instructional projects on the middle level.

Beane, J. E. (1990). *A middle school curriculum: From rhetoric to reality.* Columbus, OH: National Middle School Association.

This monograph provides a recent proposal for the development of a middle level curriculum based on personal and social issues of young adolescents.

California State Department of Education, Middle Grades Task Force. (1987). *Caught in the middle.* Sacramento, CA: California State Department of Education.

The task force provides an excellent framework for establishing a middle level curriculum.

Eichhorn, D. (1972). The emerging adolescent school of the future—Now. In J. G. Saylor, Ed. *The school of the future—Now.* Washington, DC: Association for Supervision and Curriculum Development.

Eichhorn, D. (1966, 1987). *The middle school.* New York: The Center for Applied Research in Education. Reprinted by National Middle School Association Columbus, OH, and National Association of Secondary School Principals, Reston, VA.

Eichhorn provides an in-depth analysis of the middle school curriculum, instruction, and modifications that were undertaken in the Upper St. Clair School District, Pennsylvania.

REFERENCES

Alexander, W., & George, P. (1981). *The exemplary middle school.* New York: Holt, Rinehart and Winston.

Alexander, W., Williams, E., Compton, M., Hines, V., Prescott, D., & Kealy, R. (1969). *The emergent middle school.* New York: Holt, Rinehart and Winston.

Arnold, J. (1990). *Visions of teaching and learning: Eighty exemplary middle level projects.* Columbus, OH: The National Middle School Association.

Barr, R., Smith, V., & Burke, D. (1976). *Alternatives in education: Freedom to choose.* Bloomington, IN: Phi Delta Kappa.

Barth, R. (1974). *Open education and the American school.* New York: Schocken Books.

Beane, J. A. (1990). *A middle school curriculum: From rhetoric to reality.* Columbus, OH: National Middle School Association.

Beane, J. A. (1991). The middle school: The natural home of integrated curriculum. *Educational Leadership 49 2,* 9–13.

Beauchamp, G. (1981). *Curriculum theory* (4th ed.). Itasca, IL: Peacock.

Benjamin, S. (1989). An ideascape for education: What futurists recommend. *Educational Leadership, 47(1),* 8–14.

Berman, L., & Roderick, J., Eds. (1977). *Feeling, valuing and the art of growing: Insights into the affective.* Washington, DC: Association for Supervision and Curriculum Development.

Block, J. H., Efthim, H. E., & Burns, R. B. (1989). *Building effective mastery learning schools.* New York: Longman.

Bobbitt, F. (1918). *The curriculum.* Boston: Houghton Mifflin.

Bremer, J., & Von Moschzisker, M. (1971). *The school without walls: Philadelphia's parkway program.* New York: Holt, Rinehart and Winston.

Bronfenbrenner, U. (1979). *The ecology of human development.* Cambridge, MA: Harvard Press.

Bruner, J. (1960). *The process of education.* Cambridge, MA: Harvard University Press.

Bush, R., & Allen, D. (1964). *A new design for high school education.* New York: McGraw-Hill.

California State Department of Education, Middle Grades Task Force. (1987). *Caught in the middle.* Sacramento, CA: California State Department of Education.

Carnegie Council for Adolescent Development. (1989). *Turning points: Preparing American youth for the 21st century.* Washington, DC: Author.

Caught in the Middle. (1987). Sacramento, CA: California State Department of Education, Middle Grades Task Force.

Children's Defense Fund. (1988). *Making the middle grades work.* Washington, DC: Children's Defense Fund.

Combs, A. (1982). *A personal approach to teaching.* Boston: Allyn and Bacon.

Combs, A., Aspy, D., Brown, D., Clute, M., & Hicks, L. (1975). *Humanistic education: Objectives and assessment.* Washington, DC: Association for Supervision and Curriculum Development.

Curtis, T. E., & Bidwell, W. W. (1977). Curriculum and instruction for emerging adolescents. Reading, MA: Addison-Wesley.

Dewey, J. (1938). *Experience and education.* New York: Macmillan.

Doll, R. C. (1989). *Curriculum improvement: Decision making and process.* Boston: Allyn and Bacon.

Educational Policies Commission. (1944). *Education for all American youth.* Washington, DC: National Education Association.

Eichhorn, D. H. (1972). The emerging adolescent school of the future—Now. In J. G.

Saylor (Ed.). *The school of the future—Now.* Washington, DC: Association for Supervision and Curriculum Development.

Eichhorn, D. H. (1966, 1987). *The middle school.* Originally published in New York by The Center for Applied Research in Education. Reprinted by the National Middle School Association, Columbus, OH, and the National Association of Secondary School Principals, Reston, VA.

Freire, P. (1985). *The politics of education.* Amherst, MA: Bergin and Garvey.

Gage, N.L. (Ed.). (1976). *The psychology of teaching methods.* Chicago, IL: University of Chicago.

Gagné, R. (1967). Curriculum research in the promotion of learning. In R. Tyler, R. Gagné, & M. Scriven, Eds. *Perspectives of curriculum evaluation.* Chicago: Rand McNally.

Giroux, H. (1981). *Ideology, culture and the process of schooling.* Philadelphia: Temple University Press.

Goodman, P. (1970). *New reformation.* New York: Random House.

Great Britain Central Advisory Council. (1967). *Children and their primary schools.* A report of the Central Advisory Council for Education (England), Vols. 1 and 2. London: Her Majesty's Stationery Office.

Greene, M. (1978). *Landscapes of learning.* New York: Columbia University, Teachers' College Press.

Holt, J. (1972). *Freedom and beyond.* New York: Dutton.

Jacobs, H. H., (Ed.). (1989). *Interdisciplinary curriculum: Design and implementation.* Alexandria, VA: Association for Supervision and Curriculum Development.

Jacobs, H. H. (1991). Planning for curriculum integration. *Educational Leadership 49 2,* 27–28.

Kaufman, R. A. (1972). *Educational system planning.* Englewood Cliffs, NJ: Prentice-Hall.

Klausmeier, H. J. (1977). *Individually guided education in elementary and middle schools: A handbook for implementors and college instructors.* Reading, MA: Addison-Wesley.

Kohl, H. R. (1969). *The open classroom.* New York: Random House.

Kohlberg, L. (1971). Stages of moral development as the basis for moral education. In C. Beck, B. S. Crittenden, & E. Sullivan (Eds.). *Moral education: Interdisciplinary approaches.* Toronto: University of Toronto Press.

Kozol, J. (1972). *Free schools.* Boston: Houghton Mifflin.

Lessinger, L. (1971). Accountability for results. In L. Lessinger, & R. Tyler (Eds.). *Accountability in education.* Worthington, OH: Charles Jones.

Lipsitz, J. (1984). *Successful schools for young adolescents.* East Brunswick, NJ: Transaction.

Lounsbury, J. H., & Vars, G. F. (1978). *A curriculum for the middle school years.* New York: Harper & Row.

MacDonald, J.B. (1978). Curriculum theory. In J. R. Gress and D. E. Purpel (Eds.). *Curriculum: An introduction to the field.* Berkeley, CA: McCutchan.

Maslow, A. H. (1970). *Motivation and personality.* New York: Harper & Row.

McNeil, J. (1990). *Curriculum: A comprehensive introduction.* Glenview, IL: Scott, Foresman.

Metcalf, L. E., (ed.). (1971). *Values education.* Washington, DC: National Council for the Social Studies.

Moss, T. (1969). *Middle school.* New York: Houghton Mifflin.

Myers, C. B., & Myers, L. K. (1990). *An introduction to teaching and schools.* Fort Worth, TX: Holt, Rinehart and Winston.

Newmann, F. M. (1988). *Higher-order thinking in high school social studies: An analysis of classrooms.* National Center on Effective Secondary Schools. Madison, WI: University of Wisconsin.

Ornstein, A. C., & Hunkins, F. P. (1988). *Curriculum: Foundations, principles, and issues.* Englewood Cliffs, NJ: Prentice-Hall.

Phenix, P. (1961). The use of the disciplines as curriculum content. *Educational Forum, 26 3,* 273–280.

Popham, J. W., & Baker, E. (1970). *Systematic instruction.* Englewood Cliffs, NJ: Prentice-Hall.

Popham, J. W., Eisner, E. W, Sullivan, H. J., & Tyler, R. L. (1969). *Instructional objectives.* Chicago: Rand McNally.

Raths, L. E., Harmin, M., & Simon, S. B. (1978). *Values and teaching.* New York: Merrill/Macmillan.

Redfern, G. B. (1980). *Evaluating teachers and administrators: A performance objectives approach.* Boulder, CO: Westview Press.

Rogers, C. K. (1983). *Freedom to learn in the 80's.* New York: Merrill/Macmillan.

Rogers, V., & Church, B. (Eds.). (1975). *Open education: Critique and assessment.* Washington, DC: Association for Supervision and Curriculum Development.

Saylor, J. G., Alexander, W., & Lewis, A. (1981). *Curriculum planning for better teaching and learning.* New York: Holt, Rinehart & Winston.

Schwab, J., & Brandwein, P. F. (1962). *The teaching of science.* Cambridge, MA: Harvard University Press.

Shapiro, S. B. (1987). The instructional values of humanistic educators: An expanded empirical analysis. *Journal of Humanistic Education and Development, 24 (3),* 155–170.

Simon, H. (1957). *Models of men.* New York: John Wiley.

Squire, J. R. (Ed.). (1972). *A new look at progressive education.* Washington, DC: Association for Supervision and Curriculum Development .

Sternberg, R. J. (1985a). Critical thinking: Its nature, measurement, and improvement. In F. R. Link, Ed., *Essays on the intellect.* Alexandria, VA: Association for Supervision and Curriculum Development.

Sternberg, R. J. (1985b). *Beyond IQ: A triarchic theory of human intelligence.* New York: Cambridge University Press.

Stratemeyer, F., Forkner, H., Margaret, G., McKim, M. G., & Passow, H. (1957). *Developing a curriculum for modern living.* New York: Columbia University, Teachers' College Press.

Taba, H. (1962). *Curriculum development: Theory into practice.* New York: Harcourt Brace Jovanovich.

Tanner, D., & Tanner, L. (1980). *Curriculum development: Theory into practice.* New York: Macmillan.

Toffler, A. (Ed.). (1974). *Learning for tomorrow, the role of future in education.* New York: Random House.

Turning points: Preparing American youth for the 21st century. (1989). Washington, DC: Carnegie Council for Adolescent Development.

Tyler, R. (1949). *Basic principles of curriculum and instruction.* Chicago: University of Chicago.

Tyler, R. (1956). The curriculum—Then and now. In *Proceedings of the 1956 invitational conference on testing problems.* Princeton, NJ: Educational Testing Service.

Van Til, W., Vars, G. F., & Lounsbury, J. H. (1967). *Modern education for the junior high school years.* Indianapolis, IN: Bobbs-Merrill.

Vars, G. F. (1969). A contemporary view of the core curriculum. In G. Vars, Ed., *Common learnings: Core and interdisciplinary team approaches.* Scranton, PA: International Textbook Company.

Vars, G. F. (1987). *Interdisciplinary teaching in the middle grades.* Columbus, OH: National Middle School Association.

Wann, F., Lamprey, A., Merritt, J., Sansbury, A., & Splittgerber, S. (1991). *Relationships.* Columbia, SC: Irmo Middle School, Campus R.
Weinstein, G., & Fantini, M. D. (1970). *Toward humanistic education: A curriculum of affect.* New York: Praeger.
Wiles, J., & Bondi, J. (1986). *The essential middle school.* Tampa, FL: Wiles & Bondi.
Zais, R. (1976). *Curriculum principles and foundations.* New York: Thomas Crowell.

CHAPTER OUTLINE

- Overview
- Interdisciplinary Approaches
  - Planning Integrated Curriculum Units
  - Contexts for Planning the Middle Level Curriculum
- Social Studies
- Language Arts
  - Developmentally Appropriate Instruction
- Science
- Mathematics
- Integration of Curriculum Dimensions and Contexts
- Summary
- Exploration
- Suggested Readings
- References

The Middle Level Curriculum

social studies, language arts, science, and mathematics

7

OVERVIEW

The responsive middle level school provides developmentally appropriate curricular areas and instructional practices designed to enhance young adolescents' academic, social, and personal growth. So far, we have discussed the general principles of curriculum design and have seen the importance of integrating the middle level curriculum into the personal lives and expanding social world of young adolescent learners. This curriculum framework also provides the means to connect social studies, language arts, science, and mathematics content into an integrated whole for the middle level learner.

In this chapter, the focus is on innovative and exemplary practices in each content area. Our recommendations will use as the starting point the standards and guidelines of the National Council for the Social Studies (Social Studies), the National Council of Teachers of English (Language Arts), the American Association for the Advancement of Science and National Science Teachers Association (Science), and the National Council of Teachers of Mathematics (Mathematics). This chapter will assist middle level educators in providing requisite integrated educational experiences in these basic content areas. A middle level curriculum in which personal, social, and academic experiences are integrated into the home, school, and community environments of the young adolescent should foster the development of a learning community.

In this chapter, you will read about:

1 Directions that middle level social studies, language arts, science, and mathematics will take during the 1990s and beyond.
2 Goals of social studies, language arts, science, and mathematics curriculum.
3 Content and skills appropriate for social studies, language arts, science, and mathematics curriculum.
4 Current issues in social studies, language arts, science, and mathematics.
5 The implications of computers and other technological advances for social studies, language arts, science, and mathematics curriculum.
6 Values imparted by social studies, language arts, science, and mathematics to young adolescents.
7 Interdisciplinary approaches that are most appropriate for integrating social studies, language arts, science, and mathematics.

INTERDISCIPLINARY APPROACHES

We saw in Chapter 6 that the middle level curriculum is divided into three dimensions—personal, academic, and social. To integrate these dimensions into a balanced curriculum framework requires interdisciplinary topics, themes, or units from the various subject matters. In addition, it involves the establishment of interdisciplinary teams and a team organization. An integrated approach uses interdisciplinary content so that young adolescents experience an integrated, holistic viewpoint of content and skills.

Integrated units are recommended as the means to connect the academic content of a middle level curriculum with the personal needs and social concerns of young adolescents. According to Vars (1987), some criteria that might help in the planning of an integrated unit could include: (1) understanding by teachers and learners, (2) interest expressed by learners and teachers, (3) the necessary instructional resources, (4) activities involving field trips and experiments, and (5) units six to eight weeks in length. Figure 7.1 includes some guidelines that could be employed in planning an integrated unit.

Units can be designed as topics or themes for infusion into the existing courses of study. This approach permits content to be added systematically, and the topics and themes eventually become an integral part of the curriculum. The disadvantages are that it is difficult to select what standard content may be omitted, and also, in-depth treatment of specific themes may not be possible which could result in spotty and uneven coverage of important topics and concepts.

Another strategy is to make integrated units an extension of existing units. This approach adds interdisciplinary content to the lessons in traditional courses and allows flexibility in the placement and length of topics and themes. The disadvantage is the fact that superficial and unsystematic treatment of interdisciplinary content could result.

Integrated units should:

1 Review goals and objectives for that grade level and/or subject
2 Review the curriculum scope and sequence
3 Determine the type of integrated unit that will be attempted: correlated, fused, or purely problem centered
4 Brainstorm themes, topics, or problem areas that are interdisciplinary and appear relevant to students
5 Involve students in all stages of planning, with teachers and students arriving jointly at decisions
6 Select one or two themes, topics, or problem areas for further development
7 Explore the contributions of each subject area to the unit, including pertinent content, skills, and learning activities
8 Develop an overall framework or outline of the unit
9 Invite students to help in locating learning materials and other resources
10 Plan procedures for evaluating student learning
11 Determine logistics, including time frame, student groupings, rooms, and equipment
12 Implement the unit while seeking student participation at all points
13 Evaluate the unit

FIGURE 7.1 Guidelines for planning integrated units *(Adapted from* Interdisciplinary Teaching in the Middle Grades *by G. F. Vars, 1987, Columbus, OH: National Middle School Association. Adapted by permission of NMSA.)*

The creation of entire separate interdisciplinary units is another approach. This method may raise the issue of whether these units should be elective or part of the regular curriculum. A separate unit approach organizes the content into interdisciplinary units and permits in-depth, coherent, and sustained study of various interrelationships among the academic subjects. These units must be carefully constructed so that the basic and important concepts of the various disciplines are learned. The disadvantage of this approach is that it may be difficult to sustain because resources for staff development are lacking, because of constant mandates from the various academic disciplines and state education departments for the inclusion of certain content, and because of the complexity of organizing content selected from various disciplines. There is no broad theory of knowledge that incorporates existing academic disciplines into integrated units. In Chapter 6, we have provided an ecological orientation that we hope will serve as a foundation for a comprehensive, integrated curriculum.

Another approach is to have language arts teachers go across the grades found in a given middle level school. Under this approach, language arts is taught by teams from different grades. It is also possible to have students from grades 6, 7, and 8 have combined instruction in a content field. There is more variability in the interdisciplinary team that functions across grade levels than within a grade level. For example, teachers from four different subject areas can form a team to provide instruction across sixth, seventh, and eighth grades at a given time in a particular schedule. Usually, a theme is identified and each teacher may have a part of the lesson.

In the past, interdisciplinary courses have been poorly organized with teachers and students floundering from the lack of knowledge and firsthand acquaintance with the concepts of the various disciplines. Without some framework for understanding the various disciplines, it is difficult to determine which content is important. Teachers may become overwhelmed because integrated materials require a tremendous range of knowledge, teaching materials, planning, and support.

PLANNING INTEGRATED CURRICULUM UNITS

To develop an integrated curriculum, an action plan is needed. According to Jacobs (1991), such a plan has four phases. Phases one and two are planned and implemented during the first year. Phase three is conducted during the second year and phase four during the third year. In *phase one,* teachers concentrate on an internal investigation of their current knowledge of curriculum and also investigate external approaches from the field. The prospective teacher might want to review the literature and visit some middle level schools to see how the curriculum is organized as a part of a practicum experience. For experienced teachers on the middle level, an internal investigation is conducted by teachers currently organized into grade levels, departments, or interdisciplinary teams. The school calendar is broken down into units of study taught during each month of the school year. Each teacher outlines his or her monthly units of study. The result should be to: (1) have a scope and sequence of when students are studying subjects, (2) realign subjects that would benefit from concurrent teaching, (3) reduce repetition from year to year, and (4) identify possibilities for multidisciplinary or interdisciplinary units of study (Jacobs, 1991). In addition, the eight contexts we discussed in Chapter 6 may be used as a guide to assess how well the current curriculum is meeting young adolescents' needs.

The external investigation expands teachers' awareness of the various relevant curriculum projects going on in the middle level. Through conferences, site visits, and in-service courses, teachers are encouraged to investigate best practices and options for integrating the curriculum. Possible topics that might be chosen for further study might include team-building processes, scheduling alternatives, exploratory options, and cooperative learning. Several of the contexts may need to be studied in more depth in order for integrated units to take place.

In *phase two,* a proposal is brainstormed for integrating the curriculum. The contexts in Figure 6.3 and Table 6.5 could be used as an approach for planning an integrated curriculum. Based on previous work in phase one, potential areas are identified for multidisciplinary or interdisciplinary work. The starting-point is usually to take an existing unit and integrate several disciplines into a two- to six-week unit. A pilot unit is designed to cover a specific time frame. The proposal must include budget, time lines, teachers' responsibilities, and how the unit will be evaluated. There is a need to provide a long-term agenda so that the experimental nature and short-term pilot program can be seen as being integrated into the curriculum. Each of the contexts in Chapter 6 should be used to assess the progress of the pilot program.

During the second year, in *phase three,* implementation and monitoring take place. Most pilot units are planned for two to six weeks. During the pilot, teachers evaluate student learning, decision-making, relationships that develop between team members, time allocations, and resource materials. According to Jacobs (1991), one possible outcome is collegial collaboration. Another result of the pilot is essential feedback on student growth. Teachers are continuously assessing student outcomes during the program. The data collected from the pilot unit assist the staff members in planning revisions to the unit.

In *phase four,* staff members are able to make revisions in the program based on the pilot data and then adopt the program as a permanent part of the curriculum. To adopt the pilot, there must be a modification or replacement of whatever was offered previously. For instance, the middle level course guide will state that this is an environmental unit instead of separate science, social studies, or technology courses.

CONTEXTS FOR PLANNING THE MIDDLE LEVEL CURRICULUM

As part of organizing the middle level curriculum, eight contexts are embedded in all curricula at the middle level to ensure the personal, social, and intellectual development of young adolescents. Each context should be used as a guide in planning a developmentally appropriate curriculum for young adolescents. These contexts are used as planning indicators in curriculum development. At the end of the curriculum and instruction sequence, the same contexts serve as evaluative indicators to assess student learning outcomes (See Table 6.5 in Chapter 6 for more detailed information).

SOCIAL STUDIES

The National Council of Social Studies has recently articulated a definition of social studies as "the integration of history, the social sciences and the humanities to promote civic competence" (McGuire, 1992, p.1). The term *civic competence* implies a broad interdisciplinary content basis for connecting this essential goal of schooling in a democratic society. Civic competence incorporates the role of a citizen in the broadest context and is the primary purpose for social studies. Because of the increasing diversity of our nation and the interdependence of all of the nations of the world, civic competence is essential to the survival of this country. The global citizen must have a broad base of knowledge and understand the personal and social issues facing each person individually, and the world collectively, as the twenty-first century approaches.

There continues to be concern over how far-reaching the integration of social studies subject matter should be. If the definition is expanded too far, social studies may lose its identity. However, social studies may be the key to integrating the middle level curriculum. Currently, when social studies teachers teach, they already are drawing on interdisciplinary subject matter from various disciplines. Students can see the connections between various subject matter areas because of the interdisciplinary nature of social studies. A major goal of social studies on the middle level is to have an integrated curriculum at every level (McGuire, 1992).

As social studies prepares citizens for the future, there appear to be many challenges facing middle level programs. According to Davis (1987), the social studies curriculum is occasionally based on developmentally appropriate needs and interests of young adolescents. The current middle level social studies curriculum has been influenced by the innovative curricular projects developed over the last three decades and by today's insistent demands for basic skills instruction and higher standards of student achievement. Research in social studies has suggested that social studies is one of the least interesting and most irrelevant subjects in the school curriculum. Student dislike increases with each grade level (Shaughnessy and Haladyna, 1985). This lack of interest may be in part due to the heavy emphasis on reading, the endless questions to be answered at the end of the chapter, and the repetitive nature of certain courses, such as American history.

Developmental Needs

The National Council for the Social Studies, Task Force on Social Studies in the Middle School (1991) recommended that the social studies curriculum be organized around the unique developmental needs of the young adolescent in order to provide a more relevant curriculum. The NCSS Middle School Task Force identified three areas of developmentally appropriate needs. These were physical, social/emotional, and intellectual characteristics. The physical needs are focused on physical changes such as hormonal imbalances that might affect the development of self-esteem and sense of self-identity. Social/emotional needs suggested that the search for independence and self-identity among young adolescents is challenged by a sense of dependence on adults and peers and by the wish to conform to the peer group. In conforming to peer groups, young adolescents may run counter to the social expectations of their parents and other adults. Young adolescents' assessment of their personal self-worth is based on their perception of their acceptance by adults and peers, their academic and athletic success, and their appearance. Lastly, the intellectual needs of young adolescents are characterized by variations in thinking and attention spans, curiosity, imagination, and a wide range of interests.

Motifs for Integrating Social Studies Content

In planning the social studies curriculum utilizing the three categories of developmentally appropriate needs, the NCSS Task Force on Social Studies in the Middle School (1991) recommended four basic themes for an integrated curriculum. To avoid confusion with the term "theme", the term *motif* was used. The four motifs are categories of concern shared by individuals and the larger society. These motifs should function throughout the curriculum to personalize academic instruction, to increase the relevance of the curriculum for young adolescents, and to connect classroom instruction to societal imperatives. The first motif is *concern with self: development of self-esteem and a strong sense of identity* (NCSS Task Force, 1991, p. 288). This motif addresses concerns related to self-esteem, physical growth and change, and relations with peers within the contexts of history, culture, and humanities.

The second motif focuses on *concern for right and wrong: development of ethics* (NCSS Task Force, 1991, p. 288). Ethics questions have become a major concern of business and government. For the young adolescent, the middle level represents an environment in which the personal standards, values, and beliefs are molded that will guide their decisions and actions now and later in their lives and, thus, influence society. The middle level may well represent the last best chance to provide a strong sense of right and wrong to guide students toward problem solving and decision making that internalize the highest ethical standards.

The third motif centers on *concern for others: development of group and other-centeredness* (NCSS Task Force, 1991, p. 289). Students become responsible members of a society through interacting with other adults and peers from diverse backgrounds. Concern for minorities and oppressed people is natural at this age, and with encouragement can lead to a commitment of community service. Among the most effective methods for promoting skills and values of civic competence is service to school and community.

The fourth motif is directed toward the young adolescent's *concern for the world: development of a global perspective* (NCSS Task Force, 1991, p. 289). A global perspective includes an awareness of the pluralistic, interdependent, and changing nature of the world community. To develop this global perspective, middle level students must be engaged in an examination of persistent global issues and the elements of human values and cultures as well as global systems and history. These motifs should help integrate the personal, social, and academic dimensions already proposed in Chapter 6. These social studies motifs could serve as the personal and social themes for organizing integrated units across the various academic content.

The middle level social studies program should be broad-based and should extend over many content areas, including: (1) interrelated knowledge from social sciences, humanities, natural sciences, and media, (2) informational and technical skills, (3) democratic values, and (4) social participation opportunities. Through the cooperative efforts of teachers, students, parents, administrators, and community, the middle level social studies programs should provide content of compelling interest; a broad spectrum of skills that empower young people to think creatively, critically, and independently; values education programs that emphasize the development of competent, confident, and committed citizens; and learning experiences designed to enhance the social, personal, and intellectual development of young adolescents.

Recent statements from the National Council for the Social Studies have classified social studies goals into *knowledge, beliefs, skills,* and *social participation.* Historically, knowledge has been the primary focus of middle level social studies, with the high schools dictating the content selection for the middle level. The importance of skills in the middle level social studies curriculum is difficult to determine. Skills and knowledge support each other, and the emphasis on basic skills has not left time for the logical development of social studies skills. The beliefs and values of middle level learners have ranged from unquestioned acceptance of imposed adult beliefs to questioning of traditional beliefs and values. Because of the difficulty of structuring social action experiences outside of the classroom and the overemphasis on academic content, social participation has not been widely accepted as a goal on the middle level. As a goal, social participation should be one of the essential developmentally appropriate areas of the middle level curriculum.

Goal 1: Knowledge. This goal provides the facts, concepts, and generalizations that help young adolescents understand human beings and their needs. Knowledge provides the basis for values and beliefs and is the vehicle for the development of skills. Traditionally, social studies has grouped concepts by the disciplines they represent, such as psychology, sociology, anthropology, geography, economics, political science, and history. History and geography are the major content emphases found in social studies. In addition, the California *History and Social Science Framework* (1988) stresses essential learnings by developing student literacy in history, geography, economics, sociology, political science, and humanities, including ethics.

Middle level social studies knowledge must be organized to reflect the developmentally appropriate needs of young adolescents. One approach in the middle level is to organize these diverse subject matter areas into a conceptual framework. Concepts are defined as mental constructs and/or abstractions that enable students to classify ideas, information, and experiences. Concepts usually are organized and classified around subject matter areas and are arranged from simple to complex. Understanding these concepts and their characteristics is essential to the development of interdisciplinary units. In interdisciplinary units, students would be asked to compare and contrast social science terms, ideas, and information taken from these fields. Once the social sciences have been understood, concepts could be expanded across other subject areas such as science, language arts, fine arts, etc. An understanding of concepts and how to conceptualize enables the young adolescent to solve problems, to interpret aspects of the physical and social setting, and to develop generalizations in social studies as well as other content areas. It is important that middle level social studies teachers employ concept-based teaching strategies that will enable young adolescents to develop competence and confidence in this essential element of higher-order thinking.

Goal 2: Democratic Beliefs and Values. This second category forms another basis from which middle level social studies goals are selected. Beliefs and values are essential to the development of a citizen. Values provide the criteria by which young adolescents judge the appropriateness of their individual behavior and group behavior. In the middle level, values can be organized into four categories: (1) rights of individuals (right of life, liberty, and security), (2) freedoms of individuals (freedom of worship, thought, and assembly), (3) responsibilities of individuals (respect for human life, respect for the rights of others, and tolerance), and (4) beliefs concerning societal conditions and governmental responsibilities (dissenting minorities are protected, and government is elected by the people) (NCSS Task Force, 1989, p. 383). Values are seen in terms of criteria for establishing degrees of goodness, worth, or beauty that guide the thoughts, feelings, and actions of individuals. Beliefs denote commitments to these values. The teaching of values, beliefs, and ethics is a very important area of study for the middle grades. Values education has been an integral part of the middle level social studies program. Values, attitudes, and beliefs have traditionally been taught by *transmission,* the inculcation by adults of the key values necessary for the survival of society. Teachers taught the cherished values and beliefs of the society to students who were passive recipients. In recent years, values instruction has become more open-ended, with students having more opportunities to discuss, select and accept, or reject values. Confusion and conflict often develop and teachers need to be careful not to favor one set of values over another and must clarify that point. Teachers should present values, allow students discussion time, and attempt to bring closure to the discussion.

Values education is an essential element of the middle level social studies program. During the 1960s and 1970s, *valuing* and *values education* using the processes of values inculcation, values clarification, values analysis, moral reasoning, and morality emerged as techniques employed in analyzing value questions, making value judgments, internalizing values, and making appropriate value decisions (Naylor & Diem, 1987). Strategies such as values inculcation, value analysis, values clarification, moral reasoning, and morality are important skills and processes that young adolescents need for effective social involvement, including peer group relationships.

In summary, values education needs to be considered as an essential ingredient for the development of beliefs, attitudes, and values in young adolescents. The controversial nature of values education makes it difficult to maintain continuity in the program. Is the middle level school responsible for the teaching of values, or is the home, or are other institutions in the community responsible? It would appear that there is a societal need for teaching right and wrong, but parents still want to preserve the right to teach certain values in the home. Teachers must strive to expose young adolescents to broadly accepted patterns of behavior while still respecting parental rights to teach certain values. The middle level school's primary responsibilities are to aid in the socialization of the young adolescent and promote the learner's self-concept. Since individuals base decisions on the rationality and objectivity of prior experiences that have shaped their values, beliefs, and behavior, it is important to have active involvement or simulated experiences in the development of values. Middle level social studies teachers need to take advantage of the many opportunities to teach beliefs and values that occur in the ordinary daily life of school and need to plan experiences where personal involvement can take place (NCSS Task Force, 1984; NCSS Task Force, 1989).

Goal 3: Skills. It is difficult to draw a sharp distinction between knowledge and skills because they are so interrelated. Skills mean finding, organizing, and making use of knowledge. A skill is defined as the ability to do something proficiently in repeated performances (NCSS Task Force, 1989, p. 378). Skills are essential to young adolescents in learning concepts, searching for information, and gaining insight into values and beliefs.

Skills essential to citizen participation in civic affairs for the middle level can be grouped as follows: acquiring information (this includes reading skills, study skills, reference skills, technical skills); organizing and using information (this includes thinking skills, decision-making skills, and metacognitive skills); and interpersonal relationships and social participation (this includes personal skills, group interaction skills, and social and political participation skills) (NCSS Task Force, 1989, pp. 386–387). These three categories of skills should guide middle level teachers in developing skill competencies for problem solving and decision making in their students. Each category of skills should appear in some form in the social studies curriculum of the middle grades. Because skills are important to learning concepts, information processing, problem solving, and decision making, social studies skills should be analyzed at the middle level for the interpretation of content, the promotion of civic participation, and the development of value and social interaction strategies.

Goal 4: Social Participation. This area should be the focal point for social studies on the middle level. A democracy can only be effective with the direct involvement of its citizens. Parker (1991) suggested that "participatory citizenship is the sustained opportunity to talk frankly about pressing public issues" (p. 77). One approach to active participation in the middle level is "to focus content and instruction more directly on how most people participate in society—how they spend their time and where they put their energy" (Morrissett, 1982, p. 118). This program utilizes the various roles that characterize a person's social life, such as citizen, worker, consumer, family member, friend, member of social groups, and self. Each of these defines a distinct area of social life in which nearly all young adolescents participate. The roles imply a specific set of interrelated relationships and functions. On the middle level, social participation is essential to the development of the personal and social aspects of young adolescents. In fact, *Turning Points* (1989) recommended that community service credits be awarded for service activities provided by young adolescents in the community.

Social studies programs offer numerous opportunities for social participation where young adolescents can engage in the kind of exploratory activities that are essential for the development of citizenship. Additionally, social studies involves much knowledge and many skills that students will need in varying degrees. There are, however, ideas, activities, and areas of study in social studies that appeal to students, and which they want to study in more detail. Those students who want to study a particular exploratory topic focus on that topic while other students may elect to study other topics. These exploratory topics may or may not be curriculum essentials or needs but they do represent topics that evoke interest in learners so that they *want* to study in those areas. Exploratory activities enable young adolescents to learn independently and collaboratively.

Effective social studies instructional practices on the middle level must be appropriate to the personal, social, and academic needs of young adolescents. The NCSS Task Force on Social Studies in the Middle School (1991) recommended that appropriate instructional practices included experiential learning, integrated curriculum units, cooperative learning, heterogeneous groups addressing controversial issues, performance-based assessment, decision making strategies, and extending the classroom into the community. Social studies content can be adapted to many organizational patterns which may be utilized for exploration, such as independent study, small-group discussion, research teams, advisor–advisee sessions, values seminars, and mini-courses. Other activities, such as social science fair projects, debates, socio-drama, journals, and community projects have provided students with cognitive and affective learnings of an exploratory nature. Some middle level students may choose to participate in values-related seminars, personal improvement courses, and classes emphasizing the development of social participation skills. Social studies is a relevant and humane curriculum area with practically limitless possibilities for exploratory study.

In summary, the goals of content knowledge, democratic values and beliefs, skills, and social participation are essential elements of a dynamic and interactive middle level social studies program. It is imperative that each of the four goals be fully represented in teaching and learning situations because of their importance in the personal, social, and academic development of young adolescents.

It appears from these findings and research results over the past two decades that a concerted effort is needed on the middle level to have an interactive, holistic, interdisciplinary approach to social studies. The National Council for the Social Studies Task Force (NCSS, 1989) recommended an interactive, holistic approach, stating that

> content at *any* grade level should be presented in ways that provide, in so far as possible, a comprehensive view of a complex whole. Topics may be regarded as part of an interacting network that often extends worldwide. People everywhere arrange themselves in social groups and engage in basic social processes. The earth is the home of human beings no matter where they live individually. Potentially, all human beings can share in the legacies derived from all cultures. Subject matter

at all grade levels needs to be taught from a global perspective. This approach is *interactive* because everything relates to everything else; it is *holistic* because it casts events in their broadest social context.*

An interactive, holistic approach, that looks for common relationships in the broadest knowledge and social contexts—language arts, social studies, mathematics, science, and fine arts—might provide a meaningful curriculum for all learners, especially middle level learners. Middle level schools are in a unique position to accomplish this type of change.

Scope and Sequence

The term *scope* refers to the range of substantive content, values, skills, and learner experiences that should be included in a middle level social studies program. Ideally, the scope should define the parameters of content, values, skills, and learner experiences found in the curriculum. In contrast, the *sequence* is the order in which the components appear in the curriculum. Generally, topics that are spatially, temporarily, or psychologically close to learners have traditionally appeared early in the program. This "expanding horizons" approach of arranging topics, from the familiar to the far away and from the here-and-now to the past, has been used in elementary social studies curricula with resulting impact on the scope and sequence of the middle level.

Scope and sequence for social studies programs are characterized by the similarity of course offerings in middle level schools throughout the United States, with some variation caused by local mandates. The dominant patterns are Grade 5—United States History, Grade 6—World Cultures and Western Hemisphere, Grade 7—World Geography and/or World History, and Grade 8—American History and/or state history.

Social studies in *Grade 5: People of the Americas: The United States and its Close Neighbors* focuses on the development of the United States as a nation in the Western hemisphere, with particular emphasis on its guiding principles, its diversity, and those individuals who have made significant contributions. The geography and history of Canada and Mexico are included (NCSS, 1991, p. 289). Global education advocates a thematic approach to U.S. history, with special attention to the concepts of interdependence, conflict, scarcity, and human rights, as well as the thoughts that make the United States unique.

Grade 6: People and Cultures: Representative World Regions centers on selected peoples and cultures of the eastern hemisphere and Latin America, representative of major geographic regions, levels of economic development, historical development, and political and value systems (NCSS, 1991, p. 289). Global education focuses on Africa, Latin America, and Asia, with emphasis on concepts of change, culture, conflict, interdependence, and development. The relationship of the world region to the United States is examined throughout the year.

---

*Reprinted from "In Search of a Scope and Sequence for Social Studies" by the NCSS Task Force on Scope and Sequence (1989). *Social Education, 53*(6), p. 379. Copyright © 1989 by The National Council for Social Studies. Reprinted by permission of NCSS.

Social studies curriculum for *Grade 7: A Changing World of Many Nations: A Global View* looks globally at geographic features such as climate, land use, population, natural resources, boundaries, cultures, nations, and the history of selected countries from a historical perspective and from modern geopolitical contexts. This content is usually a continuation of the Grade 6 curriculum. At least one semester is devoted solely to Latin America, either at Grade 6 or 7. Global education stresses functions of major global systems, with the first semester focused on economic systems and interdependence and the second semester stressing the political system. In addition, the history, geography, and government of the middle level learner's home state may be studied in Grade 7 (NCSS, 1991, p. 289).

Social studies in *Grade 8: Building a Strong and Free Nation: The United States* covers the chronological development of the United States as an independent democratic nation. It includes exploration, colonization, formation of the government, westward movement, growth of industries and cities, slavery and the Civil War, and the United States as a world power. The primary emphasis is on social history, economic development, global affairs and international relations, and the personal side of history—such as how ordinary people carry on their family life, work, and leisure. Global education begins with an analysis of the basic values of the society of the United States: individual freedoms and rights, work ethics, majority rule, and equity. It then takes a similar approach to the study of non-Western traditions. State history may be included in this grade level, depending on various state requirements (NCSS, 1991, p. 289).

Developmental research suggests that middle level learners should be able to make observations about their environment, hypothesize about cause-and-effect relationships, and begin to consider alternatives and their consequences for problem solving. Concepts, skills, and values should be introduced at entry levels and should be continually reinforced and applied by extending, expanding, and providing more depth as the learner is ready. Middle level scope and sequence deals with relating content, values, skills, and learner experiences.

The National Council for the Social Studies Task Force on Scope and Sequence (1989) suggested criteria for the selection of a scope and sequence. These criteria range from stating the purpose and rationale of the program to being internally consistent, integrating skills and knowledge across subject areas, reflecting a global perspective, building self-esteem, incorporating thinking skills and interpersonal skills at all levels, providing opportunities for learning, and practicing the skills of participation that have the potential to excite students. Three scope-and-sequence models were identified that most closely met these criteria: the *goals model*, based on knowledge, values, skills, and participation; the *thematic model*, utilizing themes of cultural heritage, global perspectives, tradition and change, technology, citizenship, etc.; and a *global model*, emphasizing the study of systems, human values, and persistent issues and problems. However, the task force did not recommend any one scope and sequence and did little to clarify the scope and sequence issue on the middle level.

On the middle level, it needs to be clarified whether the emphasis should be on American history or state history in grade 8. Also, continuing questions over emphasis between geography and world history in grades 6 and 7 need to be analyzed. The fact that elementary textbook series usually are designed through grade 6, with grades 7 and 8 organized as separate disciplines more closely tied to the high school curriculum, causes serious scope-and-sequence problems for middle level grades. Due to recent reforms at state and national levels, the focus on the basic skills of reading, writing, and arithmetic in the elementary school through the middle level has reduced the amount of time devoted to teaching social studies.

Although students tend to characterize social studies as boring and irrelevant, Goodlad in *A Place Called School* (1984) found social studies to have great human interest, with many topics seemingly high in interest to young adolescents. However, in his study of actual schools, he found student interest low. He observed that social studies classroom activities focused on listening, reading textbooks, doing workbooks and worksheets, and taking quizzes. Goodlad concluded that students lack interest in social studies because the human interest has been removed and the content reduced to dates and places that young adolescents have to memorize. Parker (1991) suggested that students' interest could be promoted by making social studies more relevant to their present experiences and career interests and more exciting by designing the lessons to become more engaging. In summary, middle level educators need to develop a social studies curriculum based on the social, personal, and academic needs of young adolescents that is relevant, exciting, and challenging. It is beyond the scope of this book to study all the issues involved in scope and sequence, but helpful references are provided in Figure 7.2.

Education for Citizenship in a Democracy

Citizenship has meant different things to different people at different times, due to diverse beliefs about the proper relationship of a citizen to the larger society. On the middle level, the debate continues over whether the emphasis should be on knowledge, on skills, on values, or on social participation, in order to promote the development of essential democratic behavior. Identifying what democratic behavior is necessary does not have one simple answer. In a complex, culturally diverse society like the United States, there are many groups, institutions, and ideologies competing for the allegiance of the young adolescent. Since schools probably cannot be the primary source of knowledge about citizenship, and the social sciences are hesitant to deal directly with citizenship, there is a need to establish appropriate means to develop democratic behavior in school and community settings (Longstreet, 1985). Other scholars, such as Leming (1989), have argued that it is difficult to justify citizenship as the sole province of social studies because citizenship goals overlap other subject areas, such as science. Leming maintains that teachers and theorists disagree on how to define the purposes of social studies. For example, what political participation of a citizen is desirable has been debated not only by political theorists, but also to a limited extent by social studies theorists. One promising trend in this area is the social-psychological perspective of citizenship (Hastie, 1986; Fishbein &

Bradley Commission on History in the Schools. (1988). *Building a history curriculum: Guidelines for teaching history in schools.* Washington, DC: Educational Excellence Network.

California State Board of Education. (1988). *History-social science framework.* Sacramento, CA: California State Department of Education.

Hartoonian, H. M., & Laughlin, M. A. (1989). Designing a social studies scope and sequence for the 21st century. *Social Education, 53*(6), 388–398.

National Commission on Social Studies in the Schools. (1989). *Charting a course: Social studies for the 21st century.* Washington, DC.

National Council for Geographic Education. (1984). *Guidelines for geographic education: Elementary and secondary schools.* Washington, DC: National Council for Geographic Education and the Association of American Geographers.

National Council for the Social Studies, Task Force on Social Studies in the Middle School. (1991). Social studies in the middle school. *Social Education, 55*(5), 287–293.

National Council for the Social Studies, Task Force on Scope and Sequence. (1989). In search of a scope and sequence for social studies. *Social Education, 53*(6), 376–385.

FIGURE 7.2 Scope and sequence in the social studies curriculum: useful sources

Ajzen, 1975; Rumelhardt & Norman, 1978). This approach to citizenship is primarily concerned with social influences on citizen's action and behavior. However, there continues to be a lively debate as to the most appropriate activities to develop citizens in the middle level social studies program.

Global Perspectives

As social studies aspires to prepare young adolescents for their future roles as citizens in an interdependent world, the emphasis should be on themes of global interdependence, the world environment, dependence on human beings throughout the world, and the need for a "world citizen" who views issues and events in a global perspective. In a position statement for global education in social studies, Chapman et al. (1982) stated that "social studies should assume a major role in providing students with opportunities (1) to learn to perceive and understand the world as a global system, and (2) to see themselves as participants in that system, recognizing the benefits, costs, rights and responsibilities inherent in such participation" (pp. 36–37). In a more recent statement, Kniep (1989) suggested that the themes for global perspectives were: (1) interdependence (how citizens live in a world of interrelated systems in which people interact to make a unified global perspective); (2) change (the process of movement from one state to another is universal and an inevitable part of global living); (3) culture (the environment and systems of beliefs, values, tradition, language, customs, and institutions are a way of meeting human demands in a given physical environment through interaction with other cultures); (4) scarcity (an imbalance exists for deciding how scarce resources are distributed for unlimited wants); (5) conflict (nations and individuals have differing values and opposing goals that result in tension and violence, requiring skills to maintain coexistence). Middle level social studies should stress global interdependence; provide transnational and cross-cultural experiences; provide supplementary materials that incorporate an analysis of mass media, e.g., films, television, newscasts, and newspaper articles; and utilize relevant community resources.

One current difficulty is to modify textbooks to reflect this global perspective of citizens more accurately. At the present time, while the global perspective has improved over the past two decades, textbooks still continue to reflect preferences toward American traditions and ethnocentrism (Cortes & Fleming, 1986). Middle level teachers need to take steps toward making global perspectives an integral part of the social studies program for young adolescents.

Many of the world's culturally diverse ethnic groups are represented within the United States. The middle level curriculum should focus on the necessity for young adolescents to understand their own cultural and ethnic heritage in order to appreciate and respect the cultural and ethnic heritage of others. The intent is to reduce prejudice toward the various cultural groups and specific ethnic groups within American society by establishing a curriculum that is multicultural and multiethnic. The outcome is to provide students from various ethnic groups with equal educational opportunities and to encourage them to explore cultural diversity. Banks (1991), one of the primary advocates of multiethnic education, defined the term as encompassing the total educational environment, including ethnic cultures and experiences. Ethnic studies provide the scientific and humanistic study of histories, cultures, and experiences of the ethnic groups within society. Ethnic studies provide an opportunity at the middle level for interdisciplinary involvement and exploratory activities, by combining the content of art, music, drama, reading, literature, home arts, science, and mathematics with the individual's attitudes, beliefs, and values.

In summary, as the social studies curriculum approaches the twenty-first century, it is imperative that the curriculum be integrated. Middle level learners must see the connections between personal concerns, social issues, and global concerns that face every individual in the world. The interdependence of each individual's and nation's survival is dependent on cooperation and collaboration that is undertaken to resolve major environmental, political, social, and economic problems.

Essential Considerations in the Social Studies

There would appear to be many immediate challenges in designing middle level social studies programs that consist of a definition of citizenship, selection of content, a meaningful scope and sequence, teaching thinking, the role of computers and technology, and the future for social studies in general. The cooperative efforts of teachers, students, parents, and administrators are needed to develop dynamic social studies programs in the middle level.

Essential considerations include:

1 A clearer definition of citizenship in light of global interdependency, cultural diversity, and increasing social problems of drugs, crime, and violence.
2 An integrated social studies curriculum based on personal needs and social concerns of young adolescents in order to reduce general dislike of social studies and the feeling that it is boring and irrelevant.
3 A curriculum that provides content of compelling interest; a broad spectrum of skills that empower young people to think creatively, critically, and independently; values education programs that develop competent, confident, and committed citizens; and participation opportunities for personal, social, and intellectual development of young adolescents.
4 An integrative curriculum that permits young adolescents to explore, experience, and develop a meaningful perspective of the world, but at the same time responds to the global concern of preparing competent and compassionate citizens.

LANGUAGE ARTS

Middle level schools should include in developmentally appropriate language arts the areas such as reading, listening, speaking, and writing as interrelated areas. They should also emphasize communication skills that learners can actually use. This expanded view of language arts is appropriate for young adolescents who are making a transition into an expanding social world which requires an increased ability to communicate with others. Our society places importance on language and one's ability to communicate effectively. Language arts programs providing appropriate communicational experiences also contribute to the young adolescent's self-concept and developing sense of identity.

Educators implementing developmentally responsive language arts instruction for middle level students should plan learning experiences that complement young adolescents' intellectual and psychosocial development. Goals of language arts programs include addressing young adolescents' increasing need to read and comprehend written material; to communicate in written form; to listen effectively; and to speak in formal and informal speech situations.

DEVELOPMENTALLY APPROPRIATE INSTRUCTION

Educators planning instruction in reading, writing, listening, and speaking will want to select curriculum content and instruction approaches that are developmentally appropriate for 10- to 14-year-olds. Young adolescents' desire for socialization and independence, their abilities to think and reason, their abilities to see a whole concept rather than only parts, and their recognition that learning can cross subject area lines, allow for integrated language arts approaches, i. e., a lesson that interrelates reading, writing, listening, and speaking. Likewise, language arts programs can be greatly enhanced by interdisciplinary approaches in which instruction occurs "across the curriculum" in such areas as social studies, science, and mathematics. Although these represent only a few means of developing appropriate instruction, perceptive middle level educators, without doubt, will plan other curriculum experiences that reflect young adolescents' intellectual and psychosocial development.

Reading

Reading in the middle level is usually a continuation and extension of the reading program commonly found in the elementary school. Reading, often taught as remedial instruction to young adolescents with inadequate skills, also has other significant roles as learners continue to develop cognitively and become more independent. Specific goals for the middle level include: developing an appreciation for reading; strengthening basic reading skills; shifting attention from learning to read to reading to learn; beginning to read new and more difficult materials in various content areas; and extending appreciations to include literature (Karlin & Karlin, 1987).

Early (1984), a respected reading expert focusing on grades 5 to 12, presents a general overview of the major characteristics of middle level readers. Given the widespread influence of her work on reading at the middle level, her basic descriptions seem worth noting. First, Early suggests that oral reading is fairly accurate and fluent among young adolescents. She suggests that the basics of decoding have been mastered. Limitations in oral reading or word identification are very likely due to limitations in word meaning rather than in "skills for decoding per se." This conclusion is not to suggest that there are not some young adolescents who have problems with reading or decoding. Second, Early concludes that basic reading comprehension skills have been mastered by the time students reach middle level school. Readers at this level deal well with literal aspects of comprehension and can connect details that are rather obviously related. She also points out: "They tend to be literal minded and may, therefore, be confused by metaphors and symbols, and to miss historical and literary allusions because they haven't read widely. They can think critically about text which refers to concrete experiences; they have trouble dealing with abstraction" (p. 83).

Early also concludes that once basic reading skills have been mastered, the need to apply these skills to content area texts should be considered. Dupuis (1984) edited a volume that reviewed available research on reading in the areas of English, social studies, science, foreign languages, mathematics, music, physical education, and health. We cannot comprehensively address Dupuis' extensive work here; however, because this is an issue of vital concern to teachers of young adolescents, interested readers should consult it.

Third, Early (1984) cites as the chief characteristic of middle level readers the fact that they read little. She maintains that their reading is limited because of restricted backgrounds that they bring to the reading of many texts, and their background remains restricted because they fail to use reading as a tool for extending and adding to that background.

In reading, the middle level student is typically beyond the need to attend to word identification or decoding demands and can now focus on more critical and abstract aspects of reading, although the data that exist are very discouraging as to how far students at this level actually do meet the higher-level demands of reading. There is also incontrovertible evidence of an enormous range of reading abilities among young adolescents. Some young adolescents still cannot deal with the most fundamental, decoding aspects of reading, while others are able to make a very advanced, mature response to reading (Pikulski, 1991).

Young adolescent readers can be motivated to read if the material satisfies their personal needs. In spite of Early's observation that young adolescents do not read extensively, there is little evidence to show that they cannot be motivated to read. Given the wide range of individual differences and the rapid changes young adolescents are undergoing, teachers need to present a wide array of books and topics in order to appeal to any one young person's interests (Pikulski, 1991).

Literature-based reading instruction, a significant innovation in language arts and reading programs, will continue into the next decade. Providing the basis for the reading curriculum, literature-based approaches can lead to an appreciation of reading and to a better understanding of self and others through experiences with literature. These programs can also contribute to an awareness of literary characteristics that influence the quality of writing. Learning to read through literature can help young adolescents apply ideas about writing to their own compositions and also contributes to oral communication abilities (Monson, Taylor, & Dykstra, 1988).

Reading in the Content Areas. Reading instruction on the middle level should make definite provisions for refining and extending the reading skills learned in the lower grades. Such instruction should also include provisions for developing ability to read in the content areas, since middle level learners will be required to do most of their reading in these subject areas.

Reading in the content areas (e. g., mathematics and social studies) differs significantly from reading narrative stories. First, content area materials contain a greater number of concepts, and a thorough understanding of each important concept is essential to an understanding of the whole. Second, the vocabulary used in content area materials differs from stories. While the story may have a common core of words, content material may have a specialized vocabulary list. Third, for successful reading in the content areas, learners need a systematic approach for previewing, reading, and reflecting (DeHaven, 1988).

Developmentally Appropriate Recreational Reading. Do middle level students read for pleasure? Manna, Misheff, and Robitaille (1988) conducted a research study and found that 71% of the boys and 84% of the girls responded that they read books for pleasure. Book types included mystery, romance, adventure, biography, poetry, science fiction, and historical fiction.

An objective of the language arts curriculum is the promotion of lifelong interest in reading. A comprehensive language arts program will include elements which contribute to the development of leisure-time reading habits. Learners who are successful in their reading and enjoy reading are more likely to read than less proficient students (Karlin & Karlin, 1987). Independent or recreational reading of books, magazines, and other reading materials should be an integral aspect of the reading program. Research has found that time devoted to silent reading in the classroom is positively related to reading achievement, whereas time spent on skill sheet activities does not relate positively (Anderson, Hiebert, Scott, & Wilkerson, 1985). The recreational reading program should include a variety of materials from which students may select, a time and place for reading without distractions, and opportunities for students to talk informally about their books with the teacher and with other students (Smith & Barrett, 1979).

One way to provide recreational reading time is to implement a classroom "USSR" (uninterrupted sustained silent reading) period. The entire class might read for ten or fifteen minutes at the beginning of the period designated for reading instruction. In addition to USSR, teachers might schedule learners to read at different times during the reading period or language arts period. For example, while the teacher is working with one group, another group may be enjoying recreational reading (Monson, Taylor, & Dykstra, 1988).

Writing

The teaching of writing has changed dramatically during recent decades. Traditionally, writing was viewed as a product; little emphasis was placed on teaching the actual writing process. Learners were expected to learn to write, yet teachers placed little emphasis on what successful writers actually do. Contemporary perceptions view writing as a process during which writers think, write, and then engage in editing and proofing.

Teaching middle level learners to write presently focuses on "what writers do" rather than the writer's "finished product." In other words, the writing process is a series of stages that writers move through. The extensive work of Graves (1983) and Murray (1984) has contributed significantly to an understanding of how successful writers actually write. The writing process basically consists of three stages, each having specific activities contributing to the completed product. *Exploring* and *planning*—usually considered the first stage of the process—consists of thinking, listing, talking to oneself and others, and searching for information. The next stage, known as *drafting*, consists of the actual writing; often without regard to accuracy, writers in this stage put their thoughts on paper. The third and final stage, *revising*, is when the writer makes corrections in content and general writing (Petty, Petty, & Becking, 1989). Various interpretations of the writing process exist; for example, Hoskisson and Tompkins (1987) propose a slightly different series of stages: prewriting, drafting, revising, editing, and sharing. Regardless of one's analysis of the writing process, the basic tenet remains the same: The student's writing process is more important than the finished product.

The National Assessments of Educational Progress (NAEP) conducts five-year assessments of children's and adolescents' writing ability, at ages 9, 13, and 17. The NAEP includes informative, persuasive, and imaginative writing. Although the results of the NAEP in the area of writing are not dismal, they are certainly not positive. Young adolescents remain very limited in their ability to deal with the three types of writing tasks called for in the NAEP; it is particularly disappointing to see the small percentage of students whose writings are rated as adequate. In a more detailed analysis of the 1984 NAEP writing results, Applebee, Langer, and Mullis (1988) note that students do well in responding at a minimal or surface level to writing tasks, but they reach the very important conclusion that, "(w)hen the tasks became more complex, requiring more extended reasoning in order to plan and carry out the writing, only small percentages of students at any grade were able to perform adequately" (p. 17). In summary, it appears that overall achievement for young adolescents has been stable over the last decade, with some periods of inconsistency. As with students at other grade levels, it appears that young adolescents do reasonably well with simple writing tasks, but evidence suggests considerable difficulty with tasks requiring higher-order thinking.

Listening

Listening has been a neglected area, despite the fact that—as educators know—students listen for many hours of the school day. The traditional low priority placed on listening instruction may have been based upon the myth that listening ability develops naturally or the misconception that listening skills could not be taught. The need for listening instruction has been a concern to educators, considering the repetition of many directions, explanations, and warnings during a typical school day. Statements such as that "elementary school students spend more than 57 percent of their classroom time listening . . ." (McCormick, 1981, p. 37) and Wilt's (1950) classic assertion 40 years ago that elementary school children spend about two and a half hours of a five-hour school day listening, clearly document the need for listening instruction. One can easily conclude that middle level students listen even more than their elementary counterparts.

Devine's (1978) review of fifty years of research and theorizing cleared up many misconceptions, myths, and erroneous opinions that have impeded the progress of teaching listening skills. Devine concluded: (1) that listening can be defined; (2) that listening can be taught effectively; and (3) that "evidence exists . . . that listening seems to be measurable" (Devine, 1978, p. 298).

Middle level educators should focus attention on several aspects during listening instruction. First, educators should recognize that young adolescents might not have had listening instruction during the elementary grades, and also, this age group might be far more concerned with their changing bodies and personalities than with classroom activities. Second, educators should focus on teaching students to listen with a purpose rather than just passive listening. In addition, educators should make students aware that there are various types of listening (critical, detailed, or appreciative) and that skills are needed in each area. Also, individual differences deserve consideration and should form the basis of instruction. Lastly, teachers should also strive to model effective listening skills by listening to young adolescents' concerns and comments.

Speaking

A basic tenet of middle level language arts instruction during the foreseeable future will be, as now, a focus on process rather than product. Language arts, no longer perceived as "an end in themselves", should provide young adolescents with active opportunities to speak and communicate. Perceptive educators should look to learners' developmental needs; for instance, their increasing socialization and the corresponding need for effective speaking skills.

The National Council of Teachers of English formulated the following goals for the speaking program. Students should learn:

1. to speak clearly and expressively about their ideas and concerns
2. to adapt words and strategies according to varying situations and audiences, from one-to-one conversations to formal large-group settings
3. to participate productively and harmoniously in both small and large groups
4. to present arguments in orderly and convincing ways
5. to interpret and assess various kinds of communication, including intonation, pause, gesture, and body language that accompany speaking (Maxwell, 1988)

Several aspects, that are already integral aspects of effective middle level schools, can be integrated into language arts teaching and learning. Communication during advisor–advisee sessions can be an excellent means of reinforcing language arts skills. Other means of teaching or providing opportunities to communicate can be to encourage young adolescents to work independently or to provide mini-courses of interest, to provide interdisciplinary units emphasizing language and speaking skills which cross subject area boundaries, and to take advantage of language arts approaches that encourage all forms of speaking.

The young adolescent's budding self-concept and developing identity call for educators to give special attention to multicultural, bilingual, and dialectical issues. Language, a valued aspect of one's culture, will be a significant factor in determining self-worth. Approaches emphasizing active speaking should demonstrate genuine acceptance for one's language or dialect as well as the teacher's commitment to help young adolescents develop proficiency in English.

Whole Language

Young adolescents' increasing cognitive abilities allow higher levels of thought, the conceptual ability to integrate "parts" into "whole," and the ability to recognize relationships between entities. These abilities allow middle level educators to incorporate interdisciplinary and integrative approaches into teaching the language arts, rather than teaching reading, writing, speaking, and listening in isolation from each other and from other subject areas.

Whole language instruction, an increasingly popular instructional approach during the 1990s, encourages learners to view language as a whole rather than an array of disparate and meaningless fragments of information (Froese, 1991; Watson, Burke, & Hartse, 1989; Goodman, 1986). Whole language has been defined "as a child-centered, literature-based approach to language teaching that immerses students in real communication situations whenever possible" (Froese, 1991, p. 2). Some think of whole language as an approach or method, while others consider it as a belief or philosophy. There is, however, agreement that the emphasis shifts away from the teacher to the student (Froese, 1991).

Basic tenets of whole language approaches include: learners being empowered as language users; oral language receiving greater prominence; reading being considered as thinking; the whole text being emphasized rather than the parts; writing being taught as a process; the curriculum being integrated; and reading and writing being closely connected (Fountas & Hannigan, 1989).

From the teacher's perspective, advocates believe that language is a naturally developing human activity and a genuine part of the environment of young learners. Rather than separating the language arts into isolated areas, teachers organize instruction into large blocks of time and may even include other subject areas such as science, social studies, and mathematics. Likewise, the classroom is a rich learning environment which provides learners with personalized instruction based on their individual needs. Organization of learners may include individual instruction or small- or large-group instruction, depending on the purpose; however, collaborative learning among students is encouraged (Froese, 1991). Whole language teachers see themselves as active readers and writers who actually model the processes they want their students to use (Manning & Manning, 1990).

How might middle level educators take advantage of whole language approaches? While teachers should examine their own individual instructional situation, several strategies will be appropriate for the middle level: writing activities, shared book experiences, mini-lessons usually lasting no longer than seven minutes, reading conferences, author studies, independent reading, and the application of reading and writing across the curriculum (Manning & Manning, 1990). Also, whole language approaches meet young adolescents' increasing ability to think critically. Similarly, these approaches encourage collaborative efforts that contribute to 10- to 14-year-olds' increasing needs for socialization with peers.

While whole language will be a viable instructional method during the 1990s and beyond, middle level educators also need to recognize the importance of "whole curriculum" approaches, whereby all subject areas are integrated rather than only areas of selected courses. The 10- to 14-year-old is at an ideal developmental period for such subject matter integration to begin. Such developmental characteristics as an increasing ability to think and recognize relationships, and the move toward independence and an expanding social world, provide many opportunities for middle level educators to show interrelationships between the various subject areas.

We offer here some representative suggestions that incorporate whole language concepts. Perceptive middle level educators can plan other activities designed to empower young adolescents as language users. Readers wanting additional information on whole language approaches are referred to the Suggested Readings at the end of this chapter.

Essential Considerations in the Language Arts

A number of essential considerations underly all language arts programs and contribute to their overall effectiveness. Several of these are unique to effective language arts programs, while others are unique to the middle level concept; however, all contribute to the degree to which the language arts programs meet young adolescents' developmental needs. Essential considerations for language arts include:

1 Reading, both for acquiring knowledge and for pleasure, should receive major emphasis during the middle level and should build upon strengths acquired during the elementary school years.
2 Writing should be valued as a process as well as a product, with major emphasis on teaching young adolescents to think, organize thoughts, and write effectively.
3 The increasing social contacts of young adolescents call for planned and developmentally appropriate instruction in speaking skills that promotes confidence in speaking situations.
4 Language arts should be perceived as a learning tool which contributes to achievement in other subject areas.

SCIENCE

The period of early adolescence can be an exciting time in science education. Middle level science instruction can provide a bridge between the introduction of science as a set of accessible activities and science as a sophisticated form of intellectual inquiry. According to the National Center for Improving Science Education, it must introduce the power, excitement, and utility of formal scientific systems without communicating to children that real science is only comprehensible to the brightest students, the mathematically precocious, or boys (National Center for Improving Science Education, 1990). Here, we examine the goals of middle level science in our fast-changing, technological world and provide an overview of contemporary science instruction, underscoring the need for developmentally appropriate science instruction for young adolescents.

The National Science Teachers' Association (NSTA) maintains that science instruction at the middle level has suffered for several reasons. First, rather than providing young adolescents with opportunities to explore science in their lives, science curricula have been watered-down versions of traditional secondary school courses. Second, science has sometimes been taught as if the goal was to make all middle level students into scientists. A third problem has been that some science teachers of 10- to 14-year-olds have little science background because their professional training was in elementary education, while others have a background in secondary education, which may not provide an understanding of the developmental characteristics of young adolescents (NSTA position statement, 1986).

The American Association for the Advancement of Science, in their report *Project 2061: Science For All Americans* (1989), presented recommendations on the scientific knowledge, skills, and attitudes that all students should acquire. Recommendations cover the nature of science, the nature of mathematics, the nature of technology, the physical setting, the living environment, the human organism, human society, the designed world, the mathematical world, historical perspectives, common themes, and habits of mind. The report urged educators to use interdisciplinary approaches, to base learning on systematic research and well-tested practice, and to emphasize thinking skills over specialized vocabulary and memorized procedures. Specifically, the report (American Association for the Advancement of Science, 1989) suggested that teachers begin with questions about nature, engage students actively, concentrate on the collection and use of evidence, provide historical perspectives, insist on clear expression, use a team approach, and deemphasize memorization.

A determination of the goals of the middle level science program should include a consideration of young adolescents' developmental characteristics, such as their increasing ability to think critically and abstractly, to recognize relationships, and to understand difficult concepts previously impossible to recognize. Specifically, developmentally appropriate middle level science programs should develop scientific attitudes; critical thinking skills; an understanding of the relationship between science, society, and technology; an awareness of developing bodies; and the acceptance of personal and cooperative responsibility for the earth and its natural resources.

Scientific Attitudes. A collection of attitudes comprise the ethical tradition of the scientific and technological communities: desiring knowledge; clarifying skepticism; relying on valid data; accepting ambiguity; willingness to modify explanations; cooperation in answering questions and solving problems; respecting reason; and being honest. Equally important are attitudes toward science and the self. A strong science program can contribute to the development of scientific attitudes and to the development of children's positive attitudes about science and technology, about the study of science in school, and about themselves (NCISE, 1990).

Critical Thinking. A major aspect of the middle level science program should focus on developing and enhancing the 10- to 14-year-old's newly developed thinking skills. Moving from Piaget's concrete operations stage to the early formal operations stage, learners are increasing in their abilities to reason, to think, and to deal with abstract operations. Science in the middle level school is an excellent place to build upon already existing mental capacities and newly acquired abilities and skills.

The relationship between science, society, and technology. Middle level school educators should emphasize the importance of teaching both science and technology and connections between them, and engage students in activities relating to science and technology.

In the upper elementary and middle level grades, students can further enhance their understanding of science and technology by interacting with their teachers and by reading science texts. But even at this level, learners should spend most of their time constructing and refining their developing scientific concepts by designing experiments to answer questions they have raised themselves (NCISE, 1990).

Goals of science and technology education at the middle level include developing young adolescents' ability to identify and clarify questions and problems about the world; broadening young adolescents' critical thinking skills for answering questions and making decisions; developing young adolescents' knowledge base; developing understanding of the history and nature of science and technology; and advancing young adolescents' understanding of the possibilities and limits of science and technology in explaining the natural world and solving human problems (The National Center for Improving Science Education, 1990).

Developmentally Appropriate Instruction. The National Science Teachers' Association (NSTA) calls for science instruction based on young adolescents' developmental characteristics. According to the NSTA position paper on science education for middle level students, young adolescents are cognitively beginning to make a transition from concrete to formal modes of thinking. However, middle level educators should remember that most 10- to 14-year-olds do not complete this transition until the secondary school years. Middle level students continue to need hands-on physical experiences with the scientific processes in order to master scientific concepts. Also related to development are the physical changes of early adolescence—i.e., the changes in height, weight, muscular size, and sexual maturity. These changes, and the fact that the rate of development varies among individuals, can be an excellent basis for science instruction. Likewise, young adolescents' social and emotional changes should be considered as teachers plan teaching-learning experiences (NSTA position statement, 1986).

Curriculum, Instruction, and Resources

Primary functions of science education at the middle level include providing students with an opportunity to explore science in their lives and to become comfortable and personally involved with science. Without doubt, science curricula and instructional experiences at the middle level should reflect society's goals for scientific and technological literacy and should emphasize the role of science for personal, social, and career use, as well as prepare students academically (NSTA position statement, 1986).

Curriculum. While specific content areas vary with the grade level, certain guidelines hold true for the science curriculum regardless of grade level. Young adolescents' developmental characteristics as well as school district curriculum guides should form the basis for curricular decisions; however, generally speaking, the science curricula for middle level students should focus on the relationship of science to: life, physical, and earth sciences with frequent interdisciplinary references; process skills, such as experimenting, observing, measuring, and inferring; personal use in everyday problem solving; social issues involving individual responsibilities; career goals of young adolescents; and the necessity of respecting differing points of view (NSTA position statement, 1986).

Instruction. Science instruction in middle level schools calls for activities that are appropriate for young adolescents' developmental levels. It should include making extensive use of laboratory experiences in developing student skills with the tools of science while stressing safety measures; using models, simulations, computer/student interactions, and concrete manipulations; providing instructional strategies that accommodate various student cognitive levels and learning styles; being responsive to students' short attention spans; making use of interdisciplinary approaches; involving students in experiences with the natural world; and making optimal use of community resources.

In addition, science instruction should reflect several social and personal aspects, such as emphasizing science as an endeavor in which people of both sexes and all cultures can participate successfully; balancing student and teacher-directed learning; providing many opportunities for positive experiences which allow social interaction and build student self-confidence; and allowing changes in instructional group size and composition (NSTA position statement, 1986).

Resources. To maximize the chances of success of all young adolescents, the science curriculum and instructional program must be supported with adequate resources. To provide legitimate curricular and instructional experiences, for the middle level science program, programs should follow these guidelines.

1 Teachers should have time to plan activity-oriented courses.
2 Students should attend at least 225 minutes per week of science classes.
3 Class size should never exceed twenty-five students.
4 Science classrooms and labs should be safe and well ventilated, as well as being properly equipped with tables, water, electricity, heat sources, and a movable table or desk for each student.

5 Teachers should be assigned only one classroom.
6 Financial resources should be available for field trips (NSTA, 1986).

Health and an Awareness of Developing Bodies. The current emphasis on exercise, proper nutrition, and keeping physically and mentally fit will interest many middle level students because they are at a developmental stage when many maturational changes are occurring. Also, their enhanced intellectual abilities allow them to understand the changes in their bodies and understand better how nutrition and exercise affect developing bodies. Young adolescents should demonstrate intense interest and motivation during instruction on health and the body, especially since this age group often experiences dramatic physical, psychosocial, and intellectual changes. Likewise, this age group is usually curious about their bodies and how these changes will affect their overall appearance.

Because the body breathes, grows, and responds to stimuli, science educators should encourage learners to observe their bodies and use it as a first-hand source for developing concepts of its construction, how it functions, what it needs, and how it keeps healthy. Through study of their own bodies, youngsters can add to their understanding of all living things. The increased emphasis on the school accepting responsibility for addressing sex education places an even greater emphasis on helping learners understand the human body (Blough & Schwartz, 1990).

Essential Considerations in Science

Contemporary science instruction includes considering the learners' personal and social experiences as well as the rapidly changing social and technological world. The key to effective science programs during the 1990s and the next century will be to provide developmentally appropriate instruction and to address several considerations which are essential to effective science programs for all learners.

Essential considerations for science include:

1 While learning content and factual information will continue to be a significant goal of the middle level science program, students need active learning approaches in order to "learn how to learn," using such scientific processes as observing, experimenting, hypothesizing, communicating, measuring, classifying, generalizing, and predicting.
2 The middle level school science program should be developmentally based and should reflect learners' differing levels of cognitive and psychosocial developments.
3 Young adolescents should understand the growing role of science and technology in everyday life. Science and technology should be viewed as a positive means of solving problems and making personal and social decisions.

4 The science program should reflect the contemporary emphasis on health and physical fitness of all age groups.

MATHEMATICS

The world that middle level students now live in and will eventually live and work in is a mathematical world. Students can no longer elect or not elect to study mathematics based on their career choices. Dramatic changes in technology, American society, and the global economy have resulted in an escalating need for mathematics in practically all occupations and professions. There is a growing need for all students to study mathematics intensively and effectively every year they are in school.

School mathematics gained national attention with the advent of the "New Math," occasioned by the former Soviet Union's launching of *Sputnik* in 1957. The "New Math" movement brought some positive and lasting changes to mathematics programs, such as new topics in the curriculum, manipulative materials, active learning strategies and greater application of math to real-world problems. Our recent past in middle level mathematics has been exemplified by a concern for mastery of basic skills and pressure for better mathematics performance by our students, especially the academically gifted, caused by competition from students in other nations who seem to outperform American students. Increasingly, school programs have been expected to provide teaching and learning experiences in mathematics that provide for success and achievement for all students.

Although the topics on the middle level have traditionally represented a broad body of mathematics knowledge, there are problems related to how much new mathematics content has been typically presented to middle level students, with the result that many students have been allowed to fall far short of their potential. Flanders (1987) studied the amount of new mathematics content in three popular textbook series for grades K–9. Flanders counted a page in a book as new if any new material, i.e., material not presented at a previous grade level, was presented on that page. Flanders reported that the average percentages of new pages in the three textbook series for the middle level grades were as follows: Grade 6—38%, Grade 7—36%, and Grade 8—30%. The textbooks of elementary grade students typically contained higher percentages of new material than middle level books, and in the ninth grade, due to the study of algebra, the percentage of new material increased to 88 percent. Flanders also reported that the organization of textbooks generally placed old material in the first half of the book and new math content in the last half of the book. The students would then start each year with a long review of math they had previously studied. Since the textbook forms the basic structure of what is taught, this combination of "dumbing down" the middle level curriculum (Willoughby, 1990) and enervating the creative instincts of students by reviewing and reteaching old material every year before presenting any new content (Flanders, 1987) has resulted in the non-spiral, non-cumulative learning reported by McKnight et al.

(1987) in *The Underachieving Curriculum.* Too many middle level students see the mathematics curriculum as boring, routine, and irrelevant. Teachers have usually emphasized computational skill at the expense of a comprehensive integrated study of mathematics. Such a mathematics program fails to represent the vitality of the content or the unique characteristics of the middle level learner (National Council of Teachers of Mathematics, 1989).

Like the middle level school itself, the mathematics curriculum for middle grade students is undergoing rapid and dramatic changes. Mathematics education is in the process of a massive restructuring of the curriculum with a concern for developing numeracy and mathematical power in all students. The role of the middle level school in this time of change is to be involved actively in developing content and instruction appropriate for middle level students. In this section we shall focus on the latest research, scholarly writing, and publications of national councils and associations, addressing: (1) what mathematics should be taught, (2) how it should be taught, (3) how it can be applied to real-life situations, and (4) how math can be connected to other subject areas in the curriculum.

Curriculum Philosophy and Framework

The critical importance of mathematics in the present and future lives of students makes a compelling argument that "mathematically" everybody counts, and should have the opportunity to study the best possible mathematics. However, it is imperative that in our society everybody does count, everybody does matter. Programs cannot groom some children for success, doom some to failure, and leave others along the way, half-equipped for living their lives.

Mathematics has frequently served as the subject of rigor which filters students out of "too demanding" scientific and professional career programs and often out of school itself. Today, society requires and ethical fairness demands that mathematics must change from a *filter* which moves some students toward success and dooms many students to failure and become the *pump* which moves all students toward success in American education (National Research Council, 1989). It is especially important that the success pump replace the failure filter for middle level students, who often experience so much frustration, anxiety, and failure in mathematics.

Recent reports have emphasized that mathematics should actively involve young adolescent students in the study of math, should enable students to develop mathematical power, should introduce important new topic areas and technology to the math program, should connect math to other school subjects and real-world problems, and should emphasize an array of practices that emphasize the significance of mathematics for every child at school. While addressing the total range of the K–12 curriculum, the ideas presented in these reports are of particular significance to middle level students who need mathematics programs that involve, challenge, stimulate, and help them (National Research Council, 1989, 1990).

The Mathematical Science Education Board (MSEB) addressed the problems posed by dramatic changes in American society and urgent demands for the reform of mathematics curriculum and instruction in *Reshaping School Mathematics* (National Research Council, 1990). The premise of the report was that mathematics curriculum and instruction must undergo complete restructuring and redesign, and that merely changing topics, goals, and textbooks would be completely insufficient to the challenges and opportunities facing modern mathematics in our fast-changing world. In developing the theoretical framework for restructuring school mathematics, the MSEB considered mathematics in the contexts of technology and research. Technology, primarily in terms of computers and calculators, has influenced what mathematics should be taught, how it should be taught, and how much emphasis certain mathematics topics should be given. Research on ways students learn mathematics, methods for teaching mathematics more effectively, the importance of problem solving in the math curriculum, and the efficacy of connecting math to other subjects and to real-world problems have yielded significant findings that can dramatically change mathematics curriculum and instruction.

While extensive treatment of specific curriculum models was beyond the scope of this report, the board did make general recommendations relevant to middle level mathematics programs. Some goals that appeal to young adolescents were: (1) to use calculators and computers in mathematics teaching and learning, (2) to make relevant connections and applications to other subjects and real-life situations, (3) to develop problem-solving and problem-posing skills, and (4) to emphasize the practical power of mathematics in everyday life situations (National Research Council, 1990).

Curriculum Standards

Mathematics for the middle level is in dire need of change. Middle level students need mathematics to be a practical, relevant, lively, and creative subject. Instead, it too often has been characterized by repetition of content and topics year after year and by instruction that promotes active teacher behaviors and passive student responses. The curriculum has represented the "dumbing down" curriculum characteristics found in the Flanders (1987) research, and uninspired and routine teaching that attends to neither the academic nor developmental needs of young adolescents.

The comprehensive mathematics program needed to prepare young adolescents for the challenges and changes in present and future society was presented in standards developed by the National Council of Teachers of Mathematics (NCTM) in *Curriculum and Evaluation Standards for School Mathematics* (1989). Curriculum standards for mathematics for elementary school (K–4), middle level (5–8), and high school (9–12) were formulated in the report. While divided into three classification categories, the NCTM preferred that the curriculum standards be treated as K–12 standards. Standards and goals for mathematics curriculum reflected the necessity of numeracy or mathematical literacy for all students. To meet these standards, the NCTM developed five general student goals stressing that students should learn to value mathematics, become confident in their mathematics ability, become problem solvers in mathematics, learn to communicate mathematically, and learn to reason mathematically (NCTM, 1989, p. 5). Additionally, fourteen evaluation standards were developed to assess the extent to which students were experiencing success with the mathematics curriculum standards. The evaluation standards were divided into three categories: general assessment, student evaluation, and program evaluation. The rationale for assessment was that it should be broad-based, aligned to the curriculum, related to student learning, and appropriate for instructional strategies (NCTM, 1989).

The new NCTM standards call for a broadened curriculum that goes far beyond basic skills mastery to a broader, conceptual, relevant mathematics curriculum. Additionally, the standards advocate sweeping changes, from the traditional teacher-talking-and-testing mode to active learning approaches that foster optimum opportunities for teacher–student and student–student discussions and individual and small-group work. The standards assume that the classroom would be well supplied with materials that complement effective mathematics teaching and learning. Those materials would include a variety of manipulatives and teaching supplies, calculators available for every student, and at least one computer available in each classroom (NCTM, 1989).

In developing the standards, the two primary considerations were the mathematical context and the activities students would do in learning mathematics. The mathematical context emphasized that: (1) active doing is essential to knowing; (2) mathematics is applicable to other disciplines; and (3) technology is changing mathematics and the ways it is used. Student activities should grow out of problem situations, and active involvement with mathematics should be the primary learning process. Student activities and classroom instruction should include (1) relevant project work, (2) group and individual assignments, (3) classroom discussions, (4) guided and independent practice, and (5) teacher-directed instruction (NCTM, 1989).

The NCTM presented thirteen standards for the middle grades. Four of those thirteen standards are broad in nature and apply to grades K–12. They are *problem solving, communication, reasoning,* and *mathematical connections.* These four standards, while common to all grade levels, would receive special attention across the range of the middle grades.

General Standards

The four general NCTM standards that extend across the K–12 curriculum are problem solving, communication, reasoning, and connections. For each standard, the content is explicated and the student activities in studying the mathematics are delineated. For *problem solving,* the main content emphases are studying open-ended problems, pursuing extended-problem projects, and being able to formulate and work through problem situations. Student activities in this standard focus on the study of problems that arise in mathematics and on applying mathematical solutions to real-life situations. The *communication* standard emphasized that middle grade students should learn *to communicate* mathematics as they learn *to do* mathematics. Mathematics is viewed as a language as well as a science. In this standard, students discuss, read, write, and listen to mathematical ideas to increase meaning and understanding. In *reasoning,* opportunities are provided for reasoning in spatial contexts, proportions, graphs, and inductively and deductively. Students' reasoning ability changes during the middle level, so experiences and activities in concrete to formal reasoning, appropriate to their cognitive development, are presented. It is important for middle level students to validate their thinking in individual and group processes without relying on the teacher or textbook as the sole authority in mathematics ideas. The *connections* standard relates mathematics to other subjects and to the real world. The emphasis is on connectedness of topics, rather than on isolated learning skills out of context. Through group work, projects, and technology, students learn to relate mathematical ideas to other information learned and to situations outside of the classroom. For middle level students, this standard emphasizes the practical nature of mathematics as more than a subject to be studied, as concepts and information to be used in their world (NCTM, 1989).

These four general standards were important in their own right, but additionally, they were to be stranded throughout the specific middle level standards. Problem solving, reasoning, communicating, and making connections would be integral to the study of other mathematics topics, such as algebra, geometry, measurement, and statistics.

Number, Operations, and Computations Standards

In the NCTM classification, standards five, six, and seven relate to number and operations with number. Standard five contains content about *number and number relationships.* The content emphasizes number sense, the development of the concepts of ratio, proportion, and percent, and multiple representations for fractions, decimals, ratios, and percents. Students explore and create relationships through number lines, area models, and graphs. Working as individuals and in small groups, students generate, read, and use multiple representations of number quantities.

Number systems and number theory (standard six) demonstrate the unifying structure of mathematics. This content extends beyond whole numbers into other number systems. In the middle level, students recognize the need for numbers beyond whole numbers. Students use informal explorations and technology to infer reasons why numbers occur. They explore and share experiences with number theory that illustrate the structure, logic, and aesthetics of math and its deep human dimensions.

Standard seven contains topics on *computation and estimation.* This content is noteworthy because it deemphasizes memorization of rules and algorithms, monotonous drill procedures, and practicing procedures and computations out of context. Middle level students learn to use computations to solve problems. Students also learn to select and use appropriate mental arithmetic, paper-and-pencil, calculator, and computer options in using computation and estimation to solve mathematics and real-world problems (NCTM, 1989).

Standards for Algebra, Geometry, and Other Advanced Topics

These standards (8–13) continue and develop concepts and ideas from grades K–4 and introduce certain new principles and concepts for middle level students. *Patterns and functions* represent a central theme of mathematics. On the middle level, the study of patterns shifts to an emphasis on the exploration of functions. The focus is on the analysis, representation, and generalization of functional relationships. Student activities in this standard are informal and related to real-world situations. Students use tables, graphs, and rules to represent pattern and function situations. Middle grade students observe and describe patterns in their worlds and apply patterns and functions to solve problems.

Standard nine deals with the study of *algebra* in the middle level. The content emphasizes the study of algebra concepts and processes through informal exploration. The middle level mathematics curriculum has served as a bridge between the concrete, informal mathematics experiences of the elementary school to the abstract, formal mathematics curriculum of the high school. It is imperative for middle level students that the study of algebra follow this informal, developmentally appropriate practice. This gradual transition will enable middle level students to grow in their power of abstract thinking and be prepared for more formal algebra study in grade 8 or 9.

On the middle level, the mathematics curriculum should include explorations in *statistics*. Information and technology require an increased ability for data collection and analysis. The content also emphasizes the power of statistics for prediction and decision making. Statistics is a natural area for motivating middle grade students to original, creative, and purposeful study. Key decisions in the school, community, and society are based on data and statistical procedures, and middle level students need to understand the steps of the statistics process, from gathering data to communicating results.

Probability theory is essential to understanding the modern world, ranging from situations as routine as weather forecasts to which team will win the World Series to prediction of presidential elections. Middle level students are intensely interested in probability when it is related to areas that spark their interest. Student activities in studying this content area would involve discussion, group and individual work, model situations, arranging experiments, and a myriad of practical approaches to experimental and theoretical probabilities.

On the middle level, the study of *geometry* should allow students to identify, describe, compare, and classify geometric figures of one, two, and three dimensions. The geometry standard seeks to foster in students an appreciation of geometry as it represents the physical world. Instead of memorizing formulas, facts, vocabulary, and relationships, middle level students should develop an understanding of geometric objects and relationships and should use geometry in solving problems. An informal exploration of geometry can be quite meaningful and productive for middle level students.

Standard thirteen, *measurement*, is replete with practical applications for the middle level student in and out of school. The new focus of this standard is on the development of understanding, not on rote memorization of formulas. Measurement connects to other math topics, to other subjects, and to real-world settings. Students work together to use measurement units and tools to describe and compare mathematical situations and geometric objects and to use measurement formulas and procedures to solve problems (NCTM, 1989).

A comprehensive attempt is under way to reform the teaching and learning of mathematics. Mathematics is presented as a growing, expanding body of knowledge not only to be *learned* by students but also to be *applied* by students to real-world situations and problems. The focus is on being mathematically literate and mathematically powerful in a rapidly changing world where mathematics itself is changing. The "new" math for the 1990s calls for all students to experience the full range of mathematics topics in the K–12 curriculum, while actively involving students individually and in groups in exploring, doing, and applying mathematics in mathematical contexts and real-life situations. The teacher operates as a facilitator of learning, not just as a dispenser of information. Teachers and students utilize manipulatives—learning objects—for developing concepts, calculators for problem solving, and computers for exploration to learn math concepts. Teachers and students study mathematics across the curriculum, which promotes interdisciplinary approaches to learning mathematics. Mathematics should be required for all students every year. This necessitates that the mathematics curriculum and instruction provide for creativity, high level of expected performance, use of technology, communication, shared learning, and applications to real-life situations (Steen, 1989).

Developmentally Appropriate Mathematics

Mathematics should provide for the unique developmental characteristics of young adolescents. Students in the middle level are going through significant changes in their intellectual, emotional, and social development. These students are growing in their ability to think at higher levels and reason abstractly. Students also develop increased problem-solving skills. Consequently, problem situations should accommodate the developmental growth of the learners. Math concepts change in relation to the changes in maturity and experiences of the learners.

Changes in social characteristics of middle level learners denote that students should be afforded greater opportunities for social learning. The young adolescent needs to experience group learning because it is an effective way to learn and it contributes to positive social and emotional development. Mathematics educators do not advocate any single approach to learning, favoring a variety of methods to attain the academically and developmentally appropriate program needed by young adolescents. Some approaches that have been supported by research are cooperative learning, computer-assisted instruction, inquiry, and direct instruction.

In recent years, research on effective learning and teaching have concluded that middle level students learn best when they are actively involved in their learning and when they are provided opportunities to explore, discuss, and apply mathematics to their lives. Young adolescents need mathematics programs that empower them to learn the most mathematics possible in the best ways possible. Some of these best ways enable middle level students to have open-ended experiences in mathematics which allow them to construct their own meaning, ask their own questions, and prescribe their own solutions. Mathematics has come to be viewed not only as a science but as a language; as a means of knowing and learning about the world, not merely as a set of formulas, calculations, computations, and procedures. Student discussion, cooperative group work, and individual efforts all focus on an approach to mathematics that extends beyond arriving at correct answers to word problems and/or rote computations. The goal of the teacher should be to focus the learner on making meaning out of mathematics and developing ways of applying mathematics to real-life situations.

Two concerns outweigh all others in planning for a developmentally appropriate mathematics curriculum. The first is getting a mathematics curriculum in place which is effective for all children and which makes American mathematics education the best in the world. The second is modifying and improving instruction so that students are stimulated to learn mathematics. In summary, the right math taught and learned in the right ways.

Improving Mathematics Teaching

To reach the goal—a situation where all students possess mathematical power—will take very dramatic changes in the ways that mathematics is taught. Rather than forced drill, memorization, and computation, effective teaching relates to the teacher's ability to motivate and stimulate the students to learn mathematics. Students learn best when they are actively involved, working cooperatively, and making meaning of mathematical situations. Teacher-directed instruction still has its place in the math classroom. However, student-directed words such as "examine," "apply," "prove," "discuss," "demonstrate," and "communicate" must replace teacher words like "lecture," "drill," "test," and other teacher-active–student-passive words (National Research Council, 1989, pp. 58–59).

Teachers must stop teaching a nineteenth-century mathematics curriculum to boys and girls who will spend their adult years in the twenty-first century. Additionally, teachers must use methods that promote reasoning, the use of technology, and solving problems cooperatively. It will be up to teachers to prepare students mathematically for the future (Pejouhy, 1990).

To implement the mathematics reforms that are needed will necessitate substantive changes in what teachers and students do in math classrooms. The process of teaching needs to be subordinated to the process of learning so that students initiate, direct, and evaluate *their* learning. Teachers are in classrooms to facilitate learning, and methods that enhance learning potential must be emphasized. To enable all students to attain mathematical power, teachers need to shift to teaching–learning situations that promote discussing, exploring, reasoning, connecting, inventing, problem-solving, and problem-posing in cooperative classroom communities (NCTM, 1991, p. 30).

The improvement of mathematics instruction will require the commitment to change by personnel at the building and school district levels, as well as innovations effected by individual classroom teachers. It will take professional and staff development efforts through teaching teams that combine teachers, administrators, and curriculum specialists to initiate the broad-based changes that are needed to make mathematics happen for teachers and students (Martin & McGrevin, 1990).

Essential Considerations in Mathematics

Middle level teachers face the prospect of preparing young adolescents to live in a world where the only constant is the constancy of change. The preeminent concern for the middle level mathematics curriculum and the middle level mathematics teacher is to teach mathematics in a way that equips young adolescents to live in a world of change. Essential considerations for middle level mathematics include:

1. Students learn more effectively when they can see connections between mathematics and other content areas, connections within mathematics topics, and connections between mathematics and real-world situations (Willoughby, 1990).
2. There is a consensus among mathematics educators that the teaching of mathematics needs to change dramatically. Mathematics classrooms should be learning communities where discussion, cooperation, communication, reasoning, exploration, and other learner-focused strategies are utilized.
3. Math anxiety relates to the fear of failure experienced by teachers, adults, young adolescents, and children when presented with mathematics concepts and problems. The issue of math anxiety and all of its attendant problems requires serious study in the middle level.
4. Gender differences favoring men over women become more pronounced the longer that students are exposed to the math curriculum at school. Studies of gender differences indicate that most of the differences observed are caused by sex-role experiences in the home, school, and society (National Research Council, 1989). It is imperative that middle level teachers, administrators, and guidance counselors develop plans to eliminate the gender gap by providing academic programs and counseling that foster successful mathematics experiences and broader career choices for young adolescent girls.

INTEGRATION OF CURRICULUM DIMENSIONS AND CONTEXTS

As discussed in Chapter 6, the curriculum should be a major focus of the middle level school. Organization and guidance are there to carry out the curriculum and instructional decisions. The curriculum has three dimensions of equal importance: personal, social, and academic. For too long, the emphasis has been on academic subjects without regard for the personal and social dimensions. The lack of a comprehensive framework incorporating these three dimensions has made it difficult to provide integrated units and developmentally appropriate content. Usually, the subjects are seen as separate, but in order to serve the personal and social needs of young adolescents, it is essential to balance the academic dimension with the other two dimensions. Interdisciplinary content enables the young adolescent to observe an integrated, holistic viewpoint of content and skills as well as appreciate the value of separate disciplines.

The Use of Contexts in Evaluation

Each context should be employed to assess the three dimensions in the middle level curriculum around young adolescents' learning. There is no notion that one of these contexts is more important than another. The greater the degree of utilization of these contexts in the middle level for planning and evaluation, the more likely the curriculum will provide for the felt needs and interests of young adolescents. These contexts provide teachers, learners, parents, and community leaders with a framework for authentically assessing the curriculum. Learning outcomes become effective when student indicators are linked to the program of instruction. Authentic assessment consists of evaluation tasks that replicate behaviors students perform in their daily lives. Portfolios would contain such typical student academic work as sample reports, writing, and speeches that could be used to document young adolescents' progress. Evaluation of the portfolios should determine appropriate developmental levels and should assess cognitive abilities, maturation, and backgrounds. Student products, resulting from both independent and group efforts, should be included as a part of the evaluation process.

Evaluation of middle level curriculum should focus attention toward the attainment of all program goals and should include the students' personal involvement with content areas as well as the learning of specific knowledge. The curriculum objectives, materials, and strategies would be assessed in a formative manner during instruction to determine how well students are learning and to make adjustments in objectives, materials, and strategies if necessary. At the end of instruction, summative evaluation would be utilized at the end of the instructional sequence to determine how well students had mastered an instructional sequence, but these evaluation results would also be part of the portfolio of each learner. Evaluation provides a short-term and long-term means of reporting student progress, and provides the basis for future curricular and instructional decisions. The extreme importance often placed on one or two evaluation instruments provides a sound argument for expanding the number of evaluation items used to assess student progress. For example, a learner's reading achievement scores may offer little clue to his or her abilities. Likewise, the tremendous diversity among young adolescents makes generalizations about subject matter achievement even more difficult. When evaluating achievement in content areas, student portfolios should form the basis for evaluation. Rather than base decisions on one score, i.e., an achievement test score, it is better to have students put together a collection of work which can include reading tests, written papers and reports, examples of individual effort, projects, evidence documenting the student's ability to engage in learning, and the student's contribution to a group project. Portfolios lessen the possibility of a student being penalized or assessed incorrectly just because a particular test grade did not reflect her or his potential or achievement. When appropriate, test results would be discussed with the entire school community, including students, parents, teachers, and community leaders.

Two powerful issues that must be considered a dominant part of middle level curriculum evaluation are assessing equity and excellence. Equity issues relate to providing a broad range of educational opportunities, accessible to all students, which enable students to capitalize fully on their unique abilities, interests, needs, and efforts. Excellence requires that students be expected and assisted to perform at their best and achieve to their highest potential. The educational community needs to be reminded that schools are for children, all children, and consequently, that the curriculum is for learners, all of the learners. Ideas of equity and excellence and the affirmation that everybody counts and matters are principles that must gain national and local acceptance in all middle level schools. In summary, each of the following contexts serves as an indicator for assessing whether the curriculum is addressing the personal, social, and academic dimensions of the middle level curriculum, and of the success in establishing a learning community in the middle level school.

Developmentally Appropriate Context. This context evaluates whether developmentally appropriate needs—intellectual, psychosocial, emotional, and physical needs and ethical standards of conduct—are incorporated into the middle level curriculum. These needs include the establishment of a healthy self-concept toward peers and adults in order to cope with an impersonal society and large schools, which make it difficult to develop a wholesome personal identity. An assessment would include whether the curriculum is addressing the needs of the academically diverse range of learners found in the school. Does the curriculum focus on mainstreaming handicapped and learning-disabled students? Exceptional learners may need extensive hands-on activities, observing and working individually and/or in small groups. Likewise, special attention should be given to creative and gifted learners. It is important for middle level educators to identify students with special interests, aptitudes, and talents. Is there a challenging curriculum for gifted, talented, and at-risk students? Does the middle level curriculum provide for equal access to the most advanced levels of the curriculum based on the potential and interests of young adolescents? Does the middle level curriculum ensure that an academically diverse range of learners is connected to the total school program? A healthy self-concept should be promoted in all subject matter through active learning that prepares the young adolescent for the changing nature of society. An integrated curriculum should result in intellectually reflective learners who are literate, can think critically, behave ethically, engage in a lifetime of meaningful work, and assume roles and responsibilities of citizenship (*Turning Points,* 1989).

Exploratory Context. A fundamental principle undergirding the curriculum of the middle grades should be to assess whether the learning climate encourages learners to initiate learning based on their needs, experiences, interests, and future careers. As young adolescents are developing intellect, expanding their curiosity about the world around them, and increasing their ability to study independently, do middle level educators provide appropriate exploratory opportunities? With curricular areas discussed in this chapter, are learners provided exploratory opportunities to see the interconnectedness that exists in social studies, language arts, science, and mathematics for career awareness and for the personal satisfaction of learning? Are exploratory opportunities provided to young adolescents for active teaching and learning strategies such as advisor–advisee sessions, independent work, real-life and/or simulated experiences, mini-courses, community exploration experiences, and field trips? This exploratory context should encourage middle level students to explore and select topics based on special academic, personal, social, and career interests. Students should be provided opportunities to explore and define who they are, what they believe, and what they can do and want to do.

Technology Context. As technological advances become commonplace events in our daily lives, it also becomes important to assess technological literacy in middle level classrooms. A perusal of the myriad of technological advances, such as computer software packages available to middle level teachers, indicates that these materials can be used in different educational modes and can serve many needs and purposes (Blough and Schwartz, 1990).

The *drill and practice* mode is by far the most common application of computer-assisted instruction (CAI). A software package that utilizes the drill-and-practice mode should be evaluated for tailoring the instructions to the needs of an individual and providing a management section to show the teacher how well the young adolescent is doing. The best programs not only tell a student that the answer is incorrect, but also offer a short remedial lesson. Since many software packages are available but are of varying quality, it is essential to investigate drill and practice programs.

Tutorial lessons should be assessed for enrichment or remediation. A successful tutorial program should introduce new concepts or reinforce previously learned concepts to students. The program should test students for their comprehension of what they have learned. Part of the assessment should analyze state-of-the-art graphics' capabilities to teach the lessons, motivate students, and provide for reteaching of material that is not learned.

A *simulation* should be assessed on whether young adolescents are provided with learning experiences that approximate real-world situations, in a mode that compresses time from days and years to minutes and seconds. This genre of programs should be evaluated carefully for their ability to provide meaningful learning experiences.

Problem-solving programs should be able to take a set of data, teach the learner how to organize the information, come up with a scientific rule, and solve the problem presented. Software programs should be assessed for employing a wide range of problems, from simple to complex, along with methods for showing the resolution to the problem.

One of the best uses for computers is to gather data and present information in a logical order. *Microcomputer labs* should be assessed for probes, sound CD-ROMs, and other pieces of equipment that gather measurements, put the information in a table or chart format, and allow for an interpretation of the data.

When it is impossible to schedule a class in the library to do research, it might be possible to rely upon data stored in a computer format, either as software or CD-ROM disk. *Databases* should be assessed as to their reliance upon other programs and equipment needed to access that data (Blough & Schwartz, 1990).

Videodiscs permit visual and sound images to be recorded and played back later. Interactive video systems using cable television also have been put into operation in many localities. Viewers can respond from their home to stimuli shown on television. The assessment should be directed toward determining equipment needed and the ability of disks to provide meaningful learning experiences.

A difficulty in making use of computers and technology is how to involve teaching staff. First, many teachers have not planned time for computers and technology in the classroom. Some teachers may feel threatened by computers and technology. Another problem concerns the availability and accessibility of computers and technology equipment. While more school districts are buying computers and technological equipment, many teachers still do not have access to them. In addition, the type of instructional software and technology programs available in a district or school determine their effectiveness for classroom use.

While technology and computers have enriched our lives, it is important to use the new technologies in a meaningful manner with young adolescents. The new century will demand citizens with technological and computer literacy. The computer will have an impact on society, schools, and young adolescents, and utilization must emphasize the potential strengths of computers while neutralizing their limiting features.

Cultural Diversity Context. This context analyzes whether the curriculum develops respect for cultural diversity and promotes the equity and dignity of all cultures in an interdependent society, nation, and world. In the next several decades, educators will undoubtedly experience an increase in culturally diverse populations. One prediction is that the minority school population will soon exceed 50% in several southwestern states (Norton, 1985). The multiethnic dimensions of middle level curriculum must be evaluated for the personal and social development of young adolescents. Because the 10- to 14-year-old developmental period is crucial for self-concept development and identity formation, learners' perceptions of cultural differences and their opinions of other cultures must be investigated for the significant role these play in the successful development of self-worth and self-image. Care should be exercised not to discriminate against students with differing ability levels and interests. Every student should be provided with at least one area of success in subject content areas.

For culturally different learners, language problems can occur that result in learning problems and decreased academic achievement. A student who speaks English at school and his or her native language at home and in the community will possibly experience problems with content areas. Likewise, the young adolescent speaking a dialect might have a problem reading textbooks written in standard English. Determining instructional approaches can often be challenging, especially when one's second language or dialect hinders content and skill development. The teacher's attitude toward working with culturally diverse children will be of paramount importance. The learner's communicational effectiveness and overall success in content areas will have a significant impact on the learner's personal and cultural identity. An examination of teachers' instructional approaches should be undertaken to determine whether they are enhancing classroom learning or contributing to the young adolescent's learning problems, for instance by overemphasizing content and written exercises or by using the wrong types of motivation.

Advisory Context. This context would assess the provision of guidance information, personal counseling, and advisor–advisee opportunities. Guidance has long been accepted as a major contributor to effective middle level schools and should be assessed to determine whether young adolescents develop confidence in the various content fields. Guidance program specialists should be assessed for their assistance in content areas through helping students to realize and accept their ability levels, potential, and limitations; suggesting career options; assisting students with both the confidence needed to work independently and the social skills needed to work cooperatively; helping classroom educators with the coordination of efforts in the development of interdisciplinary units and the establishment of advisor–advisee programs. As advisors, teachers should provide each young adolescent with an identification to one adult with whom they can secure personal, academic, and social support. Does every young adolescent have access to an adult advisor (advisor–advisee)? Does the advisory program seek to promote the parents' commitment to the school program through greater involvement in school governance, open communication concerning their child's performance, and increased opportunities to support their child's learning at home and at school?

Family context. This context assesses whether the curriculum contributes to engaging parents in the learning of their young adolescent and establishes effective parent–child relationships. What indicators does the school have that parents promote the basic systems of morality, positive attitudes toward school and self, appropriate ways to demonstrate behavior, and the development of personality attributes such as honesty, integrity, caring, and compassion? It is essential to determine the ability of the school to maintain positive communication with parents. The curriculum should be analyzed for programs dealing with single parenting, effects of divorce on school achievement and behavior, latchkey children, and nutrition. Does school reconnect the family with the school to reduce the at-risk factors found among young adolescents, such as drug use, child abuse, violence, crime, school dropouts, teenage pregnancies, and sexually transmitted diseases, including AIDS? In summary, the school should reconnect the family with the school, and parents should be responsible for their young adolescent's learning and behavior.

Community context. This context assesses the degree of collaboration and cooperation among school, home, and community. Do school and community agencies collaborate on improving the health and fitness of young adolescents? Does the family take an active part in the education of their children? Do the school and community collaborate on providing connections for young adolescents between schools and the community through social action and community service projects? Does the curriculum foster a learning community in which middle level learners would value relevant and meaningful social action and community service projects? The community context should promote collaboration and cooperation to have a dynamic learning community.

SUMMARY

Educators during the 1990s and into the twenty-first century will continue to experience considerable ferment in social studies, language arts, science, and mathematics. Middle level educators must prepare young adolescents to live in a world of constant change.

In preparing young adolescents for the challenges of the twenty-first century, educators in social studies, language arts, mathematics, and science need to consider interactive, holistic, and integrative approaches to the development of curricula appropriate for middle level students. New directions in social studies, language arts, mathematics, and science for the next century hold the promise of fulfilling the mission of the middle level. This mission has been to provide learning experiences related to the unique personal, social, and intellectual development of young adolescents.

Language arts educators must seek a balance in reading, writing, literature, and listening skills and will be challenged to implement literature-based curriculum and whole-language approaches. Likewise, educators will find social studies competing with other subject areas for emphasis and will be challenged to reaffirm the importance of social studies, especially for the development of young adolescents as citizens. Mathematics will need to prepare young adolescents to think mathematically, to relate mathematics to their other content areas, to link mathematics to real-world problems, and to utilize technology. A strong science curriculum is necessary for the development of scientific understanding and a positive student attitude toward science and technology, which can enable the middle level learner to make intelligent decisions regarding ethical issues found in science and technology. The role of computer and technological advances in social studies, language arts, science, and mathematics must be clearly defined.

■ ■ ■

EXPLORATION

1 Middle level students in many inner-city schools represent a wide range of cultural diversity. Survey a class of middle level learners in a large inner-city school. What are the cultural breakdowns? e. g., how many students are African-, Hispanic-, and Asian-American? Interview several of each culture to determine language problems and other problems associated with living in a pluralistic society. In order to have interdisciplinary units and topics, what specific social studies, language arts, science, and mathematics experiences will help these culturally different learners?

2 Recreational reading can play a vital role in whole-language approaches. Develop a list of books in several categories (e. g., realistic fiction, historical fiction, sports, biography, and informational books) that will be appropriate for middle level students. Remembering the need for interdisciplinary instruction, place an asterisk by books that are appropriate for social studies, language arts, mathematics, and science classes.

3 Social studies is considered by many middle level learners to be reading the textbook, listening to lectures, answering questions from teachers and in textbooks, and filling out worksheets. How can students become actively involved in social studies, both in the classroom and outside of the classroom? What activities could be employed to generate active involvement in the classroom? Outside of the classroom? What assistance could the community, computers, and technology provide?

4 How do the concerns and issues stated in question 3 relate to the science curriculum?

5 Provision needs to be made to meet the unique needs of exceptionalities such as handicapped, remedial, and gifted and talented learners. What content, instructional methods, activities and skills in social studies, language arts, mathematics, and science should be developed for these diverse learners?

6 Math anxiety is a real problem in American education in comparison with many other cultures. Identify elements of American society and culture that might contribute to this phenomenon. Identify specific classroom practices that might lead to math anxiety and math avoidance and suggest ways to reduce math anxiety in the classroom.

7 *Everybody Counts* (National Research Council, 1989) says that all students should be successful in mathematics; that mathematics is the *pump* that pro-

pels students to success. Specify how we need to modify curriculum, instruction, and organization to support the idea that everybody counts.

SUGGESTED READINGS

Froese, V. (1991). *Whole language: Practice and theory.* Boston: Allyn & Bacon.

In this edited collection of essays on whole language, Froese and his colleagues examine such issues as literature, drama, reading, writing, organization, assessment, and involving parents.

Jacobs, H. R. (1982). *Mathematics: A human endeavor.* San Francisco, CA: W. H. Freeman.

A stimulating anthology of mathematics ideas, puzzles, games, and other topics for people who don't like math.

Manna, A. L., Misheff, S., & Robitaille, N. (1988). Do middle school students read for pleasure? *Middle School Journal, 19*(4), 28–30.

This research study describes young adolescents' reading interests.

National Center for Improving Science Education (1990). A blueprint for elementary school science. *Streamlined Seminar* (National Association of Elementary School Principals), *8*(5), 1–8.

This document includes a special section on science and technology goals for middle schools.

National Council for the Social Studies, Task Force on Social Studies in the Middle School. (1991). Social studies in the middle school. *Social Education, 55* 5, 287–293.

This task force report contains valuable information for integrating social studies curriculum on the middle level.

National Council for the Social Studies, Task Force on Scope and Sequence. In search of a scope and sequence for social studies. (1984, 1989). *Social Education, 48,* 249–262 and *Social Education, 53* 6, 376–387.

These reports by a special NCSS task force examines the scope and sequence of the social studies.

National Research Council. (1989). *Everybody counts: A report on the future of mathematics education.* Washington, DC: National Academy Press.

This is a compelling status report and call to action to reform mathematics from pre-school to college.

Parker, W. C. (1991). *Renewing the social studies curriculum.* Alexandria, VA: Association for Supervision and Curriculum Development.

This monograph reviews the social studies curriculum, suggesting that social studies is important for the development of participating citizens.

Ravitch, D., & Finn, C. (1987). *What do our 17-year-olds know? A report on the first national assessment of history and literature.* New York: Harper & Row.

This provocative study reports what 17-year-olds know about history and literature and has implications for language arts and social studies in middle level.

Steen, L. A. (1990). *On the shoulders of giants: New approaches to numeracy.* Washington, DC: National Academy Press.

These essays present a vision of deep mathematical ideas and their implications for numeracy for all students at all levels of schooling.

Special Issues:

The Middle School Journal (November, 1987) focuses on interdisciplinary instruction;

The Middle School Journal (August, 1987) looks at language; and

The Middle School Journal (March, 1991) has several articles on teaching science in the middle level school.

The Middle School Journal (November, 1991 and January, 1992) focus on middle level curriculum.

REFERENCES

American Association for the Advancement of Science. (1989). *Science for all Americans: A Project 2061 report on literacy goals in science, mathematics, and technology.* Washington, DC: Author.

Anderson, R. C., Hiebert, E. H., Scott, J. A. & Wilkinson, I. A. (1985). *Becoming a nation of readers: The report of the commission on reading.* Washington, DC: National Institute on Education.

Applebee, A. N., Langer, J. A., Mullis, I. V. (1988). *Who reads best? Factors related to reading achievement in grades 3, 7, and 11.* Princeton, NJ: Educational Testing Service.

Banks, J. A. (1991). *Teaching strategies for ethnic studies.* (5th ed.). Boston: Allyn & Bacon.

Barr, R., Barth, J., & Shermis, S. S. (1977). *Defining the social studies.* Washington, DC: National Council for the Social Studies, 1977.

Beane, J. A. (1990). *A middle school curriculum: From rhetoric to reality.* Columbus, OH: National Middle School Association.

Blough, G. O., & Schwartz, J. (1990). *Elementary school science and how to teach it.* Fort Worth, TX: Holt, Rinehart & Winston.

Bowers, R. S. (1991). Effective models of middle school science instruction. *Middle School Journal, 22*(4), 4–9.

Bradley Commission on History in the Schools. (1988). *Building a history curriculum: Guidelines for teaching history in schools.* Washington, DC: Educational Excellence Network.

California State Board of Education. (1988). *History-social science framework.* Sacramento, CA: California State Department of Education.

California State Department of Education. (1987). *Caught in the middle.* Sacramento: California State Department of Education.

Carnegie Council for Adolescent Development. (1989). *Turning points: Preparing American youth for the 21st century.* Washington, DC: Author.

Chapman, J., Becker, J. M., Gilliom, M. E., & Tucker, J. (1982). Position statement on global education: National Council for the Social Studies. *Social Education, 46*(1), 36–38.

Children's Defense Fund. (1988). *Making the middle grades work.* Washington, DC: Children's Defense Fund.

Cortes, C., & Fleming, D. (1986). Global perspectives in textbooks. *Social Education, 50*(5), 376–384.
Davis, J. E. (1987). *Teaching economics to young adolescents: A research-based rationale.* San Francisco: Foundation for Teaching Economics.
DeHaven, E. P. (1988). *Teaching and learning the language arts* (3rd ed.). Glenview, IL: Scott, Foresman.
Devine, T. (1978). Listening: What do we know after fifty years of research and theorizing? *Journal of Reading, 21*(5), 262–267.
Dupuis, M. M. (1984). *Reading in the content areas: Research for teachers.* Newark, DE: International Reading Association.
Early, M. (1984). *Reading to learn in grades 5 to 12.* New York: Harcourt Brace Jovanovich.
Finn, C., & Ravitch, D. (1988). No trivial pursuit. *Phi Delta Kappan, 69,* 559–564.
Fishbein, M., & Ajzen, I. (1975). *Belief, attitude, intention and behavior: An introduction to theory and research.* Reading, MA: Addison-Wesley.
Flanders, J. R. (1987). How much of the content in mathematics textbooks is new? *Arithmetic Teacher, 35,* 18–23.
Fountas, I. C., & Hannigan, I. L. (1989). Making sense of whole language: The pursuit of informed teaching. *Childhood Education, 65,* 133–137.
Froese, E. (1991). Introduction to whole-language teaching and learning. In V. Froese (Ed.), *Whole language: Practice and theory* (pp. 2–16). Boston: Allyn & Bacon.
Galbraith, R., & Jones, T. (1976). *Moral Reasoning.* Anoka, MN: Greenhaven Press.
Glatthorn, A. A. (1987). *Curriculum leadership.* Glenview, IL: Scott, Foresman.
Goodlad, J. I. (1984). *A place called school.* New York: McGraw-Hill.
Goodman, K. (1986). *What's whole in whole language?* Richmond Hill, Ontario: Scholastic-TAB.
Graves, D. H. (1983). *Writing: Teachers and children at work.* Exeter, NH: Heinemann.
Hartoonian, H. M., & Laughlin, M. A. (1989). Designing a social studies scope and sequence for the 21st century. *Social Education 53* (6), 388–398.
Hastie, R. (1986). A primer of information-processing theory for the political scientist. In R. R. Lau & D. O. Sears (Eds.). *Political cognition.* Hillsdale, NJ: Lawrence Erlbaum.
Hoskisson, K., & Tompkins, G. E. (1987). *Language arts: Content and teaching strategies.* New York: Merrill/Macmillan.
Jacobs, H. H. (1991). Planning for curriculum integration. *Educational Leadership 49*(2), 27–28.
Karlin, R., & Karlin, A. R. (1987). *Teaching elementary reading* (4th ed.). San Diego, CA: Harcourt Brace Jovanovich.
Kerekes, J. (1987). The interdisciplinary unit is here to stay. *The Middle School Journal, 18*(4), 12–14.
Kniep, W. M. (1989). Social studies within a global education. *Social Education, 53*(6), 385, 399–403.
Leming, J. S. (1989). The two cultures of social studies education. *Social Education, 53*(6), 404–408.
Longstreet, W. (1985). Citizenship: The phantom core of social studies. *Theory and Research in Social Education, 13,* 21–29.
McCormick, K. (1981). Good listening skills help kids learn. *American School Board Journal, 168*(9), 37, 42.
McGuire, M. (1992). Board seeks members' comments. *The Social Studies Professional, 110,* 1.
McKnight, C. C., Crosswhite, F. J., Dossey, J. A., Kifer, E., Swafford, J. O., Travers, K.

J., & Cooney, T. J. (1987). *The underachieving curriculum: Assessing U.S. school mathematics from an international perspective.* Champaign, IL: Stipes.

Manna, A. L., Misheff, S., & Robitaille, N. (1988). Do students read for pleasure? *The Middle School Journal, 19*(4), 28–30.

Manning, G., & Manning, M. (1990). Here they come! *Teaching K-8, 21*(3), 48–51.

Martin, K., & McGrevin, C. (1990). Making mathematics happen. *Educational Leadership, 47*, 20–22.

Massalias, B., & Cox, C. B. (1966). *Inquiry in the social studies.* New York: McGraw-Hill.

Maxwell, J. C. (1988). Essentials of English. *Language Arts, 60*, 245–248.

Metcalf, L. E. (Ed.). (1971). *Values education: Rationale, strategies and procedures.* Washington, DC: National Council for the Social Studies.

Monson, D. L., Taylor, B. M., & Dykstra, R. (1988). *Language arts: Teaching and learning effective use of language.* Glenview, IL: Scott, Foresman.

Morrissett, I. (1986). Status of social studies: The mid-1980s. *Social Education, 50*(4), 303–310.

Morrissett, I. (Ed.). (1982). *Social Studies in the 1980s.* Alexandria, VA: Association for Supervision and Curriculum Development.

Murray, D. (1984). *Write to learn.* New York: Holt.

National Center for Improving Science Education (NCISE). (1990). A blueprint for elementary school science. *Streamlined Seminar* (National Association of Elementary School Principals), 8(5), 1–8.

National Commission on Social Studies in the Schools. (1989). *Charting a course: Social studies for the 21st century.* Washington, DC: Author.

National Council for Geographic Education. (1984). *Guidelines for geographic education: Elementary and secondary schools.*

National Council for the Social Studies, Task Force on Scope and Sequence (NCSS). (1984, 1989). In search of a scope and sequence for social social studies. *Social Education, 48*(4), 249–262; *Social Education, 53*(6), 376–387.

National Council for the Social Studies, Task Force on Social Studies in the Middle School (NCSS). (1991). Social studies in the middle school. *Social Education, 55* 5, 287–293.

National Council of Teachers of Mathematics. (1989). *Curriculum and evaluation standards in school mathematics.* Reston, VA: The Council.

National Council of Teachers of Mathematics. (1991). *Professional standards for teaching mathematics.* Reston, VA: The Council.

National Research Council. (1989). *Everybody counts: A report on the future of mathematics education.* Washington, DC: National Academy Press.

National Research Council. (1990). *Reshaping school mathematics: A framework for curriculum.* Washington, DC: National Academy Press.

National Science Teachers' Association (NSTA). (1986). Position statement: Science education for middle and junior high school students. *Science and Children, 24*(3), 62–63.

Naylor, D., & Diem, R. (1987). *Elementary and middle school social studies.* New York: Random House.

Newmann, F. M. (1988). *Higher-order thinking in high school social studies: An analysis of classrooms.* National Center on Effective Secondary Schools. Madison, WI: University of Wisconsin.

Newmann, F. M. (1989). Reflective civic participation. *Social Education 53*(6), 357–360.

Newmann, F. M., Bertocci, T. A., & Landness, R. M. (1977). *Skills in citizen action: An English-social studies program for secondary schools.* Niles, IL: National Textbook Co.

Norton, D. (1985). *The effective teaching of language arts* (2nd ed.). New York: Merrill/Macmillan.

Parker, W. C., (Ed.). (1989). Participatory citizenship. *Social Education 53*(6), 353–374.

Parker, W. C. (1991). *Renewing the social studies curriculum.* Alexandria, VA: Association for Supervision and Curriculum Development.

Pejouhy, N. H. (1990). Teaching math for the 21st century. *Phi Delta Kappan, 72*(1), 76–78.

Petty, W. T., Petty, D. C., & Becking, M. F. (1989). *Experiences in language: Tools and techniques for language arts* (5th ed.). Boston: Allyn & Bacon.

Pikulski, J. J. (1991). The transition years: The middle school. In J. Flood, J. M. Jensen, D. Lapp, and J. R. Square (Eds.), *Handbook of research on teaching the English language arts* (pp. 307–319). New York: Macmillan.

Rest, J. (1983). Morality. In P. Hussen (Ed.), *Handbook of child psychology.* New York: Wiley & Sons.

Rumelhardt, D. E., & Norman, D. (1978). Accretion, tuning and restructuring: Three modes of learning. In J. W. Cotton & R. Klatsky (Eds.), *Semantic factors in cognition.* Hillsdale, NJ: Lawrence Erlbaum.

Schwartz, L. L. (1984). *Exceptional students in the mainstream.* Belmont, CA: Wadsworth.

Shaver, J. (1985). Commitment to values and the study of social problems in citizenship education. *Social Education, 49,* 194–197.

Shaughnessy, J. M., & Haladyna, T. M. (1985). Research on student attitude toward social studies. *Social Education, 49*(8), 692–695.

Simon, H. (1957). *Models of men.* New York: John Wiley.

Smith, R. J., & Barrett, T. C. (1979). *Teaching reading in the middle grades* (2nd ed.). Reading, MA: Addison-Wesley.

Steen, L. A. (1989). Teaching mathematics for tomorrow's world. *Educational Leadership, 47,* 18–21.

Sternberg, R. J. (1985a). Critical thinking: Its nature, measurement, and improvement. In F. R. Link (Ed.), *Essays on the intellect.* Alexandria, VA: Association for Supervision and Curriculum Development.

Sternberg, R. J. (1985b). *Beyond IQ: A triarchic theory of human intelligence.* New York: Cambridge University Press.

Superka, D. (1974). Approaches to values education. *Social Science Education Consortium Newsletter, 20,* 1–4.

Taylor, R. (1980). *Computers in the schools: Tool, tutor, and tutee.* New York, NY: Columbia University, Teachers' College Press.

Turning points: Preparing American youth for the 21st century. (1989). Washington, DC: Carnegie Council on Adolescent Development.

Vars, G. F. (1987). *Interdisciplinary teaching in the middle grades.* Columbus, OH: National Middle School Association.

Watson, D., Burke, C., & Hartse, J. (1989). *Whole language: Inquiring voices.* Richmond Hill, Ontario: Scholastic-TAB.

Willoughby, S. S. (1990). *Mathematics education for a changing world.* Alexandria, VA: Association for Supervision and Curriculum Development.

Wilt, M. (1950). Study of teacher awareness of listening factors in elementary education. *Journal of Educational Research, 43*(8), 626–636.

Zaharias, J. A. (1983). Microcomputers in the language arts classroom: Promises and pitfalls. *Language Arts, 60,* 990–996.

CHAPTER OUTLINE

The Middle Level Curriculum

exploratory, elective, and career options

8

OVERVIEW

The middle level is an appropriate time for students to explore careers, general interests, hobbies, learner interests, and physical fitness. Exploratory programs provide young adolescents with insight into the personal, social, and academic dimensions of the middle level curriculum. Exploratory courses are required for grades 6, 7, and 8 for short periods of six to eight weeks. The middle level curriculum needs to focus its design and implementation on the creativity, exploration, aesthetic awareness, imagination, problem solving, and self-identification of young adolescents as part of the academic core. In developing exploratory activities, factors such as the student's reading levels, achievement levels, aptitudes, thinking levels, attention spans, special interests, individual characteristics, and mental and physical abilities must be considered. While the emphasis should focus on the "here and now," it is vital to prepare middle level youth for the challenges and career opportunities of the future. In considering the future, students should assess their individual roles by exploring career opportunities that complement their aptitudes and interests. The provision of exploratory activities in arts education, foreign languages, health, physical education, home economics, and technology education through personal experiences, electives, and career education opportunities will continue to be an essential component of the middle level curriculum. These content areas are the means for developing personal interests, talents, creativity, aesthetics, and career opportunities to further enhance the self-concept and self-understanding of young adolescents.

In this chapter, you will read about:

1. A rationale for arts education.
2. Developmentally appropriate art experiences, goals, and objectives to be addressed when planning and implementing art programs.
3. Creative writing that enables students to enjoy writing as a process from pre-writing to publishing.
4. Dance education providing all young adolescents with opportunities to develop an appreciation and understanding of dance as an art form.
5. Media arts programs that utilize the technology and techniques of the electronic age.
6. Developmentally appropriate music experiences, goals, and objectives to be addressed when planning and implementing music education programs.
7. A theater curriculum that utilizes drama/theater experiences as a means to develop self-awareness and self-concept.
8. The place of foreign languages as exploratory, elective, and required credit options.
9. Health education that promotes positive health attitudes and behaviors of young adolescents.
10. Physical education as a balanced perspective between competitive sports and physical fitness.
11. The framework for home economics/home arts curriculum.
12. Developmentally appropriate experiences, goals, objectives, and content for technology education.
13. The purposes of current and proposed career education initiatives.

EXPLORATORY PROGRAMS

How does an exploratory program provide experiences for arts, technology education, home economics/home arts, and careers? Exploratory themes might include the cultural impact of the technological era in such areas as communication, transportation, industry, manufacturing, and computers. In art education, there have been trends toward aesthetics, increasing requirements for visual arts courses, and the introduction of visual design and computer graphics. In music, expanding music instruction for everyone is suggested, with emphasis on lifelong learning and music for listening and enjoyment. In physical education, increased attention should be devoted to education and training for lifetime participation in leisure sports, with new emphasis on aerobics, weight training, and activities for young adolescents of differing physical abilities. Health education could provide young adolescents with investigations concerning drugs, pregnancies, suicide, and nutrition. In home economics, some topics that might be considered are the impact of technology on home, work, and the environment and the challenges confronting families in maintaining a family unit in the face of drugs, divorce, latchkey children, and how to manage money and achieve financial stability.

Exploratory activities provide significant opportunities for students to learn in different ways using unique skills such as artistic expression, utilization of imagination, and career awareness. The integration of content with personal and social concerns is an essential part of any middle level curriculum. Perhaps nowhere does the young adolescent have more opportunity to learn to accept his or her uniqueness than in an exploratory program designed to meet each student's specific needs. These needs must address individual needs that result from the dynamic and many-sided changes occurring in the young adolescent. Exploratory programs provide opportunities for students to participate in activities that interest them. These activities should be as diverse as the interests of the young adolescents and should utilize a variety of approaches, including clubs, electives, fairs, and exhibits. Because middle level learners vary widely in their maturation rate, intellectual range, and achievement level, a wide range of exploratory offerings must be planned.

The length of an exploratory program may follow different schedules. Some middle level schools have experimented with a regular period every day, some with a half hour several days a week, others have scheduled one hour a week, and still others have scheduled two or three full days per semester or year. It is important that all young adolescents have varied exploratory activities each year.

The key to setting up exploratory activities is to know the needs of middle level learners; to plan effectively so that the constraints of time, volunteers, and space do not restrict the program; and to gain the support of the faculty, students, parents, and community. More attention needs to be directed toward recognizing personal and social dimensions that will contribute to success at school, regardless of grades or levels. If opportunities for exploration are not provided, many young adolescents will be denied meaningful learning experiences. Responsive middle level schools will not be fully achieved until the needs of all middle level youth have been addressed through a curriculum with exploratory opportunities.

ARTS EDUCATION

The emphasis on academic achievement and the value attached to testing and accountability have compromised the status of arts education in American schools. Basics education and competency testing programs implemented in most states to remedy the problems of student deficiencies in basic skills have narrowed the focus of the school curriculum, often resulting in a curriculum that is culturally deficient. Bloom in *The Closing of the American Mind* (1987), Hirsch in *Cultural Literacy* (1987), and Ravitch and Finn in *What Do Our 17-Year-Olds Know?* (1987) have deplored the cultural level of the school programs available in the humanities and the arts. Middle level schools have had to struggle to maintain humanities and arts programs in a system driven by test score results.

In an effort to revitalize the role of the arts in education, Congress in 1985 called for a study of the status of arts education in American schools. The study group, the National Endowment for the Arts (NEA), submitted its report, *Toward Civilization: A Report on Arts Education*, as an open letter to the American people, including the education sector and the arts community. The report suggested four purposes for arts education in the school curriculum: (1) to give a sense of civilization to young people, (2) to foster creativity, (3) to teach communication through the languages of all the arts forms, and (4) to provide tools for critical assessment of what one reads, sees, and hears (NEA, 1988).

In the middle level setting, arts education has consisted mainly of art and music. In many schools, the arts education program has been expanded to include dance, drama, and creative writing. In *Toward Civilization*, the National Endowment for the Arts (NEA) defined basic arts education as including the "disciplines of *language* (from the art of writing); *visual art and design* (from the arts of painting, sculpture, photography, video, crafts, architecture, landscape and interior design, product and graphic design); *performing arts* (from the arts of dance, music, opera, musical theater, and theater); and *media arts* (from the arts of film, television, and radio)" (1988, p. 13). Under this expanded notion of basic arts education, middle level schools would provide programs for art, creative writing, dance, media arts, music, and drama/theater.

The importance of arts education in the total development of the learner was recognized in a position paper developed by the Association of Childhood Education International (ACEI) (Jalongo, 1990). The following precepts were considered essential to solidifying the place of the arts in a comprehensive middle school curriculum:

1 Every young adolescent has the right to opportunities for imaginative expression.
2 Educating the young adolescent's imagination is education for the future.
3 The educated imagination is the key to equity and intercultural understanding.
4 Young adolescents' creative productivity is qualitatively different from that of adults.
5 Creative expression should permeate the entire curriculum.
6 Imagination is the key to artistry in teaching and excellence in our schools.
7 Schools must be refashioned to reduce the use of textbooks, tests, and rigid schedules, to provide learners with more opportunities to reflect upon experiences, and to understand their own imaginative processes, as well as those of others (Jalongo, 1990).

Discipline-Based Art Education

The Getty Center for Education in the Arts was organized to determine why arts education was held in such low esteem in American schools. The center examined programs in visual arts education throughout the United States and found a primary emphasis placed on developing creative expression and artistic skills. The center's report, *Beyond Creating* (1985), sought to solidify the relative position of the visual arts in the school curriculum by expanding the content beyond creative expression. It recommended that for art to be accorded higher status in the curriculum, the content of the visual arts program should be broadened to include art history, art criticism, and aesthetics.

This new rationale for the visual arts gave an academic orientation to art education. The movement to teach the arts as content is known as Discipline-Based Art Education (DBAE). DBAE programs are intended to provide systematic, sequential teaching that involves students in creating, studying, and experiencing the arts. DBAE programs enable all students, not just those gifted and talented in art, to engage in the things people do with the arts: they make works of art, they appreciate art, they learn to understand art in relation to cultures, and they make judgments about the arts. These translate into four program areas: art production, art criticism, art history, and aesthetics. DBAE differs from other art programs in its focus on getting learners involved in the making of visual imagery, which is not synonymous with learning to see visual images. While most learners will not become professional artists, all students can learn to appreciate not only the arts but the visual forms of the environment in which they live. Rather than trying to make artists of all learners, DBAE focuses on the things most people actually do with art (Brandt, 1987/1988).

DBAE has been characterized as boring and as having a narrow vision; however, DBAE is based on sound learning theory and provides high degrees of active participation by students, self-structuring individual learning experiences, and the internalizing of aesthetic qualities which are exhibited in students' production (Cowan & Clover, 1991).

The nature of early adolescence and the rapidly occurring developmental changes can lead to an almost constant evaluation of self-concept. DBAE can make a positive contribution to young adolescents' self-concepts, another major focus promoted by the middle level education. In fact, Cowan & Clover (1991) suggested that learners in a school environment which encourages creative expression of emotion and allows opportunities to talk about feelings will tend to be accepting of their own feelings and those of their classmates. The benefits may be greatest for those students with the lowest self-concepts; however, DBAE has the potential for helping all young people learn about art, their world, and themselves in ways that create security, personal worth, and accomplishment.

Since the advent of Discipline-Based Art Education, other expressive arts areas such as music, dance, theater, creative writing, and media arts have assumed a DBAE format. Some specialists in music, dance, and theater urge caution in joining the rush to discipline-based approaches. Many educators still view the studio, the museum, and the stage as the central focus of arts education. There were concerns that the discipline-based approach with its "bias in favor of intellect" sacrificed too much creative expression to gain academic status (Ewens, 1986).

Many states are developing comprehensive arts programs combining formal study and creative expression in the expressive arts of art, drama, creative writing, dance, and music. One state, South Carolina, has developed a far-reaching program, the Arts in Basic Curriculum project, to provide every child with an arts education program comparable to programs in other basic subject areas. Curriculum guidelines were developed for art, dance, music, and theater with emphasis on creative expression, aesthetic perception, cultural heritage, and aesthetic valuing. The intent of the Arts in Basic Curriculum program is to make the study of the arts a basic component of the school curriculum, on a par with other basic academic subjects in the sciences and humanities (South Carolina Arts in Basic Curriculum, 1987).

A Student-Centered Approach to Arts Education

In *Creative and Mental Growth* (1987), Lowenfeld and Brittain effectively develop the relationships between cognitive development and creative and artistic expression. Primary themes are the importance of art in education, art as a means of understanding growth and development, the development of creativity and aesthetic awareness, and the theory that creative expression develops in stages from childhood to adolescence. Learning through the senses fosters interaction between the learner and the environment. Education in the three broad areas of knowledge, the humanities, the arts, and the sciences should emphasize the development of perceptual sensitivity. Mental growth is enhanced by rich, relevant, and diverse experiences that learners have with the total environment. The curriculum of the middle level school needs to be broadened beyond basic skills and factual information to promote opportunities in all subject areas for creative expression, aesthetic awareness, critical thinking, problem solving, and self-identification. In this learner-centered approach, the teacher's role is to provide a stimulating environment which facilitates the learner's creative self-expression.

Artistic expression, enjoyment, and motivation change as the young adolescent proceeds through developmental stages. During the middle level years, young adolescents enter a pseudo-naturalistic stage characterized by reduced spontaneity, critical evaluation of their art products, and increased self-consciousness. Young adolescents who perceive that they do not draw or paint well will lose much of their confidence and consequently their motivation for and enjoyment of artistic expression. During the middle level years, young adolescents are struggling with diverse and pervasive problems related to self-identification. The goals of the school art program should focus on (1) the interests, needs, and concerns of students, (2) the process of creating art, not the end products, and (3) a wide variety of artistic modes, including drawing, painting, sculpting, crafting, media arts, and other forms (Lowenfeld & Brittain, 1987, pp. 353–356).

While the theories and suggestions in the book deal with art, they are applicable to other areas of arts education such as music, dance, theater, and creative writing. Arts education can be such a satisfying study for young adolescents that teachers must be cognizant of the contributions that arts education can make to the total development of the learner.

Artistic Intelligences

Gardner (1990) sees the arts emanating from a framework of multiple intelligences. From his studies of cognition and human development, Gardner proposed the existence of a number of discrete kinds of human intelligences. He defined intelligence as the ability to solve problems or to fashion a product, such as a poem or a play, that is valued in one or more cultural settings. This notion that making a product exemplifies intelligence is a striking departure from the traditional theory of intelligence. The theory of multiple intelligences has significant implications for studying, experiencing, and creating in the arts.

The seven intelligences have implications for school reform, for the ways we regard human capacities, and for curriculum development. They consist of the following: (1) linguistic, (2) logical–mathematical, (3) musical, (4) spatial, (5) bodily kinesthetic, (6) interpersonal, and (7) intrapersonal. Gardner maintains that the schools place a very high premium on linguistic and logical–mathematical intelligences because they promote performance in the essential subject areas of language, mathematics, and science. Gardner maintains that it is critically important to use and refine the artistic intelligences.

Gardner does not establish specific ways that multiple intelligence may be used in schools. He suggests that just as people look different and have different personalities, they also have different minds and different ways of demonstrating their intelligence. Recognizing the differences in human minds calls for individual-centered schooling which allows learners to find something they are good at and fashion something that has value and importance to them and others.

Eisner (1990) suggests that multiple intelligences have implications for curriculum balance. He describes two kinds of balance—culturally-referenced balance and personally-referenced balance. The culturally-referenced curriculum includes those subject areas and skills that all children must master. All students need to learn to read, write, compute, and study content such as history and science. The personally-balanced curriculum enables students to follow their intellectual interests, their fantasies, and their feelings. The artistic intelligences enable students to attain this curriculum balance of academic, social, and personal development.

Artistic intelligences have significant implications for curriculum and instruction in middle level schools. The guiding philosophy of the middle level proposes that what is taught and the way it is taught should meet the unique developmental needs of young adolescents. The theory of multiple intelligence gives credibility to forms of intelligence other than linguistic and logical–mathematical. The theory of artistic intelligences enables teachers to teach young adolescents as individuals, not as a collective group labeled with a specific IQ score.

The Arts and an Interdisciplinary Curriculum

The goals advocated by national associations for the arts are compatible with the educational goals of the humanities and the sciences. The middle level curriculum offers opportunities to connect subject areas to each other toward a confluence of meaning. Students are encouraged to link these broader meanings and understandings of integrated subject areas to real-world situations and settings. William Bennett maintains that the arts give "coherence, depth and resonance to other academic subjects" (1988, p. 4). The arts have the capacity to add sparkle and effervescence to what at times can be a mundane and unspirited curriculum.

Middle level teachers can enhance their own subject area by integrating the arts into their learning activities. Teachers should also share with students their appreciation and knowledge of the arts as content to study, create, and experience. Classroom teachers and specialists in art, theater, dance, and music should plan together to maximize the learning experiences in academic core subjects, exploratory and elective courses, and class sessions in art, music, dance, and theater (Farrell, 1991).

The possibilities for integrating the arts into middle level subject areas are limitless. The humanities, sciences, and arts should never be viewed as discrete, autonomous content areas. On the contrary, the three broad areas of knowledge and experience are connected, interdependent, and overlapping.

Language arts teachers are examining connections "between the visual and verbal arts, between seeing and responding, envisioning and composing" (National Council of Teachers of English, 1989, p. 13). Language arts and literature-based reading afford excellent opportunities for creative writing. The ability of middle level student authors to create their own stories is enhanced by reading stories of peers and adult writers. Visual arts, music, drama, and dance may provide prompts that facilitate the writing process. Popular music, folk music, and classical music may be listened to and studied in relationship to themes from novels, their own experiences, and the experiences of other students. Visual arts and drama can evoke deep feelings, values questions, and evaluative responses from young adolescents (Farrell, 1991).

Social studies holds rich potential for infusing the arts into the various social science disciplines. Music, drama, dance, and art are produced in all cultures. Artistic expression shapes a culture and the culture shapes artistic expression. The arts, the humanities, and the sciences can be studied in an interdisciplinary manner, but also from a sociological, political, historical, geographical, and other social science perspective. Social study is the examination of human experience in all of its literary, artistic, and scientific dimensions. In like manner, the arts can be integrated into science, health, physical education, mathematics, and other content areas. Integrated study enriches meaning, understanding, and humaneness.

Developmentally Appropriate Arts Education Experiences

Educators have long recognized the futility and dangers of providing reading, mathematics, or other subject area experiences that do not meet young adolescents' readiness levels. Failure, frustration, and blows to the self-concept can occur when young adolescents are faced with learning tasks for which they are not physically, psychosocially, or intellectually ready. Providing appropriate experiences in arts education is equally important. Educators must match young adolescents' development with aesthetic perception, creative expression, arts heritage, and aesthetic valuing.

Young adolescents must have reached a particular level of intellectual functioning to make aesthetic judgments, to recognize and compare artistic productions, to appreciate the cultural heritage of the different areas, and to compare themes and symbols. Young adolescents' quest for increased freedom and independence can contribute significantly to their broadening arts interests and the transferring of personal experiences into artistic forms. Likewise, the physical manipulations, movements, and methods of the art form should match young learners' physical development and psychosocial development. Teachers' expectations should include the learners working alone, in pairs, or in small groups in cooperative efforts toward a particular goal.

Assessment of Arts Performance, Abilities, and Skills

The primary goal of assessing and evaluating arts education should be to help teachers improve their instructional programs. Evaluation should include student performance portfolios, interviews, reports, and projects rather than the items relating to recall, identification, and definitions. Likewise, evaluation of the student progress should focus on school districts, as opposed to state and national assessments. Such evaluation approaches assess student artistic production in relation to individual teacher objectives (Topping, 1990).

Essential Considerations in Arts Education

1 The arts program should reflect the tenets of effective middle level practice espoused in such documents as *Turning Points* (1989) and *This We Believe* (NMSA, 1992).

2 Middle level arts programs should be developmentally appropriate and should reflect aesthetic perception, creative expression, arts heritage, and aesthetic valuing.

3 All young adolescents should have equal access to arts experiences, whether for appreciation or actual doing, regardless of their artistic ability.

4 The arts program should be considered an integral aspect of the middle level curriculum and the total education program.

ART

Educators need to reach an agreement on what art programs should teach and the directions of effective programs. Topping (1990) advocated that the art curriculum should include art production, art history, aesthetics, art criticism, and knowledge concerning civilization. While some debate has focused on the term *creative self-expression*, Topping believed the art program should include the creative process which demands reflection, analysis, and synthesis. Likewise, Topping suggested that the art program requires structure and sequence, and the mastery of skills involving perception, composition, and consideration of techniques of the medium. Other objectives include developing an awareness of what is beautiful in student art work; the work of artists and the environment; an appreciation and knowledge of historical and contemporary art of North and South America, Asia, Africa, and Europe; and an awareness of the relationship of art to the total culture (Topping, 1990).

Middle level educators can play vital roles in promoting, planning, and implementing art programs for young adolescents. Rather than perceiving art programs as being a frill or a curricular area of lesser worth, educators must provide a developmentally appropriate art program which has an established scope and sequence for each middle grade level, as well as one which reflects the research on effective middle level practices.

Organization of Knowledge. Instruction in the visual arts can be included throughout the interdisciplinary learning experiences commonly found in the middle level school. Line, shape, color, texture, form, space, light, and motion are concepts generally taught in art. How these concepts are organized involves balance, emphasis, continuity, proportion, and patterning. For these terms to become meaningful, they need to be organized in the framework of a larger unit proposal decided upon by teachers and students in the interdisciplinary setting of the middle level school. For example, one way for educators to present the concept of line is to see its meaning in nature and also to see how architects use lines in their drawings and blueprints. Once young adolescents understand the concept of line, art activities may include using lines to create space and can take an interdisciplinary approach by including sociology, economics, language arts, and mathematics.

Basic Skills. The teaching of the basic skills can be accomplished by integrating art and other subject area disciplines. The young adolescent's communication skills, analytic skills, and technical skills can be addressed through a carefully considered art education program. Communication skills can be taught throughout the integrated curriculum approach and can also stress art as an important tool in the inquiry process for solving problems. Analytic skills relate to logic and thought processes and include such skills as gathering data, analyzing, synthesizing, and evaluating. Art experiences can include selecting subject matter, comparing sizes, planning compositions, and extracting meaning. Technical skills in art involve developing psychomotor skills in perfecting craftsmanship and, specifically, such skills as using and caring for tools, media, and art equipment.

Personal Development Through Art. Career awareness, visual perceptual development, and art appreciation are areas where art can contribute to the personal development of the young adolescent. Interdisciplinary problems concerning the world of work can prepare the middle level learner with knowledge of career choices. Art offers choices of the teaching profession, commercial design, interior design, art history, and industrial design as well as other career options. The middle level art program should emphasize visual perception and should base curricular and instructional decisions on the learner's development stage. The dramatic changes in thinking that occur during early adolescence allow learners to see details and to draw more realistically (Glenn, 1986).

Basic Art Skills for the Middle Level Years. Basic art skills[1] can be broken down into four components: aesthetic perception (visual and tactile); creative expression (artistic knowledge and skills); visual arts heritage (historical and cultural); and aesthetic valuing (analysis, interpretation, and judgment). Also, specific objectives for the middle level school can be suggested for each skill.

1. *Aesthetic perception* includes such objectives as (1) increased aesthetic awareness of visual and tactile qualities in works of art, and (2) seeing the physical world directly and metaphorically in terms of images and symbols that are unique to the visual arts.
2. *Creative expression* includes such objectives as (1) acquiring artistic skills to express and to communicate responses to visual experiences, (2) recognizing the importance of personal experiences and respecting one's work as well as the work of others, and (3) developing manipulative and organizational skills in using arts media effectively to translate ideas, feelings, and values.
3. *Visual arts heritage* includes such objectives as (1) studying a variety of art works and accomplishments from contemporary, historical, and prehistorical cultures, (2) understanding that art reflects, records, and shapes history and plays a role in every culture, (3) gaining an understanding of one's own creative abilities and heritage within the context of a comprehensive world view, and (4) clarifying one's own values and learning to appreciate differences in the aesthetic values of others.
4. *Aesthetic valuing* includes such objectives as (1) making informed responses

---

[1]Adapted from *Basic Art Skills: the South Carolina Framework for Visual Arts Education*, 1987, Columbia, SC: South Carolina Department of Education. Adapted by permission.

to works of art, (2) deriving meaning and value from experiences, and (3) using analysis, interpretation, and judgment about visual relationships based on learned aesthetic values to improve art production (South Carolina Department of Education, 1987).

CREATIVE WRITING

There is a growing movement throughout the United States to revitalize instruction in the "second R." Reading enables learners to absorb the thoughts and ideas of other people. Writing, the "second R," allows students to think through their own ideas and express them. Writing practices and programs are gaining acceptance in schools and colleges and hold promise for elevating writing performance for all of our children (Silberman, 1989).

VARIOUS WRITING APPROACHES

Contemporary issues regarding creative writing include writing across the curriculum, whole language programs, National Writing Project (NWP), literary arts, the reading–writing connection, cultural literacy, and collaboration between and among languages, sciences, humanities, and arts. A pantheon of writer educators such as Lucy Calkins, Donald Graves, James Gray, and Nancie Atwell have helped teachers become more proficient and more creative writers. It has been suggested that teachers who write will value writing and consequently will be more effective in teaching children to write.

Assessments of writing achievement (NAEP, 1986) indicate that 75% of the young people who took the test displayed a general understanding of grammar, punctuation, and spelling. However, knowing the rules for writing has not helped students to write well. Most students could not organize their ideas and express themselves with style, wit, or interest (Silberman, 1989).

At the middle level, creative writing seeks to remedy this situation by helping students to write with meaning and style. Various approaches being utilized—"students as writers," whole language, writing across the curriculum, and classrooms as literate communities, for instance—hold promise for improving writing performance. Creative writing emphasizes process as instrumental in creating a piece of writing. Experts in writing usually arrange the processes into the following elements: pre-writing, drafting, redrafting/revising, writing additional drafts, editing/proofreading, and evaluating/publishing (Mueller, 1989).

RESOURCES

Two noteworthy books that help teachers introduce the writing process to their middle level classrooms are Nancie Atwell's *In the Middle: Reading, Writing and*

Learning with Adolescents and Tom Romano's *Clearing the Way: Working with Teenage Writers.* These two writer–teachers turned their middle level classrooms into writing workshops using dialogue journals, response groups, writing conferences, literature study groups, and various other techniques to promote writing, reading, learning, and thinking. A fundamental principle of these innovative writing strategies is to provide young adolescents with ownership of the writing process. A sense of ownership empowers young adolescents to take a measure of control and responsibility for the choices they make; the way they use their time; the responses they make to literature and writing; the approaches they take to evaluating others and themselves; and their personal development as writers.

Nancie Atwell Model

There is growing evidence that thousands of middle level teachers throughout the country have patterned their classrooms on the Nancie Atwell workshop model. Teachers have modified the experiences, accounts, and methods Atwell described in *In the Middle,* to make them work in their own classrooms in concert with their own particular teaching styles (1989). Dudley (1989) adapted the elements of the writing process model to make it work for her students, who, because of their diverse minority backgrounds, their wide ranges of abilities, and their lack of a writing process program in elementary school, required more structured exercises and student accountability to ensure writing success. Connell (1990) used relevant events, media presentations, brainstorming study groups, and significant poets to involve her students in enjoying poetry and writing their own poems.

Reading good fiction, nonfiction, plays, and poems is an important ingredient in producing creative writing. Many teachers have realized the importance of choosing books with an adolescent or young adult theme rather than only "classics". It is important for the teacher to read these books too, so that there can be a mutual sharing of ideas, themes, impressions, and understandings about them. Students respond very positively when teachers show that they value the literature of young people's lives and living (Atwell, 1987; Dionisio, 1991; Gilles, 1989; and Rakow, 1991).

For creative writing to become an activity that many young adolescents can enjoy, teachers need to share the writing process with students. Students need to go through all the steps of the writing process—brainstorming, drafting, rewriting, and publishing. They need to experience the magic of writing (Roop, 1990).

DANCE

Several national commissions for the arts and humanities have maintained that the arts and humanities should occupy a place of similar importance to science, mathematics, and technology in contemporary American society and in the schools. A broader view of arts education places dance, theater, and creative writing with art and music in middle level curriculum design and implementation. Many states have developed arts programs that require teaching dance to all students in the K–12 school program.

PURPOSES

The purpose of dance education at the middle level is to provide *all* young adolescents with opportunities to develop an understanding and appreciation of dance as an art form. Dance education should include experiences that enable students to develop the skills necessary to create dance expression and to obtain meaning from observing dance performances. Current trends in dance education are extending the content of dance education beyond performing and creating. For complete acceptance as a subject, dance must be viewed as an intellectual process fostering higher-level thinking skills as well as a physical one (Hanstein, 1990).

Children can communicate through movement. Movement can be functional (walking) or expressive (dancing). Dance in its simplest form is expressive movement. The content for dance in middle level schools focuses on (1) movement skills and elements, (2) creating and performing, and (3) social, cultural, and historical perspectives (Lehman, 1988).

DANCE EDUCATION CURRICULUM

The dance education curriculum is being influenced by the discipline-based arts curriculum suggested by the Getty Foundation in *Beyond Creating* (Getty Center for Education in the Arts, 1985). A discipline-based dance curriculum would have an academic focus. The content would include an emphasis on dance history, dance criticism, aesthetics, and valuing in addition to dance performance (Schwartz, 1990). Some dance educators are alarmed by this overt academic focus and want to continue dance performance and creative expression as the core of the dance experience (Ewens, 1989).

At the middle level, dance becomes an area of more specialized study. Topics of study include (1) knowledge and care of the body as the instrument of dance, (2) traditional dance steps from many varieties of dance, (3) evaluation and criticism by students of their own and other dance performances, (4) improvisation and dance composition, (5) the integration of dance with other subject areas, such as history and social sciences, and (6) the importance of dance in the context of their own and other cultures (Lehman, 1988). Dance should be of high interest to young adolescents, particularly with the advent of dance video and the popularity of dance in the adolescent subculture.

IMPLICATIONS FOR MULTICULTURAL EDUCATION

Dance education has significant implications for multicultural education. All cultures have a propensity to express themselves through dance movement. Students can study dance in other cultures as a means of studying history and culture. Multicultural studies of dance enhance aesthetic awareness, humaneness, and creative expression. Through dance, students can understand and appreciate cultural differences, and in the process clarify their own values and more freely accept the values of others (Schwartz, 1991).

Dance education is demanding a larger share of the arts education schedule in the K–12 curriculum. Dance is now considered an important and relevant area of study and creative expression for all students in school. At the middle level, successful dance programs have been implemented in magnet schools stressing the performing arts. However, middle level curriculum reform must include dance education in the program of study for all young adolescents.

MEDIA ARTS

At the middle level, young adolescent interest in art expression through the traditional visual arts diminishes as they become more self-conscious and critical of their art products. However, interest in various types of media arts increases in middle level school and continues through high school. While for young adolescents there is not a popular art culture comparable to popular music culture, media arts are a satisfying form of art expression. Photography becomes an acceptable part of the art experience through imaging, processing, editing, enlarging, and other production processes. Film, television, and video production provide opportunities for young adolescents to utilize the artistic expression of the electronic age. Computers are becoming increasingly popular in the art program, both for studying and for producing art.

FORMS OF MEDIA ARTS

There are many forms that media arts programs can take. Middle level students can film their own television news programs to telecast in their own schools, as well as commercial productions to be shown in other settings. While student-produced film, television, and video productions are most often found in high schools, such creative and technical activities would be completely appropriate and acceptable in middle level schools. Some schools are now producing video yearbooks instead of the traditional print media yearbooks. While video yearbooks are a costly process, they have some definite applications to the school setting (Hargis, 1990).

Video art has become a popular form of media arts expression in recent years. Video art uses this art form to examine, analyze, and criticize commercial television programs. The advent of portable video equipment has revolutionized video art. In this medium, as in photography, films, and computers, the artist uses electronic technology to produce art (Tully, 1989).

Media arts programs involve students that traditional visual arts programs might not attract. Media arts combine immediacy, aesthetics, unlimited creative opportunities, and a pop-culture relevance that appeal to young adolescents.

MUSIC

Music has been an important creative process throughout history and may have the broadest popularity of all the arts in contemporary America. Millions of young adolescents play instruments, sing in a variety of choirs, spend enormous sums on recordings, watch MTV by the hour, attend concerts, and in other formal and informal ways participate in and listen to music. Nearly everyone likes some type of music expression (Music Educators National Conference, 1986). Music needs to be included in the curriculum of *all* young adolescents in the middle level school.

A RATIONALE FOR MUSIC IN THE MIDDLE LEVEL SCHOOL

The music curriculum changes in the middle level school. The prescribed curriculum distinguishes between students headed for careers in music and those who will continue to enjoy music for leisure purposes. The middle level program may provide: (1) study of piano, voice, string classes and applied study of specific instruments, and theory and composition, (2) performance opportunities in bands, choirs, ensembles, and orchestras, and (3) general music classes to promote recreational music (Choksy et al., 1986).

In the middle level school, students must be pleased with their performance. Students who have musical ability may continue on with the music program in bands, orchestras, and choral groups. Those students who have less musical ability or interest generally take the general music course. Quite often, the general music course causes students to build up a dislike for what they consider school music as opposed to popular music. Music also is provided as an exploratory activity for those who want to study a specific aspect of music or who want to sharpen their musical skills. These situations, which separate music education so pointedly by interest or ability, need to be modified to enable *all* middle level students to create, study, appreciate, and perform music. To remedy this middle level problem, a comprehensive and continuous K–12 music program, like the programs in most academic areas, must be developed for music education (Choksy, et al., 1986).

Such a comprehensive music education program would enable students from all backgrounds and all grade levels to discover and attain their music potential, to facilitate the practice and performance of music, and to appreciate music for its importance to personal and social development. The school music program should produce individuals who

1. are able to make music, alone and with others
2. are able to improvise and create music
3. are able to use the vocabulary and notation of music
4. are able to respond to music aesthetically, intellectually, and emotionally
5. are acquainted with a wide variety of music, including diverse musical styles and genres
6. understand the role music has played and continues to play in the lives of human beings
7. are able to make aesthetic judgments based on critical listening and analysis
8. have developed a commitment to music
9. support the musical life of the community and encourage others to do so
10. are able to continue their musical learning independently (Music Educators National Conference, 1986, pp. 13–14).

MIDDLE LEVEL SCHOOL MUSIC CURRICULUM

Early adolescence is a developmental period characterized by individual growth, self-identification, independent behaviors, and the need for discovery, exploration, and challenge. Music provides opportunities for young adolescents to pursue their own individual paths to music learning. It is important both to study music for its intrinsic value, and to integrate it into other content areas. Additionally, music should be connected to real-world settings. Greater effort is needed to include popular music in the school music program, not only because much contemporary music, such as jazz, rock, blues, soul, pop, and other forms, are worthy of study but also because popular music has such potential to motivate young adolescents. Music from different cultures and ethnic traditions should be included in the curriculum to enable students to understand and appreciate the artistic contributions of different groups in the United States and other countries. Music as a celebration of cultural diversity helps develop self-esteem, self-awareness, and self-discovery. The music curriculum for the middle level school encompasses the broad categories of performing/reading, creating, listening/describing, and valuing (Music Educators National Conference, 1986).

Many students on the middle level elect to participate in bands, orchestras, or choral groups. These students should be expected not only to gain the content and performance outcomes of the standard music program, but also to develop deeper knowledge and skills. These students should demonstrate increased ability to use the expressive qualities of music.

The school music program has a unique opportunity to enrich the learning opportunities of middle level students. Music has a great appeal to young adolescents. Music as an elective course and exploratory study enables students to use music to further their academic, social, and personal development.

DRAMA/THEATER

Theater as a middle level subject provides young adolescents with opportunities for self-exploration and self-understanding. Theater enables young adolescents to understand human behavior, to live vicariously, to explore thoughts and feelings, and to develop personal and interpersonal skills. Theater is an emotional and intellectual experience. By the middle level, theater should contain an academic focus, but should also develop the personal and social dimensions of the curriculum.

DIFFERENCES BETWEEN DRAMA AND THEATER

Theater educators distinguish between drama and theater. Drama is usually seen as less formal study and performance than theater. Drama is concerned with the educational values of the dramatic experience or activity. Young adolescents gain satisfaction from participating in plays, inventing their own creative drama, developing realistic socio-drama situations, and demonstrating a wide range of feelings, emotions, actions, and interpretations. Informal and formal drama opportunities should be available to all middle level students. Middle level students should be able to perform appropriate plays, adapt plays from literature or their own stories, improvise dramatic situations spontaneously, and use voice, language, and movement effectively to convey mood and feeling (Lehman, 1988).

Theater is a more formal study of the discipline, involving intellectual and analytical as well as emotional aspects of performance. Theater usually results in a dramatic performance by actors before an audience. The middle level student, building on the drama experiences of the elementary school, should experience a wide range of plots, stories, characterizations, and interpretations in plays, television shows, movies, creative drama, and role playing. Theater allows young adolescents opportunities to release emotions, to understand human behavior, to examine how television shows and films are similar and different from real-life situations, to sharpen their communication skills through writing and/or performing plays, and to evaluate theater productions. The learning outcomes for students in drama and theater are (1) to develop personal skills, (2) to create, and (3) to understand drama and theater (Lehman, 1988).

DRAMA AND THEATER ACTIVITIES

Drama and theater afford young adolescents opportunities for active, hands-on involvement. Reading plays and performing the roles increase student motivation to read, increase reading comprehension, and sharpen higher-order thinking skills. Drama has appeal for students from pre-school through high school and for all types of learners. Drama attends to the academic, social, and personal dimensions of curriculum and instruction. Discipline-based theater provides for the study of theater history, aesthetics, evaluation, and performance. Dramatic activities develop social skills through cooperation, collaboration, and conflict resolution. Drama promotes personal development in areas such as student confidence, self-esteem, and success (Yaffe, 1989).

DRAMA AND THEATER CURRICULUM

Representative of drama and theater curriculum programs in other states, the South Carolina Department of Education developed the South Carolina Framework for Drama/Theater Education as part of its Arts in Basic Curriculum (ABC) Project. The framework contains general and enabling objectives and skills, attitudes, and understandings for drama and theater in six developmental age levels ranging from Level One—kindergarten to Level Six—Grades 9 to 12 (specialized). The components for educating students in drama and theater are:

1 Aesthetic Perception–Concept Development (sensory perception, dramatic involvement, and responsiveness).
2 Creative Expression–Skills Development (independent and collaborative expression, performance, and production.)
3 Drama/Theatre Heritage–Historical and cultural (relating drama/theatre to self and society.)
4 Aesthetic Valuing–Applying knowledge and understanding (analyzing and judging). (South Carolina Framework for Drama/Theater Education, 1990).

Theater experiences have enormous appeal to young adolescents, who themselves play so many different roles as they strive for self-identification, social acceptance, and self-esteem. Theater provides rich opportunities to engage young adolescents in processes of cooperating, collaborating, evaluating, valuing, and making meaning in home, school, community, and peer group situations.

FOREIGN LANGUAGE

Foreign language instruction in American schools is an expanding movement in public education. Nationally and internationally, there is awareness that American mono-lingualism is a handicap economically, politically, diplomatically, and socially. Americans need foreign language proficiency in world affairs, but also, in this country, language and ethnic diversity increase the need for second-language skills. Additionally, foreign language is an appealing area of study to students, whetting their interest, curiosity, and motivation.

Foreign language at the middle level combines aspects of foreign language instruction in both elementary and secondary school. In the elementary school, foreign language instruction emphasizes communication and understanding the language in its cultural context. In the secondary school, foreign language is a proficiency-based curriculum, emphasizing what the student can do with the language. The K-12 curricula is organized into various contexts and purposes in which the student communicates both in oral and written form (Met, 1988).

FOREIGN LANGUAGE CURRICULUM

At the middle level, foreign language includes vocabulary development and grammar instruction. The goals of the program are to use vocabulary and grammar to promote communication and to study language in the social and cultural context of the foreign language country. Successful learning makes the second language meaningful, relevant, and personally and socially rewarding to the young adolescent. Students should develop proficiency in listening, speaking, reading, and writing the language. The greater the degree of social interaction, the more likely students are to develop foreign language skills. The culture of a language incorporates customs, lifestyles, beliefs, and values of the native speakers. Students should also be exposed to the literary, artistic, scientific, and historical elements of the people. Foreign language study affords young adolescents opportunities for academic enrichment, appreciation of their culture and other cultures, and purposeful interaction with their peer group.

Middle level philosophy requires that curriculum should relate to the developmental characteristics and needs of young adolescents. Application of this student-centered philosophy to middle level foreign language curriculum would stress concrete rather than abstract instruction in subject matter. Additionally, foreign language study should be available to all students rather than a select few students. The foreign language program works most effectively when it is integrated with other subject matter, school activities, and student experiences. Foreign language has the potential for improving student attitudes, for enriching study in other subject areas, and for enhancing the personal and social development of young adolescents (Freeman & Gregory, 1990).

Students enter the middle level school with diverse backgrounds in foreign language experience. Some have had no foreign language study, others have had an extensive elementary school program, while others may speak a second language in the home. Student backgrounds and interests may require different options for language study. An exploratory option may be used to motivate students to further language study based on the success they obtain from their cultural, communicative, and personal experiences with the language. A cultural awareness focus would develop an appreciation for the culture of the people who speak the language. Such cultural studies promote chances for young adolescent learners to explore and enrich their own value systems. A language proficiency approach would enable students to gain competence in listening, speaking, reading, and writing the foreign language. In areas where two languages are used in the community, a language option might focus on developing listening skills to promote bilingual competence (Freeman & Gregory, 1990).

Contemporary middle level programs may utilize more than one of the options delineated above in developing appropriate curricula for students. Grades 6 and 7 may provide exploratory courses in foreign language study. Students in grade 8 may study proficiency-based language programs. Effective foreign language programs provide various types of components to involve learners in meaningful and purposeful ways. These include language proficiency, language structure, and cultural, interdisciplinary, linguistic, and study skills. Scheduling foreign language courses may include such formats as daily instruction in semester or year-long courses, language laboratory centers, short-term exploratory or introductory course offerings of a few weeks in duration, and interactive audio–video formats. The type of components and schedules provided would vary according to the experiential background and the developmental needs of the learners (Freeman & Gregory, 1990).

Freeman and Gregory (1990) made specific recommendations for designing and implementing foreign language programs. They recommend that exploratory courses should not exceed nine weeks and should be composed of communication, cultural, linguistic, study skills, and interdisciplinary components. Students with appropriate experiences and skills in foreign languages may study advanced courses requiring more in-depth study and abstract reasoning skills.

Essential Considerations for Foreign Language

1 Foreign language instruction has enormous appeal for middle level students and should be an integral part of the middle level program.
2 Foreign language classes should be available to all students.
3 Foreign language study in grades 6 and 7 should emphasize elective/exploratory study.
4 Foreign language content should be integrated into other middle level subject areas.

HEALTH EDUCATION

Turning Points (1989) postulated a direct relationship between the health of young adolescents and their school success. While the school cannot meet every need of its students, health bears so directly on student performance in the learning process that middle level schools must accept substantial responsibility for guaranteeing student access to needed health services. Additionally, the middle level must be a health-promoting environment. Health education should improve the academic performance of young adolescents and should serve to prevent or lessen the impact of health-related problems on their personal and social development.

A RATIONALE FOR HEALTH EDUCATION

Health educators feel that today's students need a comprehensive and sequential K–12 health education curriculum. This would provide students with the information, skills, and coping strategies to keep them healthy.

Health instruction is critically important for young adolescents, who are confronted with a more bewildering array of threats and hindrances to their physical, mental, and emotional well-being than any previous generation—among them, alcohol and drug use, early and unplanned pregnancies, violence, depression, suicide, low levels of physical fitness, and sexually transmitted diseases, including AIDS (Willis, 1990).

National Adolescent Student Health Survey (NASHS). Indicative of the range of troubling attitudes and behaviors were the results of the National Adolescent Student Health Survey (NASHS). The NASHS study surveyed more than 11,000 eighth- and tenth-graders nationwide on eight health topics: AIDS, injury prevention, violence, suicide, consumer health, sexually transmitted disease, nutrition and alcohol, and drug and tobacco use. Student responses revealed adequate knowledge and information about many health problems. However, in many cases, possession of information did not help students measurably in making correct and appropriate health decisions. Figure 8.1 reports some of the health behaviors identified in the NASHS study.

- 56% of teens did not wear seat belts;
- 44% of tenth-grade students had ridden in a car in the past month with a driver who was under the influence of drugs or alcohol;
- 39% had been in a fight in the past year;
- 11% of boys and 18% of girls had attempted suicide;
- 61% of girls and 28% of boys had dieted to control weight; many used unsafe methods;
- 89% of tenth-grade students had tried alcohol, and 38% drank more than five drinks at one time within the two weeks before the survey;
- 51% of eighth-grade students had tried alcohol;
- 35% of tenth-grade students had smoked marijuana, and 15% did so regularly;
- 8% had used cocaine;
- 86% knew that condoms reduced the risk of getting AIDS from sexual intercourse; 51% thought that washing after sex would decrease the risk of sexually transmitted diseases; and 39% did not know an adult they could talk to about an STD

FIGURE 8.1 National Survey of health behavior of students in grades 8 and 10 *(Adapted from National Adolescent Student Health Survey (NASHS): Highlights of the Survey by American Alliance for Health, Physical Education, Recreation, and Dance.* Health Education 19 *(4), pp. 4–8. Copyright 1988 by American Alliance for Health, Physical Education, Recreation, and Dance. Adapted by permission of AAHPERD.)*

Data contained in the National Adolescent Student Health Survey (1988) reveal a profile of young adolescents at health risk. The primacy of the health problems in the lives of young adolescents seriously compromises student achievement, self-esteem, positive behavior, and personal health. To a great extent, the risk behaviors and risk conditions result from personal decision making and lifestyle choices. Since the students control so many of the health-risk situations, there is an urgent need to teach students specific skills and strategies for analyzing health problems and making appropriate health decisions. The school can play a pivotal role in revising risk-taking behavior such as drug use, sexually transmitted diseases, poor nutrition habits, mental depression, and other adolescent behaviors.

There is evidence that health education does produce changes in behavior. A 1988 national survey funded by the Metropolitan Life Foundation polled parents, teachers, and over 4,500 students in grades 3–12 concerning their views on the effects of comprehensive health education. The survey found that students who had participated in health education programs possess greater knowledge, reflect better attitudes, and demonstrate more positive behavior than student with little or no health education. Students with three or more years of health education showed decreases in risk-taking behavior. The report concluded that continuous health education over many years does affect behavior patterns and decision making (Harris, 1988).

In a study of health education programs in grades 4–7, Walberg et al. (1986) found that sizeable gains in health knowledge could be achieved after as little as 15 hours of instructional time. Large knowledge gains could be effected quickly, but 45–50 hours of instruction were needed to influence health attitudes and practices. The effect of instruction tended to level off between 50 and 60 hours. However, research analysis showed that a second, or follow-up, year of health instruction achieved positive effects on the health attitudes and practices of fifth- and sixth-grade students. These findings suggest the efficacy of planning two- or three-year health sequences for the middle level school.

MIDDLE LEVEL SCHOOL HEALTH CURRICULUM

School health education has traditionally received low priority and status both as a subject matter and as a school service. However, the urgent health risk facing many young adolescents requires the development of a K–12 comprehensive school health program addressing the physical, social, emotional, and mental health of students. A comprehensive middle level education program has three components: health service, a healthy school environment, and health instruction. Middle level health services are provided to assist in disease prevention, screening for health problems and rendering emergency care, and follow-up referrals. These services are carried out by doctors, dentists, nurses, teachers, and other health personnel. A healthy school environment considers the psychosocial and physical environment for students and school personnel. Schools must be clean, safe, and facilitate learning and teaching. The topics in a comprehensive program of health instruction include: Community health, Consumer health, Environmental health, Family life, Growth and development, Nutritional health, Personal health, Prevention and control of disease and disorder, Safety and accident prevention, and Substance use and abuse (Schlaadt, 1988).

While all of the curriculum topics must be addressed in the K–12 health curriculum, some types, such as sex education, drug education, AIDS prevention, emotional health, and nutrition and fitness, are of compelling interest and concern for young adolescents. At the middle level, curriculum topics may be taught as a separate course, with a certified health teacher as course instructor. Another approach integrates health education content into core subjects, especially science. Some educators advocate both the separate course and integrated approaches to health curriculum and instruction. At the middle level, health should be taught as a separate course for half a year and should also be integrated into other subject areas (Willis, 1990).

Controversial Health Education Content

The controversial nature of certain health content such as sex education, AIDS education, and drug education raises red flags to parents and school administrators. Middle level teachers who teach these topics must receive careful and specific training to deal with the controversial nature of the content. Sex education contains many sensitive topics, such as homosexuality, contraception, and abortion, that young adolescents want and need to know about but find very few informed adults who will talk to them about these subjects. Such information is essential but is deemed completely inappropriate for school discussion by many parents. National surveys show alarming ignorance and misconceptions in areas such as contraception, AIDS prevention, and sexually transmitted diseases. These issues are serious business for young adolescents. The school, home, and community must work together to prevent the incidence of pregnancy, disease, and addiction. No other subject matter in the curriculum bears as heavy responsibility for the present and future well-being of young adolescents as does health education (Willis, 1990).

In middle level health education, where you are not only teaching information but attempting to change attitudes, practices, and behaviors of young adolescents, the person who does the teaching and how it is taught become almost as important as what is taught. Health educators are concerned about the preparation of teachers who can teach more than facts. Many earlier attempts to teach sex education and drug education to young adolescents were not very successful because mere information was not enough. Teachers need to arrange for discussion groups, cooperative learning teams, values education sessions, and media presentations, as well as direct instruction, to help young people change their attitudes and behaviors. Students need courses that will help them make decisions, resist peer pressure, examine their values, and evaluate the consequences of health-risk behaviors. Teachers must be role models for students by refraining from alcohol and tobacco use, practicing proper nutrition and fitness behaviors, and being accessible to students who need an adult to listen to their concerns in a non-judgmental manner. They must provide relevant health information to students and promote the school as a healthy workplace.

The middle level health curriculum presents students with health information, strategies for decision-making and valuing, and processes for modifying health attitudes and behaviors. Teachers, parents, and students must work collaboratively to develop health programs of prevention, intervention, and remediation to help young adolescents to achieve mental, physical, and emotional health.

Essential Considerations for Health Education

1 *Turning Points* (1989) and the National Adolescent Student Health Survey (1988) identify health as an essential concern of middle level education.
2 Decision-making skills, strategies for resisting peer pressure, and values education should be stressed in addition to health information.
3 The school, home, and community must cooperate to prevent young adolescent health problems.
4 Teachers need to be role models for good health practices for their students.

PHYSICAL EDUCATION

The social context of physical education shows two important trends with implications for young adolescents and society. One trend, the sports industry, has dramatically changed the emphasis of sports programs. The fitness trend has escalated health promotion in the schools. These two trends of sports and fitness yield some interesting descriptions of physical education. Americans love sports—just look at the time, attention, and adulation granted to sports heroes—but we are increasingly becoming a nation of spectators rather than participants. The strong attachment to sports often elevates athletes to heroes and role models for young American adolescents. The results of a 1990 World Almanac poll, which asked young people to name their heroes, underscored the emerging status of athletes. In the poll, the female receiving the most votes was the mother of those surveyed. The male receiving the most votes for hero was Michael Jordan, the high-flying basketball star. Another situation shows that while large numbers of the population are involved in fitness and wellness activities, equally large numbers are not physically fit. Kenneth Cooper, the physical fitness expert, noted that kids in 1986 were heavier, fatter, and less conditioned aerobically than those in 1976. Cooper suggested four reasons for the decline in physical fitness:

1 reduced emphasis on physical education in schools
2 less active daily lives

3 physical inactivity resulting from countless hours watching TV
4 a fast-food diet high in salt, fats, and cholesterol. (Dart, 1990, p. 1d)

Physical education programs have traditionally emphasized the development of sport skills and physical fitness. Frequently, sport skills have been stressed at the expense of fitness (Johnson, 1985). School programs are undergoing changes that will enable all middle level students involved in physical education to attain physical fitness. To promote physical fitness, body development, and movement education, the overemphasis on sports in physical education programs will need to be lessened. However, it is important that a balanced middle level program should maintain sports skills in conjunction with greater emphasis on fitness activities, because most young adolescents enjoy participating in sports and games. Survey data showed that the main reasons for adolescent participation in sports are fun, skill development, excitement and personal challenge, achievement and status, fitness, friendship, and energy or tension release. In the survey, boys participated to gain achievement and status, while girls generally valued fun and friendship (Gould, Feltz, & Weiss, 1985).

The middle level physical education program does not currently stimulate enough physical activity for young adolescents at school and away from school. This pattern continues into high school and into adulthood. The United States Public Health Service reported that 20% of adults exercise beneficially, 40% exercise sporadically, and 40% do not exercise (Health-Care Costs, 1989). While the data concerning physical fitness are disquieting, there are promising trends in physical education.

Templin (1987) reported similar findings concerning physical fitness and activity. He reported that one out of every six American children is so unfit as to be categorized physically underdeveloped, that American youth have gotten fatter over the last 20 years, and that only 50% of the students in grades 5–12 exercise sufficiently for effective cardiovascular functioning. Relating to school physical education programs, he found that only 36% of students have daily physical education and that while students like physical education they rank it low in importance and difficulty.

While the data concerning physical fitness are disquieting, there are promising trends in physical education. Kneer (1987) reported that emphasis on sports is being reduced to provide instructional units in conditioning, aerobic exercise, track and field, and life survival skills. Information about nutrition and exercise is being emphasized as instrumental to fitness. There is an increased awareness that students need daily physical education. Batesky (1991) reported that emphasis in physical education is shifting toward physical activities and skills that promote lifelong participation.

A RATIONALE FOR PHYSICAL EDUCATION

Physical education is concerned with all aspects of human movement. The content of physical education can be arranged into three categories: fitness, motor skills, and movement. Each content category can be divided into performance skills and conceptual knowledge.

The performance dimensions of the fitness curriculum are health-related fitness and skill-related fitness. Health–fitness skills, such as strength, flexibility, and aerobics, improve cardiovascular functioning and reduce the risk of injury. Skill–fitness components, such as coordination, agility, and speed, relate to the ability to perform various motor tasks. The number and type of skill-related tasks vary from football to volleyball to dance. Health–fitness skills are more broadly applicable to individuals than skill–fitness components. Conceptual knowledge in the fitness dimension include principles of training and exercise, and socio-cultural perceptions of health and the body. An ultimate goal is to enable students to become aware of the need for fitness and thereby develop their own lifelong fitness programs (Bain, 1988).

The second area of the physical education curriculum is motor skills. The motor skills component includes an enormous number and variety of skills. Motor skills instruction often concentrates on using the skills in sports and games. However, teachers must provide for a broad foundation of skill development. The conceptual knowledge in this category includes the study of movement qualities, mechanical principles, and socio-cultural perceptions of skill development (Bain, 1988).

The two primary components of the movement forms category of physical education content are sport and dance. To be proficient in a sport requires competence in skills, strategies, and traditions of that sport. A necessary part of a sports program is that players not only learn to participate but that they become knowledgeable and responsible spectators. In like manner, dance education incorporates behaviors such as performance, creative expression, and responding to an audience. The knowledge component of sport and dance is concerned with aesthetic principles, socio-cultural perceptions of sport and dance, and factors such as appropriate competition and sportsmanship. An important goal of movement education is to help students develop skills in sports and dance that they will be able to enjoy throughout their lives (Bain, 1988).

Specifically, the middle level physical education program has lacked clear direction in establishing the major goals of the physical education curriculum. The ultimate goal for the middle level program is to get students to lead an active lifestyle and to possess the physical skills required for lifelong participation. The agenda for curriculum reform at the middle level revolves around whether you want to expose students to a wide variety of activities or develop strong physical skills in a limited number of activities. Whatever the curricular approach, the middle level physical education program is a critical part of the total education of young adolescents for now and later (Batesky, 1991).

Batesky (1991) suggests a three-year scheduling plan that would accommodate both exposure and skill development. In his three-year schedule, students would select 18 out of a possible 36 activities. Students would take 6 activities per year instead of the current practice of 11 or 12. Each activity would incorporate a 15-day instructional period which would allow for skill development. The three-year program would enable students to select activities that are appropriate to them, and the 15-day instructional schedule would provide enough practice time to allow students to feel successful.

INTERSCHOLASTIC COMPETITION VS. INTRAMURALS

One issue that continues to confront middle level educators is the placement and emphasis of athletic programs in the middle level school. Young adolescents are in a transitional and highly variable stage of development. This holds significant implications for the types and degrees of athletic programs made available to young adolescents in the school setting. Quite often, adults in the community, high school coaches, and middle level students themselves actively promote middle level interscholastic competition in football, basketball, baseball, soccer, and track. Most middle level educators and health care specialists feel that interscholastic competition should be limited in the middle level school and very carefully evaluated as to its impact on the personal and social development of young adolescents. The primary focus of the athletic program would be intramural (Hovland, 1990; Gentry & Hayes, 1991).

The intramural activities program should teach competence and personal responsibility, and should promote self-esteem and socialization skills. General guidelines for the intramural program reflect (1) a concern for participation by all students, (2) an emphasis on playing for fun and enjoyment over winning, (3) an emphasis on physical exercise, (4) the importance of teamwork and the contributions of others to the activity, and (5) the provision of a wide range of activities, with teams which are organized fairly by weight, age, or height (Hovland, 1990; Gentry & Hayes, 1991). Hovland (1990) further stressed that all-star teams and tournaments should not be allowed. Gentry and Hayes (1991) advocated no interscholastic sports prior to grade 8. They recommended that individual or team sports should be taught in a classroom setting rather than a competitive setting. A strong case was made to integrate athletics into the total program of the school rather than viewing athletics and academics as disparate entities. There seems to be a strongly positive link between an effective athletics curriculum and improved student academic achievement, behavior, attendance, and parental support (Hovland, 1990).

Physical education integrates the cognitive, affective, and psychomotor domains into meaningful movement forms such as dance, sport, exercise, gymnastics, and other activities. The middle level physical education program is an essential component in the process of the education for young adolescents.

Essential Considerations for Physical Education

1 Physical education programs should reflect the tenets of good practice advocated in *Turning Points* (1989) and *This We Believe* (1992).

2 Physical education programs should be developmentally appropriate for middle level students.

3 Personal fitness and lifelong physical skills should be priority concerns of physical education.

4 Intramural sports with high student participation should predominate over interscholastic sports for a small select student population.

HOME ECONOMICS

From the passage of the Smith Hughes Act in 1917, home economics programs have focused on homemaking. In the Carl Perkins Vocational Act (1984), the legislation focused on improving consumer and homemaking skills. This legislation called for increased spending on managing family resources, managing home and work responsibilities, improving responses to family crises, strengthening parenting skills, and improving nutrition. Today, home economics focuses on the consumer and homemaking. Home economics or home arts is the primary curriculum area that focuses on family and preparation of young adolescents for family and home living (Smith, 1988). The content areas found in home arts would be consumer education, clothing and textiles, housing, family living, personal and family development, food and nutrition, and health. Each of these broad headings could be broken down into such topics as interpersonal skills, marriage, pregnancy, parenting, budgeting, consumer buying guidelines, nutrition, cooking, and sewing.

In home economics, the continuing emphasis needs to be placed on family life. In a survey conducted by Home Economics Association of contemporary American teenagers' concerns and issues on self-perceptions and adequacy of school preparation, the youth identified their major concerns as money, future, and health (Schultz, 1988–1989). Approximately one-third were concerned with not being able to pay for college, not earning enough money to live adequately, or making the wrong decisions about their future. Students surveyed indicated that the schools were doing only an adequate job in teaching them the skills necessary for becoming a responsible and productive adult. Highest ratings were given to preparation by schools in life skill areas of health (substance abuse, human sexuality, and AIDS), choosing a career, and making important life decisions. Teenagers suggested the least prepared areas were family life skills such as parenting, choosing a marriage partner, and dealing with family crises such as death and divorce.

Exploratory experiences varying in length of time rather than separate courses should be provided for all young adolescents in every grade at the middle level. Home economics is not just for girls and teaches more than cooking or sewing. The current home economics curriculum also includes budgeting, nutrition, sexuality, parenting skills, interpersonal skills, marriage, pregnancy, and consumer buying guidelines. Schultz (1988–1989) suggested that as many as 75 to 79% of teenagers have not taken an adult roles and functions course, family living course, life skills management course, or child development/parenting course. All these courses are essential to the development of the young adolescent as a family member and consumer.

TWO CONTEXTS FOR HOME ECONOMICS CURRICULUM

Two approaches have been suggested for organizing the home economics curriculum: a task analysis approach and a competency-based model. In task analysis, a study of a given occupation yields a list of tasks. These become the basis for course content and student preparation. The list is verified with employers and skilled workers to ensure students are adequately prepared. Examples are found in Brink, Apt, and Horell (1986) and Downey and Kizer (1986).

In contrast, the competency-based models have been mandated by several states, but are frequently criticized for their emphasis on current practice and lack of attention to future goals (Smith, 1988). Examples of competency-based models developed by various states through state departments of education or universities are those of Missouri (Van Buren, 1989), South Carolina (Pough, 1989), and Louisiana (Drier, 1986). These comprehensive middle level instructional units include home economics exploratory courses, objectives, competencies, and activities. The recent school reform proposals have increased the number of academic course requirements; this reduces the number of elective courses available. Thus, today's students do not have life skill courses they can choose. For a number of years, home economics has claimed to teach such basic skills as food science, for which science credit is given, or mathematics for consumers, in which general mathematics credit is granted. Home economics can provide special assistance to reinforce the basics, but care should be exercised to maintain the integrity of the home economics curriculum.

In summary, the emphasis on family life education is a critical part of home economics or home arts. For young adolescents, it is important to explore health, food, nutrition, parenting, and interpersonal skills. Home economics offers a unique opportunity for young adolescents and is essential for the exploration of the personal and social dimensions in the middle level curriculum.

Essential Considerations in Home Economics

1. A holistic interdisciplinary curriculum which integrates the basic skills and knowledge of academic courses with personal and social challenges facing young adolescents.
2. The establishment of a middle level home economics curriculum which explores personal, social, and academic concerns of family and individual.
3. This curriculum should focus on current societal needs, personal interests, and career awareness but also prepare young adolescents for making a contribution in their adult lives and careers.
4. Because of the personal challenges facing young adolescents—pregnancies, substance abuse, careers, suicide, and stress—young adolescents should have exploratory experiences every year on the middle level.

TECHNOLOGY EDUCATION

During the 1980s, a transition has occurred from industrial arts to technology education. Oakes (1989) reported that approximately 40 states are now offering courses in technology education, and more than 30 states have changed their agency names to reflect technology education. In a study conducted in 1986 by Scarborough (1989) to identify technology programs throughout the United States, 67% of 297 respondents and 26 state or regional directors indicated that technology education programs existed on the middle or junior high level and 30% indicated young adolescents are required to take a course (p. 6). An average of 60% of the respondents believed that their middle level or junior high school programs are technology-education oriented. A large number of states are developing technology education curriculum guides with activities organized around four major contexts: manufacturing, communications, construction, and transportation. Several states also have passed technology literacy laws guaranteeing technology education for all children.

Ritz (1991) suggested that a recent review of technology education found in the nation's schools indicated that six types were observed: (1) shop (emphasis on material usage and tool skill development), (2) industrial arts (development of knowledge and skills of processes used by industry (drafting, wood working, metal working, etc.), (3) industrial technology (modern industrial arts, i.e., computers, lasers, digital electronics, etc.), (4) design technology (problem-solving skills, with technology content secondary), (5) technical systems (application of modern systems of communication, production, manufacturing, and transportation), and (6) technology education (studying and applying of the systems of technology, including communication, transportation, and production).

ORIGINS OF TECHNOLOGY EDUCATION

Technology education as a concept is not new. Some documents that might help develop an understanding of technology education begin with the *Jackson's Mill* report (Hales and Snyder, 1982). This report outlined the theoretical foundations of technology education by explaining how the content should be reorganized into transportation, construction, manufacturing, and communication. A second helpful document is *Perspectives* from the International Technology Education Association (ITEA, 1985). The report defines goals, objectives, and components and establishes standards for a quality program.

In 1990, the past frameworks of *Jackson's Mill Industrial Art Curriculum Theory* (Hales & Snyder, 1982) and ITEA *Perspectives* (1985) were reviewed, and a revised document was prepared that addressed technological method and content model of technology education (Savage & Sterry, 1990a). Technology was defined as "a body of knowledge and the application of resources using a systematic approach (the technological method to produce outcomes in response to human needs and wants" (Savage & Sterry, 1990b, p. 7). The revised mission of technology education was "to prepare individuals to comprehend and contribute to a technologically based society" (Savage & Sterry, 1990b, p. 7). Finally, this revised approach could be best implemented through the technological method.

TECHNOLOGICAL METHOD

Technological method helps young adolescents to acquire knowledge and experience for becoming technologically literate. The technological method goals focused on human needs and wants (lifetime roles a person undertakes and means needed to continue learning); problems (doubts, uncertainty, and difficulties) and opportunities (future, planned, and anticipated); resources (personnel, tools/machines, data, materials, energy, capital, and time); technological knowledge (bio-related, communication, production, and transportation technologies); technology processes (analyze, realize, test, and feedback); evaluation (output of technological method is judged against design requirements and original problem statement); solutions and impacts (personal, environmental, and social); and lastly, management (planning, organizing, directing, and controlling). Each technological method and subcategory forms essential goals for the development of a technologically literate person.

CURRICULUM DEVELOPMENT

The study of technology is centered on a dynamic action-oriented program. The new emphasis should reflect the diversity of needs, ranging from gifted young adolescents to those with unique learning needs. All children must have an opportunity to be educated and to live as full and informed a life as possible. The challenge is to be able to develop and utilize a significant portion of an individual's potential. The instructional content and methods of technology education must consider the diverse learning styles of learners in order to provide the opportunity for maximum individual development. Instructional strategies should include problem solving, exploratory activities, cooperative learning, verbal activities, interdisciplinary and multidisciplinary activities, and a broad range of assessment strategies, including portfolios, project work, and individual and group work. These revised recommendations proposed that technology education become "process education," employing the technological method previously discussed. This approach requires students to analyze and act on solutions based on systematic higher-level thinking processes. Balistreri (1986) stated that "technology is a product of humans. Humans are influenced by technology: In a sense we are 'products' of technology" (p. 18).

The ultimate outcome of the technology education curriculum is that all students begin to develop their innate talents, attitudes, and skills to live better in a technological world. Problem solving, career orientation, and learning for tomorrow's adaptive environment are cornerstones of technology education.

Grades 6 to 7 should provide an introduction to industrial and technological systems. The ITEA recommended that this course be required of every young adolescent for one semester. In grades 8 and 9, elective courses one semester in length should be established in systems of communication, construction, manufacturing, and transportation. Students should be encouraged to take any one of the one-semester elective courses or all four of the courses. The possible topics from which the middle level exploratory experiences could be selected are: Communication, Construction, Power Division, Transportation, and Manufacturing (ITEA, 1985).

Essential Considerations in Technology Education

1 The middle level technology education curriculum must be holistic, interdisciplinary, and integrated with other academic disciplines to promote technological literacy.

2 On the middle level, technology education must be exploratory, activity oriented, multi-sensory, and related to career awareness, personal, social, and academic interests of young adolescents.

3 Technology education can provide a foundation for young adolescents who are developing into a technologically literate work force, enabling them to compete on an international level, make a contribution to society, and enjoy life.

4 All young adolescents should be required to take an exploratory technology education course in Grades 6 and 7 and to be provided elective courses in Grade 8.

CAREER EDUCATION

Career education focuses on the young adolescent's exploration of personal interests, career awareness, and career possibilities, which will assist him or her to develop feelings of self-respect and self-worth. Rosessler (1988) suggested that any career education program in the public schools must provide a functional curriculum that stresses an integrated curriculum of career and vocational experiences and have a community-based delivery system to make those experiences relevant. Tewel and Lacey (1988) suggested that career education is a more inclusive term than vocational education, basic skills instruction, and guidance counseling. Career education includes "studying how to choose an appropriate career field, how to function within an organization, how to develop good work habits, and how to cultivate a healthy attitude toward working" (Tewel & Lacey, p. 26). Career education requires a shift from the traditional academic curriculum to a process-oriented curriculum which is based on the realities of the workplace and focuses on how each student's learning style and motivation can be utilized best. The primary emphasis of the curriculum is on career development and personal skills, with the acquisition of knowledge and information as supportive. Career education integrates concepts and materials into traditional subject matter. Skills required to function more effectively as a consumer, producer, learner, and citizen would be as important as subject-matter knowledge and basic skills. Career education provides more varied experiences, so that students can have a greater understanding of the relationship of education to an occupation, workplace, and personal desires.

By comparison, vocational education teaches occupational skills inherent in the different crafts, trades, businesses, home economics, or agriculture. The primary purpose is to prepare young people to be employable. While the term *vocational* has come to mean to prepare young people to be employable, the Committee for Economic Development (1985) suggested that the term *vocational education* must be more narrowly defined than to just prepare young people to be employable. The Committee proposed that:

> The term *vocational education* should be limited to those programs that are specifically designed to prepare students to enter a field upon graduation. All other forms of nonacademic instruction should be identified by a different term to avoid confusing them with curricula designed to impart specific job skills (p. 30).

Typically, vocational education does not extend into the middle level school unless there is career exploration of vocational and technology education programs. Vocational education tends to be more directed toward learning specific occupational performance skills for employability. Typically, the concept is limited to the secondary level rather than encompassing the entire curriculum for grades K–12. In this discussion, the term *career education* will be used as the inclusive term to describe career development and vocational and technical programs for the middle level.

PURPOSES OF CAREER EDUCATION

First, in establishing a middle level career education program, it is important to separate out employability and exploration from specific occupational preparation. Second, it is necessary to ensure that there is a commitment by teachers, administration, parents, and community to develop personal, social, and career aspects with the support of academic preparation and skills for a successful career/vocational program and the education of all learners. Third, before students are allowed to complete occupationally specific training, they should be expected to demonstrate successful academic achievement. While there may need to be an adjustment for students with learning disabilities or disadvantaged youth, general academic standards should be expected of all students. Fourth, young adolescents' self-concept and self-esteem in life are related to satisfaction with their careers. Career awareness and exploratory opportunities are necessary to make intelligent career decisions. As leisure time increases, with many vocations requiring less work time, there needs to be a wide variety of activities which develop alternative talents and abilities and provide the young adolescent with constructive recreational activities that are individually satisfying.

As technology continues to have impact on society and careers, career education programs must provide training and exposure to application of lasers, advanced electronics, robotics, and microcomputer applications in the business community. It is proposed that as computers and robots become tools of production, a number of manufacturing jobs requiring high-level skills may be reduced. But at the same time, a variety and level of skills needed to design, sell, and service the manufactured products will continue. More employment opportunities will exist in service areas rather than in manufacturing.

MODELS FOR CAREER EDUCATION

In the 1990s, the primary role of career education is to facilitate concepts, attitudes, and skills related to career development. The secondary role is to help facilitate the development of basic skills through an infusion of work-related concepts and activities into academic content. Five approaches have been utilized to develop career education: (1) experience-based, (2) developmental, (3) contextual, (4) life-centered, and (5) the approach of the Secretary of Labor's Commission on Achieving Necessary Skills (SCANS).

The *experienced-based* career curriculum is a school-based and/or community-based program relating career education concepts and academics to real work experiences. The school-based program linked academics with job site activities but did not provide a salary to students. These career education proposals involved the youth at various grade levels in awareness, exploration, or actual experiences in the community. The school leadership formed various collaborative efforts with various businesses in the community that represented these career education experience areas (Great Falls Schools, ED 151–507; Northeast Tri County Intermediate Unit, ED 163–166); and Roseville Schools, ED 164–770).

Contextual career curriculum, a refinement of experienced-based career curriculum, focuses on engaging unemployed and at-risk youths in urban areas in community-based, highly individualized programs which offer hands-on experiences for youth to learn about themselves in relation to community employment. Because contextual career education does not focus on academics, it is appropriate for both in-school and out-of-school programs. It pays the youth for his or her employment and relates the classroom component to employment-related skills and issues (Taymans et al., 1990).

Developmental career education curriculum has developmental tasks broken down into specific tasks for the middle level. On the middle level grades, Bailey (1985) recommends orientation rather than exploration experiences because of his belief that exploration requires intellectual skills that a majority of young adolescents do not yet possess and forces middle level students to make choices that should be left for high school. His premises are that, first, young adolescents are confronted with the necessity of making decisions about which curriculum to choose when they get ready to enter high school. This choice is in reality a career choice. Second, behavioral changes in grades 7 and 8 are more affective and social than cognitive. At stake is the establishment of an identity and the shifting of roles from dependence and derived status of parents to independence and primary status for emerging adolescents. Opportunities for career choices help to establish experiences with independent decision making and the development of self.

The *life-centered* career education curriculum has three domains: (1) daily living skills (homemaking or home managing, marriage, parenting, finances, leisure, recreational, and civic activities); (2) personal-social skills (independence, self-confidence, maintaining personal friendships, and socially acceptable behaviors); and (3) occupational guidance and preparation (development of the individual's potential, awareness of various occupations, essential skills, work experiences, and wise decision-making in career choices). These are further divided into 22 competencies, which in turn are each further subdivided into 97 specific competencies under the three headings (Brolin, 1988). Instruction in the academic areas is supportive to the development of the skills in the area. Without academic knowledge and skills, these three domains cannot be implemented. This model proposed that academic studies be integrated with the student's need for instruction in acquiring each competency. Each middle level school that selects this approach will need to decide how to best infuse the life-centered competencies into the traditional subject matter.

In preparing career education for the middle-level curriculum, the life-centered approach has the critical ingredients to ensure a curriculum that meets the personal, social, and academic needs of young adolescents. A competency-based curriculum is centered on those competencies that are essential to function as a consumer, producer, learner, and citizen. The life-centered curriculum recommends that career development goals be integrated into current subject matter content and be based on student needs. This approach has been suggested as a worthwhile approach for mainstreaming exceptional children. The program can continue beyond the high school for handicapped youth to acquire the competencies needed for community living. A detailed discussion of approaches, competencies, resources, and sample curricula are presented by Brolin (1988). Another source for annotated bibliographical resources on career education is found in Drier (1987).

A fifth initiative on career education has been proposed by the Secretary of Labor's Commission on Achieving Necessary Skills (SCANS, 1991). SCANS (1991) proposed that "what we call workplace *know-how* defines effective job performance today" (p. xv). This know-how has two career education contexts: competencies and a foundation. This report identifies five competencies: resources, interpersonal, information, systems, and technology. Three aspects included in the foundation context are basic skills, thinking skills, and personal qualities (SCANS, 1991).

The Commission maintains that these eight requirements are essential career preparation for all students, both those going directly to a workplace and those planning further education. Thus, the five competencies and three foundations should be taught and developed in an integrated fashion that reflects the workplace contexts in which they are applied. Learning objectives are established within a real work environment, rather than insisting that students first learn in the abstract what they will be expected to apply. These requirements of a career education initiative are part of the proposed strategy to reach national goals by the year 2000 which were presented by President Bush to the nation's governors in 1989 (Bush, 1991). The implications of these five competencies and three foundations for curriculum, instructional materials, school organization, and teacher training will be implemented by SCANS and appear to be the next career education initiative from the national level.

Essential Considerations in Career Education

1 Systematic career development or holistic life planning programs need to be implemented that would include looking at the preferred life roles, personal, physical, psychosocial, intellectual, emotional, and spiritual needs as well as vocation/career needs of young people.

2 A process-based curriculum should be designed that links work, family, education, future employment opportunities, and leisure and recreational activities with academic content and basic skills, but that is based on interests, hobbies, and recreational interests of young adolescents.

3 Developmentally appropriate courses and experiences are established and maintained that ensure the maximum opportunity for the development of diversity found in young adolescents, including gender differences, ethnic and religious minorities, disabled learners, at-risk youth, unemployed youth, and other socioeconomic groups, through cooperative planning among students, teachers, parents, industrial, and business leaders.

4 The career education program is a regular part of the curriculum offered to all young adolescents during every middle level year and begins to develop occupational skills, attitudes, work habits, and appreciation of the career opportunities available to young adolescents.

SUMMARY

In summary, exploration, electives, and career education reflect developmental processes that occur throughout school and during an individual's entire life. They attempt to seek a balance among educational goals in which subject matter, awareness of work, exploration of work, and preparation for work are seen as major educational goals. Through infusion of career education and exploratory goals into the regular curriculum, there has been an attempt to reduce the separation between content, work, and personal interest. These experiences are relevant to all persons in their search for self, career awareness, exploration, and preparation for work. The middle level should provide career awareness opportunities for young adolescents to explore their future roles as citizens, family members, and employees. A comprehensive middle level exploratory program should include an exploration of the arts, foreign language, health, physical education, home economics/home arts, technology education, occupational preparation, understanding employment opportunities and training requirements, hands-on experiences, career decision-making skills, and lifelong career development. Career education, electives, and exploratory activities are a part of the total middle level curriculum concept that encompasses personal, social, and academic dimensions of the young adolescent. The curriculum includes occupational activities in the workplace as well as throughout a young adolescent's life. Career education, electives, and exploratory activities should infuse academic skills, self-awareness, career exploration, coping skills, and problem-solving tools to better prepare students for the future.

■ ■ ■

EXPLORATION

1 Using an arts education topic, show how a lesson could be developed into an integrated curriculum or lesson plan using mathematics, language arts, science, social studies, and music. Also explain what evaluation methods and products would be appropriate for evaluating the integrated project.

2 Complete a survey of middle level schools in your area to determine equal access to the arts education program. For example, do all students have access to *both* appreciation and participation activities in art, music, theater, and dance? Are all students encouraged to participate in arts education activities, regardless of their skills and abilities? Are all students encouraged to display their work in public places and perform for the public?

3 Analyze the health education curriculum available in middle level schools in your area. Are topics such as drugs, sex education, and nutrition in the program?

4 Complete a survey of physical education in the middle level schools in your locale. Are all students allowed to participate, or a select few? Does the curriculum provide for fitness as well as sports performance?

5 Visit the home extension agent in your community to determine what programs are available and what types of problems they observe in family and homemaking for young adolescents in your locality.

6 Secure a curriculum guide from a middle level school and analyze what technology education offerings are available. How would you classify the activities and/or courses? Are the activities and/or courses exploratory, required or elective?

7 Conduct a survey of what industrial firms, businesses, and research organizations are found in your community and determine if the school district has sent graduates for employment, and the reaction of employers to the preparation of these graduates.

8 Arrange visits to industries and businesses, especially those that utilize high technology. Determine what the prospects are for future employment in those high-technology firms and organizations.

9 Propose a list of possible career opportunities that could be made available to young adolescents in your school and community. Once you have your list, decide which opportunities are already being provided and how you would provide classroom and community exploratory and on-site experiences in career education.

SUGGESTED READINGS

Atwell, N. (1987). *In the middle: Writing, reading and learning with adolescents.* Portsmouth, NH: Boynton Cook.

An excellent book that uses the workshop model to turn middle school students and teachers on to writing, reading, and learning.

Bain, L. L. (1988). Curriculum for critical reflection in physical education. In R. S. Brandt (Ed.), *Content of the curriculum.* Alexandria, VA: Association for Supervision and Curriculum Development.

An excellent source for current trends and programs in physical education.

Brandt, R. S. (1987/1988). On discipline-based art education: A conversation with Elliot Eisner. *Educational Leadership, 45* (4), 6–9.

Brandt's interview with Elliot Eisner focused on DBAE, in particular defining DBAE and examining its differences from existing programs, articulation problems, curriculum considerations, and the critics of the program.

Brolin, D. E. (1988). *Life centered career education: A competency based approach,* (3rd ed.). Reston, VA: The Council for Exceptional Children.

An excellent source for implementing a life-centered career education program that will meet the guidelines for handicapped and at-risk as well as regular learners.

Committee for Economic Development, Research and Policy Committee. (1985). *Investing in our children.* New York: Committee for Economic Development.

An excellent monograph outlining recommendations concerning what schools and businesses should do to improve the employability of the nation's youth.

Drier, H. N. (1987). Resources abound for career educators. *Journal of Career Development, 13* (3), 78–91.

The author provides an annotated bibliography of recent publications on career education.

National Endowment for the Arts. (1988). *Toward civilization: A report on arts education.* Washington, DC: U.S. Government Printing Office.

This report makes the case for arts education as an essential element of a total school curriculum.

Savage, E., & Sterry, L. (1990 a, b). A conceptual framework for technology education (two-part series). *The Technology Teacher,* (a) *50* (1), 6–11; (b) *50* (2), 7–11.

This resource contains a revision of the competencies, goals, and objectives of technology education.

Smith, J. B. (1988). Reconceptualizing the home economics curriculum. In R. S. Brandt, (Ed.), *Content of the Curriculum.* Alexandria, VA: Association for Supervision and Curriculum Development.

An excellent resource. References are provided for the development of a home economics curriculum.

REFERENCES

American Alliance for Health, for Health, Physical Education, Recreation, and Dance. (1988). National Adolescent Student Health Survey (NASHS): Highlights of the Survey. *Health Education,* 19(4), 4–8.

Atwell, N. (1987). *In the middle: Writing, reading and learning with adolescents.* Portsmouth, NH: Boynton Cook.

Atwell, N. (1989). After in the middle. *English Journal, 78* (1), 52–54.

Bailey, L. J. (1985). *Career education for teachers and counselors: A practical approach.* Cranston, RI: The Carroll Press.

Bain, L. L. (1988). Curriculum for critical reflection in physical education. In R. S. Brandt (Ed.), *Content of the curriculum.* Alexandria, VA: Association for Supervision and Curriculum Development.

Balistreri, J. P. (1986). *Impact of technology.* Reston, VA: International Technology Education Association. ED305–505

Batesky, J. (1991). Middle school physical education curriculum: Exposure or indepth instruction. *Middle School Journal, 22* (3), 7–11.

Bennett, W. J. (1988). Why the arts are essential. *Educational Leadership, 45* (4), 4–5.

Bloom, A. D. (1987). *The closing of the American mind.* New York: Simon & Schuster.

Brandt, R. S. (1987/1988). On discipline-based art education: A conversation with Elliot Eisner. *Educational Leadership, 45* (4), 6–9.

Brink, C., Apt., P., & Horell, D. (1986). Occupation of homemaking task analysis and competency-based design: Colorado curriculum project. In J. Laster, & R. Dohner, (Eds.). *Vocational home economics education: State of the field.* Peoria, IL: Macmillan, Bennett & McKnight Division.

Brolin, D. E. (1988). *Life centered career education: A competency based approach,* (3rd ed.). Reston, VA: The Council for Exceptional Children.

Bush, G. (1991). *America 2000.* Washington, DC: U.S. Department of Education.

Carnegie Council on Adolescent Development. (1989). *Turning points: Preparing American youth for the 21st century.* Washington, DC: Author.

Choksy, L., Abramson, R., Gillespie, A., & Woods, D. (1986). *Teaching music in the twentieth century.* Englewood Cliffs, NJ: Prentice-Hall.

Committee for Economic Development, Research and Policy Committee. (1985). *Investing in our children.* New York: Committee for Economic Development.

Connell, M. E. (1990). CLICK: Poets at work in the middle school. *English Journal, 79* (6), 30–32.

Cowan, M. M., & Clover, F. M. (1991). Enhancement of self-concept through discipline-based art education. *Art Education, 44* (2), 38–45.

Dart, B. (January 19, 1990). Exercise urged for youngsters. *News and Observer,* p. 1D.

Dionisio, M. (1991). Responding to literacy elements through mini-lessons and dialogue journals. *English Journal, 80* (1), 40–44.

Downey, J., & Kizer, J. (1986). Homemaker tasks-based independent modules: V-TECS consortium project. In J. Laster, & R. Dohner, (Eds.). *Vocational home economics education: State of the field.* Peoria, IL: Macmillan, Bennett & McKnight Division.

Drier, H. N. (1987). Resources abound for career educators. *Journal of Career Development, 13* (3), 78–91.

Drier, H. N. (1986). *Exploratory homemaking curriculum development,* Bulletin 1776. Thibodaux, LA: Nicholls State University.

Dudley, M. (1989). The writing workshop: Structuring for success. *English Journal, 78* (1), 28–32.

Eisner, E. W. (1990). Implications for artistic intelligences for education. In W. J. Moody (Ed.) *Artistic intelligences.* New York: Teachers' College Press.

Ewens, T. (1986) Beyond Getty: An analysis of beyond creating. In T. Ewens (Ed.), *Discipline in art education: An interdisciplinary symposium.* Providence, RI: Rhode Island School of Design.

Ewens, T. (1989). Discipline: Science and art on reflective activities. *Design for Arts in Education, 90* (4), 2–14.

Farrell, G. E. (1991). Drawbridges and moats: The arts and the middle school classroom. *Middle School Journal, 22* (5), 28–29.

Freeman, L. M., & Gregory, L. L. (1990). Language programs at the middle level. *NASSP Bulletin, 74* (530). 75–81.

Gardner, H. (1990). Multiple intelligences: Implications for art and creativity. In W. J. Moody (Ed.), *Artistic intelligences.* (pp. 11–27) New York: Teachers' College Press.

Gentry, D. L., & Hayes, R. L. (1991). Guidelines for athletic programs in the middle school. *Middle School Journal, 22* (3), 4–6.

Getty Center for Education in the Arts. (1985). *Beyond creating: The place of art in America's schools.* Los Angeles: Getty Center.

Gilles, C. (1989). Reading, writing and talking: Using literature study groups. *English Journal, 78* (1), 38–41.

Glenn, D. D. (1986). The middle school: Art, the transescent child, and the role of the teacher. *Art Education, 39* (5), 4–7.

Gould, D., Feltz, D., & Weiss, M. (1985). Motives for participating in competitive youth swimming. *International Journal of Sports Psychology, 16,* 126–140.

Great Falls Public Schools (1976–1977). *An exemplary career education program in the Great Falls Public Schools (K–14), first interim report.* Great Falls, MT: 191 pages, ED151–507

Hales, J., & Snyder, J. F. (1982). Jackson's Mill industrial arts curriculum theory: A base for curriculum derivation (two-part series). *The Technology Teacher, 41* (5), 6–10; and *41* (6), 6–8.

Hanstein, P. (1990) Educating for the future: A post-modern paradigm for dance education. *Journal of Physical Education, Recreation and Dance, 61* (5), 56–58.

Hargis, M. (1990). The video yearbook. *Media and Methods, 26* (5), 20–21.

Hargis, M. (1989, September). Health care costs push company toward fitness. *USA Today,* 3B.

Harris, L. and Associates, Inc. (1988). *Health you've got to be taught: An evaluation of comprehensive health education in American public schools.* New York: Metropolitan Life Foundation.

Heroes of young america: the tenth annual poll. *World Almanac and Book of Facts.* (1990). Englewood Cliffs, NJ: Prentice-Hall, 32–34.
Hirsch, Jr., E. D. (1987). *Cultural literacy.* Boston: Houghton Mifflin.
Hovland, D. (1990). Middle level activities programs: Helping achieve academic success. *NASSP Bulletin, 74* (530), 15–18.
International Technology Education Association (ITEA). (1985). *Technology education: A perspective in implementation.* Reston, VA. ED305–506
Jalongo, M. R. (1990). The child's right to the expressive arts: Nurturing the imagination as well as the intellect. *Childhood Education, 66* (4), 195–201.
Johnson, M. W. (1985). Physical education—Fitness or fraud? *Journal for Health, Physical Education, Recreation and Dance, 56* (1), 33–35.
Kneer, M. E. (1987). A new emphasis on physical fitness. *Educational Leadership, 44* (5), 93–94.
Lehman, P. R. (1988). What students should learn in the arts. In R. S. Brandt (Ed.), *Content of the curriculum.* Alexandria, VA: Association for Supervision and Curriculum Development.
Lowenfeld, V., & Brittain, W. L. (1987). *Creative and mental growth* (8th ed.). New York: Macmillan.
McNeil, J. (1990). *Curriculum: A comprehensive introduction.* Glenview, IL: Scott, Foresman.
Met, M. (1988). Tomorrow's emphasis in foreign language: Proficiency. In R. S. Brandt (Ed.), *Content of the curriculum.* Alexandria, VA: Association for Supervision and Curriculum Development.
Mueller, L. Z. (1990). Implications for creative writing. In W. J. Moody (Ed.), *Artistic intelligences* (pp. 116–122). New York: Teachers' College Press.
Music Educators National Conference. (1986). *The school music program* (2nd ed.). Reston, VA: Music Educators National Conference.
National Assessment of Educational Progress. (1986). *The writing report card.* Princeton, NJ: National Assessment of Educational Progress/Educational Testing Service.
National Council of Teachers of English. (1989). EJ forum: English and art. *English Journal, 78* (1) 13–36.
National Endowment for the Arts. (1988). *Toward civilization: A report on arts education.* Washington, DC: U.S. Government Printing Office.
National Middle School Association (1982, 1992). *This we believe.* Columbus, OH: Author.
Northwestern Tri-County Intermediate Unit 5. (July, 1976). *A project to demonstrate incremental improvements in K–12 career educational program through an exemplary mode.* Edinboro, PA: Northeastern Tri-County School System, 191 p. ED 163–166
Oaks, M. M. (1989). Making the change: Key issues in moving to technology education. *The Technology Teacher, 48* (5), 5–8.
Pough, C. R. (1989). *South Carolina guide for middle school home economics.* Columbia, SC: South Carolina State Department of Education. 666 p. ED313–514
Rakow, S.R. (1991). Young-adult literature for honors students? *English Journal, 80* (1), 48–50.
Ravitch, D., & Finn, Jr., C. E. (1987). *What do our 17-year-olds know?* New York: Harper & Row.
Ritz, J. M. (1991). Technology education: Where might our changes lead us? *The Technology Teacher, 50* (5), 3–4, 12.
Romano, T. (1987). *Clearing the way: Working with teenage writers.* Portsmouth, NH: Heinemann.
Roop, P. (1990). The magic of writing: How a writer teaches writing. *Childhood Education, 66* (5), 281–284.

Roseville Area School District 623. (1975–76). *Secondary career education project, final performance report.* Roseville, MN: Roseville Area School District 623. 90 pp. ED164–770.

Rosessler, R. T. (1988). Implementing career education: Barriers and potential solutions. *The Career Development Quarterly, 37*(1), 22–30.

Savage, E., & Sterry, L. (1990 a, b). A conceptual framework for technology education (two-part series). *The Technology Teacher,* (a) *50* (1), 6–11; (b) *50* (2), 7–11.

Scarborough, J. D. (1989). The changing content of technology education curricula. *The Technology Teacher, 48* (7), 5–8.

Schlaadt, R. G. (1988). School health education. In R. S. Brandt (Ed.), *Content of the curriculum.* Alexandria, VA: Association for Supervision and Curriculum Development.

Schultz, J. B. (1988–1989). Trends: Home economics. *Educational Leadership, 46* (4), 92.

Schwartz, P. (1990). Curriculum design for dance—Integrating creative and historical studies. *Journal of Physical Education, Recreation and Dance, 61* (7), 27–30.

Schwartz, P. (1991). Multicultural dance education in today's curriculum. *Journal of Physical Education, Recreation and Dance, 62* (2), 45–48.

Secretary's Commission on Achieving Necessary Skills (SCANS). (1991). *What work requires of schools: A SCANS report for America 2000.* Washington DC: U.S. Department of Labor.

Silberman, A. (1989). *Growing up writing.* New York: Times Books.

Smith, J. B. (1988). Reconceptualizing the home economics curriculum. In R. S. Brandt, (Ed.). *Content of the Curriculum.* Alexandria, VA: Association for Supervision and Curriculum Development.

South Carolina Department of Education. (1987). *Basic art skills: The South Carolina framework for visual arts education.* Columbia, SC: SCDE.

South Carolina Framework for Drama/Theater Education. (1990). Columbia, SC: South Carolina Department of Education.

Taymans, J., Lewis, K., & Ramsay, A. S. (1990). Contextual career education for urban youth: A new look at experience-based career education. *Journal of Career Development, 16* (4), 283–295.

Templin, T. J. (1987). Some considerations for teaching physical education in the future. In J. D. Massengale (Ed.), *Trends toward the future in physical education.* (pp. 51–67) Champaign, IL: Human Kinetics.

Tewel, K. J., & Lacey, R. (November, 1988). We won't build a strong work force by giving career education short shrift. *The American School Board Journal, 175,* 26–27.

This we believe. (1982, 1992). Columbus, OH: National Middle School Association.

Topping, R. J. (1990). Art education: A crisis in priorities. *Art Education, 43* (1), 20–24.

Tully, P. (1989). Video art. *School Aids, 89* (4), 23–27.

Turning Points: Preparing American youth for the 21st century. (1989). Washington, DC: Carnegie Council on Adolescent Development.

Van Buren, J. B. (1989). *Documentation of core competencies and key skills in the Missouri home economics curriculum.* Columbia, MO: University of Missouri. 459 pp. ED316678

Walberg, H. J., Connell, D. B., Turner, R. B., & Olsen, L. K. (June 1986). Health knowledge and attitudes change before behavior: A national evaluation of health programs finds. *ASCD Curriculum Update,* 4–6.

Willis, S. (November 1990). Health education: A crisis-driven field seeks coherence. *ASCD Curriculum Update,* 1–8.

Yaffe, S. H. (1989). Drama as a teaching tool. *Educational Leadership, 46* (6), 29–32.

CHAPTER OUTLINE

Organization for Teaching and Learning at the Middle Level

9

OVERVIEW

A responsive middle level organization must be student-centered, focusing on the unique developmental needs of learners. As the middle level organization has evolved, interdisciplinary teams have emerged as the dominant organizational pattern. Through interdisciplinary teams, curriculum and instruction are presented effectively to middle level learners.

The key educational elements that interdisciplinary teams make possible are meeting the developmentally appropriate needs and individual interests of learners; establishing a curricular balance among content, instruction, and skills required for general, career, and fine arts education; creating a positive school environment that emphasizes caring, respect, success, and interdependence; and finding teachers committed to teaching young adolescents (*This We Believe,* 1992). Organizational features such as core, exploratory activities, and flexible scheduling, together with specialized learning environments, such as cooperative learning, may be utilized to achieve the goals and objectives of the middle level school.

In this chapter, you will read about:

1 Vertical and/or horizontal organization features for facilitating learning.
2 Interdisciplinary teams.
3 The supportive research on team approaches.

4 Implications of grouping and tracking on middle level learners.
5 The significance of a core program for meeting the developmentally appropriate needs of middle level learners.
6 Approaches to flexible scheduling.
7 Essential features of exploratory programs.
8 Specialized learning environments.

DESIGNING AND IMPLEMENTING A RESPONSIVE MIDDLE LEVEL ORGANIZATION

For a middle level school to operate well, the organization must be responsive to the unique needs of learners and committed to the belief that all learners can learn. The organization must be able to blend developmental needs of young adolescents and curricular and instructional requirements into an effective instructional plan that provides for student learning. Interdisciplinary teams are recommended as the best plan to promote a responsive organization for the teaching and learning experiences of middle level students.

DEVELOPING A RATIONALE FOR INTERDISCIPLINARY TEAMS

Learner-centered School. As one begins the task of designing a middle level organization, the first important point to consider is that the school must organize the curriculum around the developmental needs of middle level learners. Learning should be personalized and revolve around individual learners' needs for personal and social adjustment and self-acceptance during early adolescence. Administrators and teachers should provide a wholesome school environment (caring, understanding, supportive, helping, and fair) that allows the individual learner to feel wanted, needed, and worthy. Students must perceive school personnel as genuinely concerned for them regardless of differences in achievement and behavior. The middle level school represents a systematic effort to organize the school experience around these characteristics for all young adolescents. At the same time, another key consideration is the realization that each individual has personal needs. If the curriculum and instruction in the middle level are to keep pace with the learner and serve all students, the instructional design must be matched to the learner's development and personal needs. The instructional design must permit individuality, be multidimensional, and reflect the extent of learning as well as the rate of learning.

Integrated Curriculum. Another consideration is what content to select and how to deliver the content and skills to the students through instruction. In selecting the content, it is necessary to integrate subjects and meet defined state requirements and those of accrediting agencies and legislative mandates, as well as the needs of the middle level learner. It is important that the curriculum be balanced between core subjects, career exploration, and societal mandates such as the basics, higher achievement test scores, higher-order thinking, and career education. Students must be able to observe the interconnectedness of various subjects in the curriculum. The relevance of an integrated curriculum is demonstrated to young adolescents through interdisciplinary teams.

ORGANIZING INTERDISCIPLINARY TEAMS

A gradual evolutionary process led middle level schools from informal team planning to teaching teams. Team approaches have been an essential characteristic in the development of middle level schools. These approaches were designed to provide flexibility in the curriculum, better utilize teachers' and students' time, and improve instruction (Howard & Stoumbis, 1970). Better use of time and a curriculum designed around the overall developmental needs of young adolescents became major objectives of the emerging team organization patterns of the middle level school.

The interdisciplinary team was an organizational pattern first suggested by Alexander et al. (1969) and then reaffirmed by Alexander and George (1981). These authors defined teams as "a way of organizing faculty so that a group of teachers share: (1) the responsibility for planning, teaching, and evaluating curriculum and instruction in more than one academic area; (2) the same group of students; (3) the same schedule; and (4) the same area of the building" (p. 115). These authors maintained that when these four criteria were present, no more was needed to have a team organization. Over the past decade, interdisciplinary teams have developed as the focal point of middle level organizational patterns.

ORGANIZATIONAL PATTERNS

Interdisciplinary teams are organized with two or more teachers into one of the following patterns: (1) at least two subjects are combined, such as social studies–language arts or science–mathematics; (2) four or more subjects are combined, such as language arts–mathematics–science–social studies; or (3) these four subjects are combined with art, music, physical education, etc. This organizational approach permits learning to evolve through the development of units integrated across the curriculum. Content is easily integrated and instruction is focused on the development of the individual middle level learner. Opportunities for flexible grouping patterns are facilitated. Block, revolving, and modular scheduling can facilitate curriculum and learner needs. Other teaming possibilities can be organized whereby all teachers share in the content of (1) language arts, social studies, mathematics, science, and/or reading, or (2) language arts, social studies, mathematics, science, fine arts, technology education, home arts, special education, and guidance. Special education, fine arts, technology education, home arts, and guidance staff members should be considered an integral part of all teams. For middle level teachers, the term should imply team planning with various members of the interdisciplinary team responsible for presenting instruction. Teachers must recognize their responsibilities as team members and be comfortable with expectations. It is not recommended that a hierarchical organizational pattern be established of individual faculty member's roles on interdisciplinary teams. This arrangement usually does not make the teams function effectively and may cause conflict among the teaching staff.

ORGANIZATIONAL CONSIDERATIONS

Essential considerations for establishing interdisciplinary teams are:

1 The provision for a smoother transition between elementary school and high school.
2 All students taught by qualified teachers whose expertise and strengths can be utilized by the team.
3 More instructional planning time and additional resource materials.
4 The focus on individual student developmental needs.
5 Interconnectedness among the various content areas understood by middle level learners.
6 The need for the development of a flexible schedule.
7 The coordination of all school personnel, parents, and community agencies.
8 The need for interdisciplinary teams to integrate all subject areas such as music, art, drama, home economics, technology education, and physical education.
9 Provision for security and companionship among middle level students during the young adolescent years.

To use interdisciplinary teams successfully involves administrative and teacher commitment, staff development and team planning both ahead of time and on-going, continuous adjustments—when problems arise for students or teachers—and lastly, financial and material resources—which may not be available. The most critical concern is providing adequate time for team planning. Without adequate planning time during the school year and prior planning beforehand, it is very difficult to implement interdisciplinary teams. In addition, the success of interdisciplinary teams may depend in part on whether the personalities of teachers on the teams are compatible. Another factor is whether the teachers were trained as elementary teachers or secondary teachers. Secondary teachers almost always represent strengths in one particular area and they may desire to teach only this subject to the students assigned to the team. In contrast, elementary teachers have a general content preparation which enables them to teach several areas, but they may not have enough in-depth preparation required to teach in all subjects effectively. Planning staff development programs will need to take all of these variables into account. Thus, teams may teach two, three, or four different subjects in various collaborative arrangements with their team members depending on the academic preparation and personal desires of team members.

Since no two teams will function in the same way, an operational definition of an interdisciplinary team must be alert to the perceptions of teachers, administrators, students, and parents in a given school setting. As teams become more experienced in interdisciplinary planning, team members can organize interdisciplinary units around themes where each subject specialist contributes to the topics selected for the unit. Themes such as "The Roaring Twenties" or "World War II" could include all the traditional subject matter as well as music, art, physical education, and home arts. Effective teams utilize teachers' strengths in planning across disciplines and in designing and organizing the units. However, interdisciplinary teams often need more extensive planning and intensive staff development than is required for typical in-service activities during a given school year. Because interdisciplinary team teaching is essential to an effective middle level organization, careful attention must be devoted by administrators to providing adequate time and resources for planning and staff development.

COMMUNICATING WITH STUDENTS AND PARENTS

It is important to explain the value of interdisciplinary teams to students and parents. Teams are important for students' self-concept in larger schools because it is often difficult to have an identity. A team has the potential to provide a group of 100–140 students with a better sense of personal identity. A sense of identity is critical to having successful middle level experiences for young adolescents. Students also must be able to better realize the interconnectedness of the curriculum. For parents, the term *interdisciplinary team* has not always been defined operationally, because their own school experiences usually did not include instruction through teams of teachers. Parents may be more willing to support a team approach if they have positive experiences in communicating with team members, if orientation programs occur periodically through PTA programs or special events, and if learners are positive about their school experiences. It is essential to maintain constant communication with parents so that a more optimal learning and teaching environment for young adolescents can be sustained.

Today, interdisciplinary teams require the integration of organizational, curricular, and instructional elements to ensure young adolescents' learning. A middle level organization serves as the umbrella for facilitating interdisciplinary teams through team planning and types of organizational patterns such as flexible scheduling, core programs, and exploratory programs. Interdisciplinary teams must focus on building school morale and improving interpersonal relationships among students, teachers, administrators, parents, and the community. Involving students in the team planning helps them to improve their thinking and decision-making skills. Interdisciplinary teams provide opportunities for integration of content and skills of the curriculum into meaningful learning experiences for students.

GUIDELINES

Some guidelines on how to organize learning into interdisciplinary teams on the middle level are contained in Figure 9.1. In summary, key elements of middle level school programs are concerned with the total development of the middle level learner and are focused on the individual needs and interests of the learner. They integrate content, skills, and values required for general education and career awareness. The emphasis is on the success and personal growth of learners through a responsive organization which utilizes interdisciplinary teams to support instruction through core programs, exploratory activities, flexible scheduling, and specialized learning environments, such as cooperative learning and advisor–advisee programs.

An organization with interdisciplinary teams can be configured into various combinations. The idea is to free professional staff members for the tasks in

A responsive middle level organization should:

- Recognize and respond to the unique needs (physical, emotional, intellectual, social, and spiritual) of each learner.
- Accommodate the wide diversity of the values, personality, and experiences of each learner.
- Recognize students' learning styles by providing meaningful learning activities suited to the learner.
- Integrate knowledge, skills, and values through team organization into meaningful learning experiences.
- Provide interactive learning activities through varied teaching and organizational approaches, such as teaching teams and flexible scheduling.
- Use student interests and abilities as the basis of individualizing teaching and learning.
- Consider teachers as guides or facilitators of learning.
- Use the total professional staff as a team for accomplishing learning.
- Utilize interdisciplinary, technological, and exploratory approaches to learning.

FIGURE 9.1 Guidelines for organizing interdisciplinary teams

the instructional framework from which teams can be organized within grades and instructional units, or across grades and instructional areas. Interdisciplinary teams can vary in size, roles, and responsibilities of teachers, student composition, teacher autonomy, and the ways that the schedule and time are structured for the team. Depending on the degree of flexibility provided by a school and its student population, the possibility may exist of utilizing smaller, more structured classrooms in some situations and teacher teams of varying size, composition, students, and curriculum focus in other situations. Teams also vary in utilization of large- and small-group instruction, the number and use of paraprofessionals and community consultants, and the degree of involvement of administrative staff and district personnel.

Although there are many approaches to teaming, it has become one of the essential attributes of organizational practice at the middle level. George and Oldaker (1985) found 90% of the sample of 100 schools in their study employed some type of teaming. By comparison, Lounsbury and Johnston's (1988) investigation indicated that 67% of the middle level schools in the study used some form of teaming at the sixth grade.

THE ESSENTIALS

Team Planning. Various approaches to team planning have been suggested. Each team with administrative input decides how to accomplish their instructional goals. A common time is provided for team planning. Other aspects of team planning should include team meetings with parents, subject and reading specialists, and guidance counselors to plan instructional needs of students and team members. Team planning provides the necessary bridge between team members and young adolescents. Planning teams of four teachers are the most common, probably because the academic curriculum is configured around the four basic subject areas of science, mathematics, language arts, and social studies. However, the fine arts, physical education, technology education, and home arts also should be considered in team planning to provide for diverse interests of young adolescent learners. These special subject teachers have significant contributions that can strengthen interdisciplinary team planning. With the mandated basics program found in many states, it has become necessary to have reading, special education, language arts, or mathematics teachers serve as team members and consultants to all teams.

The variations in team planning and the opportunities for organizing a teaching team are unlimited. However, without adequate organization and planning, chaos could result. Teaming demands a closer working relationship among teachers and causes each teacher to be aware of each other's ideas, attitudes, and desires which must be considered and shared. Opinions from team members are an essential part of the professional obligation of team planning. Another dividend is the focus on students and the pooling of information in support of young adolescents. Thus, the more learner information that can be shared, the more likely learning problems can be anticipated and reduced. The more individual student information that a teacher possesses, the more likely an effective classroom environment can be established for meeting the unique needs of each middle level learner.

Team planning should provide students with a wide variety of resource persons. A team of teachers will bring a much greater field of expertise and pooled knowledge to meet the wide-ranging demands that arise from young adolescents' expanding interests. The academic specialists need not surrender their content but can now employ their specialization to a wider audience. Teachers have the freedom to incorporate their individual talents and interests in the planning process. Each teacher's own personal interests which might normally be outside the range of school subjects can be used in such areas as film-making and photography. Team planning provides an opportunity for teacher talents to reach greater numbers of students.

Team planning also reduces potential personality conflicts that could arise between teachers and learners. Effective teams require dedication to planning an individualized student program if teaming is to reach its maximum potential. Thus, continuous planning must be provided over several years for the development of effective teams to occur. To increase team members' effectiveness, it is essential that team planning result in wise use of their instructional time, and reduction of personality conflicts between learners and teachers.

Resource Personnel. Another essential decision is how resource personnel will be utilized on teams. Resource personnel usually include the guidance counselor, administrators, librarian, school nurse, paraprofessionals, and any other specialized personnel. Teams which include resource personnel need to work out the expectations of the individual members on the team. Key concerns involve attendance at team meetings, contributions of resource persons to the team's effectiveness, and assistance provided by team members to help each resource person's talents increase the team's potential. Another variation is to emphasize each subject separately, and establish special resource rooms for those youth who need extra assistance with basic subjects. Guidance responsibilities may be assigned to the team through the guidance counselor serving as a consultant to the team or actually being involved in the team, depending on the number of guidance counselors available and the type of guidance program desired. Guidance functions should be considered an integral part of team planning in order to utilize fully the advisor–advisee approach. In this type of arrangement, the principal and assistant principals also serve as valuable members of the teams for planning student needs and guidance support services.

Team Leadership. In the formulation of teams, the team organizational goals and objectives need to be identified and articulated. Any team pattern must consider which organizational patterns will provide the leadership to facilitate learning and effectively utilize the existing school personnel. If a team leadership concept is used, care must be taken to ensure that the responsibilities assigned to the position, such as status and salary supplement, do not restrict effective interpersonal relationships between the team leader and team members. Because of rewards and professional jealousy, team members may let more responsibilities fall to the team leader. One option to reduce the potential for professional conflicts is to rotate the position of team leader among the team members. If the leader rotates, the potential for conflict may be lessened, but long-range planning may be more difficult to accomplish. As effective team leadership evolves, it is essential that teachers on the teams perceive themselves as making specific contributions. Teachers' recognition of their individual contributions to the team reduces the potential for personal conflicts and improves instructional effectiveness.

The Principal. Each principal has several options for organizing and being involved in the teams. One approach may be to have lead or master teachers meet with the principal. Another is to have the teams communicate objectives and goals to the principal on a regular basis. Yet another option is to have each office administrator (depending on number of administrative staff) assigned to one or more of the teams. The important point is that the principal continues to function as the instructional leader regardless of what team involvement is proposed.

Principals need to encourage teachers to make their own decisions regarding curriculum and instruction. The strength of any team is directly related to the degree of decision-making that teachers enjoy. Providing adequate time for team planning is one of the key requirements of any successful team organizational pattern. Policies need to be established on how to cope with individual students in the framework of the middle level setting. The administrative framework needs to be flexible in order to meet the challenges of education and also meet the responsibilities required by the school district and state.

While teachers on the teams will have many duties, it is essential that team members (1) know their specific responsibilities regarding curriculum and instruction, (2) communicate effectively, (3) participate in collaborative decision-making, (4) plan and schedule instructional time for students and team members, (5) arrange for building and space utilization, and (6) select appropriate instructional materials. In selecting team members, principals should pay close attention to their leadership potential and compatibility. This involves selecting teachers with inherent leadership traits who are excited about middle level learners and teaming.

Scheduling. Constructing the master schedule is the first consideration of scheduling. Second, the schedule must be flexible and achieved through the use of block, revolving, and modular scheduling or any combination of these schedules. Under team approaches, the teachers can have flexibility in their schedules to make better use of time for instruction and planning. Teachers usually are assigned a number of students to teach. The team, depending on its size, would be responsible for subject content and other electives if these members are part of the team. Team members should be involved actively in scheduling students. For example, teachers of language arts, social studies, science, and mathematics might decide to block their class periods together for a specific period during the morning, afternoon, or several periods in the morning or afternoon. The scheduling process should be able to accommodate this type of need.

Staff and Building. Another important aspect is the involvement of the professional staff in planning the design of the middle level teams for teaching and learning. Planning with the staff is essential in organizing teams for the middle level. All too often, the program is in place and the staff has had little or no chance to be involved.

In addition, the existing building may not be the most architecturally sound building for the development of middle level learners. The building may be the old high school or other surplus building that has been converted or will be converted into a middle level school. Many middle level schools have portables, which make it more difficult to provide for various kinds of planning and learning activities that involve large groups or require specialized equipment. Teachers who travel from room to room may make it more essential that common planning areas be provided. The use of existing buildings makes it even more imperative that there be staff planning in the development of middle level teams.

In summary, the principal remains the instructional leader of the school. Whatever interdisciplinary team approach is used, it must include the instructional responsibilities of the principal in order for the team and the administration of the middle level school to be successful. Management responsibilities cannot be delegated beyond a reasonable point. A collaborative management plan is developed to ensure the success of a team organization. Without the involvement of staff in all aspects of planning, there will not be an effective middle level program. Because the training of staff for the unique demands of the middle level may be so varied, it is suggested that a staff development program be instituted over several years through workshops, retreats, or summer workshops. While there is a tendency to rush staff planning and development, care must be exercised by the school administration to plan carefully the implementation of successful middle level interdisciplinary teams. An organization with interdisciplinary teams is an evolving process which utilizes each middle level school setting to provide the most effective learning, planning, and utilization of personnel.

CRITERIA FOR SUCCESS

In Figure 9.2, Merenbloom (1986) gives some guidelines for determining a successful interdisciplinary team. This excellent evaluation instrument was developed by Merenbloom (1986) to determine whether an interdisciplinary team was successful. Merenbloom suggested the following questions: (1) Who will evaluate the effectiveness of our team? (2) Will we have the opportunity to participate in a self-evaluation as part of the overall plan for evaluation? If so, how? and (3) What instrument will we use to evaluate the effectiveness of our teams?

An interdisciplinary team is successful when:

- Team members enhance the self-concept of the learner through concern for personal needs of individual students.
- Flexibility exists in student and master schedules.
- Team members explore their roles and functions.
- The school and district administration support the team's efforts.
- Organized subject matter and skill development are correlated.
- Parents are an integral part of a team.
- There is adequate time for team planning and that time is used productively.
- Resource persons are available to the team.
- Team members feel free to share thoughts, ideas, and responsibilities.
- Pupils are in various grouping arrangements during the day.
- Staff development activities are provided.
- Team members practice effective human relations skills.
- Students feel good about themselves.
- Teachers believe in the middle school concept.

FIGURE 9.2 A successful interdisciplinary team *Adapted from* The team process in the middle school: A handbook for teachers *by E. Merenbloom, 1986, p. 177. Columbus, OH: National Middle School Association. Adapted by permission from NMSA.*

How will the instrument be used? Thus, the purpose of assessment is to help teams improve student learning.

RESEARCH FINDINGS ON INTERDISCIPLINARY TEAMS

Arhar, Johnston, and Markle (1988) investigated interdisciplinary teams and concluded that "the team has important effects on the organizational climate of the school, the satisfaction and professional development of teachers, and collaboration within the workplace" (p. 24). They also found that teams can provide small groups of students with a more caring environment and the opportunity for improving their personal growth. However, the authors urge caution in jumping to conclusions. Teaming may result in major instructional changes. Teaming provides the opportunity for the development of interaction and cohesive groups, but does not guarantee that instructional changes will take place. The authors stated that "while a team arrangement may allow collaboration to occur, it cannot compel it. Nor can it compel cross-disciplinary planning or instruction" (Arhar, Johnston & Markle, 1988, p. 24).

In a study of 100 middle level schools, George and Oldaker (1985) found that interdisciplinary teams made a meaningful contribution to staff morale. The research findings indicated positive results for interdisciplinary team arrangements.

CASE STUDIES OF INTERDISCIPLINARY TEAMS

Lipsitz. In Lipsitz's (1984) account of successful middle level schools, interdisciplinary teaming was a common element in each of the four schools studied. The level of team interdependence varied from school to school. In some schools, team teachers met only to solve student scheduling problems, but did not work on curricular and instructional problems. In only one of the four schools studied did teachers identify the team structure as the most representative feature of the school. This school, Noe Middle School, had academic teams which shared the responsibility for learning experiences with 150 students. Teachers, assisted by principals and team leaders, used team planning to make decisions on grouping, departmentalization, interdisciplinary units, allocation of time, intramurals, teacher-based guidance, and team rules. Teaching performance was not a function of personal qualities and characteristics alone. The joint efforts and actions of highly motivated and competitive groups resulted in improved teaching performance.

Lipsitz suggested that teaching styles tended to be more alike on teams. Since the team selection process was not described, uniformity may have to do with teacher self-selection into the most comfortable teaching. Uniformity was not the ideal consequence of team instruction. A final conclusion reached from the study was that teachers with decision-making power perceived themselves as professionals. The ability to discuss and reach some type of consensus removed the feeling of teachers being alone. Lipsitz (1984) concluded: "Organizational structure establishes continuity in adult-child relationships and opportunities for the lives of students and adults to cross in mutually meaningful ways. In each school, students express their appreciation for being cared about and known. They are actively aware of being liked, which is notable only because in most schools, young adolescents are generally disliked" (p. 181).

Ashton and Webb. As a part of determining the relationship between teachers' sense of efficacy and teaching teams, Ashton and Webb (1986) studied two different middle level schools with sixth, seventh, and eighth grades. A traditional junior high with departmentalization, single-age grouping, and a homeroom was compared to a middle level school with interdisciplinary teams, multi-age grouping, and the advisor–advisee program. The study showed the differences in attitudes associated with collaborative and noncollaborative organizational structures. The study hypothesized that a school organization that encourages collegial interaction may enhance teacher efficacy while lowering isolationism. The results indicated that the organizational differences created quite different relationships among teachers. Teams produced a sense of community and forged strong collegial relationships. Sharing of student responsibilities, classroom practices, and planning time gave teachers a commonality of accomplishment and a sense of professional and emotional support. Teaching in interdisciplinary teams was viewed as a communal enterprise. In contrast, the departmentalized school staff considered themselves as independent members, each doing separate tasks, sharing few responsibilities, relying on their own successes, and valuing their perceived autonomy. In conclusion, the team structure resulted in greater interdependence. Teachers were rewarded by the support and approval of their colleagues.

EFFECTS OF TEAMING ON STUDENT ACHIEVEMENT

Because of the popularity of teaming, does the instructional organizational approach really benefit students? Until recently, several studies correlating the causal relationship between student achievement and teaming have not demonstrated that teaming has any effect on student achievement (Armstrong, 1977; Cotton, 1983). Organizational arrangements may not be as important as the conditions under which teaming and traditional arrangements were found or the effect of some specific characteristic of learners. George and Oldaker (1985), in a study of 100 best middle schools, compared traditional and teaming organizational patterns and reported consistent academic improvement on achievement tests and observed increased teacher confidence in those schools with team organizations. They concluded that, "62% of the respondents in this study described consistent academic improvement" and "85% observed that teacher confidence in students' abilities had increased, which, many suggested, led to higher expectations and greater student productivity in academic classes" (George & Oldaker, 1985, p. 20).

In a more controlled study, Bradely (1988) found after studying interdisciplinary teams and departmentalized arrangements in mathematics and reading achievement that teaming was more effective in fostering mathematics achievement. Both organizational arrangements were equally effective in developing reading achievement. In addition, students from all ability levels received higher mathematics scores than did students in departmentalized settings. Team-taught students in heterogeneously grouped levels did as well in reading as homogeneously grouped, departmental learners. In conclusion, interdisciplinary teams have a positive impact on student learning outcomes. It would appear that teaming fosters positive student–teacher relationships which in turn facilitate individual student motivation and learner success.

AFFECTIVE AND SOCIAL OUTCOMES OF TEAMING

When middle level schools utilize teaming, students demonstrate more enthusiasm about learning than students in schools with departmentalization. When teachers model cooperative behavior, it would appear that similar behavior is encouraged from students. George and Oldaker (1985) found that school discipline was improved and that disruptive behavior, office referrals, and suspensions were reduced as a result of teaming. Arhar, Johnston, and Markle (1988) concluded that it would appear that "team arrangements reduce teacher isolationism, increase satisfaction and improve individual teachers' sense of efficacy. Teaming is also more likely to promote discussions of individual student needs and the operational details of teaching, a finding that parallels very closely George's description (1984) of the early stages of development teams go through" (p. 25).

ASSESSING THE EFFECTIVENESS OF INTERDISCIPLINARY TEAMS

The team's success depends upon continuous assessment. George (1982) proposed a model for examining and assessing interdisciplinary teams called the Four-Phase Model. According to the model, an instructional team may progress through four hierarchical stages toward becoming fully operational and effective. Figure 9.3 outlines the four-phase model. The first stage is *organizational*. In this stage, the essential characteristics are (1) utilizing the same schedule and physical space with teachers responsible for instruction, (2) restricting student movement, and (3) providing close interaction with students and parents. These criteria are the essential developmental elements for expanding any team concept. Stage two, a sense of *community*, is provided for young adolescents to identify with a small group in the school and to be known by several adults. Stage three is focused on *instruction*, with interdisciplinary teams grouping students for instruction and collaboratively planning integrated curriculum units. Stage four, the *administrative* level, utilizes shared decision-making with the school's administration. At this final level, the team is "the central unit of school level

Level	Description
Organizational	In this phase, the same schedule and physical space are shared by a group of teachers and students, student movement is minimized throughout the school and opportunities are provided for close interaction with students and parents. Teachers are responsible for instructing students.
Community	In this phase, the opportunity is provided for young adolescents to identify with a small group in the school and to be known by several adults. A sense of identity is illustrated by various types of indicators such as team names, colors, buttons or clothing. Team contests and field trips are held, often with parent involvement.
Instruction	During this stage, interdisciplinary teams group students for instruction, design and implement integrated curriculum units. Collaboration in planning is an essential feature.
Administrative	At this level, decision-making is shared with the school's administration. The team resolves problems and is central to policy development decisions.

FIGURE 9.3 The four-phase model *(Adapted from "The interdisciplinary team organization" by K. Plodzik & P. S. George, May 1989,* Middle School Journal, *20, pp. 15–17.)*

problem solving and policy development, even though appropriate decisions do involve these other levels" (Plodzik & George, 1989, p. 15). Team representatives meet with administrators on a regular basis to resolve problems and discuss issues.

To determine the degree to which an interdisciplinary team in a middle level organization fits these four stages, a follow-up study of seventh-grade New England middle schools was conducted during the 1985–1986 school year (Plodzik & George, 1989). The study found the four stages of team organization in varying degrees in middle level schools surveyed. A significant relationship existed between a specific stage of team development and the access to staff development courses on the middle level for teachers and administrators. Effective team teachers were competent in their subject matter content, flexible, willing to be a team member, and aware of the needs of young adolescents. The study suggested that schools reached a more sophisticated stage of development when principals encouraged teams in their schools, stressed the importance of teaming, provided common planning time, and established goals for teams to meet.

ORGANIZATIONAL PATTERNS FOR INTERDISCIPLINARY TEAMS

The following organizational patterns provide more opportunities for interdisciplinary teams to meet the developmental and personal needs of young adolescents. Approaches such as core programs, flexible scheduling, exploratory programs, and learning centers are considered an essential part of the evolving process of attaining and maintaining interdisciplinary teams. Specialized learning environments such as cooperative learning, learning laboratories/resource rooms, and a technology center provide specialized learning climates for middle level learners. A brief outline of these patterns is provided in Table 9.1.

Most middle level organizations decide to implement one or more these patterns depending on financial resources, instructional staff, commitment of instructional personnel and building principal, and support of the school district and community. Care should be exercised to ensure that the organizational development does not cause any of those involved, including staff, district personnel, and the community to lose confidence in the reorganization efforts of the middle level school.

CORE OPTIONS

Definition and Purposes. Traditional content areas of language arts, social studies, mathematics, and science usually form the essential subjects in the school's academic curriculum. These academic subjects represent the general education content and skills required for all middle level learners. Various core approaches can be seen as a continuum going from a gradual curricular change of integrating two subjects to a comprehensive curriculum revision as represented by interdisciplinary units. These interdisciplinary units could be developed around

TABLE 9.1 Organizational Patterns for Interdisciplinary Teams

Organizational Pattern	Description
Core options	These options provide for flexibility in content, ranging from integration of separate disciplines to learner-based content.
Flexible scheduling	Three types—block, revolving, and modular—provide flexibility for time frames, grouping, teams, large and small groups.
Exploratory programs	Activities that provide for a wide range of diverse learner needs and interests, e.g., career exploration and drug education. Students given opportunity and responsibility to explore, think, investigate, and study on their own in any area that the learner has a particular interest.
Learning centers	Learners permitted to work at own pace on an appropriate skill level while learning through a variety of modalities. Four types of centers are skills, discovery, listening, and creativity.
	SPECIALIZED LEARNING ENVIRONMENTS
Cooperative learning	Three approaches to cooperative learning are (1) structure approach, (2) curriculum specific approach, and (3) social interdependence.
Learning laboratories/ resource rooms	These facilities provide study areas and function as a workroom where resources and materials of particular subjects are accessible.
Technology centers	Computers and multimedia are utilized for instructional purposes (drill, tutorial, simulations, etc.) to motivate learners and permit exploratory activities.

broad themes such as energy, pollution, careers, family, school, government, and international relations. These broad themes would include relevant content from the various areas such as mathematics, writing, social studies, and language arts.

As used in this textbook, the core concept is broader than just general education and can include a problem-centered curriculum utilizing variable groups, interdisciplinary content, and individual and group guidance. When considering the continuum of options, middle level educators should select and design core options that best suit their situations. In determining the combination of options that might be selected, consideration should be given to the following criteria. First, the flexibility of the school's schedule must be explored. A review of the flexible schedule section may help determine if the needed flexibility is provided in the current schedule. Second, the enthusiasm of the staff for the various core options must be considered. If instructional staff members do not see the reasons for restructuring, then the chances for revision are minimal. The greater the change, the greater the need for planning time with the faculty. Gradual change may be more realistic than full-scale curricular changes. Third, the nature of the curriculum requirements vary from grade to grade and state to state depending on requirements of the state. Fourth, caution needs to be exerted to provide careful planning time so that units are meaningful and carefully orchestrated. Careful planning must be devoted to address community concerns, state and school curriculum requirements and at the same time enrich the curriculum of the specific middle level school. Fifth, additional staff and funds are required usually to sustain team efforts and ensure success of the teams. Sixth, parents have difficulty accepting the value of interdisciplinary programs because few have had prior experiences with this approach in their own schooling. More time may be needed to inform the community about the beneficial features of these options. Seventh, caution should be exercised not to make assumptions about which subjects lend themselves to interdisciplinary units.

Positive Outcomes for Teaching and Learning. Effective core programs must consider (1) a wide variety of teaching techniques, such as large- and small-group instruction, field trips, debates, role playing; (2) opportunities for students to explore important contemporary issues of interest while fusing the skills and concepts of two or more subject areas into one topic; (3) the relationships that exist among other subject areas, concepts, or skills; (4) efficient use of instructional time; and (5) increased motivation of young adolescents based on exploring their own personal interests and social concerns.

Personal problems and needs of pupils become important in programming the subject matter. Personal information on students' needs, interests, problems, and values is better able to be addressed. Problems growing out of interpersonal relations can be worked out through units studying real problems and participating in various types of group work. Core programs provide increased opportunity for the adviser–advisee program to work. Also, the potential exists for increased teacher involvement in guidance.

FLEXIBLE SCHEDULING

Flexible scheduling permits flexibility in the scheduling process to provide for varied size instructional groups and personalized instruction. There has been a great deal of confusion and misunderstanding about flexible scheduling. In its simplest form, the class periods may all be the same length (block schedule) but there is a possibility for variation both in length, number of periods, and/or times of day (daily extended periods) in which instruction will be offered. A revolving schedule changes the times for each period and rotates the periods during the week for shorter or longer time frames. The varied time frames for each period remain the same, with the periods rotating from day to day. In contrast, modular scheduling is based on the premise that the schedule of each day does not have to be the same as the previous day either in time frame or number of periods, that class size and length will vary according to the specific subject matter being presented, that teachers and content will require different amounts of time, and that young adolescents differ in the amount of time required to learn something. Thus, the class size, duration of the class, number and type of weekly meetings required, aptitudes and interests of the middle level learners, the nature of instruction, the content area, and the outcomes of teaching are all variables of modular scheduling.

Flexible schedules provide opportunities to investigate a wide range of special interests among middle level learners and still spend the needed amount of time on content. Approaches such as independent study and core programs are other possibilities. Flexible schedules allow adequate time for acquisition of knowledge and variation in activities for extended content requirements and can better accommodate differences in students' attention spans.

The typical schedule consists of six to eight periods, depending on the length of each period and the number of students enrolled. The typical time frame is class periods of 45 to 60 minutes. Flexible scheduling in its most simplified form arranges class periods of the same length, but there is opportunity for variation both in length and the time of day when they are taught. A revolving schedule breaks the traditional periods into time frames of 20, 30, 50, 60, and 100 minutes but retains these time frames throughout the week. In contrast, a modular schedule breaks the same units of time—20, 30, 50 minutes etc.—with variations in time over each day of the week, depending on what is needed to meet the subject and state mandates. It should be noted that any flexible schedule permits an instructional staff to move into team teaching and large-group or small-group instruction and provides the flexibility to address young adolescent needs.

Block Schedule (Period By Period). This schedule is the easiest format to move from a regular schedule of six periods into scheduling each content area into blocks or periods back to back. In the Type A block schedule shown in Table 9.2, each teacher has two or more blocks and/or periods by pairing Language Arts (Teacher A) with social studies (Teacher B) or science (Teacher C) and mathematics (Teacher D) or any other combination of all four. Teacher A has the same group of students the first period, and Teacher B could have the same students during the second period, Teacher C, third period, and Teacher D, fourth period. If all sections offered each period are composed of the same subject matter and teachers, i.e., Mathematics, Science, Social Studies, and Language Arts, various types of grouping and regrouping opportunities as well as teams may exist over periods scheduled in this manner. This type of schedule permits from two to four teachers, depending on how the schedule is arranged, to provide opportunities for teams and team planning of various class schedules. If periods three and four were included, the potential could be even greater for various

TABLE 9.2 Type A Block Schedule—Period by Period

Period	Time	Teacher A	Teacher B	Teacher C	Teacher D
1	55 minutes	Language Arts	Social Studies	Science	Mathematics
2	55 minutes	Language Arts	Social Studies	Science	Mathematics
3	55 minutes	Language Arts	Social Studies	Science	Mathematics
4	55 minutes	Language Arts	Social Studies	Science	Mathematics

TABLE 9.3 Type B Block Schedule—Daily Extended Periods

Period	Time	Monday	Tuesday	Wednesday	Thursday	Friday
1	55 minutes	**1**	1	1	1	2
2	55 minutes	**1**	**2**	2	3	3
3	55 minutes	2	**2**	**3**	**4**	**5**
4	55 minutes	4	3	**3**	**4**	**5**
5	55 minutes	5	4	4	5	**6**
6	55 minutes	6	5	6	6	**6**

learner groupings. Additional flexibility can be provided by having a block of time scheduled in the afternoon.

Type B (Extended Periods Each Day). Another variation of the standard block schedule, shown in Table 9.3, is the daily extension of periods for two or more periods by block scheduling each subject one day a week (bold numbers daily) for a double period. The other four days it would meet for one period. In each instance, one period of a given content area would not meet one day of the week.

Type C (Additional Period Block Schedule). Another modification of daily extended periods is found in Table 9.4. Type C uses the same six-period day but adds a seventh period so that six-subject areas each have double periods one day of a week and the seventh period is ten minutes longer (bold numbers daily). The same amount of classroom time is provided over six days for six periods. The advantages are that more time can be devoted to content matter and more flexibility can be provided in the schedule over the six days by adding another period.

Revolving Schedule. In the revolving schedule (see Table 9.5), both the time and length of class are different every day (bold number daily) but each period time frame remains the same during the cycle of the schedule until the required number of minutes is met for each content area to incorporate the essential curricular and instructional requirements. The schedule recycles itself when all time

TABLE 9.4 Type C Additional Period Block Schedule—Daily Extended Periods

Period	Time	Monday	Tuesday	Wednesday	Thursday	Friday
1	55 minutes	**1**	1	1	1	1
2	55 minutes	**1**	**2**	2	2	2
3	55 minutes	2	**2**	**3**	3	3
4	55 minutes	3	3	**3**	**4**	4
5	55 minutes	4	4	4	**4**	**5**
6	55 minutes	5	5	5	5	**5**
7	65 minutes	**7**	**7**	**7**	**7**	**7**

TABLE 9.5 Revolving Schedule

Period Length	Monday	Tuesday	Wednesday	Thursday	Friday	Monday
30 minutes	**1**	2	3	4	5	6
45 minutes	2	3	4	5	6	**1**
100 minutes	3	4	5	6	**1**	2
75 minutes	4	5	6	**1**	2	3
50 minutes	5	6	**1**	2	3	4
30 minutes	6	**1**	2	3	4	5

frames are met, with the schedule beginning over on Tuesday with the same format as previously indicated on Monday of the first week. The previous schedule allows every teacher and class to have lessons and activities that take more or less than the standard period of time. Additional periods can be added to make the schedule recycle every week.

Modular Schedule. The final variation, modular scheduling, assumes that the schedule is made up of modules of time 15 minutes, 20 minutes, or 30 minutes long. Several features of a modular schedule are that a student would spend varying amounts of time in daily classes and would be involved in self-guided study (Independent Study). Large-group and small-group activities could be included. The modular schedule in Table 9.6 does not reflect all the variables, but indicates the flexibility that can be provided by a modular schedule.

In the block schedule shown in Tables 9.2 and 9.3, there are six or seven courses of 55 minutes meeting at the same time each day. In the modular schedule (Table 9.6), the student could have six courses; however, the length of classes varies from 40 minutes to 60 minutes and the schedule is different each day in the weekly cycle. The average for each class, including the Independent Study period, is 48 minutes. Usually, in order to attain a class day schedule, the master schedule needs to be divided into a larger number of modules. Rather than a six-hour day divided into six or seven periods of approximately 55 minutes, the flexible day might be arranged into 18 modules of 20 minutes or 24 modules of 15 minutes each during the same six hours. Schedules may be arranged so that Monday is scheduled for content and would not offer some of the electives. On Tuesday, the schedule offers exploratory activities, career guidance, humanities, fine arts, and practical arts. Next Monday and Tuesday could be scheduled in a different manner, or recycled. If it is important to provide 55 minutes for each class, the school day can be extended or begun earlier.

In summary, Figure 9.4 provides some general guidelines for scheduling to assist middle level principals and teachers. The right combination of traditional, block, revolving, and modular scheduling will vary according to the type of curriculum and instructional patterns that have been planned and the unique needs of middle level learners. Teachers must be involved in the schedule construction. However, it is important to develop the curriculum first, then orga-

TABLE 9.6 Modular Schedule (20 Minute Modules)

Time	Module	Monday	Module	Tuesday
8:00	1 (20 min.)	Homeroom	1 (20 min.)	Homeroom
	2	Social Studies	2	Foreign Language
	3	" "	3	" "
	4	Science	4	Independent Study
	5	"	5	" "
	6	"	6	Exploratory-Science
	7	Mathematics	7	" "
	8	"	8	Lunch
	9	Lunch	9	Advisor/Advisee
	10	Recreation Period	10	" "
	11	Language Arts	11	Mathematics
	12	" "	12	"
	13	" "	13	"
	14	Fine Arts	14	Language Arts
	15	" "	15	" "
	16	Physical Education	16	" "
	17	" "	17	Social Studies
3:40	18	" "	18	" "

nize the schedule. The schedule is one means to providing a responsive middle level organization with interdisciplinary teams.

EXPLORATORY PROGRAMS

A brief summary of exploratory programs is provided in Table 9.1. Exploratory activities enrich interdisciplinary teams by offering an exploration of topics which are of interest to young adolescents. *This We Believe* (1992) suggested that brief interest-based activities are necessary due to the short attention spans, difficulty in concentration, and restlessness found in middle level learners. Ideally, much of the curriculum at the middle level should be exploratory, with the acquisition of new knowledge and competencies as the primary goal. The curriculum design should organize the academic content and exploratory programs around exploring the students' interests in order to learn more about the implications of their future. Exploration is more than an academic core and nonacademic work. There is a need for young adolescents to be involved in activities

Master schedules take time to construct, but scheduling can be made easier by considering the following factors.

1 Classes with only one section must not be scheduled at the same time, to avoid conflicts such as band and foreign language.
2 Priority must be given to other requirements, such as teachers who travel or state mandates for certain number of minutes for each class.
3 Scheduling becomes easier if the school forgets chronological grade lines and mixes students of differing interests and abilities. If the school employs a graded schedule, all subjects of one grade should be scheduled before beginning another grade.
4 Teachers must be involved in the schedule construction. In fact, if certain types of teams are planned, the teachers might be the developers of the schedule.
5 The schedule should be constructed on the availability of rooms and special facilities.
6 Balancing the sections, and the number of students in each class, e.g., 30, is not as important as the program being offered. First develop a curriculum, then shape the schedule to fit it.
7 Alternative courses should be scheduled every period of the school day, if enrollment is large enough. Even with a schedule possessing some flexibility, it is not good practice to have only French and advanced mathematics as choices to home economics.
8 The bell system should be curtailed and flexibility should be built in wherever possible.

Remember the schedule is an instructional and administrative tool to provide a meaningful education for middle level learners!

FIGURE 9.4 Guidelines for scheduling

that meet for approximate time periods and are tied to special interests. Traditionally, the emphasis has been on a course format.

Typical Exploratory Program Offerings. Courses in business, keyboarding, choirs, band, homemaking, unified arts, and print making would be typical electives or course offerings. The emphasis of the curriculum framework has been on exploratory and elective courses, special interests activities, service clubs, and independent activities. The typical exploratory program provides several required choices ranging from homemaking, industrial arts, word processing, and cooking in each of the middle level grades. The number of electives and exploratory activities are limited by the middle level school schedule and curriculum. The classes usually run from 40 to 50 minutes, depending on how much time is allotted to each period. The range of electives might include band, choir, drama, dance, art, and music appreciation. A homeroom and a last-period class for special activities, guidance, and service clubs are possible options. A homeroom allows for the traditional routine that begins a day to take place (attendance, announcements, and motivational activities for self-concept). If careful attention is paid to the amount of time for each period, it is possible to have a flexible period for exploratory activities. The length of an exploratory program is usually from one-half hour to several hours on one day for several weeks (six weeks to ten weeks) to several different days a week of one or more hours a week (during a semester or for a specified number of weeks) or two or three days a semester. The time of day may be important for individuals and businesses to volunteer their expertise and services. Volunteers may be available only in the morning, over the lunch hour, during the afternoon, or only in the evening. Several middle level schools have experimented with a half hour several days a week, others have scheduled one hour a week, and still others have scheduled two or three days per semester or year. Careful attention must be directed toward the utilization of the last period of the day. The last period can be set aside for bringing students together for guidance or special activities. Small-group discussions on divorce, separation, death, or computer instruction are some of the possible options. Counselors can have time to assist youth on several days during the week. Planned activities and club meetings of students can take place during this period.

Exploratory Activities for Young Adolescents. Exploratory activities must be thought of in a broader context than courses and electives and service clubs. The following list outlines procedures in establishing student-centered exploratory activities:

1. Young adolescents in consultation with teachers identify exploratory experiences which are personally interesting and intellectually stimulating.
2. Firsthand experiences are provided wherever possible, either in the school or community.
3. The planning of exploratory classroom activities is based on knowledge acquired through the learner's experiences.
4. Teachers serve as guide, resource, and coach.
5. Learners assume the responsibility for organizing their experiences and sharing their observations with other students.

Individuals and small groups of students need to explore topics that are of personal interest and contain intellectual integrity. The learner is viewed as the focal point of exploration, rather than a topic or subject. It is difficult to challenge students to study traditional content without first engaging the learner. Learning must be viewed as procedural steps resulting from a variety of experiences. Exploration implies first-hand experiences utilizing the learners' natural curiosity about their environment as the means to support and enrich the traditional curriculum. First-hand experiences suggest both intellectual and physical engagement between the young adolescent's experiences and the academic knowledge. Thus, exploration represents an opportunity to assist young adolescents to discover their interests, aptitudes, and capabilities and, at the same time, satisfy their natural desire to explore their surrounding environment. When student activities explore personal interests and concerns, the potential for learning increases because of the personal involvement of the young adolescent.

The classroom is a starting place to survey students for their personal interests and concerns. Questions such as: "What activities do you enjoy doing?" "What activities are you involved in at the present time?" could generate exploratory activities for individuals and small groups. These types of questions might indicate student interests in hobbies, sports, and music. Another technique might be to use a brainstorming technique to identify topics of interest to young adolescents. It should be noted that it is difficult to outline a detailed plan for structuring student learning experiences. Detailed planning of exploratory activities usually does not match young adolescent learners' interests and their need for direct involvement. As the knowledge gained from exploratory experiences occurs, the plans for organizing and presenting the study can be outlined. Young adolescents are responsible for judging what processes are significant for understanding their study. Learners are expected to organize their insights about their experiences and share their observations with other students. The process of synthesizing, evaluating, prioritizing, and sharing the experiences with others assures that the learner becomes engaged in the study.

Teachers' Roles. The teacher serves as a guide, resource, and coach. While the teacher can provide support and clarification, it is difficult for teachers to know when to keep hands off guiding or directing the experience. As teachers, we are trained to tell students what to do. Teachers need to be very skilled in knowing when to be responsive in helping students successfully accomplish their exploratory activities. Because some young adolescents may have difficulty making independent choices in exploratory activities, the teacher may need to assist the learner directly. Teachers also need to guide the selection of exploratory activities in order to ensure that student interests, community resources, family interests, and characteristics of the locale will sustain a given exploratory activity. Constraints such as schedule, space, transportation and the cost of the activity may be essential components for teachers to review. Young adolescents may need encouragement due to the length of time required for completing the exploratory project.

Constant monitoring and assessing of young adolescents' progress are essential to the success of exploratory activities. In some instances, the teacher may need to serve as a sounding board to help students formulate their ideas. While teachers are free to spell out assessment criteria, the emphasis should be placed upon individual learner's perception and internalization of the experiences. Students must go through the sorting process, exercising personal decisions and organizing experiences to share with others. Part of the learning process is to learn how to present the material gained from first-hand experiences. The personal interpretation of these experiences rests solely on the learner. Young adolescents judge the value of the knowledge learned from the experience and decide where the emphasis should be placed in the presentation.

The greatest challenge is to capture the potential educational experiences outside of the middle level school and, yet, maintain a balance between exploratory activities and required studies. Exploratory activities must focus on changing societal conditions and rethink the content and packaging of appropriate learner activities. Exploratory strands must become permanent scheduled times in the schedule. In maintaining a balance between supporting student exploratory interests and following the required scope and sequence of state and local mandates, care must be exercised not to judge the worth of students solely on a prescribed course of study. All learning must be considered exploratory. Through exploration, young adolescents' interests become centered on the various aspects of the experience. As young adolescents become aware and challenged by new learning experiences, their motivation to achieve higher levels of mastery of school subjects is enhanced. Thus, exploratory activities are a basic essential to any organizational pattern.

In recent reform movements, great attention has been directed toward changing requirements for graduation or adding programs to increase learning time for academic content. More attention needs to be directed toward recognizing learner exploratory experiences which will contribute to the success of all learners, regardless of grades or levels. If exploratory opportunities for diverse needs of young adolescents are not provided, some individuals will be denied sufficient learning experiences. Interdisciplinary teams provide a unique opportunity for facilitating the learner's selection of exploratory activities.

Independent Study. In independent study, individual students are given the opportunity and responsibility to explore, think, investigate, and study on their own any subject in which they have a particular interest at a given time. Independent study presumes that essential knowledge, skills, and values of a subject are enriched as a result of the student's individual discovery. It is presumed that what individuals do independently helps them to understand their unique personalities. Students exercise self-discipline, pursue in-depth projects of their choice, learn to budget and use time wisely, make use of material resources, and strive for continual improvement. As a result of independent study, every learner should be challenged to demonstrate the highest levels of thinking and inquiry.

Independent study should be student-initiated with minimal teacher guidance. The teacher serves as a coach by guiding the student to explore a designated topic independently. Independent study may be an individual activity or may involve two or more pupils working together on a project. Young adolescents may be assigned to study a specific topic requiring considerable research. This approach is usually integrated with class assignments where possible. Young adolescents will need help in identifying community resources that will assist them in their project. Independent study can be used to promote community service projects where students are assigned to businesses, shops, offices, social agencies, and government agencies for career exploration or community service. Usually, students are encouraged to complete projects that will help them to explore career possibilities and understand better the community in which they live. Independent study can be beneficial to students of varying abilities and should be considered a privilege earned by students who have demonstrated wise use of their own time, effort, and behavior.

LEARNING CENTERS

Learning centers are helpful in the development of learning. Figure 9.5 provides a brief description of learning centers, showing the four main types. Centers can be established in a classroom or as a separate facility. A strong argument must be made for including the library in the design of learning centers. Most learning centers are either self-paced or teacher-directed. To understand the potential of learning centers, teachers should identify first their roles in the learning center. If teachers consider themselves disseminators of information, then learning centers may not be successful. In contrast, if teachers portray themselves as facilitators or guides of a student's learning, there are many advantages to learning centers, including: reducing paper and pencil seatwork, permitting students to be self-paced, permitting instruction to be based on students' learning styles, providing individual teacher assistance to learners, developing self-responsibility and self-discipline of young adolescents through accomplishment and success, and providing immediate self-assessment. Some instructional uses of centers are for skill development, reinforcement, independent study, practice, enrichment, and remedial purposes. If the centers are to be used for reinforcement and remediation of instruction, teachers will want to monitor the student's work closely. This concern does not mean that the centers cannot be flexible in allowing students to select materials. Centers designed for enrichment should have activities that allow students to explore subject-matter-related areas and are based on student interests.

Skills centers	Include appropriate practice and drill in mathematics, reading, dictionary use, and so on. The center should have activity cards that state goals, objectives, pretest and post-test criteria.
Discovery or enrichment centers	Include advanced activities in higher-order thinking and problem solving and content areas such as mathematics, science, and thinking.
Listening centers	Provide lessons on tape, supplemental instruction in another format, and leisure listening.
Creativity centers	May include art, music, crafts, mathematics, social studies, or language arts activities.

FIGURE 9.5 Types of learning centers

If carefully planned, learning centers can be effective for all learners, permitting students the opportunity to work at their own pace and at an appropriate skill level while learning through a variety of modalities. Thus, each learning center should have a specific focus and provide opportunities for the extension and remediation of learning. If the learning centers are based on the knowledge and skills learners need, the centers will serve an important function in the development of the self-concept of middle level learners. In summary, learning centers can be useful in exploratory programs, interdisciplinary teams, and enrichment of any classroom.

SPECIALIZED LEARNING ENVIRONMENTS

Specialized learning environments can facilitate interdisciplinary teams. Table 9.1 contains a brief outline of the three patterns—cooperative learning, learning laboratories/resource rooms, and technology centers, that can facilitate interdisciplinary teams.

Cooperative Learning. Cooperative learning permits small groups of students to work together and share successes. Cooperative learning is a means of improving classroom management on interdisciplinary teams because students' experience of success motivates them to get involved in the learning process. A competitive learning environment is replaced by students cooperatively sharing the responsibility for completing the academic goals. The achievement of the group is rewarded. Cooperative learning is a basic instructional method which emphasizes student cooperation instead of competition. This strategy stresses positive interdependence, individual accountability, shared leadership, social skills, and group problem solving.

Table 9.7 outlines three major approaches to cooperative learning that may occur in classrooms. They are: (1) the structure approach (Kagan, 1985, 1989); (2) the curriculum-specific approach (Slavin, Madden, & Stevens, 1990); and (3) the social interdependence approach (Johnson & Johnson, 1989).

In the *structure approach,* the teacher is free to select any method which is free of a given curriculum or curriculum materials. The structures can be used for any grade level. The focus is on teacher behaviors that are important in structuring a classroom. Some of the more common types of structured patterns are Jigsaw (Aronson et al., 1978; Kagan, 1989; Slavin, 1987b) Student Teams–Achievement Divisions (STAD) (Slavin, 1980), Teams–Games–Tournament (TGT) (DeVries & Slavin, 1978) and Group Investigation (Sharan & Sharan (1989–1990). Many other derivations of these approaches are discussed by Kagan (see Table 9.7). The different structures are useful for different functions, depending on curriculum and outcomes desired (such as individual vs. group participation).

In contrast, the *curriculum-specific approach* selects instructional methods based on specific curricula and curricular materials (see Table 9.7). But the focus is still centered on teacher behaviors that are important in structuring a class-

TABLE 9.7 Cooperative Learning Approaches

Method/Proponent	Description
STRUCTURE APPROACH	
Student Teams–Achievement Divisions (STAD) (Slavin, 1987b)	In four student learning teams (mixed in performance levels, sex, and ethnic issues), the teacher presents the lesson, students in teams help others master material. Students then take quizzes and team rewards are earned.
Teams–Games–Tournament (TGT) (DeVries & Slavin, 1978)	Using the same teacher presentation and teamwork as STAD, TGT replaces the quizzes with weekly tournaments in which students compete with members of other teams to contribute points to team scores. Competition occurs at "tournament tables" against others with similar academic abilities, which provides all students with equal opportunity for success. Team rewards are earned.
Jigsaw (Aronson et al., 1978)	Students are assigned to 6-member teams to work on academic material that has been divided into sections. Each member reads a section; then members of different teams meet to become experts. Students return to groups and teach other members about their sections.
Jigsaw II (Slavin, 1987b)	Students work in 4- or 5-member teams. Rather than specific parts, students read a common narrative (e.g., a chapter). Students become an expert on a topic. Learners with the same topics meet together as in Jigsaw, and then teach the material to their original group. Students take individual quizzes.
Group Investigation (Sharan & Sharan, 1989/1990)	Groups are formed according to common interest in a topic. Students plan research, divide learning assignments among members, synthesize/summarize findings, and present to entire class.

room. Slavin, Madden, & Stevens (1990) organized cooperative learning programs for a particular subject and grade level. Two programs, Team Assisted Individualization (TAI) in mathematics and Cooperative Integrated Reading and Composition (CIRC) were designed and developed at Johns Hopkins University. TAI combined cooperative learning strategies with an individualized learning program for students not ready for a full algebra course (Slavin, Leavey, & Madden, 1986). By comparison, the CIRC used research on reading and writing in combination with cooperative learning to provide for a reading and writing program for the elementary level. Three primary elements found in the CIRC are basal-related activities, direct instruction in reading comprehension, and integrated language arts/writing. In the CIRC program, students worked in heterogeneous learning teams (Slavin et al., 1990).

In the *social interdependence approach* outlined in Table 9.7, strategies are utilized to improve the cooperation among schools, family, and community. Cooperation, or positive social interdependence, is at the heart of family life, economic systems, legal systems, and global activities. Positive interdependence implies sharing common goals, striving for the benefit of all members, having

TABLE 9.7 Cooperative Learning Approaches (*continued*)

Method/Proponent	Description
CURRICULUM-SPECIFIC APPROACH	
Team-Assisted Individualization (TAI) (Slavin, Leavey, & Madden, 1986)	TAI uses 4-member mixed ability groups but differs from STAD and TGT in combining cooperative learning and individualized instruction. Learners take a placement test, work independently, and proceed at own pace. Team members check one another's work and help with problems. Without help, students take formative tests scored by student monitors. Weekly, the teacher evaluates and gives team scores/rewards. Applies to mathematics in grades 3–6.
Cooperative Integrated Reading and Composition (CIRC) (Madden, Slavin, & Stevens, 1986)	CIRC is designed to teach integrated reading and writing in upper elementary grades and assigns students to different reading teams. The teacher works with one team (four students), while other teams engage in cognitive activities: reading, predicting story endings, summarizing stories, writing responses, practicing decoding, and learning vocabulary. Team members are paired with two from top group and two from lower group. Teams follow the sequence of teacher instruction, team practice, pre-assessments, and quizzes. Advanced students monitor student work. Each learner has independent reading. Quizzes are taken when team feels the student is ready. Team rewards are given.
SOCIAL INTERDEPENDENCE APPROACH	
Learning Together (Johnson & Johnson, 1987, 1989/1990)	Learning Together has five basic elements: positive interdependence (students believe they are responsible for both their learning and the team's); face-to-face interaction (students explain their learning and help others with assignments); individual accountability (students demonstrate mastery of material); social skills (students communicate effectively, build and maintain trust, and resolve conflicts); group processing (groups periodically assess their progress and how to improve effectiveness). Uses 4- or 5-member heterogeneous teams.

shared identity and a long-term perspective of mutual support. Each member of the group is mutually responsible and obligated to other members for their support. Cooperative learning is essential for providing a positive learning environment which supports young adolescents on interdisciplinary teams.

Learning Laboratories/Resource Rooms

It is recommended that specialized facilities be accessible to all learners on interdisciplinary teams. Since these facilities may be an integral part of independent study, interdisciplinary team teaching, flexible scheduling, and core programs, they need to be flexible for all learners to participate. Laboratories/resource rooms can have two functions: first, they can serve as a study area where pupils read, write, listen, view, think, and at times talk with others; and second, they can function as a workroom where resources of a particular subject are kept. These areas should be considered places where any student can receive enrichment or remedial assistance. An important issue is how the laboratories or resource rooms are staffed and whether appropriate materials are available. Laboratories with chemicals or dangerous equipment must be staffed for safety reasons. The rooms should be equipped with study carrels and such resources as videotape players, records, computers, software, maps, books, and projectors. Sound equipment should have earphones to avoid disturbing other students. One arrangement for resource rooms is by content areas. Another pattern would be to have these specialized areas tied to the library and/or laboratories in the school.

The facilities, staffing, and funding will determine limitations on the type of programs that can be considered. With appropriate teams and resource staff, it is possible to provide meaningful opportunities for assisting learners with exploratory programs, skills, and content materials. The important point is to make the facilities flexible when designing the areas.

Technology Center

Because computers and multimedia have become an essential part of our daily lives, it is important to decide how these components will be utilized for instructional and administrative purposes in middle level education. A technology center can support the instruction and curriculum required on interdisciplinary teams. A careful needs assessment, involving the teams of middle level teachers and administrators, must be implemented to determine how best to utilize computers and multimedia for instructional and administrative purposes. Assuming that most middle level schools already have several computers and various types of media, it is important to make sure to utilize these elements effectively.

Computers can be used to teach new concepts, to provide databases for study, practice, and drills, and to simulate situations requiring problem solving and higher-order thinking. The computer can assist with administrative tasks such as scheduling, record keeping, grade reporting, word processing, and managing instruction. Certainly, computers can be used in the school library for filing as well as accessing library databases. They are a useful tool for all young adolescents, including learners with handicaps as well as gifted youth. Thus, the potential uses of computers are unlimited. The advantages would appear to be speed, reliability over long time periods, accuracy if programmed correctly, storage of large amounts of data, and unlimited potential for problem solving and decision making if sufficient data are available. There are also disadvantages: The complexity of new programs may make computers not cost efficient. At the present time, the cost of constant updating of hardware and software may make it impossible for schools to fund computers adequately. It is also a mistake to believe that computers make no errors. Computers cannot determine the value or worth of something. Other considerations in using computers include the problem of compatibility of different computer hardware manufacturers, and where to locate the computers for easy use while protecting hardware and software. If computers are not readily available for classroom instruction, they will not be used. If hardware and software are not secured, there will be system failures, loss of data and programs, and frustration on the part of students and teachers.

Multimedia in a technology center should be considered a valuable resource that can be utilized by teachers on the middle level to motivate middle level learners. Multimedia includes chalkboards, television, film, overhead projectors, tape players, record players, videotape recorders, cameras, computers, CD-Roms, and video laser disks. Multimedia also should include video disks, photographs, software, bulletin boards, maps, and video and software programs developed by students. Integration of multimedia, including computers, holds promise for challenging middle level learners. Teachers need to be trained to utilize multimedia and computers effectively in their classroom instruction. Middle level learners will need teachers to help facilitate their understanding of computers and multimedia. Because computers and media are being utilized in society and they are interactive, they have an important role in business and education. The difficulty is to make sure that computer and multimedia programs are based on sound educational principles.

TRADITIONAL MIDDLE LEVEL ORGANIZATIONAL PATTERNS

Traditional vertical and horizontal organizational plans also have been proposed for promoting learning on the middle level. Typically, horizontal patterns suggest self-contained and departmentalization as possible options. In contrast, the vertical organization has been concerned with policies and procedures for moving learners through the curriculum from an entry point to complete the requirements for promotion and/or graduation. The intent is to provide for a continuous upward progression of all learners, while at the same time accommodating the wide range of differences that exists among them. While the typical American pattern has been to use grades as a means for vertical progression, the graded approach often has not addressed the wide range of pupils' abilities which continue to expand at different rates, and has not factored in the wide variation in developmental characteristics, interests, and intellectual abilities that exist among learners. Alternatives that have been proposed are grouping, tracking, ability grouping, and house plans.

CONVENTIONAL MIDDLE LEVEL ORGANIZATIONAL PATTERNS

The traditional organizational patterns for the middle level usually suggest some combination of either a self-contained classroom with one teacher responsible for all instruction in all subject areas, a departmental organization with different teachers for each subject, or some type of disciplinary subject teams. Variations of self-contained classrooms and departmental approaches may evolve into in-

evolve into interdisciplinary teams as a natural result of thinking through how to combine self-contained and departmental approaches for the middle level learner who is in a gradual transition. Several variations of these organizational patterns can result in the formulation of interdisciplinary teams. Another outcome might be differentiated staffing, which may be considered in conjunction with variations of interdisciplinary teams.

Self-contained. In self-contained classrooms, each teacher has sole responsibility for teaching all subject areas to a group of students. Possible exceptions might be music, art, or physical education. Thus, the teacher would teach English, social studies, reading, mathematics, and science to the same group of young adolescents. This teacher has great latitude as to what will be taught and what methods will be employed. A great deal depends on the individual teacher. This approach is popular at the primary level because it is believed that it provides for the security and development of young learners. In the transition to the middle level school, there is a need to ensure that there is a functional transition between self-contained and middle level team organizational patterns.

Departmentalization. When young adolescents enter the middle level, they are often confronted with departments based solely on subject matter. Each department represents an academic discipline staffed with a group of teachers with specific subject matter preparation and certification. Teachers teaching in the various academic disciplines have specialties such as biology, American history, or mathematics. The teacher works with other members in the department on specific content. Students usually are promoted on the basis of passing subjects. This pattern is usually found on the junior high school and high school levels where teachers have been trained in academic disciplines. The fact that departmentalization was found to be the dominant pattern in junior high schools does not mean that there is a continuing need for subject specialists to dominate middle level subject areas. In implementing middle level interdisciplinary teams, departmentalization must be modified before a smooth transition can take place. The challenge to any middle level school is to provide an interdisciplinary team organization that integrates the subject matter curriculum for a smooth transition from elementary to high school.

Disciplinary Teams. Disciplinary teams usually are organized around two or more teachers who teach the same subject and cooperate to present that course to two or more scheduled sections on the same days and times. Each team member has unique strengths which can aid in the teaching of the content in specific subject areas. Teachers have an opportunity to specialize in a specific subject. The course would be broken down into content areas where each teacher's specialization could be utilized better. In the disciplinary team, close attention would be paid to advanced planning for the delivery of content and the resource materials to be used. The advanced planning is better in this approach than that usually found in the departmentalized classroom. With careful planning, several variations in organizational groups can be planned for meeting the needs of different learning styles of middle level learners in the specific disciplines. The major purpose is to find the best way of teaching the subject matter and meeting the needs of students assigned to those sections. Some students should be encouraged to conduct self-directed study either on the basis of teacher assignment in the unit studied or initiated by students and their classmates. In contrast, other learners may require more direct supervision, which can be facilitated by the disciplinary team.

With disciplinary teams, there can be a team concept, team planning, and an effort to integrate curriculum, but it is more difficult to integrate subject matter curriculum. Disciplinary teams must be analyzed as to aspects that keep them from being effective. Learners may be asked to adjust to many different teachers and classroom learning environments. Too often, the totality of student needs may be sacrificed for specialization of content areas. Because less emphasis is placed on personal development, there may be a tendency for teachers to focus on the content of the instructional program rather than the developmental needs of the learner. Young adolescents may not see the integration of various content areas and skills across academic subjects.

GROUPING AND TRACKING

Most middle level schools have various types of groups depending on the interdisciplinary team organizational framework. The middle level should facilitate the grouping and regrouping of students. Reasons for grouping and regrouping are to focus on the needs of middle level students who are undergoing a series of developmental changes or need specialized learning groups. Additionally, for a healthy self-concept to develop, the middle level learner needs exposure to a variety of learning opportunities. There may be a need to explore other subject areas and provide other learning experiences through heterogeneously grouped instructional approaches.

Grouping. Grouping implies scheduling students into classes on the basis of some criteria such as grades, home background, readiness, skills, interests, physical abilities, emotional maturity, teacher recommendations, test scores, and student need. As interests, motivation, physical abilities, emotional maturity, and growth patterns change, students would be placed in different groups than their initial placement.

Various groupings within interdisciplinary teams can be established for the middle level. In each organizational structure, students may be grouped initially by assignment to teams and then regrouped within the teams as needed. Middle level schools should organize students for instructional groups as part of the overall scheduling process. It is critical that teachers understand the organizational and scheduling options and the implications for initiating instructional groups. Students should not remain in the same groups for the entire day or year. Changes in growth, improved academic progress, and skills may warrant moving students to different groups.

Parents and students must be made aware of the grouping options. Building principals and teachers need to explain to parents in an orientation at the beginning of school how students are placed and grouped on teams. Parents should be familiar with the grouping procedures used in each team as well as the approaches for regrouping. Changes and adjustments made must be clearly communicated to the learners and should be perceived as positive and non-threatening to their self-concepts. Special activities that will require regrouping, such as reading, spelling, or advisor–advisee, should be posted on bulletin boards and announced by teachers.

Subjects must be heterogeneously grouped on interdisciplinary teams. Heterogeneous grouping means that students will be placed on teams without concern for different academic abilities, aptitudes, physical abilities, emotional maturity, varying interests, and motivation. In this arrangement, teachers should feel free to make student section changes or even design an individual schedule for students who should be in several different sections. Team members are responsible for monitoring student progress and can make the necessary grouping adjustments. For example, a special education student could be mainstreamed into several sections and, depending on specific learner's needs, be provided intensive special education classes.

In an interdisciplinary organizational structure, the school may assign a block of 100–120 students to a group of teachers. Pupils may be placed in instructional groups according to skill level, previous experience, performance level, or interests. In this arrangement, teachers can be paired for teaching specific interdisciplinary units. Groups can be brought together and the interdisciplinary units can be taught concurrently. Those students who mastered the test would be given enrichment, and remedial work could be given to other students not mastering the test. Once the majority of the students had mastered the unit test, then learners would be regrouped for the next unit. Regrouping should be based on cumulative achievement, student needs, interests, and maturity.

Another variation (for purposes of smaller groups), the school-within-a-school option—also referred to as houses, clusters, or pods—has been a successful organization that the public has identified as being part of a responsive middle level school. This approach is designed to reduce the impact of a large number of students in a single school with little identity by dividing students into sub-schools or smaller units, each with its own faculty, who may be responsible for scheduling, teaching, and grouping. One major objective of the school-within-a-school is to provide for successful transition from the self-contained single-teacher classroom found in many elementary schools to the larger departmentalized school environment usual in secondary schools. Another goal may be to specify smaller groups of students with unique needs and design a specific type of program to address their common characteristics.

While middle level schools continue to group students with similar aptitudes by ability, academic abilities, physical abilities, and emotional maturity, it is not recommended as a way to provide for the developmental needs of middle level learners. If ability grouping is practiced, students would be assigned to mathematics, science, social studies, and language arts sections primarily based on their academic ability, but also on factors such as interests, maturity, and physical development. The number of sections depends on the number of teachers assigned to teams and the number of groups, i. e., gifted and talented, college preparatory, regular, basic, or remedial.

Tracking. In tracking, students are grouped homogeneously on readiness, academic abilities, skills, teacher recommendations, physical abilities, and test scores. In fact, ability grouping and tracking have often been used interchangeably, not always to the best interest of young adolescents. Tracking is not recommended for interdisciplinary teams in middle level schools. According to George (1988), tracking represents one of the most important unresolved issues on the middle level. On the surface, tracking would appear to be a practical solution to a difficult problem. Placing students into different groups based on a measure of students' prior achievement with differentiating learning has been tried in the majority of the school districts in this nation. It has been assumed that reducing the wide range of intellectual and/or achievement differences should assist teachers. However, most research studies have found little evidence that tracking by ability improves student learning.

In two recent studies conducted by Slavin (1987a) in elementary and middle level schools and by Gamoran and Berends (1987) in junior high and secondary schools, expected gains in academic achievement did not occur. In both studies, there were few, if any, gains in student achievement, with the exception of tracking favoring the highest tracks. After reviewing 1,000 studies on school achievement and school desegregation, Hawley and Rosenholtz (1987) maintained that the chances of achieving a quality integrated education in schools that rely on grouping by ability, tracking, or whole class are minimal. Perhaps one reason for the failure of tracking to improve learning was the process used for placement of students into groups. The dominant reliance on intelligence and achievement test scores for placement may not discriminate clearly what students know. Another reason for the failure of tracking may be that students are assigned to classes on socioeconomic criteria which may have little relationship to their academic ability and consequently may result in resegregation within schools.

While there may be positive affective outcomes from tracking and ability grouping to the top 10% in the highest academic group, the research evidence suggests that grouping tends to have a negative effect on the remainder of students, especially on those assigned to lower tracks. George (1988) concluded that tracking and ability grouping fail because of the power of expectations. Teachers and students in the lower track classes tend to settle for a less demanding academic curriculum. Also, teachers tend to behave differently toward low-track students, often expecting a lower level of academic performance and slowing down the instructional pace. As a result of altered teacher behavior and reduced expectations, students in lower tracks fall further behind and learn less each year. The emphasis in the lower tracks is on conformity, working quietly, and passive learning.

Recent research evidence also suggests that teachers prefer to be assigned to high-track classes, work to secure these classes, and guard their monopoly of those classes (Gamoran and Berends, 1987). Teachers are motivated to spend more time on class preparation in the high-track classes, vary their instructional strategies, exert more pressure for learning, employ less overt disciplinary procedures, and have higher expectations of the learners. In fact, Gamoran and Berends (1987) indicated that "both teachers and students become demoralized by remaining at the bottom of the school status hierarchy. Thus, not only may low-track students receive inferior teachers compared to their high-track peers, but their teachers may worsen over time" (p. 424). George (1988) concluded that students tend to polarize into pro-school and anti-school groups because of the failure of the less successful students to find success and self-esteem by the time they reach the middle level.

Because schoolwide tracking provides few benefits to all groups of learners, George (1988) concluded at the middle level that "it appears that only the top ten percent of the students may learn more when tracking is utilized, and the remaining ninety percent may actually learn less" (p. 27). If tracking cannot be supported by research in the very best middle level schools and only a small group of high ability students benefit from tracking, why is the practice continued? George suggested that it is because tracking benefits the children of most articulate and politically powerful adults. Educators may be bowing to the pressure exerted by elitist parents who want the schools to benefit their children at the expense of other children. A more basic reason may be the difficulty of many teachers in the management of instruction for heterogeneously grouped classes. With the pressures being exerted on teachers, the added burden of heterogeneously grouped students makes it more difficult to teach. George (1988) concluded that "homogeneous grouping is more difficult for most students, and heterogeneous grouping is more difficult for most teachers; here is a real educational dilemma, and reason why teachers and administrators resist practices that they are told are better for their students" (p. 27).

According to *An Imperiled Generation*, a report by the Carnegie Foundation for the Advancement of Teaching (1988),

> [tracking] has a devastating impact on how teachers think about students and how students think about themselves. The message to some is, *you are the intellectual leaders; you will go on to further education*. To others it is: *you are not academic. You are not smart enough to do this work.* Students are divided between those who think and those who work, when, in fact, life for all of us is a blend of both.
> (pp. 3)

It is essential that middle level schools consider ways of deemphasizing tracking in developing interdisciplinary teams. One approach to reduce the negative effects of tracking is an interdisciplinary team format in which students are placed heterogeneously. The focus of interdisciplinary teams is on positive identification of the individual student with a specific group. It should be remembered that team arrangements are not limited to one grouping approach. A school might decide to modify variations of several grouping patterns. Students should be regrouped according to their needs. Regrouping for instructional purposes from one teaching section to another for certain school subjects, such as science, mathematics, chorus, or physical education, is one approach to regrouping. Another approach is to regroup students in special activities like reading and writing skills, labs, and home-base or advisor-advisee programs. These programs provide additional opportunities for improving functional communication skills and personal learner concerns. Consideration should be given to implementing changes in heterogeneous classes to expand students' learning opportunities, to provide teachers with useful techniques such as cooperative learning, and to ensure successful learning environments for all students. Teachers must be assisted to develop skills that will make them more effective instructors in heterogeneous classes. Current efforts utilizing small-group activities and cooperative learning show promise. Other provisions that show promise are peer-assisted instruction and advisor–advisee strategies, but these approaches will require additional staff planning time and additional financial resources.

OTHER ORGANIZATIONAL STRATEGIES FOR SPECIALIZED LEARNER POPULATIONS

To assist individual learners with specialized developmental needs, various strategies—mainstreaming, acceleration, enrichment, and at-risk programs—have been recommended. Each of these strategies can be designed to complement the interdisciplinary team middle level organizational pattern discussed above.

MAINSTREAMING

Mainstreaming is the practice of placing students with emotional, physical, and/or mental handicaps in regular classes. It implies educating children with handicaps in an environment as nearly normal as possible. The most important act was Public Law 94-142 (The Education for All Handicapped Children Act of 1975, now called the Individuals with Disabilities Education Act). The act assured that all children with handicaps have available a free, appropriate education provided under public supervision and direction. Handicapped children were defined as "mentally retarded, hard-of-hearing, deaf, speech impaired, visually handicapped, seriously emotionally disturbed, orthopedically impaired, other health impaired, deaf-blind, multihandicapped, or as having specific learning disabilities" (U.S. Office of Education, 1977, p. 42478).

For organizational purposes, special education was defined as "specifically designed instruction, at no cost to the parent, to meet the unique needs of a handicapped child, including classroom instruction, instruction in physical education, home instruction, and instruction in hospitals and institutions" (U.S. Office of Education, 1977, p. 42480). The criteria for the individualized education program (IEP) were specified, and the IEP must be developed in consultation with one or both parents. The implementation of the IEP can be used to provide education for children with handicaps in the least restrictive environment. This provision of the law, sometimes referred to as *mainstreaming,* is open to various interpretations. Nowhere in P.L. 94-142 or in federal regulations does the word *mainstream* or *mainstreaming* appear. *Least restrictive environment* appears only in the regulations, not the law. It is assumed that not all children with handicaps can participate fully in the educational mainstream, but it is expected that some children can be removed from segregated settings into less isolated or less restrictive settings where they can interact more freely with their peers.

Organizational Features. The three key features for organizing mainstream opportunities are: (1) the importance of effective classroom management systems, (2) the need to provide a continuum of instruction and related services, and (3) the establishment of school-based program delivery systems (Stainback, Stainback, and Forrest, 1989). Effective management systems include efficient monitoring of the program. Teachers need student information available so that effective instructional decisions can be made and corrective feedback given to students (Wang and Walberg, 1986). The instruction and related services continuum provides for a variety of instructional strategies and service activities. The essential features include instruction based on the assessed characteristics and capabilities of each student; the availability of a variety of materials and alternative learning sequences; instructional procedures that permit mastery of subject matter content at a pace suited to individual abilities and increased interests; students taking on responsibility for planning and monitoring their own learning; and support services, i.e., psychologists, nurses, and special facilities to assist learners. In school-based delivery models, the entire school staff is involved. The classroom teacher is the central figure. The school principal is a key member of the instructional team, and schoolwide support teams include counselors, psychologists, nurses, special education teachers, and aides who have the responsibility for serving all students. Some essential features are needs assessment, curriculum developed for individual differences, effective management, organizational patterns including multi-age grouping, peer-assisted instruction, interdisciplinary teams, cross-age grouping, staff development, and program evaluation (Stainback et al., 1989).

In summary, care should be exercised not to assume that there is one best pattern for mainstreaming students, but rather that the best middle level interdisciplinary team organization is the one that serves the needs of learners, school, and community most effectively. The plan should provide for maximum professional and instructional involvement among all staff to assist young adolescents in their development. The middle level organization is essential only as a means of ensuring the opportunity for every learner to learn.

ACCELERATION

Acceleration is any strategy that permits more rapid advancement of young adolescents through the regular curriculum of the public schools. Many teachers do not understand fully the potential of accelerated programs. Youth need to be considered as whole entities in the establishment of program guidelines. Academic skill levels, interests, skills, emotional maturity, social acceptance, health and motivation, and teacher's acceptance are factors that should be included (Feldhusen, 1989).

There are three principles of acceleration for organizing middle level schools. First, acceleration involves the time (rate of learning) that it takes for learners to progress through the curriculum of the school at their own pace. Second, acceleration is based on the individual student's learning rate, not teaching to the average or middle. Teaching to the middle loses both gifted and handicapped learners. Third, teachers attend to students who finish early. Programs may include early school entrance, grade skipping, planned completion of three primary grades in two years, fast-paced or accelerated classes (honor classes), ungraded classes, summer classes, advanced placement program, or completion of any regular school program in less than the normally required time. The idea has been applied primarily to gifted learners and has not become well accepted or a permanent feature of school programs (Clark, 1983).

In summary, all learners should be provided a learning environment that encourages them to reach their potential. A part of the middle level accommodating acceleration may be realized by vertical or horizontal enrichment.

ENRICHMENT

Enrichment is classified as either vertical or horizontal. Vertical enrichment implies moving students ahead, as in continuous progress programs. The emphasis is on acquiring greater knowledge across a wide range of subjects. In contrast, horizontal enrichment emphasizes a breadth of knowledge within a particular topic or content focus. It also refers to outside classroom activities that can enhance the unit. By popular usage, enrichment usually means what the regular classroom teacher does to provide a differentiated curriculum within a regular classroom. The program must include classroom materials, consultant assistance, library resources, and community resources.

Enrichment is for all learners to extend their learning and show progress toward developing effective learning strategies including those whose original instruction was mastered or needed remediation. All young adolescents should be given the opportunity to enrich, extend, or remediate their learning. Essential characteristics of enrichment activities are that they are rewarding learning opportunities and are challenging to learners. The activities are not busywork or simply a repetition of previous classroom activities, but must be motivational. Students are more motivated to reach mastery of the content earlier if they are rewarded and the opportunities are perceived as exciting. The second essential characteristic is that the enrichment activities must be challenging to young adolescents. Enrichment activities provide the opportunity to involve students in higher-level cognitive tasks (analysis, synthesis, or evaluation). These activities should be designed to stimulate and motivate all learners. All learners who finish early should be given incentives for early completion of learning units (Guskey, 1985).

Enrichment activities provide an opportunity to broaden and expand learning. A variety of instructional strategies should be employed, and extensive materials appealing to a broad range of young adolescent interests should be provided. Some activities should be designed for learners who are self-directed, and thus do not require as much structure. Students are encouraged when they are given some choice and flexibility. Other activities should be designed for learners who are dependent on teacher assistance. A variety of activities which are rewarding and challenging must be provided.

Economic, physical, and staffing limitations will restrict the range of enrichment activities available. Although enrichment activities have been criticized for holding back students who could benefit most from constant exposure to new content and material, these activities, if properly designed, hold promise for satisfying individual needs of middle level learners.

AT-RISK PROGRAMS

At-risk learners need to have the middle level organization focus on student-centered problems as a means for improving their performance. If at-risk student problems can be identified, the middle level can greatly reduce the effects of these behaviors and problems by considering changes in school organization, curriculum, and instruction. Some indicators of at-risk learners would be lower grades, test scores, and retention in one or more grades. Other key indicators are that at-risk learners have more discipline problems, higher truancy rates, more absences, tardiness, detentions, and higher suspension rates. Given these types of behavior indicators, middle level at-risk learners are usually dissatisfied with school, see little relevance in school, and are less satisfied with themselves and their accomplishments. School size also may contribute to a sense of alienation. In addition, the middle level students' self-concept becomes an important determinant in their academic performance in school and their involvement in extracurricular activities. An analysis of methodology, school environment, teacher involvement, and student participation in classrooms and the school setting should be factors utilized to develop a better self-concept for middle level learners.

Student-centered problems that might be targeted in organizational decisions for at-risk students on the middle level include: (1) limited attention to academic tasks, (2) negative school attitude, (3) difficulty with reading, or minimal reading ability, (4) slow learning ability, (5) poor reading and listening comprehension, (5) a high rate of absenteeism, (6) inadequate written expressive ability, (7) withdrawn or passive behavior, (8) unusually high activity level, and (9) a failure orientation. Each problem or set of problems identified for a specific at-risk learner would require different adaptations of the school organization, curriculum, and instruction. No one approach will work for every learner with similar learning problems.

Outside of the classroom, different approaches to attendance in regular classes may be necessary for some youth. There may be a need for self-contained classrooms, a different school location, personalized environment, and special resource rooms for students who need different learning environments. Variation in individual student's learning pace, topics to be covered, and activities to sustain interest may be important organizational considerations. Other examples of alternative learning environments that may improve the school climate and the self-concept of at-risk students are classroom and work experiences in the community with businesses (for credit), independent student investigations of topics they have chosen, or attendance at other educational institutions in the community. The most important consideration may be that when students are successful, they will be motivated to continue learning.

SUMMARY

In developmentally responsive middle level schools, the school organization does make a difference in student achievement and behavior. An exemplary school organization includes a clear philosophy of the expectations for students and staff on the middle level. Where students accept the expectations, structure, school attendance policies and rules, and the staff accepts the behavior of young adolescents, the potential to achieve responsive middle level schools can be realized. The middle level focus must be on learning and student responsibility for learning.

Exemplary middle level schools identify appropriate approaches that school organizations can undertake. A responsive middle level interdisciplinary team school organization promotes competence and achievement of middle school learners. Relevant interdisciplinary teams are evident when students participate in their school and community activities and are enthusiastic about their learning. The principal as the instructional leader usually establishes the tone of a responsive school environment and determines the direction that curriculum and instruction should take. Administrative decisions essential for the determination of responsive middle level schools should include teacher empowerment, interdisciplinary team organization, flexible scheduling, exploratory activities, and specialized learning environments. The principal also serves as a resource person and actively participates as a team member in curricular and instructional decisions. Finally, the principal and staff members must remain receptive to change. Willingness to change includes self-evaluation and being responsive to changing needs at all levels of the school organization, including principals, teachers, support staff, parents, school board members, and district administrators.

Because the school organization must be responsive to developmental needs of the young adolescent, the need for interdisciplinary teams, flexibility in scheduling, exploratory activities, and learning centers are essential factors. The scheduling should be flexible and capable of being modified for interdisciplinary study. A balanced curriculum of core subjects, motivating exploratory courses and a diversity of extracurricular activities are designed to ensure that each student can be successful. Responsive middle level schools offer numerous exploratory opportunities for students to become involved in their learning and relate their schooling to what they have experienced. Middle level schools become a tool for young adolescents to explore new knowledge, skills, and values and can provide meaningful experiences through student-initiated study and activities in school and community projects. In the communities, students can participate by working with community leaders and agencies in various service capacities. Positive social interaction with adults is extremely important to cope with the changing relationships that occur among young adolescents. Adult interactions should be provided through advisor–advisee relationships, staff participation in activities, and informal contact between students and staff inside and outside the school with adults in the community. Involvement with adults provides the opportunity for self-exploration and self-definition, with new understanding reflecting itself through improved social skills. Every teacher must believe that each learner can learn. The interdependence of these needs demands that responsive middle level schools encourage school principals, teachers, parents, and communities to design responsive school organizations that encourage learning and healthy growth in young adolescents.

In closing, middle level organizational patterns should be utilized to promote the best learning and teaching environment. A school organization is only as good as the personnel who are committed to that organization and take a personal interest in the success of learners. The basic purpose of any organization is to support the professionally qualified individuals for those tasks in the instructional framework for which they are best qualified.

▪ ▪ ▪

EXPLORATION

1. Given the concept of mainstreaming, design a plan for your classroom that would include grouping patterns, learning activities, scheduling, and cooperative learning for all mainstreamed students assigned to your room.
2. Describe a core curriculum plan including rationale, pattern, and types of units you would include.
3. Identify the characteristics of an interdisciplinary team organization that would best serve middle level learners, your subject matter, and your personality.
4. Describe an exploratory program. What features would you deem essential to include in your exploratory proposal?

5 Develop a plan for a technology center for all teachers that would include staff development, needs, equipment, software, location, and student and teacher access.

SUGGESTED READINGS

Bitter, G. G., & Camuse, R. A. (1988). *Using a microcomputer in the classroom*. Englewood Cliffs, NJ: Prentice-Hall.

This book presents the middle level administrator and teacher with an excellent set of guidelines for decisions about microcomputers. Some special features are evaluation of software, computer literacy, designing and integrating lessons for subject matter, including special education.

Bradely, E. (1988). The effectiveness of an interdisciplinary team organizational pattern in a selected middle level school setting. An unpublished doctoral dissertation, State University of New York at Buffalo.

The study investigated seventh-grade student achievement, grouped by ability levels into interdisciplinary teams and departmental arrangements.

Dunn, R., Beaudry, J. S., & Klavas, A. (1989). Survey of research on learning styles. *Educational Leadership, 46* (6), 50–57.

An excellent report of the research over the past decade on matching instructional methods to student learning styles.

George, P. S. (September 1988). Tracking and ability grouping. *Middle School Journal 20*, 21–28.

An excellent article on the effects of ability grouping and tracking. It includes current research and will help the practitioner consider the advantages and disadvantages in ability grouping, heterogeneous grouping, and tracking approaches.

Johnson, D. W., & Johnson, R. T. (1989). *Cooperation and competition: Theory and research*. Edina, MN: Interaction Book.

This book is a meta-analysis of all research conducted in the area of cooperative and competitive strategies and provides a rationale for the use of cooperative techniques in classrooms.

Johnson, D. W., Johnson, R. T., & Holubec, E. J. (1990). *Cooperation in the classroom*. Also: *Advanced cooperative learning*. (1988). Edina, MN: Interaction Book.

The first book helps structure classrooms for cooperative learning and provides a set of practical strategies for cooperative learning. The second book focuses on teaching students cooperative leadership, trust, and communication skills. The address is Interaction Book Company, 7208 Cornelia Drive, Edina, MN 55435 Telephone: (612) 831-9500. A cooperative learning center network for schools may be joined by writing: The Cooperative Learning Center, 150 Pillsbury Drive, SE, Minneapolis, MN 55455. Telephone: (612) 624-7031.

Johnston, J. H., & Markle, G. (1986). *What research says to the middle level practitioner.* Columbus, OH: National Middle School Association.

This monograph reviews the research on organization, classroom groups, ability grouping, computer-assisted instruction, effective schools, and middle level principals. It is available from the National Middle School Association, 4807 Evanswood Drive, Columbus, OH 43229.

Merenbloom, E. (1986). *The team process in the middle school: A handbook for teachers.* Columbus, OH: National Middle School Association.

This monograph helps review the characteristics and needs of adolescent learners, curriculum, grouping, leadership, staff development, scheduling, planning, and evaluation for the development of an effective team process in the middle level school. It is available from the National Middle School Association, 4807 Evanswood Drive, Columbus, OH 43229.

Weller, L. D., Brown, C., Short, M., Holmes, C. T., DeWeese, L., & Love, W. G. (1987). *The middle school.* Athens, GA: University of Georgia, Bureau of Educational Services.

The booklet is developed to help practitioners implement a middle level school. It contains information on rationale, components and curriculum of a middle school, converting to a middle level philosophy, school guidance, and implementation of flexible scheduling, and team teaching. It can be ordered from Bureau of Educational Services, G-9 Aderhold Hall, College of Education, University of Georgia, Athens, GA 30602 for $6.50, which includes postage and handling.

REFERENCES

Alexander, W., & George, P. S. (1981). *The exemplary middle school.* New York: Holt, Rinehart and Winston.

Alexander, W., Williams, E., Compton, M., Hines, V. Prescott, D., & Kealy, R. (1969). *The emergent middle school.* New York: Holt, Rinehart and Winston.

Arhar, J., Johnston, J. H., & Markle, G. (July 1988). The effects of teaming and other collaborative arrangements. *Middle School Journal 19,* 22–25.

Armstrong, D. (1977). Team teaching and achievement. *Review of Educational Research, 47* (1), 65–86.

Aronson, E., Blaney, N., Stephan, C., Sikes, J., & Snapp, M. (1978). *The jigsaw classroom.* Beverly Hills, CA: Sage.

Ashton, P. T., & Webb, R. B. (1986). *Making a difference: Teacher's sense of efficacy and student achievement.* New York: Longman.

Bitter, G. G., & Camuse, R. A. (1988). *Using a microcomputer in the classroom.* Englewood Cliffs, NJ: Prentice-Hall.

Braddock J. H., & McPartland, J. (1990). Alternatives to tracking. *Educational Leadership, 47* (7), 76–79.

Bradely, B. M. (1988). The effectiveness of an interdisciplinary team organizational pattern in a selected middle level school setting. An unpublished doctoral dissertation, State University of New York at Buffalo.

Cafferty, E. (1980). An analysis of student performance based upon the degree of match between the educational cognitive style of the teachers and the educational cognitive style of the students. An unpublished doctoral dissertation, University of Nebraska.

Carnegie Foundation for the Advancement of Teaching. (1988). *An imperiled generation.* New York: Carnegie Corporation.

Cartwright, C. P., Cartwright, C. A., & Ward, M. E. (1989). *Educating special learners* (3rd ed.) Belmont, CA: Wadsworth.

Clark, B. (1983). *Growing up gifted* (2nd ed.). New York: Merrill/Macmillan.

Cooper, D. H., & Sterns, H. N. (1973). Team teaching, student adjustment and achievement. *Journal of Educational Research 66,* 323–327.

Cotton, K. (1983). *Effects of interdisciplinary team teaching, research synthesis.* Portland, OR: Northwest Regional Lab. ED 230 533

Curry, L. (1987). *Integrating concepts of cognitive learning style: A review with attention to psychometric standards.* Ontario, Canada: Canadian College of Health Service Executives.

Curtis, T., & Bidwell, W. (1977). *Curriculum and instruction for emerging adolescents.* Reading, MA: Addison-Wesley.

DeVries, D. L., & Slavin, R. E. (1978). Teams-games-tournament (TGT). *Journal of Research and Development in Education 12,* 28–38.

Dorman, G. (1985). *The middle grades assessment program.* Carrboro, NC: Center for Early Adolescence, University of North Carolina, Chapel Hill.

Elkind, D. (1988). Mental acceleration. *Journal for the Education of the Gifted 11* (4), 19–31.

Feldhusen, J. F. (1989). Synthesis of research on gifted youth. *Educational Leadership 46* (6), 6–11.

Gabel, C. (November 1985). Exploratory activities—Adapting to the 80's. *Middle School Journal 17,* 22–24.

Gamoran, A., & Berends, M. (1987). The effects of stratification in secondary schools: Synthesis of survey and ethnographic research. *Review of Educational Research 57,* 415–435.

George, P. S. (1982). Interdisciplinary team organization: Four operational phases. *Middle School Journal 13* (3), 10–13

George, P. S. (1984). Middle schools instructional organization: An emerging consensus. In J. Lounsbury (Ed.), *Perspectives: Middle school education, 1964–1984.* Columbus, OH: National Middle School Association.

George, P. S. (September, 1988). Tracking and ability grouping. *Middle School Journal 20,* 21–28.

George, P. S., & Oldaker, L. L. (1985). *Evidence for the middle school.* Columbus, OH: National Middle School Association.

Good, T. L., & Brophy, J. E. (1991). *Looking into classrooms* (5th ed.) New York: Harper Collins.

Guskey, T. R. (1985). *Implementing mastery learning.* Belmont, CA: Wadsworth.

Hawley, W. R., & Rosenholtz, S. J. (1987). *Achieving quality integrated education.* NEA Professional Library, cited in *R&R Preview, 1* (4).

Howard, A., & Stoumbis, G. (1970). *The junior high and middle school: Issues and practices.* Scranton, PA: Intext Educational Publishers.

Jacobs, H. H. (1989). *Interdisciplinary curriculum: Design and implementation.* Alexandria, VA: Association for Supervision and Curriculum Development.

Johnson, D. W., Johnson, R. T., & Holubec, E. J. (1988). *Advanced cooperative learning.* Edina, MN: Interaction Book.

Johnson, D. W., Johnson, R. T., & Holubec, E. J. (1990). *Cooperation in the classroom.* Edina, MN: Interaction Book.

Johnson, D. W., & Johnson, R. T. (1987). *Learning together and alone: Cooperative, competitive and individualistic learning.* Englewood Cliffs, NJ: Prentice-Hall.

Johnson, D. W., & Johnson, R. T. (1988). *Leading the cooperative school.* Edina, MN: Interaction Book.

Johnson, D. W., & Johnson, R. T. (1989). *Cooperation and competition: Theory and research.* Edina, MN: Interaction Book.

Johnson, D. W., & Johnson, R. T. (1989/1990). Social skills for successful group work. *Educational Leadership 47* (4), 29–33.

Johnston, J. H., & Markle, G. (1986). *What research says to the middle level practitioner.* Columbus, OH: National Middle School Association.

Kagan, S. (1989). *Cooperative learning resources for teachers.* San Juan Capistrano, CA: Resources for Teachers.

Kagan, S. (1985). Dimensions of cooperative classroom structures. In R. Slavin, S. Sharan, S. Kagan, R. Hertz-Lazarowitz, C. Webb & R. Schmuck (Eds.), *Learning to cooperate, cooperating to learn.* New York: Plenum.

Kagan, S. (1990). The structured approach to cooperative learning. *Educational Leadership, 47* (4), 12–15.

Levine, D. E., Levine, R. F., & Eubanks, E. (1984). Characteristics of successful inner-city intermediate schools. *Phi Delta Kappan, 65,* 707–711.

Lipsitz, J. (1984). *Successful schools for young adolescents.* New Brunswick, NJ: Transaction Books.

Lounsbury, J. H., & Vars, G. E. (1978). *A curriculum for the middle school years.* New York: Harper and Row.

Lounsbury, J. H., & Johnston, J. H. (1988). *Life in three 6th grades.* Reston, VA: National Association of Secondary School Principals.

McPartland, J. M. (1987). *Balancing high quality subject matter instruction with positive teacher student relations in the middle grades,* Report 15. Baltimore, MD: The Johns Hopkins University Center for Research on Elementary and Middle Schools.

McPartland, J. M., Coldiron, R., & Braddock, J. H. (1987). *A description of school structures and classroom practices in elementary, middle and secondary schools,* Report 14. Baltimore, MD: The Johns Hopkins University Center for Research on Elementary and Middle Schools.

Madden, N. A., Slavin, R. E., & Steven, R. J. (1986). *Cooperative integrated reading and composition: Teachers' manual.* Baltimore: Johns Hopkins University, Center for Research on Elementary and Middle Schools.

Merenbloom, E. (1986). *The team process in the middle school: A handbook for teachers.* Columbus, OH: National Middle School Association.

Merenbloom, E. (1988). *Developing effective middle schools.* Columbus, OH: National Middle School Association.

National Middle School Association. (1982, 1992). *This we believe.* Columbus, OH: Author.

Oakes, J. (1985). *Keeping track: How schools structure inequality.* New Haven, CT: Yale University Press.

Plodzik, K., & George, P. S. (May, 1989). The interdisciplinary team organization. *Middle School Journal 20,* 15–17.

Scanlon, R. G., & Brown, M. (1970). Inservice education for individualized instruction. *Educational Technology, 10* (2), 62–65.

Shaplin, J., & Olds, H., Jr. (Eds.). (1964). *Team teaching.* New York: Harper & Row.

Sharan, Y., & Sharan, S. (1989/1990). Group investigation expands cooperative learning. *Educational Leadership 47* (4), 17–21.

Sinclair, R. (1980). The effect of middle school staff organizational patterns on student perceptions of teacher performances, student perceptions of school environment, and student academic achievement. An unpublished doctoral dissertation, Miami University.

Slavin, R. E. (1987a). Ability grouping and student achievement in elementary schools: A best evidence synthesis. *Review of Educational Research 57*, 293–336.

Slavin, R. E. (1987b). *Cooperative learning* (2nd ed.). Washington, DC: National Education Association.

Slavin, R. E. (1980). *Using student team learning.* Baltimore: The Center for Social Organization of Schools, Johns Hopkins University.

Slavin, R. E., Leavey, M. B., & Madden, N. A. (1986). *Team accelerated instruction—Mathematics.* Watertown, MA: Mastery Education Corporation.

Slavin, R. E., Madden, N. A., & Stevens, R. J. (1990). Cooperative learning models for the 3 R's. *Educational Leadership, 47* (4), 22–28.

Stainback, S., Stainback, W., & Forrest, M. (Eds.). (1989). *Educating all students in the mainstream of regular education.* Baltimore: Paul Brookes.

Stanley, J. C., & Benbow, C. P. (1982). Educating mathematically precocious youths: Twelve policy recommendations. *Educational Researcher, 11* (5), 4–9.

This we believe. (1982, 1992). Columbus, OH: National Middle School Association.

United States Office of Education. (August 23, 1977). Implementation of Part B of the Education of the Handicapped Act. *Federal Register, 42,* 42474–42518.

Van Til, W., Vars, G. F., & Lounsbury, J. (1971). *Modern education for the junior high school years.* Indianapolis, IN: Bobbs-Merrill.

Vars, G.F. (1987). *Interdisciplinary teaching in the middle grades.* Columbus, OH: National Middle School Association.

Wang, M. C. & Walberg, H. J. (1986). Classroom climate as mediator of educational inputs and outputs. In B. J. Fraser (Ed.), *The study of learning environments 1985.* Salem, OR: Assessment Research.

Waxman, H. C., Wang, M. C., Anderson, K. A., & Walberg, H. J. (1985). *Adaptive education and student outcomes: A quantitative synthesis.* Pittsburgh: University of Pittsburgh, Learning Research and Development Center.

Weller, L. D., Brown, C., Short, M., Holmes, C. T., DeWeese, L. W., & Love, W. G. (1987). *The middle school.* Athens, GA: University of Georgia Bureau of Educational Services.

Wright, G. (1958). *Block-time classes and the core program in the junior high school,* Bulletin 1958, No. 6. Washington, DC: Government Printing Office.

CHAPTER OUTLINE

Guidance in the Middle Level School

10

OVERVIEW

Because the guidance program has been a major tenet of the middle school movement since its inception, it will continue to play a major role in the middle level during the 1990s and beyond. Responsive guidance programs must address concerns and problems that may result from contemporary societal changes and must also be aware of the rapid physical, psychosocial-emotional, and intellectual changes during early adolescence. Consistent with the team approach inherent in middle level philosophy and practice, the guidance program should focus on the cooperative efforts of teachers, counselors, administrators, young adolescents, and parents working together in a caring manner to meet the needs of students. This chapter examines the team approach to the guidance program, the advisor–advisee program, and the special needs of at-risk young adolescents.

In this chapter, you will read about:

1 The rationale and functions of the middle level guidance team.
2 How effective team approaches operate.
3 The complementary roles of counselors, teachers, and administrators.
4 The roles of parents, families, and the community in middle level school guidance programs.

5 Advisor-advisee programs and how they function.
6 At-risk young adolescents and their special needs.
7 How the middle level school guidance team can identify at-risk young adolescents.
8 How the middle level school guidance team can prepare young adolescents to cope with contemporary concerns in the 1990s and beyond.

THE ROLE OF GUIDANCE IN THE MIDDLE LEVEL SCHOOL

The developing nature of young adolescents and the transitional nature of the middle level school result in the need for a guidance program that differs from elementary and secondary programs. Contemporary pressures—the overemphasis on success, the push to grow up too fast, and health-related issues—undoubtedly take a toll on young adolescents. This may warrant professional intervention or other special attention.

A myriad of social, personal, and academic problems beset young adolescents, compromising their academic success, career opportunities, and social and personal adjustment. The hectic and intense pressures of contemporary society make the future uncertain for many young adolescents (see Figure 10.1).

Research has shown that a set of hierarchical needs must be met before learners can attain positive academic, social, and personal adjustment. Havig-

1 The child will be exposed to divorce, the child will live with a single parent, the child's mother will work outside the home, and the child's major activity will be watching television (Frost, 1986).
2 The United States has the highest rate of teenage drug use of any industrialized nation. Nearly 60% of American youth have experimented with an illicit drug before finishing high school, more than two-thirds have used cigarettes, and 91% have used alcohol (Falco, 1988).
3 Each year's class of school dropouts will, over their lifetime, cost the nation about $260 billion in lost wages and taxes. Unemployment rates for high school dropouts are more than twice those of high school graduates (*Turning Points,* 1989).
4 Almost 10,000 pregnancies annually occur in young adolescents under the age of 15 (Millstein, 1988). The United States spends billions each year in payments for health care and nutrition to support families begun by teenagers. Babies born to teen mothers are at heightened risk of low birth weight. Of teenagers who give birth, 46% will go on welfare in less than four years; of unmarried teenagers who give birth, 73% will be on welfare in four years (*Turning Points,* 1989).

FIGURE 10.1 The certainty of an uncertain future

hurst (1952) outlined developmental tasks appropriate for each life-span period, while Thornburg (1980) looked more specifically at developmental tasks for the young adolescent years.

MacIver (1990) summed up the rationale for the middle level guidance program as:

> One major challenge facing educators in the middle grades is how to provide early adolescents with the social and emotional support they need to succeed as students. As young adolescents strive for autonomy, as they grapple with learning how to regulate their own behavior, and make responsible choices, their need for close, caring adult supervision and guidance is paramount (p. 458).

By planning and implementing activities and experiences which are developmentally appropriate for 10- to 14-year-olds, effective middle level guidance teams can provide experiences and activities that address the specific developmental tasks of early adolescence (see Figure 10.2).

Early Adolescence Development. Middle level guidance programs must meet the challenges of the early adolescence developmental period, which has its own developmental tasks, psychosocial crises, and challenges. Often faced with the difficult situation of feeling too old to be children and too young to be adolescents, middle level learners may feel caught in the middle between adult and peer expectations. Responsive guidance programs which demonstrate caring and positive approaches can help young adolescents understand their changing world, cope with their developmental changes, and help them attain wise and age-appropriate decisions.

Concern over body development, the desire for social acceptance, the seemingly inevitable conflict with adult norms and expectations, the desire to try out new ideas and beliefs, and the desire to experiment with a heightened intellectual ability all point to the need for an intensive and extensive guidance program (*This We Believe,* 1992).

1 Becoming aware of increased physical changes
2 Organizing knowledge and concepts into problem-solving strategies
3 Learning new social and sex roles
4 Recognizing one's identification with stereotypes
5 Developing friendships with others
6 Gaining a sense of independence
7 Developing a sense of morality and values

FIGURE 10.2 Early adolescence: developmental tasks

THE FUNCTIONS OF GUIDANCE

Several functions emerge in guidance programs designed to meet the needs of middle level students. First, the guidance professional's role should address the specific needs of 10- to 14-year-olds and be more than disciplinarian, test interpreter, or assistant to the principal. A second function is to balance psychological–personal, social, and career education needs. Thus, guidance professionals must be prepared to deal with a variety of issues, as well as perceive problems or concerns from the young adolescent's perspective. Third, the program functions to promote a team approach which includes teachers, counselors, administrators, parents, young adolescents, and the community. Recognizing the resources of each person and group from the vantage point of several perspectives increases the possibility that the young adolescent's problems can be addressed adequately. A fourth function of the middle level guidance program is to explain the roles of counseling and guidance services and how this program meets specific psychological and social needs of young adolescents.

Suggesting there is a powerful relationship between intellectual, physical, and emotional health, the California State Department of Education suggested that middle grades should play a fundamental role in furthering the development of young adolescents' minds and enhancing their academic goals (*Caught in the Middle,* 1987). Effective middle level schools must provide collaborative, specialized guidance support, access to on-site professionally trained counselors, scheduled access to school-related health support services, and outreach programs designed to meet the intellectual and physical developmental needs of young adolescents.

In general, an effective middle level guidance program addresses both the affective and cognitive needs of young adolescents. Using the teacher-as-counselor concept, teachers can help learners in several areas: self-concept, values clarification, career exploration, questions and concerns about development, academic problems, and other school-related or personal problems (Weller et al., 1987). The teacher-as-counselor philosophy fulfills the concern expressed in *Turning Points* (1989) that each student should be known by at least one adult. This report by the Carnegie Council on Adolescent Development recommends providing access to counseling services that should include each young adolescent being known by at least one adult in the school, an advisor–advisee program involving all of the professionals in the school, and an adequate number of guidance counselors to meet the needs of all young adolescents.

> Students should be able to rely on that [one] adult to help learn from their experiences, comprehend physical changes and changing relations with family and peers, act on their behalf to marshal every school and community resource needed for the student to succeed, and help to fashion a promising vision of the future. (*Turning Points,* 1989, p. 40)

Guidance counselors should retain a central role in assisting with the advisor–advisee program, consult with advisors concerning student problems, counsel students with problems that go beyond the teacher's expertise, and connect students and their parents with professional resources in the community. Advisors working with young adolescents should receive both pre-service and in-service training in young adolescent development and principles of guidance.

A TEAM APPROACH TO GUIDANCE

The needs of young adolescents are diverse enough to warrant a team approach to middle level guidance and counseling. Teachers, counselors, administrators, parents, and people in the community should understand the 10- to 14-year-old learner and the need to work together for his or her overall welfare. Teachers observe the learner's academic and study habits; counselors have the professional expertise to intervene appropriately; administrators place priorities and allocate funds; parents provide the family-home-perspective; and the community and service agencies provide a wealth of resources.

The efforts of the middle level team should focus on the developmental needs of young adolescents rather than only slightly modifying the approach of elementary or secondary schools. In determining appropriate areas to address, effective teams need to look to the most current and reliable research on young adolescent development. Several areas stand out as being especially appropriate: personal development and self-concept, improving socialization skills, and exploring career roles and options.

Young adolescents are subject to rapidly changing self-concepts. The young adolescent's perception of self is paramount, and the guidance team needs to recognize that the young adolescent might exhibit extreme behavior in order to feel worthy or to gain equal status with others. Second, the widening social world, in which young adolescents begin to shift emphasis from parents and immediate family to peers, warrants the attention of the middle level guidance team. Working closely with the family, the team should plan programs that recognize the importance of friendships during early adolescence and that provide direct attempts to improve social skills. Third, although young adolescents do not yet need to choose a career, they need opportunities to examine and explore areas of interest.

The above are not an exhaustive list, but are examples of areas the middle level guidance team should address. It is the responsibility of the team to consider individual young adolescents and decide which other areas need to be addressed.

In summary, the guidance and counseling program in the middle level grades should address the specific needs and concerns of young adolescents: their concern with their body development, their desire for social acceptance, their conflicts between their own needs and wishes and adult norms and expectations, and their desire to experiment with new ideas and beliefs. As a result, guidance counselors should play many roles in effective middle level schools: coordinating the guidance efforts of teachers, administrators, and parents to ensure a team approach, working with young adolescents in both individual and group settings, helping to implement parent education programs and programs for at-risk learners, and designing a program that addresses the specific cognitive and psychosocial-emotional needs of each young adolescent.

TEACHERS

Classroom teachers, knowingly or unknowingly, "advise" throughout the day. The planned advisor–advisee program and other sessions coordinated with the guidance counselor represent only one form of advisement. Through structured and unstructured advisement, teachers model affective attitudes, whether caring or uncaring, during all interactions with students. Students benefit from teachers genuinely demonstrating the attitudes and behaviors suggested in guidance sessions. However, teachers also are called upon in unforeseen or unpredictable situations where prior planning may be difficult. Students feeling a sense of anonymity or having family problems call for immediate action. Although it may be impossible to prepare for all advisement situations, teachers can develop a heightened empathy and caring.

The teacher working daily with students may provide several counseling services in several ways. First, the teacher can be a listener who simply listens to students and their concerns. The teacher serving in this function may serve as a sounding board for the young adolescent desiring a means of talking out issues with a significant adult. Second, the teacher is in the position to know the learner's strengths and weaknesses and can facilitate personal and career development.

The Teacher's Role. The role of the teacher in the middle level guidance program should be more personal than for either elementary or secondary school. Teachers participate in the guidance program by providing a warm and caring environment, planning and implementing advisory activities, assisting advisees in monitoring their academic progress, being a listener for young adolescents, communicating with parents and guardians, maintaining appropriate records, and encouraging advisee's personal and social development (James, 1986). The classroom teacher also serves as the initial contact with the students and has the greatest interaction with them during the school day. Although classroom teachers should not be expected to be guidance experts, they should attempt to detect potential problems, to handle immediate problems (e. g., a crying and troubled student or a fight), and to work with the guidance counselor to prevent and solve both short-term and long-term problems.

Caught in the Middle (1987), California's educational reform for young adolescents, called for peer advising programs, which involve mentoring relationships between students of the same or different ages. Peer advisors have firsthand knowledge of contemporary problems and can provide young adolescents with an opportunity to discuss problems with a person who might be more empathic or understanding. Likewise, some 10- to 14-year-olds might feel uncomfortable revealing problems to an older person, even though the person genuinely cares about young adolescents and their problems. Perhaps as the first professional to recognize potential problems, the teacher can function in the unique position of encouraging and allowing time for peer counseling. In essence, the young adolescent with a problem knows that a peer wants to help, and perhaps, has experienced and dealt with similar problems.

Several suggestions have been offered for teachers working in counseling roles:

1 Know each child as an individual.
2 Develop a secure and comfortable classroom atmosphere.
3 Try a degree of self-disclosure to show students that a teacher has problems, satisfactions, and challenges.
4 Never downplay a student's problem or concern.
5 Organize some units of learning with the students.
6 Try some "What's bugging me" sessions. (Brough, 1985)

Improving Self-Concept. Among suggestions for improving self-concept in the literature (Kostelnik, Stein, & Whiren, 1988), a positive verbal environment has been reported as having a particular significance. Negative verbal environments cause children to feel unworthy, incompetent, or insignificant as a result of what adults say or do not say. The worst examples are obvious: screaming at children or making fun of them or using ethnic slurs. Yet, more common adult behaviors may include showing little or no interest in children, speaking discourteously, or dominating verbal exchanges that occur daily. In positive environments, verbal comments aim at satisfying children's psychological needs and making them feel valued. In speaking situations with children, adults should focus not only on content but also on the affective impact of their words (Kostelnik et al., 1988). Establishing a positive verbal environment has special relevance for middle level teachers. The following are ways to provide a positive learning environment for young adolescents:

> 1 Teachers should use appropriate words to show affection for students and should invite children to interact positively.
> 2 Teachers should speak courteously to students and should listen attentively to what they have to say.
> 3 Teachers should plan or take advantage of spontaneous opportunities to talk with each student informally and should use students' interests as a basis for conversation.
> 4 Teachers should avoid making judgmental comments about children either to them or within their hearing. (Kostelnik, Stein, & Whiren, 1988)

COUNSELORS

Young adolescents need access to on-site, professionally trained counselors. For maximum counseling effectiveness and for the most productive relationships to occur, students should remain with the same counselor throughout their middle level years (*Caught in the Middle,* 1987). Learners functioning in the unique young adolescent developmental period demand responsive, professionally trained guidance counselors. The counselor plays a pivotal role in coordinating the advisor–advisee programs, working with parents, and counseling in individual and in small- and large-group settings. Professionally trained counselors are responsible for overseeing the entire guidance program and for providing assistance to students, parents, and teachers. Similarly, guidance counselors assist advisors with the development of group activities for the advisory period, consulting with advisors concerning students' problems, counseling students with problems that extend beyond the advisor's expertise, and connecting students to appropriate community resources when the middle level school is unable to respond adequately to their needs.

Counselors also serve in teaching roles. First, counselors work with large groups discussing topics of interest to students or teaching developmentally appropriate areas, e.g., moral reasoning situations, socialization skills, or dealing with peer pressure. A second teaching role is the counselor serving as a curriculum specialist and actually providing instruction in developmentally appropriate topics such as growth and development, career information, or communication skills. Decision-making processes and values clarification are other appropriate areas for the guidance counselor, either in small groups, with a classroom group, or teamed with the subject area teacher. Likewise, the counselor serves as teacher resource by helping other faculty locate and implement career education and personal developmental programs and by assisting with the development of exercises to be conducted by teachers in advisor–advisee groups.

Small- and Large-Group Counseling. Since children already function as members of groups in their families and with peer groups and in classroom settings, some counselors prefer group counseling because this mode represents a natural setting. The first group session should be devoted to setting ground rules and agreeing on guidelines for the group. Students may want to know about confidentiality and the possibility of removing themselves from the group. Generally speaking, group counseling sessions may include (1) involvement meetings, (2) rules meetings, (3) thinking meetings, (4) values-clarification meetings, (5) hypothetical problem-solving meetings, (6) actual problem-solving, and (7) group councils (Thompson & Rudolph, 1988). One topic especially suited for group sessions is career counseling, where information can be shared with a number of learners. After career information has been given to the group, more specific information may be given in individual settings (Peterson & Nisenholz, 1987).

Although large-group activities may not provide sufficient opportunities for student participation and may contribute to a loss of individuality among students, such activities may have a place in the middle level guidance program. Introductory aspects of topics such as developing bodies, peer pressures, and at-risk conditions may be discussed in large-group situations provided appropriate small-group or individual sessions follow to allow students an opportunity for offering their comments. Teachers may coordinate activities to allow the homeroom teacher to initiate discussions in larger groups. Similarly, teachers can seek the advice and assistance of the counselor in using large-group models and in the most effective utilization of large-group dynamics.

Scheduling times for small- and large-group counseling sessions can be arranged with a team effort of counselors, teachers, and administrators. First, homeroom and advisory responsibilities may be combined so that after homeroom business and morning announcements, students may meet in a group session. Second, having about thirty minutes at the beginning of the day and about fifteen minutes at the end allows time for groups to meet and may also provide an opportunity for smaller group sessions. Other possibilities include meeting in a large group in the mornings and meeting individually or in smaller groups throughout the school day (Alexander & George, 1981).

Improving Socialization Skills. Young adolescents' constantly expanding world results in the need for enhanced socialization skills. As discussed in Chapter 3, many psychosocial changes occur during early adolescence: social change is a factor contributing most to this developmental period (Jones, 1981); 10- to 14-year-olds become socially curious beings and strive for companionship and social interactions, while establishing a strong desire for peer approval (Thornburg, 1983); allegiance and affiliation shift from parents to peers (Alexander & George, 1981); and friendship formation is crucial to social development (Crockett, Losoff, & Petersen, 1984).

Effective middle level guidance and counseling teams can play significant roles in improving the social skills of their learners. Despite the current hue and cry for more academic rigor, middle level educators cannot forget social development and its accompanying skills. The guidance team can serve important functions in the socialization of young adolescents by teaching social skills, encouraging friendships and social interaction through clubs, and allowing friends or potential friends to study or work cooperatively together. Directions or suggestions for middle level schools to take include:

- Recognize, understand, and encourage social development and the skills needed for interaction in young adolescents through worthwhile and appropriate activities.
- Realize that young adolescents are complex and diverse individuals and that all do not develop socially at the same rate.

- Remember that assertiveness, aggressiveness, and boisterous behavior are often a facade and the young adolescent's means of assessing independence or autonomy.
- Respond appropriately when young adolescents complain of having few friends or no friends, since friendships constitute a vital aspect of social development.
- Realize that the middle level guidance team may be the most stable and secure force in the lives of many young adolescents. (Manning & Allen, 1987)

As with other aspects of the guidance program, addressing the social development and skills of young adolescents should be a complementary task with the parents. Socialization does not end when the young adolescent leaves school. Peer interactions and the development of friendships continue at home and in the community. The young adolescent who may appear anti-social or a loner at school may appear quite well-adjusted at home (or vice versa). The guidance team working constructively and positively with the family can develop a more realistic picture of the learner and the area of socialization needing attention.

Career Education: Choices and Options. Another responsibility of the middle level guidance and counseling team is to respond to and build upon young adolescents' increasing interest in career education. Rather than the guidance team's goal being only "telling the students what they can do when they complete high school," efforts should include realistic expectations and the interrelated aspects of life, work, job, and self. Likewise, an appropriate response includes broadening the concept of career education to include leisure time activities.

California's educational reform for young adolescents suggested that teachers, counselors, and administrators should provide multiple opportunities for all middle level students to understand their human potential more fully. Suggested means to stimulate and sustain commitment to academic and career goals included parent–student–staff conferences; group guidance activities under the co-sponsorship of middle level and high school counselors and teachers; conversations with successful persons whose experiences convey identification with the value struggles and personal aspirations of young adolescents; motivational assemblies that inspire and encourage commitment to positive educational values and personal ideals; printed materials which show the relationship between relative levels of success in the middle level and access to academic options; and developmentally appropriate advisor–advisee programs (*Caught in the Middle*, 1987).

> Academic counseling should be provided through planned procedures which ensures that middle grade students have timely access to critical information about

> the school curriculum and its personal implications in terms of future academic options and career choices. (*Caught in the Middle*, 1987, p. 48)

Because young people grow vocationally just as they do chronologically, emotionally, socially, and academically, they need appropriate career education activities which promote appropriate attitudes, values, and beliefs in relation to their future. More than just learning about careers and the job market, goals of the career education program may include developing positive self-concepts, interpersonal skills, decision-making and problem-solving abilities, economic awareness, occupational information, and the habits, attitudes, and skills necessary for any work role. While large group sessions may deal with introductory information and create interest about career possibilities, the guidance team may extend student learning (both cognitive and affective) through the advisor–advisee program, exploratory programs, special interest sessions, and cooperative learning activities (Duffey, 1989).

ADMINISTRATORS

Whether the middle level guidance program adequately addresses the needs of young adolescents depends significantly on the administrator's understanding and support of the program. Acting as the instructional leader, the administrator's support for the guidance team and related counseling activities includes establishing priorities and allocating funds so that the guidance program complements and coordinates the entire middle level school. Other roles include the administrator assuming responsibility for scheduling and coordinating school–community–home relations.

As with elementary and secondary schools, strong administrative support is essential for a fully functioning and effective guidance and counseling program. Not only must support be shown for the teachers and counselors, the administrator must voice public support in the community for programs that might otherwise be misunderstood by parents and other community members. Also, support is visible when administrators accept an advisor–advisee group or become directly involved with counselors and teachers in guidance efforts.

PARENTS AND THE FAMILY

Interested parents and the community can complement the efforts of the middle level guidance program and extend efforts outside the school setting. The guidance team, consisting of administrators, counselors, and teachers, is responsible for guiding and extending efforts to help young adolescents. Group sessions with parents sometimes can be conducted in a central location away from the school and can focus on developmental concerns of young adolescents, ways to encourage career exploration, and how to cope with 10- to 14-year-olds. Such contact has the potential for improving parent–child communication as well as school–community relations. As parents begin to allow their developing young adolescents more freedom and independence, parents can benefit from and also contribute to the effectiveness of guidance programs.

The Complementary Roles of Schools and Families. Helping young adolescents understand the family, its purpose, and how it works are essential aspects of the counselor's role. Prior to implementing any program designed to enhance family dynamics, several factors warrant consideration. First, increasing numbers of divorces, leading to alternative family arrangements, make it necessary for counselors to understand nontraditional family dynamics. Second, counselors must recognize cultural differences, such as the emphasis on extended families in some cultures or the tendency not to respect egalitarian family roles.

Among issues that counselors of young adolescents might encounter are understanding changing role relationships, understanding and accepting young adolescents' increasing quest for independence, and handling family disruptions resulting from peer pressure. Appropriate intervention might include working directly with parents when an individual's family situation affects school routines or progress, planning parent education programs and workshops, and arranging appropriate community and professional support.

Above all, the counselor should understand (and convey to the entire guidance team) how family and home problems affect a learner's self-concept, motivation, and academic achievement. Similarly, the family's potential as a support system should not be overlooked or under-utilized. Engaging the family as an integral part of the guidance team can address both issues. While the family's problems can contribute to a better understanding of the young adolescent, having the family's participation and support on the guidance team results in enhanced guidance efforts.

Roles of Parents in Assisting Young Adolescents. Working closely with the teachers and counselors, parents can play a significant role in the middle level guidance team. Parents can serve complementary roles by encouraging and showing support for guidance efforts and directions. Similarly, parents can help young adolescents by coordinating efforts with services of community support agencies which have the potential for providing professional help that schools may be unable to provide. As with other school areas, just having parents' support of the guidance program shows students that guidance efforts are valued and efforts are worthwhile. Also, parents working closely with the guidance counselor can continue and reinforce efforts at home which were initiated at school. Several recent reports, including *Turning Points* (1989) and *Caught in the*

Middle (1987), have emphasized the importance of getting families involved in and committed to the education of their children.

> Reversing the downward slide in parent involvement and closing the gulf between parents and school staff with mutual trust and respect are crucial for the successful education of adolescents. Middle grade schools can reengage families by:
>
> - Offering parents meaningful roles in school governance;
> - Keeping parents informed; and
> - Offering families opportunities to support the learning process at home and at school. (*Turning Points*, 1989, p. 67)

Planning and Implementing Parent Education Programs. Parent education programs should be planned to inform parents of typical young adolescent behaviors and to provide strategies and techniques designed to help parents deal effectively with problems associated with development and the transition to the middle level grades. Specific objectives should include:

1. To provide parents with knowledge of young adolescent development
2. To inform parents about behaviorally related problems associated with development
3. To suggest and demonstrate various strategies and techniques designed to assist parents in dealing with young adolescents
4. To involve parents in the education of their children
5. To provide parents with opportunities to interact with recognized professionals who can offer advice and suggestions
6. To provide parents with an opportunity to share common concerns and problems
7. To obtain support for the school system and its educational programs. (Batsell, 1983)

Similarly, parent education programs may result in improved learner behavior and academic achievement as a result of better parental understanding of problems associated with early adolescence (Batsell, 1983). Through careful planning, parent education programs can address the concerns of parents (e.g., the increasing socialization of young adolescents and their growth from dependence to independence) and also build a closer relationship with parents and middle level schools.

As with all areas of the guidance team, parent education should reflect the input and opinions of teachers, counselors, administrators, and young adolescents. What specific roles can the middle level counselor play in parent education? First, the counselor should seek input from other professionals and eventually reach a decision whether the parent education should be based upon a pre-packaged program or whether an individual school program should be developed. Second, the counselor with the advice of the guidance team should decide on the most effective means of promoting the program. Third, the counselor should assume major responsibility for developing the guidelines for the program: leadership techniques, session times, format, and materials to be distributed (Huhn & Zimpfer, 1984).

COMMUNITY

Responsive middle level professionals involve the community whenever possible, e.g., as resource people for the guidance program. Volunteers can be particularly helpful in special interest areas such as mini-courses, advisory activities, and career exploratory programs. Community people with nontraditional work roles or who have been particularly successful when life conditions indicated otherwise may inspire or motivate middle level students either to achieve academically or to improve in some needed area.

Community Resources. Probably, the first step after deciding to use community resources is to identify what resources are possible. Procedures may include requesting input from parents, placing newspaper and other media advertisements, and requesting information on sheets sent home. Upon identifying community resources, information and commitment forms should be ready for distribution to interested community members. Forms should request such information as areas of expertise, available times, and any special restrictions or requests. Although the guidance team should not burden community people and organizations with undue time-consuming activities, time and effort should be planned to provide sessions to acquaint community volunteers with school policies and practices.

ADVISOR–ADVISEE GUIDANCE PROGRAMS: AN ESSENTIAL

Schools have grown increasingly impersonal during the past several decades. As suggested in *Turning Points* (1989), "many large middle schools function as mills that contain and process endless streams of students. Within them are masses of anonymous youth" (p. 37). Factors helping to make the school impersonal are likely to include lack of knowledge of the early adolescence developmental period, large classes, and unrealistic counselor–student ratios. One way to make the school less impersonal is to develop effective guidance programs, especially the advisor–advisee program, which allows the classroom teacher to interact with small groups and individuals. Referring to the Shoreham-Wading River Middle School, Maeroff (1990) showed the caring philosophy underlying advisor–advisee programs:

> Having an advisor means that each child has an adult in the school to whom to turn. Each advisory group seems to develop its own personality, but what the groups share is the sense of being havens, safe ports in the storm of early adolescence. Often the advisor functions as a kind of personal ombudsman, contacting other teachers on a student's behalf (p. 507).

GOALS AND FUNCTIONS

Student–teacher relationships and student personal development have been primary goals of the middle level school movement. One means of reaching these goals is the advisor–advisee program, which focuses on small group and affective education programs. The advisor–advisee program basically consists of every teacher, including specialists, and a small group of students who meet as a group for a scheduled time during the school day. During these sessions, the teacher functions as the advisor, school expert, and affective guide for the group (Doda, 1981). An effective advisor–advisee program can provide a means to achieving the suggestion that "every student should be known by at least one adult" (*Turning Points,* 1989, p. 40). While the most important function of the advisor–advisee program is to conduct small-group sessions designed to provide students with an opportunity to interact with one another, other functions include orientation activities, academic scheduling, record-keeping, referral services, career education, and extra-curricular activities (Henderson & La Forge, 1989) (see Figure 10.3).

The Teacher's Role in the Advisor–Advisee Program. The teacher, the primary determiner of the success of advisor–advisee sessions, has responsibilities in

Advisor-Advisee Programs: Why, What, and How (James, 1986) published by the National Middle School Association suggests:

1. Guidance and counseling will continue to be an essential aspect of effective middle schools during the 1990s and beyond.
2. The advisor–advisee program is a vital element of effective middle schools and deserves the attention and support of all professionals working in schools.
3. Educators designing an effective advisor–advisee program should allow sufficient lead time for planning and implementation, should design programs which differ clearly from academic classes, should involve parents, and should include appropriate in-service training for all program participants.

FIGURE 10.3 Advisor–advisee programs

three major areas. First, the teacher is the academic expert for each advisee and assists with exploratory activities, communicates with parents, maintains cumulative records, and, generally speaking, helps the student adjust to the middle level grades and to the challenges of early adolescence. Second, the advisor is the students' school advocate and guide. Specific activities include building a trustful and caring relationship with each advisee, helping the learner develop a positive self-concept, and being responsible for parent–school communication. Third, the advisor is the person most directly responsible for the social and emotional development and maturation of the advisees. Other roles include establishing a personal, caring relationship with advisees, being readily available to discuss matters of concern and interest to students, conferring with students and their parents, and serving as a first-line source for referrals (McEwin, 1981).

The Counselor's Role in Advisor-Advisee Programs. The counselor has the responsibility for determining a realistic profile of the characteristics, purposes, and possible outcomes of the advisor-advisee program. Possible problems should be identified and clearly addressed by everyone involved in the program. Upon reaching a decision to initiate the program, the counselor should work closely with the administration to develop appropriate in-service training for teachers. The emphasis should be on preparing teachers to become advisors to small-group sessions. Therefore, the counselor has the task of both clarifying the difference between advisor–advisee guidance sessions and other academic classes, and of training other teacher-advisors to create the difference between advisor–advisee guidance sessions and academic classes (Henderson & La Forge, 1989).

The Administrator's Role in Advisor-Advisee Program. As with other aspects of the middle level school, the advisor-advisee program cannot become a reality without administrative support. To demonstrate such support, administrators must designate time for the program in the master schedule, provide paid in-service training for faculty members, and allocate a reasonable budget for materials and equipment (Henderson & La Forge, 1989). Other administrator roles include:

1 Generating a total school philosophy that supports the advisor-advisee program
2 Promoting the advisor-advisee program within the school and the community
3 Developing a management system for the program
4 Allocating time and space for planning and implementing the program. (James, 1986)

The best evidence of support for the guidance program includes the administrator's provision of adequate space, staff, and materials. Giving the guidance program a workable time in the master schedule shows both support and commitment and the acceptance of professional responsibility. Such a commitment includes the effective utilization of personnel, the acquisition of special materials and other resources to assist teachers and students, and the provision of sufficient space for testing and counseling (James, 1986).

GUIDELINES FOR ADVISOR-ADVISEE PROGRAMS

Guidance professionals have a major responsibility to develop successful advisor-advisee programs. Several guidelines for effective programs include:

1 Staff development, an important prerequisite, should include teachers and students knowing the purposes of the programs, their roles, and how effective results are best achieved.
2 Classes should be smaller than the average academic class. Smaller class sizes may be reached by assigning every available adult an advisor role.
3 Classes should meet every day at a regularly scheduled time so that students may have a chance to deal with home and family problems. Some educators indicate that when programs are scheduled early in the morning, students do not view the sessions as "free time." This also provides students with a time to discuss problems before the school day actually begins.
4 Class length should range from 20 to 35 minutes. More time may be needed if schoolwide announcements and paperwork cannot be avoided.
5 Advisors should have the freedom and flexibility to design their programs.
6 Counselors should play vital roles in initiating and maintaining complete affective education programs (Doda, 1981).

It is important to note that schools, like learners, differ and require individual consideration. Asking these questions will provide the direction the school and ultimately the advisor-advisee program might want to take: What is the nature of young adolescents' problems? How can team efforts be most effectively coordinated to address learner concerns and needs? What specific topics should be addressed during sessions? What resources (kits, speakers, community agencies) can be sought to assist with the program? How can staff development needs be assessed and how can advisors be best trained? The reader is directed to sources which describe specific programs, such as the Shoreham-Wading River Middle School (James, 1986) (see Figure 10.5).

Believing children entering the middle school for the first time need adults they can trust, Shoreham-Wading River Middle School on Long Island created an advisory system that assigns an adult advisor–advocate to each student. Virtually all school staff serve as advisors, so the ratio of advisors to students is never more than one adult to ten students. The program makes it possible for young adolescents to develop a supportive relationship with an adult who is not a parent.

Advisor–advisee groups start the day and provide opportunities for advisors to meet with their group for ten minutes to discuss school issues and students' activities. Later in the day, students and their advisors eat lunch together. Advisors meet twice a month with each student on a one-to-one basis in small groups. The advisor, assigned for the entire year, observes the student in classes and after school activities and discusses the student with other faculty and staff. The advisor–advisee groups provide for a close personal relationship with at least one adult in which students get to know one adult well, and learn that there is at least one person at the school with the time to hear out the student's side of things.

Advisors meet twice a year with parents to discuss students' grades and progress in school. The Shoreham-Wading River Middle School advisory system includes every student rather than only students demanding attention or earning special recognition.

FIGURE 10.4 Shoreham-Wading River Middle School—building relationships of trust *(From* Turning Points: Preparing American Youth for the 21st Century. *(1989) by the Carnegie Council on Adolescent Development. New York: Carnegie Corporation.)*

ACTIVITIES AND TOPICS

Although some activities may be appropriate for nearly all young adolescents, teachers should select (with the assistance of the guidance counselor) activities and topics based on individual school needs and priorities. Suggested activities and topics include:

Peer Pressure	Young Adolescent Development
Tobacco/Alcohol/Drugs	School Rules
Friendships	Understanding Parents
Health-related Issues	Contemporary Issues
Career Exploration	Leisure Time Activities

As previously stated, individual school and student concerns should be considered. Probably, one of the best ways is to seek suggestions from the students about contemporary issues which may cause concern and alarm. Contemporary issues such as AIDS and other health-related concerns, developmental changes, pressures to experiment with drugs and alcohol, pressures to grow up too fast, and stresses caused by an overemphasis on academic achievement might be possible topics.

GUIDING AND COUNSELING AT-RISK YOUNG ADOLESCENTS

Middle levei students today face many problems and frustrations: changing bodies, shifts in family relationships, divorce and one-parent homes, pressure to excel academically and to grow up quickly, increased peer pressures to engage in sexual behaviors, drug abuse, and other forms of misbehavior. In addition, yet another challenge facing middle level guidance and counseling is to help developing young adolescents achieve a positive self-concept and feel competent to function in their expanding social world. The middle level guidance team has a responsibility to guide and counsel all young adolescents through this potentially difficult developmental period, however, some students may be classified as at-risk and may need additional assistance in specialized areas. This section looks at improving self-concepts and several at-risk conditions which affect many young adolescents.

The middle level guidance team must be on the lookout for at-risk students who, for one reason or perhaps a combination of reasons, might experience more serious problems than the average middle level learner. Just to provide representative examples, these students may include lower academic achievers, drug users, sexually active students, potentially suicidal students, or any number of conditions that might prevent students from developing and achieving. Hartley and Braciszewski (1988) described the problems facing at-risk youth and the difficulty addressing their needs as:

> The plight of the at-risk population is too broad, too important to be ignored. It's also such a complex problem that we become frustrated in our attempts to solve it and often find it difficult to get to the heart of the issue. (p. 16)

At-risk conditions appear in many forms: exceptional learners, school dropouts, alcohol/drug/tobacco use, depression and suicide, and pregnancy/AIDS/other health-related issues, just to name representative examples. The precarious situation of students today is a cause for concern, especially those youth experiencing changing family structures, being pressured by society trying to rob their young adolescent years, and undergoing undue frustrations with their school experiences. When dealing with these students' challenges, the guidance team undoubtedly requires combined efforts of counselors, classroom teachers, parents, and the community.

The Association for Supervision and Curriculum Development (ASCD) has established the Urban Middle Grades Network as a project designed to assist middle level schools in developing performance-oriented systems for at-risk urban disadvantaged young adolescents. The project initiative is targeted to make major revisions in the way middle level schools educate disadvantaged students. ASCD will help school personnel to develop and implement strategic plans incorporating promising research practices that have demonstrated a capacity to improve student success. The project identified as the 3-High Achievement Model intends to develop a collaborative program between school personnel and community members that addresses developmental needs of young adolescents (An ASCD Focus Area: At-risk students, 1989/1990, p. 94).

EARLY ADOLESCENCE: AN AT-RISK DEVELOPMENTAL PERIOD

The possibility of the early adolescence period, itself, being at-risk should concern the middle level guidance team. Some evidence leads one to conclude that young adolescents might be hurried into adolescence and eventually into adulthood: changes in the American society (Frost, 1986); the changing family (Ayers, 1989); and rushing children through the childhood years (Elkind, 1981; Postman, 1982). Evidence indicating that young adolescents are being rushed into adolescence and adulthood include: competitive sports, pressures to achieve academically, and boy–girl dances and parties where emphasis is placed on physical development, attractiveness, and one's financial ability to dress in the most popular fashions.

The middle level guidance team can influence young adolescents, parents, and school policymakers to recognize early adolescence as a worthy and unique developmental period between childhood and adolescence—a special time in which youngsters develop identities, gain independence, learn appropriate sex roles, understand their developing bodies, learn about the positive and negative aspects of peer pressure, and the other myriad aspects characterizing the developmental period.

RECOGNIZING AT-RISK CONDITIONS AND LEARNERS

It is important to note that practically all young adolescents may be considered to be at risk, due to the many physical, psychosocial, and intellectual changes associated with the 10- to 14-year-old developmental period. Rapidly changing bodies, a widening social world, and a wide array of intellectual developments all have the potential for placing young adolescents in at-risk situations. The challenge is for educators and families to identify learners with at-risk conditions before it is too late to take action. It also includes the middle level guidance and counseling team working with families to find ways to reduce the at-risk conditions.

Several clearly visible at-risk conditions need the attention of families and educators: The United States has the highest rate of teenage drug use of any industrialized nation, and at least one study has indicated that 36% of 9- to 12-year-old children view drug users as popular (Falco, 1988). Escalating at-risk conditions include the high school dropout rate and its overall cost to society (*Turning Points,* 1989). Other at-risk conditions include the incidence of depression and suicide among young people (Johnston, Markle, & Coey, 1987); the financial and emotional costs of teenage pregnancy (*Turning Points,* 1989); and the increasing prevalence of AIDS in children younger than 13 (Wishon, Swaim, & Huang, 1989). Causes of such at-risk conditions may be family breakdown, the unwillingness or inability of schools and government agencies to respond appropriately, the increasing permissiveness of American society, or the absence of values in the home. These students have been referred to as a domestic

"Third World"; they are perceived as being unproductive, underdeveloped, and noncompetitive (Pellicano, 1987).

At-Risk Learners: Implications for the Middle Level Guidance and Counseling Team. Guidance and counseling teams in middle level schools should attempt identification of at-risk young adolescents, work closely with families to assist (and to seek assistance), and plan appropriate intervention strategies. Offering solutions for each at-risk condition is an impossible task and extends beyond the scope of this text. However, middle level educators should be on a constant lookout for at-risk conditions and either arrange for (or help the family to seek) appropriate school and community professional resources. While many families recognize or suspect a problem, deciding on appropriate action may be another issue. Middle level guidance and counseling teams can offer professional and emotional support to families trying to help their young adolescents overcome at-risk conditions.

It is imperative that the guidance and counseling team accept the fact that young adolescents are at school only a relatively short time and that gains are often difficult and slow since the young adolescent leaves the school only to return to a situation which may have contributed to the at-risk condition. Still, however, responsive middle level schools have the responsibility, if possible, to address learners' needs and to work with parents to reduce or, if possible, to eliminate the at-risk condition.

> For many students, the middle grades may represent their last substantive educational experience. As noted earlier, the dropout statistics accelerate rapidly during the early years of high school. A solid philosophy of middle grades education can blunt these statistics and move large numbers of at-risk or potentially at-risk students into the future with a spirit of courage and hope. (*Caught in the Middle,* 1987, p. 68)

Depending on the at-risk condition, some directions the middle level guidance and counseling team might take include:

Exceptional Learners. Although all learners are exceptional and deserve individual attention, some learners have more exceptional differences and deserve extra professional attention and expertise. Guidance and counseling teams can plan activities which are appropriate for the type and degree of exceptionality.

School Dropouts. Although most dropouts occur during the high school years, the middle level guidance team can be on the lookout for at-risk indicators such as pregnancy, being over-age, school failure, dislike of school, poor attendance habits, family problems, suspension/expulsion, and signs of involvement with alcohol or drugs.

Depression and Suicide. The middle level guidance team might be the first to recognize signs of depression or suicidal tendencies: pregnancy, rejection by a friend, fear of being caught in a delinquent act, serious illness (Johnston,

Markle, & Coey, 1987). Other conditions might include: loneliness, shyness, withdrawal, tenseness, extreme perfectionism, impulsivity, hyperactivity, and restlessness (Seibel & Murray, 1988).

Pregnancy, AIDS, and Other Health-Related Issues. The issues are clear: teenagers in the United States under the age of 15 are fifteen times more likely to give birth than their peers in other Western nations (Buie, 1987). Numbers of children under age 13 who have been infected with the virus that causes AIDS continues to grow at an alarming rate. Other health-related issues include venereal diseases, obesity, bulimia, and anorexia nervosa (Papalia & Olds, 1989). With the assistance and input of families, middle level guidance teams can provide developmentally appropriate sex education and other health-education programs.

Middle level schools can plan and implement other programs that focus attention toward specific at-risk populations. Designing viable programs includes targeting a specific at-risk group, planning the program to meet certain behavioral and developmental needs, and engaging parents for support to continue the program's objectives at home.

The importance of counselors, teachers, administrators, and parents working together as a team cannot be overemphasized. Parents are often the first adults to recognize potential problems, yet they may not know how to respond or may assume the middle level school is working toward a solution. A plan to reduce or possibly eliminate the at-risk condition should not be "school efforts" and "parents' efforts" but "combined efforts" of professionals and parents working toward the same goals. Such an approach not only provides the expertise of everyone involved, but also demonstrates to the young adolescent a feeling of genuine caring and concern.

SUMMARY

An effective guidance program will continue to be an integral aspect of the middle level during the 1990s and beyond. Essential to the middle level concept and contributing to the psychological well-being of the young adolescent, the guidance program faces many challenges: counseling young adolescent learners, assisting with the advisor–advisee program, working with middle grade learners demonstrating at-risk conditions, and contributing to the various types of literacy. Rather than working in isolation, guidance professionals will continue to have the major responsibility for coordinating students, teachers, administrators, and parents into an effective guidance team.

▪ ▪ ▪

EXPLORATION

1 Study several young adolescents who have low self-concepts to determine the reasons for their negative feelings. Examine their physical development rates, their degree of socialization, and their academic achievement. Design an individual plan to increase the self-concept of each learner.

2 Survey 10 to 15 young adolescents to determine topics they want addressed in advisor–advisee groups. Upon reaching a consensus, plan advisor–advisee sessions for each, list goals for each session, and list possible professional resources and developmentally appropriate materials.

3 Choose a type of at-risk condition and develop a checklist or scale for predicting whether a particular young adolescent will be at risk. What steps can middle level educators take to reduce the factors or conditions that make this specific learner at risk?

4 Survey several middle level schools which have successfully included parents in the guidance program. What specific steps did these schools take? In a plan for involving parents in middle level guidance programs, list specifically goals, rationale for wanting to include parents, specific activities in which parents will be included, and a means of evaluating the plan.

5 Plan a career education program which is appropriate for middle grade learners. Specifically, list what such a program should include in the middle level and what the student should do or learn. How does the career education program in the middle level school differ from programs commonly found in elementary and secondary schools?

SUGGESTED READINGS

Ayers, W. (1989). Childhood at risk. *Educational Leadership, 46 (8)*, 70–72.

Ayers believes that the precarious situation of children today should provoke educators to informed action. Issues such as children and families, society, schools, and the restoration of childhood are examined.

Bingham, C. R. (1989). AIDS and adolescents: Threat of infection and approaches for prevention. *The Journal of Early Adolescence, 9*, 50–66.

Bingham, believing the adolescent population is currently behaviorally and biologically at risk of contracting AIDS, suggests modification of at-risk behaviors, anonymous blood testing, and development of support services.

Educational Leadership, (March 1988), *45 (6)*.

This theme issue deals with youngsters coping with life and focuses particularly on such issues as drugs, alcohol, tobacco, suicide, and sex education.

Henderson, P., & La Forge, J. (1989). The role of the middle school counselor in teacher-advisor programs. *The School Counselor, 36,* 348–351.

Henderson and La Forge examine the role of the middle level school counselor in advisor–advisee programs and focus on such issues as assessing the school's readiness, forming teacher advisory committees, and preparing teachers for their roles.

James, M. (1986). *Advisor–Advisee programs: What, why, and how.* Columbus, OH: National Middle School Association.

James provides a rationale and specific guidelines for implementing effective advisor–advisee programs. Also included are descriptions of six successful ongoing programs.

MacIver, D. J. (1990). Meeting the needs of young adolescents: Advisory groups, interdisciplinary teaching teams, and school transition programs. *Phi Delta Kappan, 71,* 458–464.

In this article, MacIver describes "Group Advisory Periods," provides a sound rationale for middle level school guidance, and shows how young adolescents can benefit from such programs.

McEwin, C. K. (1981). Establishing teacher-advisory programs in middle level schools. *The Journal of Early Adolescence, 1,* 337–348.

McEwin examines several aspects of the advisor–advisee program responsibility, goals and functions, roles, and activities.

Maeroff, G. I. (1990). Getting to know a good middle school: Shoreham-Wading River. *Phi Delta Kappan, 71,* 505–511.

Maeroff takes an in-depth look at a middle level school which has virtually perfected its advisor–advisee program—a school "pervaded by a sense of community, a place where students and teachers actually look forward to each day" (p. 505).

St. Clair, K. L. (1989). Middle school counseling research: A resource for school counselors. *Elementary School Guidance and Counseling, 23,* 219–226.

This review of the research will prove helpful to readers wanting available research and implications for middle level schools. The author divided the research into several areas: behavior, affect, imagery or feelings, cognition, and interpersonal relations.

Sportsman, S. J. (1987). What worries kids about the next level. *Middle School Journal, 18* (3), 34–35.

Sportsman allowed sixth- and eighth-grade students to write about their concerns and worries about the next level of schooling. Sportsman provides separate and interesting lists of concerns for both boys and girls.

Thompson, C. L., & Rudolph, L. B. (1988). *Counseling children* (2nd ed.). Pacific Grove, CA: Brooks/Cole.

This text represents a comprehensive attempt to understand children and their counseling needs. Although their text addresses all phases of counseling, Thompson and Rudolph focus attention on school-related issues such as homework, classroom meetings, school phobia, and school dropouts.

REFERENCES

Alexander, W. M., & George, P. S. (1981). *The exemplary middle school.* New York: Holt, Rinehart, & Winston.

ASCD focus area, An: At-risk students. (1989/1990). *Educational Leadership, 47*(4), 94.

Ayers, W. (1989). Childhood at risk. *Educational Leadership, 46*(8), 70–72.

Barber, L. W., & McClellan, M. C. (1987). Looking at America's dropouts: Who are they? *Phi Delta Kappan, 69,* 264–267.

Batsell, G. (1983). Parent education—a planned program pays off. *Middle School Journal, 15*(1), 10–11.

Blyth, D. A., & Traeger, C. M. (1983). The self-concept and self-esteem of early adolescents. *Theory Into Practice, 22*(2), 91–97.

Brough, J. (1985). Teacher as counselor: Some considerations. *Middle School Journal, 16*(4), 4, 8–9.

Buie, J. (1987). Teen pregnancy: It's time for the schools to tackle the problem. *Phi Delta Kappan, 68,* 737–740.

California State Department of Education, Middle Grades Task Force. (1987). *Caught in the Middle: Educational reform for young adolescents in California public schools.* Sacramento, CA: California State Department of Education.

Carnegie Council on Adolescent Development (1989). *Turning points: Preparing American youth for the 21st century.* Washington, DC: Author.

Caught in the middle: Educational reform for young adolescents in California public schools. (1987). Sacramento, CA: California State Department of Education.

Crockett, L., Losoff, M., & Petersen, A. (1984). Perceptions of the peer group and friendships in early adolescence. *Journal of Early Adolescence, 4,* 155–181.

Doda, N. (1981). *Teacher to teacher.* Columbus, OH: National Middle School Association.

Duffey, P. L. (1989). Skills for life: Fitting career awareness into the curriculum. *Instructor, 98*(6), 36–38.

Edelman, M. W. (1989). Defending America's children. *Educational Leadership, 46*(8), 77–80.

Elam, S. M., & Gallup, A. M. (1989). The 21st annual Gallup poll of the public's attitudes toward the public schools. *Phi Delta Kappan, 71,* 41–54.

Elkind, D. (1981) *The hurried child.* New York: Collier.

Falco, M. (1988, June). Preventing abuse of drugs, alcohol, and tobacco by adolescents. (Working paper). Washington, DC: Carnegie Council on Adolescent Development.

Frost, J. (1986). Children in a changing society. *Childhood Education, 62,* 242–249.

Gastright, J. F. (1989, April). Don't base your dropout program on somebody else's problem. *Research Bulletin* (Phi Delta Kappa), *8,* 1–4.

Hahn, A. (1987). Reaching out to America's dropouts: What to do? *Phi Delta Kappan, 69,* 256–263.

Hartley, R., & Braciszewski, B. (1988). Incentives for at-risk youth. *Thrust, 17*(6), 16–18.

Havighurst, R. L. (1952). *Developmental tasks in education.* New York: McKay.

Hein, K. (1988). AIDS in adolescence: A rationale for concern. (Working paper). Washington, DC: Carnegie Council on Adolescent Development.

Henderson, P., & La Forge, J. (1989). The role of the middle school counselor in teacher–advisor programs. *The School Counselor, 36,* 348–351.

Horton, L. (1987). Alcohol use and abuse. *Middle School Journal, 18*(3), 8–10.

Huhn, R., & Zimpfer, D. G. (1984). The role of middle and junior high school counselors in parent education. *The School Counselor, 31,* 357–365.

James, M. (1986). *Advisor–Advisee programs: What, why, and how.* Columbus, OH: National Middle School Association.

Johnston, J. H., Markle, G., & Coey, P. (1987). What research says about—suicide. *Middle School Journal, 18*(2), 8–10.

Jones, R. M. (1981). Social characteristics of early adolescents upon entering middle school. *Journal of Early Adolescence, 1,* 283–291.

Kenny, A. M. (1987). Teen pregnancy: An issue for schools. *Phi Delta Kappan, 68,* 728–736.

Kostelnik, M. J., Stein, L. C., & Whiren, A. P. (1988). Children's self-esteem: The verbal environment. *Childhood Education, 65,* 29–32.

Larsen, P., & Shertzer, B. (1987). The high school dropout: Everybody's problem? *The School Counselor, 34,* 163–169.

MacIver, D. J. (1990). Meeting the needs of young adolescents: Advisory groups, interdisciplinary teaching teams, and school transition programs. *Phi Delta Kappan, 71,* 458–464.

McEwin, C. K. (1981). Establishing teacher-advisory programs in middle level schools. *The Journal of Early Adolescence, 1,* 337–348.

Maeroff, G. I. (1990). Getting to know a good middle school: Shoreham-Wading River. *Phi Delta Kappan, 71,* 505–511.

Manning, M. L., & Allen, M. G. (1987). Social development in early adolescence: Implications for middle school educators. *Childhood Education, 63,* 172–176.

Millstein, S. G. (1988). The potential of school-related centers to promote adolescent health and development. (Working paper). New York: Carnegie Council on Adolescent Development.

Myrick, R. D., Highland, M., & Highland, B. (1986). Preparing teachers to be advisers. *Middle School Journal, 17*(3), 15–16.

National Middle School Association. (1982, 1992). *This we believe.* Columbus, OH: Author.

Otte, F. L., & Sharpe, D. L. (1979). The effects of career exploration on self-esteem, achievement motivation, and occupational knowledge. *The Vocational Guidance Quarterly, 28,* 63–70.

Papalia, D. E., & Olds, S. W. (1989). *Human Development* (4th ed.). New York: McGraw-Hill.

Pellicano, R. R. (1987). At Risk: A view of the "social advantage." *Educational Leadership, 44*(6), 47–49.

Peterson, J. V., & Nisenholz, B. (1987). *Orientation to counseling.* Boston: Allyn & Bacon.

Postman, N. (1982). *The disappearance of childhood.* New York: Delacorte.

Purkey, W. W. (1970). *Self concept and school achievement.* Englewood Cliffs: Prentice-Hall.

Reed, S. (1988). Children with AIDS. *Phi Delta Kappan, 69,* K1–K12.

Seibel, M., & Murray, J. N. (1988). Early prevention of adolescent suicide. *Educational Leadership, 45*(6), 48–51.

Sportsman, S. J. (1987). What worries kids about the next level. *Middle School Journal, 18*(3), 34–35.

St. Clair, K. L. (1989). Middle school counseling research: A resource for school counselors. *Elementary School Guidance and Counseling, 23,* 219–226.

Sylwester, R., & Hasegawa, C. (1989). How to explain drugs to your students. *Middle School Journal, 20*(3), 8–11.

This we believe. (1982, 1992). Columbus, OH: National Middle School Association.

Thompson, C. L., & Rudolph, L. B. (1988). *Counseling children* (2nd ed.). Pacific Grove, CA: Brooks/Cole.

Thornburg, H. D. (1982). The total early adolescent in contemporary society. *The High School Journal, 65,* 272–278.

Thornburg, H. D. (1983). Can educational systems respond to the needs of early adolescents? *Journal of Early Adolescence, 3,* 32–36.

Toepfer, C. (1986). Suicide in middle level schools: Implications for principals. *NASSP Bulletin, 70*(4), 55–59.

Turning points: Preparing American youth for the 21st century. (1989). Washington, DC: Carnegie Council on Adolescent Development.

Weller, L. D., Brown, C. L., Short, M. L., Holmes, G. T., DeWeese, L. S., & Love, W. G. (1987, Winter). *The middle school.* Athens, GA: University of Georgia.

Wishon, P. M., Swaim, J. H., & Huang, A. (1989). AIDS. *Middle School Journal, 20*(3), 3–7.

Yarber, W. (1987). *AIDS education: Curriculum and health policy.* Bloomington, IN: The Phi Delta Kappa Educational Foundation.

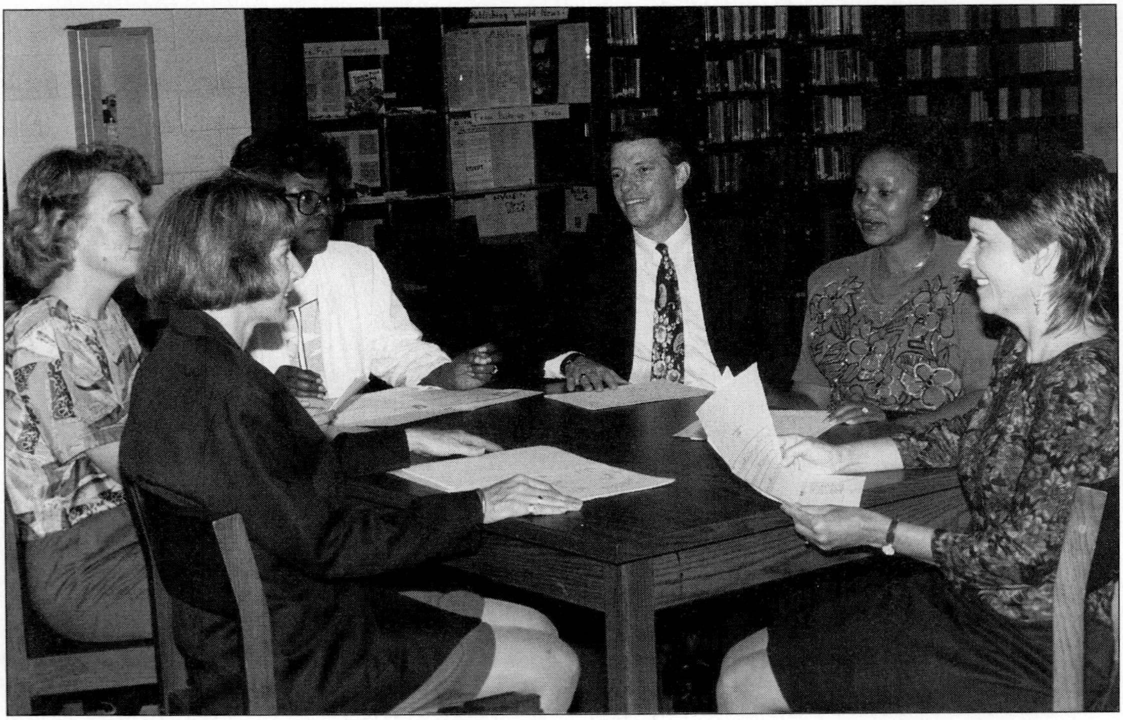

CHAPTER OUTLINE

Home, Community, and the Middle Level School

11

OVERVIEW

There has been a growing awareness that connections need to be forged between and among school, home, peer group, and community to provide the experiences and activities that complement the education of young adolescents. Of the eight recommendations in the *Turning Points* report, three had to do with improving home, school, and community relationships. One recommendation called for interagency cooperation to improve the health and fitness of young adolescents. A second recommendation sought to reengage families more directly in the education of their children. The third recommendation proposed to establish connections between schools and community organizations. In combination, the home, school, and community work together to promote success for *all* young adolescents in school, to create more relevant learning situations by community service and social action experiences, and to provide a comprehensive system of health education, health services, and fitness education.

In this chapter you will read about:

1 The role of the home in the education and care of the young adolescent.
2 The role of the community in the education and care of the young adolescent.
3 The role of the school in coordinating efforts of the home, school, and community.

4 The collaborative efforts of the home, school, and community in special areas such as health care and dropouts.
5 The advent of community service projects into the curriculum of the middle level school.

THE CHANGING FAMILY STRUCTURE

Middle level schools today face the challenge of educating students with many serious problems. Family trends and practices have important implications for a child's social and academic behavior. Hofferth (1987) presented a research perspective for several aspects of family life and their implications for children. She examined marriage and divorce, women's employment outside of the home, and poverty.

Marriage and Divorce

Almost half of American marriages end in divorce. The frequency of divorce is twice what it was 20 years ago. The increase of parental separation and divorce has had a major impact on children. Research has shown that parental divorce reduces the child's achievement and chances for high school graduation. Divorce increases the probability of early sex experiences, pregnancy, and marriage. Divorce seems to affect boys more strongly than girls. Research seems to indicate that for some children the effects of divorce diminish after a year or two. However, for many children divorce has long-term negative effects. For the achievement and behavior of middle level students, divorce has serious social, personal, and educational implications.

Working Mothers

Over the last 15 years, there has been a significant increase in the number of women in the work force. The percentage of working mothers with school-age children is expected to reach 75% by 1995, and the percentage of working mothers with children under the age of six could reach 66%. The latch-key child is a present reality in our society. Adequacy of child care for younger children and proper supervision for older children are serious social, emotional, and educational concerns. Maternal employment has not been found to produce positive or negative effects on children. There has been an enormous capacity by young people to adjust to the reality of working mothers, busy schedules, and fluctuating family arrangements.

Poverty and the Home

Poverty is a problem with enormous present and future consequences. Data show that more and more families in this country are slipping into poverty circumstances. Many homes are now headed by women; these homes are more likely to be poor than traditional families with father and mother present. Poverty has serious implications for success in school. Poor children have more serious health problems, more illness-related absences from classrooms, and inadequate nutrition for health and fitness. Poverty usually equates with a low level of educational attainment by parents, which correlates strongly with the school performances of their children.

There are many other social, emotional, and academic problems that place many of our children in at-risk situations. The school, the home, and community agencies must develop strategies for prevention, intervention, and remediation.

THE CHANGING SOCIETY

From a demographic standpoint, American society is not only changing but in many ways it is being transformed. Many of these changes have enormous implications for schools and the society. Over the next decade, we will become an increasingly older nation with a rapidly increasing minority population. Caucasian males will occupy a minority position in the work force, as more than half the young workers reentering the work force by the year 2000 will be Hispanic, African-American, or Asian. Many of the new workers will be women, and the two-income household will become the standard. The next years will see a continuation of the decline in birth rate, which will result in smaller numbers entering the job market. Poverty conditions will proliferate, with increasing numbers of children born into poverty. While poverty is very high in minority groups, two-thirds of poor Americans are Caucasian. The gap between the very rich and very poor has widened significantly and is continuing to widen.

Changing Student Population

In the young adolescent subculture, the situation closely corresponds to the patterns of the general population. Young people are spending far more time watching television than attending school during the course of their K–12 school careers. Functional illiteracy is high for young adolescents, especially minority students. Technological illiteracy is high due to lack of access to computers and technology programs and student apathy toward technological change. Twenty-three of the 25 largest school systems in the United States are attended by minority students and seriously underfunded. Patterns of delinquent behavior, drug use, early sex experiences, and school problems are increasing among 10- to 17-year-olds. So many young people are in volatile situations that 50% of major crimes in this country are committed by 10- to 17-year-olds, large numbers (135,000) carry a gun to school each day, a great amount of criminal activity occurs in and around school, and surprisingly large numbers of young people admit to having seen a shooting or stabbing at some time in their lives. While not all young adolescents live in such high at-risk situations, too many young people do, with devastating effects on their success, happiness, and self-development (O'Neil, 1991; Reed & Sautter, 1990; Templin, 1987).

The family, the society, the workplace, and the school are changing dramatically. The school must transform itself to do a much better job of teaching young people whom it has traditionally not been very effective in teaching. The challenges of the 21st century will require long overdue changes in curriculum, instruction, organization, and the general mission and objectives of the school. There will need to be collaboration among all elements of society involved in the care and education of young adolescents to effect the changes needed to maintain and improve the living and working conditions of young people in our society.

THE CHANGING MIDDLE LEVEL SCHOOL

The middle level school must change to meet the pressing needs of young adolescents. The middle level school should become a community of learners building on the diversity of its student population to provide curriculum and instruction programs that emphasize relevance, initiative, competence, and humaneness. As a learning community, young adolescents and their teachers would not only learn the content of the curriculum but would learn from each other and about each other.

Integrated Curriculum

Classrooms and schools need to be restructured to make them learner-friendly. The middle level school would modify the organization, instruction, and student support services to facilitate learning opportunities for *all* young adolescents. Middle level curriculum design would be directed toward integrating the curriculum. Beane (1991) has presented five key elements of this promising approach to middle level curriculum. In the curriculum, Beane advocated students would play a critical role in developing curriculum which addresses questions and concerns they have about themselves, others, the social order, and a range of self-emanating issues, topics, and themes. Secondly, curriculum is viewed as something to be constructed by students from their knowledge, experience, and questions rather than a course of study to be imposed on students. A third aspect of this curriculum is that it is knowledge-rich. A fourth feature of the curriculum is that it integrates affect and cognition in ways that young adolescents can experience, think about, and act upon personal and social issues. Finally, the integrated curriculum becomes the whole curriculum of the middle level school.

A Learning Community

Utilizing the integrated approach, the middle level school could become a learning community developing a community of learners. The learners in the middle level learning community would want to make contacts with the real community. Middle level learners value relevant, meaningful and effective connections with the community.

The Need for Home-School Community Relationships

Young children interact with relatively few elements of the home, school, and community. By early adolescence, students become involved with a wider variety of religious, peer, school, and community groups. The school in the middle is not only in the middle of the student's development—childhood to adolescence—but is also in the middle of many different kinds of group relationships. Students need to interact with a large number of groups because of the richness that interaction with diverse groups adds to a student's curriculum. Additionally, the contributions of diverse groups can help more students experience success, stay in school till graduation, and become more effective citizens.

Parents as Partners, Volunteers, Helping Teachers at Home

There are so many ways that parents are the most important teachers their children will ever have. Parents teach their children basic systems of morality, positive attitudes toward self and school, appropriate ways of behaving, attributes of personality such as honesty, integrity, kindness, and sensitivity, and so many first lessons that affect the social, emotional, intellectual, and personal development of young people. Due to the problems of single-parent families, the rigors of the modern work schedule, the omnipresence of television and other forms of media, and the powerful influence for good and/or bad of the peer group, many parents are having trouble maintaining a functioning parent–child relationship. The school, community agencies, and parent groups need to mount an organized effort to improve these important relationships.

HOME–SCHOOL RELATIONSHIPS

One of the main recommendations of *Turning Points* was to reengage families in the education of young adolescents. Three ways were suggested for middle level schools to get parents directly connected to the education of their children. One was to offer parents meaningful roles in the governance of the school. Schools need to make a major effort to reach out to parents to get them involved in planning the school program. Parent advisory councils can dramatically improve education if they are really given a role in shared decision-making. These councils should represent the cultural diversity of the school and should be composed of parents, students, professional staff, community members, and the principal as an ex-officio member. Most parents want only one thing of the school—a good education for their children (Jennings, 1989).

Another important aspect of getting parents reengaged in their child's learning is for the school to keep parents informed. This is one area in which schools need to show rapid and dramatic improvement. There should be frequent, coherent, positive communication between home and school. This communication needs to continue throughout the K–12 grade span. There has been a tendency for communication to decrease every year after the elementary school years. The advisor–advisee program of the middle level school affords many opportunities to inform parents about rules and procedures, explain the expectations that schools have of parents, and provide parents with status reports about their children.

Parent–teacher conferences are an effective means of communicating with parents. While it would be ideal to interact with all parents in such a format, there may not be enough time or energy available for such an undertaking. Parent–teacher conferences should focus on vulnerable students who are at some type of risk. These at-risk factors could be misbehavior, chronic absenteeism, physical health problems, low academic achievement, low motivation, poor self-esteem, and a range of other target problems. Parents are usually eager to obtain information about their child's school performance. Teachers need to provide such information in a consistent, fair, relevant, and accurate manner. Teachers should prepare carefully for conferences and conduct them with positive goals in mind (Wolf & Stephens, 1989). Conferences are powerful tools to share knowledge of the child, note mutual concerns for the child, and develop a mutual plan for the child's performance at school.

A third way of getting parents more involved in the education of young adolescents is to help parents support their child's learning at home and at school. Parents can be effective helping teachers at home. They can tutor their children, read to them and listen to them read, monitor their homework, and help them study for assignments and tests. Parents are important teachers. Schools should be an experience that parents and children can share, enjoy, and work on together. Parents must view their efforts to support their child's learning as an opportunity not a requirement, a blessing not a burden, and something to be cherished not resented.

Another way that parents can support their child's learning is to be a school volunteer. Children like to see their parents valuing and supporting education. Volunteering at school is a visible demonstration of support. Hunter (1989) maintains that volunteer parents in the classroom can enrich the curriculum of the school by sharing their knowledge and experience in careers, their skills in hobbies and crafts, and their cultural knowledge. Schools need to have active programs to get "par-aides" (parent aides) involved in the school program. With this recruitment should be a training program to maximize parent contributions to the school through effective presentations in classrooms. The interpersonal gains are substantial in that parents feel good about volunteering and their children appreciate the show of support. Additionally, the enormous potential for curriculum enrichment is of great benefit to the school program.

THE ADVANTAGES OF PARENT INVOLVEMENT

Joyce Epstein through her research at Johns Hopkins University in the Center for Research in Elementary and Middle Schools (CREMS) and the Center for Research on Effective Schooling for Disadvantaged Students (CDS) has studied parent involvement and the effects of family–school relationships on students, parents, and teachers. She has found that parents want to be more involved in their children's learning, in that they want to help their children at home and want clear directions from the school about goals, roles, and responsibilities (Brandt, 1989).

Positive Home Environments. Epstein (1989) has classified parent involvement into five major types or categories. Type one of parent involvement is concerned with parenting. In this type, the goal is to build positive home environments to support learning. The school helps parents satisfy their basic obligations as parents to promote health and safety, to prepare children to enter school ready to learn, and to develop the skills to supervise, guide, and discipline children at each age level. Through workshops, videotapes, newsletters, and other forms of communication, the school gets parents to participate in programs to improve their parenting skills.

Improving Communication. The second type of parent involvement is directed toward improving the ways that schools communicate with parents. The goals are to inform parents about school programs and what these programs mean to them and to their children, and also to inform parents about their child's status and progress in school. Teacher–parent conferences are effective ways of communicating with parents. Folders containing the child's work should be sent home on a regular basis and interview reports should be sent to parents concerning their children's academic performance.

Volunteering. Volunteering is the third type of parent involvement. Parents are recruited and trained to serve as volunteers who assist in the instructional program of the school. Volunteering also incorporates parents as community resources, helpers on field trips, participants in school events, and other school or non-school events such as clubs, sports programs, and community programs such as Boy and Girl Scouts, YMCA/YWCA, 4-H, and other options. The school needs to conduct comprehensive surveys to ascertain the skills and availability of all the parents.

Teacher's Helpers. The fourth type has to do with ways of getting parents to be helping teachers for their children. Epstein in her research has found that this type of involvement—supporting and helping their children at home—is what is of great interest to parents. Teachers plan ways to get parents actively involved in their child's homework assignments, studying for tests, doing projects together, reading to the child, and listening to the child read. Parents need to provide a quiet time and place to study, monitor homework and study sessions, interact with the child as a student at home, and show interest in what the child is doing and learning at school.

Advisory Roles. Type five relates to parent involvement in governance and advocacy. Governance, advocacy, and leadership involve smaller numbers of parents. In this category, parents represent the larger population of parents in parent–teacher associations, school advisory councils, school improvement committees, and other special needs committees. The schools need to recruit and train these parent volunteers for their leadership roles. Additionally, the school must strive to assure that the leadership group represents the cultural diversity of the school. Parents typically want a good education for their children and this type of involvement gives them a chance to initiate, to influence, and to evaluate the education program.

FOSTERING SCHOOL—HOME CONNECTIONS

There are many areas in which the school can help in the home. Various opinion polls have shown that parents would like for the school to help them in areas such as managing their children's behavior, motivating them to better achievement, helping them to understand their social and emotional problems, and a variety of other educational, social, and personal concerns.

One specific area that the school should work on is promoting family literacy. There are still too many young adolescents who live in families where parents possess low literacy skills. Parents need to be encouraged to develop their reading skills, to promote reading for their children, to visit the local library, to limit the amount of television, and in general to cultivate a literate environment. All middle level students would benefit from a literate environment, but it is a necessity for students from less advantaged backgrounds.

The middle level school must develop a strategy to help parents understand how to be helping teachers for their children at home. This approach means that parents will have to get excited about learning for themselves as well as for their children. Schools will need to employ positive strategies to promote family literacy programs. Student and parents benefit when more literate home environments are fostered. These approaches can range from helping to improve the circumstance of parent(s) who may be illiterate to improving the home situation of families who do not support the academic goals of the schools. Schools can promote family literacy by some of the following efforts:

1 Making classrooms "print-rich" environments
2 Encouraging young adolescents to read at home
3 Informing parents about adult literacy programs
4 Providing schedules and resources of the local library

5 Making home visits to determine interests and resources
6 Promoting family projects for cooperative work
7 Providing enrichment types of homework. (Rosow, 1991)

Family literacy is one overture the school can make to the home, but there are others in important areas such as self-esteem, values, and taking responsibility. In many cases, teachers get along better with young adolescents than any other positive adult role model. The middle level school should share some of that expertise to improve family relationships when such help is requested. The school–home connection should be strengthened because this will result in better education and care of young adolescents.

Every report of any consequence over the last 30 or more years has called for increased parental involvement in their child's learning at home and at school. Research findings substantiate that parent involvement directly relates to academic, social, and emotional success for their children. The time for the schools to become active in involving parents in many types of school–parent participation and commitment is now.

STRUCTURING PARTNERSHIPS TO HELP YOUNG ADOLESCENTS AT RISK

Moynihan (1989) calls for broad-based reform to serve America's children. He observes that children should never be neglected by society; much less should 20% of our children be allowed to live in poverty. He asks the question that a responsive society (and middle level school) must answer, "Can we expect children growing up in misery to mature into adults capable of maintaining, much less improving, American society?" (p. 341).

Joy Dryfoos (1990) applied social, economic, and educational concerns to adolescent behavior. She found that as many as half of the 10- to 17-year-old population could be classified as moderate to very high-risk because of their involvement in a range of problems, including substance abuse, early sexual activity, low educational achievement, and delinquent behavior. Her studies point to the rise of an adolescent subculture, tuned out to society and turned off to schools, who are strongly at risk of not only jeopardizing their success and happiness as young adolescents but of not being able to develop into responsible adults.

One of the most critical roles of school, home, and community relationships is to structure interagency partnerships to deliver comprehensive services to children and families. The *Turning Points* report recommended that the school and community should organize a comprehensive delivery system of health services to young adolescents. Another recommendation called for connecting young adolescents to the communities in which they live in meaningful, purposeful, and tangible ways.

THE SCHOOL AND COMMUNITY

The school is the educational and cultural center of the neighborhood and of the community. School and community are inescapably intertwined. The success of one is not possible if the other is perceived as failing. You cannot have good communities and poor schools and vice versa. In the 1990s, communities must take more responsibility for the education of their children and stand ready to help students when problems arise. Schools have to promote community involvement, use people in the community in meaningful ways, and adapt what is taught and the ways it is taught to students rather than expecting all of them to adapt to traditional school practices and programs. If the ambitious national goals for the year 2000, or even the more specific goal of parents and schools, are to be met we must gear up to use all the resources of the school, community, and home to meet the challenge facing our young people today.

As has been described in previous chapters, early adolescence is a developmental stage where many at-risk conditions of physical and mental health—such as drug use and abuse, violence, school dropouts, teenage pregnancy, sexually transmitted diseases, and other socio-educational concerns—occur with increasing frequency. Data reveal an alarming profile of young adolescents who follow a deficient physical health regimen, including poor nutrition, low physical fitness, increasing use of tobacco, alcohol, and other drugs, and an assortment of general health factors. In mental health, young adolescents are more susceptible to tendencies toward depression, suicide, alienation from parents, teachers, and other adults, feelings of rejection, and low self-esteem than at any time in their previous development.

Being cognizant of these problems, the home, school, and community must work together to help young people develop more effective physical, mental, and emotional health habits. Research shows that knowledge and information about appropriate health practices does not cause young adolescents to modify their health attitudes and behaviors. Students will need to be helped with developing more positive values systems, strategies for decision-making, and ways for resisting peer group pressure.

SCHOOL DROPOUTS

While students actually drop out of school most typically in the high school years, the problems related to dropouts start in the elementary school and exacerbate during the middle level years. A profile of dropouts shows that they have lower grades and test scores, are more likely to have been retained, are more likely to be discipline problems in schools, are more likely to have been truant, suspended, or expelled, and are more likely to be placed in a lower ability track and vocational curriculum. Dropout students experience greater feelings of failure at schools, less counseling about career goals, lower levels of parent and teacher expectations, and lower levels of participation in informal and complementary learning experiences, sports and extracurricular activities, and community service activities (*Before It's Too Late*, 1988).

Statistics show that approximately 27% of our students drop out prior to graduation from high school. Dropout rates in certain urban areas are as high as 50%. The dropout rates of minority youth are very high. However, poverty plays a more significant role even than race. When socioeconomic status is controlled, African American and Caucasian students drop out of school at comparable rates. One exception to this is the high dropout rate of language-minority Hispanic children. Lack of proficiency in English seriously limits the school success of Hispanic students (*Before It's Too Late*, 1988).

Fine (1986) used self-report techniques to determine the reasons that students themselves gave for leaving school early. The responses are clustered into five categories:

1 Perceived low values of a high school diploma
2 Competing responsibilities of family and school
3 Undermined self-esteem
4 School "pushout" practice
5 Pregnancy

Based on her research, which included interviews with and observations of students, Fine concluded that the reasons for dropping out of school were related to students' educational, social, and economic situations rather than in individual deficits related to ability or desire to learn.

Overwhelming evidence points to a combination of factors which accumulate for vulnerable students coming into conflict with inflexible school practices to force the youngsters out of school. Young adolescents who are at risk academically get these negative messages at a time when they are seeking self-identification and self-esteem. Wehlage and Rutter have accurately observed, "The process of becoming a dropout is complex because the act of rejecting an institution as fundamental to the society as school must also be accompanied by the belief that the institution has rejected the person" (1986, p. 5). There must be a collaborative effort by home, school, and community to solve the problem of school dropouts both for the welfare of individual students who are being denied their full rights as students and the welfare of society which is being cheated out of the contributions these young people could make if they were more powerfully educated.

Standardized testing usually works against dropout-prone students. Such tests are usually based on reading skills, which are traditionally weak areas for vulnerable students. Test results are often misused to track or place students in ability groups. All students need to be evaluated to determine progress in the school program. However, the tests should be multi-purpose and closely related to the skills and abilities of *all* young adolescents.

The standard curriculum of mathematics, science, language, and social studies with its teacher-active and child-passive instructional system is inadequate for all middle level students, but it is especially inappropriate for potential dropouts. Low-achieving students benefit from hands-on experiences in their school studies in addition to basic skills mastery. The curriculum needs to provide integrated study of the subject areas, high interest exploratory or elective courses, and learning activities that allow students to make connections to real-world situations.

Elements of Successful Middle Level Schools. Schools that recognize the unique developmental needs of young adolescents do exist, and the elements that make them successful can be described. Lipsitz (1984) found in her case studies of four successful middle level schools that these schools were academically effective as well as developmentally appropriate. Particular organizational features that would enhance the performance of vulnerable students are (1) interdisciplinary team teaching in a school-within-a-school model; (2) an integrated, interdisciplinary curriculum incorporating basic skills, exploratory courses, cooperative learning, and self-directed learning; (3) flexible block scheduling; and (4) teacher-based guidance (*Before It's Too Late*, 1988, pp. 24–26).

Inhibiting Factors in Middle Level Schools. School practices which aggravate the problems that lead to leaving school early are non-promotion, tracking, misuse of tests, and standardized curriculum and instruction. By the middle level, one of the most severe procedures practiced by middle level schools is retention in grade. Alternative approaches to non-promotion must be considered because holding students back directly contributes to dropping out of school.

Tracking and ability grouping become particularly destructive of academic achievement, self-esteem, and the development of social skills for vulnerable students in the middle level grades. By the middle levels, the results of inflexible tracking and ability grouping patterns have seen a widening of the achievement gap between high-achieving and low-performing students. Low-achieving students realistically assess their situation and realize their prospects of achieving at school are bleak. Many students drop out of active, purposeful study of the school curriculum years before they are able to leave school legally (*Before It's Too Late*, 1988).

SCHOOL-LINKED SERVICES

A vast array of agencies, institutions, people, and programs compose the comprehensive delivery system needed to coordinate services that young adolescents need in health areas, juvenile justice, educational programs, family relations, child care, and other sectors of youth policy. Historically, two problems have characterized youth service delivery: under-service and fragmentation of services (McLaughlin & Smrekar, 1988).

Reasons and Solutions for Under-service and Fragmentation. Reasons that cause under-service and fragmentation are known and need to be addressed.

One problem is that our service system is crisis-oriented. We need to emphasize prevention. It is cheaper and more effective to stop problems before serious harm is done. Second, the youth service system divides problems into distinct and separate categories that fail to account for the interrelated nature of the problems. Solutions must cut through the bureaucratic red tape to provide for coordinated solutions, with many agencies cooperating to provide meaningful and broad-based services. A third reason for the failure of youth services has been the lack of communication between agencies. This sets up a situation in which agencies concentrate on services they provide rather than focusing on what the clients need. School–agency coordination of services should operate on a client-need basis as their operational procedure for providing services to young adolescents. Another reason for inadequate youth services has been that these services are inadequately funded. Schools and community agencies must press for much more significant funding of programs to provide health, educational, and counseling services to young adolescents (Melaville & Blank, 1991).

Services in a Comprehensive System. There is a need for an expanded national effort in the total lives of children and families. While we are restructuring education to provide more relevant curriculum and on-site management techniques, we need to restructure schools to provide the comprehensive services that young adolescents need for successful academic, social, and personal development. School-linked comprehensive service programs should incorporate more than health services in its comprehensive delivery system. Some of the services provided are as follows:

1 Development of academic and social skills which will contribute to better performance in school (e.g., dropout prevention programs)
2 Development of basic life skills which will contribute to a more enjoyable, rewarding life
3 Preparation for the world of work
4 Enrichment of the educational process through experiences in environmental education, recreation, cultural arts, and other areas, including enrichment for special school audiences such as the handicapped
5 Provision of supervised recreation and child care services
6 Access to specialized services, including those which help youth to prepare to return to or stay in the formal school setting (e.g. parenting, substance abuse counseling and rehabilitation). (McLaughlin & Smrekar, 1988, pp. 12–13)

In our society, schools have more direct and sustained contact with children than any other institution. However, schools do not have the human resources or financial resources to provide the broad range of services needed by young people and their families. Alliances of parents, social service agencies, and educational institutions need to form to provide the health care, social services, child care, child protection, parent education, and the host of other services needed to assist young people. Kirst (1991) suggests that any efforts to coordinate services must build upon a history of failed attempts and an unpromising current status. Kirst advocates providing services that focus on prevention, continuity, comprehensiveness, equity, and accountability (p. 617).

There is a sense of emergency to this situation, so Kirst (1991) advocates short-run improvement approaches that (1) group multiple services in one place (a school) or several locations, (2) engender a sense of collaboration by several agencies to improve comprehensive services without any one agency being solely responsible, and (3) assess the effectiveness of the collaboration processes by issuing a child-care report card to determine whether the programs have made a difference.

For long-term improvements to be made in a comprehensive services delivery system, there will need to be broad-based legislation at the state and federal levels. Legislation will develop procedures and regulations for child care services which will be implemented in the local schools and communities (Kirst, 1991).

A Failed Effort

Just identifying the problems and developing initiatives will not solve society's health problems, family poverty, educational deficits, and an array of staggering social and economic problems. The failure to attain the 20 health care goals for infants and children for 1990, postulated by the United States Surgeon General in 1980, illustrates the emptiness of establishing national goals without enlisting a deep commitment from the school, the home, the community, and the business sectors. A study conducted by the American Academy of Pediatrics (Reed & Sautter, 1989) found that only one goal—that of reducing the neonatal mortality rate, had been achieved out of 20 health care goals established for 1990. Nineteen other goals of significant concern for schools and society had not been accomplished. The study reported two health nations in the United States. One nation was prosperous with the best of health care readily available for adults and children. The other nation has health care similar to a Third World nation (Reed & Sautter, 1990).

Success must come from our experiences with failure. Young adolescents, their families, and society will pay too heavy a price if the year 2000 proclaims similar failed efforts. There are health, education, family, and personal development trends of early adolescence that must be revised for the present and future well-being of young adolescents.

Societal Imperatives for Collaboration

Society expects more and more of its schools. Beyond responsibility for the academic instruction of young adolescents, the middle level school is increasingly being held accountable for a wide range of social, emotional, and health needs of young people. It is essential that other agencies should be organized to help in meeting the diverse and demanding needs and problems of a youth subculture that is moving toward potentially destructive at-risk conditions.

There have been many past attempts at collaboration. Some localized efforts have been successful, but comprehensive state and national efforts have been less successful. Guthrie and Guthrie (1991) have identified principles that need to be included in streamlining interagency collaboration for young adolescents at risk. The first element to facilitate collaboration is that it must be *comprehensive,* even to the point of cutting across the protocols and procedures of bureaucracy. A comprehensive approach offers a wide variety of essential services that should emphasize early prevention as opposed to later intervention. Another element of collaboration is to assure that it is person-centered rather than service- or program-centered. Child-centered services enable agencies to attend to the growing diversity of needs and problems of early adolescence. The problems of young people need to be addressed in a holistic fashion, not compartmentalized into discrete categories such as dropouts, drugs, teenage sex, and AIDS.

The delivery of needed services carries the weight of a mandate. The problems of the young adolescents are so acute and the available home and school services are so fragmented that collaborative efforts are required to prevent the society from becoming at-risk. However, the mandate is just one side of the complex problem. There is also a pressing need for businesses, industries, commercial institutions, communication groups, and a wide spectrum of community agencies to establish a broad network of work sites to connect young adolescents to the total life of the community. Young adolescents need to study the community, need to value the community, and need to contribute to the community. The adopt-a-school movement has been popular, but there is a need for students to adopt a business or community cause. Such community programs add relevance, interest, and satisfaction to school learning. When community education programs are operated effectively, they increase student feelings of competence, confidence, and caring. A very strong developmental need of young adolescents is the need to be needed. Community service is an imperative for the academic, social, and personal development of young adolescents.

COMMUNITY SERVICE AND THE MIDDLE LEVEL SCHOOL

One of the refreshing aspects of the community service movement is that it is a reform initiative that is bubbling up from schools and communities all over the country and is not a trickle-down or top-down pronouncement. Community service renews a theory by John Dewey that schools should be democratic, social laboratories that are directly tied to community needs. The interaction between school and community results in active learning of meaningful, relevant content (Nathan & Kielsmeier, 1991).

The best youth service programs are developed at the local school setting. Teachers and students need to have a great deal of latitude in selecting service projects. Additionally, service adds strength to the school program when service/social action programs are integrated into the school curriculum. The complete range of subject areas, including the sciences, the humanities, and the arts, can be designed to include service activities. Service learning programs provide opportunities for improving communication skills, for solving problems, for critical thinking, and for utilizing higher-order thinking skills (Nathan & Kielsmeier, 1991). The service/social action curriculum has application from elementary to high school but is a particularly powerful tool for the middle level school.

Service Programs in the School. Another aspect of social service is to apply it to the school setting through school improvement projects, tutoring programs, and peer helping programs for drug education, sex education, and school problems. These programs can be within the peer group and across age groups. Cross-age teaching programs of middle level students tutoring primary grade children in math and reading have been popular and successful for many years. A positive benefit of cross-age teaching programs has been that both the helper and the one being helped derive positive gains (Hedin, 1987). Peer helping programs have been most effective in reducing drug use (Tobler, 1986).

Conrad and Hedin (1991) conducted a review of the research on school-based community service. In the literature, they found a thread running from the Progressive Education of Dewey and Kilpatrick, through the activism of the 1960s and 1970s, culminating in recommendations for community service in national reports such as Goodlad's *A Place Called School* (1984), Boyer's *High School* (1983), the Carnegie report *Turning Points* (1989), and the Grant Foundation report *The Forgotten Half* (1988). Boyer advocated that high schools should require 120 hours of community service as a primary educational need of middle grade students. *The Forgotten Half* strongly urged that non-college bound students should be involved in community service programs. This concern at the national level culminated in 1990 when President George Bush signed into law The National and Community Service Act of 1990. This legislation, which drew broad-based support from liberals and conservatives, provided funds for community service programs in schools and colleges and support for the creation of a full-time service corps that students can be involved in after high school.

Research on Community Service. In their review of quantitative research studies, Conrad and Hedin (1991) found an increase in personal and social responsibility, more positive attitudes toward adults, more active exploration of careers, enhanced self-esteem, and other aspects of intellectual and social-psychological development resulting from community service. They did not find that service participation resulted in higher scores on tests of general knowledge, with the exception that the achievement scores of students who served as tutors increased.

Conrad and Hedin (1991) conducted a qualitative analysis of the learning outcomes of service and social action projects. A consistent finding of qualitative research is the high degree to which participants say they learned a great deal from service activities. In reviewing the journals of high school students involved in service projects, 95% of the students indicated that they learned more in service activities than they had learned in regular classrooms. They concluded that service warrants the serious consideration of practitioners and policy makers to be continued as a part of the school program.

COMMUNITY SERVICE FOR YOUNG ADOLESCENTS

There once was a time in American society that young adolescents emerged from childhood with a well-defined social role. These young people were closely integrated into the life of the family, the work of the family, and the workings of the community. In the last decades the roles of young adolescents have diminished, causing them to become more isolated and quite often alienated from the community (Schine, 1989). Howe maintains that youth have increasingly been denied chances to be involved in work that is important to them and to others. Consequently, the rewards that such useful work produces have been denied to them (Howe, 1986).

Contemporary Problems of Rolelessness. Nightingale and Wolverton (1988) address the problem of adolescent rolelessness in modern society. While they do have certain roles prescribed by their parents, teachers, and peers, adolescents do not have active, positive, productive roles that connect them to the adult world. The authors maintain that adolescents have no established status in society that is appreciated or approved. This lack of acceptance makes it hard to develop a sense of identity and self-esteem.

A growing number of middle level educators feel that this sense of isolation can be remedied by programs that give young people opportunities for community service. There are several personal and social benefits to volunteer community service. The young person gets a real boost in self-esteem as well as a sense of accomplishment. Community service allows for career exploration, for experiencing the values and attitudes of the workplace, for connecting school experiences to the real world, and for learning skills of cooperation, collaboration, and compromise (Schine, 1989). An opportunity for community service as a young adolescent may very well translate into a commitment to community service in adulthood.

Community service is a developmentally appropriate behavior for young adolescents. The research of Lipsitz (1984) and Toepfer (1988) have confirmed that young adolescents are realizing feelings of altruism and idealism. They are reaching out to adults other than parents and teachers for meaningful role participation. A sense of belonging to a community larger than school, family, and peer group emerges in this developmental stage.

Using the work of researchers in this field, Schine (1989) has compiled some of the needs of young adolescents that are satisfied by community service. They include:

- To develop a sense of competence, testing and discovering new skills
- To discover a place for themselves in the world, to create a vision of a personal future

- To participate in projects with tangible or visible outcomes
- To know a variety of adults, representative of different backgrounds and occupations, including potential role models
- To have the freedom to take part in the world of adults, but also to be free to retreat to a world of their peers
- To test a developing value system in authentic situations
- To speak and be heard, to know that they can make a difference
- To achieve recognition for their accomplishments
- To have opportunities to make real decisions, within appropriate limits
- To receive support and guidance from adults who appreciate their problems and their promise. (p. 3)

Appropriate Roles and Settings for Young Adolescents. Schine (1989) reports general agreement that the most meaningful roles for young adolescents in community service are in the areas of interpersonal relationships. The developmental needs of young adolescents indicate that they benefit from working with the very young and with aging adults. They particularly enjoy working with people who are different from them—the handicapped, the homeless, the disadvantaged, and shut-ins. The warm receptions they receive and the feeling of making a difference make such community service activities successful ventures for young adolescents.

There have been successful service programs for young adolescents for many years. The Early Adolescent Helper Program in New York City has been placing young adolescents in helping relationships with pre-school, school-age, and elderly people in a variety of case settings since 1982. This model has been replicated in other cities in the United States (Schine, 1989).

Quite often, it is more difficult to place middle level students in community settings than high school students. In the early years, the focal point of service might be the school setting. School improvement projects, peer tutoring, cross-age teaching, and peer-helping programs may be instituted within the school. Many schools try to provide a community-based service project by the completion of Grade 8.

Additionally, service projects may be provided by such non-school groups as Boy Scouts, Girl Scouts, Boys Clubs, Girls Clubs, church groups, and other community groups. These complementary educational opportunities add richness and diversity to the experience of young adolescents (Saxe, 1972).

Service is organized into the school program in several different ways. In some schools, it is a club activity. For some students it becomes an exploratory or elective credit. Other schools have integrated service activities into the interdisciplinary curriculum. However, it is placed in the school curriculum, service, which teaches the importance of giving, has become an important element of the middle level school experience. For such programs to be successful, the home, school, and community must work together to develop the richest possible service and social action program.

THE MIDDLE LEVEL SCHOOL AND THE COMMUNITY

Community organizations can make significant contributions to the emotional, social, and experiential development of young adolescents. Community organizations represent a positive convenient alternative support system beyond the traditional family and school support systems. Community youth-serving organizations, such as churches, civic clubs, sports organizations, youth clubs, and social clubs provide opportunities for *complementary education;* complementary education facilitates learning in settings other than school (Saxe, 1972).

Youth and Community Organizations

Heath and McLaughlin (1991) found that most young people were not involved in any community-based activities on a regular basis. For many young adolescents, this lack of participation indicates lack of opportunity to become involved due to a shortage of facilities, funds, and sponsoring organizations. However, in many cases, programs are available but do not attract the participation of young people. Those who work with young people report that the major problem is gaining and maintaining the involvement of young people in their programs.

Heath and McLaughlin (1991) found that traditional organizations such as Boy and Girl Scouts, YMCA and YWCA, Boys and Girls Clubs, Future Farmers of America, sports clubs, and church youth groups did not attract the involvement of young people by automatic response to what these clubs are and what they stand for but attracted young people because of the relevance of the program and how the program was operated. Successful youth-serving organizations were characterized by some of the following features:

1. Insistence that members feel that they belong to the group
2. Activities which are developmentally appropriate to the young people who attend
3. Approaches that are firm and flexible, which empower and manage and which individualize and socialize
4. An atmosphere that is similar to a functional family life, in that it supports, extends, holds accountable, etc.

The resources and opportunities available through community organizations quite often are just what young adolescents need to help with social, emotional, peer, or parent problems that are pressing in on them. The middle level school must become more responsive to the needs of young adolescents. However, the school cannot provide the broad-based services and activities that young people require. Community organizations provide young adolescents with another support system to help them function effectively in their high-risk environments.

Roth and Hendrickson (1991) found that the collaborative efforts of school and community-based youth organizations were successful in helping young adolescents deal with self-destructive behaviors, such as substance abuse, early sexual activity, and sexually transmitted diseases. The school has traditionally been responsible for teaching as much information and values as the family, the church, and the state would permit. That the school has been less than successful in its efforts can be found in the low status these drug and sex education programs have in school and the prevalence of the harmful behaviors in young adolescents.

Some programs have been successful in placing responsibility for addressing some of the harmful behaviors of early adolescence on youth service organizations. Additionally, these community groups have not *taught* the information or values to the young people but have enlisted young adolescents themselves to help their peers develop skills and strategies to steer clear of the self-harming behaviors which are so tantalizing to young adolescents.

School/Business Partnerships

School and business partnerships are a growing trend in American education. Merenda (1989) reported that more than 140,000 education partnerships are in operation throughout the nation, with the number still growing. While the partnerships of today have a new twist, they are built on a foundation of volunteer efforts going back to the 1950s. Burt and Lessinger (1970) traced the relationship between the world of school and the world of work. They specified ways that programs of voluntary industry involvement in public schools could be initiated.

School partners range from individuals and small companies to large corporations or government agencies. Partners include banks, bakeries, law firms, insurance companies, professional sports teams, and a host of other business concerns. The most common pattern of partnership is that of volunteer workers from a company going to the school to provide a variety of instructional, tutorial, management, motivational, and career services. The business–school partnership programs typically consist of techniques for increasing employability status, studies of school management, drug education courses, and opportunities for employment to students in the school.

MacDowell (1989) cautioned the business community that they might have to wait longer than they might want before realizing a return on their investment. A student's school career is a long one, and companies will need to be patient enough to let the partnership process ferment. The business community possesses the skills, relevant work situations, personnel resources, and the finances to provide greater opportunities for students to learn about careers, connect their academic learning to the real world, and learn from mentors and role models other than teachers.

SUMMARY

This chapter has examined the connections between and among school, home and community. By early adolescence, students have become involved with a wider variety of religious groups, peer groups, school groups, and community organizations. The middle level school is not only in the middle of the student's development, between childhood and adolescence, but it is also in the middle of the student's network of social and educational connections.

The need for home, school, and community relationships is an essential consideration given the enormous problems that exist in areas such as dropouts, health-related concerns, and dramatic changes in family conditions. There has been some tradition of interaction among the home, school, and community but a much more proactive effort is required. Too often, home, school, and community relationships have been more talk than action. The crisis situations facing young adolescents in society call for immediate, collaborative efforts to improve school and community settings for young adolescents. School–business partnerships, community youth associations, and community service programs are promising trends to promote more effective learning and living situations for young adolescents.

■ ■ ■

EXPLORATION

1 Read Kozol's *Savage Inequalities.* Develop a position on the role that individuals should play in developing good schools for rich and poor children.

2 John Gardner, in his book *Excellence,* asked "Can we be excellent and equal too?" What are the implications of that question today? How does equity relate to excellence and equality?

3 Organizations like the Children's Defense Fund are persuasive advocates for the well-being of young people. Compile a list of local, state, and national child-advocacy organizations. Assemble material representing the positions that these groups take on important child issues.

4 Interview teachers and principals in your community to determine the types and extent of community service programs in their schools. Try to identify strengths, weaknesses, obstacles, etc. to such programs.

SUGGESTED READINGS

Dryfoos, J. (1990). *Adolescents at risk: Prevalence and prevention.* New York: Oxford University Press.

This is a revealing account of the problems, prospects, and preventions for adolescents at risk.

Kozol, J. (1991). *Savage inequalities.* Southbridge, MA: Crowne Publications.

This text is a galvanizing report on the disparity between schools for the rich and schools for the poor.

Lewis, B. A. (1991). *The kid's guide to social action.* Minneapolis: Free Spirit.

An experienced teacher tells how to get young people turned on to and successful in social action projects.

National Commission on Children. (1991). *Beyond rhetoric: A new agenda for children and families.* Washington, DC: U.S. Government Printing Office.

This commission issued a call to action to rescue the millions of children whose lives and dreams are in jeopardy.

Slavin, R. E, Karweit, N. L., & Madden, N. A. (1989). *Effective programs for students at-risk.* Boston: Allyn & Bacon.

The authors present research on programs which work for compensatory education students.

William T. Grant Foundation, Commission on Work, Family and Citizenship. (1988). *The forgotten half: Non-college-bound youth in America.* Washington, DC: William T. Grant Foundation.

This report reminds us that the non-college bound students need programs that promote success and self-esteem.

REFERENCES

Beane, J. A. (1991). Middle school: The natural home of integrated curriculum. *Educational Leadership, 49*(2), 9–13.

Before it's too late. Dropout prevention in the middle grades. (1988). Boston: Massachusetts Advocacy Center.

Boyer, E. L. (1983). *High school.* New York: Harper & Row.

Brandt, R. (1989). On parents and schools: A conversation with Joyce Epstein. *Educational Leadership, 47*(2), 24–27.

Burt, S., & Lessinger, L. (1970). *Volunteer industry involvement in public education.* Lexington, MA: D. C. Heath.

Carnegie Council on Adolescent Development (1989). *Turning points: Preparing American youth for the 21st century.* Washington, DC: Author.

Conrad, D., & Hedin, D. (1991). School-based community service: What we know from research and theory. *Phi Delta Kappan, 72*(10), 743–749.

Dryfoos, J. (1990). *Adolescents at risk: Prevalence and prevention.* New York: Oxford University Press.

Fine, M. (1986). Why urban adolescents drop in and out of public high school. *Teachers College Record, 87*(3), 393–409.

Gardner, J. W. (1961). *Excellence: Can we be excellent and equal too?* New York: Harper & Row.

Goodlad, J. I. (1984). *A place called school.* New York: McGraw-Hill.

William T. Grant Foundation, Commission on Work, Family, and Citizenship (1988). *The forgotten half: Non-college-bound youth in America.* Washington, DC: William T. Grant Foundation.

Guthrie, G. P., & Guthrie, L. F. (1991). Streamlining interagency collaboration for youth at risk. *Educational Leadership, 49*(1), 17–22.

Heath, S. B., & McLaughlin, M. W. (1991). Community organizations as family: Endeavors that engage and support adolescents. *Phi Delta Kappan, 72*(8), 623–627.

Hedin, D. (1987). Students as teachers: A tool for improving school climate and productivity. *Social Policy, 17*(3), 42–47.

Hofferth, S. L. (1987). Implications of family trends for children: A research perspective. *Educational Leadership, 14*(5), 78–84.

Howe, H. (1986). *Can schools teach values?* Remarks at Lehigh University.

Hunter, M. (1989). Join the "par-aide" in education. *Educational Leadership, 47*(2), 36–41.

Jennings, W. B. (1989). How to organize successful parent advisory committees. *Educational Leadership, 47*(2), 42–45.

Kirst, M. W. (1991). Improving children's services: Overcoming barriers, creating new opportunities. *Phi Delta Kappan, 72*(8), 615–618.

Lipsitz, J. (1984). *Successful schools for young adolescents.* New Brunswick, NJ: Transaction Books.

MacDowell, M. A. (1989). Partnerships: Getting a return on the investment. *Educational Leadership, 47*(2), 8–11.

McLaughlin, M. W., & Smrekar, C. (1988). *School-linked comprehensive service deliver systems for adolescents.* Washington, DC: Carnegie Council on Adolescent Development.

Melaville, A. I., & Blank, M. J. (1991). *What it takes: Structuring interagency partnerships to connect children and families with comprehensive agencies.* Washington, DC: Education Human Services Consortium.

Merenda, D. W. (1989). Partners in education: An old tradition renamed. *Educational Leadership, 47*(2), 4–7.

Moynihan, D. P. (1989). Welfare reform: Serving America's children. *Teachers College Record, 90*(3), 337–341.

Nathan, J., & Kielsmeier, J. (1991). The sleeping giant of school reform. *Phi Delta Kappan, 72*(10), 739–742.

Nightingale, E. O., & Wolverton, L. (1988). *Adolescent rolelessness in modern society.* Washington, DC: Carnegie Council on Adolescent Development.

O'Neil, J. (1991). A generation adrift? *Educational Leadership, 49*(1), 4–9.

Reed, S., & Sautter, R. C. (1990). Children of poverty: The status of 12 million young Americans. Kappan Special Report. *Phi Delta Kappan, 71*(10), K1-K12.

Rosow, L. (1991). How schools perpetuate illiteracy. *Educational Leadership, 49*(1), 41–44.

Roth, J., & Hendrickson, J. M. (1991). Schools and youth organizations: Empowering adolescents to confront high-risk behavior. *Phi Delta Kappan, 72*(8), 619–622.

Saxe, R. W. (Ed.). (1972). *Opening the schools: Alternative ways of learning.* Berkeley, CA: McCutchan.

Schine, J. (1989). *Community service for young adolescents: A background paper.* Washington, DC: Carnegie Council on Adolescent Development.

Templin, T. J. (1987). Some considerations for teaching physical education in the future. In J. D. Massengale (Ed.), *Trends toward the future in physical education.* (pp. 51–67). Champaign, IL: Human Kinetics.

Tobler, M. S. (1986). Meta-analysis of 143 adolescents drug prevention programs. *Journal of Drug Issues, 16*, 537–567.

Toepfer, C. F. (1988). What to know about young adolescents. *Social Education, 52*(2), 110–112.

Turning points: Preparing American youth for the 21st century. (1989). Washington, DC: Carnegie Council on Adolescent Development.

Wehlage, G., & Rutter, R. (1986). Dropping out: How much do schools contribute to the problem. *Teachers College Record, 87*(3), 385.

Wolf, J. S., & Stephens, T. M. (1989). Parent/teacher conferences: Finding common ground. *Educational Leadership, 47*(2), 28–31.

CHAPTER OUTLINE

Implementing the Middle Level School

12

OVERVIEW

Socrates said that "an unexamined life is not worth living." By the same token, an unexamined school is not worth having. By examining middle level school theory and practice—those exciting, creative, responsive, and appropriate programs that many educators have done and are doing—we can develop responsive middle level schools worth having and worthy of our children. The challenge facing middle level educators is to get on with the task of implementing the exemplary middle level school programs we need for tomorrow—today.

In previous chapters, the essential components of developmentally appropriate middle level schools have been presented. This chapter looks at the dimensions of middle level schools which represent some practices that need to be implemented. The contexts and levels which serve as decision points in the implementation process are examined. The need for a systematic plan to implement the recommendations in national and state reports is developed.

In this chapter you will read about:

1. The roles that national research centers can play in implementing effective middle level schools.
2. The ways that legislation in Florida, California, and Maryland can serve as models for state initiatives in middle level reform.

3 The levels and sources of implementation decisions for middle level schools.
4 Suggestions for implementing the recommendations in the *Turning Points* (1989) report.
5 A systematic model, *Planning for Success,* for implementing changes in middle level schools.

THE IMPLEMENTATION PROCESS

Changes in curriculum, instruction, organization, and philosophical assumptions occur in a complex societal setting—the school system. In many schools, established and proven school patterns and practices are hard to dislodge in favor of innovations. The process of implementation is a political process as well as a personal, social, and institutional one.

Fullan and Park (1982) identified some factors which are characteristic of implementation. Implementation is a process, not an event. It happens to individuals and is usually complex, often requiring adaptation and variation. Implementation usually has to resolve questions of ethics, values, and professional responsibility. Not only must the implementation process work for a specific curriculum or instructional innovation, but teachers, principals, parents, and others must develop competence in the process so that future implementation can be successful. In summary, implementation should be a dynamic, interpersonal, future-oriented process which is directed toward being responsive to the needs of students and the society.

Fullan (1985) developed a three-part model for the change process. The model includes (1) the psychological elements of the change process, (2) the limitations of available research relative to the change process, and (3) alternative, complementary strategies to foster change. Psychological factors such as change taking place over time, the anxiety and uncertainty involved in the change process, and the necessity for interaction between teachers and administrators impact on successful change. The leadership team must recognize the human dimension in the implementation process and allow for anxiety, misunderstanding, and resistance to change as typical behaviors in the change process.

The Fullan Model provided a checklist of alternative strategies to direct the change process.

1 Develop a plan.
2 Invest in local facilitators to implement suggestions of outside consultants.
3 Allocate resources for the change.
4 Select schools for pilot projects.
5 Develop the principal's instructional leadership role.
6 Focus on instruction.

7 Emphasize staff development.
8 Plan for maintenance and dissemination.
9 Review potential for future change.

A school district should undertake the implementation plan in a very careful and deliberate manner. Williamson and Johnston (1991) indicate that one of the most critical steps in the change process is developing a "plan to plan." The first formal step in their plan is to form the groups that will be involved in the implementation process. A second step is to assemble information about the innovation being considered. In this plan, the appropriate groups conduct surveys of effective practices, expert knowledge, and related research studies for middle level education. The planning team should conduct an internal review to determine what the district is already doing in middle level education. This internal review would determine the best middle level practices for the school or school district. An external survey would compile significant books and journals, research studies, publications of national associations, data from other districts, and relevant programs from the various state departments of education related to middle level schools. Additionally, consultants would be selected to assist the implementation of the targeted innovation in the school or school district.

For changes in middle level school curriculum, organization, instruction, and student services to be implemented, it is imperative that the best of middle level practice be studied by the various committees involved in the implementation process. Careful examinations must be made of the significant books, research studies, guidelines, and mandated programs prior to making decisions as to what to implement and how to do it.

EXAMINATIONS OF MIDDLE LEVEL SCHOOLING

In previous chapters, we delineated the contributions of the junior high school and the middle school in the development of middle level education. The junior high school established a new level between elementary and secondary education to provide for a smoother transition from elementary to high school. There are many institutions named *junior high school* in the United States that must participate in the necessary reform of middle level education. The capacity for change will be essential to the dynamics of the junior high school as a functional entity in the lives of young adolescents. Van Til, Vars, and Lounsbury were instructive and insightful when they asserted that "the final word on the functions of the junior high school has not been written and, hopefully, never will be. As the world changes, as society and environment change, education must change, too, and with it the functions of the junior high school" (Van Til, Vars, & Lounsbury, 1967, p. 35).

The middle level school has deemphasized some of the more overtly secondary elements of the junior high school in developing responsive middle level

Nelson Bossing and Roscoe Cramer. (1965). *The Junior High School.* Boston: Houghton Mifflin.
Donald Eichhorn. (1966). *The Middle School.* New York: Center for Applied Research in Education.
William Van Til, Gordon Vars, and John Lounsbury. (1967). *Modern Education for the Junior High School Years.* Indianapolis: Bobbs-Merrill.
William Alexander, et al. (1969). *The Emergent Middle School.* New York: Holt, Rinehart and Winston.
William Gruhn and Harl Douglass. (1971). *The Modern Junior High School.* New York: The Ronald Press.
Thomas E. Curtis and Wilma W. Bidwell. (1977). *Curriculum and Instruction for Emerging Adolescents.* Reading, MA: Addison-Wesley Publishing Company.
John Lounsbury and Gordon F. Vars. (1978). *A Curriculum for the Middle School Years.* New York: Harper and Row.
William M. Alexander and Paul S. George. (1981). *The Exemplary Middle School.* New York: Holt, Rinehart and Winston.
Paul George and Gordon Lawrence. (1982). *Handbook for Middle School Teaching.* Glenview, IL: Scott, Foresman and Company.
Joan Lipsitz. (1984). *Successful Schools for Young Adolescents.* New Brunswick, NJ: Transaction Books.
James Fenwick. (1986). *The Middle School Years.* San Diego: Fenwick Associates.
Jon Wiles and Joseph Bondi. (1986). *The Essential Middle School.* Tampa, FL: Wiles, Bondi and Associates.
Judith L. Irvin. (Ed.). (1992). *Transforming middle level education.* Boston: Allyn & Bacon.
Rosemary G. Messick and Karen E. Reynolds. (1992). *Middle Level Curriculum in Action.* New York: Longman.
K. Denise Muth and Donna E. Alverman. (1992). *Teaching and Learning in the Middle Grades.* Boston: Allyn & Bacon.
Chris Stevenson. (1992). *Teaching Ten to Fourteen Year Olds.* New York: Longman.

*Books listed by date of publication.

FIGURE 12.1 Recommended books examining middle level schools*

schools. Building on such positive features of the junior high school as core curriculum, guidance, and socialization experiences, the responsive middle level school has implemented such representative practices as interdisciplinary team organization, advisor–advisee programs, integrated curriculum, and exploratory activities which have been proven by research to actualize the student-centered philosophy.

Alexander, Eichhorn, Lounsbury, George, Lipsitz, Wiles, Bondi, and others have given definition and direction to the middle level school movement. The essential theme of their work was that the middle level school should organize, instruct, and guide, with the learner as the central focus. Elements such as interdisciplinary team organization, advisor–advisee, exploratory programs, and active learning reflected the student-oriented philosophy of the middle level school.

The junior high school and the middle school have long championed many of the causes which recently have become so popular in middle level education. The literature of middle level education is characterized by numerous articles, monographs, studies, and programs that exemplify successful school theory and practice. Figure 12.1 contains a selected listing of some books that have presented a systematic examination of junior high school, middle school, and middle level education.

GUIDELINES FOR IMPLEMENTING MIDDLE LEVEL SCHOOLS

While many different forces and issues have given impetus to the middle level school movement, a general consensus has evolved concerning representative functions and characteristics. These characteristics broadly defined the curriculum, organization, instruction, and student services found in middle schools. Middle school curriculum was characterized by integrated curriculum; interdisciplinary units; basic core subjects, exploratory study; community education; and physical, social, and creative experiences. Organizational patterns consisted of interdisciplinary team organization, flexible scheduling, continuous progress, and variable grouping. Instruction emphasized orientations such as individualization, cooperative learning, active participation, discovery, peer teaching, and team learning. The academic, social, and personal needs of young adolescents were attended to by personalized evaluation, advisor–advisee programs, guidance and counseling, and the above-stated curriculum, instruction, and organizational practices.

This synthesis of knowledge, experience, and information prepares the planning groups to proceed to the next stage of the implementation process. A helpful source is the Williamson and Johnston monograph, *Planning for Success* (1991), an insightful step-by-step explanation of the phases and decision points of the implementation process. *Planning for Success* is a very detailed account of how a district goes through the entire implementation process.

The implementation described in the rest of this chapter deals with many different levels, sources, and contexts of the change process. Statements of rationale such as *This We Believe* (1992), assessment guides such as the *Middle Grade Assessment Program* (1985), state initiatives such as Maryland's *What Matters in the Middle Grades* (1989), and national reports such as *Turning Points* (1989) are suggested as appropriate sources and guides to plan best middle grade practice.

MAKING MIDDLE LEVEL IMPLEMENTATION WORK

The reports, studies, and research related to middle level school improvement are numerous and growing at a rapid pace. The sadly repetitive story of innovation in American schools has been that after the initial excitement has gone it has been hard to sustain viable educational reform. The educational landscape is dotted with programs and practices initiated with vigor and enthusiasm only to fade into disuse. The needs of young adolescents are so pressing that society can no longer tolerate such a haphazard, hit-or-miss, trial-and-error approach to school improvement. The middle level school of tomorrow is needed today.

Cuban (1989) prepared a background paper to suggest ways that the recommendations in the *Turning Points* (1989) report could be implemented at federal, state, and local levels. As he addressed the problem, Cuban focused on three issues: the nature of the change, negotiating the complexities of governance systems in public education, and deeply engaging the infantry of reform—teachers and principals—in the process of implementation. Additionally, Cuban examined the process of implementation at the macro-level (social, economic, political, and historical factors), middle-level (federal, state, and district policy systems), and micro-level (schools and classroom).

In addressing the nature of the changes recommended in the report, Cuban differentiated between the sweeping changes in curriculum, instruction, governance, and organization called for in the Carnegie Council report and the incremental nature of changes called for in most reform efforts. Cuban presented an historical analysis of implementation strategies used in movements such as the kindergarten, the junior high school, the open classroom, and post-*Sputnik* curriculum reform. He concluded that (1) given the proper climate, reform could be locally implemented with minimal federal and state involvement, (2) the time span of reform took a decade or more, not years, (3) persistent conflicts simmered for years, and (4) reforms that call for changing teacher attitudes and behaviors were the most difficult to implement and sustain.

Regarding procedures for navigating the complex and interlocking governance systems of public education, Cuban synthesized his beliefs about recent efforts in federal, state, and district reform. He suggested that research and experience show that successful implementation is local and context-driven. Implementation is heavily dependent upon individual and group initiatives and develops through stages, yet remains uncertain in its course. Policy makers must develop strategies that involve teachers, principals, and parents significantly and personally in the implementation process.

As a final note on implementation, George (1986) contended that "Certain programs, when present, strengthen everything else in the school. In middle schools, it's whatever gives you smallness within bigness" (p. 81). The programs to be implemented are known. It is time to develop middle level schools that are academically effective and developmentally responsive for young adolescents.

CONTEXTS OF IMPLEMENTATION

Implementation must be orchestrated at the national, state, district, school, and classroom level. Implementation decisions for middle level schools necessitate a variety of contexts. Important contexts for middle level schools are the societal, socio-personal, institutional, and professional (see Figure 12.2).

There have been many statements of the societal contexts influencing middle level education. Among the most eloquent and pressing are the ones developed by the Carnegie Task Force in their *Turning Points* report which stated what 15-year-olds would be like who had been well served by their middle level schools (*Turning Points,* 1989).

Middle level schools are for young adolescents. They must be established and organized so that the socio-personal dimensions of young adolescents are realized. The individual as a person and as a member of a peer group is of central importance in the school and in the society. The young adolescents' relationship, adjustment, and contributions to the home, family, and the community

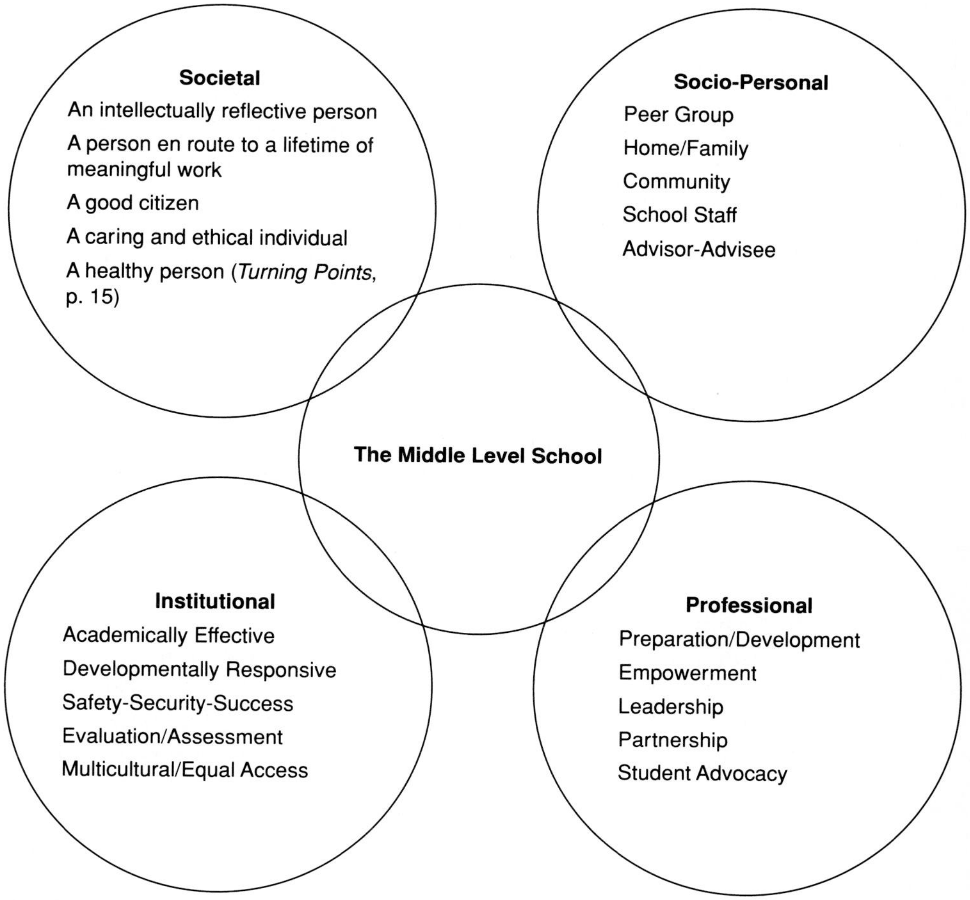

FIGURE 12.2 Contexts of middle level implementation

are of paramount importance to their total development. The entire school staff, and especially the advisor–advisee program, are carefully placed to provide the personalized support and direction each individual student needs to optimize his or her social, personal, and academic development.

In recent years, various research studies have focused on attributes of effective schools. Research has reinforced the importance of middle level schools becoming developmentally responsive to their students. Other institutional contexts which must be guaranteed are personal safety and emotional security; success in academic, vocational, and personal development programs; attention to multicultural elements; and equal access for all students to all aspects of the school program. Evaluation and assessment procedures must be established to assure that all of these institutional contexts function as they should.

The involvement and commitment of professional educators in the implementation of effective middle level practice is absolutely indispensable. The need for competent, confident, and caring middle level teachers and principals has been a fundamental ingredient which differentiates successful middle level schools from their less effective counterparts. In recent years, issues and developments have emerged that hold bright promise for the education profession. The profession has been approaching consensus on the primacy of attributes such as specialized middle level preparation for professional educators, the empowerment of teachers and principals, and the efficacy of leadership through collaboration. The pinnacle of professional development is a commitment to student advocacy where professional educators, parents, students, and citizens will be empowered to lead through partnership models in developing responsive middle level schools.

The reader is referred to Figure 1.2 in Chapter 1 to review the essential dimensions of middle level schools. The student is at the center of all changes in middle level programs. The dimensions which relate to the development of academically effective and developmentally responsive programs are the curricular, the instructional, the organizational, and the supportive. Each dimension has important elements that need to be considered by schools which may not have implemented some of the specific program elements. These dimensions, in concert with the societal, socio-personal institutional, and professional contexts, represent boundaries and directions for middle level implementation.

LEVELS AND SOURCES FOR IMPLEMENTATION

Once the dimensions of middle level schools are determined and the contexts driving implementation are attended to, the advocates of middle level improvement must determine the level at which the decisions affecting implementation may most appropriately and effectively be made. Decision points for middle level implementation efforts are the national, the state, the district, the school, and the classroom levels (Figure 12.3). At each level, different sources and influences bear on the ultimate decision points of implementation—the school and the classroom.

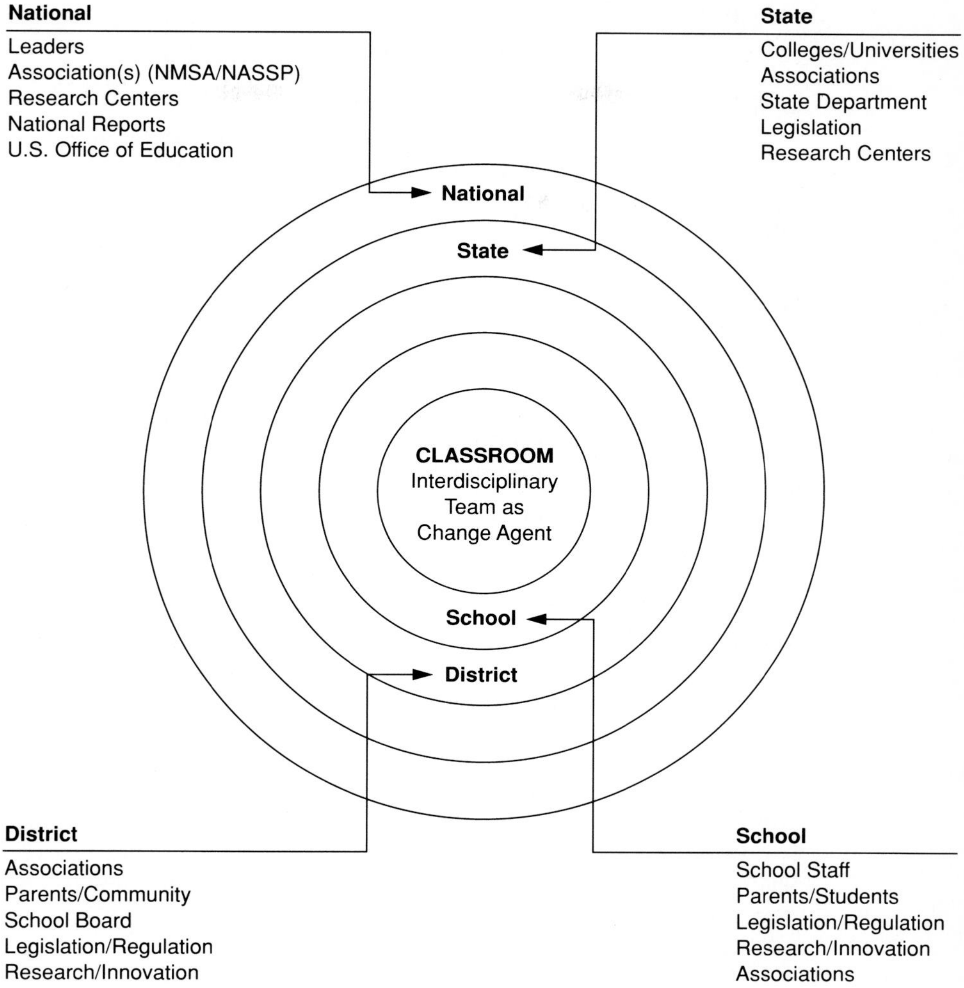

FIGURE 12.3 Levels and sources for middle level implementation

National

At the national level, reports such as *Turning Points* have served to galvanize national debate and concern and to stimulate changes in middle level education. The *Turning Points* report has possibly generated more substantive changes in schools due to the clout of the Carnegie Council and to the fact that financial grants have been made to states, districts, and schools to implement aspects of the recommendations. Schools have also been encouraged to conduct research studies which will generate broad-based data about effective curricular and instructional practices.

National associations such as the National Middle School Association and the National Association of Secondary Schools Principals give direction, dimension and impetus to needed changes in establishing the best schools possible for young adolescents. The scholarly writing and research of recognized national leaders play an important role in advocating schools which serve young adolescents.

Reports from national research centers are instrumental in pointing out exemplary school practice. Epstein (1990) reported research from *Education in the Middle Grades: A National Survey of Practice and Trends* related to establishing goals and implementation of "signature" practices for middle level education. In the survey, principals were asked to rank seven goals according to their importance for *all* students. Principals in middle level schools—middle schools, grades 7–8 schools, and junior high schools—ranked the seven goals in the following order:

1 Basic skills (reading, math, writing, speaking, and subject-matter mastery)
2 Personal growth and development (self-esteem, self-knowledge)
3 Work habits (self-discipline, autonomy, and self-direction)
4 Attitudes and commitment (positive attitudes about school, participation in class, school activities)
5 Human relations (getting along with others, good race relations, multicultural education)
6 Higher-level skills (reasoning, problem solving, critical and creative thinking)
7 Citizenship (including service to the school and community) (p. 440)

All schools ranked basic skills first. However, principals of middle level schools gave a higher priority to personal growth and development than principals in K–8 and 7–12 schools. The goals established and the priority given by middle level principals to basic skills and personal growth and development influenced decisions about curriculum, instruction, student services, and teacher–student relationships.

Epstein (1990) also reported findings on the likelihood of middle level principals to implement key practices in middle level schools. Practices that principals indicated that they were most likely to implement over the next three years were:

- Interdisciplinary teams of teachers
- Common planning time for teams of teachers
- Flexible scheduling
- Students assigned to the same homeroom or advisory teacher for all years spent in the middle grades
- Cooperative learning as an instructional approach
- Exploratory courses and minicourses

- Parent involvement in workshops on early adolescence
- Parents as volunteers in the middle grades. (p. 443)

The Epstein research study and other research being done at national research centers are proving that certain practices, when implemented, do indeed result in positive academic, social, and personal improvement. Since the principal as instructional leader of the school is such a widely-held precept, it is imperative that principals working with implementation teams of teachers, parents, citizens, and students be given the resources to actualize these important practices into middle level schools.

The Office of Educational Research and Improvement of the United States Department of Education serves the function of identifying, collecting, and disseminating research and innovation to middle level schools. At this writing, a national agenda for education in the United States for the year 2000 has been issued with implications for middle level education. The national goals which came out of an education summit in Charlottesville, Virginia in 1989 related to (1) children being ready to start school, (2) increased high school graduation rates, (3) competence in basic subject areas, (4) U.S. students being first in the world in science and mathematics, (5) 100% adult literacy, and (6) safe, drug free schools (*National Goals for Education,* 1990, p. 1).

While these national goals are entirely laudable and important for the United States, middle level educators must be alert to how these goals are implemented. National reports such as *A Nation at Risk* (National Commission on Excellence in Education, 1983) and the national and state push for comprehensive testing programs can place certain middle level programs in jeopardy. Zealous efforts for basic skills, higher academic performance, pupil assessment, and teacher evaluation can lead to the erosion and even the elimination of practices such as exploratory curriculum, advisor–advisee programs, integrated curriculum, and other student-centered programs. The curtailment or elimination of these developmentally appropriate practices for any extended period of time would serve to place the middle level school at risk. If middle level educators are prudent and responsible, these important national goals can be achieved in the context of exemplary middle level schools. Meeting the demands placed on the schools by the society in combination with the challenges exerted by international competition will make it difficult to keep in our middle level schools those programs that are best for the total development of young adolescents. Providing those schools will be a worthy challenge for the 1990s and beyond.

State

Implementation at the state level tends to assume a more direct role as legislatures, sometimes on their own initiative but frequently using the research and information provided by colleges and universities, state and national associations, research centers, and the State Department of Education enact legislation which causes changes in middle level schools. Examples of enlightened and comprehensive state legislation are the PRIME program in Florida, Maryland's *What Matters in the Middle Grades*, and the *Caught in the Middle* report from California. These three states provided excellent models of the procedures to follow for enacting appropriate legislation. In the *Turning Points* report, critical issues for a state task force on middle level education to consider are summarized as follows:

- Determine whether technical assistance is available to divide large schools into several sub-schools or houses and to create teams
- Review the core curriculum
- Examine curriculum frameworks and requirements and textbook selection procedures
- Examine expectation levels for students reflected in test requirements, grade-retention standards, and policies toward between-class ability grouping
- Consider school governance standards
- Evaluate the physical and mental health of the 10- to 15-year-old population
- Inventory community resources to identify local organizations and individuals willing to work with schools in a supportive role
- Examine certification standards
- Evaluate the nature and character of staff development for experienced teachers
- Consider incentives that attract teachers to service in middle grade schools
- Assess the role parents are allowed in the middle level program
- Assess the morale of teachers and students in the middle level program. (p. 83)

The checklist developed by the *Turning Points* (1989) committee to direct the efforts of a state task force on middle level education represents a good beginning point for reviewing middle grade programs and practices. Task force groups at the state and/or district level need to be cautious not to attempt too much change too quickly. Small steps taken in a thoughtful, deliberate manner yield more positive results than trying to effect sweeping changes.

School District and Schools

At the district and school levels, middle level education is influenced and directed by state legislation, school board policies, local associations, and parent/community forces. An invaluable instrument to assess and improve the status of middle level schools is the *Middle Grades Assessment Program* (Dorman, 1985). As the result of the review and evaluations conducted by the assessment team using MGAP standards and criteria, the individual middle level school is able to obtain an assessment of current curriculum and instruction and suggested areas for improvement. The *Middle Grades Assessment Program* would assist any school in assessing its program, determining strengths and weaknesses, and indicating needed improvements.

Networks of schools have emerged as an effective means of exchanging information, sharing resources, and providing support during the reform phases. At the district and state levels, networks of schools provide a horizontal dimension to reform and innovation.

In 1987, the Office of Middle Grade Support Services of the California State Department of Education established the Regional Networks of Foundation and Partnership Schools. In this plan, ten regional networks, each network consisting of 10–12 partnership schools and one foundation school, would facilitate the development of state-of-the-art middle grade schools. Partnership schools are dedicated to implementing the reforms embodied in the *Caught in the Middle* (1987) report. Foundation schools are already considered to be exemplary middle grade schools, representing state-of-the-art middle grade theory and practice. These foundation schools provide leadership to the partnership schools in the network. At the same time, the partnership schools network with each other to disseminate effective practice (Jackson, 1990).

Partnership and foundation schools share a commitment to:

- Plan and implement innovative strategies, programs, practices, and policies which facilitate middle grades education reform.
- Systematically evaluate activities and report findings related to instructional issues.
- Make a multi-year commitment to allow planning, implementation, and evaluation of new programs and practices.
- Create linkages among people, institutions, and organizations that allow a continuous exchange of ideas and information and the sharing of resources.
- Serve as a catalyst for middle grades education renewal and reform, and use the network to disseminate findings and recommendations to all levels of public education. (p. 2)

Something like the partnership and foundation school model could likely work in other states and districts. States and school districts need to develop similar models over which they have feelings of creation, ownership, and evaluation. It is important that procedures be established so that the best practices attained by certain middle level schools can be disseminated to middle level schools who need to implement these practices.

Classroom

The classroom is the focal point of implementation. All levels and sources converge so that developmentally responsive curriculum and instruction can be implemented into middle level classrooms. Additionally, should implementation decisions from other levels and sources not develop or fail to effect the changes needed for effective teaching and learning, there are opportunities for implementation to occur in classroom settings based on the actions of interdisciplinary teams of teachers. Many active learning experiences for students can be developed at the classroom level without involving the entire school or other schools. Implementation starts and stops at the school and classroom. Leadership teams representing the entire school can institute curricular and instructional change for the whole school. Interdisciplinary teams of teachers can introduce needed changes in their classroom units and in their teams. The significance of school and classroom implementation as an internal process must not be lost on middle level educators.

There have been increasing numbers of sources for implementation of middle level reforms. National associations, foundations, research centers, and state departments of education have directed experimentation in middle level education. Organizations and groups which have developed programs and technical assistance to promote improvements in middle level schools are located in Appendix A.

BEGINNINGS

During the last one hundred years, educators have been occupied with efforts to develop a school in the middle. Professional organizations such as the National Middle School Association and the National Association of Secondary Principals and middle school theorists such as Alexander, Eichhorn, George, and Lounsbury have given dimension and direction to the middle level school. In recent years, researchers have conducted several studies which have proven specific practices that enhance middle level education. State initiatives in Florida, California, and other states have legislated improvements and reform in middle level schools.

The philosophy of a student-oriented school has challenged the junior high and middle school. Great strides have been made in implementing aspects of best middle level practice, but there is still much to be done to make the promise of middle level education a reality. Middle level education is at a crucial, yet promising, turning point. The middle level reform movement, while not at the beginning of the end, can assuredly be plotted as successfully closing in on the end of the beginning. The rest of this decade will surely provide opportunities for the implementation of effective, appropriate, and responsive middle level schools for young adolescents.

▪ ▪ ▪

EXPLORATION

1 There have been several reports advocating changes in the junior high and middle school. The Association for Supervision and Curriculum Development published two such reports: *The Junior High We Need* (1961) and *The Middle School We Need* (1975). Read these two reports and compare their recommendations to those being made currently about middle level education in the national reports included in this chapter. In what ways are the recommendations alike? In what ways are they different?

2 Of the various recommendations made by the national reports and in state legislation, select the twelve that you think are most significant for middle level schools. Write a short paper justifying your twelve selections. Compare your list with another member of the class.

3 The United States Department of Education prepared effective schools reports highlighting the best efforts of "hypothetical" *James Madison Elementary School* (Bennett, 1988) and *James Madison High School* (Bennett, 1987). Why was there not a report on James Madison Middle School? What problems and concerns does this raise for middle level education?

4 Develop a plan that will make it more likely that the *Turning Points* report will truly represent a turning point in the lives and education of young adolescents. Identify specific steps to include parents, students, and community groups in the process. Identify ways that teachers may be empowered to lead the reform movement.

5 Middle level theory and research should emphasize the developmental needs of young adolescents. Read about the developmental needs of young adolescents in Chapters 3 and 4. Study an assessment guide such as the *Middle Grades Assessment Program* (Dorman). Be able to discuss ways that societal needs and adolescent developmental needs may be reconciled into "the middle level school we need."

SUGGESTED READINGS

Alexander, W. M., & McEwin, C. K. (1989). *Schools in the middle: Status and progress.* Columbus, OH: National Middle School Association.

The current status of the middle level school is examined through a comprehensive national research study.

California State Department of Education, Middle Grade Task Force. (1987). *Caught in the middle: Educational reform for young adolescents in California public schools.* Sacramento, CA: California State Department of Education.

In this comprehensive report, the California plan to implement effective middle school programs for *all* of its young adolescents is discussed.

Carnegie Council on Adolescent Development (1989). *Turning points: Preparing American youth for the 21st century.* (1989). Washington, DC: Author.

This report is an eloquent statement of the uncertain future of young adolescents in America and an urgent call for establishing schools to meet the academic, social, and personal needs of young people.

Cuban, L. (1989). *Background paper on implementing the task force's report on educating young adolescents.* Washington, DC: Carnegie Council on Adolescent Development.

This paper suggests ways that the recommendations of the *Turning Points* report may be implemented at national, state, district, and school levels.

Dorman, G. (1987). *Improving middle grade schools: A framework for action.* Carrboro, NC: Center for Early Adolescence, University of North Carolina–Chapel Hill.

This monograph documents the school improvement efforts of 11 middle level schools that participated in piloting the *Middle Grades Assessment Program.* Case studies of the schools describe their efforts to be safe and secure settings, academically effective, and developmentally responsive.

George, P., & Oldaker, L. (1985). *Evidence for the middle school.* Columbus, OH: National Middle School Association.

Data and research to support the advocacy of middle schools are presented in compelling fashion.

Lipsitz, J. (1984). *Successful schools for young adolescents.* New Brunswick, NJ: Transaction Books.

This case study approach examines what four middle level schools did to make their environments developmentally responsive and academically effective for their students. Describes the human dimensions involved in true school improvement.

Maryland Task Force on the Middle Learning Years. (1989). *What matters in the middle grades.* Baltimore: Maryland State Department of Education.

This report contains recommendations for making middle level education emanate from the characteristics and needs of young adolescents.

Phi Delta Kappan, (February, 1990), *71*(6).

The six articles in this issue report research by the Center for Research on Elementary and Middle Schools at Johns Hopkins University.

REFERENCES

Alexander, W. M., & McEwin, C. K. (1989). *Schools in the middle: Status and progress.* Columbus, OH: National Middle School Association.

Association for Supervision and Curriculum Development (ASCD). (1961). *The junior high school we need.* Washington, DC: Association for Supervision and Curriculum Development.

ASCD Working Group on the Emerging Adolescent Learner. (1975). *The middle school we need.* Washington, DC: Association for Supervision and Curriculum Development.

Bennett, W. J. (1987). *James Madison high school.* Washington, DC: United States Department of Education.

Bennett, W. J. (1988). *James Madison elementary school.* Washington, DC: United States Department of Education.

California State Department of Education, Middle Grade Task Force (1987). *Caught in the middle: Educational reform for young adolescents in California public schools.* Sacramento, CA: California State Department of Education.

Carnegie Council on Adolescent Development. (1989). *Turning points: Preparing American youth for the 21st century.* Washington, DC: Author.

Children's Defense Fund (1988). *Making the middle grades work.* (1988). Washington: Author.

Council on Middle Level Education. (1985). *An agenda for excellence at the middle level.* Reston, VA: National Association of Secondary School Principals.

Cuban, L. (1989). *Background paper on implementing the task force's report on educating young adolescents.* Washington, DC: Carnegie Council on Adolescent Development.

Dorman, G. (1985). *Middle grades assessment program.* Carrboro, NC: Center for Early Adolescence, University of North Carolina–Chapel Hill.

Epstein, J. (1990). *Education in the middle years: A national survey of practice and trends. Phi Delta Kappan 71*(6), 435–469.

Florida Program in Middle Childhood Education (PRIME). (1984). §§230.2319.

Forgotten years, The. (1984). Tallahassee: Speaker's Task Force on Middle Childhood Education.

Fullan, M. (1985). Change processes and strategies at the local level. *Elementary School Journal, 85*(5), 391–421.

Fullan, M., & Park, P. (1982). *Curriculum implementation.* Toronto: Ontario Ministry of Education.

George, P. (1986). Comments made at the annual conference of the New England League of Middle Schools, March 24–25. In A. Wheelock (Ed.), The way out: Student exclusion practices in Boston middle schools. Boston: Massachusetts Advocacy Center, 81.

Gruhn, W. T., & Douglass, H. R. (1971). *The modern junior high school* (3rd ed.). New York: The Ronald Press.

Jackson, A. (1990). Turning points. *Middle School Journal, 21*(3), 1–3.

Lipsitz, J. (1984). *Successful schools for young adolescents.* New Brunswick, NJ: Transaction Books.

Maryland Task Force on the Middle Learning Years. (1989). *What matters in the middle grades.* Baltimore: Maryland State Department.

National Commission on Excellence in Education (1983). *A nation at risk: The imperative for educational reform.* Washington, DC: U.S. Government Printing Office.

National goals for education. (February 2, 1990). *Education Daily, 23*(38), 1–2.

National Middle School Association (1982, 1992). *This we believe.* Columbus, OH: National Middle School Association.

Resolutions. (1989). *Middle School Journal, 20*(3), 18–20.

This we believe. (1992). Columbus, OH: National Middle School Education.

Turning points: Preparing American youth for the 21st century. (1989). Washington, DC: Carnegie Council on Adolescent Development.

Van Til, W., Vars, G., & Lounsbury, J. (1967). *Modern education for the junior high school years.* Indianapolis, IN: Bobbs-Merrill.

Williamson, R., & Johnston, J. H. (1991). *Planning for success: Successful implementation of middle school reorganization.* Reston, VA: National Association of Secondary School Principals.

Appendix A
sources for implementation of middle level education

ASSOCIATIONS

Association for Supervision and Curriculum Development
1250 N. Pitt Street
Alexandria, VA 22314-1403

National Association for Core Curriculum
316 White Hall
Kent State University
Kent, OH 44242

National Association of Elementary School Principals
1015 Duke Street
Alexandria, VA 22314

National Association of Secondary School Principals Council on Middle Level Education
1904 Association Drive
Reston, VA 22091

National Middle School Association
4807 Evanswood Drive
Columbus, OH 43229

FOUNDATIONS

Early Adolescent Helper Program

Center for Advanced Study in Education (CASE)
City University of New York
33 West 42nd Street
New York, NY 10036

Making the Middle Grades Work

The Children's Defense Fund
25 E Street, N.W.
Washington, DC 20001

Middle Grades Improvement Program

Lilly Endowment Inc.
Indianapolis, IN 46208

New Futures Program

Annie E. Casey Foundation
31 Brookside Drive
Greenwich, CT 06830

Program for Disadvantaged Youth

The Edna McConnell Clark Foundation
250 Park Ave.
Room 900
New York, NY 10017

Turning Points

Carnegie Council on Adolescent Development
Carnegie Corporation of New York
11 DuPont Circle, N.W.
Washington, DC 20036

Urban Middle Grades Network

Association for Supervision and Curriculum Development
1250 N. Pitt Street
Alexandria, VA 22314-1403

Youth Services Program

National Association of State Boards of Education
701 N. Fairfax Street
Alexandria, VA 22314

STATE DEPARTMENTS OF EDUCATION

Florida Progress in Middle Childhood Education Program (*PRIME*) (1984)
The forgotten years (1984)
Florida State Department of Education
Tallahassee, FL 32301

Foundations and Partnership Schools
Office of Middle Grades Support Services
State Department of Education, Sacramento, CA 94244

Maryland Task Force on the Middle Learning Years. (1989). *What matters in the middle grades.* Baltimore, MD: Maryland State Department of Education.

Middle Level School Task Force. (1989). *Paths to success for middle level education in Minnesota.* St. Paul, MN: Minnesota Department of Education.

Middle Level Task Force. (1988). *Success in the middle.* Augusta, ME: Maine Department of Education and Cultural Services.

Superintendent's Middle Grade Task Force. (1987). *Caught in the middle.* Sacramento: California State Department of Education.

RESEARCH CENTERS

Center for Early Adolescence
University of North Carolina at Chapel Hill
Suite 223
Carr Mill Road
Carrboro, NC 27510

Center for Research on Elementary and Middle Schools
The Johns Hopkins University
3505 N. Charles Street
Baltimore, MD 21218

Effective Middle Schools Program
Center for Research on Elementary and Middle Schools
The Johns Hopkins University
3505 N. Charles Street
Baltimore, MD 21218

National Middle School Resource Center
University of South Florida
College of Education
4202 Fowler Ave.
Tampa, FL 33620

Office of Educational Research and Improvement
United States Department of Education (USDE)
555 New Jersey Avenue, N.W.
Washington, DC 20208-5571

Glossary for Middle Level Schools

Advisor–advisee program: A program in which each student has the opportunity to interact with peers and staff about school and personal concerns. The program helps each student to develop a meaningful relationship with at least one adult in the school.

At-risk programs: Programs provided by the school to address deficit needs in the development of young adolescents in areas such as reading, family relationships, health education, drug awareness, self-concept, etc.

Basic skills: Those skills considered to be essential to the students' development, as well as to successful functioning in society. Examples of basic skills are reading, writing, mathematics, and computers.

Block scheduling: A procedure that provides large blocks of time in which individual teachers or teacher teams can organize and arrange groupings of students for varied periods of time. This organizational approach enables teachers to plan for specific instructional needs without affecting the schedule of the entire school.

Common planning time: A regularly scheduled time during the school day when teachers who teach the same students meet for joint planning, parent conferences, materials preparation, and pupil evaluation. Common planning time allows teachers to plan a more comprehensive educational program which appropriately integrates subject areas, skills, and individual needs.

Continuous progress: An instructional procedure that allows students to progress at their own pace through a sequenced curriculum. This approach allows for wide variations in development, individual learning styles, varied academic placement, and self-pacing.

Cooperative learning: A teaching–learning strategy that allows small teams of students to work together, share ideas, and solve problems while still being evaluated and tested individually. Cooperative learning stresses student cooperation, positive interdependence, individual accountability, shared leadership, social skills, group problem-solving, and active involvement.

Core (academic) curriculum: The subject areas generally considered essential for all students in the middle level school. These areas typically are language arts, social sciences, mathematics, science, health, and physical education.

Core (integrated) curriculum: The integration of topics, themes, and subject areas to promote interdisciplinary learning which allows students to connect learning from one subject area to another, to real-world situations, and to their own experiences.

Counseling: Professional assistance given to students by school counselors. The services include academic counseling, career counseling, family adjustment, peer problems, crisis intervention, and other student problems.

Curriculum: A program of study which includes all the planned, guided, and intended experiences available to students during their years in the middle level school.

Departmentalization: A plan which arranges courses by discipline (e.g., mathematics, English, science, social studies, etc.). This type of organization usually requires teachers to be subject-matter specialists who teach only in that subject or closely related subject areas.

Departmentalized team: A team that consists of specialists for each subject area but that allows for team teaching, team planning, and team evaluation of students.

Developmental age characteristics: A set of common characteristics that occur for virtually all young people between 10 and 14 years of age. They consist of the physical, social, emotional, and intellectual characteristics which, when considered as a whole, indicate an individual's development relative to others during this life span.

Developmental needs of young adolescents: A set of needs unique and appropriate to the physical, emotional, social, and intellectual development of young adolescents. These needs should be accommodated in the total school program developed for young adolescents.

Early adolescence: The developmental stage young people go through as they approach and begin to experience puberty. This stage usually occurs between 10 and 14 years of age and deals with the successful attainment of the appropriate developmental age characteristics for this period of life.

Ecological curriculum orientation: This approach attends to the personal, social, and academic needs of young adolescents holistically in all of their interrelated environments of family, school, peer group, church, and community. This orientation establishes an ecological relationship between curriculum elements and environmental systems.

Elective: High-interest or special-needs courses that are based on student selection from various options.

Equal access: A term denoting a concern for equity, so that all students may have access to any of the curriculum and programs of the middle level school.

Exploratory curriculum: Courses designed to help students explore curriculum experiences based on their felt needs, interests, and aptitudes.

Flexible scheduling: Organization of classes and activities in a way that allows for variation from day to day, as opposed to a fixed schedule that is the same every day.

Guidance: Special assistance given to young adolescents by all school personnel to help students experience success in their transition from childhood to adolescence.

Heterogeneous grouping: A grouping pattern which does not separate learners into groups based on their intelligence, learning achievement, or physical characteristics. This approach indicates that students can learn together even though there are wide ranges in ability and achievement.

Homogeneous grouping: A grouping pattern which usually separates students into groups based on their intelligence and/or achievement. Schools use this approach to narrow the range of differences in ability and achievement and thereby increase student learning. Rigid application of this approach can lead to tracking, which is a practice of concern to middle level advocates.

House plan: An organizational approach that groups students based on factors such as age, interest, grade level, etc., enabling them to work together in smaller learning communities (see School-within-a-school).

Independent study: An instructional strategy which allows the student to select a topic, set the learning goals, and work alone to attain the goals. The teacher advises and guides the student during the study.

Integrated/interdisciplinary programs: Instructional programs that combine subject matter usually taught separately, such as history, literature, or science, into integrated learnings under a single curriculum structure.

Interdisciplinary team organization: An organizational pattern of two or more teachers representing different subject areas. The team of teachers shares the same students, schedule, areas of the school, and the opportunity for teaching more than one subject. This approach uses block scheduling and places curriculum planning, grouping, and scheduling decisions with the team of teachers who accommodate instruction to the developmental needs of the students.

Intermediate school: An organizational approach for the middle level grades; usually grades 7–8 or 5–7, that typically follows the elementary school model in curriculum, instruction, organization, and learning activities.

Interscholastic sports: Athletic competition between teams from two different schools.

Intramural program: Activities that feature events between individuals or teams from the same school. These may include athletics, academics, games, or the arts.

Junior high school: An organizational approach for grades, typically grades 7–9, usually following the high school model in terms of curriculum, schedule, activities, instruction, and organization.

Learning center: An instructional strategy which utilizes activities and materials designed to teach one concept, objective, or content area. Students usually work individually to complete the activities. Learning centers facilitate self-pacing, individual mastery, and self-evaluation.

Learning resource center: The central location in the school where instructional materials and media are stored, organized, and accessed by students and staff.

Learning styles: Indicators of a consistent pattern of how students respond to learning and instructional strategies. Research shows a positive relationship when preferred learning styles are equated with teaching–learning activities.

Magnet school: A school with a specialized curriculum (the arts, a humanities strand, etc.) or special program (computers, technology) designed to pull students to the school from a large population area.

Mainstreaming: The practice of assigning students with emotional, physical, and/or mental handicaps into the regular classroom in the least restrictive environment.

Mentoring: A strategy of pairing students with adults or other students to promote successful experiences in school, work, and interpersonal relationships.

Middle level curriculum: The integration of planned or intended learning experiences formulated and organized around (1) knowledge, (2) the commonly shared concerns of young adolescents for their personal development, and (3) the serious global, social issues experienced by them and the world.

Middle level education: The school unit between elementary and high school based on the unique developmental needs of young adolescents. This term seeks to include all schools (middle, intermediate, and junior high school) in the agenda of middle level school theory and practice.

Middle school: An organizational approach for the middle level grades; usually Grades 6–8, sometimes Grade 5; advocating curriculum, instruction, and organization appropriate to the developmental characteristics and needs of young adolescents.

Mini-courses: Short-term, variable-length courses (academic and personal interest) usually found within an exploratory program. Mini-course offerings usually focus on a particular activity or topic such as computers, guitar, chess, dance, drama, video games, or video production.

Multi-age grouping: A grouping pattern which places students from more than one grade or age level in the same class to facilitate academic, social, and personal progress and develop long-term interpersonal relationships between teachers and students and among students themselves. This grouping better attends to the achievement, interest, physiological development, social maturity, emotional readiness, and intellectual levels of students than grouping based solely on chronological age.

Multicultural (multiethnic) education: Middle level students study multiethnic education to understand their own cultural and ethnic heritage and to appreciate and respect the cultural and ethnic heritage of others.

Multidisciplinary teaching: An approach which brings the perspectives of different disciplines to the unified study of problems, topics, or themes. Relationships and connections between and among disciplines are explored but the disciplines are kept distinct and separate.

Multiple intelligences: Theory which presents a number of different intelligences rather than one general intelligence. The other intelligences identified to date are linguistic, musical, logical-mathematical, spatial, kinesthetic, interpersonal, and intrapersonal.

Peer tutoring: An instructional strategy which places students in a tutorial role. Students who have learned successfully help students who have not yet learned a particular subject. Research shows that the knowledge and skills of both tutor and tutee are enhanced.

Portfolio assessment: An alternative approach to evaluation which assembles representative samples of a student's best work (project, papers, tests, creative work) as a basis for assessment. Students determine the contents of the portfolio and students and teachers review the portfolio together. The credo of this approach is that the best measure of a child's work is that child's actual work.

School-within-a-school: An organization known variously as houses, clusters, or pods. The grouping pattern is designed to reduce the impact of large numbers of students in a single school by dividing students into little schools, each with its own faculty. This approach improves the transition from elementary school to high school for young adolescents.

Self-contained classroom: Grouping pattern resulting in one teacher teaching all or most subjects to one group of students. This approach has never been prominent in middle level schools.

Service learning: A collaborative program that extends the school into the community by utilizing community service activities to enhance the learning experience of young adolescents. These programs connect school learning to community, promote leadership and responsibility, and enhance confidence and caring for students.

Team planning: An arrangement in which a group of teachers plan instructional objectives, evaluation procedures, and management strategies appropriate to the students in their team.

Team teaching: An arrangement in which two or more teachers share responsibility for planning, teaching, and evaluating learning experiences for a team of students. Team teaching emerges from team planning, but team teaching extends this into planned classroom strategies and activities.

Transescence: A term describing the unique developmental characteristics of the 10- to 14-year-old. A *transescent* is the term for the 10- to 14-year-old student in this developmental stage.

Transition: Transition offers opportunities to adjust to a new learning environment for the learner. Major transitions occur when students move from the elementary grades to the middle level school and again when they move from the middle level to a high school setting.

Unified arts/allied arts: A curriculum program that provides learning experiences and activities in the humanities, the practical arts, and the fine arts. This is an essential element of a responsive middle level school program.

Young adolescent: A 10- to 14-year-old experiencing the developmental stage of early adolescence.

Name and Title Index

Subject Index

About the Authors

Harvey A. Allen is the Associate Dean for Administration in the College of Education at the University of South Carolina—Columbia, where he teaches courses in middle level curriculum and instruction and social studies education to undergraduate and graduate students. He taught in an intermediate school for six years and was an intermediate school principal for two years. He earned his MAT and PhD degrees at the University of North Carolina at Chapel Hill. His current research and academic interests include improving teacher education for the middle level school, middle school restructuring initiatives, cooperative learning, effective teaching practices, providing appropriate educational programs for at-risk learners, and establishing community service programs. He has conducted and supervised national and state research surveys in middle level education aimed at determining best middle level school practice. He has written monographs and numerous articles and reviews for *Phi Delta Kappan*, *Peabody Journal of Education*, *Clearing House*, and *Teacher's College Record*. He enjoys reading, writing, traveling, teaching, and vacationing at the beach with his family.

Fred L. Splittgerber teaches undergraduate and graduate middle level and high school courses and supervises doctoral students in the Department of Instruction and Teacher Education at the University of South Carolina—Columbia. Previously, he has taught in secondary schools. He earned his MA in History from the University of Omaha and his Ed.D. from the University of Nebraska at Lincoln. His current research interests include the integration of middle level curriculum, middle school organizational patterns, effective teaching strategies, social studies methods, science, technology and society issues, and improving teacher education for the middle grades. He has co-authored three books and several chapters in books, and has authored numerous articles in *Social Education, Phi Delta Kappan, School Business Affairs, Educational Technology,* and *Catalyst for Change.* He has had grants from the Rockefeller Foundation and National Endowment for the Humanities. Currently, he serves as Chairman of the Science and Society Committee of the National Council for the Social Studies, as board member of the Southeast Regional Social Studies Conference, as a member of the statewide advisory committee on middle level education in South Carolina, as well as on advisory groups to several middle schools. In his leisure time, he enjoys writing, reading, and running.

M. Lee Manning teaches middle level school courses and language arts in the Department of Educational Curriculum and Instruction at Old Dominion University in Norfolk, Virginia. He taught 5th, 6th, and 7th grade language arts for five years. He earned his M.Ed. from Clemson University and his PhD from the University of South Carolina. Professor Manning's current research interests include young adolescent development, effective middle level school practices, cultural and gender differences in 10- to 14-year-olds, providing appropriate educational experiences for at-risk learners, and improving teacher education for the middle grades. He has co-authored two books and has authored or co-authored nearly 100 articles and book reviews in journals such as *Phi Delta Kappan, Childhood Education, Middle School Journal, NASSP Bulletin, Action in Teacher Education,* and the *Journal of Early Adolescence.* He currently serves on the publications committee of the Association for Childhood Education International and also serves on the advisory panel for the Center of Early Adolescence's project to strengthen teacher education preparation for the middle grades. He enjoys writing, traveling, and walking on the beach with his wife and children.

ISBN 0-675-21347-9
90000>
9 780675 213479